3 8002 01432 8456

C

COVENTRY LIBRARIES

**Please return this book on or before
the last date stamped below.**

PS130553 Disk 4

KU-410-989

11-9-18

09 FEB 2007

21 MAR 2007

1 8 APR 2007

19 AUG 2007

8 JAN 2008

13-10-15

Th

Pat

Coventry City Council

To renew this book take it to any of
the City Libraries before
the date due for return

COVENTRY CITY LIBRARIES

781·5707

Published in Great Britain by:
Jazz Services Limited, 132 Southwark Street, London SE1 0SW
Copyright © 2003 Jazz Services Limited
ISBN 0-9519380-7-X

Information Management: Celia Wood
Layout and Typesetting: Steve French & www.naughtymutt.com
Drawings: Alastair Graham
Proofing: Biddy Samuels
Cover Design: A3 Design
Printing: Leiston Press, Suffolk 01728 833003

With thanks to all of the following for their contributions and hard work in helping
with the compilation and updating of the contents: Frances Haran, Sara Bailey,
Julie Staplehurst, Biddy Samuels, Charles Beale, Louise Gibbs and Alastair Graham
for his kind permission to reproduce his drawings

All entries supplied by individuals, groups and organisations were deemed correct
at the time of compilation. The publishers take no responsibility for any errors,
omissions or inaccuracies.

This book was made possible through lottery money approved and administered by
Arts Council England.

SUPPORTED BY
THE NATIONAL LOTTERY
THROUGH
THE ARTS COUNCIL
OF ENGLAND

Jazz Services is a company limited by guarantee No 946244
registered charity No 258044.
www.jazzservices.org.uk

Contents

Part IV: Youth Jazz Orchestras, School Bands And Rehearsal Bands 356

Part V: Disability Arts Organisations 385

Part VI: International

Index

Introduction

Welcome to the first edition of the Jazz Education Book, published by Jazz Services. It is aimed at anyone wanting to learn jazz, and also includes advice for anyone wanting to teach it.

Perhaps you are looking for a jazz piano teacher in your area. Perhaps you are a non-specialist primary music teacher looking for a musician to come and do some workshops. Are you a parent with a child who won't stop improvising? Or perhaps you're a self-taught jazz musician, who now feels the need for a bit more support and perhaps a qualification which might lead to a University place too. Perhaps you're doing a project, and just need some directions or guidance on where to go for information.

We hope this book will fulfil a need by providing a directory of individual tutors and courses available across the country region by region, to help you find a jazz teacher or course in your area suitable for your needs. Through articles written by professionals, it also paints a picture of the growing range of jazz education found across the UK.

Jazz education is currently a burgeoning field in the UK. The jazz degree courses that seemed so new even only ten years ago are now producing a generation of committed and enthusiastic jazz musicians who have a comprehensive musical knowledge backed up by systematic training. From Leeds and Glasgow to London, there are courses producing graduates specialising in jazz, many of whom will earn part of their living teaching or running groups in schools.

As with other areas of music education at the moment, jazz education is also in a state of flux. New kinds of ever more confusing qualification, funding and teaching structures are coming on stream every year. Do you know about the new jazz exams? What about the Associated Board and Guildhall, BTECs, GCSEs, NVQs, OCN programmes, LGSMs? We hope this book will translate some of the gobbledegook into English, clear up any confusion and help you to find the qualification and teaching which suits you. We hope too to allay some fears, and also to help you decide whether you just need to learn to play.

There are reference sections, full of useful information of other kinds. It includes a list of useful books and textbooks on jazz, information on jazz related organisations, awards and possible sources of funding, archives both in the UK and internationally.

Professor Charles Beale
MA (Cantab.), PhD, LGSM, PGCE, Jazz piano

Professor Charles Beale is one of the most interesting and articulate jazz educators in the UK today. He was the main moving force in the construction of the Associated Board's Jazz Piano exams and one of its best exponents of the exams abroad, holding workshops demonstrating the possibilities of learning jazz piano and improvisation through a structured exam syllabus.

About This Book

Part I: General Information

This section includes guidance notes on educational levels and qualifications for those starting out on jazz education. As jazz in education is a comparatively new phenomenom a brief review has been included as to its growth and those who (in the UK) championed the tuition of jazz. A review of the Associated Board's jazz exams has been included and as these are very new, many students and parents may not be aware that jazz can be graded and awarded a qualification. Louise Gibbs suggests ways into teaching opportunities for the jazz musician. The rest of Part I lists information to help locate funding and other organisations who have an involvement with jazz education.

Jazz Services receives a lot of requests from students wanting information on jazz, from its history to the current viability of the music and its market. For those trying to locate source material about jazz history we have a list of archives. There is also a short list of favourite books (from the last 50 years) that have been suggested by teachers and musicians.

Part II: Tutors

Are you primarily interested in private lessons, perhaps with a one-to-one teacher or in a small group outside a teaching institution? If so, this is the place to look.

Tutors are listed in an index by region and within that by instrument, followed by individual musician details in alphabetical order by surname.

Each tutor was invited to give a personal statement outlining their approach and attitude to teaching jazz as well as their past and present experience in teaching jazz. The range of experience is very varied. Some are full-time teachers, others are primarily players who also teach. All the information here was provided by the tutors themselves.

Part III: Courses

Do you need something more substantial or long term? Perhaps some musicianship training to get your ears together, some theory or harmony work? An opportunity to play in group with others of the same level, or to learn about recording or using computers to make music? If so, look in the section on courses. Courses have been divided into Full Time, Part Time, Workshops, Short courses, Summer schools *for each region*. Within these catagories broad levels of experience have been outlined:-

Beginner and recreational

These are courses for the relative novice. They may include workshops at your local Further Education (FE) college or school, along with other playing in your local area or rehearsal bands. Perhaps you just want to dip your toe in the water as an improviser, as a classical musician, or you are interested in jazz but have to learn an instrument from scratch too. If it's mixed ability grooves you're after, this is the level for you.

Good amateur or semipro

This level would be of interest for those who already have some skill, and are possibly already in a band. This area includes Summer schools and Access courses. You may already be earning some money from playing, or perhaps you just love the music and want to learn more.

Aspiring professional, degree level and above

This level includes degree and post-graduate level courses across the country and internationally, and is designed for those who see themselves as earning a living full-time from music making or teaching jazz.

Music technology courses

Some of these courses have been listed for those musicians who are increasingly using computer technology and pre-recorded material in their compositions. Some electroacoustic courses also appear under this heading as some jazz musicians have moved into this realm. Remember that some of these courses may also be available part-time too.

Part IV: Youth Jazz Orchestras

This is only a sample of the many big bands that operate from schools, colleges and music centres for young people at various stages of their early musical development. Also included in this list are a few of the many rehearsal bands that have been formed by musicians, at semi-professional or professional levels, who enjoy playing in a big band situation but don't necessarily run the band on a commercial basis. Many give public performances, often raising money for charity.

Part V: Disability Arts/Music Organisations

This section is not jazz specific, but many of the organisations will work with musicians who use improvisation when developing and teaching their students musical skills.

Part VI: International

This section includes general information on jazz organisations, research sources, competitions and awards in Europe and the USA. There are far more educational courses, at all levels, in the USA in particular. We have only listed a few of the most respected university and conservatoires. The International Association for Jazz Educators (IAJE) offers detailed information on courses throughout the USA in its membership publication.

Background Information

Bill Evans
Waltz for Debby / Original Jazz Classics OJC 210

Choosing A Tutor; Choosing a Course

This section of the directory lists jazz tutors. We 'questionnaired' as many as we could find, and, as you will see, some offered fuller accounts of themselves than others. All have at least offered a current name, address and home phone number, and a sentence about what they do. Before you plunge into the names themselves, here are some things to think about when choosing a tutor:

What region are you in? How far are you prepared to travel for lessons?

There is an index of tutors by region, name and instrument for you to choose from those nearest you. Within your regional list, you might have to think carefully about how far you want to go for lessons. Some regions, as you'll see, are well served, while in others you may need to travel further to find someone who meets your needs.

What instrument do you play?

You may already play and have some jazz experience, or perhaps you have a classical technique but you want explore improvising or some other aspect of jazz; you may find that you could have worthwhile lessons with someone who doesn't play your instrument. Working on bebop vocabulary, for example, it might be useful to find a Charlie Parker specialist, likely to play alto sax, even if you yourself are a pianist or singer.

What level are you at?

It may seem strange to start the process of finding a teacher by asking yourself questions, but you can save yourself a lot of time and effort by choosing a teacher who is appropriate for your particular needs.

Think about whether you are a total beginner in jazz, or whether you have some experience but need more depth, or whether you need to work with someone more experienced, perhaps to develop a new approach or because they use some vocabulary you'd particularly like to explore.

If you are a total beginner, then professional experience gigging may be less useful to you. Look perhaps for someone with some education qualifications, or at least someone who has a couple of years' experience working with less experienced learners. Some musicians are fantastic players, but are less good at communicating that knowledge so that it makes sense to others. The less you know yourself, the more useful it will be to find someone who knows how to teach as well as they play.

If you're already in a band or have been playing a couple of years, you may need to find someone who will stretch you further, or take you into new areas. Perhaps you've heard of all the different styles of jazz, but have only been able to play one or two. At this stage, you'll need to find someone with in-depth knowledge, who can point you at particular repertoire. At this stage, too, it may be useful for you to get yourself into a group playing these kinds of music (the Big Bands and workshops listed in the directory may be of help).

Finally, you may already be gigging occasionally, even regularly, and want to brush up your changes, explore more contemporary approaches or work on your technique. If you are in the last category, you will need a specialist.

How many lessons do you need? And how often?

It is often good to have regular weekly lessons, since this provides you with a motivation to do regular practice and leads to steady improvement.

But your needs may be more clearly defined, and so may be their way of working. Do you perhaps need two or three consultation lessons, to see how you fit in with the teacher? Are you only going to be able to afford one lesson a month? Perhaps your teacher is particularly busy, and can usually fit in a 3 hour lesson every few weeks, with a long cup of tea and some jazz jokes in the middle. Do you only need an adviser at the moment, who can monitor your development every few months, while you work away at things on your own?

Your own self discipline will be a key factor here too, as well as your level of prior experience. It's unwise to take regular lessons if you are not prepared to do the necessary practice in between them. You won't get anywhere if you don't put in regular and preferably daily work. A weekly lesson will not necessarily provide you with the motivation you need.

On the other hand, you need to ask yourself whether the person who will teach you is going to be able to motivate you. Do you think they will actually care about your playing? Will they be demanding enough? Do they provide a clear structure with goals to aim for week by week?

This brings us to a list of questions you should ask your prospective tutor. Don't be afraid to quiz them, as they are providing you with a service for which you are likely to be paying.

Firstly – what kind of jazz do you teach?

Jazz means different things to different players. It can include anything from Louis Armstrong or Charlie Parker right through to the smooth and commercial sounds of Kenny Gee and the harsh angular intensity of Cecil Taylor. Your idea of jazz may not be the same as that of your prospective teacher, and you'll have to decide how far you want to learn the kind of jazz they offer.

Look carefully at the listings, to get a feel for what kind of musician they seem to be. Some tutors specialise in particular types of jazz, whilst others perhaps offer a range of styles, and may also offer music theory, the more general 'improvised music' and the possibility to explore other styles too.

Listening to one of their performances or CDs may help here, as may asking them questions about what and how they teach. Find out how much they use stave notation, particularly, and ask if they use any methods or course books.

Ask – have you ever worked in schools and had, or even failed, the standard police check? Would you object if a standard police check was made on you?

We certainly wouldn't want you to approach your prospective jazz tutor assuming anything about their past history. Long gone are the days when jazz musicians deserved any kind of reputation for particularly outlandish, or even bohemian behaviour. Some jazz clubs are now non-smoking environments after all, and jazz musicians are usually business people as well as creative people!!

But if you are a parent, for example, looking for a private tutor for your child, you should certainly consider running a police check under the Children's Act. It will reveal any past convictions which you might want to know about, and will certainly set your mind at rest. Those working currently in schools should have had a police check done on them automatically. Jazz Services are unfortunately not able to verify the details presented to us by the listed musicians.

Ask – how much do you charge?

Prices vary enormously from tutor to tutor and from institution to institution these days. The MU recommended private teacher rate for Autumn 2003 is £22.20 per hour. But rates also vary a great deal from geographical area to area on the private market. In London, in a wealthy area (like Hampstead) a jazz piano tutor may ask anything up to £30 or £35 an hour, whilst an equivalent pianist in, say Lewisham, will charge half of that.

From the other side of the coin the Musicians' Union minimum rate for visiting music teachers in Independent and Maintained Schools is £17.97 to £19.39 at Entry Level, which is for newly qualified teachers on entry into the profession; £20.92 to £22.66 at Standard Level which takes into account FHE and other relevant specialist musical qualifications and a minimum of two years' relevant experience; £23.50 to £25.27 for Credit Level which allows for recognition of further teaching experience, quality and additional qualifications, experience and status as a performer; at Advanced Level for those teachers who do specialised work or who have additional duties or responsibilities like Head of Department at least £26.21 per hour.

Ask – where do you teach?

Wherever possible we have asked where tutors teach but if this isn't listed do check if they teach at their home. If so, check the room for comfort, size and evidence of regular teaching going on.

Others may work from institutions where they teach part time, or even hire a studio space to teach in. Each approach has its pros and cons, in terms of how much you can get to know the teacher, how convenient it is to get to, how private the room is, how much teaching is supervised etc. Again, ask, and if possible check out the space. If you're a pianist, do you like their piano? If you're a drummer, do you have to bring your own kit? Is an amp provided? Do vocalists have to bring their own mic?

Ask – are you more experienced at group teaching or one to one?

When you look at the listings, you'll see some tutors tend to work more with groups. They may run a local Big Band, or do workshops, which often means facilitating improvising rather than giving one to one advice on one instrument in particular. Look out for someone who has special skills and a genuine love of one to one teaching.

Choosing a Course

The directory lists courses by region, in broad types – Full time, Part time, Short courses, Workshops, Summer schools, Music Technology, Teacher . . .

If you're a complete beginner or if you simply want to play for fun, then look at short courses, workshops or Summer schools. If you're beyond that stage and already have good playing skills in areas other than jazz look at Access courses that would lead to a qualification towards taking up a full time university, college or conservatoire course.

Practical/Theoretical : Academic/Vocational

Courses often have a number of different emphases, and it is important that you find one that suits your needs and your previous experience. In particular, think carefully about whether you want a course that is primarily practical or theoretical, and whether it is primarily academic or vocational.

Practical courses, obviously, involve a more hands-on use of instruments and equipment and you learn by doing – through playing, composing, listening. The advantage of this emphasis is that you become good at performing the music but sometimes these courses can lack the range of knowledge and tend to focus you on your own interests.

In courses where the emphasis is more theoretical, more time is spent on reading about music, discussing, researching and writing essays. Here the danger is the opposite: that you know a lot about the music, but don't develop the skills to actually be a musician.

At HE level, for example, conservatoire courses are often highly practical, involving long hours of practice and ensemble work – the aim is to produce specialists in performance, albeit with a smattering of all round knowledge. They are very intensive, but some also have a reputation of producing narrow prima donnas who are less good at interacting with others and have no skill in areas other than music, should the promised career as a concert pianist or top session musician fail to materialise.

University courses tend to be more theoretical in their approach, and develop deeper knowledge about history, analysis and the social background of music. Here you are studying where it came from, what histories there are to tell about it and how we decide whether the music we listen to is any good. Writing and critical skills are more to the fore, which are particularly useful if you want to be a journalist, a teacher at FE or HE level or generally work around music, as well as in it. You often get good at discussing, and can talk a good game, but may not then be able to play as well as you talk.

Most good courses at any level will contain some of both of these ways of learning – they are not mutually exclusive, and many courses also allow considerable flexibility. It's a matter of emphasis.

There is also a divide currently between academic courses and those with a more vocational emphasis. Academic courses tend to be designed to develop knowledge, skills and understanding in a particular subject area, like Baroque music or bebop. Vocational courses are more focused on what's called the 'world of work' and on the knowledge, understandings and skills necessary to have a job. They tend to have more elements of work experience, and are often assessed through the production of evidence that you can fulfil a job role and apply your knowledge, rather than whether you simply know a lot about something.

Vocational courses have been coming on line a lot in the last few years. NVQ and GNVQ qualifications are on the increase, and tend to be more appropriate for less academic, though not necessarily less skilled learners. They are not easier, whatever anyone says, but test different kinds of abilities and are often assessed through the production of evidence rather than through old fashioned exams or essays.

In practice, the academic/vocational split is not always clear. Some academic courses at universities also develop professional playing or music technology skills, for example, and many NVQs and other vocational courses involve extensive production of written portfolios of evidence which have to demonstrate critical skills and knowledge of the area concerned. Most educationalists think that at every level, learning about music has to have elements of the practical and the theoretical. You can't learn to play a jazz repertoire relevant to the world of work without understanding its history and the theory of how harmony works, for example.

The main thing is to think carefully about what you want your course to contain, and find one that suits your needs.

Think short term: what can I do already? What are my interests? Will I stay the course for three years?

But also think long term: what are all the possible things I might want to do later? What are main career options that lead from the qualification I get? What flexibility will I gain?

There are a number of other skills that we will all need in coming years and which, as a professional musician or someone wishing to work in the area of music, you will do well to check your course provides.

Computer skills; reading, writing and numbers; study skills. Computer skill is the most important of these, and sometimes the least familiar to musicians. The internet is already a crucial part of many musicians' lives and will become more important as we learn to buy, sell, market research and write about music on the web. So too is music technology; the ability to record, compose and perform using computers and electronics.

As a professional musician, or a teacher, journalist or writer, you will need to be able to use a word processor to write professional letters, use a database, perhaps do your accounts on a spreadsheet, and so on. Some colleges insist that all assignments are word-processed, for example, and will provide you with the support to achieve this free or as part of your course.

These are all resources which most schools, colleges and universities provide to greater or lesser extent – some have fantastic facilities while others only do the minimum. You will need to find out what support is available to you, and how to access it.

The other area to consider, particularly if, in common with many musicians, school was not the most profitable or balanced time of your life(!), is to update your literacy and numeracy skills.

Perhaps you took a break before you decided to take your education further, because you were in a band or whatever. But these days a GCSE or O level in Maths and English really is a minimum requirement for many kinds of work. If you plan to be self-employed, it's even more crucial to make sure you have these skills.

Luckily, many colleges and universities have Access courses for older learners, and opportunities to re-sit, retake or otherwise update – they want your business. Others will require you to have these skills before you arrive, so it's worth checking and then taking appropriate evening classes at your local college if necessary first, at least to show willing on interview.

If you plan to do a course higher than Level 2, and you've been out of education for a while, think about preparing yourself for the routines and work-styles of education by doing a study skills course first. This is particularly worthwhile, if you're returning to study.

Many college and universities offer the chance for you to learn how to study – to practise reading efficiently and productively, taking notes, writing essays, discussing with fellow students, and so on. Sometimes, your institution will provide you with one in your first term anyway. What follows this introduction is the directory of courses, by alphabetical list of institution name.

Music Technology Courses

Music Technology is an area none of us musicians can avoid these days. It is the medium through which we hear music, and it changes the way we approach it. Even the most acoustic and non-technical of players use music technology almost every time they play or listen to music – microphones, amplifiers, speakers, cables, CDs, tape machines, digital recording – the list is endless.

There are several kinds of music technology course. Some courses are purely music technology based. These are for real specialists, and you often need Maths or Physics A level and an interest in science to make the most of them. Others you might call more music business based. They tend to begin with the assumption that you want to be an engineer in a studio recording popular musical styles, sometimes including jazz. Again these are specialist courses, which probably go into more depth than you need simply to be a musician who knows a bit about music technology.

Others combine music technology with other aspects of music, while still calling themselves music technology courses. Some combine music technology with composition or performance, others with a knowledge of the music business, production, management and finance. Some integrate music technology well with the rest of the course, while others stick it out on a limb, as the 'technical bit'.

Finally, there are now relatively few music courses with no music technology elements in at all, certainly within colleges and universities and at level 3 or HE level. Some have only a single unit or module that will give you the basics, while others may be developing a whole pathway in music technology alongside a general musical training which might include the possibility to do a range of styles of music and to perform, compose, analyse and write about musical styles and their history.

So ask yourself the questions as to the level of music technology expertise you need as a jazz musician. Perhaps you only need to know enough to prevent feedback on acoustic gigs, or to choose a good microphone to give you the sound you need as a horn player or vocalist. Enough perhaps to talk knowledgeably with the engineer when they ask you about your sound, and about the reverb and EQ. Or perhaps you need something more substantial, and want to really get into composition with computers, sampling and engineering.

Write-ups on each course will help give you an idea of how much music technology they contain, but check out the reality first, before believing the hype and if possible talk to a student on the course at open days. Remember that music technology is now the shop window item that attracts students to courses, so institutions will sell themselves hard.

Look carefully in the prospectuses of those that interest you, the text as well as the glossy pictures of the posing smiling students. Make a point of going to visit their facilities too, to check out their level of equipment and the number of students that use it. Ask how many hours a week or term students get access to equipment and what technical support is available. Look for a balance between flash gear that sings and dances, and lots of available cheap four-tracks and computers that all students can use to learn the basics. Other pitfalls, are courses with loads of gear, but no access to it for all but the most advanced and trusted students. Or courses where everyone gets access, but there's no money for maintenance, so the computers always crash and leads don't work. Watch for gathering dust on flash-looking gear, and for the number of computers not working on your visit.

International Jazz Schools

The UK isn't the only place to go to study jazz. In fact many musicians say they benefited from time studying abroad, which brings new challenges but also new confidence on your return to England. The same rules apply as for home courses – think carefully about the level of the course you want and about whether you want a full time course, or perhaps just a set of lessons with a key guru player in New York who you know will fulfill your needs and be a lot cheaper.

If you do decide you want to study abroad, there's a huge range of courses for you to choose from. Starting with the States, the Performing Arts Major's College Guide is a good place to start your search – it recommends around 25 full time jazz courses. There are the big campus universities like North Texas and also city universities like Berklee in Boston or the New School in New York. There's the East and West coast issue to consider, and what kind of an environment you want to work in. There is also the cost to take into account, with high tuition fees, accommodation and living expenses as well as health care insurance and flights to and from the UK.

Bear in mind too that the educational style of US courses is very different. Many of the universities have fantastic facilities compared to the UK ones, with huge libraries, acres of performing facilities, instruments, recording studios and concert halls. Many also have many hundreds of students in each subject, so individual attention can sometimes be limited, and assessment is often more mass-student related, with multiple choice jazz history tests and essay writing the order of the day.

Also check out the level of the student entry. Even places with top reputations to maintain, like Berklee, will take virtually anyone who can pay the fees if they come from abroad. Then they put them in Aural class 7 and Improv. Band 9, and the experience they get may not be with the top teachers. At the other end of the scale, the level of playing at the top colleges is fantastically high. In areas like knowledge of the mainstream repertoire and sheer playing facility, the general standard is much higher than in the majority of colleges and universities in the UK. US jazz players have to compete with literally millions of others – they invented the music, so they know the repertoire virtually from the womb, and, as a whole, they also work phenomenally hard on their technique from very early on, sometimes, in some educators' views, at the expense of the individuality of the final performance.

In short the US experience is not for everyone, though it gives some the confidence and facility they need. It can be costly and, like all foreign countries, you have a lot to learn about the culture as well as about jazz. On the other hand, if you know what you want, the States is so huge and varied that there is almost certainly somewhere or someone who can definitely provide it, and the US can provide a kind of quality of resources, teaching and learning that UK jazz learners can only dream about, albeit at a price.

European jazz education is equally varied. Again costs can be high, and another consideration is language, since teaching in Holland, for example, even though many people speak English, will obviously be in Dutch throughout. But there are world class outfits out there, from the Hilversum School of the Arts 5 year degree programme with six Big Bands, through to others in Northern and Southern Europe.

Professor Charles Beale

MA (Cantab), PhD, LGSM, PGCE (Jazz Piano)

Levels and Qualifications – Guidance notes

The qualifications picture in the UK has become increasingly complex over the past two or three years. The variety, names and combinations of qualifications and levels can seem confusing to all except the hardened qualifications 'anorak'. This situation is not helped by the fact that jazz education in the UK is still a relatively new area. Educationalists are still working out what the different levels mean specifically for jazz. This section of the guide will hopefully clear up some of the confusion.

Happily the government have been aware of the problem for some time and have started to organise the national structure. It is called the National Qualifications Framework - and eventually most qualifications will fit into one clear overall structure and set of levels:

Level 1

This is an initial or preparatory level, designed for programmes dealing with basic and introductory concepts and to lead on to further learning. In some kinds of qualification, there is also a Level E, for Entry, mainly used for adults with learning disabilities. It is very rare to find jazz courses at Entry Level and Level 1.

Level 2

This level is comparable to the standard of work expected at GCSE level (the old O Levels). The average 16-year old should be able to pass this level after 5 years of study. Other qualifications at this level include General National Vocational Qualification (GNVQ) Level 2 (taught school/college based courses), National Vocational Qualification (NVQ) Level 2 (work based qualifications built around an occupational role) and Open College Network (OCN) Level 2 (locally devised and/or nationally developed programmes based on learner need and demand).

Level 3

This level is comparable to the standard of work expected at A level. Level 3 is the pre-university (degree) entry level and so includes many Access and Foundation courses too. Other qualifications at this level include GNVQ Level 3, NVQ Level 3 and OCN Level 3. Some of these qualifications can be 'kite marked' as Access to Higher Education programmes too. These qualifications are designed by the Open College Network, specifically for adults who wish to enter Higher Education (normally degree courses). Not only do they develop the necessary subject-based skills, knowledge and understanding, but also the necessary 'key skills' required by all degree students. Most forward thinking university/college based jazz degree courses will look upon a 'mature' (21 plus) musician with an Access to Higher Education Certificate from a music programme *very* favourably. There are some jazz courses that rarely take applicants straight school with little or no 'professional' or 'industry' experience. So don't worry if you don't have A Levels, an Open College Network (they cover the whole of the UK) accredited jazz programme at Level 3, with an Access to Higher Education Certificate attached to it plus industry experience will often put you on at least an equal footing with the 18-year-old with A Levels.

Degree Level

Above Level 3 comes degree level work, which usually takes place in Universities or Colleges of Higher Education, but some are also available from Further Education Colleges. Most degrees take three years, and each university year is often also confusingly labelled Level 1, 2 and 3. But within the national Qualifications Framework they will be grouped together as Level 4. However, for Degree qualifications begin with the letter B for Bachelor, and include Bachelor of Arts (BA), Bachelor of Science (BSc.), Bachelor of Education (BEd.) and Bachelor of Music (BMus.). A BMus. tends to be more specialised towards a particular area or style of music than a BA in music, which is broader and usually less stylistically focussed. Many BA degrees often allow more study of a second subject, which may or may not relate to the arts.

Sometimes HE courses can be more than three years long. BEd. degrees, for example, integrate three years' study of a degree subject with an extra year's worth of education study (normally related to the teaching of primary or secondary aged pupils), to qualify you as a teacher as well, the all important Qualified Teacher Status (QTS).

If you leave your degree course after one or two years, the institution may give you a Certificate of Higher Education (1 year) or Diploma Higher Education (2 years), this acknowledges your successful learning, work and achievement at Level 1 (HE) or Level 2 (HE), but is not a full degree.

There are also two levels of Post-Graduate work: Masters and Doctorates, at Levels 4 (HE) and 5 (HE). Masters degrees begin with M, and as with Bachelors degrees above, you can get MA, or MSc. Doctorates often begin as PhD, or DPhil., though some institutions also have other names for these qualifications. These are usually research-based, though in some cases performance and composition can count as research too.

It is also possible for a 'professional' musician to work towards a National Vocational Qualification (NVQ) at Level 4 (Level 1 and 2 HE) in Music Performance. This qualification is not just for jazz musicians. Rather than attending a taught degree course as a student, you work in the industry as a musician and develop a portfolio of evidence and are observed 'in action' by a qualified assessor. This qualification assesses your professional or vocational competence and is therefore only available at Level 4. The qualification has been developed and co-ordinated by Metier, the National Training Organisation (NTO) for the Arts and Entertainment Sector. To find out the name and contact information for your nearest accredited NVQ Assessment Centre contact Metier on (01274) 738 800 or try www.metier.org.uk or, www.netgain.org.uk.

There are also a range of post graduate qualifications leading to Qualified Teacher Status or 'QTS'. QTS allows you to teach in either a primary or secondary school and be paid as a qualified teacher at the appropriate pay level and not as an 'instructor'. In addition to the BEd. mentioned above, there are two other main routes that will allow you to gain QTS. Firstly the Post Graduate Certificate of Education (PGCE) which is a one-year, university-based taught course for musicians who already have a degree. Secondly, through a School Centred Initial Teacher Training (SCITT) Programme, a school based training route. The Graduate Teacher Training Registry can provide you with a list of PGCE courses (01242) 544 788. The National Secondary Music SCITT Group runs a SCITT Programme leading to QTS specifically designed for professional musicians from all stylistic backgrounds who can demonstrate graduate equivalence. They can be contacted on Freephone (0800) 281 842. All one year teacher training programmes, leading to QTS, now offer a £6,000 'Training Salary'.

Mike Welsh

Access to Music

Review Of History Of Jazz In Education USA And UK

USA

Jazz, it is generally agreed, was born and spent its early years in New Orleans at the beginning of the 20th century. The definitions of what jazz 'is' are varied, but most agree that its' rhythmic roots are African and it evolved out of Negro work songs, spirituals and the blues. At each stage of its evolution it has acquired a new descriptive signature – New Orleans, Dixieland, Traditional (Trad), Boogie-woogie, Chicago, Mainstream, Swing, Bebop, West Coast, Hard-Bop, Post-Bop, Modern, Free/Improvised, Contemporary, Jazz-Rock-Fusion, Acid Jazz, Jazz Funk. Most of these styles continue to exist simultaneously.

Most jazz musicians learnt by listening to others and by live performance (which is still the core component of any jazz course); it didn't appear as a 'formally' taught subject in the USA until the late 1940s. In fact the 'establishment' music educators in the 1930s and 40s in America strongly believed that jazz shouldn't be taught and it was inappropriate to include jazz in their music curricula. Classical music was 'serious' music but jazz was thought to have a degenerative effect on 'serious' music students.

In the USA attitudes started to change towards jazz in the education system during the 1950s when there were more than 30 colleges and universities that had intro-duced jazz courses to their curriculum and by the end of the decade, jazz courses were also included in many Summer Camp programmes.

With this change music publishers began to produce graded parts for school jazz Big Bands and by the 1960s method books and educational material had started to emerge, especially from jazz musicians who had become involved in teaching. By the 60s jazz was beginning to be seen as 'art' music and gradually accepted by the formal music education community.

High school and college jazz bands increased enormously in the 1960s and by the mid-70s the classroom tuition of jazz was established in hundreds of colleges.

With these increases came a surge in dubious quality jazz teaching materials in America and partly in response to this, the National Association of Jazz Educators was formed in 1968. The members pooled resources and aimed to set standards and authenticate education materials. This association became international in the 1990s – IAJE – and now has over 8,000 members world-wide.

Jazz education in America has now become a major business with thousands of students participating in jazz courses at schools and colleges (but of course not all of them are studying to become professional jazz soloists). Graham Collier in his *Churchill Report on Jazz Education in America* (1993) observed that the main bias of much American jazz education (and what the IAJE has been talking about at most of their conventions) has been the Big Band in High Schools and colleges. There are literally thousands of 'stage bands' (a euphemism for 'Big Band' first designed to get fledgling jazz programmes past the vigilant certifying bodies). Ten years ago he found that many of these bands' repertoire was musical theatre with little jazz content. In the case of the IAJE this is gradually changing. In 1993 after he had visited a number of major jazz schools in the USA, he concluded that there were two approaches to jazz education: "That of preparing the all-round musician and that of preparing the people who will contribute to jazz's development".

UK

Until the 1950s most musicians learnt the rhythms, harmonies and melodies of jazz from '78s' and other jazz musicians or developed their techniques by playing live. Eddie Harvey, who has become one of the UK's best known jazz educators, cites one of his early sources of jazz information as the walls of a London jazz club, where Dennis Rose wrote out 'jazz changes' for him. During the war years, when jazz recordings were scarce, he learnt a number by heart, from the ration of one release a month. It took many years for music schools and conservatories to open their doors to jazz as a taught 'serious' music. The following charts some of the key people and events that developed the provision of educational opportunities for the aspiring jazz player in the UK.

Up until the mid-1950s in the UK there was no real funded support for jazz education but probably one of the first Local Education Authorities in the UK to support a jazz course was in 1955 for a course at Hendon College run by Owen Bryce. Over the next year his course was extended to other South London colleges. He went on, in 1958, to set up a week-long jazz course as part of the Summer Music School at Wortley Hall (near Sheffield) organised by the 'Workers Music Association' which ran for the next 21 years.

1960s

1965 the London School Band, set up by Bill Ashton, appeared on TV which resulted in an approach by the London Youth Service (who part-funded them) to perform and give classes at Youth Centres throughout London. Out of this band came the National Youth Jazz Orchestra (NYJO) which has inspired the creation of many other Youth Jazz Orchestras around the country.

Also in 1965, at Leeds Music Centre, Jo Stones became the new director, with a brief from the local education authority to develop the existing part-time recreational classes and to introduce full-time courses. He initiated a course with a strong jazz content.

By 1979 the department had grown to eleven staff and the course had more than 90 students – but it was still called the 'Jazz AND Light Music Course'. As Richard Hawdon (Head of the department from 1967 until 1992) explained "we had to make it look as if it wasn't jazz. In 1965/6 it was the first full-time jazz education course in Europe. The colleges at Manchester and London Guildhall pooh-poohed it at first. They soon realised we were on to a winner. The Leeds Music Advisor thought it was disgraceful and did his best to put the mockers on it, but Jo Stones steamrollered over everything!"

1965 Michael Garrick (pianist and qualified teacher who holds an Open Fellowship to Berklee College of Music Boston USA) set up the 'Travelling Jazz Faculty'. It consisted of a pool of professional musicians available for projects that used pieces specifically designed to combine juniors and seniors, as well as adult learners, to foster cross-curriculum work.

1966 Barry Summer School (that became Glamorgan Summer School) set up by Pat Evans. In the late 1960s the 'Jazz Centre Society' was set up to provide touring, information and education nationally.

1970s

The Wavendon All Music Plan was established by John Dankworth and Cleo Laine with jazz workshops introduced at The Stables, their music venue in Milton Keynes. The Spring and Summer courses became known as the best short jazz courses in the UK.

1972 Pat Kelly set up Berkshire Youth Jazz Orchestra (BYJO) which is still going strong under the name of Pendulum.

During the same period the Camden and Bracknell Jazz Festivals, organised by Serious Productions, included Musicians' Union funded jazz workshops.

1976 Ian Darrington set up the Wigan Youth Jazz Orchestra, which still provides a training ground for young jazz musicians throughout the region.

1979 Digby Fairweather and Stan Barker set up 'Jazz College' which aimed to "bring the art of improvisation into the school curriculum". Stan Barker subsequently became the Director of the Royal Northern College of Music (Manchester). Digby Fairweather, as well as being a busy and high profile musician and bandleader, also became involved in jazz broadcasting for Jazz FM and subsequently the BBC.

1980s

1982-84 Cornwall Youth Jazz Orchestra set up.

1983 – Jazz Services was set up as the national body for jazz development – touring bands, providing information on education and jazz related contacts in the UK.

1983 onwards – Regional Jazz Organisations (RJOs) grew up in the South, South West, Midlands (Central) East, North West and North East (Jazz Action). All became involved in jazz education in their regions, initiating workshops and master classes.

1983 -87 'Jazz in Education Pilot Scheme' initiated and funded by the Arts Council of Great Britain (now Arts Council England), the Regional Arts Associations (now regional offices of the Arts Council England), Musicians' Union, local education authorities and organised and co-ordinated by the Regional Jazz Organisations (RJOs) which are no longer in existence, apart from Jazz Action in NE region. The scheme lasted four years, with fourteen experimental projects with schools in all the RJO regions. The aim was to develop the knowledge, understanding and practice of jazz and to stimulate a deeper awareness of the contribution of jazz to music education.

1985 Community Music (London) set up to provide services in music education, training, therapy, information, job creation and advice. They provided (and still do) workshops and courses in London to those who would not normally have access to professional music guidance. John Stevens devised a teaching method 'Search and Reflect' that has had a long term influence on the teaching of improvisation.

1986 First National Jazz Education conference held at Goldsmiths College (London) to discuss methodology and approachs within jazz.

1986 Jazz Action was set up as a joint initiative between Yorkshire and Humberside Arts and Northern Arts.

1987 Second National Jazz Educational conference held in Sheffield organised by Jazz Services.

1989 Full time four year jazz course started at Royal Academy by Graham Collier.

1989 The Report and Education Directory of the 'Jazz in Education Pilot Schemes' compiled by Mary Greig and distributed by Jazz Services. The report noted that there had been a proliferation of educational activity relating to jazz and improvised music during the 1980s, where previously it had been confined to jazz musicians combining their performing careers with teaching. The scheme led to the 1986 jazz education conference and the continuing involvement of some local authorities in jazz education funding support.

1990s

Della Rhodes introduced a formal jazz course 'ear training for vocalists' at the City Lit Institute (London) where Eddie Harvey had been running jazz workshops until 1987.

A steady increase in the inclusion of jazz modules, at all levels of music education, as well as music degrees specialising in jazz from year two. These now include the Royal Academy of Music, Trinity College, Barnsley College, Brunel University College, Birmingham Conservatoire of Music, Truro College, Goldsmiths College and the post graduate course at the Guildhall school of Music and Drama.

1999 The Associated Board of the Royal Schools of Music brought out the first ever validated jazz exams in the UK for piano followed by exams for jazz ensemble and in 2003 the jazz horns exam.

Associated Board Exams

Associated Board Overview

The Associated Board have been running their jazz piano and jazz ensemble exams in the UK since January 1999, and since then over 1,780 people a year have taken an examination with them. The syllabus for the eams was developed over a number of years, in consultation with key jazz performers and teachers, and includes works written especially for the exams, as well as well-known standards from a wide selection of styles and composers.

Great care has been taken in developing the Associated Board Jazz syllabuses to make it suitable for all students of jazz; both those already playing or studying the genre, who have never before had access to performance assessment of this kind, and also those who have gained their existing experience and knowledge from the study of classical music. Equally important has been the desire to be true to the free spirit at the heart of jazz style and to keep the elements of spontaneity and enjoyment alive in all sections of the exam. Through a structed and progressive framework which encourages disciplined style of the rich variety of jazz tradition, all players will have the opportunity to express themselves and gain the freedom, confidence and understanding to develop their own personal direction in jazz performance.

Currently it is possible to take jazz piano exams at grades 1 to 5; however, plans are being developed for higher graded exams through to grade 8. Jazz ensemble exams are available at three levels: Initial, Intermediate and Advanced, and are open to any combination of instrumentalists and/or singers. In the summer of 2003 the Board launchs the next set of jazz syllabuses for trumpet, trombone, clarinet and alto and tenor saxophone.

In addition to the examinations, the Associated Board also run a series of workshops and courses for teachers interested in jazz. One-day workshops form a progressive series and are mostly aimed at teachers who do not have much experience of working with jazz. These are run at venues up and down the UK, and can take the form of general introductions to jazz playing and teaching, or more in-depth sessions on one particular aspect of jazz (e.g. rhythm, improvisation). We also run a jazz summer school at the Benslow Music Trust in Hitchin (Herts) in August each year. This is an in-depth introduction to the skills necessary for jazz playing and teaching. A residential weekend takes place in the Autumn, usually aimed at people who are already playing and/or teaching jazz.

Jazz Piano

Publications and CDs to work towards the new Jazz Piano syllabus, with advice on the various components of the exams. Grades include specially arranged Blues and Jazz Standards as well as pieces specially composed by contemporary jazz musicians.

Available - Jazz Piano Pieces Grades 1-5, Aural tests Grades 1-3 and 4-5, Piano scales Grades 1-5, Quick Studies Grades 1-5, Jazz Piano Grades 1-5, Jazz Piano from Scratch (book and CD by Charles Beale). For the detailed content of each Grade see the website: www.abrsm.ac.uk/jazzpiano

Jazz Works for Ensembles

Collection of compositions for jazz ensembles at three levels: Initial, Intermediate and Advanced. Includes original compositions by leading jazz composers, parts for flexible ensembles from duo to large band (C, B flat and bass-clef instruments, rhythm section of piano, bass guitar and drums). Also includes separate Teachers Books and CDs with complete performances of all pieces.

Jazz Clarinet, Alto and Tenor Sax, Trumpet and Trombone
New syllabuses launched mid 2003 for Grades 1-5 in all the above instruments;

Exam dates for Practical Grades

UK and Ireland early March

Scotland and Ireland early June

England and Wales early June

UK and Ireland early November

The Associated Board have been running Piano Seminars to introduce the syllabus throughout the UK as well as One Day Kick Start Workshops for teachers and a Jazz Summer School (one week residential course) for teachers with little experience of jazz who want to develop their skills in a supportive group environment and to find out how to incorporate jazz into their teaching.

NB These did not take place in 2003 (due to the launch of the new Jazz Horn syllabus), it is hoped they will resume in 2004.

Cool Keys

A collaboration between the BBC, Jazz Services, the Associated Board of the Royal Schools of Music and Yamaha to produce a unique resource introducing jazz and improvisation to teachers and pupils.

It has been specifically designed to fit in with the UK music curriculum requirements at Key Stages 3 and 4. It is an entertaining and informative way for teachers to explore jazz with their students for first time.

The Cool Keys video includes a wide range of interviews and music from those well known in jazz as well as music 'icons' Sir Paul McCartney, Ray Charles, Herbie Hancock, George Shearing and Julian Joseph.

These musicians talk about the music and demonstrate examples and explanations of jazz styles and techniques. Julian Joseph gives a fascinating Master Class which even inspired two members of the BBC production team to rush out and take piano lessons.

The pack consists of a 60-minute video, an audio CD with examples of a range of jazz styles for class listening and sample tracks and ideas for class work. The booklet includes background information and explanations on jazz, listening ideas and material, starting points and ideas for workshops and worksheets.

Teachers' resource pack for Cool Keys available from PO Box 50, Wetherby, West Yorkshire, LS23 7EZ, at £24.99.

Horses For Courses - A Review Of The Associated Board Jazz Exams

I recently read an article discussing the Associated Board's jazz work that was so provocative that I thought I would share it with you. To summarise, the author suggested that the jazz grades start at the level of Grade 3 'classical' and that, whatever the Associated Board says to the contrary, Grade 1 Jazz 'really' equals Grade 3 in classical music.

It is one of the Associated Board's most remarkable achievements to have established a progressive and clearly structured set of levels for jazz musicians – currently Grade 1 to Grade 5. In terms of Grade 1 jazz, it is surely possible to find music that can be played by someone who has been playing jazz for about 18 months and has achieved a basic competence, and mark them on their ability to play it. And there is no reason to suppose that classical music is the only place to start as a musician. There are professional musicians in many styles for whom learning classical repertoire and technique was not part of their early experience. Seeing classical music as the only starting point implies a stylistic rigidity which is hard to sustain in today's more interactive musical world.

A convential classical training has many undoubted strengths, and I speak as someone who experienced that training. It gives you the ability to play with technical fluency and, often, to make a good sound. Via stave notation, it opens the doors to an emotionally rich and structurally complex cornucopia of fantastic music. At the same time, all educational systems have their blind spots. For example, classical musicians often criticise themselves for being overly re-creative and unable to survive without the printed music. Jazz educators also observe what they see as rhythmic inflexibility in some classical players, which they call 'first beat of the bar' syndrome.

Like all bodies of work, the classical repertoire of the 18th and 19th centuries is the product of a particular time and place and has its own norms – its rhythmic clichés and approaches to dynamics, articulation and phrasing, for example. In their own educational tradition, these norms are not problematic. What can be a problem, though, is when norms associated with one style begin to dominate in the educational traditions of another. Often my pupils' main task is to un-learn the rhythmic clichés and the dynamics, articulation and phrasing habits of other styles, rather than simply to learn jazz. Of course this makes jazz seem harder.

So is Grade 1 jazz really harder that Grade 1 classical? Well, if you start from the assumption that improvising and learning music by ear is harder than reading from notation, then possibly. If you think clapping on beats 2 and 4 is harder than feeling downbeats on 1 and 3, then maybe. But I can point to any number of 'untrained' 9-year olds who could demonstrate the opposite. For some of the South London children involved in the original Jazz Piano plot, working by ear was easier than working from stave notation, clapping on 2 and 4 was the obvious way to indicate a pulse and improvising was far easier and more natural than trying to copy the sounds of others.

For me, a plurality of educational practices and standards is a natural consequence of a plurality of musical styles. And this leads to a plurality of definitions of easy and hard, which are then reflected in Associated Board exams. A musical effect defined as easy in one style may turn out to be harder in another because it occurs less often – it's horses for courses. So Grade 1 jazz, like Grade 1 classical music, usually takes a year and a half or so to achieve. But the musical journey your pupil goes on to get there is likely to be different.

Professor Charles Beale

(from Libretto *magazine 2002)*

Teaching Opportunities For Jazz Musicians

The launch of graded jazz piano examinations and the proliferation of teaching materials with 'jazz' in the title is a sure sign that the idea of jazz, if not the music, has made inroads into mainstream music education. As a consequence there's a growing demand for jazz teachers. Musicians who can fulfil the roles of instrumental teachers or workshop leaders are finding themselves crossing between the bandstand and the classroom. Some have already discovered that teaching is an attractive addition to their portfolio career. Certainly, it's one financially remunerative way of continuing to work with music and get to see daylight hours. But what perhaps is the surprising thing about teaching is the very high degree of personal satisfaction that it can give.

But is teaching for everyone? This chapter prompts you to consider your suitability, and gives some advice about what jazz teaching work is available and how you could go about getting it.

What do I need to become a teacher?

Being a competent, even brilliant, jazz musician is no guarantee that you are going to be an effective teacher. Teaching requires commitment, personal qualities and skills that are additional to your musical expertise. If you're not sure whether you have what it takes to be a teacher, try this quick self-assessment. If you can answer 'yes' to most of the questions, then teaching is an avenue worth exploring.
• Are you interested in music (not just jazz)?
• Are you interested in and curious about people?
• Are you interested in sharing your musical expertise with others?
• Could you be described as having patience and calm?
• Do you have a generally positive and constructive outlook on life?
• Do you care about treating people as you yourself want to be treated?
• Are you intellectually curious?
• Are you reliable?

Having discovered that you have most of the personal qualities of a potential teacher, you can think about the kinds of professional knowledge and skills needed for teaching. Looking at the lists below you should already have 'A' list skills. 'B' list skills you can acquire through a teacher preparation course and/or first hand experience of teaching. 'C' list skills will help you be business-like.

A List skills (essential prerequisites)
• musical competence and performing experience
• knowledge of your instrument, jazz repertoire and history, improvisation practices
• music theory and notation reading

B List skills (essential and can be acquired through experience and/or training)

- diagnostic skills (how to find out about and match your student's capabilities to what they need to learn and what you can offer)
- planning skills (how to organise and prioritise a progressive sequence of learning activities for the time available)
- instructing and communicating skills (how to convey information and motivate learners)
- assessing and evaluating skills (how to monitor student progress and monitor your teaching effectiveness)

C List skills (not essential but highly desirable and can be acquired)

- organisational and time-management skills
- business and promotional skills

What kinds of teaching opportunities are available for jazz musicians and what qualifications are needed?

Where provision is statutory, as for class music in state primary and secondary schools, Qualified Teacher Status (QTS) is required. For one-off workshops, peripatetic instrumental teaching in state or private schools, in higher education institutions, and for private teaching, formal qualifications are desirable but not mandatory. However, this situation is likely to change as increasingly jazz musicians become formally trained and qualified. When there is a choice between two equally good musicians, one with a degree and one without, employers are likely to settle for the former.

For those seeking to work in higher education, occasional and casual teachers may escape the requirement of formal qualifications for music or teaching, but those who want an academic teaching post will need postgraduate qualifications of some kind, and also a record of research or a body of creative work behind them. There are also recent moves to require teachers in higher education to have a teaching endorsement.

How do I become experienced and qualified?

Institutions looking for workshop leaders will want good musicians who can motivate and keep groups of students (often of highly variable ability) interested and learning. Anyone recruiting a jazz musician-teacher looks for teaching experience. The Catch-22 here is that you cannot get a job until you have experience and generally you cannot get experience until you get a job! The best way to gain teaching experience is to be attached ('apprenticed') to a working teacher. You can learn a great deal by observing and assisting. And though you are not likely to be paid, you may have the opportunity to deputise or be recommended for work.

Another enterprising way of getting teaching experience is by setting up your own workshops or learning bands, especially if you have identified a local need for jazz tuition or a group of learners. This approach needs considerable chutzpah and determination and will call upon your organisational as well as musical skills.

At present there is no specialist professional training available for jazz teachers in the UK. Musicians would need to tap into existing professional development initiatives and adapt these to the teaching, for instance, of jazz repertoire, style and improvisation. The best courses will provide opportunities for guided teaching practice and mentoring. You might look into:

ABRSM Certificate in Teaching for private teachers

Training initiatives by community music providers (including Community Music London)

Certificates in Music Teaching to Adults and Music Workshop Skills (both at Goldsmiths College, University of London)

MA in Music Education' at Trinity College of Music

MTTP at University of Reading

Summer courses for teachers at Guildhall School of Music

LiTMus Programme at the Royal College of Music (for teachers already working in HE)

If you are interested in general school music teaching and obtaining Qualified Teacher Status (QTS) either through on the job training or a postgraduate route you should contact the Teacher Training Agency (TTA) at: teaching@ttainfo.co.uk and 0845 6000 991

How do I make or find teaching work: setting up a private teaching studio

It is surprisingly easy to get started with private teaching. However, only by taking a professional approach can you attract and keep students. If you are to take private teaching seriously it is recommended you acquire most of the following teaching resources:

- comfortable teaching space (adequate soundproofing, ventilation, warmth, light)
- reliable instrument(s) in good repair and adjustable seating
- tape/CD/minidisk player and recorder
- repertoire albums, fake books and instrumental tutor books, jazz theory and improvisation books
- CD collection, listening compilations, reference books, music and music teaching journals/magazines
- student/teaching record keeping notebook
- practice advice and work sheets for students
- music stands, mirror, metronome, white board and non-permanent pens
- piano or pre-recorded play-along resources, small percussion instruments
- accounts and receipt books
- public liability insurance (important if using your home as studio)

Attracting students

You will find that most prospective students for jazz are adults. Initially, they will make enquiries because they have heard you perform. If you can maintain the interest and progress of these initial students your reputation will grow through word-of-mouth, the cheapest and most effective advertising. Another way to get started is to advertise in the music (not necessarily jazz) or local press. However, you need to be clear about the publication's readership as advertising can be expensive. For example, if you want to attract adult beginners, then a magazine like *Time Out* might be more effective than *Jazz Journal* which is more likely to cater for specialised interests and experienced players. If you are interested to teach children then advertise in the tuition column of the local rag or place a card with local notice boards and schools to alert interested parents and teachers. Don't forget to place your details with the Teachers' Lists of Jazz Services and the Musicians Union. The Incorporated Society of Musicians (ISM) has a list of registered teachers which goes to every library in the country. Entry, however, is by application and referral.

Incorporating workshops into your performing tours

This not only ensures a knowledgeable and enthusiastic audience for your tour dates, but also stimulates participants to continue learning – maybe even taking private lessons. You need to have a clear idea of what your workshop is attempting to achieve, have a way of communicating effectively, and be able to deal with the various levels of ability, experience and cooperation you're likely to find in any group of unknown participants.

Applying to schools

If you have workshop leading and teaching experience you can approach state and private primary and secondary schools with a music making project or workshop. This entails more than just performing to the students. You will need to convince schools (usually through the Head Teacher or Head of Music) that you can motivate and maintain the interest of (large) groups of children, not to mention offering professional development to staff. A good way to do this would be to show how your workshop might deliver some of the music learning targets of the National Curriculum, especially those to do with creative work. If you have devised any written materials or work sheets send a sample copy (with your name and contact details stamped obviously on the page).

Don't forget that schools also have a programme of instrumental and vocal teaching that is usally carried out by peripatetic teachers. Saxophone, keyboard and guitar teachers will find themselves in demand. Draw attention to any group instrumental teaching experience that you have, and any special approach to incorporating improvising and composing into your teaching. You will need to approach schools individually or through a local education authority or music teaching agency.

Adult and community education

If you have a good idea for a workshop or a course, you can approach various organisations and institutions offering adult and community education (See the annual guide *Floodlight* for adult education, and *Sounding Board* for community education). When applying 'cold' to any organisation, do your homework, considering how your proposal would fit into the existing programme. Don't just offer the title of a new course proposition; provide, say, a 10-week plan of it stating likely learning outcomes. This shows that you have some idea of how to effect progress.

Further education, conservatoires and universities

Many colleges now offer jazz courses ranging from introductory 'tasters' to special-

Teaching Oportunities	Where	Qualifications needed
Instrumental, vocal tuition and/or jazz musicianship (improvisation/arranging/theory)	Private (studio and/or home visit)	None
Instrumental, vocal tuition and/or jazz musicianship (improvisation/ arranging/theory)	Peripatetic service in primary and secondary schools, adult education colleges, conservatoires, universities	Music degree or equivalent is required, teaching experience is essential
Workshop leading (Introducing jazz, small bands, improvisation) local self-managed groups	Primary and secondary schools, peripatetic service, adult education, youth and community service, colleges, conservatoires, universities	No formal qualifications but music degree or equivalent and teaching experience is highly desirable
Ensemble directing (Big Bands, jazz choirs)	Local self-managed groups secondary schools, adult education, colleges, conservatoires, universities	Band directing experience is highly desirable
Lecturing (jazz theory, history, repertoire) and Practical Masterclasses	Colleges, conservatoires, universities	Music degree or equivalent is required, teaching experience is highly desirable. Band directing experience is highly desirable
Classroom music teaching (National Curriculum)	primary and secondary schools, (state and private sector)	Bmus/BA and PGCE (QTS)
Professional development of music teachers	primary and secondary schools, colleges and universities	Music degree or equivalent is required, teaching experience is essential

ist undergraduate degrees and postgraduate jazz programmes. Because these courses are certificated, teaching will involve student assessment. This can be particularly challenging for courses involving improvisation. Opportunities to teach at further and higher education level do not come up often. However, if you have something special and additional to instrumental tuition to offer, a slant on aural training, music technology, arranging, or composition, your position becomes more attractive. Whether applying 'cold' or to an advertised position, do your homework on the institution and make a case for what you have to offer that enhances (or improves) any existing provision. A record of performance and research is particularly relevant to university positions.

Making professional contacts

Getting to meet other musician-teachers (whether working in jazz or otherwise), finding out what they do and sharing what you know raises your profile. Attend conferences, read teaching journals, join relevant professional organisations, and participate in professional development events. You can also ask an experienced teacher if you might observe or assist with their lessons or classes, or you can open up your studio for teachers to observe what you do. As well as recommending new students, your musician-teacher colleagues can be a great source of support and advice.

Relevant Organisations

Associated Board of the Royal Schools of Music (ABRSM) – 24 Portland Place, London W1B 1LU, Tel: 020 736 5400, abrsm@abrsm.ac.uk

Department for Education and Employment (DFEE) – Sanctuary Buildings, Great Smith Street, London SW1P 3BT, Tel: 020 7925 5000.

Incorporated Society of Musicians – 10 Stratford Place, London W1N 2AE, Tel: 020 7629 4413, www.ism.org

International Centre for Research in Music Education – University of Reading, Bulmershe Court, Woodlands Avenue, Reading, RG6 1HY, Tel: 0118 931 8221.

LiTMus (Learning and Teaching in Music) programme, Woodhouse Centre, Royal College of Music, Tel: 020 7591 4392, www.litmus.rcm.ac.uk

Musicians Union – 60-62 Clapham Road, London SW9 0JJ, Tel: 020 7582 5566, www.musiciansunion.org.uk

National Association of Music Educators – Tel: 01494 473 410, www.name.org.uk

Trinity College of Music, Mandeville Place, London W1 – Tel: 020 7935 5773

Useful Resources

GIBBS, Graham (1988) Learning by Doing: a guide to teaching and learning methods (London: Further Education Unit)

GIBBS, Louise (1998) PTDP Scheme Study Pack (Southampton: University of Southampton, Performance Teachers' Development Project) Materials also at: www.litmus.rcm.ac.uk

HALLAM, Susan (1995) Professional musicians' orientations to practice: implications for teaching, British Journal of Music Education 12, no1, pp3-20.

HALLAM, Susan (1998) Instrumental Teaching: a practical guide to better teaching and learning (Oxford: Heinemann Educational Publishers)

HARRIS, P and R. CROZIER (2000) The Music Teacher's Companion: a practical guide (London: ABRSM)

HEAD, Louise (Ed) (2000) Music Education Yearbook 2000-2001, 17th Edition (London: Rhinegold Publishing Ltd)

INCORPORATED SOCIETY OF MUSICIANS (1998) Employment of Music Teachers: key principles (London: ISM)

MUSIC TEACHER – published monthly, Rhinegold Publishing

TIMES EDUCATIONAL SUPPLEMENT (TES) - published weekly (Friday)

TIMES HIGHER EDUCATIONAL SUPPLEMENT (THES) - published weekly (Friday)

Louise Gibbs is a jazz vocalist and recording artist. She teaches voice and improvisation at Goldsmiths College, University of London, and is also Director of the LiTMus (Learning and Teaching in Music) Programme which provides continuing professional development for teaching staff at the Royal College of Music and for performance teachers in higher education.

louise@jazzmine.co.uk
website: www.louisegibbs.co.uk
lgibbs@rcm.ac.uk : LiTMus Programme website: www.litmus.rcm.ac.uk

Part I: General Information

Thelonious Monk
Big Band/Quartet in Concert / Columbia 476898

UK Awards

BBC Radio 2 and 3 Jazz Awards

Now in its third year (2003) over one hundred and fifty people in the UK jazz industry are polled to vote for – Best Band, Best Rising Star, Best Instrumentalist, Best Vocalist, Best New Work, Best Innovation and Best CD. The three most popular nominees go forward to the final awards ceremony held at the QEH on the South Bank with live performances from some of the nominees. Listeners can vote for the best out of the three nominated albums on BBC website. An award is also offered to an indivual considered to have made a major contribution to jazz in the UK.

BBC Radio 2 National Big Band Competition

Ray Harvey, Producer, 34 Riefield Road, Birmingham, West Midlands (020 8850 5788) organised by Ray Harvey (now retired from the BBC) for the past 28 years

1. Open to classic Big Band form of 5 saxes, 4 trumpets, 4 trombones and a rhythm section, with a minimum of 15 and a maximum of 20 players. Mixed front lines are not acceptable.
2. Senior bands are limited to 6 fully professional musicians.
3. Junior bands must be under 22 at the time of recording. Signed declaration from band leader to this effect.
4. Competing musicians may play with one band only.
5. Musical Directors may direct one band only.
6. Previous winning bands are excluded from the competition for two years unless junior bands move into senior band.
7. Only the first 10 minutes of the recording will be heard by the jury.
8. Deadline end of March 2003 (for 2004 TBC)

In 2002 rules changed. Previous juries had found difficulty in judging bands on extracts of performances, so now recordings sent in must be played in their entirety. One item only may be faded to a minimum time of 3 minutes to assist bands in keeping to the 10 minute maximum duration rule. Also changed is the limitation of the total number of players to a maximum of 20 players. The aim is to encourage bands to have one player on each part. All the players are paid full MU rates for the broadcast and extra players on the same part makes for contractual problems. There is also a limitation of 6 fully professional players in the senior bands (fully professional is defined as those musicians that earn the majority of their income from performing music). For an application form and full set of rules contact the Producer.

Prizes awarded: 1st and 2nd in Senior Section, 1st and 2nd in Junior Section, Best Soloist; Most Outstanding Musician; Best Arrangement; John Dankworth Trophy to Most Promising Musician under 22; Don Lusher Trophy to Best Trombonist; Kenny Clare Trophy to Best Drummer.

Previous year's winners: Senior: Fat Chops Guildhall Jazz Band

Junior: Aylesbury Music Centre Dance Band, Northamptonshire County Youth Big Band.

Carleton Granbery Award

Guildhall School of Music and Drama, Silk Street, Barbican, London EC2Y 8DT 020 7628 2571.

Carleton Granbery was a keen jazz pianist and the awards at Guildhall were established by his family to celebrate his life and love of jazz.

Available to two or three students *who have been offered a place on the one year Jazz Post Graduate course at the Guildhall School of Music (London)* according to talent and financial need. There are two other 'Career Development' awards to students finishing the course. Students are provided with application forms. The Career Development awards are based on achievement and excellence throughout the course and their performance at the finals.

Creative Collaborations in Music Awards

Nelson Fernandez, Head of Performing Arts and Training, Visiting Arts, 11 Portland Place, London W1N 4EJ 020 7389 3017, nelson.fernandez@britishcouncil.org www.britishcouncil.org/visitingarts

British-based music organisations can apply having identified the foreign composer. Venues and festivals can also apply on behalf of a specific music group if they are partners. Residencies should be up to 8 weeks duration. Music genres should reflect modern contemporary music. Priority countries include - Bangladesh, Barbados, China, Ghana, Grenada, India, Jamaica, Kenya, Nigeria, Pakistan, Trinidad and Tobago, South Africa, Uganda and Zimbabwe. Also N. Africa, Middle East, E. and S.E. Asia, Central and South America. Partnership funding also needs to be found. Applications initially should be submitted on no more than 3 sides of A4 and should identify UK partners and foreign composer with some background information. Proposed dates for the residency. Details of the facilities that will be provided for the visiting artist.

To provide composers and music creators from the UK and their counterparts from overseas, through a UK residency, with the opportunity to work together. Up to 6 awards (max £6,500 each) available.

Hamlet British Jazz Awards

Big Bear Music, PO Box 944, Edgbaston, Birmingham, West Midlands B16 8UT (0121 454 7020) www.bigbearmusic.com

Panel of jazz critics and the 'great and the good'. Nominations invited from circulated forms of suggested names in each category. Previous years' winners not eligible for following year. Award ceremony held (Pizza Express Dean St London) with press coverage. No cash benefits but a certificate issued. This year marks the 16th anniversary of the British Jazz Awards. 2002 winners: Trumpet – Gerard Presencer, Alto Saxophone – Peter King, Guitar – Jim Mullen, Miscellaneous instrument (Baritone Sax) – Alan Barnes, Big Band – National Youth Jazz Orchestra, Trombone – Mark Nightingale, Tenor Sax – Tommy Smith, Bass – Dave Green, Vocals – Claire Martin, Rising Star – Steve Fishwick, Clarinet – Tony Coe, Piano – Dave Newton, Drums – Clark Tracey, Small Group – Jazz Couriers Celebration, Arranger/Composer – Alan Barnes, Best New CD – Jazzizit for Spike Robinson/Derek Nash, Best Re-issue CD – Sony Jazz Billie Holiday. John Dankworth Awards Longstanding talent – Tommy Whittle, Talent Deserving wider recognition – Julian Siegel, Special Awards – Services to British Jazz – Peter King. Jazz Writer of the Year – Alyn Shipton

Marion Montgomery Awards

Dorothy Cooper. MUM(UK), PO BOX 5063, Milton Keynes, Bucks MK5 7ZN (01908 670 306) www.jazzdivas.freeeuk.com

First award for jazz vocalists given in 2002 in association with the Montgomery Holloway Music Trust and the Ventnor Jazz Divas Festival. Before her death Marion Montgomery agreed to endorse these awards designed to encourage and support emerging jazz vocalists. The awards are dedicated to her memory. Finalists for the awards are selected by a panel of judges – Dorothy Cooper (jazz agent), Laurie Holloway (musician and Marion's husband), Antonia Couling (editor of the *Singer Magazine*) Abigail Holloway Hellens (daughter), Chris Walker (Radio Solent Jazz presenter) and Sue Gouch (artist). The finalists will be chosen at a series of auditions. Finalists will be booked to appear at the Ventnor Jazz Divas Festival 12 to 14 September 2003. Winners will receive a promotional package made up of :-

- A photographic publicity portfolio
- A promotional web page
- A commissioned one-off glass trophy
- Auditions for a London Jazz Club venue

Application forms available from the website www.jazzdivas.tv or Ventnor Jazz Divas, the Wintergardens, Ventnor, Isle Of Wight or from Dorothy Cooper. Completed application forms should be returned to Dorothy Cooper and should be accompanied by a CD or tape containing three tracks of standard jazz classics and a cheque for the entry fee - £35. Application forms available from January 2003 and the deadline is 31 March.

Trinity College of Music

King Charles Court, Old Royal Naval College, Greenwich, London SE10 9JF (020 8305 3888) info@tcm.ac.uk www.tcm.ac.uk

Archer Scholarship - Entitles a postgraduate to approximately £900 worth of lessons with a tutor/s of their choice, in return for which they must play with the college Big Band for six hours of rehearsals a week and all gigs.

Spike Robinson Scholarship - Available, through audition, to a Baritone, Tenor or Alto Saxophone student studying at Trinity College of Music - pays £1000 towards the recipient's fees (BMus or Postgraduate) and in addition covers the cost of a week's accommodation in and flight to USA plus a year's Musicians' Union membership.

The fund has been set up in memory of Spike Robinson, who died in 2001. He played equally in the UK and the USA (where he was born) and contributions to the fund, through a tax free Gift Aid scheme, have and will continue to come from both sides of the ocean and through donations from benefit jazz events.

This scholarship is also available to a student at the University of Colorado, Boulder USA, to visit Trinity for a week with accommodation provided by Trinity and the opportunity to play in the Greenwich Festival and in a variety of jazz clubs during their stay.

Peter Whittingham Jazz Award

Sue Dalton, Musicians Benevolent Fund, 16 Ogle Street, London W1P 8JB (020 7636 4481 Fax 020 7637 4307) www.mbf.org.uk

Musicians Benevolent Fund administer the Peter Whittingham charitable trust founded by his family in 1989. Individuals under the age of 26 on the closing date may apply for projects to be undertaken independently or with others. Where an application is made on behalf of a group the average age of the group members should also be under 26. The project can be a recording, composition or performance and must be in the 'cutting edge' field of jazz. Non-British nationals must have lived in UK for 3 years. Applicants should complete the application forms and enclose a cheque for £10 payable to Whittingham Award.

Closing date 24 October 2003. Candidates should enclose a CD or cassette (and may also include a manuscript) with a letter of recommendation supporting the project. Shortlisted candidates will be invited to interview in November 2002. The recipient must undertake the chosen project during 2003. Award is up to £4,000. Awards - 1998 Martin Speake tour, Andy Scott - commission. 1999 Tim Whitehead award, 2001 Tom Arthurs for a recording, 2002 Paul Towndrow.

Worshipful Company of Musicians

c/o Keith Howell, 24a Langton Road, West Molesey, Surrey KT8 2HX (020 8941 6610, keithhowell@btinternet.com)

2001 offered sponsorship for 3 years to National Youth Jazz Orchestra. In 2000 this City of London Livery Company (Guild) celebrated its 500th anniversary, when it will launch 'Funding a Future' to provide financial support for the most talented young musicians in the UK, in the crucial years between college and the establishment of a professional career. Main focus is the support of classical musicians. However two jazz awards established in 1992. Silver Medal - awarded to established musicians for outstanding services to British jazz. Usually by recommendation. Winners so far John Dankworth 1993; Ronnie Scott 1994; Humphrey Lyttelton '95; Bill Ashton '96; Stan Tracey '97; Dame Cleo Laine '98; George Shearing '99, Don Lusher 2000, Chris Barber 2001, Tony Coe 2002. Bronze Medal - awarded to exceptionally talented young (up to 35 years) British jazz musicians. Bronze winners - Tina May '92; Andy Panayi '93; None in 1994 Mark Nightingale 1995; Tim Garland 1997; Jim Watson 1998; Steve Brown 1999, 2000, 2001, 2002. Musicians can apply for Bronze by sending a tape/CD to KH. Bands invited to play in November (for a flat fee) at the Pizza on the Park where members of the city livery vote at the performance. Winner decided by the New Year and presented with their medal at a Summer gig (also at Pizza on Park), with their own band. In 2002 there were five lunch time concerts in Finsbury Circus as part of the City of London Festival 24-28 June, which included a variety of past winners. John Dankworth and Cleo Laine gave two concerts 7 July at Wavendon and 8 July at the Globe Theatre. The CD of the 2000 Jazz at the Globe event was available in 2002.

Other Sources For Funding And Funding Advice

Arts Council England

Alan James, Music Officer, 14 Great Peter Street, London SW1AP 3NQ (020 7333 0100; direct line 020 7973 6494; Fax 020 7973 6590, Alan.james@artscouncil.org.uk) www.artscouncil.org.uk

Arts Council's regional offices are able to provide funding, information and advice to artists and arts organisations

Regional offices

Arts Council London, Andrew McKenzie, Music Officer, 2 Pear Tree Court, London EC1R 0DS (020 7608 6100, Fax 020 7608 4100, Textphone 020 7608 4101) info@artscouncil.org.uk

Arts Council East, John Davidson, Eden House, 48-49 Bateman Street, Cambridge CB2 1LR (01223 454400, Fax 0870 242 1271, Textphone 01223 306893) east@artscouncil.org.uk Areas covered - Bedfordshire, Cambridgeshire, Essex, Hertfordshire, Norfolk and Suffolk and the non-metropolitan authorities of Luton, Peterborough, Southend-on-Sea, and Thurrock

Arts Council East Midlands, James Burkmar,St Nicholas Court, 25-27 Castle Gate, Nottingham NG1 7AR (0115 989 7520 Fax 0115 950 2467) eastmidlands@artscouncil.org.uk Areas covered - Derbyshire, Leicestershire, Lincolnshire (excluding North and North East Lincolnshire), Northamptonshire, Nottinghamshire; and unitary authorities of Derby, Leicester, Nottingham, Rutland

Arts Council North East, Mark Monument, Music Officer, Central Square, Forth Street, Newcastle upon Tyne NE1 3PJ (0191 255 8500, Fax 0191 230 1020, Textphone: 0191 255 8500) northeast@artscouncil.org.uk Areas covered - Durham, Northumberland; metropolitan authorities of Gateshead, Newcastle upon Tyne, North Tyneside, South Tyneside, Sunderland; and unitary authorities of Darlington, Hartlepool, Middlesbrough, Redcar and Cleveland, Stockton-on-Tees

Arts Council North West, Eddie Thomas, Manchester House, 22 Bridge Street, Manchester M3 3AB (0161 834 6644, Fax 0161 834 6969, Textphone 0161 834 9131) and Graphic House, 107 Duke Street, Liverpool L1 4JR (0151 709 0671 Fax 0151 708 9034 Enquiries 0161 834 6644) northwest@artscouncil.org.uk Areas covered - Cheshire, Cumbria, Lancashire; metropolitan authorities of Bolton, Bury, Knowsley, Liverpool, Manchester, Oldham, Rochdale, St Helens, Salford, Sefton, Stockport, Tameside, Trafford, Wigan, Wirral; and unitary authorities of Blackburn with Darwen, Blackpool, Halton, Warrington

Arts Council South East, Trevor Mason, Music Officer, Sovereign House, Church Street, Brighton East SussexBN1 1RA (01273 763 000) southeast@artscouncil.org.uk Music Officer - Trevor Mason. Areas covered - Bournemouth, Buckinghamshire, East Sussex, Hampshire, Isle of Wight, Kent, Oxfordshire, Surrey and West Sussex, the non-metropolitan districts of Bracknell Forest, Brighton and Hove, the Medway Towns, Milton Keynes, Portsmouth, Reading, Slough, Southampton, Swindon, West Berkshire, Wiltshire, Windsor and Maindenhead and Wokingham

Arts Council South West, Moragh Brooksbank, Music Officer, Bradninch Place, Gandy Street, Exeter, Devon EX4 3LS (01392 218188, Fax 01392 229229, Textphone 01392 433503) southwest@artscouncil.org.uk Areas covered: Cornwall, Devon, Dorset, Gloucestershire, Somerset, Wiltshire; unitary authorities of Bath and North East Somerset, Bournemouth, Bristol, North Somerset, Plymouth, Poole, South Gloucestershire, Swindon, Torbay

Arts Council West Midlands, Val Birchall, Music Officer, 82 Granville Street, Birmingham B11 2LH (0121 631 3121, Fax 0121 643 7239, Textphone 0121 643 2815) westmidlands@artscouncil.org.uk Areas covered Shropshire, Staffordshire, Warwickshire, Worcestershire; metropolitan authorities of Birmingham, Coventry, Dudley, Sandwell, Solihull, Walsall, Wolverhampton; and unitary authorities of Herefordshire, Stoke-on-Trent, Telford and Wrekin

Arts Council Yorkshire, Music Officer, 21 Bond Street, Dewsbury, West Yorkshire WF13 1AX (01924 455555, Fax 01924 466522, Textphone 01924 438585) Area covered: North Yorkshire; metropolitan authorities of Barnsley, Bradford, Calderdale, Doncaster, Kirklees, Leeds, Rotherham, Sheffield, Wakefield; and unitary authorities of East Riding of Yorkshire, Kingston upon Hull, North Lincolnshire, North East Lincolnshire, York

South East Music Schemes

Judith Clark, 2 The Oast House, Crouch's Farm, East Hoathly, Lewes, East Sussex BN8 6QX (01825 841 302), judithaclark@fsmail.net

The purpose of the scheme is to help stimulate new work, new ideas and new groups in the South and South East. All genres of music are included: jazz, blues, classical, folk, contemporary, world and traditional. Between three to six groups are selected each year and their work/ideas are marketed to 800 promoters, venues, festivals and educational establishments in the S and SE by a series of newsletters, an interactive website and showcase events.

Incentive grants are offered for up to 10 concerts with each group. Each group/band is appointed to the scheme for a period of two years from the selection date. It aims to encourage promoters to take new music that they may not have previously experienced. The incentive grant lowers the cost of the concert. SEMS also works in collaboration with schools and colleges, Making Music, Youth Music and other agencies.

Candidates are selected initially by an application form, recordings and written references. A percentage of the best applicants are invited to a live audition in February 2003, when the final selection is made. The main area covered by the scheme is for those musicians resident in the South and South East including Berkshire, Hampshire, Kent, Oxfordshire, Surrey, East Sussex, West Sussex. Special consideration is given to musicians who are resident in, or who can demonstrate a connection with, the South and South East. This does not preclude the success of other applications from external groups who provide an essence of the new, unusual and otherwise unavailable. Closing date for applications end December.

Arts Council of Northern Ireland

MacNeice House, 77 Malone Road, Belfast BT9 6AQ (028 9038 5200, 028 9066 1715) www.artscouncil-ni.org.

Arts Council of Northern Ireland and An Chomhairle Ealaion jointly fund a place at the Summer Jazz Institute of Skidmore College (USA) usually held June/July. Open to applicants from Northern Ireland and the Republic of Ireland. Deadline 28 February 2003

Arts Council of Wales

Holst House, 9 Museum Place, Cardiff CF1 3NX (02920 376500) www.ccc-acw.org.uk.

Scottish Arts Council

12 Manor Place, Edinburgh EH3 7DD (0131 225 9833) www.sac.org.uk.

British Council, COA

John Keiffer, Head of Music, 10 Spring Gardens, London SW1A 2BN 020 7389 3087 Fax 020 7389 3088, john.keiffer@britishcouncil.org) www.britishcouncil.org

The British Council promotes educational, cultural and technical cooperation between Britain and other countries. Its work is designed to establish long-term, worldwide partnerships to improve international understanding.

The Music team in the Performing Arts department is the expert link between British music and the Council's global network. They liaise with colleagues to plan, resource, deliver and evaluate high-impact arts projects – tours, education/community programmes, international collaborations, etc. Also works with all forms of music, including jazz.

BC is not a funding body, but occasionally provide some financial assistance to British-based artists who have been invited overseas. The group/musician must be of the highest artistic standard, with an established or emerging national reputation in their field. Proposals must show the strong commitment of promoters or local partners, usually demonstrated by a willingness to cover a substantial proportion of the costs. Acceptance of a proposal depends on the Council's specific aims in that overseas country, the quality of the work in question, and whether funds are available.

There are no application forms and no deadlines, but as much information as possible is needed 12-18 months in advance. This should include a project description and outline itinerary, together with a realistic budget. Proposals should be made by the overseas partner who has issued the invitation and should be sent to their local British Council office. The music project managers based in London, who specialise in particular regions, are available to discuss the proposals

Council for International Education

9-17 St Albans Place London N1 0NX (020 7288 4330 Fax 020 7288 4360)

www.ukcosa.org.uk

Seeks to protect the interests of students from abroad studying in the UK and students from the UK wishing to study abroad. Membership includes all UK universities most further and higher education institutions with international students and student unions. Main area of activity is a specialist advice service offering information and guidance on topics related to international education. Service is mainly used by its member institutions but deals with many thousands of queries from prospective students worldwide on subjects like immigration and employment law, financial aid and regulations on fees and grants. Telephone service Mon-Fri 13.00 to 16.00 (GMT) for students on 020 7107 9922.

Department for Education and Skills

Sanctuary Buildings, Great Smith Street, London SW1P 3BT (020 7925 5000)
www.dfes.gov.uk

Produces a guide to financial support for students – which gives details of grants available from LEAs

Educational Grants Advisory Service

Family Welfare Association, 501-505 Kingsland Road, London E8 4AU (020 7249 6636) www.fwa.org.uk

Sources of financial help. Advice for parents and students on negotiating with LEAs and can provide contact with educational charities.

National Foundation for Youth Music

1 America Street, London SE1 0NE 020 7902 1075, info@youthmusic.org.uk
www.youthmusic.org.uk

Established in 1999 with lottery funding from the Arts Council of England. The intention was to make music making more accessible to children and young people who might not otherwise get a chance. Their funding complements music in the national curriculum by supporting activities held mainly out of school hours. It aims to establish a legacy of music making opportunities, improve the overall standards of music making and prove that music has a positive effect on children and young people by the end of 2005 when their present funding ends.

National Union of Students

Nelson Mandela House, 461 Holloway Road, London N7 6LJ (020 7272 8900)
www.nus.org.uk

Offer information pack that includes grant information, awards and alternative assistance.

PRS Foundation

29/33 Berners Street, London W1P 4AA (020 7580 5544, david.francis@prsf.co.uk)
www.prsf.co.uk

Charitable, non-profit making organisation funded by the Performing Right Society, whose aim is to encourage, promote and sustain music creation and its performance - of all genres and at all levels of activity with financial support. PRS is the UK's largest independent funder solely for new music. Its main aims are to encourage, promote and stimulate the creation and performance of all genres of new music and to help people have a positive experience of new music. Funding schemes include – Composers in Education; Performance Groups; Festivals; Live Connections; Music Creators in Residence; New Works; Organisations; Promoters; Special Projects and scholarships for Post Graduate students.

UCAS

Rosehill, New Barn Lane, Cheltenham, Gloucester GL52 3LA (01242 227788)
www.ucas.com

Clearance house for university places in their scheme (your school has to be a member of scheme). Early applications considered if received by 15 January for the following September intake. Late applications considered up until 30 June for same year. After that, applications go into a pool for late consideration.

www.ucas.com - website has information on clearing vacancies for current academic year, applicant enquiries, course search for next academic year. Advice for students, schools, higher education staff which covers the whole application process with information on courses, finance, deadline dates.

Women in Music

Alison Lea, 7 Tavern Street, Stowmarket, Suffolk IP14 1PJ (01449 673 990 Fax 01449 673 990 info@womeninmusic.org.uk) www.womeninmusic.org.uk

Formed in 1987. National membership organisation. Aims are to promote the awareness of the imbalance that exists between the sexes in the art and science of music and to redress this imbalance; to encourage public awareness of the role and achievements of women in all aspects of music making; to advance, improve and maintain the musical education and career prospects of women to enable women to fulfil their musical potential at all levels; to establish a focus and forum for women's work and achievements in all areas of music. Has developed an archive and information resource, networked and lobbied, organised festivals and events and fund raised.

Second round of funding available to enable the creation of new music by women. A small number of new projects will receive up to £7,000 towards the costs of their work. All styles and genres of music are eligible and WiM invites proposals from composers, performers or promoters or any combination of these.

Main criteria: Projects must be visionary, innovative and radical; raise the profile of women in music; produce new music – they will not fund proposals solely for performance or recording of pre-existing work; culminate in a quality public event – they will not fund proposals for composition of new music without plans for distribution; must contribute to the artistic and/or professional development of those involved – should clearly show how you anticipate the future work and career of all participants to benefit from a WiM award; will attract partnership funding – you need to indicate how you intend to cover the total costs of your project. WiM will not fund proposals which solely rely on their funding support; will take place mainly in the UK with national and/or international distribution – applications for projects based in Scotland, Wales and Northern Ireland as those in England. They will not fund work which mainly takes place outside of the UK or which takes place purely at a local level in UK. Closing Date is 3 August 2002. Contact Clare Adams for an application pack.

Grants awarded through WiM Commissioning Fund which is financially supported by the PRS Foundation and the Esmee Fairbairn Foundation. The commissioning fund is part of the Creative Renewal project funded by the European Social Fund through the EQUAL programme to address issues of labour market inequality in the arts with respect to gender, race and disability.

UK Jazz Related Organisations

Afro Caribbean Music Circuit

Charles Easmon, ACMC House, Unit 5, Ellerslie Square, Lyham Road, London SW2 5DZ (020 7733 8897 Fax 020 7924 9520, info@themusiccircuit.com)

www.themusiccircuit.com

Exists to raise standards in the quality and awareness of music from African, Caribbean and Latin American people, to a national and continental audience. They arrange tours of the highest calibre artists from Africa and the Caribbean, provide education and training activities within a variety of cultural and artistic setting in the UK, work with British based African and Caribbean musicians to forge new partnerships to reach the widest possible audience in UK and Europe. They aim to develop the infrastructure and logistics that will enable the organisation to become a central point for co-ordination of national activities for "live" black music and education on black history through music. They work with Regional Arts Boards, promoters, venues, festivals, local authorities and artists to develop a touring network that meets the needs of promoters and audiences.

Asian Music Circuit

Ground Floor Unit E, West Point, 33/34 Warple Way, London W3 0RG (020 8742 9911 Fax: 020 8749 3948, katerina@amc.org.uk) www.amc.org.uk

The Asian Music Circuit provides a wide variety of music, celebrating cultural identity by focusing on traditional music, developing a new generation of talent, entertaining the public and aiming to inform and educate with recording, videos and exhibitions. As well as presenting and touring world-famous artists, the AMC has also been responsible for the first international tours and are active promoters of the next generation of Indian classical musicians.

They commission new music as an important aspect of their work setting up collaborations such as Zakir Hussain and John McLaughlin and new compositions from UK-based Asian artists. They also manage educational projects for schools and colleges around the country, and present public workshops and lecture-demonstrations by touring artists.

Caber Enterprises (established by Caber Music)

47b Bridge Street, Edinburgh EH21 6AA 0131 653 2203 www.cabermusic.com
Caber Music have developed educational CDs to introduce children to the fun of improvising and jazz and folk music. The CD is accompanied by a explanatory booklet with some ideas for basic improvisation, musical concepts with stories and games. It features some of Scotland's best musicians – Tom and Phil Bancroft, Brian Kellock, Freddie King and Mario Caribe. At the moment support workshops are available in Scotland at schools. This service will shortly be available in England once the necessary adjustments have been made in line with the differences in curriculums between Scotland and England.

Community Music

Alison Tickell, Development Director, 82 Southwark Bridge Road, London SE1 0AS
(020 7633 0550 Fax 020 7261 1133) www.cmonline.org.uk

Dedicated to the creation of new music through structured access and artist development. It works as an alternative to mainstream provision by targeting young people who do not have the opportunity to learn and musicians who do not have recognised qualifications. The music reflects the synergy created by combining learning and opportunity in a creative environment.

Community Music Ltd. (CM) is the largest independent music access project in London. Formed in 1983, to give young people the chance to develop skills, accreditation and employment within a dynamic, inclusive and creative environment.

Through structured access, training and professional development offer a number of different pathways to learning and accreditation including National Vocational Qualifications, Open College credits, Open University and City and Guilds certification. Also have an extensive outreach programme with young people around London, running workshops on estates, in special schools, youth and disability centres and training projects - anywhere young people meet who want to make music.

Community Music East

70 King Street, Norwich NR1 1PG (01603 628 367 Fax 01603 767 863,
enquiries@cme.org.uk) www.cme.org.uk

Not specifically a jazz organisation but it has been associated with various jazz and percussion workshops. It was established in 1985 to develop and run programmes for a range of disadvantaged people. They also train practising musicians in the necessary skills and techniques to become workshop tutors. Develop core work with specific user groups, as well as running a public programme of workshops. It is developing a Community Music Centre and recording studio for Norfolk and Norwich.

The Music Life Project and workshops are targeted at young people in disadvantaged communities in Great Yarmouth, North Walsham, areas of Norwich, Thetford and Wayland. Young people are able to write music and create their own music using a range of instruments such as guitars, drums and keyboards. This enables them to develop confidence, team building and communication skills. Younger children are using rhythm and percussion instruments to create stories and develop listening skills.

Duke Ellington Society UK

Derek Else, 47 Yoxley Drive, Illford, Essex IG2 6PX, (derekelse@desuk.fsnet.co.uk)
www.dukes-place.co.uk

Membership Society founded in 1994 to promote wider appreciation of the music of Duke Ellington and Billy Strayhorn.

Free/Improvised music site, based Sheffield University

www.shef.ac.uk/misc/rec/ps/efi/ehome.html

European Free/Improvised music site – not strictly jazz but contains excellent biographies and discographies of improvising musicians and very comprehensive independent record label list. Peter Stubley regularly updates news items.

JazzDev – The Jazz Development Trust

Jonathan Abbott, 18 Carthew Road, London W6 0DX (020 8741 1752, jonathan@jazzdev.demon.co.uk) www.jazzdev.org

JazzDev exists to improve the position of British Jazz and jazz in Britain, by developing the audience for jazz, through greater jazz access, participation and education for the general public, young people and music teachers, decision makers, opinion formers and the media.

In September 2000 JazzDev organised a jazz industry conference in Manchester to present a study of the audience and potential audiences for jazz in Birmingham, Leeds, Liverpool and Manchester. It included the profile of the jazz audience and barriers to attendance with ways of overcoming these. In association with Arts Council of England and the Regional Arts Boards the results of the study with development ideas were presented in a series of seminars. Intended to be of interest to jazz club organisers, promoters and would be promoters, arts centre programmers, venue managers, musicians intending to organise their own gigs. They have been tied into festivals or jazz related events. In 2002 these were at Cheltenham May 3 at jazz festival, June 29 Milton Keynes at the Stables at Wavendon, July 15 Wigan Jazz festival, August 23 Coventry Jazz Festival, September 18 Maidstone Pizza Express, September 21 Lancaster Jazz Festival, Darlington Arts Centre. Panellists include Tony Dudley-Evans (Birmingham Jazz and Cheltenham Jazz Festival), John Holland (New Jazz 5, Lincoln), Lucy Power (Manchester Jazz Festival) and Jonathan Abbott (JazzDev).

Jazz Piano Teachers' Association

(webbmadd@britishlibrary.net) www.jazzpianoteachersassociation.org.uk

Robert Webb has founded an association for jazz piano teachers. Publishes newsletter on 15 February and November each year, the Jazz Piano Teachers' Association (JAPTA) welcomes enquiries from ISM members with a special interest in jazz piano - from either experienced jazz piano teachers or from classical piano teachers intending to convert to the jazz syllabus.

Jazz Research Network

www.jazzservices.org.uk/extras

Registration form on website or contact education@jazzservices.org.uk

The network was set up to foster and coordinate research and scholarly activity in jazz and related musics. To act as a forum for the exchange and dissemination of ideas and developments in jazz research. To liaise as appropriate with other jazz organisations and promote collaboration between jazz researchers. To seek recognition for jazz research by government and statutory bodies. To foster and maintain contact with other related research organisations.

Jazz in Scotland

15 Windsor Square, Penicuik, Midlothian, Scotland EH26 8ES (0196 8679 299, Fax: 0196 8679 299, admin@jazz-in-scotland.co.uk) www.jazz-in-scotland.co.uk

website for all aspects of jazz activity in Scotland listing gigs, venues, musicians, education.

National Youth Jazz Orchestra of Scotland

Mike Hardy, 13 Somerset Place, Glasgow G3 7JT (0141 332 8311, mikehardy@nyos.co.uk) www.nyos.co.uk

The NYOS provides a comprehensive and cohesive network for young music students to develop their musical skills in jazz, with an emphasis on contemporary and modern jazz. The courses and workshops are open to students of varying degrees of ability and the extensive outreach workshop programme extends from beginners to advanced music students. It also runs a summer jazz course.

Jazz Umbrella

Peter Watson, Membership Secretary, c/o The Crypt, 81 Camberwell Church Street, Camberwell, London SE5 8RB (020 7701 1016, info@jazzumbrella.com) www.jazzumbrella.com

Jazz Umbrella is a musicians' collective with a 250-strong membership. Their main aims are to promote jazz events and workshops in the London area and thereby promote awareness and understanding of jazz and improvised music. The programming, fundraising and workshop organisation are undertaken by the membership. Organise Friday night gigs at the Crypt in Camberwell.

Ken Colyer Trust

John Long, 83 Beaconsfield Road, Langley Vale, Epsom, Surrey KT18 www.kencolyertrust.org

To preserve and protect the memory of Ken Colyer and his music. See website for Archives, Library, Membership, Band, Trust events, Fund raising and their 'Special relationship' with New Orleans.

London Musicians Collective

Ed Baxter, Unit 3.6 Third Floor, Lafone House, London SE1 3HN (020 7403 1922, Fax: 020 7403 1880, lmc@lmcltd.demon.co.uk) www.l-m-c.org.uk

Musicians Collective for Experimental and Improvised music. Promote at a range of venues with an annual festival. Magazine - *Resonance*. From April 2002 for a year have been given a broadcasting licence on the 104.4FM waveband, broadcasting from Bankside London SE1 with a radius of 5 kilometres - covering central London.

Serious

Chapel House, 18 Hatton Place, London EC1N 8RU 020 7405 9900 (020 7405 Fax: 020 7405 9911) info@serious.org.uk www.serious.org.uk

Known as the main jazz promoters in the UK working in the largest London venues they organise the November London Jazz Festival plus seasonal programmes at the South Bank. Since the days of the Camden and Bracknell Festivals (produced by Serious Productions) they have created programmes of workshops.

In 2001 they facilitated a residency with the Lincoln Centre Jazz Orchestra and Wynton Marsalis at the Barbican (London) with workshops and lectures. When the orchestra was on tour, in Newcastle, Leicester and Birmingham, the musicians gave Big Band workshops for youth jazz orchestras.In 2002 Serious organised a national workshop tour with Courtney Pine and two DJs combining jazz and hip-hop. Courtney Pine was also part of the 'Count Yourself In', an education tour run in tandem with 'On Track', a national concert tour. 'Dubbing the Jazz' started in 2000 and is still running as a series of DJ workshops in London boroughs.

Tomorrow's Warriors

Unit 1, 73 Canning Road, Harrow HA3 7SP (Tel 020 8424 2807 Fax 020 8861 5371, jazz@tomorroswarriors.org.uk) www.tomorrowswarriors.org.uk

Established in 1992 by Jazz Warriors double bassist - Gary Crosby. They have now received core funding until 2004.

Provide apprenticeships and performance/educational workshops for young jazz musicians and organise and coordinate concerts as well as other public performances by young jazz musicians nationally and internationally.

It is an artist resource for other arts organisations and music industry professionals wishing to collaborate and/or work with jazz musicians and a local, national and international information/co-ordination/advisory resource for promoters, musicians, arts organisations, production companies, print/broadcast media, venues and others (for example, enterprise training centres).

Since its inception, Tomorrow's Warriors has helped many young musicians to launch successful professional careers in jazz and the organisation is now widely regarded as one of the key organisations in the UK for the professional development of young jazz musicians.

Tomorrow's Warriors exists to encourage and develop young people aspiring to become professional jazz musicians. This is achieved through the provision of performance workshops and informal jam sessions held at a variety of venues throughout the country. Not only does this enable young musicians to have an opportunity to work with professional musicians, but also it provides a relaxed environment and a superb performance platform on which individuals can build confidence, improve technique, and network with a broad group of people working in the music industry. A hugely popular and successful project, Tomorrow's Warriors has spawned a number of award winning artists including Gary Crosby's Nu Troop (Best International Ensemble 1998 - Jazz a Vienne, France), J-Life (European Young Jazz Artist 1997 - Intl Jazz Federation; Best Young Ensemble 1998/Best Young Vocalist 1998 - Perrier Jazz Awards) and Denys Baptiste (An Album Of The Year 1999 - Technics Mercury Music Prize; Best Jazz Act 1999 - MOBO Awards)

Other UK Music Related Organisations

British Academy of Composers/Songwriters
26 Berners Street, London W1T 3LR (020 7636 2929, info@britishacademy.com) www.britishacademy.com

The Academy represents the interests of music writers across all genres providing professional and artistic advice. It administers a number of events, including the Ivor Novello Awards and publishes a quarterly magazine – *The Works.*

The organisation is an amalgamation of the Association of Professional Composers (APC), the British Academy of Songwriters, Composers and Authors (BASCA) and the Composers' Guild of Great Britain.

Largest composer/songwriter organisation in the world, representing over 3,000 UK music writers.

British Music Information Centre
10 Stratford Place, London W1N 9AE (0171 499 8567 (12-5pm), Fax: 0171 499 4795) www.bmic.co.uk

A resource centre for contemporary classical composers and their works.

British Music Rights
26 Berners Street, London W1T 3LR (020 7306 4446) www.bmr.org
Established in 1997 to represent the composer, songwriter and music publisher members of the Academy, MPA, MCPS and PRS.

Federation of Music Services
6 Berwick Courtyard, Berwick St Leonards, Salisbury, Wilts SP3 5SN (01747 820 042, fms@musiced.fsnet.co.uk) www.federationmusic.org.uk

Approximately 127 Local Education Authority Music Services are members of the Federation representing some 500,000 pupils and 10,000 teachers

The Federation organises professional development courses at both regional and national level, also less formal occasions for sharing expertise and experience

Generator North East
Black Swan Court, 69 Westgate Road, Newcastle NE1 1SG (0191 245 0099 Fax 0191 245 0144, mail@generator.org.uk) www.generator.org.uk

Music Business advice and information for the Rock, Pop and Indie sector. Website covers contacts for national media, A and R, NE studio, agent, promoters, support organisations, UK region touring information packs, making your own record, dealing with the media, marketing, live gig tips. Also has an extensive organisation list for pop, rock and Indie under the network title of META www.metamusic.org.uk

International Intelligence on Culture

4 Baden Place, Crosby Row, London Bridge, London SE1 1YW (020 7403 7001, enquiry@intelculture.org) www.intelculture.org

The organisation has two main roles – one is the provider of a free enquiry service, and the other is as the national filter/contact point for a European Foundation which provides grants to the cultural sector.

International Intelligence on Culture is a dynamic consultancy which brings together a highly-experienced multi-national group of experts to work with and for the international cultural sector. Activities include: policy intelligence; research; consultancy; training; and information services. There is an email, journal and web-based subscriber service International Cultural Compass will keep you up-to-date with international developments, policies and programmes relating to culture. There is a free enquiry service for advice and information on international cultural policies, contacts, funding etc.

The European Cultural Foundation (ECF) is an independent non-profit organisation that promotes cultural cooperation in Europe. Grants are available under each of its three priorities for specific activities under four categories: individual travel grants; project grants; evaluation and communication grants and partnership grants for advocacy projects. Applications should be submitted online via the ECF website www.eurocult.org. Enquiries can be directed to the UK Committee.

Making Music – National Federation of Music Societies

7-15 Roseberry Avenue, London EC1R 4SP (0870 872 3300) www.makingmusic.org.uk

Represent and support amateur and semi-professional music groups, including choirs, orchestras and music promoters, throughout the United Kingdom. Provide a comprehensive range of artistic and administrative services, development and training opportunities. Making Music also lobbies on behalf of members to national and local government and other agencies. December 2001, new Making Music Eastern scheme (with funding from RALP) which will run for 3 years – divided into two overlapping 18-month phases. Aim to increase the level of contemporary music promoted and performed by voluntary music groups in the Eastern Region. All genres of music. Project seeking to select two artists/ensembles for touring engagements between January/July 2003 and January/July 2004. Deadline for application end of January 2002.

MCPS/PRS

29/33 Berners Street, London W1P 4AA (020 7306 4003) www.mcps-prs-alliance.co.uk

These two organisations remain separate in terms of membership and the rights they licence. Music Copyright Protection Society (MCPS) collects and distributes 'mechanical' royalties to its composer and music publisher members. These are generated from the recording of the music onto to many different formats. They publish an excellent booklet *On the Right Track* which is an introduction to the Music Business. It covers Creation, The Next Step, Production, Manufacture, Marketing and Distribution and Protection.

The Performance Right Society (PRS) collects licence fees for the public performance and broadcast of musical works. It distributes this money to its members – writers and publishers of music.

Merseyside Music Development Agency

70 Hope Street, Liverpool, Merseyside L1 9EB (0151 709 2202, 0151 709 2205, info@mmda.org.uk) www.mmda.org.uk

This is a free music enterprise service (not particularly jazz) which works with people who have music projects and businesses to help them to develop and achieve their action plans.

Information – they hold in hard copy and on-line information about the music sector – industry contacts, local service providers, market research, availability of training, sources of financial assistance available.

Business Advice and Guidance – MMDA employs experienced business counsellors who can help develop a viable music business idea. Advise on finance, marketing, personnel, operations, property management etc and can, where appropriate refer you to specialist solicitors/accountants.

Financial Assistance – offer a financial packaging service which helps identify and draw down grant and loan funding.

META – see Generator

Metier

Glyde House, Glydegate, Bradford, West Yorkshire BD5 0BQ (01274 738 800)

This is the main office; there is also one in London:33 Southampton Street, Covent Garden, London WC2E 7HE

This is the training organisation for the arts and entertainment industry – this includes vocational training and education. It develops and implements NVQs (National Vocational Qualifications) and SVQs (Scottish Vocational Qualifications) It also researches the labour market and skills needs; develops website guidance, learning and information; develops programmes in modern apprenticeships and foundation degrees; provides career information at both entry level and for graduates; provides information on best training practice. Their remit includes arts administration and management; arts development and teaching; performing arts; technical stagecraft.

MusicEd

www.musiced.org.uk

Not specifically a jazz site but compiled with the demands of the National Curriculum for Music in mind. Teacher notes available on most features for use in classroom, specialist articles and information about music services nationwide including 'The Power of Music' - study by Professor Sue Hallam of the strength of music's influence on our lives. Did you get paid last month? a look at copyright issues, Composing and improvising in the classroom, a booklet published by the National Association of Music Education, Arts education in secondary schools: effects and effectiveness - summary of the key findings

Musicians' Union

London Office, 60-62 Clapham Road, London SW9 0JJ (020 7840 5533, info@musiciansunion.org.uk) www.musiciansunion.org.uk

The Musicians' Union (MU) is the only trade union solely representing musicians. With over 40,000 members, it is the largest musicians' organisation in Europe. The

MU has members in all areas of music; performing, writing, arranging and teaching. It is affiliated to the various trade union groups in the entertainment industry, and is a member of the Performers' Alliance, the National Music Council and other bodies in arts and entertainment.

The services offered to members include sickness and accident benefit, a media rights collection and distribution service and a music business and legal advisory service.

Structure - The Union has 120 local branches and an elected executive committee; Union policy is decided by a delegate conference every two years. There are specialist sections within the Union, such as Session Musicians, the Arrangers, Composers and Copyist sections, the Jazz section, the Music Education and Teaching section, as well as consultative committees for BBC Orchestras, Symphony Orchestras, etc.

National Music Council

Fiona Penny, 60/62 Clapham Road, London SW9 0JJ (020 7820 9992) www.music-council.org

The NMC was set up as the UK arm of the International Music Council - a UNESCO body. It has a Royal Charter and broadly aims to act as a coordinating body for musical activity in the UK.

P@MRA

Richard Steele, 3rd Floor, 161 Borough High Street, London SE1 1HR (020 7940 0400, office@pamra.org.uk) www.pamara.org.uk

Organisation of 'Performing Artists' Media Rights Association' the UK's collecting society for performers, which means they pay out money to qualifying performers for the broadcast of their recorded performances. The right to receive royalities for recorded performances was only introduced into UK law in 1996. For more detailed information check their website.

SPNM – Society for the Promotion of New Music

18-20 Southwark Street, London SE1 1TJ (020 7407 1640, jill@spnm.org.uk) www.soundinventors.org.uk

Brings the work of composers at the start of their careers to the attention of a wider public through concerts, workshops, lectures and seminars with top professional musicians throughout the UK and Europe

Visiting Arts

Nelson Fernadez, Bloomsbury House, 74-77 Great Russell Street, London WC1B 3DA Tel 020 72911600 Fax 020 7291 1616 email information@visitingarts.org.uk www.visitingarts.org.uk

Visiting Arts is a joint venture of the Arts Council of England, the Scottish Arts Council, the Arts Council of Wales, the Arts Council of Northern Ireland, the Crafts Council, the Foreign and Commonwealth Office and the British Council.

Visiting Arts promotes and facilitates the inward flow of foreign arts into England, Scotland, Wales and Northern Ireland.

UK Archives

Archive Museum of Black History

Sam Walker, Director, 378 Cold Harbour Lane, Brixton, London SW9 8LF (020 7738 4591, yejide@archivemuseumblackheritage.org.uk) www.archivemuseumblackheritage.org.uk

Not specifically jazz but it does have some jazz and Calypso 78s. The collection is, at the moment, somewhat ad-hoc and includes 19th century photos, work by Sam Coleridge Taylor, sculptures, newspaper cuttings. Researchers welcome by appointment.

American Music at Exeter University

Julie Gray, Archivist, Exeter University Library, Stocker Road, Exeter, Devon EX4 4PT (01392 263860)

Open 9.00 – 5.30pm week days during term time and is open to outside researchers as well as the students of the University. The collection forms part of the Audio-Visual department in the University library which has 123,000 slides and 10,500 videos with seminar rooms, DVD and editing suites. University runs 14 film courses. The American Music collection covers the full range of American music; American Indian, Country, Cajun, Zydeco, shaker, salsa, soul, rock, punk and classical, but the main specialisation is jazz and blues. Jazz artists particularly well represented are Duke Ellington, Art Tatum, Thelonius Monk and Miles Davis. The collection also includes a collection of rare early Blues recordings. There are thousands of recordings on vinyl, cassette and CD. The recordings are supported by an excellent book collection, a wide variety of American music periodicals, and a clippings file on American musicians from the 1950s to now.

The founder of the collection – Nick Eastwood – left in the summer 2002, after 32 years. It is the biggest music resource in Europe and the fastest growing. It is hoped that the BMus Jazz course currently running at Truro College, will relocate to Exeter in the next 3 years.

BBC Written Archive Centre

Caversham Park, Reading, Berks RG4 8TZ (01189 486 281)

Open Wed/Friday 9.45 to 5pm with an appointment. Store information on microfich, film, card index, files. Includes written jazz material from 1935 to now.

British Institute of Jazz Studies

Graham Langley, 17 The Chase, Edgcombe Park, Crowthorne, Berks RG45 6HT (01344 775669)

Founded in the 60s this has one of the largest reference collections of jazz literature in the country, including books, magazines, programmes, newspaper cuttings for use by students and researchers.

The strength of the collection is the holding of British Magazines dating back to the 30s and estimated to be over 80% complete. It is not funded and is non-profit making body, incorporated under the Charities Act to further education and interest in jazz and popular music throughout the British Isles.

Make an appointment to visit the collection. The Institute has a large collection of duplicate jazz literature available for sale - in the region of 400 books and many magazines. Contact Graham on his email for lists.

EMI Record Archive
Central Research Lab, Dawley Road, Hayes, Middlesex UB3 1HH1 (020 8848 2000)

Open 9-5pm by appointment indicating the nature of your research, Tuesday to Thursday (inclusive). Every EMI record ever made since 1897. Items not listed on a database but by card index system with catalogue numbers. This now includes Blue Note and Verve labels.

Institute of Popular Music
Dr Sara Cohen, Liverpool University, Roxby Building, PO BOX 147, Liverpool, Merseyside L69 3BX, sara@liv.ac.uk)

The collection is part of the archive of the Institute of Popular music which is part of the University of Liverpool but is accessible to the public for consultation by prior arrangement.

The archive is in excess of 35,000 LPs of which jazz forms about about 4,000 vinyl records, dating from the 1950s to the 1980s. There is also a smaller collection of blues LPs and a significant collection (approx 5,000) of 78s of British Dance Band music of the 1930s. Selection of discographies, back issues of *The Wire, Jazz Monthly* and *Jazz Journal*.

Donations gratefully received.

John R T Davies Vintage Jazz Archive
1 Walnut Tree Cottage, 53 Britwell Road, Burnham, Bucks (0162 860 4811)

Over 100,000 sides of jazz recordings. The earliest 1898 through to the present day, but with the main emphasis on the period between the wars, ie 1918 to 1939.

The collection is available to archivists, researchers and musicians.

John Davies has 50 years of experience in restoring jazz recordings and working with small re-issue labels.

Leeds College of Music Archive
3 Quarry Hill, Leeds LS, Gwyneth Allatt – Librarian (g.allatt@lcm.ac.uk)

Launched in 1987 the archive was initially started with their own small collection of material, but it has now attracted a large number of donations, to the point where they are looking for more spacious accommodation.

The balance of the collection is approximately 65% jazz to 35% popular music.

As the CLCM has always been at the forefront of education in jazz and popular music (see Education Section for courses) this resource is appropriately placed but it is also available to the public, with prior arrangement.

National Sound Archive
Andrew Simons, Jazz Curator, British Library, 96 Euston Road, London NW1 2BD (020 7412 7434, andrew.simons@bkl.uk)
www.bl.uk/collections/sound-archive/jazz.html

The Jazz Section of the NSA holds published recordings in all formats, unpublished live and studio sessions, broadcasts and jazz oral histories. This is complemented by a reference library in the Humanities 2 Reading Room, which includes artist and record company discographies, periodicals, record company catalogues, and CADENSA, the catalogue to the archived sounds. Further, the Listening Service plays anything free of charge, by appointment. For jazz enquiries, contact either Andrew Simons (0207-412-7434) or Paul Wilson (0207-412-7446).

A Readers Pass is available at Reader Admissions, as you enter the building. You will need to bring a form of ID and provide specific reasons why you require access to British Library materials for your research, which are not available elsewhere. Such research materials might include runs of the *Melody Maker* or *Radio Times*, or the CADENSA catalogue and Listening Service.

Hours: Monday 10-8pm; Tuesday to Thursday 9.30-8pm; Friday/Saturday 9.30-5pm.

The National Sound Archive also has ties with the National Jazz Foundation Archive at Loughton Public Library and the British Institute of Jazz Studies, which also have extensive book and periodical collections.

NSA produce a bulletin, 'Playback', which covers new additions and developments.

National Jazz Foundation Archive

David Nathan, Jazz Librarian, Loughton Central Library, Traps Hill, Loughton, Essex IG10 1HD (020 8502 0181)

Opened in 1988, the National Jazz Foundation Archive, was the brainchild of Digby Fairweather - jazz musician and broadcaster.

The intention, right from the beginning, was to form a national archive which could accommodate and positively encourage the donation of collections of jazz material for study by researchers - from TV companies to students!!

Digby Fairweather took the original idea to Jazz Services and with their involvement, a committee was formed.

The collection is housed at Loughton Central Library with Essex County Council providing staff and buying all newly published jazz books, as well as most of British Jazz Magazines. The Archive has grown with bequests/donations from Brian Priestley, Chips Chipperfield, George Webb and the late Charles Fox amongst many others. On permanent loan is John Blandfords' bound collection of *Melody Maker* 1926-41, making a complete run up to 1981. As well as books and magazines, the Archive holds fanzines, programmes, photographs and other memorabilia.

The archive now has a permanent jazz archivist - David Nathan, who works at the archive four mornings a week.

Hours: Monday/Tuesday/Wednesday/Friday 10-1pm

Women In Jazz

Jen Wilson, Director, Room 1-3 First Floor, Queens Buildings, Cumbrian Place, Maritime Quarter, Swansea SA1 1TW (01792 456 666, jenjazzarchive@aol.com) www.jazzsite.co.uk/wja

The Women's Jazz Archive re-launched in February 2002 as Women in Jazz. It is the only archive in the UK specialising in women's jazz music. It is a valuable resource centre for researchers, students and the general public wishing to increase their knowledge of British women jazz musicians and singers.

The Archive contains oral history tapes, records, CDs and cassettes relating to women jazz musicians and a growing library of books, catalogues, publications, sheet music and indexes. The Archive is indebted to the Calouste Gulbenkian Foundation, Swansea Leisure Services, PRS and the Welsh Arts Council, with additional grant assistance from the Foundation of the Sport and The Arts.

The Women's Jazz Archive opened officially on June 26th 1993 with the Crissy Lee Big Band and contributions and donations are increasing on an almost weekly basis.

Recommended Jazz Reference Books

Jazz History Books

Jazz Styles, History and Analysis. Mark Gridley. Prentice Hall. ISBN 0-13-509134-9 voted best jazz history book by the (8,000) members of International Association for Jazz Educators

Early Jazz. Gunther Schuller OUP ISBN 0-19-504043-0

The Swing Era. Gunther Schuller OUP ISBN 0-19-504312-X

Hear Me Talkin' To Ya. Nat Shapiro and Nat Hentoff. Penguin, 1962. Old, but wonderful.

Arranging the Score. Portraits of the Great Arrangers. Gene Lees. Cassell 2000 ISBN 0-304-70488-1

Lost Chords. White Musicians and their Contribution to Jazz, 1915-1945. Richard M. Sudhalter. OUP 1999. ISBN 0-19—3505585 Award winning, excellent.

The Oxford Companion to Jazz. Bill Kirchner. Oxford University Press 2000. ISBN 0 19 512510 X

The New Grove Dictionary of Jazz. Barry Kernfeld. A new edition of this is about to be published.

Music is my Mistress Ellington, Edward Kennedy 'Duke'.1980. New york: Da Capo.

Miles Davis: A Biography. Ian Carr. 1984. New York: Quill.

Jazz Styles Gridley, Mark C. 1985. Englewood Cliffs NJ: Prentice Hall.

As Serious As Your Life Valerie Wilmer, 1977. London: Quartet.

Harmony and Theory

Harmony With Lego Bricks. Conrad Cork. Tadley Ewing Publications. ISBN 0-96515795-3-3

The Jazz Theory Book. Mark Levine. Sher Music. ISBN 1-883217-04-0 Thorough compendium of jazz information and theory, but with no guidance on improvising.

The Jazz Piano Book. Mark Levine. Sher Music

Jazz Theory and Practice. Lawn and Hellmer. Wadsworth. ISBN 0-534-19596-2

The Lydian Chromatic Concept of Tonal Organisation. George A Russell. 1959. New York: Concept

Jazz Keyboard Harmony by Phil DeGreg. Aebersold

20th Century Harmony. Vincent Persichetti.

Practical

A Method for Developing Improvisational Technique. David Baker. 1977. DB Workshop Publications. Chicago. There are innumerable other titles in this series - many of them very useful. For all instruments. Develop technique and aural ability simultaneously.

Metamorphosis- Transformation of the Jazz Solo. Sam Most. 1980. California: Century Music. Examples of how a jazz solo can be transformed step by step, using chord tones, 3rds, 4ths, etc. Good models for learning for all instruments.

Modern Chord Progressions. California : Ted, Greene.1976. Dale F. Zdenek. For guitarists wanting to really explore chord progression and voicings.

Ear Training for Improvisors- A Total Approach. Thom D Mason. 1986. California: Alfred Publications.

Ear training using 'sol fa'. Good for developing interval knowledge and aural memory.

Handbook of Chord Substitutions. Andy, Laverne.1991. New York : Ekay Music. Excellent outline of different ways to create and use chord substitutions. Written for piano, but useful to all instrumentalists.

Interaction - Opening Up the Jazz Ensemble, Graham Collier. 1995. Tubingen: Advance Music.

Jazz Workshop - The Blues. Graham Collier.1988. London : Universal Edition. Both books are very useful for practical workshops or rehearsals with ensembles.

Super Chops - Jazz Guitar Technique in 20 weeks. Howard Roberts. !978. Washington: Playback Music. If you can stick to it, this really works, and can quite easily be adapted for any instrument.

Chord Melody. Howard Roberts.1972. Washington: Playback Music. Good introduction to a wide range of chord melody techniques most useful to guitarists only.

Thesaurus of Scales and Melodic Patterns. Nicolas Slonimsky. 1947. New York : Coleman – Ross. Inspirational scales and melodic fragments to build solos and compositions from. Used by Coltrane et al.

Jamey Aebersold Series of Play Along records and books (at least 80). Very thorough and effective in the 'right hands'. Beginners to advanced.

Improvising

How To Improvise - A Guide to Practising Improvisation by Hal Crook published by Advance. Quite simply the best book written about practising jazz.

Ready, Aim Improvise! Exploring the Basics of Improvisation. Hal Crook published Advance. Excellent and comprehensive explanation of ingredients, skills, and processes.

Musical Improvisation- It's Nature and Practice in Music. Derek. Bailey, 1980. Ashbourne England and Englewood Cliffs N J: Prentice Hall.

Thinking in Jazz - The Infinite Art Of Improvisation. Paul F Berliner. 1994. Chicago University Press.

Ways of the Hand: The organisation of Improvised Conduct. David. Sudnow. 1978. Cambridge: Harvard University Press.

Creative Improvisation. Roger. Dean. 1989. Milton Keynes: Open University Press.

Improvisation - Methods and Models In Generative Processes in Music by Jeff Pressing. 1988. Ed. John Sloboda. Oxford: Clarendon.

Teaching Jazz

The Teaching of Jazz. Jerry Coker. Publisher - Advance
Thorough pedagogical explanation of a North American Jazz Programme
The Inner Game of Music. Green and Gallwey. Pan Books
Popular handbook of teaching and learning strategies (employing "Inner Game" theory that 'performance = potential minus interference.' Good chapter on instructions and language).

Search And Reflect John Stevens. Community Music (out of print).
Work book containing 'warm-up' activities, plans for group composition and collective improvisation.

The Sounding Symbol. George Odam. Stanley Thornes
Good practice in the classroom. Relating key educational wisdom to the practicalities of music making. Especially relevant to improvisors and composers.

Accelerated Learning in Practice. Alistair Smith. Network Educational Press
Easy to read with a work book for teachers presenting a number of strategies based on current knowledge of the brain.

Jazz in the Classroom by Eddie Harvey. Published by Boosey and Hawkes
Teacher's Book and CD ISMN: M060113765
One of the most widely used resources for Key Stage 2 - 3 and GCSE. New edition of the teacher's book includes an audio CD, providing backing tracks for group activities and examples of jazz styles and instruments, replacing the previously available cassette.

Sources for Publications

Jazzwise Publications, 2b Gleneagle Mews, Ambelside Avenue, London SW16 6AE
020 8664 7222 (office tel) www.jazzwise.com (internet) Wide range of books, Fake Books and Real Books, Play alongs, Orchestrations, DVDs, Videos. On-line purchasing available.

Associated Board of Royal Schools of Music 24 Portland Place, London W1B 1LU
020 7467 8283 www.abrsm.ac.uk Jazz Piano, Jazz Ensembles, Jazz Horns exam books and CDs. On-line shopping available.

Sheet Music

Boosey and Hawkes Music Publishers Ltd, 295 Regent Street, London W1B 2JH 020 7580 2060 (office tel) 020 7580 5815 (hire library) www.boosey.com (internet) Very good website where sheet music can be downloaded to your computer. Also have teaching materials available.

Stanza Music (NYJO) 11 Victor Road, Harrow, Middlesex HA2 6PT 020 8863 2717 (office tel) bill.ashton@virgin.net (email) www.nyjo.org.uk

*All current National Youth Jazz Orchestra repertoire; Non-current Big Band arrangements from NYJO's early days, including easier mate*rial suitable for schools; Small Band Arrangements; Trombone Band Arrangements; Saxophone Arrangements; Arrangements for trumpets, clarinets, guitars

Arranging

Inside the Score. Rayburn Wright. Kendor.

Miscellaneous

Drawing On The Right Side Of The Brain. Betty Edwards. Harper Collins
Although written for artists, this book provides practical experiences in aligning with the Right Brain

Free Play - Improvisation in Life and Art. Stephen Nachmanovitch Tarcher. Putnam.
Profound and insightful treatise on the deeper elements of improvisation, the internal dynamics of creating, discipline, inspiration and practice.

Conferences

International Association for Jazz Educators (IAJE)

IAJE, Chris Whitmore, PO BOX 724, 2803 Claflin Road, 66505 Manhattan, Kansas, USA (00 +1 785 776 8744 Fax:00 +1 785 776 6190, chrisw@iaje.org)
www.iaje.org

January 21st to 24th 2004 at the New York Hilton and Sheraton hotels

2003 was the 30th conference and the first event to be held outside of the USA, in Toronto. The conference is a gathering of IAJE members from all parts of the USA as well as internationally and includes some of the biggest names in jazz through to college bands. Everything from seminars and master classes to a large trade exhibition of published music parts and tuition CDs and details of University jazz courses throughout the States. Concerts take place throughout the day, spread across a variety of locations, utilising the conference facilities at large hotels to accommodate the 7 to 8,000 attenders. The intention is to provide a place and time for those involved in jazz education and players to meet and exchange ideas and knowledge.

International Association of Schools of Jazz (IASJ)

IASJ, Walter Turkenburg, Service Bureau, J van Stolberglaan 1, 2595 CA The Hague, Netherlands (+31 70 315 1400 Fax: +31 70 315 1518 (fax) servicebureau@iasj.com)
www.iasj.com

28th to 30th October 2003 at Royal Conservatory in the Hague.

2003 will be the first Jazz Education conference held by the IASJ in Europe and will be combined with organisations annual meeting for its members. The annual meeting has a programme of 6 groups, all with an international mix, who rehearse and perform. The conference will not include student 'combos' but will cover topics like – 'The value of Play-alongs'; 'The use of Real Books'; 'Top down versus Peer-to Peer teaching'; 'Jazz education and the new media'.

JYVASKYLA Summer Jazz Conference

University of Jyvaskyla, Department of Music, PO BOX 35 (M) Finland 40014 +358 14 26 01 361 Fax:+358 14 26 01 331 sjulin@cc.jyu.fi

5-7th June 2003 at University of Jyvaskyla. Conference language is English. Keynote speaker Dr Barry Kernfeld (USA) editor of the New Grove Dictionary of Jazz. His papers are Pop Song Piracy; a History of Fake Books and America's First Criminal Copyright Trials; the Making of the Real Book. Topics for the conference are 'Ethnic Influences in Jazz'; 'Jazz and World Music in Music Education'; 'Copyright and Piracy Questions'; 'Jazz Pedagogy'. The conference is held simultaneously with the Summer Jazz Festival.

Leeds Jazz Educators Conference

Leeds College of Music, 3 Quarry Hill, Leeds

In 2003 held 4 and 5 April at Leeds College of Music. 2003 focused on two main themes – 'Jazz a Way of Life' looking at the influence of jazz on other aspects of culture and society and 'Jazz in Step' exploring the close relationship between jazz music and dance. The conference consists of two intensive days of performances, workshops, talks and discussions. It features papers with a strong practical and educational emphasis, from people involved in the study of jazz, whether as lecturers at Universities or Music colleges, post graduate students, teachers or writers. High profile contributors from Europe and the USA included Nicholas Cook, Krin Gabbard, Robert O'Meally and Janice Wilson. Jazz Services hosted a presentation by Charles Beale – professor of Jazz piano and jazz history at the Royal College of Music and the person responsible for leading the development of the Associated Board (ABRSM) Jazz syllabus. Performers included Christine Tobin (voice) Jason Yarde (sax), Andrea Vicari (piano), Dave O'Higgins (sax) and the Jazzcotech Dancers, Sonora del Norte y Sud, Omar Puente, Roberto Pla.

MODAL

Celia Bell, Modal Coordinator, c/o Leisure and Community Services, Isabella Street, Nottingham NG1 6AT (0870 243 0278) celia@modaluk.uklinux.net www.modal.co.uk

11 to 14 September 2003 at Lakeside Arts Centre, Nottingham, East Midlands, UK

A convention (rather than a conference) for music 'outside of the mainstream' incorporating topics of interest and concern to those involved in folk, jazz, latin and world music, be they promoters, musicians, funders, labels or in 2003 educators.

Wayne Shorter
Nefertiti / Columbia CK 65681

Tutors Index

South East
Miners, Richard
Bassoon
London
Smith, Daniel
Yorkshire
Beck, Mick
Cello
London
Mattos, Marcio
North West
Berry, Steve
South West
Dickie, Chas
Lang-Colmer, Claudia
Silk, Rose
Clarinet
East Midlands
Iles, Trevor
Lloyd, Peter
Palmer, Matt
Trott, Malcolm
Watkins, Michael
Eastern
Hart, Frances
Jolly, Paul
Light, Patrick
Pritchard, Malcolm
Wilson, Jeffrey
London
Bartlett, Rachel
Berg, Russell van den
Blackmore, Dave
Bray, Ned
Christiane, Kelvin
Coe, Tony
Cuzner, Kate
Guttridge, Derek
Hampton, Andrew
Lammin, Dennis
Lynch, Sue
Pretty, Adam
Rendell, Don
Sharpe, Martin

Smith, Daniel
Sydor, Bob
Tomlinson, Jim
York, Clive
North East
Wood, Fiona
North West
Cox, Gary
Salisbury, Harold
Silmon-Monerri, Joe
Other
Atkinson, R. John
Bond, Lynn
Scotland
Burgess, John
Forbes, Stewart
Hall, Rob
Hallam, Dan
Moy, Norman
South East
Bernard, Bob
Biscoe, Chris
Boardman, Bruce
Bowdler, Dave
Cook, Natasha
East, Ian
Feast, Penrose
Greenway, Susan
Griffith, Frank
Nicholas, Julian
Panayi, Andy
Steele, Jan
Stuart, Don
Woods, Tony
South West
Aston, Jack
Bowles, Geoff
Forward, Thomas
Fulcher, Harry
Hearnshaw, Charlie
Ian Parsons
Jo Gurr
Johns, Larry
Mike Hopkins
Rose, Martin
Sneyd, Peter

Trevett, Julie
Wales
Butterworth, Martin
Sanders, Gareth
Sansbury, Brian
West Midlands
Crabb, Colin
Gray, Mike
Gumbley, Chris
Orton, Ken
Spiers, Stuart
Yorkshire
Smith, David S.
Cornet
London
Stevenson, Nick
North West
Elliott, Don
South East
Campbell, Duncan
South West
Harding, David
Double Bass
Eastern
Brown, Jill
Pullin, David
London
Babbington, Roy
Clyne, Jeff
Gascoyne, Geoff
Leahy, David
Manington, Dave
Mattos, Marcio
Miles, Matt
O'Neill, Bernard
Rayner, Alison
Rodel, Chris
Walkington, Julie
North East
Newton, Raymond
North West
Berry, Steve
Riley, Stuart
Willmott, Peter
South East
Garside, Gus

63

Higgins, Gerry
Ind, Peter
Kendon, Adrian
Kershaw, Steve
Silk, David
Thomas, Nigel
South West
Goodier, David
Lang-Colmer, Claudia
Miles, DavidV
Vergette, Marcus
Wales
Gardiner, Paula
West Midlands
Lilley, Terry
Drums
East Midlands
Stewart, William
Eastern
Booth, Brian
Cater, Peter
Dodd, Jonathan
Finlay, Rick
Gaines, Will
Odell, Roger
London
Altman, Darren
Austin, Wade
Bianco, Tony
Bryant, Mark
Howarth, Ian
Johnson, David
Ritchie, Stuart
Tilbury, Nigel
Tomkins, Trevor
Wellard, Gordon
North East
Dennis, Kelvin
North West
Bowman, Anna
Scotland
Goodman, Ronnie
Mathieson, Ken
South East
Austin, Dennis

Bennett, Rex
Drew, Martin
Howton, Barry
Newby, Richard
Richardson, Neal
Rushton, Steve
Webb, John
Webster, David
South West
Brian, Robert
West Midlands
Richards, Tony
Yorkshire
Fairclough, Peter
Hession, Paul
Electric Bass
London
Miles, Matt
South West
Domay, Michael
Electric Piano
Eastern
Hove, Gillian
Euphonium
London
Bennett, John
Flugel Horn
Eastern
Batson, Ray
London
Diprose, Mike
Edmonds, Paul
Speyer, Loz
York, Clive
North West
Browning, D A
South East
Campbell, Duncan
Eshelby, Paul
Hamer, Ian
Wales
Haines, Cris
Flute
East Midlands
Trott, Malcolm

Eastern
Austin-Brenes, Julia
Light, Patrick
Neighbour, Pete
London
Ballantine, Ian
Bartlett, Rachel
Christiane, Kelvin
Crumly, Pat
Elliott, Katie
Elliott, Louise
Garland, Tim
Guttridge, Derek
Lammin, Dennis
Lynch, Sue
Parker, Eddie
Rendell, Don
Sydor, Bob
Thomas, Peter
Waithe, Keith
North West
Cox, Gary
Salisbury, Harold
Silmon-Monerri, Joe
Other
Atkinson, R. John
Scotland
Burgess, John
Forbes, Stewart
Hallam, Dan
Moy, Norman
South East
Barrett, Elizabeth
Bowdler, Dave
Cheneour, Paul
East, Ian
Forsyth, Alex
Greenway, Susan
Panayi, Andy
Steele, Jan
Stuart, Don
Sutherland, Rowland
South West
Aston, Jack
Bowles, Geoff

Hume, Alastair
Gurr Jo
Johns, Larry
Sneyd, Peter
Trevett, Julie

West Midlands

Crabb, Colin
Orton, Ken
Spiers, Stuart

Yorkshire

Miller, Sue
Taylor, Jon

French Horn

London

Charlton, Kay

Fretless Bass

South West

Miles, DavidV

Guitar

East Midlands

Gardner, Christopher
McCaughern, Danny
Overon, Geoff
Parker, Christopher

Eastern

Ansell, Danny
Houlston, Robert
Walker, Crosby
Watson, Andy

London

Alexander, Charles
Bannerman, Alf Kari
Blackwell, John Keith
Chadwick, James
Davies, J P
Dux, Tim
Etheridge, John
Hannah, Tom
Jenkins, Billy
Meier, Nicolas
Naylor, Patrick
Preiss, Jonathan
Stoysin, Branco
Weinreb, Paul

North East

Birkett, James

North West

Mitchell-Davidson, Paul
Parkinson, Brian
Seaman, Peter
Thorpe, Tony

Scotland

Goldie, John
Wyness, James

South East

Barnard, Tony
Cruickshank, Ian
Fogg, Rod
Garside, Gus
Holland, Bernie
Murrell, Dave
Purcell, John
Spolia, Rajan

South West

Benham, Patrick
Domay, Michael
Rosser, Pete

Wales

Earl, Rhoderick
Stopes, Ian

Yorkshire

Hares, Paul
Jasnoch, John
Lad, Milan
Swift, Jeff

Hammond Organ

London

Moran, Paul

Keyboards

East Midlands

Callingham, Matthew
Hunter, Neil
Wain, Janet

Eastern

Adcock, Mike
Ball, Steve
Brown, Simon
Hove, Gillian
Lemer, Peter
Newman, Ron
Puddick, John
Simon Brown

Stanley, Christine
Sterling, Andrew
Strong, Barry
Walker, Crosby

London

Baldwin, Gary
Bos, Pieter Jaap
Crawford, John
Erselius, Steven
Harrod, Andrew
Ingleby, Mark
Moran, Paul
Samuels, Biddy
Veltmeijer, Angele
Webb, Robert

North East

Luck, Steven

North West

Guppy, Eileen
Harrison, Gerard
Phillips, Marlene
Seaman, Peter

Scotland

Breingan, Stan
Wood, James

South East

Cartledge, David
Chambers, Stephanie
Corbett, David
Cornick, Mike
Field, Trixi
Johnston, David
Lawrie, Martin
Mander, Derek
Mason, Janette
McEwen, Bill
Priest, John
Christopher
Robinson, Joe
Stephens, Ian
Taggart, Robert
York, Adrian

South West

Buxton, Dave
Cliff, Tony
Domay, Michael

Dunn, Julie
Taylor, Jonathan
Williams, Peter
Wood, Stephen
Wales
Bailey, Elaine
Williams, May
West Midlands
Blunn, Nick
Heeley, Roger
Woodhead, John
Yorkshire
Sharpe, Ian
Mandolin
Yorkshire
Hares, Paul
Marimba
London
Beaujolais, Roger
Midi Vibes
London
Veltmeijer, Angele
South West
Silk, Rose
Oboe
South West
Mike Hopkins
Organ
Eastern
Stanley, Christine
London
Carr, Mike
Stuckey, Bob
North East
Richardson, Gerry
South East
Johnston, David
Percussion
East Midlands
Anderson, Mat
Eastern
Ball, Steve
Booth, Brian
Finlay, Rick
Gaines, Will

London
Akingbola, Sola
Bannerman, Alf Kari
Bryant, Mark
Embliss, William
Howarth, Ian
Wallen, Byron
Yeboah, Kwame
North East
Dennis, Kelvin
North West
Jarman, Jilly
Lewis, Steve
Scotland
Dibbs, Martin
Goodman, Ronnie
South East
Austin, Dennis
South West
Brian, Robert
West Midlands
Mealing, Adrian
Richards, Tony
Yorkshire
Birkby, Peter
Piano
East Midlands
Bryce, Owen
Buxton, Helen
Callingham, Matthew
Hudson, Bob
Hunter, Neil
Iles, Trevor
Saunders, Hilary
Eastern
Adcock, Mike
Badham, Maggie
Blackwell, John
Brannan, Mick
Brown, Simon
Burn, Chris
Churchill, Pete
Clouts, Philip
Dodd, Jonathan
Garrick, Michael
Hove, Gillian

Iles, Nikki
Lemer, Peter
Newman, Ron
Oswin, John
Pritchard, Malcolm
Rose, John
Shepherd, Peter
Simon Brown
Stanley, Christine
Sterling, Andrew
Strong, Barry
Williams, Paul
Wilson, Jeffrey
London
Ballantine, Ian
Bos, Pieter Jaap
Carr, Mike
Chapman, Greg
Crawford, John
Davies, J P
Dean, Barry
Dhillon, Sara
Diprose, Mike
Edmonds, Paul
Elliott, Katie
Erselius, Steven
Franks, Ruth
Fuller, Christopher
Gruner, Alan
Gunning, Josephine
Hampton, Andrew
Harrod, Andrew
Ingleby, Mark
Johnson, David
Kemp, Josh
L'Estrange, Alexander
Lodder, Steve
Mackworth-Young, Lucinda
Maguire, Alex
Mitchell-Luker, Vicci
Moran, Paul
Nelson, Deborah
Noble, Liam
Parker, Eddie
Perrin, Roger

Perrin, Roland
Potter, Sarah
Quinton, Neill
Richards, Tim
Sharp, Tim
Sharpe, Martin
Snow, Barbara
Stuckey, Bob
Treiger, Norman
Vicari, Andrea
Ward, Chris
Watson, Pete
Webb, Robert
Weinreb, Paul
Weldon, Nick
Williams, Gareth
Williams, Kate
Yeboah, Kwame

North East
Chester, Ray
Diver, John
Luck, Steven
Peters, Pete
Richardson, Gerry
Wood, Fiona

North West
Berry, Steve
Bowman, Anna
Darrington, Ian (MBE)
Dewhurst, Robin
Escobar, Brigitte
Gray, Ian
Grew, Stephen
Guppy, Eileen
Harrison, Gerard
Jarman, Jilly
Johnstone, Margaret
Magson, Jen
Melville, Brian
Phillips, Marlene
Seaman, Peter
Sykes, Tom
Wilson, Paul
Zegelaar, Art

Scotland
Bancroft, Sophie

Breingan, Stan
Eliot Murray
Finnerty, Adrian
Hall, Rob
Michael, Richard
Trahan, Linda
Wood, James

South East
Arnold, Tim
Austin, Derek
Barrett, Elizabeth
Beebee, Dave
Boardman, Bruce
Burch, John
Carr, Judy
Cartledge, David
Chambers, Stephanie
Cook, Natasha
Corbett, David
Cornick, Mike
Cromar, Amanda
Cunningham, Philip
Ebbage, David
Field, Malcolm
Field, Trixi
Griffith, Frank
Harvey, Eddie
Hicks, Deirdre
Ind, Peter
Johnston, David
Jones, Dave
Knight, Frances
Lawrie, Martin
Leport, Jeannette
Longworth, Jocelyn
Mander, Derek
Mason, Janette
McEwen, Bill
Michael, Will
Milburn, Philip
Murray, Angus
Nash, Phil
Norchi, Alan
Powell, Patricia
Priest, John
Christopher

Purcell, John
Rawbone, Martyn
Richardson, Neal
Riley, Howard
Robinson, Joe
Seabrook, Terry
Stepney, Roger
Taggart, Robert
Williams, Geoff
York, Adrian
Young, Jeffrey

South West
Aitchison, James
Berry, John
Bilham, Andrew
Bowers, Rachel
Buxton, Dave
Cliff, Tony
Du Valle, Cecil
Dunn, Julie
Fox, Mandy
Fulcher, Harry
Gill, Peter
Haines, David
Haywood, Christine
Hearnshaw, Charlie
Iles, Elizabeth
Lees, Lesley
Peck, Mike
Positive, John
Riley, Lewis
Rosser, Pete
Silk, Rose
Spencer, Piers
Stein, Jon
Taylor, Jonathan
Walter, John
Williams, Peter
Wood, Stephen

Wales
Bailey, Elaine
Green, Paul Francis
Little, Keith
Tunley, Sarah
Walmsley, Beryl
Williams, May

West Midlands
Barron, Barbara
Beyer, Lawrence
Blunn, Nick
Bolton, Chris
Corbet, Alan
Edwards, Jane
Gumbley, Chris
Gumbley, Chris
Harvey, Margaret
Heeley, Roger
Jones, Sarah
Wetton, Carol
Woodhead, John
Yorkshire
Berwin, Lindsey
Cook, Jonathan
Eveleigh, Ray
Hopson, Yvonne
Hunter, John
Miller, Sue
Sharpe, Ian
Sherburn, Angela
Swift, Belinda
Piccolo
South East
Sutherland, Rowland
Recorder
South East
Chambers, Stephanie
West Midlands
Williams, John
Saxophone
East Midlands
Brush, Andy
Iles, Trevor
Kopinski, Jan
Lloyd, Peter
McBride, Sean
Trott, Malcolm
Watkins, Michael
Eastern
Collins, Geoff
Jolly, Paul
Light, Patrick
Pritchard, Malcolm

Pullin, David
Wilson, Jeffrey
London
Berg, Russell van den
Blackmore, Dave
Caldwell, Chris
Christiane, Kelvin
Coe, Tony
Crumly, Pat
Cuzner, Kate
Dvorak, Jim
Francomb, Roger
Garland, Tim
Guttridge, Derek
Hampton, Andrew
Khan, Sean
Lammin, Dennis
Lynch, Sue
McKenzie, Paul
Moore, Sarha
Perrin, Roger
Pretty, Adam
Samuels, Biddy
Sharpe, Martin
Smith, Daniel
Sydor, Bob
Thomas, Peter
Tomlinson, Jim
Toussaint, Jean
York, Clive
North East
Johnson, Stuart
North West
Baylis, Paul
Cox, Gary
Manship, Münch
Perry, Terry
Salisbury, Harold
Scott, Andy
Other
Atkinson, R. John
Scotland
Burgess, John
Forbes, Stewart
Hall, Rob
Hallam, Dan

MacDonald, Laura
Moy, Norman
South East
Andrews, David
Ashton, Bill
Bernard, Bob
Biscoe, Chris
Bowdler, Dave
Cook, Natasha
East, Ian
Haslam, George
Lockheart, Mark
Nicholas, Julian
Packham, Kit
Panayi, Andy
Purcell, John
Ramsden, Mark
Robinson, Joe
Steele, Jan
Stuart, Don
Woods, Tony
South West
Bowles, Geoff
Figes, Kevin
Fulcher, Harry
Hearnshaw, Charlie
Hume, Alastair
Ian Parsons
Jo Gurr
Lloyd, Jon
Mike Hopkins
Parr, Kenneth
Rose, Martin
Trevett, Julie
Wales
Butterworth, Martin
Fawcett, Andrew
Sanders, Gareth
Sansbury, Brian
West Midlands
Crabb, Colin
Dunmall, Paul
Gray, Mike
Gumbley, Chris
Gumbley, Chris
Jones, Sarah

Orton, Ken
Spiers, Stuart
Williams, John
Yorkshire
Beck, Mick
Ingham, Richard
Taylor, Jon
Soprano Sax
East Midlands
Hislam, Nick
London
Ballamy, Iain
Bartlett, Rachel
Bruer, Jason
Clahar, Patrick
Kofi, Tony
Northover, Adrian
O'Neill, John
Siegel, Julian
Smith, Harrison
Williamson, Steve
North West
Hall, Mike
Other
Finkel, Sigi
Scotland
Smith, Tommy
South East
Feast, Penrose
Forsyth, Alex
George Haslam
Wales
Stacey, Peter
Soundbeam
South East
Jackson, David
Steel Pans
London
Austin, Wade
Tabla
South West
Riley, Lewis
Tenor Banjo
London
Catchpole, Nat

Tenor Sax
East Midlands
Hislam, Nick
Eastern
Neighbour, Pete
Peploe, Brian
London
Arguelles, Julian
Atzmon, Gilad
Ballamy, Iain
Bartlett, Rachel
Bitelli, David
Bray, Ned
Bruer, Jason
Chambers, Dave
Clahar, Patrick
Elliott, Louise
Kemp, Josh
O'Higgins, Dave
O'Neill, John
Rendell, Don
Siegel, Julian
Smith, Harrison
Williamson, Steve
North West
Hall, Mike
Silmon-Monerri, Joe
Scotland
Eliot Murray
Gilmour, Mary
Smith, Tommy
South East
Crooks, Dick
Feast, Penrose
George Haslam
Greenway, Susan
Pells, Roger
Tompson, Mike
Whitehead, Tim
South West
Aston, Jack
D'Aiello, Renato
Johns, Larry
Other
Finkel, Sigi

Wales
Manby, Glen
Stacey, Peter
Yorkshire
Miller, Sue
Trombone
East Midlands
Crouch, John
Eastern
Alex Moore
Lewis, Jeremy
London
Bennett, John
Charlton, Kay
Embliss, William
Nash, Michael
Smith, Malcolm
North East
Chester, Ray
North West
Elliott, Don
Melville, Brian
Nelson, Ian
Royle, Ian
Scotland
Boyd, Denis
Kenny, John
Whittaker, John
South East
Jarvis, Robert
Lusher, Don
Miners, Richard
Rawbone, Martyn
Wade, Tim
South West
Berry, John
Hicks, Keith
Munnery, Paul
Robinson, Eddie
West Midlands
Hughes, John
Yorkshire
Blenkiron, Nigel
Mansfield, Simon

Trumpet
East Midlands
  Bryce, Owen
  Fullick, Teddy
  Willan, Eric
Eastern
  Alex Moore
  Batson, Ray
  Fairweather, Digby
London
  Bennett, John
  Charlton, Kay
  Diprose, Mike
  Dvorak, Jim
  Edmonds, Paul
  Embliss, William
  Higgs, Patrick
  Lee, Chris
  Snow, Barbara
  Speyer, Loz
  Stevenson, Nick
  Wallen, Byron
North East
  Chester, Ray
  Wood, Fiona
North West
  Browning, D A
  Darrington, Ian (MBE)
  Elliott, Don
  Royle, Ian
Scotland
  Whittaker, John
South East
  Andrews, David
  Campbell, Duncan
  Eshelby, Paul
  Hamer, Ian
  Miners, Richard
South West
  Hague, Andy
  Harding, David
  Hicks, Keith
  Holmes, Christopher
  Robinson, Eddie
Wales
  Haines, Cris

  Liddington, Gethin
  Williams, Ceri
West Midlands
  Hughes, John
  Jones, Chris
  Severn, Eddie
Yorkshire
  Blenkiron, Nigel
  Cook, Jonathan
Tuba
North West
  Royle, Ian
  Waite, Glenn
South West
  Hicks, Keith
Yorkshire
  Mansfield, Simon
Vibraphone
London
  Ballantine, Ian
  Beaujolais, Roger
South East
  Jones, Dave
South West
  Brian, Robert
Violin
London
  Forrell, Gaby
  Garrick, Chris
  Johnson, David
  Thompson, Billy
North West
  Sykes, Tom
South East
  Leport, Jeannette
  Massey, Aidan
Voice
Eastern
  Alexander, Gill
  Churchill, Pete
  Foster, Clare
  Odell, Larraine
London
  Alldis, Dominic
  Dvorak, Jim
  Gibbs, Louise

  Gruner, Alan
  Kerr, Trudy
  Mitchell-Luker, Vicci
  Nicols, Maggie
  Pace, Paul
  Samuels, Biddy
  Smith, Malcolm
  Waithe, Keith
  Wilding, Adele
  Zakian, Laura
North West
  Escobar, Brigitte
  Guppy, Eileen
  Jarman, Jilly
  Lee-French, Segun
Scotland
  Bancroft, Sophie
  Duncan, Fionna
  Eliot Murray
South East
  Bentley, Alison
  Browne, Anton
  Browne, Anton
  Bundy, Rachel
  Cave, Phoene
  Field, Trixi
  Gibson, Lee
  Milburn, Philip
  Murray, Angus
  Ponsford, Jan
South West
  Dunn, Julie
  Fox, Mandy
  Karian, Karin
Wales
  Bailey, Elaine
Wind Synthesizer
East Midlands
  Brush, Andy
Woodwind
London
  Veltmeijer, Angele
West Midlands
  Barron, Barbara
Yorkshire
  Smith, David

Tutors

Adcock, Mike
(Eastern)
6 Ramsbury Road, St Albans AL1 1SL
01727 835 989, 01727 835 989 fax, mikeadcock@yahoo.com
Instruments taught: Keyboards, Piano.
Teaches 1 to 1. Age(s): under 11, 17 plus. Area(s): refresher. Place(s): own home, pupil's home.
Workshops: Speciality area(s): Primary. Improvisation. Composition. Improvisation workshop for Hertfordshire County Music. Specialisation - Introduction to Improvisation and Free Improvisation.
Schools: for 12-16 hours per week. Primary
Qualifications: PGCE. (Has been teaching for 15-20 years.) Includes improvisation. Other style(s): popular music, world music, other (Blues, Free Improvisation).
During 10 years teaching at Herts College of Art and Design, ran improvisation and composition workshops. "While I have a particular interest in improvisation, I prefer not to consider this only as an activity within jazz, as my reference points are often to other music forms from around the world. The term 'jazz' usefully describes a wide range of musical activities, but with the development of jazz as a curriculum, examinable subject its currency in the language now carries certain expectations, However, many of the methods and models I employ do relate to the history of jazz (12 bar blues, modes, free improvisation) but I do not see myself as a 'jazz tutor' only"

Aitchison, James
(South West)
Penmorvah Workshop, Garro Lane, Mullion TR12 7ED
01326 241 440
Instruments taught: Piano.
Teaches 1 to 1. Teaches Associated Board Piano Exam. Age(s): under 11, 11upwards. Area(s): reading, beginners, some knowledge, coaching. Place(s): other (I am resident teacher for Clemens Music Shop in Helston, Cornwall. I also teach at six schools - mostly complete beginners).
Schools: Primary, Secondary
Qualifications: BA MUS HONS; A MUS M; PGCE (has been teaching for 10-15 years). Other style(s): popular music, classical.
" I don't consider myself specifically a jazz only specialist. I am a fully qualified teacher (PGCE) with experience of a wide range of music including Jazz. I am a classically trained composer and performer who loves to play jazz - sometimes professionally. My experience as a composer gives me special insights into aware-ness of style, analysis of structure and musical elements –melody, harmony"

Akingbola, Sola
(London)
21 Brenley House, Tennis St., London SE1 1YG
020 7378 6488 tel/fax, gillian.evans1@tesco.net
Instruments taught: Percussion.
Teaches 1 to 1. Age(s): 11 upwards. Area(s): beginners, some knowledge. Place(s): own home, pupil's home, other (own studio).

Workshops: Amongst others has taught several workshops at the Tabernacle (Nottinghill, London). Specialisation - Hand drumming & Yoruba rhythms. "My most recent student came to me because he is a 3rd year music student (at Goldsmiths learning electric bass) and wanted to learn to become competent on percussion and has found advantages in using a private tutor"

Alexander, Charles
(London)
2b Gleneagle Mews, Ambleside Avenue, London SW16 6AE
magazine@jazzwise.com
www.jazzwise.com
Instruments taught: Guitar.
Teaches 1 to 1. Age(s): 17 plus. Area(s): some knowledge. Place(s): own home. Workshops: usually small groups. Previously and currently, Jazz Guitar classes (Saturday mornings) and Jazz ensemble workshops at Richmond Adult Community College, Parkshot Centre, Parkshot, Richmond since 1985. (Has been teaching for over 20 years). Includes improvisation.
Jazz Centre Society Summer schools in 1970s. Extensive private tuition. Co-runs the Jamey Aebersold Summer School. Also edited the book 'Masters of the Jazz Guitar' (Balafun 1999).

Alexander, Gill
(Eastern)
The Tithe Barn, Mill Lane, Needham IP20 9LD
01379 852721, 01379 852721 fax, mail@jazzangles.co.uk
www.jazzangles.co.uk
Instruments taught: Voice.
Specialises in Jazz workshops for adults, children and disabled people and was peripatetic double bass tutor for Norfolk for five years. Organises jazz concerts in her own home in aid of charity six times a year, using top jazz musicians, who also do post concert workshops. The childrens' bands are used in her lectures "Teaching jazz to children" at The Royal Academy and Royal Northern College. Runs workshops in about 30 schools a year. Holds regular jazz workshops, all over East Anglia.

Alldis, Dominic
(London)
122 Dawes Road, Fulham, London SW6 7EG
020 7381 2963, 0870 056 8106 fax, 07956 393314 mobile
dominic@dominicalldis.com, www.dominicalldis.com
Instruments taught: Voice.
Teaches 1 to 1. Age(s): 17 plus. Area(s): refresher, coaching. Place(s): own home. Workshops: vocal coaching for trained/semi-trained singers and 'singing at the piano'. Previously taught at Royal Academy of Music - Improvisation, Jazz Piano, Harmony. Jazz Academy - Jazz singing. Specialisation - Jazz Singing and accompaniment.
1985-87 teacher of jazz and improvisation at Westminster School. 1986-87 tutor at Dartington International Summer School. Professor of jazz piano, keyboards and teaching skills at the Royal Academy of Music. Also Professor of harmony and counterpoint, junior department of Royal College of Music. Has given workshops/ recitals about jazz and improvisation in schools and colleges. Currently tutors on Michael Garrick's "Piano People" and gives monthly workshops in specialist Music Schools. Author of 'A Classical Approach to Jazz Piano' (pub. Hal Leonard Corp.).

Gives occasional lessons to intermediate - advanced pianists. He also gives masterclasses and workshops at the RAM and RCM.

Altman, Darren
(London)

62 Spring Gardens, Grosvenor Avenue, Highbury, London N5 2DT
020 7704 9012, 07778 577 464,
darrenaltman@homechoice.co.uk
Instruments taught: Drums.
As well as his regular teaching in London, he has taught at the Wavendon Jazz Summer School, Glamorgan Jazz Summer School and the Laurie Holloway/Marion Montgomery Summer School. In February 2002, he was invited to Cyprus by the British Council to give workshops in jazz and to perform with the Cyprus State Orchestra.

Anderson, Mat
(East Midlands)

10 The Promenade, Victoria Park, Nottingham NG3 1HB
07919 035671, matanderson@ukonline.co.uk
Instruments taught: Acoustic Guitar, Percussion.
Has run improvisation workshops for University of Derby.

Andrews, David
(South East)

16 Pear Tree Close, Alderholt, Fordingbridge SP6 3ER
01425 654819 tel/fax, musmak1@aol.com
Instruments taught: Trumpet, Saxophone.
Teaches 1 to 1.
Workshops: small groups, large groups. Speciality area(s): large groups. Running choirs, Music courses, MD for shows etc.
Schools: for 16+ hours per week. primary (5-11), secondary (11-16).
Qualifications: GRSM, LRSM, ARCM (has been teaching for 10-15 years). Includes improvisation. Other style(s): popular music, classical, world music.

Ansell, Danny
(Eastern)

74 East Park, Old Harlow, Harlow CM17 0SD
0779 084 6999
Instruments taught: Guitar.
Teaches 1 to 1. Age(s): 11 upwards. Area(s): reading, beginners, some knowledge, refresher. Place(s): own home, other (Teaches at a converted church hall).
Workshops: usually small groups. Workshop leader. 2002 Easter workshop with Mark and Mike Mondesir and Zoe Rahman which took place before their concert at St John's Arc, Old Harlow in conjunction with Harlow Arts.
Schools: Secondary (11-16), HE/FE, special needs. Peripatetic music teacher through Essex Music Services at Colchester Institute and Harlow College.
Qualifications: Philosophy degree (has been teaching for 5-10 years). Includes improvisation. Other style(s) Indian.
Holds regular workshops but dependent on raising sufficient funding. Has experience of teaching in a variety of settings.

Arguelles, Julian
(London)
12b Balchier Road, London SE22 0QN
020 8480 0492, 020 8480 0401 fax, 07974 181 665
Jularg@aol.com
Instruments taught: Baritone Sax, Alto Sax, Tenor Sax.
Teaches 1 to 1. Age(s): 11 upwards. Area(s): some knowledge, coaching. Place(s): own home, other (colleges, cusic centres etc.).
Workshops: Previously and currently, various jazz summer Schools, RAM, RNCM, York University, Guildhall (has been teaching for 5-10 years.)
Currently teaches at Royal Academy, Trinity College and is an Associate tutor at Royal Northern College Manchester and York. Has previously taught at the Guildhall, Royal National College of Music, Middlesex University and the Glamorgan Summer school. "I try to help students to enjoy music making and to help them teach themselves."

Arnold, Tim
(South East)
Albertine Horsham Road, Hardcross, Haywards Heath RH17 6DE
01444 400643, tim.arnold@lineone.net
Instruments taught: Piano.
Teaches Associated Board Piano Exam. Age(s): under 11, 11 upwards. Area(s): reading, beginners, some knowledge. Place(s): own home, other (Teaches at Lancing College and East Sussex Academy of Music. Chinese University Hong Kong).
Workshops: ABRSM Workshops - Leeds, Cardiff, RCM, Petersfield, Malaysia, etc Specialisation - Introduction to Associated Board Jazz.
Schools: Pre-school, Primary, Secondary. HE/FE
Qualifications: B Mus (Hons) Cert GSMD (has been teaching for over 20 years).
Other style(s): popular music, classical.
"I am a 'classical' pianist and teacher who is trying to become more aware of jazz. I believe that jazz has a lot to offer instrumental teachers and would encourage all to explore its possibilities".

Ashton, Bill MBE, DipEd
(South East)
11 Victor Road, Harrow HA2 6PT
020 8863 2717, 020 8863 8685 fax, 0836 204545 mobile
bill.ashton@virgin.net, www.NYJO.org.uk internet
Instruments taught: Saxophone.
Qualifications: BA; DipEd; FCLCM (has been teaching for over 20 years). Other style(s): popular music.
As Musical Director of National Youth Jazz Orchestra, organises workshops both with and seperately from concerts. Details on request. NYJO's music is now part of the GCSE syllabus.

Aston, Jack
(South West)
40 Priory Road, Knowle, Bristol BS4 2NL
0117 9080839
Instruments taught: Clarinet, Flute, Tenor Sax.

Workshops: usually large groups. Speciality area(s): adult. Theory, Composition, Arranging.

Schools: for 1-4 hours per week. St George Community School, Bristol.

Qualifications: Cert. Ed. Has been teaching for over 20 years.

Atzmon, Gilad
(London)

07973 291 505, gilad@gilad.co.uk, www.gilad.co.uk

Instruments taught: Alto Sax, Tenor Sax.

Teaches 1 to 1 (has been teaching for 5-10 years). Includes improvisation.

Austin, Dennis
(South East)

81 West Street, Bexleyheath DA7 4BP

020 8301 0142

Instruments taught: Drums, Percussion.

Teaches 1 to 1. Age(s): under 11, 11 upwards. Area(s): reading, beginners, some knowledge, refresher, coaching. Place(s): own home, pupil's home, other (Extra music groups).

Workshops: Previously primary and secondary schools SE London and Kent. Currently people with learning difficulties and behaviour problems in Southwark area. Drum workshops in schools. "I am 63 years old and have been playing jazz since 1954. I have also served time in Royal Dragoon Guards Band. My tutor was Max Abraham and I have played all types of jazz and currently heavily involved with free improvisation."

Austin, Derek
(South East)

6 Fairplace, South Road, Wivelsfield Green RH17 7QR

01444 471567, 07774 869 418, daustin@pavilion.co.uk

Instruments taught: Piano.

Teaches 1 to 1. Teaches Associated Board Piano Exam. Age(s): 11 upwards. Area(s): beginners, some knowledge, refresher. Place(s): pupil's home.

Qualifications: Grade 8 Organ; A level music (has been teaching for 3-5 years). Other style(s): popular music.

Director of Music at Hurstpierpoint College. "I base my teaching approach according to the individual. Although a 'natural jazz musician, I also enjoyed a classical training, and use that on occasions. I have attended Dartington for the past two summers as a member of Herbie Flowers' 'Rockshop', specialising in helping classical musicians to improvise. In addition, have worked with many 'Rockshops' in schools, community centres etc, and have six private pupils (of all ages) studying jazz/blues piano. After taking grades 6 and 8 and A level Music at school, I spent two years at the London College of Music, taking a GLCM, studying Organ and Composition."

Austin-Brenes, Julia
(Eastern)

6 Riffhams, Hutton, Brentwood CM13 2TW

01277 262694

Instruments taught: Flute.

Teaches 1 to 1.

Workshops: usually small groups, large groups, classes (20+). Speciality area(s): secondary. Schools: for 16+ hours per week. Primary, Secondary. Adults. Qualifications: BA (Hons)Music/PGCE. (Has been teaching for 15-20 years.) Other style(s): popular music, classical.

Babbington, Roy
(London)
7 Sinclair Road, London W14 0NS
020 7602 3018
0771 262 2355
Instruments taught: Bagpipes, Double Bass.
Teaches 1 to 1.
Group demonstration/coaching/discussion.

Badham, Maggie
(Eastern)
51 Halleys Ridge, Hertford SG14 2TH
01992 582379
Instruments taught: Piano.
Teaches 1 to 1. Teaches Associated Board Piano Exam. Age(s): under 11, 11 upwards. Area(s): reading, beginners, some knowledge, refresher. Place(s): own home.
Workshops: Has done workshops but prefers one-to-one.
Qualifications: Experience in 'the field' (has been teaching for 5-10 years). Other style(s): popular music, classical.
"A Jazz tutor must be someone who knows and loves jazz - possibly also goes out to play it, but they must be able to convey all this to the student. This is tricky as jazz is so complex but it can be done. I hope I fullfil these criteria."

Bailey, Elaine
(Wales)
9 Victoria Avenue, Craig-y-don, Llandudno LL30 1PQ
01492 876 302
Instruments taught: Piano, Keyboards, Voice.
Teaches 1 to 1. Age(s): under 11, 11 upwards. Area(s): reading, beginners, some knowledge. Place(s): own home.
Schools: for 8-12 hours per week. Secondary.
Qualifications: Dip in Performing Arts (has been teaching for over 20 years). Includes improvisation. Other style(s): popular music.
"I am very interested in popular music and find pupils respond well to the distinctive sounds of jazz - bringing a part of themselves out through improvisation. I try to tailor the lesson to the indivual pupil."

Baldwin, Gary
(London)
75 Lincoln Road, Forest Gate, London E7 8QN
020 8471 0907 tel/fax, mitzibal@aol.com
Instruments taught: Keyboards.
For several years Gary has been teaching keyboards in two Inner London schools working within the National Curriculum which includes all modern styles of music including basic jazz.

Ball, Steve
(Eastern)

3 Hawkshead Court, Eleanor Way, Waltham Cross EN8 7XA
01992 767875, 07787 375 292, steveball@jazzexplorium.net
www.jazzexplorium.net
Instruments taught: Percussion, Keyboards.
Workshops: usually small groups, large groups. Speciality area(s): Primary, secondary, tertiary, adult. Special needs groups.
Qualifications: 30 years playing experience (has been teaching for 3-5 years).
Other style(s): popular music, classical, world music, other (Salsa).
Specialises in untuned percussive instruments. Teaches 'Groove', Working together, Self expression, Creativity and Celebration. Facilitates Drum Circles, Percussion Playshops and a 'Drumnasium' - a rhythm playshop. Not particular to jazz - more rhythm and improvisation. The drum circle sessions are based on tried and tested rhythm games and exercises last two hours. It has been used for stress-busting and team building, with teenage special needs groups, primary schools and even family get-togethers. He provides the instruments but more are always welcome. Caters for groups of 5 to 50.

Ballamy, Iain
(London)

Flat 4, Old Queen Anne House, 63 Aylesbury Road, Walworth, London SE17 2EQ
020 7708 5853 tel/fax, 07973 940020, iainballamy@easynet.co.uk,
www.ballamy.com
Instruments taught: Soprano Sax, Tenor Sax.
Teaches 1 to 1. Age(s): 17 plus. Area(s): refresher, coaching. Place(s): own home.
Workshops: Speciality area(s): small groups, adult, 'Instrumental Concepts'.
Saxophone Maintenance and Repair.
In the past has taught at Birmingham Conservatoire, Royal Northern College of Music, Bretton Hall, the Royal Academy, Trinity.
Currently teaches part-time at Royal Academy of Music and Trinity (has been teaching for 10-15 years). Includes improvisation. Other style(s): world music.

Ballantine, Ian
(London)

49a Victoria Crescent, Upper Norwood, London SE19 1AE
020 8761 1079
Instruments taught: Piano, Vibraphone, Flute.
Teaches 1 to 1. Teaches Associated Board Piano Exam. Age(s): under 11, 11 upwards. Area(s): reading, beginners, some knowledge, refresher, coaching. Place(s): own home, pupil's home.
Workshops: Previously, one off workshops in schools. Specialisation: Jazz and classical ensemble. Composition and theory.
Qualifications: Graduate City of Leeds College of Music (has been teaching for over 20 years). Includes improvisation. Other style(s): popular music, classical.
Qualified teacher who has taught music extensively in schools, including jazz. A great deal of private teaching of jazz. Runs approx 4 workshops a year. "I have taught all age groups both privately and in schools, beginners and advanced including special needs. I am able to explain complex theory in a way that can be understood by by beginners who find this difficult to understand".

Bancroft, Sophie
(Scotland)
32 Main Street, Pathead EH37 5QB
018775 320 505, sbancroft@sol.co.uk
www.jazz-in-scotland.co.uk/banlyn.htm internet
Instruments taught: Piano, Voice.
Teaches 1 to 1. Age(s): 11 upwards. Area(s): reading, beginners, some knowledge, refresher, coaching. Place(s): own home, other (Schools, Universities, Music Schools).
Workshops: small groups. Speciality area(s): 1 to 1, small groups, primary, tertiary, adult, song interpretation, improvisation, performance techniques, self esteem/confidence development. Currently is a main tutor on the Fionna Duncan vocal Jazz Workshops run in Glasgow, Edinburgh and around Scotland.
Schools: for 8-12 hours per week. secondary, HE/FE, adults.
(Has been teaching for 3-5 years). Includes improvisation. Other style(s): popular music, world music.
Former Jazz Education Development worker. Has held Jazz Vocal and composition workshops. (1999) Also runs songwriting workshops in primary schools. "As well as a strong focus on the practical and technical (vocal) elements of jazz vocals and its performance, much of my work is focusing on the development of self esteem and confidence, without which it is impossible to explore ones full potential as a creative and liberated vocalist."

Bannerman, Alf Kari
(London)
3 Blenheim Road, Stratford, London E15 1UF
020 8555 0339 tel/fax, alfredbanaman@hotmail.com
Instruments taught: Guitar, Percussion.
Teaches 1 to 1.
Workshops: Goldsmith College, Blackheath Halls, Breston Hall College.
Schools: Primary, secondary.
Workshop at International Guitarist Festival of Great Britain. Fusion of jazz with African contemporary music specifically Ghanaian hilife.

Barnard, Tony
(South East)
36 Station Road, Carshalton SM5 2LA
020 8647 1347
Instruments taught: Guitar.
Teaches 1 to 1.
Workshops: usually small groups. Speciality area(s): secondary, adult.
Schools: for 12-16 hours per week. Primary, secondary.
Qualifications: Dip Music (has been teaching for over 20 years). Includes improvisation. Other style(s): classical, world music.
Extensive teaching experience in New South Wales and Canberra Conservatoriums and workshops in Sydney, Bondi and Hayman Island.

Barrett, Elizabeth
(South East)
1 Barnard Gardens, Motspur Park, New Malden KT3 6QG
0208 942 4402, 07769 587958

Instruments taught: Flute, Piano.
Teaches 1 to 1. Teaches Associated Board Piano Exam. Age(s): under 11, 11 upwards. Area(s): reading, beginners, some knowledge, refresher, coaching. Place(s): own home.
Schools: Primary, secondary.
"I trained as a classical musician and felt my experience was lacking in the improvisation area - I have studied and been on courses and now developed knowledge and a love in this field."

Barron, Barbara
(West Midlands)

46 Merrivale Road, Stafford
01785 244147, 07971 765 940,
barbara@barron22.freeserve.co.uk
Instruments taught: Piano, Woodwind.
Teaches 1 to 1. Teaches Associated Board Piano Exam. Age(s): 11 upwards.
Area(s): reading, beginners, some knowledge, refresher, coaching. Place(s): own home.
Workshops: small groups. Speciality area(s): secondary, adult, composition, ladies Jazz Bands. Currently runs two jazz groups from home address.
Schools: for 4-8 hours per week. Secondary, HE/FE, adults.
Qualifications: LMus TCL; LTCL (GMT). (Has been teaching for 15-20 years.)
Includes improvisation.
"I have taught Jazz for twelve years to all ages. I perform regularly as a solo pianist or in a band. I am doing a Masters degree in jazz at Leeds College of Music. My pupils love their jazz studies. I work to a high standard and use two academic exam systems."

Bartlett, Rachel
(London)

21a Navarino Road, Hackney, London E8 1AD
020 7254 2829, 07989 686036, duncan.noble@btinternet.com
Instruments taught: Alto Sax, Clarinet, Soprano Sax, Tenor Sax, Flute.
Trained with Community Music under John Stevens in 1989. Teaching experience in Adult Education and schools and privately since 1989. Member of 'Transisters' performance and workshop group working in schools for the last three years.

Batson, Ray
(Eastern)

26 Broadacres, Luton LU2 7YF
01582 453419 tel/fax, ray@nostab.freeserve.co.uk
www.cljazz.co.uk
Instruments taught: Flugel Horn, Trumpet, Bass Trombone.
Teaches 1 to 1. Age(s): 17 plus. Area(s): reading, beginners, some knowledge, refresher, coaching. Place(s): own home, pupil's home.
Workshops: small groups. Speciality area(s): small groups, tertiary, adult. Jazz Improvisation Workshop, South Luton Community College, Melbourn Village College. Crayford Manor House.
Schools: for 8-12 hours per week. HE/FE, adults.
Qualifications: Certificate in Education. (Has been teaching for 15-20 years.)
Includes improvisation. Other style(s): popular music.
Also a tutor on 'CL Jazz' Easter, summer and autumn courses in Wales (see sepa-

rate entry). Attends many music courses himself to refresh his knowledge of teaching techniques and education. "Able to appreciate student and tutor view-point. See the groups that I teach as not about passing exams but as enjoyment, playing with other musicians and self improvement".

Baylis, Paul
(North West)
6 Simister Green, Simister, Prestwich, Manchester M25 2RY
0161 798 9700, 0966 538 639 mobile
Instruments taught: Saxophone.
Teaches 1 to 1. Age(s): under 11, 11 upwards. Area(s): beginners, some knowl-edge, refresher, coaching. Place(s): own home, pupil's home.
Workshops. Has been teaching the saxophone for seven years. "I am a self-taught musician who nevertheless has toured, recorded and gigged professionally since 1984. I teach people as individuals finding out what sort of 'sound' they are inter-ested in, then I proceed with the mechanics, feelings etc".

Beaujolais, Roger
(London)
Basement Flat, 12a Lower Clapton Road, London E5 0PD
020 8533 4178 tel/fax, 07909 850419
vibes-r-us@staytuned.freeserve.co.uk, www.rogerbeaujolais.com
Instruments taught: Vibraphone, Marimba.
Teaches 1 to 1. Age(s): 17 plus. Area(s): some knowledge, refresher, coaching. Place(s): own home.
Qualifications: None. (Has been teaching for 15-20 years.) Includes improvisation. Other style(s): popular music, world music, other (Funk, Latin).
"Best way to learn is by practical experience and listening. I help my students to listen and direct them in a way that helps them to understand the music".

Beck, Mick
(Yorkshire)
78 Kingfield Road, Sheffield S11 9AU
0114 258 4999, 0796 055 2087, mick.beck1@btinternet.com
Instruments taught: Saxophone, Bassoon.
Teaches 1 to 1. Age(s): under 11, 11upwards. Area(s): some knowledge, refresher, coaching. Place(s): own home.
Workshops: Improvisation, mixed ability. Specialisation - free improvisation and instant compositions.
(Has been teaching for 10-15 years). Includes improvisation. Other style(s): classi-cal.
"My interest is in teaching people about music and different ways of generating it, rather than sticking to a particular formula. I introduce people to flexible and inno-vative approaches to their instruments, developing a range of improvisation tech-niques. I mostly do this through group workshops. On teaching individual instru-ments, I have advanced technical skills on the saxophone and moderate skills on the bassoon. I share these with students preferring to give occasional lessons with lots of ideas, asking students to work on them for a while before returning".

Beebee, Dave
(South East)
17 Corsica Road, Seaford BN25 1BB
01323 894224, david.beebee@virgin.net
www.davidbeebee.co.uk
Instruments taught: Bass Clarinet, Piano.
Teaches 1 to 1. Teaches Associated Board Piano Exam. Age(s): 11 upwards.
Workshops: Saturdays 1 to 1 and groups at Blackheath Conservatoire.
Qualifications: Teaching Diploma from the Royal Academy of Music.
"I have been teaching the piano, bass, guitar, harmony theory for the last 10
years, including 5 years at Kingston University, as well as some group workshops"

Benham, Patrick
(South West)
Redmeads, Wagg Drove, Huish Episcopi, Langport BA16 OYD
01458 250278, PB@millfield.somerset.sch.uk
Instruments taught: Guitar.
Teaches 1 to 1.
Workshops: usually small groups. Speciality area(s): secondary, tertiary.
Schools: for 16+ hours per week. Secondary, HE/FE.
(Has been teaching for over 20 years). Other style(s): popular music, classical.
"I have the ability to work at the level of the student and to demonstrate improvi-
sation skills. I also compose and arrange for a school ensemble - allowing students
an input into the development of the material with the emphasis on shared explo-
ration - vocalist participation encouraged."

Bennett, John
(London)
61 Hampton Road, Forest Gate, London E7 0NX
020 8522 0058, 0976 232 452 mobile
johnbennettband@another.com
Instruments taught: Trombone, Euphonium, Trumpet.
Teaches 1 to 1. Age(s): under 11, 11 upwards. Area(s): reading, beginners, some
knowledge, refresher, coaching. Place(s): own home, pupil's home, other (Schools
and Art Centres).
Workshops: Jazz Music workshop at Brady Centre on Mondays;The Space on the
Isle of Dogs (London).
Schools: Primary, secondary, HE/FE, adults, special needs.
Has run adult music workshops in Tower Hamlets for 10 years as well as at
Goldsmiths College. "I try to keep the atmosphere open and relaxed. I use the
Blues Standards and my own compositions. I try to demystify scales and chords
and encourage anyone, at any level, to take part and to play in an ensemble".

Bennett, Rex
(South East)

1 Ellery Close, Cranleigh GU6 8DF
01483 276393, 0788 7738318
Instruments taught: Drums.
Teaches 1 to 1. Age(s): 11 upwards. Area(s): reading, beginners, some knowledge.
Experience - "A long stint as a session musician, plus an association with Big Bands and Jazz groups."

Bentley, Alison
(South East)

43 Arnold Road, Oxford OX4 4BH
01865 728275, 07711 372 846
alisonbentley@jazzmenagerie.freeserve.co.uk
Instruments taught: Voice.
Teaches 1 to 1. Age(s): under 11, 11 upwards. Area(s): reading, beginners, some knowledge, refresher, coaching. Place(s): own home.
Workshops: usually large groups, classes (20+). Speciality area(s): adult vocal techniques, harmony, improvisation.
Schools: for 1-4 hours per week. Secondary, HE/FE, adults.
Qualifications: PGCE (English/Drama); RSA Dip TEFLA (has been teaching for 5-10 years). Includes improvisation. Other style(s): popular music, world music.
"I have an interest in relating jazz songs to popular singing styles e.g. soul and an ability to teach vocal improvisation as if the voice were an instrument. I have experienced training in Estill vocal method, which is a disciplined approach to vocal technique."

Berg, Russell van den
(London)

3 Underwood Road, London IG8 7LD
020 8502 9893, 07759 790 709
russellbecky@vandenberg0.freserve.co.uk
Instruments taught: Clarinet, Saxophone.
Teaches 1 to 1. Age(s): 11 upwards. Area(s): beginners, some knowledge, refresher, coaching. Place(s): own home, pupil's home.
Workshops: small groups, classes (20+). Wavenden Summer and Winter courses. Specialisation - group interaction, band sound (colour), improvisation.
Secondary schools, HE/FE.
Qualifications: Graduate Diploma. Postgraduate Diploma (has been teaching for 5-10 years). Includes improvisation. Other style(s): popular music, classical, world music, other (Dutch speaker. Also plays the harmonica).
"I've been a student myself and realise how to communicate to a pupil and understand the personal barriers pupils need to acknowledge in order to progress beyond their present understanding of themselves musically, to allow for effortless practice and greater freedom in playing."

Bernard, Bob
(South East)

57 Ferndale, Tunbridge Wells
01892 523497, bob@nbernard.co.uk

www.bobbernard.koolhost.com
Instruments taught: Saxophone, Clarinet.
Teaches 1 to 1.
Kent County Council Music Teacher at Tonbridge and Tunbridge Wells Girls Grammar school

Berry, John
(South West)

16 Elton Road, Bishopston, Bristol BS7 8DA
0117 942 2532, berrys@jontag.freeserve.co.uk
Instruments taught: Trombone, Piano.
Teaches 1 to 1. Age(s): under 11, 11 upwards. Area(s): reading, beginners, some knowledge, coaching. Place(s): own home, other (schools).
Workshops: usually large groups. Speciality area(s): secondary. Director of North Bristol Big Band - organised by the Bristol Music Service. Currently, weekly at West Bristol Music Centre, Portway School, Penpole Lane, Shirehampton, Bristol. Portway Community School Summer Music School. Specialisation, Big Band work.
Schools: for 16+ hours per week. Secondary.
Qualifications: B.Ed. (Music Educ), M.Ed. (Bristol) ARCM (has been teaching for over 20 years).
"I have considerable experience as a player in the Big Bands of the 1950s onwards and wide professional expertise over forty years. I am still active as a player (local jazz groups and Big Bands) and teacher having spent years as a Director of Music in a comprehensive school. I have run a private teaching practice for over 30 years."

Berry, Steve
(North West)

51 Alexandra Road, Blackburn BB2 6DW
01254 673871 tel/fax, steve@room4music.com
www.room4music.com
Instruments taught: Cello, Piano, Double Bass.
Teaches 1 to 1.
Workshops: small groups, large groups, classes (20+). A lot of experience of work-shops, from reception classes (infant schools) through to leading classes at music colleges and Glamorgan Summer School (since 1991) and Burnley Summer school since 1995. Currently active leading Improvisation workshops in schools, colleges and community Schools: for 8-12 hours per week. Qualifications: None (has been teaching for 10-15 years). Other style(s): popular music, classical, world music.
First workshops on UK tour with 'Loose Tubes' in 1986. Jazz Animateur for Wigan MBC 1990-92. 'Animateur in Composition' started in 1999, for three years, at Worcester.

Berwin, Lindsey
(Yorkshire)

41 The Fairway, Leeds LS17 7PE
0113 268 4866, home@berwin.co.uk
Instruments taught: Piano.
Teaches 1 to 1. Teaches Associated Board Piano Exam. Age(s): under 11, 11upwards. Area(s): reading, beginners, some knowledge. Place(s): own home.
Workshops: EPTA Yorks on how to get started on Associated Board Jazz

Improvisation (using other teachers' pupils). Hope to be invited to do similar workshops in other areas.

Qualifications: GRSM HONS; LRAM; PGCE (has been teaching for 10-15 years). Includes improvisation. Other style(s): popular music, classical.

"I feel I am good at taking each student as an individual and 'steering' them in the direction which will help them find their own potential. I seem to be able to do this with any age group."

Beyer, Lawrence
(West Midlands)

84 Woodlands Road, Sparkhill, Birmingham
0121 7777871, lawrence-beyeer@beeb.net
Instruments taught: Piano.
Teaches 1 to 1. Teaches Associated Board Piano Exam. Age(s): 11 to 16. Area(s): beginners, some knowledge, refresher. Place(s): own home.

"As a piano teacher, I want to give my pupils as varied a choice of music styles as possible. I have a personal interest in jazz and enjoy not only teaching but also playing jazz with my pupils and listening to jazz with them."

Bianco, Tony
(London)

56 Alexandria Park Road, London N10 2AD
020 8444 4628
Instruments taught: Drums.
Teaches 1 to 1.
Taught workshops in New York City and Germany.

Bilham, Andrew
(South West)

78 Trefusis Road, Redruth TR15 2JL
01209 219581
Instruments taught: Piano.
Teaches 1 to 1. Teaches Associated Board Piano Exam.
Workshops: small groups, large groups.
Schools: for 16+ hours per week. Secondary. HE/FE, adults (21+).
(Has been teaching for 10-15 years). Includes improvisation. Other style(s): popular music.

Birkby, Peter
(Yorkshire)

PO Box 7, South Kirby, Pontefract WF9 3XJ
01977 648645 tel/fax, 07770 300 593, music@prbp.co.uk
www.prbp.co.uk
Instruments taught: Percussion.
Teaches 1 to 1.
Workshops: small groups, large groups. Speciality area(s): large groups, tertiary. Salsa Bands at Leeds College of Music and Percussion at Barnsley College.
Schools: for 16+ hours per week. Secondary. HE/FE, special needs. Barnsley College, Leeds College of Music.
Qualifications: GCLCM, LRAM. (Has been teaching for 15-20 years.) Includes improvisation. Other style(s): popular music, world music.

"My professional experience in performing jazz, pop, classical, 20th century music, salsa, samba etc has given me a diverse musical education. From this point I can relate to the student's musical roots and develop their style and listening skills, hopefully put into practise on their chosen instruments."

Birkett, James
(North East)
Faculty of Visual and Perf Arts, Rye Hill Campus, Scottswood Road, Newcastle upon Tyne NE4 7SA
0191 232 1718 tel/fax, jamesbirkett@btinternet.com
Instruments taught: Guitar.

Biscoe, Chris
(South East)
27a Crescent Road, Kingston upon Thames KT2 7RD
020 8549 4465, 020 8547 3701 home fax
Chris@biscoe.fsbusincess.co.uk, www.geocities.com/chrisbiscoe internet
Instruments taught: Saxophone, Clarinet.
Teaches 1 to 1. Age(s): 11 upwards. Area(s): reading, beginners, some knowledge. Place(s): own home, pupil's home.
Workshops: in Somerset school, others set up in Aylesbury, Blackheath, Bristol. Also with Grand Union, Mike Westbrook and his own bands. Has taught saxophone on an Eddie Harvey Course. Specialisation - structuring performance. "I have been instrumental in setting up workshops, which look at ways of introducing inexperienced (in jazz terms) musicians to improvisation through the use of melodic fragments, rhythmic devices, non-diatonic scale patterns and organised collective improvisation."

Bitelli, David
(London)
London NW10 9AP
020 8965 2624, bitelli@talk21.com
Instruments taught: Alto Sax, Tenor Sax, Baritone Sax.
Teaches 1 to 1. Place(s): pupil's home.
Workshops: Schools: One day a week at local secondary school.
2002 taught at Glamorgan Summer school. In the past has taught at Trinity College and Southampton University

Blackmore, Dave
(London)
76 Powerscroft Road, London E5 0PP
020 8533 0152 tel/fax
Instruments taught: Clarinet, Saxophone.
Teaches 1 to 1.
Workshops. Speciality area(s): large groups, primary, secondary, tertiary, adult. In 1980s ran beginners and Intermediate jazz workshops. Schools: for 4-8 hours per week. Primary, secondary.
Qualifications: Diploma in Jazz and Studio Music (Guildhall SMD). (Has been teaching for 15-20 years.) Includes improvisation. Other style(s): popular music, classical, world music.

Blackwell, John
(Eastern)
48 Victoria Street, Dunstable
01582 475674
Instruments taught: Piano.
Teaches 1 to 1. Teaches Associated Board Piano Exam. Area(s): reading, beginners, some knowledge, refresher, coaching. Place(s): own home.
Workshops: usually small groups.
Schools: for 16+ hours per week. Primary,secondary. HE/FE, adults. Northfields Upper School, Houghton Road, Dunstable, Beds.
Qualifications: Degree in Jazz Studies (Leeds College of Music) (has been teaching for 5-10 years). Includes improvisation. Other style(s): popular music.

Blackwell, John Keith
(London)
Flat 4, 212a Richmond Road, London E8 3QN
020 7254 2311, 0802 498668 mobile
Instruments taught: Guitar.
Teaches 1 to 1. Age(s): under 11, 11 upwards: reading, beginners, some knowledge, refresher, coaching. Place(s): own home.
Workshops: usually small groups. Speciality area(s): secondary, tertiary. In past has run workshops at Islington Arts Factory, Goldsmiths College, Hampstead Garden Suburb AE Institute. Schools: for 16+ hours per week. Primary and secondary, HE/FE, adults.
Qualifications: No Formal Academic qualifications (has been teaching for 10-15 years). Other style(s): popular music.
1985 to date - private tuition of jazz standards, scales and theory. Since 1987 has taught at Westminster school on individual tuition in jazz guitar. Runs workshops in Jazz Guitar Repertoire and Improvisation at Westminster. Also at Chichester on Free Improvisation (on the BTEC National Diploma) "I enjoy contact with musicians of all ages and abilities. Communication between musicians brings joy into our lives."

Blenkiron, Nigel
(Yorkshire)
c/o Sixth Form College, Sandy Bed Lane, Scarborough YO12 5LS
www.wiganjazz.net
Instruments taught: Trombone, Bass Guitar, Trumpet.
Teaches 1 to 1.
Qualifications: LTCL Cert Ed (has been teaching for over 20 years). Includes improvisation. Other style(s): popular music, classical.

Blunn, Nick
(West Midlands)
12 Showell Grove, Droitwich WR9 8UD
01905 776 688 tel /fax, 07973 7197691
nick@keypres.freeserve.co.uk
Instruments taught: Piano, Keyboards.
Teaches 1 to 1. Teaches Associated Board Piano Exam. Age(s): under 11, 11 upwards. Area(s): reading, beginners, some knowledge, refresher, coaching. Place(s): own home, pupil's home.

Workshops: small groups. Worcester Theatre Jazz Workshop (18 people). Specialisation - Group/Ensemble/Jazz/composition.
Schools: for 16+ hours per week. primary, secondary, HE/FE, adults.
Qualifications: B Ed (has been teaching for 10-15 years). Includes improvisation.
Other style(s): popular music, classical.
"I am a professional pianist and have been engaged to fulfil a variety of roles over the last twenty years. I am an examiner for the Associated Board Jazz Syllabus and currently teach thirty pianists." Currently teaches at Redditch College

Boardman, Bruce
(South East)

c/o 10 Southfield Gardens, Twickenham TW1 4SZ
07879 446879, bruceboardman@vizzavi.net
Instruments taught: Clarinet, Piano.
Teaches 1 to 1.
Teachs regularly at some schools in the Hertfordshire area, both jazz and classical
Enjoys teaching a variety of music.

Bolton, Chris
(West Midlands)

Asterton Hall Farm, Asterton, Lydbury North SY7 8BH
01588 650408 tel/fax
Instruments taught: Piano.
Teaches 1 to 1. Teaches Associated Board Piano Exam. Age(s): under 11, 11 upwards. Area(s): reading, beginners, some knowledge, refresher, coaching. Place(s): own home.
Workshops: small groups, large groups, classes (20+). Speciality area(s): small groups, secondary. Composing and arranging jazz, works for specific ensembles. Previously Jazz Central Workshops - Birmingham. Currently Shropshire Youth Jazz Ensemble, Church Stretton Schools: for 16+ hours per week. pre-school, primary secondary.
Qualifications: LGSM; G Mus, Dip Mus (has been teaching for over 20 years). Other style(s): world music.
"I have been a jazz tutor for over twenty years, both on a one-to-one basis, at workshops and running youth bands. I specialise in teaching children (3 - 18) and, in particular, improvisation. I also compose and arrange music for both solo piano and jazz ensembles."

Booth, Brian
(Eastern)

40 Butterfield Road, Wheathampstead AL4 8QH
01582 832425
Instruments taught: Drums, Percussion.
Teaches 1 to 1. Age(s): under 11, 11 upwards. Place(s): own home.
Workshops: small groups, large groups. Speciality area(s): small·groups.
Schools: pre-school, primary, secondary, HE/FE, adults, special needs.
(Has been teaching for over 20 years).
Runs small jazz group 'Your Move' from Watford Grammar school who have performed at Royal Festival Hall Foyer(London)

Bos, Pieter Jaap
(London)
pjbosman@hotmail.com
Instruments taught: Keyboards, Piano.
Teaches 1 to 1. Teaches Associated Board Piano Exam. Age(s): under 11, 11
upwards. Area(s): reading, beginners, some knowledge, refresher, coaching.
Place(s): own home, other (Schools, institutions).
Workshops: Extensive workshops in New Zealand at high schools. Specialisation -
Improvisation, Harmony.

Bowdler, Dave
(South East)
27 Station Road, Sidcup SE18 1NT
Instruments taught: Saxophone, Flute, Clarinet.
Teaches 1 to 1. Age(s): under 11, 11 upwards. Area(s): reading, beginners, some
knowledge, refresher, coaching. Place(s): own home.
Workshops: small groups. Speciality area(s): Primary. Beginners woodwind -
although not strictly jazz, using backing CDs. Jazz Workshops - Goldsmith College
Schools: for 8-12 hours per week. primary, secondary, adults.
Qualifications: L.G.S.M. (has been teaching for over 20 years). Includes improvisa-
tion. Other style(s): classical.

Bowers, Rachel
(South West)
Forge Cottage, Butcombe, Bristol BS407UT
01761 462 769, rachel@theebowers.demon.co.uk
Instruments taught: Piano.
Teaches 1 to 1. Teaches Associated Board Piano Exam. Age(s): under 11, 11
upwards. Area(s): reading, beginners, some knowledge, refresher. Place(s): own
home.
Qualifications: CT ABRSM (has been teaching for 5-10 years). Other style(s): popular music, classical.
"I am an active amateur musician with considerable performing experience in a
variety of contexts, as a piano acccompanist to choirs and drama groups, and
accordion player with folk and Irish bands. I teach both classical and Jazz piano to
children and adults at beginner and intermediate level. I aim to develop confident
practical musicianship in all my students".

Bowles, Geoff
(South West)
22 Hollis Gardens, Cheltenham GL51 6JQ
01242 236482, geoffbow@cableinet.co.uk
Instruments taught: Saxophone, Clarinet, Flute.
Teaches 1 to 1.
(Has been teaching for 5-10 years). Includes improvisation. Other style(s): popular
music, classical.
Private tuition. School teaching.

Boyd, Denis
(Scotland)
3 Gamekeepers Walk, Kinneswood KY13 7JS

01592 840877
Instruments taught: Trombone.
Teaches 1 to 1.
Workshops: small groups. Speciality area(s): 1 to 1, small groups, primary,
Schools: for 16+ hours per week. Primary, secondary.
Qualifications: HND Music Studies (has been teaching for 3-5 years). Includes
improvisation. Other style(s): classical, world music.

Brannan, Mick
(Eastern)

58 Belle Vue Road, Wivenhoe, Colchester CO7 9LD
01206 825829
Instruments taught: Alto Sax, Piano.
Teaches 1 to 1. Age(s): 11 upwards. Area(s): beginners, some knowledge,
refresher, coaching. Place(s): wherever
Workshops: small groups, classes (20+). Specialisation: Jazz, Fusion,
Improvisation. St Mary's Arts Centre, Colchester (1991). N E Essex Institute Music
School (1988).
Eastern Jazz workshop tutor 87, 88. MU workshop tutor (Eastern region). Jazz and
improvisation tutor at Essex University
Schools: for 16+ hours per week. HE/FE.
Qualifications: B.Ed (Hons)/Teacher Cert (has been teaching for 10-15 years).
Includes improvisation. Other style(s): popular music, other (Blues/Funk/Soul).
Currently Senior course tutor on Access to Music Foundation course at Colchester
Institute. "I try to tailor my approach to students' particular needs. I supply piano
backgrounds (my own and pre-recorded tapes) to make the theory 'more practi-
cal'. I supply handouts. Students need not be sight readers. The theoretical per-
spective is explored."

Bray, Ned
(London)

60 Burrard Road, West Hampstead, London NW6 1DD
020 7435 2939, 020 7794 7589 fax, 07778913701
jazzindo@k.white.dircon.co.uk, www.jazzindo.co.uk
Instruments taught: Alto Sax, Tenor Sax, Clarinet.
Teaches 1 to 1. Age(s): under 11, 11 upwards. Area(s): reading, beginners, some
knowledge, refresher. Place(s): pupil's home.
(Has been teaching for 3-5 years). Includes improvisation. Other style(s): popular
music, classical, world music.
"For many years I worked as a Creative Director in Advertising and also lectured in
Creative thinking and development. I use these techniques, together with my own
methods to bring out the potential in the student."

Breingan, Stan
(Scotland)

8 Ailsa Street, Prestwick KA9 1RH
01292 678148
Instruments taught: Piano, Keyboards.
Teaches 1 to 1.
(Has been teaching for over 20 years). Includes improvisation. Other style(s): pop-
ular music.

Brian, Robert
(South West)

29 Paul Street, Corsham SN13 9DG
01249 715473, 01249 713144 fax, 07718 225 063
rob@brian1770.fsnet.co.uk
Instruments taught: Vibraphone, Percussion, Drums.
Teaches 1 to 1. Age(s): 11 upwards. Area(s): reading, beginners, some knowledge, refresher. Place(s): pupil's home, other (schools).
Workshops: Previously Sherborne School for boys, Sherborne/St Marks School Bath/ Assembly Music Bath. Has worked for Avon and Somerset county councils as visiting teacher.

Brown, Jill
(Eastern)

11 Rowlands Close, Foxton, Cambridge CB2 6SQ
01223 872006, jil@jbrown44.fsnet.co.uk
Instruments taught: Double Bass.
Teaches 1 to 1. Age(s): 11 upwards. Area(s): reading, beginners, some knowledge, refresher, coaching. Place(s): own home.
Workshops: small groups. Speciality area(s): small groups, primary, adult. Previously, Melbourn Village College and Bottisham Village College - group sessions. Currently, Jazz workshop - Anglia Polytechnic University, Cambridge. Specialisation: beginners/elementary.
Schools: for 1-4 hours per week.
Qualifications: Teacher's Certificate, Diploma in Music Education (has been teaching for over 20 years). Available for individual tuition in harmony, and for workshop sessions. "I concentrate on explaining the basis of harmony without which improvisation is aimless and without form. Also on the listening skills: to each other and constructively to live and recorded performances. No-one can play jazz without proper listening! Beginners are then enabled to move on, form groups and play with confidence."

Brown, Simon
(Eastern)

23 Grange Road, Norwich NR2 3NH
01603 259799, mr.brown@cwcom.net
Instruments taught: Keyboards, Piano.   .
Teaches 1 to 1. Teaches Associated Board Piano Exam. Age(s): under 11, 11 upwards. Area(s): reading, beginners, some knowledge, refresher. Place(s): own home.
(Has been teaching for 5-10 years). Includes improvisation. Other style(s): popular music.
"As my experience as a jazz pianist has broadened over the last ten years, I have been able to pass this on to my students. This experience ranges from the more 'straight forward' musical issues of timing, reading, 'feel' etc to observations of on-stage scenarios - ie setting up, plugging in, using microphones, etc. I arrange jazz pieces to suit specific students, write MIDI file backing/jam tracks, prepare students for gigs, jam sessions and college auditions."

Browne, Anton
(South East)
PO BOX 1018, Croydon CR9 3YX
07966 237 099, music@handmaid.co.uk, www.handmaid.co.uk
anton@antonbrowne.co.uk, www.antonbrowne.co.uk
Instruments taught: Voice.
Teaches 1 to 1.
Produced singing practice CD - "The Sing Thing" for Hand Maid Music.
Initially ran workshops at Jenako Arts in Islington, then on to Lewisham College.
Set up the BTEC singing course(at the then brand new) BRIT School in 1991.
Currently working with Southwark College, The City Lit and continuing the association with the BRIT School.

Browning, D A
(North West)
The White House, Rotherwood Road, Wilmslow SK9 6DR
01625 527756
Instruments taught: Trumpet, Flugel Horn.
Teaches 1 to 1.
Workshops: usually 1 to 1. Speciality area(s): 1 to 1, small groups.
Schools: for 8-12 hours per week. HE/FE, adults
(Has been teaching for over 20 years). Includes improvisation. Other style(s): popular music.

Bruer, Jason
(London)
40 Beresford Road, London N8 OAJ
020 8374 7455 tel/fax, 0802 436 288 mobile
jason@bruer.fsbusiness.co.uk, www.smithandbruer.com
Instruments taught: Alto Sax, Soprano Sax, Tenor Sax.
Teaches 1 to 1.
Musical Director of the Young Music Makers in Highgate on Saturdays for 5 to 18 years see website www.youngmusicmakers.co.uk

Brush, Andy
(East Midlands)
Access to Music, 18 York Road, Leicester LE1 5TS
Instruments taught: Saxophone, Wind Synthesizer.
Teaches 1 to 1.
Qualifications: ATM, IMF, NVQ Level 3 (has been teaching for 3-5 years). Includes improvisation. Other style(s): popular music.

Bryant, Mark
(London)
2 Vassall House, Antill Road, London E3 5BS
020 8980 7839
Instruments taught: Percussion, Drums.
Teaches 1 to 1.
Teaches general drum technique and variety of basic styles that includes jazz drumming at the Centre for Young Musicians and university college school.

Bryce, Owen
(East Midlands)
58 Pond Bank, Blisworth NN7 3EL
01604 858192, owen-iris@bryceo.fsnet.co.uk
www.mysite.freeserve.com/bryceandjazz internet
Instruments taught: Trumpet, Piano.
Workshops: Teacher on many short courses which mainly concentrate on Big Band and Dixieland idioms.
(Has been teaching for over 20 years). Other style(s): popular music.
Runs practical jazz courses - includes Big Band, Jazz Improvisation and Harmony and Beginners. See Courses.

Bundy, Rachel
(South East)
Brighton
01273 604758, 07747 866 457
music@rachelbundy.co.uk, www.rachelbundy.co.uk
Instruments taught: Voice.
Distinction in jazz diploma-Chichester college

Burch, John
(South East)
55 Millstrood Road, Whitstable CT5 1QF
01227 274898
Instruments taught: Piano.
Teaches 1 to 1. Age(s): 17 plus. Area(s): beginners, some knowledge, refresher, coaching.
Workshops: City Lit Jazz Courses in London.
Original Barry Summer School Jazz tutor for 11 years from 1969. "Active Jazz Pianist for 41 years (Refer 'Groves' Dictionary of Jazz Musicians, John Chilton's 'Jazz in London of the 60s, etc.) (Also Leonard Feathers 'Encyclopedia of jazz)."

Burgess, John
(Scotland)
5 Collins Place, Stockbridge, Edinburgh EH3 5JD
01620 822 542, johnburgess222@hotmail.com
www.jazz-in-scotland.co.uk/urge2burge.htm internet
Instruments taught: Clarinet, Flute, Saxophone.
Teaches 1 to 1 in students own home. All styles. Beginners welcome

Burn, Chris
(Eastern)

11 Marks Avenue, Ongar CM5 9AY
01277 362 416 tel/fax, chrisburn@talk21.com
Instruments taught: Piano.
Workshops: Previously London Musicians Collective, Community Music,
Specialisation - Approaches to Free improvisation and large group Improvisation.
His ensemble gives improvisation workshops in schools, colleges and Universities
and he teaches at Colchester Institute. Organises 'Mopo Moso' improvised music
events with John Russell. "Vast experience in leading workshops, often with 'Chris
Burn's Ensemble' - group of eleven improvising musicians"

Burrows, Clive
(West Midlands)

67 Monkmoor Road, Shrewsbury SY2 5AT
monkmoor@compuserve.com
Instruments taught: Alto Sax.
3 years composition and saxophone tuition with the late baritone saxophonist
Ronnie Ross.

Butterworth, Martin
(Wales)

2 Rock Villa, Rifle Street, Blaenavon NP4 9QN
07811 893 353
Instruments taught: Saxophone, Clarinet.
Teaches 1 to 1.
Qualifications: None. (Has been teaching for 15-20 years.) Includes improvisation.

Buxton, Dave
(South West)

76 Snowberry Close, Bradley Stoke, Bristol BS32 8GB
01454 202347, 0771 2329159
David.Buxton7@btopenworld.com, www.musicteachers.co.uk
Instruments taught: Keyboards, Piano.
Teaches 1 to 1. Age(s): under 11, 11 upwards. Area(s): reading, beginners, some
knowledge, refresher, coaching. Place(s): own home.
(Has been teaching for over 20 years).
"I have 25 years experience as a jazz educator and professional jazz pianist, 6
years of which I toured and recorded albums with the 'Andy Sheppard Quintet'. I
provide the student with a wealth of knowledge and application, all of which I have
experienced in performance. I work on the student's mental and physical preparation before an improvisation. This enables the student to feel completely relaxed
and focused on the improvisation. I use rhythm section backing tracks on the CD
for the student to practise with, an opportunity to experience the 'feel' and the
'groove' of the music"

Buxton, Helen

(East Midlands)

6 Lakeside, Hadfield, Glossop SK13 1HW

01457 864218

Instruments taught: Piano.

Teaches 1 to 1. Teaches Associated Board Piano Exam. Age(s): under 11, 11 upwards. Area(s): reading, beginners, some knowledge. Place(s): own home, pupil's home.

Qualifications: CT; ABRSM. (Has been teaching for 15-20 years.) Includes improvisation.

"I have put myself through all 5 of the Associated Board exams to know I have achieved the required standard and to have a first hand knowledge of the exam situation."

Caldwell, Chris

(London)

Unit 317 Greenwich, Greenwich Commercial Centre, London SE10 8JL

020 8691 0569 tel/fax, 07768 076687, info@chriscaldwell.co.uk email

www.chriscaldwell.co.uk

Instruments taught: Saxophone.

Teaches 1 to 1.

Qualifications: GGSM. Includes improvisation. Other style(s): classical.

Callingham, Matthew

(East Midlands)

19 Station Road, Retford DN22 7DE

01777 708468

Instruments taught: Keyboards, Piano.

Teaches 1 to 1. Teaches Associated Board Piano Exam.

Workshops: small groups, large groups. Speciality area(s): large groups, primary, secondary, tertiary, adult.

Schools: for 16+ hours per week. Primary, secondary, HE/FE, adults

Qualifications: ABRSM Exams (has been teaching for 5-10 years). Includes improvisation. Other style(s): popular music, classical.

Weekly workshops at 1 Session Arts Support Service and Retford Music Workshops

Campbell, Duncan

(South East)

Field Gates, 29 Long Lane, Ickenham UB10 8QU

01835 674600

Instruments taught: Flugel Horn, Trumpet, Cornet.

Teaches 1 to 1.

Workshops: Psychology - towards the approach to jazz thinking.

Schools: Primary, secondary. HE/FE, adults

(Has been teaching for over 20 years). Includes improvisation. Other style(s): popular music, classical, world music.

Carr, Judy
(South East)
37 Bramley Rise Strood, Rochester MME2 3 SU
01643 718488, kelvin.carr@talk21.com
Instruments taught: Piano.
Teaches 1 to 1. Teaches Associated Board Piano Exam. Age(s): 17 plus. Area(s): beginners. Place(s): own home.
Qualifications: ATCL (Performance) LTCL (Teaching). (Has been teaching for 15-20 years.)
'I have only just begun learning and teaching jazz so I am very new to the scene. I am basically a classical teacher and hope to invest some time in learning more jazz styles. At the moment I only have one jazz student and we are enjoying experimenting with ideas simultaneously as we prepare for the ABRSM jazz exams.

Carr, Mike
(London)
39 Clitterhouse Crescent, London NW2 1DB
020 8458 1020 tel/fax, www.mikecarr.co.uk
Instruments taught: Organ, Piano.
Teaches 1 to 1. Age(s): 17 plus. Area(s): refresher. Place(s): own home.
(Has been teaching for 15-20 years.) Includes improvisation.
Wrote and produced 12" single dedicated to the jazz greats called 'Jazz Rap'. The nicknames were printed on the inside sleeve with a short biography of each. "When asked to help students with improvisation on piano or in the art of playing Hammond organ I am happy to try and help. I am basically a self-taught musician so I concentrate on this part of tuition."

Cartledge, David
(South East)
56 Margaret Road, Oxford OX3 8NQ
01865 766601
cartledgedave@aol.uk
Instruments taught: Keyboards, Piano.
Teaches 1 to 1. Teaches Associated Board Piano Exam. Age(s): under 11, 11upwards. Area(s): reading, beginners, some knowledge, refresher, coaching. Place(s): own home.
Qualifications: LRSM (Part 1) (has been teaching for 5-10 years). Includes improvisation. Other style(s): popular music, classical.
"Since gaining the Graduate Diploma (Jazz) at Leeds college of Music, I have performed in a wide variety of jazz styles. I approach jazz teaching in the broadest possible sense, incorporating listening to recordings, improvisation/composition, personal expression, technical aspects and study of the classical repertoire"

Catchpole, Nat
(London)
47 St Peter's Close, Bethnal Green, London E2 7AE
020 7739 1691, 0790 5532985, natcatchpole@hotmail.com
www.geocities.com/nathanielcatchpole internet
Instruments taught: Tenor Banjo, Baritone Sax.

Cater, Peter
(Eastern)
PO BOX 123, Borehamwood WD6 3ZG
020 8953 3830, 020 8386 8487 fax, 0831 419958
pete.cater@virgin.net, www.petecaterbigband.com
Instruments taught: Drums.
Teaches 1 to 1.
Currently teaching jazz drums, creativity and improvisation for Thames Valley University, Brunel University

Cave, Phoene
(South East)
201 Hanworth Road, Hampton TW12 3ED
07970 615241, phoene.cave@blueyonder.co.uk
Instruments taught: Voice.
Teaches 1 to 1. Age(s): 11 upwards. Area(s): reading, beginners, some knowledge, refresher, coaching. Place(s): own home, pupil's home.
Workshops: small groups, large groups. Music Therapy Sessions with children with Special Needs, 1 to 1 with adults with learning difficulties, music sessions with Pre-School children, music Reading and Writing Skills, student teacher at Goldsmiths college, Jazz Vocal Workshop, Saturday Jazz School at Richmond Adult and Community College.
Qualifications: Bachelor of Music, Diploma in Music Therapy, Cert in Music Teaching to Adults. (Has been teaching for 2-3 years). Includes improvisation. Other style(s): popular music.
"My enthusiasm is for teaching others to find their voice and have the courage to sing with confidence! I have twelve years experience as a professional singer in the world of jazz and pop, combined with 'behind the scenes' knowledge, having worked in one of London's leading theatrical agents as well as TV and Record Companies. As well as my academic qualifications I am also a qualified Music Therapist which gives me a unique understanding of the emotional and psychological aspects of music making and voice production."

Chadwick, James
(London)
20 Westview close, Grove Avenue, Hanwell, London W7 3DZ
020 8566 2836, 0771 4539663
Instruments taught: Guitar.
Teaches 1 to 1. Age(s): under 11, 11 upwards. Area(s): reading, beginners, some knowledge, refresher, coaching. Place(s): own home, pupil's home.
Workshops: Various Schools. Also jazz course at Battersea Arts Centre..
Schools: Secondary. HE/FE, adults
Likes to help people discover jazz through playing and encouraging the 'fun' part of playing.

Chambers, Dave
(London)
4 Cleve Road, London NW6 3RR
020 7624 6626, dch@mr nice.net
Instruments taught: Alto Sax, Tenor Sax.
Teaches 1 to 1. Age(s): 11 upwards. Area(s): reading, beginners, some knowl-

edge, refresher, coaching. Place(s): own home.
"I am only interested in helping people who want to learn. I can teach tone production, phrasing, timing and rhythm."

Chambers, Stephanie
(South East)
11 Henwood Crescent, Pembury, Tunbridge Wells TN2 4LJ
01892 822397 home tel
Instruments taught: Piano, Recorder, Keyboards.
Teaches 1 to 1. Teaches Associated Board Piano Exam. Age(s): under 11, 11 upwards. Area(s): beginners. Place(s): own home.
Qualifications: LTCL; PCET (has been teaching for over 20 years). Includes improvisation. Other style(s): popular music.
'I have a wide interest in most forms of music.'

Chapman, Greg
(London)
44 Adelaide Avenue, Brockley, London SE4 1YR
020 8469 0609 tel/fax, 07788 163517, gc@freeuk.com
home.freeuk.net/gc/ internet
Instruments taught: Piano.
Teaches 1 to 1. Teaches Associated Board Piano Exam. Age(s): 11 upwards. Area(s): reading, beginners, some knowledge, refresher, coaching. Place(s): own home.
Workshops: Jazz Workshops at the Four Bars Inn (Cardiff) and schools and colleges. Keyboard workshop at the Premises (London)
Qualifications: Grade 8 and BA in music (has been teaching for over 20 years). Includes improvisation. Other style(s): popular music, classical, world music.
Had 20 years experience teaching privately at schools, colleges and open workshops particularly sensitive to needs of classically trained musicians crossing over into jazz, can provide tailor made practise tapes. Deputy for Tim Richards' jazz classes at Goldsmiths and Morley College.

Charlton, Kay
(London)
19a Glenarm Road, Clapton, London E5 0LY
020 8985 2200 tel/fax, 07702 817994
Instruments taught: French Horn, Trumpet, Trombone.
Kay has worked with Greenwich and Lewisham Youth Jazz Orchestra and regularly works in schools with the 'Transisters'

Cheneour, Paul
(South East)
21b Charles Road, St Leonards on Sea TN38 0QH
01424 729569, 07980 823444
paul@redgoldmusic.com, www.redgoldmusic.com
Instruments taught: Flute.
Teaches 1 to 1.
Workshops: small groups. Speciality area(s): Primary, secondary.
Schools: for 12-16 hours per week (has been teaching for over 20 years). Includes improvisation. Other style(s): popular music, classical, world music, other (Arab,

Indian, Chinese, Japanese, Irish).
For 20 years PC has run workshops covering techniques of
Flute/Keyboards/Bassdrums, musical styles, improvising and composition along
with information on running your own band. Paul also gives Master classes in all
the above for Flute players and non musicians.

Chester, Ray
(North East)

10 Roker Park Terrace, Roker, Sunderland SR6 9LY
0191 567 3013, raychester@ukonline.co.uk
Instruments taught: Piano, Trombone, Trumpet.
Workshops: Previously Big Band for Sunderland LEA.
Qualifications: B.Ed (has been teaching for over 20 years). Includes improvisation.
Ten years teaching experience at Newcastle College. Not teaching at the moment
but interested should opportunity arise.
   "I think that my talent lies in coaching groups rather than in one-to-one teaching.
I taught on the jazz course at Newcastle College for ten years, taking early retire-
ment a few years ago. During that time I ran the Big Band and coached innumerable improvisation ensembles. I have run my own Big Band for over thirty years,
also small ensembles, and work as arranger and composer so that I have a good
insight into the way bands work. Prior to working at the College I helped to run a
Saturday morning Big Band for South Tyneside L.E.A. for a number of years so
that I have extensive experience in dealing with all age groups."

Christiane, Kelvin
(London)

8 Stella Road, London SW17 9HG
020 8682 9960, 020 7228 9160 fax, 07971 242864
kelvin@kcmusic.co.uk, www.kcmusic.co.uk
Instruments taught: Flute, Clarinet, Saxophone.
Teaches 1 to 1. Age(s): 17 plus. Area(s): beginners, some knowledge, refresher,
coaching. Place(s): own home.
Workshops, Speciality area(s): classes (20+), primary, secondary. Jazz Umbrella,
Morley college. Specialisation - jazz Improvisation.
Schools: for 1-4 hours per week. Secondary, adults
Qualifications: GDLM. (Has been teaching for 15-20 years.) Includes improvisation.
Other style(s): popular music, classical.
   "I aim to give students the confidence to try things out - make suggestions - have
huge amount of material to work from and provide a *fun* environment."

Churchill, Pete
(Eastern)

Chaucer Cottage, 57 Vicarage Lane, Kings Langley WD4 9HS
01923 269974 home tel
Instruments taught: Piano, Voice.
Teaches 1 to 1.
Workshops: small groups, large groups, classes (20+). Speciality area(s): adult.
Works with large choirs. Write pieces collectively and anything to do with working
'by ear'. Schools: for 16+ hours per week. Adults. Guildhall School Music/Drama,
Middlesex University.
(Has been teaching for 10-15 years). Includes improvisation. Other style(s): classi-
cal, world music.

Teaching at Guildhall (Post-Grad) Since 1988 has taught workshops abroad - Finland, Holland, Bulgaria and Jazz course at Leeds College of Music. Currently teaches at Middlesex University, Bretton Hall. Summer Schools - Fife, Guildhall, Glamorgan, Chelmsford, Mediterranean.

Clahar, Patrick
(London)
85 Dyers Lane, Putney, London SW15 6JU
020 8785 9243, 07802 498971, patclahar@nclworld.com
Instruments taught: Alto Sax, Soprano Sax, Tenor Sax.
Teaches 1 to 1. Area(s): reading, beginners, some knowledge, refresher, coaching. Place(s): own home.
"I try to be thorough and meticulous with all aspects of the fundamentals of jazz theory - this will really give the foundation to express yourself with clarity. In addition use the great legacy left by the masters, to influence and shape your ideas - that's what it's there for!"

Cliff, Tony
(South West)
Tremar, Trescobeas Manor, Trescobeas Road, Falmouth TR11 4JB
01326 314423 tel/fax, 07970 921993, tonycliff@talk21.com
Instruments taught: Keyboards, Piano.
Teaches 1 to 1. Teaches Associated Board Piano Exam. Age(s): under 11, 11 upwards. Area(s): reading, beginners, some knowledge, refresher. Place(s): own home.
"I have wide experience teaching piano both classical and jazz. For many years I taught degree students at the University of Salford. I also teach composition, arranging and theory. I have had many compositions published and recorded. Stainers and Bell recently published my book 'Piano Grooves' designed to assist and develop both reading and improvisation. This publication has an integral CD recording with both complete performances and backings only."

Clouts, Philip
(Eastern)
11 Rockliffe Avenue, Kings Langley WD4 8DR
01923 261 985, pclouts@yahoo.co.uk, www.zubop.com
Instruments taught: Piano.
Teaches 1 to 1. Teaches Associated Board Piano Exam. Age(s): under 11, 11 upwards. Area(s): reading, beginners, some knowledge, refresher, coaching. Place(s): own home, pupil's home.
Qualifications: LGSM (Guildhall) (has been teaching for 10-15 years). Includes improvisation. Other style(s): popular music, classical, world music.
"I always tailor my lessons according to the individual needs and interests of each pupil. I encourage creativity and I am happy to work from music or by ear. I have worked in many different fields of music and can include these whenever appropriate."

Clyne, Jeff
(London)
10 Temple Gardens, London NW11 0LL
020 8455 2893, jeffclyne@yahoo.co.uk
Instruments taught: Double Bass.

Teaches 1 to 1. Age(s): under 11, 11 upwards. Area(s): reading, beginners, some knowledge, refresher. Place(s): own home.

Co-Directs Wavendon Summer Jazz Course (contact Dorothy Cooper) Teaches at Royal Academy (repertoire) and the Guildhall (small group projects).

Coe, Tony
(London)

22 Glenton Road, London SE13 5RS

020 8549 1706 home tel

Instruments taught: Saxophone, Clarinet.

Teaches 1 to 1. Area(s): some knowledge, refresher. Place(s): own home.

Workshops: Christchurch College, Canterbury. Wavendon.

Collier, Graham
(Other)

Apartado 477, Ronda

graham@jazzcontinuum.com, www.jazzcontinuum.com

Instruments taught: Piano.

Workshops

Founder and Artistic Director of the Jazz course at the Royal Academy of Music (1989-99) Now freelance presenting workshop projects developing his ideas of 'Opening Up the Jazz ensemble'. Has recently given workshops in Perth, Sydney (Australia) Dartmouth College (New Hampshire USA), Manhattan School of Music (New York) Mannheim and Frankfurt (Germany) Lucerne (Switzerland); Linz (Austria) Kristiansand (Norway) and Trinity College (London UK) Rotterdam and Oslo.

Collins, Geoff
(Eastern)

4 Queens Road, Chelmsford CM2 6HA

01245 356192, 0771 233 6905

Instruments taught: Saxophone.

Teaches 1 to 1. Age(s): under 11, 11 upwards plus. Area(s): reading, beginners, some knowledge, refresher, coaching. Place(s): own home.

Workshops: Currently, Chelmsford Jazz Co-operative workshop. Specialisation - Post-bop Jazz styles, Improvisation/group Interaction.

Some experience running scratch workshop sessions in Basildon (Essex). "My playing background and approach to teaching combines the disciplines of Jazz Theory, reading skills and musical analysis, with the adventurousness and exploratory attitude of contemporary styles and Free-Improvisation"

Cook, Jonathan
(Yorkshire)

23 Broom Terrace, Rotherham S60 2TS

Instruments taught: Piano, Trumpet.

Workshops: classes (20+). Ensemble Direction.

Schools: for 16+ hours per week. secondary

Qualifications: PGCE Secondary Music (has been teaching for 5-10 years). Includes improvisation. Other style(s): popular music. Encourages improvisation in all areas of music cirriculum. Runs School jazz band - St Bernards Swing Band.

Cook, Natasha
(South East)

10 Chichester Court, Pevensey Gardens, Worthing BN11 5PQ
01903 504 974 home tel
Instruments taught: Clarinet, Piano, Saxophone.
Teaches 1 to 1. Teaches Associated Board Piano Exam.
Qualifications: BA QTS Music Hons. (Has been teaching for 5-10 years) Other
style(s): classical. "I enjoy learning jazz alongside my pupils and strive to achieve
high standards, whilst making lessons fun and enjoyable."

Corbett, David
(South East)

47 Fircroft Close, Tilehurst, Reading RG31 6LJ
0118 942 6559 tel/fax, 07956 132054
Instruments taught: Piano, Keyboards.
Teaches 1 to 1. Place(s): own home.
Teaches in schools

Cornick, Mike
(South East)

24 Kneller Gardens, Isleworth TW7 7NW
Instruments taught: Piano, Keyboards.
Teaches 1 to 1.
Qualifications: BA, Cert. In Education (has been teaching for over 20 years).
Includes improvisation. Other style(s): classical.

Cox, Gary
(North West)

22 Torkington Road, Gatley, Cheadle SK8 4PR
0161 428 5749, 07775 516 570
Instruments taught: Flute, Clarinet, Saxophone.
Teaches 1 to 1.
Workshops: small groups, large groups. Speciality area(s): Primary, secondary,
adult.
Schools: for 16+ hours per week. Has taught at Salford College of Music, Royal
Northern College, Cheltenham School and many other workshops including at the
Wigan Jazz Festival. Qualifications: 48-years professional to a high level and teach-
ing (has been teaching for over 20 years). Includes improvisation. Other style(s):
popular music, world music.

Crabb, Colin
(West Midlands)

41 West Drive, Pershore Road, Edgbaston B5 7RR
0121 472 3845 home tel
Instruments taught: Flute, Saxophone, Clarinet.
Teaches 1 to 1.
Workshops: small groups. Speciality area(s): Primary, secondary, tertiary, adult.
Schools: for 4-8 hours per week. Qualifications: B.Ed. L.R.A.M. (Has been teaching
for over 20 years) Includes improvisation. Other style(s): popular music, classical,
other (Klezmer).

Crawford, John
(London)
36 Avignon Road, London SE4 2JT
07721 463 723, john@vidanova.freeserve.co.uk
www.vidanova.freeserve.co.uk/jcweb.htm internet
Instruments taught: Keyboards, Piano.
Teaches 1 to 1. Age(s): 17 plus. Area(s): some knowledge, refresher. Place(s): own home, pupil's home.
John Crawford currently runs the only course in the UK for pianists who wish to learn Latin American piano styles at Goldsmith College. He specialises in teaching improvisation. He has taught at Morley College, Thames Valley University, Wavendon, Southwark College, Lewisham College. Currently writing book 'Rhythm and Independent exercises for Improvising Pianists'.

Cromar, Amanda
(South East)
12 Bredon court, Stonegrove, Edgware HA8 8HA
020 8958 3511 tel/fax
Instruments taught: Piano.
Teaches 1 to 1. Teaches Associated Board Piano Exam. Age(s): under 11, 11 to 16. Area(s): reading, beginners. Place(s): own home, pupil's home.
Qualifications: B Mus (Hons). (Has been teaching for 15-20 years.) Includes improvisation. Other style(s): popular music, world music.
"I'm certainly not a distinctive jazz tutor - as yet anyway - having only started investigating and teaching it with the start of the Associated Board Jazz exams and courses".

Crooks, Dick
(South East)
29 Nichol Road, Chandlers Ford, Eastleigh SO53 5AY
02380 260 395 home tel
Instruments taught: Tenor Sax, Alto Sax.
Teaches 1 to 1.
(Has been teaching for 1-2 years). Includes improvisation.

Crouch, John
(East Midlands)
North Kesteven School, Moor Lane, North Hykeham
07977 209381
Instruments taught: Trombone.
Teaches 1 to 1. Age(s): under 11, 11 upwards. Area(s): reading, beginners, some knowledge, refresher, coaching.
Schools: for 16+ hours per week. Pre-school, primary, secondary.
Qualifications: LGSM, GDLM, PGCE (has been teaching for 10-15 years).

Cruickshank, Ian
(South East)
31 Grimmer Way, Woodcote, Reading RG8 0SN
Instruments taught: Guitar.
Teaches 1 to 1.

Workshops: small groups. Speciality area(s): secondary, tertiary.
Schools. Benslow Music Trust, Beckfoot House, Oxford Summer School.
(Has been teaching for over 20 years). Includes improvisation. Other style(s):
world music, other (Gypsy Jazz).
Teaches/has taught at Oxford Summer School, Benslow Music Trust, Beckfoot
House, Penrith Cumbria and at the Leeds College of Music.

Crumly, Pat
(London)
89 Samuel Lewis, Vanston Place, London SW6 1BU
020 7381 3233, 020 7386 8194 fax, 07971 084354
pat@crumly94.freeserve.co.uk, www.pcjazz.co.uk
Instruments taught: Flute, Saxophone.
Teaches 1 to 1.
Qualifications: 20+ years professional performer. (Has been teaching for over 20
years) Includes improvisation. Other style(s): popular music.
Wavendon All Music Plan.

Cunningham, Philip
(South East)
Wyndwood, 6 Long Peak Close, Milton Keynes MK4 3BY
01908 506591, PandJCunnigham@Freeway.uk.com
Instruments taught: Piano.
Teaches 1 to 1. Teaches Associated Board Piano Exam. Age(s): 11 upwards.
Area(s): reading, beginners, some knowledge, refresher, coaching. Place(s): own
home, other (Schools). Workshops:
Qualifications: GLCM(Hons) LTCL; LLCM; A Mus LCM (has been teaching for 5-10
years). Includes improvisation. Other style(s): classical.
Jazz piano tuition specialising in classical - jazz changeover. Structured lessons in
improvisation and chord vocabulary. Performance opportunities for pupils in concerts and festivals. Has a high pass rate for Associated Board's jazz piano syllabus.

Cuzner, Kate
(London)
52 Turnstone Close, Upper Road, Plaistow, London E13 0HW
020 7511 5552, 07850 935 634
Instruments taught: Clarinet, Saxophone, Alto Flute.
Teaches 1 to 1.
"I run workshops and a jazz club at lunchtimes at schools where I teach, arranging
music for varying abilities and assisting in pupils' GCSE compositions/improvisa-
tion."

D'Aiello, Renato
(South West)
The Flax Mill, Mill Lane, Lopen, South Petherton TA13 5JS
01460 240189, 01460 240294 fax, 07779 305004
renatodaiello@yahoo.co.uk, www.renatodaiello.com
Instruments taught: Tenor Sax.
Teaches 1 to 1. Age(s): under 11, 11 upwards. Area(s): reading, beginners, some
knowledge, refresher. Place(s): own home, pupil's home.
Workshops: Saxophone ensembles and jazz improvisation. Jazz improvisation at

Basel Jazz School, Jazz sax reading for Big Band in Italy, jazz sax and improvisation St Gallen Jazz School.

Good aural teaching system. Direct experiences as student of 'Salnistico' (Count Basie and Woody Herman Band) and Steve Grossman, Barry Harris (as well as sharing the stage with them).

Darrington, Ian (MBE)
(North West)

Park Road, Hindley, Wigan WN1 2NB

07785 982524, ian.darrington@btinternet.com

www.wiganjazz.net

Instruments taught: Piano, Trumpet.

Teaches 1 to 1. Age(s): under 11, 11 upwards. Area(s): reading, beginners, some knowledge, refresher, coaching. Place(s): own home.

Workshops: Previously, Big Band and Brass workshops - Singapore/Australia/USA. Specialisation - ensemble playing in Big Bands.

Schools: Primary, secondary. HE/FE.

MD of Wigan Youth Jazz Orchestra since 1979. Performed Jazz/Big Band workshops for Daily Telegraph and BASBWE throughout UK. Big Band workshops in USA, Mexico, France and Eire. Advisor to Cork School of Music Big Band. Clinician at Cork International Jazz Festival. UK IAJE Representative. Advisor for Metropolitan Wigan Ed Dept. "Over the past 24 years working with Wigan Youth Jazz Orchestra and other Big Bands around the world I have formulated an approach to ensemble playing that promoted confidence and tighter ensemble work in players of all ages. It does so with the appropriate inflection and style. The positive responses that I have regularly received from the many bands that I have worked with are an indication that my methods of tutoring an ensemble are to a large degree, proving to be effective." Founder and Director of the Wigan Int Jazz Festival and Wigan Jazz Club. Has produced 11 albums with WYJO. In 1997 awarded a MA from Liverpool University where he is currently studying a PhD on 'The Evolution of the Trumpet mouthpiece Design and the effects of the design on the music of the 20th century'

Davies, J P
(London)

27 Sonia Gardens, Neasden, London NW10 1AG

020 8208 3654 tel/fax, 0966 502243 mobile, Jack__md@yahoocom

Instruments taught: Piano, Guitar.

Teaches 1 to 1. Teaches Associated Board Piano Exam. Age(s): under 11, 11upwards. Area(s): reading, beginners, some knowledge, refresher, coaching. Place(s): own home, pupil's home, other (FE College (Extra Mural Activity).

Schools: Primary, secondary, HE/FE.

"In Jazz, nothing comes easily to me: playing by ear, reading, improvising, composing, swing - it has all been a struggle. I know how learners feel, I have experienced every jealousy and frustration. But, I believe that the opportunity to play is the starting point for development."

Dean, Barry
(London)

514 Fulham Road, London SW6 5NJ

020 7736 3977, 020 7736 0699 home fax

Instruments taught: Piano.

Teaches 1 to 1.

Qualifications: Specialist Blues and Boogie Study Only (has been teaching for 3-5

years). Includes improvisation. Other style(s): popular music
Has taught complete beginners and adults blues, boogie woogie RandB rock and
jazz funk.

Dennis, Kelvin
(North East)

Cooper Centre, Beech Grove, South Bank, Middlesborough TS6 6SSU
07884 437 128
Instruments taught: Percussion, Drums.
Teaches 1 to 1. Area(s): reading, beginners, some knowledge, refresher, coaching.
Place(s): own home, other (Schools and colleges).
Workshops: small groups, large groups. 52 piece band. Previously and currently,
251 Jazz ensemble at Eston Park school. Specialisation - Style and Groove.
Schools: for 16+ hours per week. Primary, secondary, HE/FE. Tees Valley Music
Service. Has introduced 'Samba' to 10 primary schools who have a total of 250
children involved in samba bands.
(Has been teaching for over 20 years). Includes improvisation. Other style(s): pop-
ular music. Runs approx 4 workshops per year on Jazz, Rock, Pop and commercial
Music. "I have taught for 25 years. I direct a youth band - 'Band of 78' (25 years)
from which I take membership for '251 Jazz'. I play drums with my son's band, the
Noel Dennis Band which is a Be Bop - Jazz Messengers type of band. I also play
with a Trad Jazz group as well as commercial work"

Dewhurst, Robin
(North West)

Adelphi building, Peru Street, Salford M36 6EQ
0161 295 6136 tel/fax, R.Dewhurst@music.salford.ac.uk
www.music.salford.ac.uk/music2/web/index.htm internet
Instruments taught: Piano.
Workshops: classes (20+). Speciality area(s): large groups. Music of Gil Evans.
Jazz Composition/arranging at Leeds,York, Academy of Music, Paris, University of
Salford, Royal Marines School of Music. Schools: for 8-12 hours per week. HE/FE.
(Has been teaching for 10-15 years). Includes improvisation. Other style(s): popular music.
Senior lecturer in music at Salford University. Head of Jazz Performance, Musical
Director of University Big Band. Member of IAJE, Master degree focused on works
of Gil Evans. Teaches aural and transcription studies, jazz piano, jazz history, form
in jazz from Be-Bop to Third stream and beyond, contemporary arranging for jazz
orchestra, jazz and popular music songwriting, archetypes and applications of form
in jazz and popular music. External examiner for MA in Jazz at Napier University
(Eddie Severn) and Jazz, Pop and Commercial music in Newcastle College, visiting
professor at Royal Marine in Portsmouth.

Dhillon, Sara
(London)

211 North Gower Street, London NW1 2NR
020 7387 0850, 07940 541538, Sara__dhillon@hotmail.com email
Instruments taught: Piano.
Teaches 1 to 1. Teaches Associated Board Piano Exam. Age(s): under 11 upwards.
Area(s): reading, some knowledge, refresher, coaching. Place(s): own home.
Workshops: small groups. Speciality area(s): small groups, large groups, adult.
Started Morley Jazz summer School 3 years ago. Chard jazz Spring School
(Somerset) - Course leader. Currently Morley jazz Summer School, Jazz harmony

(Level 1 and Level 2), Jazz Ear training.
Schools: for 4-8 hours per week (Has been teaching for 5-10 years). Includes improvisation. Other style(s): popular music.
"Based on my own experiences and struggle when first learning how to improvise, my focus is always to communicate with students in such a way that the whole process of improvisation becomes demystified and actually becomes fun. Improvisation is about creating music in the moment and I try always to give students practical exercises and coaching to achieve this".

Dibbs, Martin
(Scotland)
3 Morgan Street, Dundee DD4 6QE
01382 453431 home tel
Instruments taught: Percussion.
Teaches 1 to 1. Age(s): 11 upwards. Area(s): reading, beginners, some knowledge, refresher, coaching. Place(s): own home.
Workshops: small groups. Speciality area(s): secondary. Musical Director, Carnoustie High School Jazz Big Band. Some workshops in area.
Schools: for 16+ hours per week
Qualifications: Diploma in Jazz Studies. (Has been teaching for 15-20 years.) Includes improvisation. Other style(s): popular music. Since 1986 has taught in Tayside region. Carries out in-service training of teachers teaching jazz.

Dickie, Chas
(South West)
2 Ropers Buildings, Weymouth DT3 5LR
01305 816151, chas_dickie@hotmail.com
Instruments taught: Cello.
Teaches 1 to 1. Age(s): 11 upwards. Area(s): refresher. Place(s): own home, pupil's home.
Workshops: small groups. Multi disciplinary workshops for stringed players wanting to improvise.
Other style(s): classical.
20 years teaching experience as well as 10 years workshop leader experience. Has also branched out into African Dance/Drummer workshops and workshops with a painter and dancer.

Diprose, Mike
(London)
Flat 3, 48a Chatsworth Road, London NW2 4BT
020 8451 0269 tel/fax, 07768 298343, sloanesquares@hotmail.com
www.geocities.com/soho/square/1896 internet
Instruments taught: Trumpet, Piano, Flugel Horn.
Teaches 1 to 1.
Kent Youth Jazz Orchestra. R.A.M. Tuition on various courses, Boston House School for the Blind, Purcell School.

Diver, John
(North East)

2 Admirals Croft, Hull Marina, Hull HU1 2DR
01482 587 432, john@phantasm.karoo.co.uk
Instruments taught: Piano.
Teaches 1 to 1. Teaches Associated Board Piano Exam. Age(s): under 11 upwards. Area(s): reading, beginners.
Workshops: In 2000 gave first Jazz piano workshop to piano teachers undertaking the ABRSM Course in Sheffield.
Qualifications: CT ABRSM; Jazz Piano Grade 5 (Distinction) (has been teaching for 5-10 years). Includes improvisation. Other style(s): popular music.
"My teaching of Jazz piano is very much informed by my own playing: over half my work is as a pianist (functions/hotels etc) where I play lots of solo Jazz piano (+ other styles). I use music technology as a teaching aid for jazz piano – keybords, sampler, musical laser beam etc"

Dodd, Jonathan
(Eastern)

43 Old Warren, Taverham, Norwich NR8 6GE
01603 868952, 07769 556525, cavefelis@tinyworld.co.uk
Instruments taught: Piano, Drums.
Teaches 1 to 1. Teaches Associated Board Piano Exam. Age(s): under 11, upwards. Area(s): reading, beginners, some knowledge, refresher, coaching. Place(s): own home.
Workshops: Arts Day Jazz workshop, St. Martins School, Brentwood, GCSE Composition workshop, Hedley Walter High School, Brentwood, History of singing, Norwich School. Specialisation - Jazz Bands; Small Combo work; Composition.
Schools: Primary, secondary. HE/FE.
Qualifications: BA Hons (has been teaching for 5-10 years). Includes improvisation. Other style(s): popular music, classical.
"Having trained classically (but played jazz for many years) with a degree in composition, I am able to teach any aspect of musicianship. This gives my pupils a solid grounding in understanding the music as well as performing it."

Domay, Michael
(South West)

20 Argyll Road, Parkstone, Poole BH12 2DR
01202 721329 home tel
Instruments taught: Keyboards, Electric Bass, Guitar.
Teaches 1 to 1. Teaches Associated Board Piano Exam. Age(s): under 11, upwards. Area(s): reading, beginners, some knowledge, refresher, coaching. Place(s): own home. "Introducing jazz into the education system can only encourage more young people to play. I've taught jazz guitar since 1980. Examination entries to Guildhall School of Music and Drama." "I have written a book entitled 'Inventive Harmony and Improvisation' developed from pupils' needs to improvise when playing guitar solos in fusion, jazz, rock or blues. Gives guidelines for young players (under 12!) on how to 'plan' a solo. This is based on twenty years teaching jazz as well as other styles and providing students with instant compositions and backing tracks. I consistently use jazz standards as a reference source for reading and improvisation purposes. For my playing experience see 'International Who's Who (Popular music) volume 2'."

Drew, Martin
(South East)

38 College Road, Wembley HA9 8RJ
020 8 908 0558 tel/fax, 07801 930 920
drums@martindrew.co.uk email, www.martindrew.co.uk
Instruments taught: Drums.
Teaches 1 to 1. Age(s): under 11, 11 upwards. Area(s): reading, beginners, some knowledge, refresher, coaching. Place(s): own home
Workshops: small groups. Speciality area(s): large groups, classes (20+), primary, secondary, tertiary, adult. Specialisation rhythm section training.
Schools: Primary, secondary. HE/FE.
Qualifications: 40 years experience. (Has been teaching for 1-2 years). Includes improvisation. Other style(s): popular music, world music.
Has taught 1 to 1 but prefers rhythm section seminars, where a wealth of experience can be used to help students and professionals improve. Has used his Quartet to demonstrate the interplay within a jazz group using audience participation. His teaching methods aim to make learning quicker and more fulfilling, as well as enjoyable and accurate. Martin has played with some of the greatest jazz musicians in the world in particular - Oscar Peterson, Ronnie Scott, Eddie Daniels, Arturo Sandoval. "I have enormous experience playing all kinds of music particularly Jazz, have worked with the world's finest musicians and can communicate this knowledge to students."

Du Valle, Cecil
(South West)

Stara Masha, East Taphouse, Liskeard PL14 4 NJ
01579 320636 tel/fax, cecil.duvalle@ic24.net
Instruments taught: Piano.
Teaches 1 to 1. Age(s): 11 upwards. Area(s): reading, beginners, some knowledge, refresher, coaching. Place(s): own home, other (Teaches Associated Board GR 2 Diploma (not piano exam) Also teaches at St Austell College A level National Diploma). Workshops: Jazz for 13 years at Baunnel School (Cornwall). Performance at Minimac Theatre - school performance, TSB Rock School for the Schools Music Association (USA) Specialisation Jazz, Composition.
Schools: Primary, secondary. HE/FE, special needs.
"I work with a system taught to me in the 1960s by Jim Amadic and Dennis Sandole (USA). I've expanded on these techniques from my experience as a touring musician (1975/83) in the USA. Some of my past students have been finalists in the 'BBC Young Musician of the Year' and Young Composer award at the Northern Schools."

Duncan, Fionna
(Scotland)

The Nest, Portincaple, Garelochhead G84 0EU
01436 810752 tel/fax, jazz@cathierae.prestel.co.uk
www.fionnaduncan-workshops.co.uk
Instruments taught: Voice.
Teaches 1 to 1.
Vocal Jazz Teacher at Napier College Jazz Course Edinburgh. Director of Vocal Jazz Course which runs in conjunction with the Glasgow International Jazz Festival in June/July. Now entering its 7th year. Also runs one and two day beginner and intermediate workshops for vocal jazz throughout Scotland during each year.

Dunmall, Paul
(West Midlands)

1 Pigeonhouse Cottages, Dingle Road, Leigh, Worcester WR6 5JX
01886 832046 tel/fax
Instruments taught: Saxophone.
Teaches 1 to 1.
Teaches at Dartington Summer school, Cardiff Welsh College of Music and Drama, Leicester University and Malvern College. Has run workshops (approx 4 a year) in Belfast and Durham whilst on tour.

Dunn, Julie
(South West)

Brompton House, Sherbourne Road, Yeovil BA21 4HQ
01935 471774, 07946 528 476, jdunn@F2S.com
Instruments taught: Keyboards, Voice, Piano.
Teaches 1 to 1. Teaches Associated Board Piano Exam. Age(s): under 11, upwards
Area(s): reading, beginners, some knowledge, refresher, coaching. Place(s): own home.
Jazz vocal workshops with Louise Gibbs, Marion Montgomery and Mark Murphy. Private piano/voice coach in jazz, classical, contemporary styles. MA Music Performance studies (Jazz improvisation and the vocalist). "Personal attention to individual needs of pupil's keeness to develop all-round musicianship (especially in singers) and encourage intelligent yet sensitive approach in interpreting jazz material. Absolutely committed to stimulating the pupil's creativity, to the best of their abilities, engendering a love of performance and communication".

Dux, Tim
(London)

79 Longton Grove, Sydenham, London SE26 6QQ
020 8778 7147, 020 8778 1529 fax, 0956 522589 mobile
Instruments taught: Guitar, Bass Guitar.
Teaches 1 to 1.
Qualifications: B.Sc Psychology (has been teaching for 10-15 years). Includes improvisation. Other style(s): popular music, world music.
Peripatetic teacher at secondary schools

Dvorak, Jim
(London)

43b Mulkern Road, London N19 3HQ
020 7281 1153, 020 7503 8417 home fax
www.musart.co.uk/dvorak-htm internet
Instruments taught: Saxophone, Trumpet, Voice.
Teaches 1 to 1. Area(s): reading, beginners, some knowledge, refresher, coaching.
Place(s): own home, pupil's home, other (Rented Studio Space - Premises - Hackwell).
Workshops: Previously Jazz and Improvisation - Islington Arts Factory, Holloway, London. Jazz and Improvisation at Community Music - Farringdon, London. Jazz and Improvisation - Jazz Days International, Balham, London. Improvisation and Listening skills at Jackson's Lane, Highgate, London. Specialisation - Improvisation - Developing Listening. "Thirty years professional Jazz trumpeter. Direct experience with the pioneers of improvised music in the UK. Has held workshops in Germany,

Holland, Italy and USA. A thorough grounding in 'Search and Reflect' programs along with ongoing live performances with top UK artists (Tippett, Dean, Moholo) make my workshops in developing listening skills enjoyably intense and relevant to today's requirement for clarity and spontaneity."

Earl, Rhoderick
(Wales)

14 Hillsboro Place, Porthcawl CF36 3BH
01656 772935 home tel
Instruments taught: Guitar.
Age(s): under 11, 11 upwards. Area(s): reading, beginners, some knowledge, refresher, coaching. Place(s): own home, pupil's home.
Private tuition in theory and practical applications of guitar using finger style. Occasional clinics at local Youth organisations.

East, Ian
(South East)

4 Spencer Street, Gravesend DA11 OPT
01474 355 214, 07958 781768
ianeastsax@hotmail.com, www.beebossrecords.co.uk
Instruments taught: Saxophone, Clarinet, Flute.
Teaches 1 to 1. Age(s): under 11, 11 upwards. Area(s): reading, beginners, some knowledge, refresher, coaching. Place(s): own home.
Workshops: Live Music Now Workshops; Blackheath Conservatoire (London); Jazz and Blues workshops in Richmond. Specialising in jazz wind instruments.
Qualifications: B Mus from the Royal Academy of Music; L R A M (Teaching Diploma in jazz). (Has been teaching for 1-2 years). Includes improvisation.
Wide experience in teaching with students of all ages. Experienced player having studied with leading teachers and players on the jazz scene.

Ebbage, David
(South East)

The chalet, 75 Claremont Road, Tunbridge Wells TN1 1TE
01892 527970 tel/fax
Instruments taught: Piano.
Teaches 1 to 1. Teaches Associated Board Piano Exam. Age(s): under 11, 11 upwards Area(s): reading, beginners, some knowledge, refresher, coaching. Place(s): own home, pupil's home, other (Music Centres or College).
Workshops: Previously, Kent Music School, Kent Youth Jazz Orchestra (Rhythm Section). Jazz Piano Styles. Specialisation - Big Band, Swing Band and Improvisation.
Schools: secondary. HE/FE. Kent Music School, College Road, Maidstone, Kent.
Tutor for Rhythm section of the Kent Youth Jazz Orchestra in the 1980s. "I have many years experience of running Big Bands directly from the piano! Also, work with singers. I have performed all of Claude Bollings Jazz works and also have my own Jazz Trio, playing concerts and clubs. With my Palm Court Orchestra, play early period Jazz from 20s, 30s, 40s and 50s."

Edmonds, Paul
(London)
85 Randolph Avenue, London W9 1DL
020 7266 5430 home tel
Instruments taught: Piano, Trumpet, Flugel Horn.
Teaches 1 to 1.
Workshops: small groups. Schools: secondary
(Has been teaching for 3-5 years). Other style(s): popular music, jazz fusion.

Edwards, Jane
(West Midlands)
46 Campion Way, Rugby CV23 OUR
01788 572912, music@counts.freeserve.co.uk
Instruments taught: Piano.
Teaches 1 to 1. Teaches Associated Board Piano Exam. Age(s): under 11, 11
upwards. Area(s): reading, beginners. Place(s): own home.
(Has been teaching for 10-15 years). Includes improvisation. Other style(s): classical.
"'Confidence-building, rhythm-making, rhythm-breaking, exciting, relaxing, frus-
trating, exhilarating, concentrating, listening, achieving, playing Music."

Elliott, Don
(North West)
White House Cottage, New Road, Laxey IM4 7HS
01624 861461 tel/fax, 07624 496 548
Instruments taught: Trumpet, Trombone, Cornet.

Elliott, Katie
(London)
196 Stroud Crescent, Putney Vale Estate, Roehampton, London SW15 3EQ
020 8789 4218 tel/fax, katie.elliott@flappingmo11usc.freeserve.co.uk
Instruments taught: Piano, Flute.
Teaches 1 to 1.
Was a facilitator for the Young Women's Band Project at Chard Festival of Women
in Music, a Song writer in Schools for the New Millenium Experience Company's
'Voices of Promise' project. Linked up with the Children's Music Workshop and was
involved in jazz projects for them in 2000. Music Educationalist/author for Boosey
and Hawkes.

Elliott, Louise
(London)
13 Tabley Road, London N7 0NA
020 7609 6489, louise.elliott@blueyonder.co.uk
www.jazzhearts.com
Instruments taught: Flute, Tenor Sax.
Teaches 1 to 1. Age(s): 17 plus. Place(s): own home.
Workshops: usually small groups.
Schools: Primary.
Teaches workshops and music courses for Local Authorities in London. Teaches in
Wandsworth Children's Music Centre.

Embliss, William
(London)
5 Blake Road, London N11 2AD
020 8374 3453 home tel
Instruments taught: Percussion, Trumpet, Trombone.
Workshops: Speciality area(s): small groups, primary. Community Groups with people crossing over these age ranges and categories.
Schools: for 1-4 hours per week. Primary (5-11), secondary (11-16).
(Has been teaching for 5-10 years). Includes improvisation. Other style(s): world music.
Has taught Stevenage Community Band as well as street band workshops for children and adults. Tuned percussion workshops for up to 15 people on creative music, rhythm and composition. Musical instrument making workshops.

England, Trevor
(N Ireland)
38 Edenberry cottages, Shaws Bridge, Belfast BT8 8RY
028 9064 1148, 07977 911264, trev.england@virging.net
Instruments taught: Bass Guitar.
Teaches 1 to 1. Age(s): 11 to 16, 17 plus. Area(s): beginners, some knowledge, refresher, coaching. Place(s): own home.
Workshops: Previously conductor with Irish Youth Jazz Orchestra. Conductor of Young Arts Jazz Orchestra. Many workshops including Arts council for NI, Antrim Borough Council. Southern Education and Library board. Belfast Education and Library Board. Specialisation. Big Band Ensemble, Improvisation.
"Graduate of the Berklee College of Music in Boston. Leader of numerous improvisation workshops throughout Ireland. Musical Director of many Big Bands including leading the Young Arts Jazz Orchestra - second place in the BBC Big Band competition. Awarded MA for Jazz composition."

Erselius, Steven
(London)
5 Oliver Avenue, South Norwood, London SE25 6TY
020 8653 6288 home tel
Instruments taught: Piano, Keyboards.
Teaches 1 to 1. Teaches Associated Board Piano Exam. Age(s): 11 to 16, 17 plus. Area(s): reading, beginners, some knowledge, refresher. Place(s): own home, pupil's home.
Qualifications: PGCE (has been teaching for 5-10 years). Includes improvisation. Other style(s): popular music, classical.
"Coming from a strong classical background, I may tend to emphasise greater accuracy in rhythmic playing, sight reading, tonal shading and correct and adequate technique. As well as the theory and history of the music."

Escobar, Brigitte
(North West)
11 Chiswick Road, Didsbury, Manchester M20 6RZ
0771 4046 833, escobarbrigitte@yahoo.co.uk
www.btinternet.com/~Brigitte.Escobar internet
Instruments taught: Piano, Voice.
Teaches 1 to 1. Area(s): reading, beginners, some knowledge, refresher, coaching.

Workshops: usually small groups, large groups, classes (20+). One-off workshops for adults.

Schools: for 12-16 hours per week. secondary (11-16), HE/FE, adults (21+). Band on th Wall, Shena Simon College, Manchester School of Music, Access to Music.

Qualifications: MGK from Danish Music Academy, Music facilitator (Access to Music) (has been teaching for 3-5 years). Includes improvisation. Other style(s): popular music, world music.

Runs weekly workshops at Band on the Wall, Manchester and runs 4 - 8 workshops a year for Access to Music. "Teach all ranges and abilities from total beginners to professional recording artists. Teaching includes learning about the anatomy of singing, physical exercises, breathing exercises, vocal warm-up and technique as well as work with songs ranging from pop and soul to jazz and blues. Lessons can also include ear training, music theory and rhythmic awareness - depending on the needs and wishes of the pupil. Lessons are led in a relaxed and good humoured manner suitable for even the most nervous pupils!"

Eshelby, Paul
(South East)

Cranleigh, 118 Preston Hill, Harrow HA3 9SJ
020 8204 1032, 020 8206 0539 fax, 0802 417638 mobile
Instruments taught: Trumpet, Flugel Horn.
Teaches 1 to 1. Age(s): 11 to 16, 17 plus. Area(s): some knowledge. Place(s): own home.
Workshops: usually 1 to 1, large groups. Speciality area(s): tertiary, adult. Previously and currently, Big Band Summer Course, Benslow Music Trust, Hitchin.
Schools: for 16+ hours per week. secondary (11-16), adults (21+).
Qualifications: LGSM, CLCM (has been teaching for over 20 years). Includes improvisation. Other style(s): popular music.
Big Band teaching - phrasing and interpretation of styles, jazz improvisation. Director of NYJO II. Professor of trumpet RCM London, Trumpet Teacher, Eton College, Trumpet Section and soloist BBC Big Band, Paul Eshelby Trio.

Etheridge, John
(London)

31 Constantine Road, London NW3 2LN
020 7435 9574 tel/fax, 07958 356324
post@johnetheridge.f9.co.uk, www.johnetheridge.com
Instruments taught: Guitar.
Teaches 1 to 1.
Workshops: usually small groups.
Schools: for 1-4 hours per week. HE/FE. Thames Valley University.
(Has been teaching for 15-20 years.) Includes improvisation.
Numerous courses taught; Wavendon, Barry, Royal Academy and Dartington College.

Eveleigh, Ray
(Yorkshire)
Pasture Lodge, West End, Kilham, Driffield YO25 4RR
01262 420060, rev@revray.co.uk, www.revraymusic.com
Instruments taught: Piano.
Teaches 1 to 1. Age(s): 11 to 16, 17 plus. Area(s): beginners, some knowledge.
Place(s): own home.
Qualifications: BSc; MA. (Has been teaching for 15-20 years.) Includes improvisation.
Author of 'Jazz Harmony and Improvisation' a ten week course. This has been used in UK and USA. Has many years teaching experience in schools and colleges in UK and USA. Has a great deal of experience in the use of music software as an aid to learning jazz.

Fairclough, Peter
(Yorkshire)
150 Knowle Lane, Sheffield S11 9SJ
0114 236 4845 tel/fax, peter.fairclough1@btinternet.com
Instruments taught: Drums.
Teaches 1 to 1. Age(s): under 11, 11 to 16, 17 plus. Area(s): reading, beginners, some knowledge, refresher, coaching. Place(s): pupil's home.
Workshops: usually small groups. Speciality area(s): secondary, tertiary, adult. Previously, Sheffield Jazz Workshops, Sheffield. Currently, 'Document 1' (a band for secondary school aged children - any instruments) Specialisation - Composition/Improvisation/Performance/Recording.
Schools: for 12-16 hours per week. Secondary. HE/FE, adults.
Qualifications: Graduate Diploma in Light Music. (Has been teaching for 15-20 years.) Includes improvisation. Other style(s): popular music, classical.
Currently Sheffield jazz workshops, tutor at Welsh College of Music and Drama. Recent work in Yorkshire Youth and Music schools workshops. In the past has taught on the Wavendon Jazz course. "As a drum teacher, I am interested in time, feel, form, reading, repertoire, movement and posture. As a workshop leader, I am interested in composing (from scratch), improvising, performing and recording."

Fairweather, Digby
(Eastern)
129 Westborough Road, Westcliff on Sea SS0 9JG
01702 435727 tel/fax, digby@digjazz.co.uk, www.digjazz.co.uk
Instruments taught: Trumpet.
Teaches 1 to 1. Age(s): under 11, 11 to 16, 17 plus. Area(s): reading, beginners, some knowledge, refresher, coaching. Place(s): own home.
Schools: Secondary. HE/FE, adults.
Co-Director of the Jazz College - educational charity founded in 1979. Co-Author The Rough Guide to Jazz. "Over twelve years Stan Baker and I formulated a methodology for jazz instruction based on aural training/written exercises for the non-profit making trust 'Jazz College'."

Fawcett, Andrew
(Wales)
Court Lodge, Aberthin, Cowbridge CF71 7HB
01446 772137, 07771 941 394

andrew@fawcett43.fsnet.co.uk, www.andrewfawcett.co.uk
Instruments taught: Saxophone.
Teaches 1 to 1. Age(s): 11 upwards. Area(s): beginners, some knowledge,
refresher. Place(s): own home, pupil's home.
Workshops: Previously at Portsmouth Polytechnic "Having been largely self taught
for over 30 years, I understand the problems facing the aspiring jazz musician.
However, in the last five years, I have received the benefit of top flight teaching
and modern teaching methods, including a semester at the prestigious Berklee college of Music in Boston. I am ready to pass this information on to others."

Feast, Penrose
(South East)
17a Goldsmid Road, Hove
01273 725105 home tel
Instruments taught: Soprano Sax, Tenor Sax, Clarinet.
Teaches 1 to 1. Place(s): own home.
Experience in teaching improvisation to special needs (Leeds/Jazz Services 1992
project), mainstream and private educational settings from one on one to large
workshops.

Field, Malcolm
(South East)
15 Mareshall Avenue, Warfield, Bracknell
01344 642331 home tel
Instruments taught: Piano.
Teaches 1 to 1. Teaches Associated Board Piano Exam. Age(s): under 11, 11
upwards. Area(s): reading, beginners, some knowledge. Place(s): own home.
Qualifications: ATCL; AMusTCL; LTCL. (Has been teaching for 1-2 years). Includes
improvisation. Other style(s): classical.
"I have a solid classical background and have qualified as a piano teacher from
Trinity College. I have been impressed by the ABRSM Jazz syllabus and (since I
don't believe in my pupils doing something I'm not prepared to!) have sat some of
the exams myself. My very high marks have confirmed my ability. My current
pupils enjoy their lessons. I believe my positive, encouraging style combined with
my musical ability and flexible approach make me an effective Jazz teacher."

Field, Trixi
(South East)
36 The Phelps, Kidlington OX5 1SU
01865 371805, 07788 774471
contactTrixifield@aol.com, www.trixifield.co.uk
Instruments taught: Voice, Keyboards, Piano.
Teaches 1 to 1. Teaches Associated Board Piano Exam. Age(s): under 11, 11
upwards. Area(s): reading, beginners, some knowledge. Place(s): own home.
Workshops: 1999 and 2000, Vocal Workshops, Skyros. Specialisation: Voice,
Improvisation, Song Writing.
Qualifications: MA (Music Education) Med (has been teaching for 3-5 years).
Includes improvisation. Other style(s): popular music, classical.
Has studied creative music making at the Orff Institute (Mozarteum, Salzburg).
Teaches jazz piano for beginners. Regular vocal and creative music workshop
leader for summer courses in Syros. Member of the Voices Foundation and
European Piano Teachers' Association. "Trixi Field is particularly effective at

introducing jazz and improvisation techniques to even very young children. Already at an early stage, she encourages improvisation and songwriting/composition alongside reading music. Equally she has helped a number of older children and adults, eager to learn jazz, to make the transition from classical with confidence."

Figes, Kevin
(South West)
64 Robertson Road, Eastville, Bristol BS5 6JT
0117 939 3555, kevin.figes4@virgin.net
Instruments taught: Saxophone.
Teaches 1 to 1. Age(s): under 11, 11 upwards. Area(s): reading, beginners, some knowledge, refresher, coaching. Place(s): own home.
Workshops. Speciality area(s): 1 to 1, small groups.has run series of workshops around Marlborough as part of Festival. Big Band in Forest of Dean; Teignmouth, Bristol Jazz workshops.
Schools: for 8-12 hours per week. Primary, secondary. HE/FE.
Qualifications: None (has been teaching for 10-15 years). Includes improvisation. Other style(s): classical.
"Teaching forms an integral part of my activities, which include performing jazz standards and my own compositions in a variety of settings. It is this link I find most important. As a jazz tutor I put in as much energy as I can, to get the most out of the pupils, who give me things to think about in return."

Finkel, Sigi
(Other)
Ferdinandstrasse 15/4, Vienna
00 43 1 212 6936 tel/fax, sigifinkel@brainwork.at
www.jazzpages.com/SigiFinkel internet
Instruments taught: Tenor Banjo, Soprano Sax.
Teaches at a Conservatory in Vienna (for past 7 years). Runs a variety of workshops.

Finlay, Rick
(Eastern)
25a Rosslyn Avenue, East Barnet EN4 8DH
020 8361 0265, 020 8368 6293 fax, 07831 376175
jeoj@macunlimited.net, www.bluebanana.com/jeoj internet
Instruments taught: Percussion, Drums.
Teaches 1 to 1. Age(s): under 11, 11 upwards. Area(s): reading, beginners, some knowledge, refresher, coaching. Place(s): own home.
Workshops: Weymouth College (1999), Rhythm Workshop. Specialisation: Samba, Rhythm, Salsa Percussion. (Has been teaching for 15-20 years.) Includes improvisation. Other style(s): popular music, world music.
Currently instrumental teacher at Middlesex University. "I've been playing and teaching jazz and related music on drums and percussion since 1983, touring and recording with 'Just East of Jazz' since 1996. My teaching draws on extensive practical experience of all aspects of the music industry, including performing in a wide variety of situations, managing a band and record label"

Finnerty, Adrian
(Scotland)
10 Brandon Drive, Bearsden, Glasgow G61 3LN
0141 943 1517, adrian.finnerty@totalise.co.uk
Instruments taught: Piano.
Teaches 1 to 1. Teaches Associated Board Piano Exam. Age(s): 11 upwards.
Area(s): reading, beginners, some knowledge, refresher. Place(s): own home, other (School).
Workshops: small groups.
Schools: for 16+ hours per week. Secondary.
Qualifications: BA(Hons), Mmus, MA Ed, Dip T Mus, ALCM. (Has been teaching for 15-20 years.) Includes improvisation. Other style(s): popular music, classical.

Fogg, Rod
(South East)
17a The Barons, Twickenham TW1 2AP
020 8892 5183, 0976 421118 mobile
Instruments taught: Guitar, Bass Guitar.
Teaches 1 to 1.
Workshops: Speciality area(s): secondary, tertiary.
Schools: Secondary. HE/FE, adults.
Qualifications: BA (Hons) Performing Arts (has been teaching for 10-15 years).
Includes improvisation. Other style(s): popular music, classical, world music.
Lecturer at Kingston University.

Forbes, Stewart
(Scotland)
2 Moorfield Avenue, Kilmarnock KA1 1TS
07960 035130, stewartwforbes@strath.ac.uk
www.geocities.com/swforbes internet
Instruments taught: Clarinet, Saxophone, Flute.
Teaches 1 to 1. Teaches Associated Board Piano Exam.
Workshops: small groups. Speciality area(s): Primary, tertiary.
Schools: for 16+ hours per week. Primary, secondary. HE/FE, adults. Stewarton Academy; University of Strathclyde; Perth College.
Qualifications: LTCL (Cert Music Berklee) (has been teaching for over 20 years).
Other style(s): popular music, classical, world music. "Believes that everyone has the ability to spontaneously create music - it's just finding the right stimulus."

Forrell, Gaby
(London)
10 Point Close, Blackheath Hill, London SE10 8QS
020 8691 8318 tel/fax, gbf@btinternet.com
Instruments taught: Violin.
Teaches 1 to 1.
Qualifications: LLCMTD, B.Ed. Music, Community Music Diploma (has been teaching for 10-15 years). Includes improvisation. Other style(s): popular music, classical, world music.
"As a graduate of 'Community Music' has learned workshop skills in improvisation. Has been a workshop leader in many institutions."

Forsyth, Alex
(South East)
14 Beacon Close, Farnham GU10 4PA
01252 792221 home tel
Instruments taught: Flute, Soprano Sax.
Teaches 1 to 1.
Workshops: small groups.
Schools: for 16+ hours per week. Primary, Secondary. HE/FE, adults.
Qualifications: PGCE (1984), LGSMD (Jazz) 1998 (has been teaching for 10-15 years). Includes improvisation. Other style(s): popular music, classical.
Full Time teacher. Also teaches individuals at schools from 10 to 18 years and workshops. Runs 'Language and Music for Life' jazz course.

Forward, Thomas
(South West)
36 Crock Lane, Bridport DT6 4DF
Theakasandbeeb@com
Instruments taught: Clarinet.
Workshops: woodwind. Beaminster Big Band, Beaminster Dorset; Gryphon Big Band, Sherborne; Three Counties Swing Band Axminster.
Schools: Primary. Secondary. Adults. Beauminster Comprehensive Dorset.
Qualifications: FTCL LTCL DIP ED EXETER (has been teaching for over 20 years). Includes improvisation. Other style(s): popular music, classical.
Student at The Royal Academy of Music in the 70's. Acquired jazz knowledge through working years, so although not strictly a jazz tutor, he is keen to expand his knowledge even further.

Foster, Clare
(Eastern)
4 Seaforth Road, Westcliff on Sea SS0 7SN
01702 431517, clarefoster@tesco.net
Instruments taught: Voice.
Teaches 1 to 1. Age(s): under 11, 11 upwards. Area(s): beginners, some knowledge. Place(s): own home, pupil's home.
Workshops: small groups, large groups, classes (20+). In past worked at Weekend Arts College London Easter Jazz School, Southend-on-Sea, Nightfly Studios. Currently at Morley College, City Lit - Jazz Singers. Specialisation - Improvising/Phrasing.
Schools: for 4-8 hours per week. Primary. HE/FE, adults.
Qualifications: Guildhall Music Diploma (has been teaching for 5-10 years). Includes improvisation. Other style(s): popular music.
Runs workshops in a variety of venues including schools and studios, where performance experience is important but not absolutely essential. Provides advice and assessment with most workshops, offering a jam session and final performance. Experience of vocal workshops in Canada and Holland ('93-'99). As a jazz educator she aims to open the vocal doors, with an approach that combines both the instrumentalist's concerns for 'sound' and 'time' with the vocalists duty to communicate the meaning of the lyric.

Fox, Mandy
(South West)

Cracklewood, 10 Doctors Hill, St. Keverne, Helston TR12 6UX
01326 280 228, 0798 98 36213
Instruments taught: Piano, Voice.
Teaches 1 to 1. Teaches Associated Board Piano Exam. Area(s): reading, beginners, some knowledge, refresher. Place(s): own home, other (Truro College).
Workshops: usually small groups. Speciality area(s): large groups, classes (20+), primary, secondary, tertiary, adult. Voice and mediation course - based mainly on Hindustani music - Helston Cornwall.
Schools: for 8-12 hours per week. Primary. HE/FE. Peripatetic teacher for Cornwall County Music Service.
Qualifications: LGSM (Jazz), PGCE (has been teaching for 10-15 years). Includes improvisation. Other style(s): popular music, world music.
Jazz improvisation workshops for peripatetic primary and secondary teachers and student teachers, community organisations, HM Prisons and theatres. Teacher of voice and jazz musicianship at Brunel University. 1996 PRS Composers in Education Award "I have a broad experience of jazz, other music and teaching, and bring that to my teaching with a very 'personal' approach. Music without the soul is meaningless".

Francomb, Roger
(London)

28 Disdale Road, Blackheath, London SE3 7RL
020 8858 3773, 07980 379 044, rfrancomb@hotmail.com
Instruments taught: Saxophone.
Teaches 1 to 1. Age(s): under 11, 11 upwards. Area(s): reading, beginners, some knowledge, refresher, coaching. Place(s): own home, pupil's home.
Workshops: 'Popular music' workshop at Croom's Hill, Greenwich (Convent School). Includes improvisation.
"If provided with a group of musicians/music students of intermediate level or above with a good range of instrumentation, I would be confident demonstrating the conventions of jazz playing - particularly fusion styles. I could enable cohesive playing where the group is paying close attention to each other."

Franks, Ruth
(London)

14 Beechwood Hall, Regents Park Road, Finchley, London N3 3AT
020 8346 5720, ruth.franks@lineone.net
Instruments taught: Piano.
Teaches 1 to 1. Teaches Associated Board Piano Exam.
Qualifications: BA Hons Jazz (has been teaching for 3-5 years). Includes improvisation. Other style(s): popular music.
"Experienced vocalist and pianist. Started as a vocalist with the National Youth Jazz Orchestra in 1977/78 as well as attending Wavendon courses with Cleo Laine. Sang with the BBC Big Band in the 80s, backing vocals for Carol Kidd, as well as performing regularly as singer/pianist in clubs and hotels. 1994/97 took a degree at Middlesex University. Enjoys teaching beginners in jazz."

Fulcher, Harry
(South West)
Lulworth, Grenville Road, Salcombe TQ8 8BJ
01548 842869, harry@limbisystem.net
Instruments taught: Piano, Saxophone, Clarinet.
Teaches 1 to 1. Age(s): under 11, 11 upwards. Area(s): reading, beginners, some knowledge, refresher, coaching. Place(s): own home.
Workshops: Previously, Kingsbridge Music Workshop, Devon.
Qualifications: A.L.C.M., L.L.C.M. (TD). (Has been teaching for 15-20 years.)
Includes improvisation. Other style(s): popular music, classical. Teaches main instruments, improvisation, harmony and Midi to individuals. 'I love music. I love people, I am a qualified instrumental teacher and perform professionally.'

Fuller, Christopher
(London)
13 Langley Crescent, Wanstead, London E11 2LZ
020 8989 0327 home tel
Instruments taught: Piano.
Teaches 1 to 1. Teaches Associated Board Piano Exam. Age(s): under 11, 11 upwards. Area(s): reading, beginners, some knowledge, refresher, coaching. Place(s): own home.
Workshops: Previously 'Jazz Appreciation' at Loughton College, Barnet College, 'Musicworks',
Schools: Pre-school, primary, secondary. HE/FE, adults. Kingsmead School, Kingsmead Way, Hackney, London. Qualifications: B.Ed (Also Master Practitioner NLP) (has been teaching for over 20 years). Includes improvisation. Other style(s): popular music, classical, other (Blues/Boogie Woogie).
"Firstly, I encourage students to memorise tune and chords separately and to sing everything that they play: Such ear training is vital for developing improvisational skills. The student should learn to sing, play, and perhaps transcribe, a favourite solo. And learn a simple two-hand accompaniment and put all this together so they are able to present a basic but satisfactory performance of the tune."

Fullick, Teddy
(East Midlands)
Flat 10 Windsor House, Redcliffe Gardens, Mapperley Park, Nottingham NG3 5AX
0115 9603450, stephen.m@virgin.net
Instruments taught: Trumpet.
Teaches 1 to 1.
Likes to encourage pupils to go to the roots of jazz, to learn basic blues and simple melodies and to value the 2/4 feel in jazz.

Gaines, Will
(Eastern)
11 Woodfield Road, Leigh on Sea SS9 1EL
01702 713333 tel/fax, 07932 580537
www.ukjtd.force9.co.uk/jazz internet
Instruments taught: Percussion, Drums.
Teaches 1 to 1. Age(s): under 11, 11 to 16, 17 plus. Area(s): beginners.
Workshops: Previously and currently, Jazz Collective London, Community Centre Broadstairs, Edinburgh Festival, Essex and Birmingham/Colleges. Specialisation - Improvisation, Rhythm.

Schools: Primary, secondary also adults. special needs.
Regular workshops in art centres, colleges and Adult Education institutes. "Bringing and advancing Improvisation skills. Encouraging young musicians 'to think on their feet'. Learning in a relaxed way. To experiment, to have courage and enjoy diverse music."

Gardiner, Paula
(Wales)

Madeline Street, Pontygwaith CF43 3LT
paula@paulagardiner.co.uk, www.paulagardiner.co.uk
Instruments taught: Double Bass.
Workshops: small groups. Speciality area(s): small groups, secondary. Composition in Schools.
Schools: for 1-4 hours per week. Secondary. HE/FE, adults. (Has been teaching for 15-20 years.) Includes improvisation.
1992 set up Blackwood jazz improvisation workshop. Regular tutor at Glamorgan Summer School. Currently teaches jazz improvisation at two centres for Cardiff University, Dept. of Continuing Education.

Gardner, Christopher
(East Midlands)

The Willows, 2 Javelin Road, Manby, Louth LN11 8UA
01507 327848, 07932 384283, chris@2javelin.freeserve.co.uk
Instruments taught: Guitar.
Teaches 1 to 1. Age(s): under 11, 11 upwards. Area(s): reading, beginners, some knowledge, refresher. Place(s): own home, other (London College of Music (Thames Valley University)).
Workshops: small groups, large groups, classes (20+). Speciality area(s): Primary, adult. Previously, Adult education guitar classes (early 90s) One day summer workshops.
Schools: for 4-8 hours per week. Pre-school, primary, special needs.
Qualifications: Cert Ed; Membership of RGT (has been teaching for over 20 years). Includes improvisation. Other style(s): popular music, world music.
Has taught improvisation basics at AEI. Teaches infants using RGT (Registry of Guitar Tutors) syllabus. Runs occasional workshops for beginners to advanced students. "School teacher with a life-long love of guitars and their music. He has made, played and tutored guitar for over 30 years. Many of his students have gained merit or honours at RGT/LCM examinations involving up to 30% improvisation. His interests and involvement are with guitar synthesis and computer assisted music"

Garland, Tim
(London)

65 Birchen Grove, Kingsbury, London NW9 8RY
020 8930 4803 tel/fax, 07960 100960 timgarland@compuserve.com
Instruments taught: Flute, Saxophone.
Teaches 1 to 1. Age(s): 17 plus. Area(s): reading, beginners, some knowledge, refresher, coaching. Place(s): own home
Workshops: Previously,Trinity, Royal Adademy; Guildhall, Leeds, Wavendon Summer School, Masterclasses in Kent, Manchester, Aberdeen (plus may abroad).
Specialisation: improvising on all instruments, Big Band, Composition.
Schools: Secondary. HE/FE, adults.

Teaches individuals as well as workshops in Richmond. Tutor at Royal Academy and Guildhall School. "I have been a teacher of what I do professionally for over ten years and tend to teach from personal experience, demonstrating myself what I am explaining. I have had considerable international experience and wish to put that back into the music community".

Garrick, Chris
(London)
112 The Avenue, London NW6 7NN
07967 560 106, fly@chrisgarrick.com
Instruments taught: Violin.
Teaches 1 to 1. Age(s): under 11, 11 upwards. Place(s): own home.
"String tutor on the annual Jazz Academy jazz course. Lots of experience with children age 5 upwards and with disadvantaged and disabled people."

Garrick, Michael
(Eastern)
12 Castle Street, Berkhamsted HP4 2BQ
01442 864989, 01442 384493 home fax
Instruments taught: Piano.
Workshops: Previously and currently, Royal Academy of Music, Jazz Academy since 1989. Tunbridge Wells and Hereford.
(Has been teaching for over 20 years). Includes improvisation.
Director of Jazz Academy Summer course since 1989. Taught in schools from 1965-88. Has taught at Wavendon All Music Plan 1975-84. Teaches one day at Trinity College and half day at the Academy. Runs a four-day course 'Piano People' at the Royal National College, Hereford. Summer School in August, at Tunbridge Wells, Beechwood Campus. "I have had 40 years experience. Initiated ABRSM jazz syllabus 1989. Individual and broad view of the jazz impulse in music."

Garside, Gus
(South East)
20 Hertford Road, Brighton BN1 7GF
01273 387487 home tel
Instruments taught: Guitar, Double Bass.
Workshops: small groups, large groups, classes (20+). Speciality area(s): People with Learning Difficulties; People with Health problems.
Schools: for 4-8 hours per week. Secondary. HE/FE, adults. University of Sussex.
Qualifications: Certificate of Education: Teaching Adults with Learning difficulties. (Has been teaching for 15-20 years.)

Gascoyne, Geoff
(London)
93 Alderbrook Road, Clapham South, London SW4
020 8673 6043, 020 8355 6905 fax, 07956 283 900 mobile
mail@geoffgascoyne, www.geoffgascoyne.com
Instruments taught: Double Bass.
Teaches 1 to 1. Area(s): refresher. Place(s): own home.
Regular teacher at Royal Academy of Music and Trinity College, as well as the Wavendon Summer School courses.

Gibbs, Louise
(London)
Flat 10, 15 Catherine Grove, Greenwich, London SE10 8BS
020 8692 0626, 020 8692 1370 home fax
louise@jazzmine.co.uk, www.louisegibbs.co.uk
Instruments taught: Voice.
Teaches 1 to 1. Workshops: Speciality area(s): small groups, tertiary. Music theory and harmony; voice; improvisation; teacher preparation.
Schools: for 12-16 hours per week. Primary, secondary. HE/FE, adults.
Qualifications: M.Ed, LTCL (has been teaching for over 20 years). Includes improvisation. Other style(s): popular music, classical. Teaches jazz vocal techniques and keyboard musicianship at Goldsmiths College, London University and Guildhall School of Music and Drama. Formerly Head of Continuing Education programme at Goldsmiths College, initiating the Certificate in Jazz and Popular music and the Postgraduate Certificate in Music Teaching to Adults.

Gibson, Lee
(South East)
Garden Cottage, 48 New Road, Penn HP10 8DL
01494 817548 tel/fax, www.leegibson.co.uk
Instruments taught: Voice.
Associate Professor at Guildhall School London teaching on post graduate course. Wavendon Summer School. Guest Lecturer University of Western Australia (Perth).

Gill, Peter
(South West)
PO box 454, Cheltenham GL50 2ZE
01242 237937, petergill@bigfoot.com
Instruments taught: Piano.
Teaches 1 to 1. Teaches Associated Board Piano Exam. Age(s): under 11, 11 upwards. Area(s): reading, beginners, some knowledge, refresher, coaching. Place(s): own home, pupil's home.
"I believe that music, be it jazz, classical or popular can be learnt by anyone and is not an elitist art. I aim to cultivate a passion in jazz and build a confidence in players to achieve more than they believed possible. I also aim to keep it 'simple' at first so that you can then build on firm foundations."

Gilmour, Mary
(Scotland)
Lismore, Avoch IV9 8RF
01381 620655, 07710 783 203, mary@tfjazz.freeserve.co.uk
Instruments taught: Alto Sax, Tenor Sax.
Teaches 1 to 1.
Qualifications: Experience as Soloist, Band member, Broadcaster (has been teaching for 5-10 years). Includes improvisation. Other style(s): popular music.

Goldie, John
(Scotland)
17 Monks Road, Airdrie ML6 9QW
01236 748711 tel/fax, 07710 516177, www.johngoldie.co.uk
Instruments taught: Guitar.
Jazz Guitar workshops worldwide. Guitar Institute (London). Royal Academy of
Music and Drama (Glasgow) Scottish Youth Jazz Orchestra Course Tutor.

Goodier, David
(South West)
68 Somerset Road, Knowle, Bristol BS4 2HY
0117 971 6785, 07903 096093, mail@davidgoodier.com
Instruments taught: Double Bass, Bass Guitar.
Teaches 1 to 1. Age(s): under 11, 11 upwards. Area(s): reading, beginners, some
knowledge, refresher. Place(s): own home.
(Has been teaching for over 20 years). Includes improvisation. Other style(s): popular music.
He has been a full-time professional bass player for 25 years and has worked with
a wide range of jazz artists. His education work has included various projects touring schools - pop, rock and jazz. He was a peripatetic bass tutor at King's College
(Taunton) for 14 years as well as bass tutor and co-director of the Bude Jazz
Summer School (mid 1990s) In 1991 he co-founded the Bristol Jazz Workshop and
was its musical director for ten years. Recently has been touring with Ruby Turner.

Goodman, Ronnie
(Scotland)
Flat 1/2, 472 Paisley Road West, Glasgow G51 1PX
0141 427 7161 tel/fax, crgdmn@globalnet.co.uk
Instruments taught: Drums, Percussion.
Teaches 1 to 1.
Workshops: small groups, large groups, classes (20+). Speciality area(s): small
groups, large groups, tertiary. Interactive Workshops.
Schools: for 16+ hours per week. HE/FE. Perth College.
(Has been teaching for 5-10 years). Includes improvisation. Other style(s): popular
music, world music.
"Through Leeds College GDLM learned some basic teaching principles for improvi-
sation and have since gone on to develop Rhythm workshops. I run occasional
(approx 4 a year) workshops specialising in Latin American music."

Gray, Ian
(North West)
84a Liverpool Road, Penwortham, Preston PR1 0HT
01772 748942, 01772 513006 fax, 07771 915497 mobile
graymusic@tinyworld.co.uk
Instruments taught: Piano.
Teaches 1 to 1. Teaches Associated Board Piano Exam. Age(s): 11 upwards
Area(s): reading, beginners, some knowledge, coaching. Place(s): own home.
Workshops: usually classes (20+). Speciality area(s): secondary. Jazz workshops
(all ages). Piano (in both Jazz and popular music styles). Currently, LCC
Woodlands/Chorley, annual jazz course, Higham Hall College, Bassenthwoite Lake,
Cockermouth, Cumbria. Specialisation - Jazz in the classroom. Jazz ensemble work,

Jazz Piano.
Schools: Secondary
Qualifications: LGSM, Cert Ed., Diploma in Light Music. (Has been teaching for 15-20 years.) Includes improvisation. Other style(s): popular music, classical, world music.

Extensive experience in schools, using improvisation as an educational tool, including work with mentally handicapped and hearing impaired children. November 1997 accepted by Associated Board to train as an examiner for the new jazz piano exams. "I have always been interested in Jazz education in its own right and in Jazz being used as a 'way in' for the teaching of other classical and popular genres; I am interested in the teaching of arranging and use an approach which complements both practical and theoretical aspects as well as placing listening at the heart of the lessons given." Project Manager for Lancs Music Services for popular music and jazz.

Gray, Mike
(West Midlands)

28 Barnes Wallis Drive, Leegomery, Telford TF1 4XT
Instruments taught: Clarinet, Saxophone.
Teaches 1 to 1. Age(s): 11 upwards. Area(s): reading, beginners, some knowledge. Place(s): own home, pupil's home, at Market Drayton Musicland, Highbury House, Market Drayton, Shropshire.

Access to Music instrumental music facilitator and improvisation teacher at Janine Knight School of Music in Market Drayton, Shropshire. "As a jazz musician with many years of experience in a variety of styles, I feel that I am able to pass on the practical knowledge I have acquired over the years to students in a friendly, informal manner which puts even the most apprehensive trainee improvisor at their ease."

Green, Paul Francis
(Wales)

42 Vancouver Drive, Newport NP20 3QT
01633 251663 home tel
Instruments taught: Piano.
Teaches 1 to 1. Teaches Associated Board Piano Exam. Age(s): 11 upwards. Area(s): reading, beginners, some knowledge. Place(s): own home.
Qualifications: B Sc Hons (Eng Science) Member of National Youth Orchestra of Wales (has been teaching for 10-15 years). Includes improvisation. Other style(s): classical.

"I regard myself as a talented amateur rather than a true jazz pianist. With a strong background in classical music (ex member of National Youth Orchestra of Wales) and teaching for 10 years I have embraced the new Jazz Syllabus enthusiastically and introduce it either from scratch (to adults who ask for it) or from about Grade 1V level (to children) (ie Grade 1 Jazz). Took the 3 exams and found them a rewarding if nerve-wracking experience!

Greenway, Susan
(South East)

27a North Street, Middle Barton OX7 7BH
01869 347 616 home tel
Instruments taught: Flute, Tenor Sax, Clarinet, Alto Sax.
Teaches 1 to 1. Age(s): under 11, 11 upwards. Area(s): reading, beginners, some knowledge, refresher.

Teaches at the Oxford Brooks University.
Qualifications: B.Mus (Hons), PGCE (has been teaching for 5-10 years). Includes improvisation. Other style(s): popular music, classical, world music.
Regular player in the Syd Lawrence Orchestra. Teaches harmony and arranging.

Grew, Stephen
(North West)
75 Wingate, Saul Road, Lancaster LA1 5DW
Instruments taught: Piano.
Teaches 1 to 1. Age(s): under 11, 11 upwards. Place(s): own home.
Workshops: Free Improvisation. Womad workshops with Peter Moser, Morecambe (Lancaster)Grammer School, St Martin College(Lancaster)
"The ability to communicate new ideas and approaches to listening and creating unique structures in music, playing with the purity of sounds, where they come from and where they ultimately go."

Griffith, Frank
(South East)
99 Eastcote Lane, Northolt UB5 5RH
020 8842 3217 tel/fax, 0976 313 224, frank.griffith@brunel.ac.uk
Instruments taught: Clarinet, Piano.
Teaches 1 to 1. Teaches Associated Board Piano Exam. Age(s): 11 upwards. Area(s): reading, beginners, some knowledge, coaching. Place(s): own home, pupil's home.
Workshops: small groups. Speciality area(s): small groups, large groups, tertiary. Organising jazz events (concerts, workshops and jam sessions) for HE students. Previously and currently, Kathy Stobart Workshop (Devon) Jamey Aebersold - Richmond (London). Specialisation - Ensembles, Master classes, Big Band.
Schools: for 12-16 hours per week. HE/FE, adults.
Qualifications: Masters degree - Music. (Has been teaching for 15-20 years.) Includes improvisation. Other style(s): popular music, classical, world music.
Lecturer at City College of New York for 10 years. Has taught ensembles, jazz improvisation and arranging. Private students. Currently teaching composition and arranging and jazz workshops at Brunel University. "My experience as an educator and player in NYC for 15 years and in the UK, allows me to combine people and pedagogical skills in a unique and effective fashion. While emphasising theoretical knowledge, my main thrust is to activate and encourage students to explore their own improvisatory proclivities."

Gruner, Alan
(London)
79 Gordon Rd, Finchley, London N3 1ER
020 8346 0159 tel/fax, alangruner@fdn.co.uk
Instruments taught: Piano, Bass Guitar, Voice.
Teaches 1 to 1. Teaches Associated Board Piano Exam. Age(s): under 11, 11 to 16. Area(s): beginners, some knowledge. Place(s): own home, pupil's home.
Workshops: Barnet. Specialisation: Mostly rock material. Schools: Pre-school, primary HE/FE, adults.
Qualifications: Self taught plus a CT ABRSM Professisonal Development (has been teaching for 5-10 years). Includes improvisation. Other style(s): popular music.
"I do not consider myself wholly a jazz tutor but the new Jazz Piano syllabus has given me a much better vehicle to express my musicality and has put me in touch

with a very good way of teaching jazz to students. I include 'jazz' music, techniques etc with my singing lessons with children and adults and also with students not studying the jazz syllabus".

Gumbley, Chris
(West Midlands)

53 Peel Terrace, Stafford ST16 3HE
07779 721717, chris.gumbley@btclick.com
Instruments taught: Clarinet, Piano, Saxophone
Teaches 1 to 1. Teaches Associated Board Piano Exam. Age(s): 11 upwards.
Area(s): reading, beginners, some knowledge, refresher, coaching. Place(s): own home.
Workshops. Speciality.area(s): small groups, secondary, adult. Previous jazz courses - include Stoke, Birmingham, Bournemouth. Current Annual jazz course: Wedgwood Memorial College, Barlaston, Stoke-on-Trent. Teaches in schools for 8-12 hours per week. Usually teaches secondary, HE/FE. Birmingham Conservatoire, Qualifications: BA (Hons) Music LTCL (has been teaching for over 20 years). Includes improvisation. Other style(s): popular music. "Extensive experience in teaching and performance in all fields. Specialist Jazz knowledge."

Gunning, Josephine
(London)

22 Whittell Gardens, Sydenham, London SE26 4LN
020 8699 9112, jo@jpalmer.demon.co.uk
Instruments taught: Piano.
Teaches 1 to 1. Teaches Associated Board Piano Exam. Age(s): under 11, 11 upwards. Area(s): reading, beginners, some knowledge. Place(s): own home.
"My commitment is to children doing what inspires them, this often takes them towards jazz. From the very first lesson I devote time to letting the child improvise freely, giving them a chance to relax and access their innate creative abilities. As they progress they are ready to be challenged by the more advanced rhythms and improvisational skills presented in the Associated Board Jazz exams. They also have an ease around creating their own compositions and songs. My main commitment is that children are excited by their music and that it is a real expression of who they are, whatever their age or ability".

Guppy, Eileen
(North West)

36 Old Lancaster Road, Catterall, Garstang PR3 0HN
01995 601884 home tel
Instruments taught: Keyboards, Piano, Voice.
Teaches 1 to 1. Teaches Associated Board Piano Exam. Age(s): under 11, 11 upwards Area(s): reading, beginners, some knowledge, refresher, coaching. Place(s): own home.
Workshops: WEA Jazz Piano at Friends' Meeting House Lancaster; Jazz/Popular vocal at Leeds College of Music Summer School. Specialisation Jazz Piano and small group work.
"I enjoy teaching beginners to improvise and find the psychology of improvising a fascinating topic. I aim to encourage the development of the mental processes involved in playing or singing jazz, so that students can make more valuable use of the time they spend practising". Teaches at Royal Northern College of Music. Open University, Walton Hall, Milton Keynes MK7 6AA (www.open.ac.uk) Taught for 10 years at Leeds College of music.

Gurr, Jo
(South West)

Purbeck View, Blandford Road, Corfe Mullen, Wimborne
07778210844, jokeonthesax@aol.com, www.scbb.org.uk internet
Instruments taught: Saxophone, Flute, Clarinet.
Teaches 1 to 1. Teaches Associated Board Piano Exam. Age(s): under 11, 11
upwards. Area(s): reading, beginners, some knowledge, refresher. Place(s): own
home, other (schools).
Schools: Pre-school, primary, secondary. Adults. East Herts Music Centre,Ingram
House.
Qualifications: LLCM (has been teaching for over 20 years). Includes improvisation.
Other style(s): popular music.
"I have been a professional musician/teacher for 40 years. Presently run a suc-
cessful student big band in Hertfordshire"

Guttridge, Derek
(London)

14 Cairn Avenue, Ealing, London W5 5HX
020 8567 3510 home tel
Instruments taught: Flute, Clarinet, Saxophone.
Teaches 1 to 1. Age(s): under 11, 11 upwards. Area(s): reading, beginners, some
knowledge, refresher, coaching. Place(s): own home.
Workshops. Speciality area(s): Primary, secondary, adult.
Schools: Pre-school, primary, secondary. HE/FE, adults, special needs.
Many years teaching and playing experience, constantly searching for new
approaches. "Apart from helping pupils devlop their skills in playing their instruments, I am very keen to help them develop their aural skills - to be able to play
the notes they require".

Hague, Andy
(South West)

PO BOX 529, Bristol BS99 3GH
0117 966 9344, andy@musicsender.com
www.musicsender.com
Instruments taught: Trumpet.
Workshops: small groups. Under the informal grouping of the Bristol Jazz
Workshops - see courses.

Haines, Cris
(Wales)

14 Felinfach, Cwmtwrch Uchaf, Swansea SA9 2XR
01639 830501 home tel
Instruments taught: Trumpet, Flugel Horn.
Teaches 1 to 1. Age(s): 17 plus. Area(s): reading, beginners, some knowledge.
Place(s): own home, pupil's home.
Workshops: small groups. Previously and currently Jazz Improvisation, Big Band,
Swansea University Campus plus outside locations in Swansea, Neath, Ammanford
area. Specialisation - understanding and applying chord/scale theory and improvi-
sation in general.
Schools: for 4-8 hours per week. HE/FE, adults.
Qualifications: LLCMTD. Includes improvisation.

"I have over twenty years experience as a working Jazz and Blues musician and have taught Jazz improvisation at Swansea University Adult Education since about 1993. As someone who taught himself Jazz theory through books and experience I understand the fears, confusion and frustrations of the beginning improvisor and can guide them through the awaiting pitfalls".

Haines, David
(South West)

88 Higher Brimley, Teignmouth TQ14 8JU

01626 779690, 07957 658863, Puzjig@aol.com

www.mercuryworkshop.co.uk

Instruments taught: Piano.

Teaches 1 to 1. Teaches Associated Board Piano Exam. Age(s): under 11, 11 upwards Area(s): reading, beginners, some knowledge, refresher. Place(s): pupil's home.

Qualifications: BA (Hons) Music (has been teaching for over 20 years). Includes improvisation. Other style(s): classical.

"The arrival of the Associated Board Jazz Syllabus brought a wonderful breath of fresh air to my piano teaching in 1999, reinvigorating both my students' interest and my own in piano playing of all kinds. As a relative newcomer to jazz piano myself, I bring the vigour and enthusiasm of the newly-converted, an excitement which has led to many Merit and Distinction passes for my pupils over the last 18 months".

Hall, Mike
(North West)

70 Barkers Lane, Sale M33 6SD

0161 973 7052, mikelane@barkerslane.freeserve.co.uk

www.mikehall.co.uk

Instruments taught: Tenor Sax, Alto Sax, Soprano Sax.

Teaches 1 to 1.

Director of Jazz Ensemble and co-ordinator of Jazz Studies, lecturing in jazz theory and history at Royal Northern College of Music; Saxophone and Improvisation techniques at City College Manchester and for the last 6 years has taught at the Manchester and Royal Academy Jazz Summer Schools. Some private pupils. Also tutors at the Cawford Summer School of Music.

Hall, Rob
(Scotland)

57 Laburnum Drive, Milton of Campsie, Glasgow G66 8JS

01360 311992, 07973 145976 mobile

rob@robhall.co.uk, www.robhall.co.uk

Instruments taught: Clarinet, Piano, Saxophone.

Teaches Associated Board Piano Exam. Age(s): under 11, 11 upwards. Area(s): reading, beginners, some knowledge, refresher, coaching. Place(s): own home, pupil's home.

Workshops: Previously Cambridge jazz course (6 years); Oxford Jazz Course; Ashford School; Skye Jazz, Portree, Isle of Skye; Sheffield jazz workshop. Cambridge Jazz course at Parkside community·College; RSAMD, Glasgow. Specialisation: Improvisation.

Schools: Secondary.HE/FE.

Qualifications: B.Mus.,GRNCM, PPRNCM, Alumnus Berklee college of Music (USA) (has been teaching for 10-15 years). Includes improvisation. Other style(s): popular music, classical. Ex-Berklee scholarship student. Founder/Director Cambridge Jazz Course which runs bi-annually for a week. "Through leading courses and workshops over many years I have developed a flexible and accessible approach to teaching jazz and improvisation, accommodating different ability levels and a wide range of instruments including those often wrongly considered as 'non-jazz' instrument (e.g. cello, oboe etc). This approach, which focuses primarily on the art of improvisation, is productive, fun, and allows for a healthy degree of spontaneity. In this way I am able to respond to the abilities of the musicians for each group whilst I'm working with them and set the musical challenges at the right level, even with a mixed ability group. My ideas and teaching style derive directly from my own experiences as an active performer".

Hallam, Dan
(Scotland)
26 Marmion Crescent, Inch, Edinburgh EH16 5QY
dan.hallam@btinternet.com
Instruments taught: Saxophone, Clarinet, Flute.
Teaches 1 to 1. Age(s): under 11, 11 upwards. Area(s): reading, beginners, some knowledge, refresher, coaching. Place(s): own home, pupil's home, other (schools).
Workshops: Band techniques/directing. Lothian regional jazz residential, City of Edinburgh Jazz Residential, City of Edinburgh Education Department Summer Jazz Course.
Vast experince of various types of Big Band groups/ages/backgrounds/ethnicities as conductor and player.

Hamer, Ian
(South East)
68 Rosehill Terrace, Brighton BN1 4JL
01273 600002 home tel
Instruments taught: Flugel Horn, Trumpet.
Teaches 1 to 1.
Qualifications: Experience (has been teaching for over 20 years). Includes improvisation.
Tutor on Wavendon All Music Course, Glamorgan Summer School, Richmond Adult Education and Richmond Youth Orchestra, Brighton Musicians Co-Operative, Sussex Youth Jazz Orchestra.

Hampton, Andrew
(London)
28 Harold Road, London N8 7DE
020 8292 8012 tel/fax
Instruments taught: Clarinet, Piano, Saxophone.
Teaches 1 to 1. Age(s): under 11, 11 upwards. Area(s): reading, beginners, some knowledge, refresher, coaching. Place(s): own home.
Workshops: usually classes (20+). Speciality area(s): small groups, large groups, classes (20+), secondary.
Schools: for 16+ hours per week. Secondary.
Qualifications: BA, LTCL, MA (has been teaching for over 20 years). Includes improvisation. Other style(s): popular music, classical.
Published a Tutor book for sax called 'Saxophone Basics' (Faber).

Hannah, Tom
(London)
133a Goldhawk Road, London W12 8EN
020 8743 9659, 020 8743 9708 fax, 07803 245518 mobile
tomhannah@zeigonmusic.co.uk, www.zeigon.demon.co.uk
Instruments taught: Guitar, Bass Guitar.
Workshops: small groups. Speciality area(s): small groups, secondary.
Schools: for 8-12 hours per week. Secondary.
(Has been teaching for 10-15 years). Includes improvisation.

Harding, David
(South West)   .
67 Audley Avenue, Torquay TQ2 7PD
01803 323801 home tel
Instruments taught: Trumpet, Cornet.
Teaches 1 to 1. Age(s): under 11, 11 upwards. Area(s): reading, beginners, some knowledge. Place(s): own home, pupil's home, other (at school).
Schools: Primary. Currently teaching trumpet/cornet within the state education system. Also provides an educational and entertaining 'demonstration band' visiting schools - which includes talks, ensemble playing, and demonstrations of wide variety of instruments and their role in jazz.

Hares, Paul
(Yorkshire)
6 Salt Pan Well Steps, Whitby YO22 4AB
Instruments taught: Mandolin, Guitar.
Teaches 1 to 1.
Qualifications: ALCM. (Has been teaching for 15-20 years.) Includes improvisation.
Other style(s): classical, world music.

Harrison, Gerard
(North West)
25 Glenwyllin Road, Waterloo, Liverpool L22 4RN
0151 920 7748 home tel
Instruments taught: Alto Sax, Keyboards, Piano.
Teaches Associated Board Piano Exam.
Workshops: small groups, large groups. Speciality area(s): small groups, large groups. 1 to 1 occasionally.
Schools: for 12-16 hours per week. Adults. Liverpool Music Centre.
Qualifications: Certificate in Education LTCL (Piano teaching) + D A S E (has been teaching for over 20 years). Includes improvisation. Other style(s): popular music, classical, world music.
Over 20 years practical experience as a performer and teacher. "I believe that anyone - given the opportunities can benefit from jazz, which I see as an approach to music as much as a style". He aims to make it an inclusive rather than inaccessible art form for a chosen few. Tries to convey his own enthusiasm

Harrod, Andrew
(London)

281 Highgate Hill, London N19 5NL
020 7263 2476 home tel
Instruments taught: Piano, Keyboards.
Teaches 1 to 1. Teaches Associated Board Piano Exam. Age(s): under 11, 11
upwards Area(s): reading, beginners, some knowledge, refresher, coaching.
Place(s): own home, pupil's home.
Qualifications: P G C E; BA Hons M A (Music Education).
"I am a keen enthusiast for the state of jazz and the future of jazz in this country.
I believe there is enough talent around to refresh and develop the art form into the
wider context of contemporary music."

Hart, Frances
(Eastern)

Oliver Road, Ipswich IP33 3JB
Instruments taught: Alto Sax, Clarinet.
Workshops: usually classes (20+).
Schools: for 16+ hours per week. Primary, secondary. Westley Middle School.
Qualifications: PGCE (has been teaching for 5-10 years). Includes improvisation.
Other style(s): popular music, classical, world music.

Harvey, Eddie
(South East)

64 Park House Gardens, Twickenham TW1 2DE
020 8892 6709, 07788 674410, eddie.harvey@btinternet.com
Instruments taught: Piano.
Teaches 1 to 1. Teaches Associated Board Piano Exam. Age(s): under 11, 11
upwards Area(s): reading, beginners, some knowledge, refresher, coaching.
Place(s): own home.
Workshops: small groups, large groups, classes (20+). Speciality area(s): Primary,
secondary, tertiary, adult. Teacher inset training -jazz in the classroom and
ABRSM. London Thames Valley University - Head of Music.
Schools: Secondary.
Qualifications: Certificate of Education (Cambs) FLCM (Hon). (Has been teaching
for over 30 years). Includes improvisation. Other style(s): classical.
Coaches teachers in teaching jazz in the classroom. Runs Jackdaws summer school
in Frome, teaches at Marine School in Portsmouth and is Director of London
College of Music and Media. Probably the best known jazz musician/educator
around. Head of Jazz Studies at Thames Valley University of Music and Media and
Richmond Adult and Community College.

Harvey, Margaret
(West Midlands)

78 Poplar Road, Smethwick B66 4AN
0121 429 2529 home tel
Instruments taught: Piano.
Teaches 1 to 1. Teaches Associated Board Piano Exam. Age(s): 11 to 16. Area(s):
beginners. Place(s): own home.
Qualifications: LRAM; ABSM (has been teaching for over 20 years). Includes improvisation.

"I am very much a beginner jazz tutor! I had to learn all about jazz to keep my pupil, Kwasi Ajare, busy in the gap before he would take Grade 6 piano while he was sampling Grade 4 and Grade 5 Theory Papers. He is my one and only Jazz pupil. I never ever thought he would be interested in Jazz - but I am - we are both, now, enthusiasts."

Haslam, George
(South East)

3 Thesiger Road, Abingdon OX14 2DX
01235 529012 tel/fax, georgehaslam@aol.com
www.members.aol.com/georgehaslam internet
Instruments taught: Saxophone.
Teaches 1 to 1. Age(s): 11 upwards. Area(s): reading, beginners, some knowledge, refresher. Place(s): other (Music and Arts Centres).
Workshops. Improvisation - Saulkrasti (Latvia). Ensemble Playing - Matrix Arts Centre. Swing Band - Abingdon Music Centre. Specialisation – Blues.
For 20 years has taught individual saxophone classes both privately and in schools. Workshops in many countries. School recitals on the National Curriculum. 1996 Masterclasses in Hong Kong; gives regular workshops called "Learning the Blues" at Bracknel Park and improvisation workshops in University of Oxford Faculty of Music. "The continued success and development of the Blues workshop at South Hill Park over the last 5 years has shown an ability to encourage and enthuse musicians - beginners and experienced - to play and learn with an open mind, leading to the joy and satisfaction of group performances".

Haywood, Christine
(South West)

21 Brookway, Exeter EX1 3JJ
01392 664705 home tel
Instruments taught: Piano.
Teaches 1 to 1. Teaches Associated Board Piano Exam. Age(s): under 11, 11 upwards. Area(s): beginners. Place(s): pupil's home.
Qualifications: BA; GLCM; LGSM; CERT ED (has been teaching for over 20 years). Other style(s): popular music.

Hearnshaw, Charlie
(South West)

Home Farm, Craddock, Cullompton EX15 3LN
01884 840015, charliehearnshaw@eclipse.co.uk
Instruments taught: Clarinet, Saxophone, Piano.
Teaches 1 to 1. Age(s): 11 upwards. Area(s): reading, beginners, some knowledge, refresher, coaching. Place(s): own home, other (Kings College, Taunton. Dartington College).
Workshops: Previously, Jazz weekend at the Beaford Centre, North Devon. Saxophone and Clarinet workshop at Exeter Arts Centre, Taunton. Big Band Workshop at King's College, Taunton. Jazz day at Danesfield School (Middle School). Specialisation - Clarinet, Saxophone, Improvisation, Advanced Jazz Improvisation, Improvisation for classical. Schools: for 8-12 hours per week. Primary,secondary HE/FE, adults.
Qualifications: DDME (Dartington Diploma of Music Education), Cert Ed (has been teaching for 5-10 years). Other style(s): classical.
In the past ran weekly workshop for Taunton Jazz Club. He has aimed some workshops at classical players who are trying to broaden their repertoire.

Heeley, Roger
(West Midlands)

126 Brooklands Road, Hall Green, Birmingham B28 8JZ
0121 777 8096 home tel
Instruments taught: Keyboards, Piano.
Teaches 1 to 1. Teaches Associated Board Piano Exam. Age(s): 11 to 16. Area(s): reading, beginners, some knowledge. Place(s): pupil's home, other (Local music shop).
(Has been teaching for 10-15 years). Includes improvisation. Other style(s): classical.
Private pupils but mainly involved in teaching beginners basics and taking pupils to GCSE standards and music grades. "I have been a Jazz musician for many years with experience in just about every style, and have also worked as a teacher for around 2 decades."

Hession, Paul
(Yorkshire)

41 Hanover Square, Leeds LS3 1BQ
0113 243 1569 home tel
Instruments taught: Drums.
Workshops. Speciality area(s): small groups, large groups, adult. Group Improvisation.
Schools: for 4-8 hours per week. Adults. Improvised Music Leeds.
(Has been teaching for 15-20 years.) Includes improvisation.
Established improvised music workshop for WEA in 1983. 1989-91 taught drumming to school children for Calderdale. Currently runs Improvised Music Leeds - workshops.

Hicks, Deirdre
(South East)

24 Raglan Road, Reigate RH2 0DP
01737 243 931 home tel
Instruments taught: Piano.
Teaches 1 to 1. Teaches Associated Board Piano Exam. Age(s): 11 to 16. Area(s): beginners. Place(s): own home.
Retired from teaching music at Reigate Grammar School. "I am not distinctive as a jazz tutor but have managed to keep one or two 14 yr old boys on board by introducing the Associated Board syllabus and this has proved very successful. I am learning too by experience. I am very keen on jazz and can help students with simple improvisation."

Hicks, Keith
(South West)

Melbourn, 61 Sidford High Street, Sidmouth EX10 9SH 01395 514446
Instruments taught: Tuba, Trumpet, Trombone.
Teaches 1 to 1.
Workshops: small groups, large groups, classes (20+). Jazz history and development.
Schools: Primary. Adults. WEA South West District.
Qualifications: Cert. Ed (has been teaching for over 20 years). Includes improvisation.

Has taught music at 6 primary schools and Head of Music in 3 of them. Concentrates on style and repertoire. Ensemble work with Big Band. Adult teaching on the History of Jazz.

Higgins, Gerry
(South East)

Flat 4, 11 Palmeira Square, Hove BN3 2JB
01273 208815, 01273 722471 fax, 07778 495 195 mobile
gerry@comprador, demon.co.uk, www.comprador.demon.co.uk
Instruments taught: Bass Guitar, Double Bass.
Teaches 1 to 1. Age(s): 17 plus. Area(s): beginners, some knowledge, refresher, coaching. Place(s): own home.
(Has been teaching for 15-20 years.)
Teaches improvisation at Richmond Upon Thames Tertiary College

Higgs, Patrick
(London)

33 Ranelagh Gardens Mansions, Fulham, London SW6 3UQ
020 7736 5733 home tel
Instruments taught: Trumpet.
Teaches 1 to 1. Area(s): reading, beginners, some knowledge, refresher, coaching. Place(s): own home, pupil's home.
Workshops: usually small groups. Speciality area(s): small groups, primary, secondary. Previously JAWS Summer Jazz course (West London Institute of Higher Learning). Henry Compton School Community Education.
Schools: for 16+ hours per week. secondary (11-16), HE/FE, adults (21+).
Qualifications: None (has been teaching for over 20 years). Includes improvisation.
For last 15 years has taught 2 adult and 3 junior jazz workshops. "40 years experience playing Mike Westbrook, Chris McGregor, Willie Garnett, Charlie Watts Big Band."

Hislam, Nick
(East Midlands)

97 Knighton Church Road, Leicester LE2 3JN
0116 270 4124, sajani@btinternet.com
Instruments taught: Tenor Sax, Soprano Sax, Alto Sax.
Adult workshops in basic improvisation skills. Some teaching of improvised percussion in primary schools. Organises jam sessions for emerging jazz musicians. Workshops organised within remit of Leicester Jazz House.

Holland, Bernie
(South East)

1 Lynn Close, Wealdstone HA3 5LP
020 8863 3223, bernieholland@freeuk.com
Instruments taught: Bass Guitar, Guitar.
Teaches 1 to 1.
Workshops: Seminars in Theory - composition - Improvisation.
Schools: for 8-12 hours per week. Primary, secondary. HE/FE, adults (21+).
Qualifications: BA(Hons) Humanities, PGCE (Music) (has been teaching for over 20 years). Includes improvisation. Other style(s): popular music, classical, world music.

Holmes, Christopher
(South West)
c/o St Martins Junior School, Shady Bower, Salisbury SP1 2RG
Instruments taught: Trumpet.
Teaches 1 to 1.
Workshops: usually small groups. Speciality area(s): large groups, primary, secondary.
Schools: for 16+ hours per week. Primary, secondary. Salisbury Area Young Musicians, Wiltshire Music Service.
(Has been teaching for over 20 years). Includes improvisation. Other style(s): popular music.

Hopkins, Mike
(South West)
3 Bramley Road, Kinson, Bournemouth BH10 5LU
01202 572407 tel/fax, jazizus@yahoo.com
Instruments taught: Saxophone, Clarinet, Oboe.
Teaches 1 to 1. Age(s): under 11, 11 upwards. Area(s): reading, beginners, some knowledge, refresher, coaching. Place(s): own home.
Workshops: Big Band, jazz improvisation. Combermere Barracks - Windsor; Lychett Minster School - Dorset; Bryanston School - Dorset; Bournemouth College - Dorset.
Schools: Primary, secondary. Adults.
Qualifications: as a player- R.M.S.M.Dip, army qualifications. (Has been teaching for 15-20 years.) Includes improvisation. Other style(s): popular music, classical, other (improvisation).
"I have over 30 years experience as a player, freelancing with many bands and orchestras. TV and radio sessions, studio work, many Big Bands. I feel I am able to pass on what I have learnt by playing, learning and listening to the many top players that I have worked with, to my younger pupils. I also run my own jazz group."

Hopper, Hugh
(South East)
29 Castle Road, Whitstable CT5 2DZ
01227 277129, 0771 3006898 mobile
hhop@ukonline.co.uk, www.musart.co.uk/hhhpage.htm internet
Instruments taught: Bass Guitar.

Hopson, Yvonne
(Yorkshire)
45 Medina Way, Barugh S75 1NF
01226 384131, yvonne.hopson@talk21.com
Instruments taught: Piano.
Teaches 1 to 1. Teaches Associated Board Piano Exam. Age(s): 11 upwards. Area(s): reading, beginners, some knowledge. Place(s): own home, pupil's home.
Qualifications: CT ABRSM (has been teaching for 5-10 years). Other style(s): popular music, classical.
"I think my ability to play and teach jazz comes from an excellent understanding of rhythms, and I have an enthusiasm which is infectious, judging from my students! Jazz is the musical equivalent to common sense!"

Houlston, Robert
(Eastern)

12 Longacres, St. Albans AL4 ODR
01727 851809, bob@houlston.freeserve.co.uk email
www.houlston.freeserve.co.uk./guitar.htm internet
Instruments taught: Guitar.
Teaches 1 to 1. Age(s): under 11, 11 upwards. Area(s): beginners, some knowledge. Place(s): own home.
(Has been teaching for 10-15 years).

Hove, Gillian
(Eastern)

Edgewood, Lark Hill Road, Canewoon SS4 3RX
01702 258200 home tel
Instruments taught: Electric Piano, Keyboards, Piano.
Teaches 1 to 1. Teaches Associated Board Piano Exam. Age(s): under 11, 11 upwards. Area(s): reading, beginners, some knowledge, refresher. Place(s): own home.
Workshops: usually small groups.
Schools: for 1-4 hours per week.
Qualifications: Assoc. London College of Music (has been teaching for over 20 years). Includes improvisation. Other style(s): popular music.
"Learnt popular music in the 60s and 70s and learnt to improvise on the electric organ in the 70s/80s. I've taught jazz electric organ and popular musician keyboards for 25 years as well as popular, classical and jazz on the piano for 20 years."

Howarth, Ian
(London)

9 Macarthur House, Tilson Gardens, London SW2 4NQ
020 8671 0967, ianhowarth@Milehouse, demon.co.uk
milehouse.demon.co.uk
Instruments taught: Drums, Percussion.
Teaches 1 to 1. Area(s): beginners, some knowledge, refresher. Place(s): own home.
Workshops: usually small groups. Speciality area(s): Primary, secondary, tertiary, adult.
Schools: for 16+ hours per week. Primary, secondary., HE/FE, adults.
Qualifications: Prof. Of Drumming, Kenny Clare School. (Has been teaching for 15-20 years.) Includes improvisation. Other style(s): other (Group Situations).
Teaches the basics of jazz drumming and cymbals.

Howton, Barry
(South East)

7 Church Street, Old Town, Bexhill on Sea TN40 2HE
01424 734 077, 0956 481415 mobile
Instruments taught: Drums.
Teaches 1 to 1.
Workshops: small groups. Speciality area(s): large groups, classes (20+), primary, secondary, tertiary, adult. Jazz via Internet.
Schools: for 12-16 hours per week. Primary, Secondary. HE/FE, adults.

Qualifications: Degree in Behavioural Studies. (Has been teaching for 15-20 years.) Other style(s): classical, other (Folk).

Teacher for many years particularly using group dynamics approach and self awareness connections with improvising, both individually and collectively.Works with disabled people. Runs weekly workshops in various schools.

Hudson, Bob
(East Midlands)

11a Worcester Road, Woodthorpe, Nottingham NG5 4HW

0115 956 7952, bob.hudson@ntlworld.com

www.homepage.ntlworld.com/robert.hudson2 internet

Instruments taught: Piano.

Teaches 1 to 1. Teaches Associated Board Piano Exam.

Qualifications: B.A.. (Has been teaching for 1-2 years). Includes improvisation. Other style(s): popular music, classical.

Teaches jazz appreciation courses at Nottingham University Adult Education department.

Hughes, John
(West Midlands)

36 Jesson Road, Walsall WS1 3AS

01922 635262 tel/fax, jh@jesson36.fsnet.co.uk

www.ostrichmusic.com

Instruments taught: Bass Guitar, Trombone, Trumpet.

Teaches 1 to 1. Age(s): 11 upwards. Area(s): reading, beginners, some knowledge. Place(s): pupil's home.

Workshops: small groups, large groups. Previously, Jazz/Rock workshop in Walsall. Currently, Jazz workshop. Contact: Forest Community Centre, Hawbush Road, Walsall. Specialisation - Composition/Improvisation (Adults).

Schools: for 16+ hours per week. Primary. Secondary. HE/FE, adults.

Qualifications: Teaching Cert (has been teaching for over 20 years). Includes improvisation. Other style(s): popular music.

"Work as Trombonist, Bass/Guitar in Big Bands and Jazz/Rock groups. Taught all Brass instruments for local Education Authority since 1972. Formed Walsall Youth Jazz Orchestra in 1975, organised American Tours, Montreux Festival concerts etc. Ex-members include Martin Shaw, Duncan McKay, Richard Iles, Julian Arguelles, Trevor Lines, Tom Porter.

Hume, Alastair
(South West)

86 Seafield Road, Bournemouth

01202 425015, vanalgeo1@tinyworld.co.uk

Instruments taught: Flute, Saxophone.

Teaches 1 to 1. Age(s): 11 upwards. Area(s): reading, beginners, some knowledge, coaching. Place(s): own home, other (School).

Workshops: small groups, large groups, classes (20+). Big Band Trainer and Arranger.

Schools: for 16+ hours per week. Primary,secondary, adults. King Alfred's Middle School, Shaftesbury Upper School.

Qualifications: GGSM (has been teaching for over 20 years). Includes improvisation. Other style(s): popular music.

1982-86 ran Leeds College Big Band. 1990-96 ran Swing Band in Shaftesbury

Hunter, John
(Yorkshire)
5 Newbury Road, Rastrick, Brighouse HD6 3PG
Instruments taught: Piano.
Teaches 1 to 1. Age(s): 11 upwards. Area(s): reading, beginners, some knowledge. Place(s): own home.
Workshops: usually large groups, classes (20+). Speciality area(s): secondary. Youth ensembles, arranging, composing, conducting. MD. Previously, Bradford University Jazz Ensemble - spring 97 + two years of coaching since/similar for Santhorpe Youth Big Band 1983 -90.
Schools: for 16+ hours per week. Secondary. HE/FE.
Qualifications: B Mus (Hons); PGCE (has been teaching for over 20 years). Includes improvisation.
"Years of playing experience and teaching in both classical and jazz fields. Experience of working with 11 year old beginners through to seasoned professionals. As a jazz bigband leader and composer for 20 years I still get excited at the prospect of gigging and teaching!!"

Hunter, Neil
(East Midlands)
32 Evesham Road, Leicester LE3 2BD
0116 2332909, neil.hunter@rrds.co.uk
Instruments taught: Keyboards, Piano.
Teaches 1 to 1.

Iles, Elizabeth
(South West)
93 Richmond Wood Road, Bournemouth BH8 9DQ
01202 301117 home tel
Instruments taught: Piano.
Teaches 1 to 1. Teaches Associated Board Piano Exam. Age(s): under 11, 11 upwards. Area(s): beginners. Place(s): own home.
Qualifications: LRAM; GRSM (has been teaching for over 20 years). Includes improvisation.
"I cannot by any stretch of the imagination call myself 'distinctive' as a jazz tutor! I try to enthuse and find a way to interest musically able students who need a change from the classical repertoire."

Iles, Nikki
(Eastern)
Chaucer Cottage, 57 Vicarage Lane, Kings Langley WD4 9HS
01923 269974 home tel
Instruments taught: Piano.
Qualifications: GDPLM, Cert Ed. (Has been teaching for 15-20 years.) Includes improvisation. Other style(s): classical.
Teaches on the BA in Jazz Studies at Middlesex University and Glamorgan Summer School, Mediterranean Summer School (see Clive Fenner).

Iles, Trevor
(East Midlands)
27 The Lawns, Collingham, Newark NG23 7NT

07939 081809, trevoriles@hotmail.com
Instruments taught: Clarinet, Piano, Saxophone.
Teaches 1 to 1. Teaches Associated Board Piano Exam. Age(s): under 11, 11 upwards. Area(s): reading, beginners, some knowledge, coaching. Place(s): pupil's home, other (schools).
Schools: Primary, secondary, HE/FE, adults and special needs.
Qualifications: BA, teaching certificate (has been teaching for over 20 years). Includes improvisation. Other style(s): world music.

Ind, Peter
(South East)
207 Amyand Park Road, Twickenham TW1 3HN
020 8744 2747, waveindjones@compuserve.com
www.jazzcorner.com
Instruments taught: Double Bass, Piano.
Teaches 1 to 1. Age(s): 17 plus. Area(s): beginners, some knowledge, coaching. Place(s): other (At PI's studio).
Workshops: Past experience includes founding the jazz course at Leeds College of music in 1967 and teaching at the Jazz Centre Society workshops. Adults.
"I first introduced the concept of how to develop as a jazz improviser when I returned to the UK in 1966. Since then the methods I taught have been copied and widely used by others!"

Ingham, Richard
(Yorkshire)
Greenroyd House, 31 Agbrigg Road, Sandal Magna, Wakefield WF1 5AB
01924 257826, 01924 219272 fax, 07889 145 745 mobile
Instruments taught: Saxophone.
Teaches 1 to 1.
Workshops: small groups, large groups, classes (20+). Speciality area(s): Primary, secondary, tertiary, adult. Saxophone - classical; Music Technology - WX7 Midi Wind controller; 20th Century History.
Schools: for 16+ hours per week. Primary, secondary. HE/FE, adults.
Qualifications: BA (Hons) LRAM, ARCM, PGCE (has been teaching for over 20 years). Includes improvisation. Other style(s): popular music, classical.
Studied music at York University, and is a member of the Northern Saxophone Quartet, with whom he has performed internationally. He has presented master-classes in conservatoires in the UK and abroad, and in his capacity as a jazz educator gives many jazz workshops and lectures throughout the country. He has recently completed a lecture tour of South-East Asia. His numerous annual residential saxophone courses have proved very popular. Visiting Professor of Jazz at the University of St Andrews, and jazz tutor and twentieth century music history tutor at St Mary's Music School, Edinburgh; a music festival adjudicator and specialist examiner and lectures at Leeds College of Music. Saxophone consultant at Wells Cathedral Music School and gives classes at the Royal Welsh College of Music and Drama. He is a mentor for the Associated Board. He was chairman of the Clarinet and Saxophone Society of Great Britain (1989-1992), and co-directed the first seven British Saxophone Congresses from 1990 to 2002. He led the 'Sounds Like a New Century' jazz education project in 2000, in conjunction with JazzDev, Yorkshire Arts and Leeds College of Music. He has given many jazz workshops for the Royal Marines Bands Service. His own saxophone studio in Yorkshire has produced the following advanced student performances: BBC Young Musician of the Year 2000 Woodwind finalist and winner of the Walter Todds Bursary, and 2002

Woodwind finalist; Finalist, Perrier Young Jazz Musician competition 2000; Winner, Royal Overseas League Woodwind and Brass Competition; UK winner and European Silver Medallist, European Music for Youth Saxophone Award.

Ingleby, Mark
(London)

50 Ivy Road, Brockley, London SE4 1YS
020 8694 8250, 020 8653 1413 home fax
ingleby@canopy.globalnet.co.uk
Instruments taught: Keyboards, Piano.
Teaches 1 to 1. Teaches Associated Board Piano Exam. Age(s): under 11, 11 upwards. Area(s): reading, beginners, some knowledge, refresher, coaching. Place(s): pupil's home.
Workshops: Jazz Workshops for Jazz Umbrella. Currently Jazz Umbrella workshops at the Crypt, Camberwell Church St. Two seasons a year of approximately 10-12 weeks. Specialisation - mixed ability/Ensemble listening and cohesion/Rhythmic development.
Schools: for 16+ hours per week. Primary, secondary. Adults.
Qualifications: PGTC (has been teaching for 10-15 years). Includes improvisation. Other style(s): popular music.
1987 Jazz workshops at 6th form level. History of Jazz for non jazz/non improvising musicians at all levels. Teaches improvisation at GCSE and Pre GCSE as a regular part of Instrumental music. Tuition in keyboards and composition at Secondary level with Jazz/Blues and Gospel being an important part of this. "Having worked during 3 years in USA with Kansas City style musician, Jimmy Cheatham and avant-gardist Anthony Braxton, my mixed ability jazz workshops pay fundamental attention to rhythm, melody and black cultural traditions, expanding out into many differing rhythmic styles across the broad range of jazz, funk, salsa, gospel styles, etc, whilst developing rhythmic/melodic counterpoint and listening by all participants. This leads to a band with a high degree of cohesion, despite mixed ability students, by the end of each course."

Jackson, David
(South East)

37 Carey Road, Wokingham RG40 2NP
0118 9790211 tel/fax, tonewall@btinternet.com
Instruments taught: Soundbeam.
Teaches 1 to 1.
Workshops: usually small groups. Speciality area(s): 1 to 1. Disabled childen and adults, and staff of special school and day centres. Previously 'Soundability' (the Soundbeam Project). Currently, freelance consultancy in Soundbeam. Specialisation - Soundbeam. (See separate entry).
Schools: for 8-12 hours per week. Pre-school, primary, secondary. HE/FE, adults and special needs. Meldreth Manor School, Meldreth, Nr Royston, Herts
Qualifications: MA, PGCE. (Has been teaching for 15-20 years.) Includes improvisation. Other style(s): popular music, classical, world music, other (Classical, Folk and rock).
"I am perhaps the leading performance artist today using Soundbeam. I am also a saxophonist, formerly with 70's legendary rock Band - Van der Graff Generator. I play 'beams, switches and horns simultaneously, but better than that is when I work with groups (of all abilities and disabilities) who play my unique array of invisible instruments." I am also a composer and Project leader and have been a Soundbeam trainer for 10 years"

Jarman, Jilly
(North West)

21 Maple Drive, Penrith, Penrith CA11 8TU
01768 866559, 07909 846581, jilly.jarman@virgin.net
www.cljazz.free-online.co.uk
Instruments taught: Voice, Piano, Percussion.
Teaches 1 to 1. Teaches Associated Board Piano Exam. Age(s): under 11, 11
upwards Area(s): reading, beginners, some knowledge, refresher, coaching.
Place(s): own home. Workshops: Previously, Islington Adult Education. Currently
Schools and Arts Projects; Residential adult course - Cumbria, Harlow, London,
Wales. Specialisation - vocal, songwriting, improvisation, general.
Schools: Primary, secondary. HE/FE, adults. Ullswater A.E., Ullswater Community
College, Penrith Eden Arts, Penrith.
Workshop tutor for the past 20 years. Enjoys facilitating risk-taking work in a sup-
portive and non-competitive atmosphere. Teaches small and large. "As a jazz edu-
cator likes to create a safe space where students can push their technical and confidence boundaries. Believes that jazz is an ideal form in which to explore one's
own voice and musicality."

Jarvis, Robert
(South East)

76 Whitstable Road, Faversham ME13 8DL
01795 531715, robertjarvis@usa.net
Instruments taught: Trombone.
Teaches 1 to 1.
Workshops: usually small groups. Speciality area(s): Primary, secondary, tertiary.
Organises and runs various music (composition) projects as a freelance animateur.
Schools: for 16+ hours per week. Primary, secondary. HE/FE.
Qualifications: BA Music and Film (has been teaching for 10-15 years). Includes
improvisation. Other style(s): classical.

Jasnoch, John
(Yorkshire)

66 Robey Street, Sheffield S4 8JF
th.jas@care4free.net
Instruments taught: Guitar.
Teaches 1 to 1.
I wouldn't say I teach jazz, I would say I teach rudiments and I encourage stu-
dents to look at improvisation.

Jenkins, Billy
(London)

18 Tremaine Close, London SE4 1YF
020 8692 3921, billyjenkins@piemail.co.uk
www.billyjenkins.com
Instruments taught: Guitar.
Teaches 1 to 1. Age(s): under 11, 11 upwards. Area(s): reading, beginners, some
knowledge, refresher, coaching. Place(s): own home.
Workshops: In the past has taught at Royal Academy Jazz Course (London);
Middlesex University music course - Big Band Director; International Freie
Kunstschule (Berlin); Moving Music (Belfast) Greenwich Youth Jazz Orchestra

(Blackheath, London). Recent work was with the Pied Piper Project - bringing creativity and Improvisation to rural areas of North Yorkshire. Specialisation - inner strengthening and improvisation, Blues, Guitar techniques, jazz appreciation classes.

Schools:Primary, secondary. HE/FE, adults.

(Has been teaching for over 20 years). Includes improvisation. Other style(s): popular music, other (Blues).

1990-96 visiting tutor in guitar technique at Lewisham College. 1995 "Big Fight" workshops Royal Academy Guest lecturer. 1996 Directing Middlesex University Jazz Ensemble "Jazz is a kinetic art form. I teach formal music - then let the pupil be shown how to 'jazz it up'. Teaching 'Jazz' *per se* is a *non sequitur*. Creation not Curation. Too much 'jazz education' has dampened and formulised the genre. I bring out the arsonist in the player. Too many theorists encourage the fireman. I teach selectively to retain that spontaneous feeling"

Johns, Larry
(South West)

Penrose, Halt Road, Goonhavern, Truro TR4 9QE

01872 573 055, larry@kornwall.co.uk , www.kornwall.co.uk

Instruments taught: Tenor Sax, Flute, Clarinet.

Teaches 1 to 1. Age(s): 11 upwards. Area(s): reading, beginners, some knowledge, coaching. Place(s): own home, other (College).

Workshops: small groups, large groups, classes (20+).

Schools: for 16+ hours per week. HE/FE, adults.

Qualifications: L R A M equivalent (has been teaching for over 20 years). Includes improvisation. Other style(s): classical.

"I have spent a lifetime playing professional jazz"

Johnson, David
(London)

10 Burntwood Close, Wandsworth, London SW18 3JU

020 8870 3450 tel/fax, cf1961@aol.com

Instruments taught: Violin, Drums, Piano.

Teaches 1 to 1.

Given workshops in UK and Switzerland. Including work with Oxford University Jazz Society, Charterhouse School, co-led youth Big Band in Tunbridge Wells for 5 years.

Johnson, Stuart
(North East)

PO Box 254, Gateshead NE8 2YR

07885 435098, stuart@silentway.freeserve.co.uk

www.homepage.ntlworld.com/silentway internet

Instruments taught: Saxophone.

Workshops: small groups, large groups. Speciality area(s): tertiary.

Schools: for 4-8 hours per week. Primary.HE/FE. University College Ripon and York St. John/Access to Music, Leicester.

Qualifications: PGCE (has been teaching for over 20 years). Includes improvisation. Other style(s): popular music, classical, world music.

Jazz Animateur in Mid-Northumberland in 1989. MD Windjammer 1986 to now. Adviser B/Tec Popular Music courses. Visiting lecturer Wakefield College Music dept. 1995 PRS composer in Education project.

Johnston, David
(South East)

36 Oakfield Road, Ashtead KT21 2RD
01372 275293, 07973 354418, david.johnston@btinternet.com
www.watermilljazz.co.uk
Instruments taught: Keyboards, Organ, Piano.
Teaches 1 to 1. Teaches Associated Board Piano Exam. Age(s): under 11, 11 upwards. Area(s): reading, beginners, some knowledge, refresher, coaching. Place(s): own home.
Qualifications: Classical Training; Jazz lessons from John Horler and Michael Garrick (has been teaching for 10-15 years). Includes improvisation. Other style(s): other (Classical).
"As a professional Jazz pianist working with many of the country's leading soloists, I have had the opportunity to practise and refine techniques which I apply to my teaching. Some of my students have themselves gone on to a career as professional musicians. I teach all jazz standards - classical pianists particularly welcome."

Johnstone, Margaret
(North West)

409 Lytham Road, Blackpool FY4 1EB 01253 402577
Instruments taught: Piano.
Teaches 1 to 1. Teaches Associated Board Piano Exam. Age(s): under 11, 11 upwards. Area(s): reading, beginners. Place(s): own home.
Qualifications: LRAM; LTCL; ATCL (has been teaching for over 20 years). Includes improvisation. Other style(s): popular music.
"I teach piano and as I include improvisation skills, I decided to offer the ABRSM Jazz Piano exams to interested pupils. Those who have taken/are taking the exams really enjoy(ed) doing so."

Jolly, Paul
(Eastern)

65-67 Bute Street, Luton LU1 2EY
07850 207346, 33jazz@compuserve.com, www.33jazz.com
Instruments taught: Saxophone, Clarinet.
Teaches 1 to 1. Age(s): under 11, 11 upwards. Area(s): reading, beginners, some knowledge. Place(s): own home, pupil's home.
Workshops: Big Band workshop at Bute Street, Arts Centre.
(Has been teaching for 15-20 years.) Includes improvisation.
"Apart from one-one instrumental teaching, I like to work with mixed ability musicians (from all musical genres) to explore group improvising and collective expression."

Jones, Chris
(West Midlands)

Lawnswood Road, Stourbridge DY8 5PQ
cjones@saltwells.dudley.gov.uk, www.edu.dudley.gov.uk internet
Instruments taught: Trumpet.
Age(s): under 11, 11 to 16.
Workshops: Getting started at improvising. Improvising for instrumental teachers. Big Band for traditional instrumentalists (both at Dudley Music Centre).

Qualifications: PGCE. Includes improvisation. Other style(s): popular music.

Jones, Dave
(South East)
341 Kingsway, Hove BN3 4PD
01273 414559 home tel
Instruments taught: Piano, Vibraphone.
Teaches 1 to 1.
Qualifications: 30 years experience, Trinity College of Music. Interested in teaching jazz appreciation. Teaches jazz by way of young group involvement.

Jones, Sarah
(West Midlands)
Farnham, 10 Tilley Road, Wem, Shrewsbury SY4 5HA
01939 233060 home tel
Instruments taught: Piano, Saxophone.
Teaches 1 to 1. Teaches Associated Board Piano Exam. Age(s): under 11, 11 upwards Area(s): reading, beginners, some knowledge, refresher, coaching. Place(s): own home.
Workshops: small groups. Speciality area(s): Primary, secondary. Children and young adults with 'special needs'.
Schools: for 1-4 hours per week. Secondary. HE/FE and special needs.
Qualifications: ABRSM Grades, A Level Music; BA Combined Hons Education (has been teaching for 5-10 years). Includes improvisation. Other style(s): popular music, classical.
"I enjoy teaching and am passionate about music, especially jazz. I played lead alto sax in a Big Band for 7 years. I have a flexible and open minded approach to teaching. I'm willing to listen to students likes and dislikes and will gear lessons to maximise their enjoyment. I also identify strengths to encourage, and weaknesses to be worked on, so that good results can be achieved. Overall my aim is for lessons and practise to be a pleasure, not a chore".

Karian, Karin
(South West)
9 Green Road, Winton, Bournemouth BH9 1DU
01202 253704 tel/fax, 07703 686982, kkq@jazz.demon.co.uk
Instruments taught: Voice.

Kemp, Josh
(London)
5 Alexandra Mansions, Chichele Road, London NW2 3AS
020 8452 2583, 020 8452 2627 fax, 07973 828884 mobile
mail@klqt.com, www.klqt.com
Instruments taught: Piano, Tenor Sax.
Teaches 1 to 1. Age(s): under 11, 11 upwards. Area(s): reading, beginners, some knowledge, refresher. Place(s): own home.
Qualifications: RGSM (Guildhall) Post Grad Diploma (Performance) (has been teaching for 10-15 years). Includes improvisation.
Teaches at Grafham Water residential jazz weekend, workshops for Cambridge Jazz Co-operative, coaching Cambridge Youth Jazz Orchestra as well as teaching in schools.

Kendon, Adrian
(South East)
25 Kenilworth Road, Bognor Regis PO21 5NE
01243 863590, adrian.kendon@chichester.ac.uk
www.jazzcollege.org.uk internet
Instruments taught: Double Bass.
Workshops: usually small groups, large groups, classes (20+).
Schools: for 16+ hours per week. HE/FE. Chichester College.
Qualifications: City and Guilds 730 (has been teaching for 10-15 years). Includes improvisation. Other style(s): world music.

Kenny, John
(Scotland)
69 Spottiswoode St., Edinburgh EH9 1DL
0131 447 3707 tel/fax, carny@mcmail.com
Instruments taught: Trombone.
Teaches 1 to 1.
Workshops: small groups, large groups, classes (20+). Theatre Direction, Stagecraft, Composition.
Schools: for 8-12 hours per week. Primary, secondary. HE/FE, adults. Guildhall School of Music and Drama, Royal Scottish Academy of Music and Drama.
Qualifications: LRAM, ARAM. (Has been teaching for 15-20 years.) Includes improvisation. Other style(s): classical, world music, other (Contemporary, Electro Acoustic).
Has worked in a variety of creative/improvisation workshops. Tutor on Scottish National Youth Jazz course. Briefly directed Edinburgh Youth Jazz Orchestra.

Kerr, Trudy
(London)
86 Churchdown, Bromley, London BR1 5PQ
020 8465 0333, 07961 382685 mobile
mail@trudykerr.com, www.trudykerr.com
Instruments taught: Voice.
Teaches 1 to 1. Age(s): 17 plus. Area(s): beginners, some knowledge, refresher, coaching. Place(s): own home, other (Colchester Institute - Mon/Tuesday). Richmond College Adult and FE - Sat Masterclass.
Qualifications: Post Grad Cert Guildhall School of Music (has been teaching for 3-5 years). Includes improvisation.
Teaching degree course at Colchester Institute - 1 to 1 teaching Jazz-pop ensemble. "As a professional singer I have a lot to offer a student in respect of performance and communication with the audience and musicians. As I studied at the Guildhall School of Music I have a sound knowledge of jazz theory too. I've also sung soul and pop for many years and have a good understanding of what is required technically for these genres of music."

Kershaw, Steve
(South East)
3 New Street, Deddington, Oxford OX15 0ST
01869 338123, 07775 943995, drspkershaw@msn.com
home7.inet.tele.dk/kjolby/stekweb internet
Instruments taught: Double Bass, Bass Guitar.

Teaches 1 to 1.
Workshops: small groups.
Schools: for 4-8 hours per week. Secondary.
Qualifications: Vocational Honors Graduate Bass Institute of Technology, Musicians Institute, Hollywood, CA, USA (has been teaching for 5-10 years). Includes improvisation.
Workshops in schools and colleges in harmony and theory, improvisation.

Khan, Sean
(London)
16 Prothero Road, Fulham, London SW6 7LZ
020 7381 8787 home tel
Instruments taught: Saxophone.
Teaches 1 to 1.
Workshops: usually small groups. Speciality area(s): adult.
(Has been teaching for 5-10 years). Includes improvisation. Other style(s): popular music, classical.
Has taken classical clarinet lessons and had private tuition in Jazz Harmony/Saxophone. Has experience in playing Salsa and funk.

Kirtlan, David
(Yorkshire)
School of Music, Thornes Park Centre, Horbury Road, Wakefield WF2 8QZ
www.wakcoll.ac.uk internet
Instruments taught: Bass Guitar.
Qualifications: Cert Ed (has been teaching for 5-10 years). Other style(s): popular music.

Knight, Frances
(South East)
40 Mandeville Road, Canterbury CT2 7HD
01227 785257, 0860 731242 mobile
Instruments taught: Piano.
Teaches 1 to 1. Teaches Associated Board Piano Exam. Age(s): 11upwards.
Area(s): reading, beginners, some knowledge, refresher. Place(s): own home.
Schools: Secondary. HE/FE, adults.
Other style(s): popular music.
Has taught and run jazz workshops for all ages since 1984 at places like Weekend Arts College (WAC), Oval House (London), Bath University. For about three years initiated, raised funding for and ran summer school in Canterbury (now finished) Peripatetic teacher in two secondary schools. (Piano, Big Band). Also teaches at Christchurch University College.

Kofi, Tony
(London)
63A Norbury Crescent, London SW16 4JS
0771 902 8058, tonydkofi@aol.com
Instruments taught: Soprano Sax, Alto Sax.
Teaches 1 to 1.
Workshops: Jazz workshops with Grand Union.

Kopinski, Jan
(East Midlands)

22 Nelson Road, Daybrook, Nottingham NG5 6JE
0115 9265484 tel/fax, 07989 463748 mobile
jankopinski@yahoo.com, www.jankopinski.com
Instruments taught: Saxophone.
Teaches 1 to 1. Age(s): 11 upwards. Area(s): reading, beginners, some knowledge, refresher, coaching. Place(s): own home.
Workshops: Go global - 16+ Jazz/Improvisation - Masterclass series - University of Salford, Manchester, Jazz and Improvisation - Bilborough College, Notts. Also workshops as part of curriculum on BA Hons popular music courses at University of Salford and Derby. Specialisation - Improvisation. Workshops with Pinski Zoo. "I have a combined experience of professional musician and educational tuition, with plenty of recording, performance and touring history. I look for the simplest and most direct way of learning and teaching improvisation and jazz harmony."

Lad, Milan
(Yorkshire)

64 Horton Grange Road, Bradford BD7 3AQ
07748 641 035, x10921@bradford.ac.uk
Instruments taught: Guitar.
Teaches 1 to 1. Age(s): 17 plus. Area(s): some knowledge, refresher. Place(s): own home.
(Has been teaching for 5-10 years). Includes improvisation.
On request available for private tuition. Has given talks to students in school/colleges about music and music business and is currently the Development Officer at the Alhambra Theatre (Bradford).

Laffan, Peter
(Yorkshire)

17 Collinfield Rise, Woodside, Bradford BD6 2SL
01274 412325, Plaffan@lineone.net
Instruments taught: Bass Guitar.
Teaches 1 to 1. Age(s): under 11, 11 upwards. Area(s): reading, beginners, some knowledge, refresher, coaching. Place(s): own home.
Workshops: In the past has taught at Bradford and Ilkley College, Huddersfield Technical College and the Academy of Contemporary Music - but not specifically jazz.
Qualifications: Grade 8 music theory/Practical; BA; PGCE. (Has been teaching for 15-20 years.) Includes improvisation. Other style(s): classical.
"I have an interest in jazz and am an able composer which ties in with an ability to improvise"

Lammin, Dennis
(London)

29 Eden Road, Walthamstow, London E17 9JS
020 8503 7491, dennis.lammin@lineone.net
Instruments taught: Saxophone, Flute, Clarinet.
Teaches 1 to 1. Age(s): under 11, 11 upwards. Area(s): reading, beginners, some knowledge, refresher, coaching. Place(s): own home.
Workshops: small groups, large groups. Speciality area(s): 1 to 1, small groups,

large groups, classes (20+), primary, secondary, adult.
Schools: for 1-4 hours per week. Primary, secondary. Special needs.
Qualifications: Certificate in Music Teaching to Adults (has been teaching for 10-15 years). Includes improvisation. Other style(s): popular music, world music.
"40 years experience playing and improvising music of black origin and world music. Teaching since 1987 to all ages and levels of experience from beginners to advanced. Subjects covered: - Harmony, Theory, Improvisation, Composition, Playing Technique, Aural Training, sight Reading, Jazz History."

Lang-Colmer, Claudia
(South West)

17 Bronescombe Close, Penryn TR10 8LE
01326 373300 home tel
Instruments taught: Double Bass, Cello, Bass Guitar.
Teaches 1 to 1.
Workshops: small groups. Speciality area(s): small groups, secondary.
Schools: Primary, secondary. Adults.
(Has been teaching for 3-5 years). Includes improvisation.
Peripetetic teacher of classical technique 3 days a week in 10 Cornish schools. Incorporates jazz into instrumental lessons, as she is an active jazz player performing in bands 4 nights a week.

Lawrie, Martin
(South East)

35 The Broadway, Sandhurst GU47 9AB
07976 712869, M.Lawrie@tesco.net, www.jazzfusioneers.co.uk
Instruments taught: Piano, Keyboards.
Teaches Associated Board Piano Exam. Age(s): under 11, 11 upwards. Area(s): reading, beginners, some knowledge, refresher, coaching. Place(s): pupil's home, Qualifications: B Ed. (Has been teaching for 15-20 years.) Includes improvisation. Other style(s): popular music, classical, other (Rock).
Currently head of keyboard at Berkshire Young Musicians Trust, implementing Associated Board Jazz syllabus and Trinity Keyboard Syllabus. Also lead jazz and improvisation workshops and training sessions for staff. Writes and delivers rock and jazz courses. "An active live jazz and rock performer. I have been teaching jazz and improvisation for many years and have developed a structured approach to the techniques and styles involved. This structured scheme of work allows even beginners to access successful improvising, developing a confident foundation on which to build."

Lawson, Steve
(London)

PO Box 13788, London N14 5ER
07966 235 072, steve@steve-lawson.co.uk
www.steve-lawson.co.uk
Instruments taught: Bass Guitar.
Teaches 1 to 1. Place(s): own home, pupil's home.
Workshops: "Recently there has been more interest in group tuition, mainly from churches or youth groups. I do run one day courses in creativity, improvising, music theory, band musicianship, arranging, working with the whole band on playing together and managing rehearsal time. I can fit into a lot of different scenarios, from church music group to metal band, so if you think that your group could do

with a bit of direction, or help with rehearsals, get in touch".

Schools: Secondary. HE/FE.

"Having played in a myriad of different musical environments, I am well placed to cover whatever stylistic preference you may have. I have taught students from every conceivable background, from thrash metal to disco, punk to mainstream Jazz, and many of my students have gone on to play and record in many different musical settings, including professional session work with Top 40 artists." "The course of study is tailor-made for the student in question - it's not a case of sticking to one book. Most of the time is spent working on the 'building blocks' of music - harmony, theory, ear-training, rhythm studies, reading etc. Other topics covered can include - Hand positioning, technique, chordal harmony, bass line construction, improvising, advanced technique (slap, tap etc.), walking bass lines, different styles (jazz, latin, reggae etc.) chord substitution, use of effects, and anything else that comes to mind during the lesson!!"

Leahy, David
(London)

626 Lyndhurst Way, Peckham, London SE15 5AP

david@daf-music.freeserve.co.uk, www.daf-music.freeserve.co.uk

Instruments taught: Double Bass.

Teaches 1 to 1.

Lee, Chris
(London)

54A, North Birbeck Road, Leytonstone, London E11 4JQ

020 8539 9873 home tel

Instruments taught: Trumpet.

Teaches 1 to 1. Age(s): under 11, 11 upwards. Area(s): reading, beginners, some knowledge, refresher, coaching. Place(s): own home, pupil's home.

Workshops: Previously Tottenham Green Youth Centre, Marylebone Resource centre, Chiswick Community School.

Schools: Primary, secondary. HE/FE, adults and special needs.

1986-Part time Jazz Course Goldsmiths, 1986-Part time Jacksons Lane workshops, 1987- Music worker course-Community Music, 1988 - workshops in many community environments, 1990-Music teaching in secondary schools. "I have twenty years experience as a gigging musician and have played music from many genres and styles. I have taught music for ten years"

Lees, Lesley
(South West)

16 Shannon Court, Thornbury BS35 2HN

01454 415319/281150, lesley@leeshome.fsnet.co.uk

Instruments taught: Piano.

Teaches 1 to 1. Teaches Associated Board Piano Exam. Age(s): under 11, 11 upwards. Area(s): reading, beginners, some knowledge. Place(s): own home.

Qualifications: Cert Ed in Music S. Katharine's Liverpool (has been teaching for over 20 years). Includes improvisation.

"Enjoy teaching pupils who are keen - when reading is hard, improvisation is a great relaxer and for some pupils, jazz seems easy to memorise."

Lemer, Peter
(Eastern)

Glebe House, Great Hallingbury, Bishop's Stortford CM22 7TY
01279 461264, 01279 461266 fax, mfinger@cix.co.uk
Instruments taught: Piano, Keyboards.
Teaches 1 to 1. Teaches Associated Board Piano Exam. Age(s): under 11, 11 upwards. Area(s): reading, beginners, some knowledge, refresher, coaching. Place(s): own home.
Workshops: Self expression, complete theoretical grounding - if that's what the student wants. Music workshop at home, lots of workshops whilst touring with Barbara Thompson and Jon Hiseman, coach and teach via .
Schools: Pre-school, primary, secondary.
(Has been teaching for over 20 years). Other style(s): world music, other (Modern, Fusion, Improvised).
"I focus on what it takes to break through to a clearing where the student gets to fully express themselves in their own unique way. I support this breakthrough with a depth of experience and technique, as needed."

Leport, Jeannette
(South East)

25 Leigh Grove, Banbury OX16 9LN
01295 255448, 07931 659 990 mobile
jeannette@ku2000.freeserve.co.uk
Instruments taught: Violin, Piano.
Teaches 1 to 1.
Workshops:
Schools: for 4-8 hours per week. Primary, secondary. Adults.
Qualifications: LRAM, Dip Ed (has been teaching for over 20 years). Includes improvisation. Other style(s): popular music, classical, other (Blues).
Private tuition in keyboards, Blues and Jazz.

L'Estrange, Alexander
(London)

Flat 3, 24 Broughton Road, Ealing, London W13 8QW
020 8930 1772 tel/fax, 07973 510235, a.j.lestrange@onet.co.uk
Instruments taught: Piano.
"I have regularly taught Jazz piano (and improvisation on other instruments) and run Jazz ensembles and bands in a number of schools (e.g. Abingdon, City of London, Christ's Hospital) ever since leaving University. I arrange and write Jazz for young players and singers, and am currently applying to become an Associated Board Jazz Examiner.

Lewis, Jeremy
(Eastern)

John Savage Centre, Fencepiece Road, Hainault, Ilford IG6 2LJ
Instruments taught: Trombone.
Qualifications: L.W.C.M.D. L.T.C.L. Cert Ed.. (Has been teaching for 15-20 years.)
Other style(s): popular music, classical, world music.

Lewis, Steve
(North West)
56 Clarence Street, Lancaster LA2 3BB
improv@btopenworld.com
Instruments taught: Percussion.
Peripatetic specialist in improvised and African musics for Lancashire Education (1989-93). Percussion teacher with 'More Music in Morecambe' Community Music residency 1995-present. Masses of freelance work including Special Needs, Open Access, other musicians and private students.

Liddington, Gethin
(Wales)
22 Clos Powys, Yorkdale Estate, Beddau, Pontypridd CF38 2SY
01443 201204, GethinLiddington@aol.com
Instruments taught: Trumpet.
Teaches 1 to 1.
Workshops: small groups. HE/FE.
Qualifications: LWCMD and AWCMD (has been teaching for 5-10 years). Includes improvisation.
Jazz trumpet at Welsh College of Music and University of Cardiff. " I believe that in today's very competitive musical world there is less room for the 'one-style' specialist. My own experience as a player (everything from Dixieland to Free Jazz and contemporary Pop) has shown me that the all-round approach is important. I try to develop my students (at all levels) to gain as broad a grounding as possible".

Light, Patrick
(Eastern)
10 Century Road, Ware SG12 9DY
01920 464825 home tel
Instruments taught: Flute, Saxophone, Clarinet.
Teaches 1 to 1. Age(s): 11 upwards. Area(s): reading, beginners, some knowledge, refresher, coaching. Place(s): own home.
Schools: Secondary. Adults. Chancellors School, Pine Grove, Broodmane Park, Nr Hatfield, Herts. Monks Walk School, Knightsfield, Welwyn Garden City, Herts
25 years as an instrument teacher now with the Herts Music Service teaching both reading and improvisation. "My interest in Jazz Improvisation started from day one. This has continued and still does as a professional musician. My work teaching adults and children has resulted in my own course of improvisation from a very early stage. This uses good practices that Jazz Educators use, no doubt, but progresses in easily achievable stages".

Lilley, Terry
(West Midlands)
0966 434195, mail@TerryLilley.com, www.terrylilley.com
Instruments taught: Bass Guitar, Double Bass.
Teaches 1 to 1. Age(s): 17 plus. Area(s): reading, beginners, some knowledge, refresher, coaching. Place(s): own home, pupil's home.
Workshops: Popular music and music technology National Diploma at South Birmingham College.

Little, Keith
(Wales)

127 Plassey St, Penarth CF64 1EQ
029 2030 1313, keith.littlejazz@ntlworld.com
Instruments taught: Piano.
Teaches 1 to 1. Age(s): under 11, 11 upwards. Area(s): reading, beginners, some knowledge, coaching. Place(s): own home.
Teaches jazz piano for Gwent CC and also has private students. Worked as a professional jazz pianist touring Europe and the USA for the last 20 years. Supported many famous American musicians and has worked with many international bands. One of the few professionals to concentrate on earlier styles of jazz.

Lloyd, Jon
(South West)

34 Portland Road, Bournemouth BH9 1NQ
01202 514 696, jon.llloyd@ic24.net , www.jonlloyd.org internet
Instruments taught: Saxophone.
Teaches 1 to 1. Age(s): under 11, 11 upwards. Area(s): reading, beginners, some knowledge, refresher, coaching. Place(s): own home, pupil's home.
Workshops: Improvisation workshops in London and Poole. Specialisation - Improvisation and contemporary composition.
Schools: Primary.
"I have introduced musicians not versed in improvisation to the world of composition, graphic score, spontaneous improvisation. I am a good motivator and can give musicians confidence to perform. I am a facilitator and catalyst."

Lloyd, Peter
(East Midlands)

Herrick Road, Leicester
Instruments taught: Saxophone, Clarinet.
Teaches 1 to 1.
Schools: Primary, secondary. HE/FE, adults and special needs.
(Has been teaching for over 20 years). Includes improvisation. Other style(s): classical.
Has an enthusiasm for the subject matter.

Lockheart, Mark
(South East)

8 Stephens Road, Tunbridge Wells TN4 9JE
mark@marklockheart.co.uk, www.marklockheart.co.uk
Instruments taught: Saxophone.
Teaches 1 to 1.
Workshops: small groups.
Schools: for 8-12 hours per week. HE/FE.
Qualifications: LTCL (has been teaching for 5-10 years). Includes improvisation. Other style(s): popular music, classical, world music.
Sax teacher at Middlesex University and Royal Academy of Music. Has led many workshops with bands 'Perfect Houseplants' and 'Matheran'.

Lodder, Steve
(London)
53c Clapton Common, Clapton, London E5 9AA
020 8806 9576, 07768 115941 mobile
slod@stevelodder.com, www.stevelodder.com
Instruments taught: Piano.
Teaches 1 to 1. Age(s): 11 upwards. Area(s): reading, some knowledge, refresher.
Place(s): own home.
Workshops: small groups. Speciality area(s): adult. Has taught workshops in UK
and abroad - South America, Africa etc.
Schools: Primary, secondary. Adults. City Lit, Goldsmiths College.
Qualifications: Post Graduate Teaching Diploma (has been teaching for 5-10
years). Includes improvisation. Private tuition. Workshops with schools and
summer courses

Longworth, Jocelyn
(South East)
Blackcat, Bolney Road, Shiplake RG9 3NT
01189 402 677, 07968 702 986 mobile
Instruments taught: Piano.
Teaches 1 to 1. Teaches Associated Board Piano Exam. Age(s): under 11, 11
upwards. Area(s): reading, beginners, some knowledge, refresher. Place(s): own
home, pupil's home, other (Gillotts School, Gillotts Lane, Henley on Thames,
Oxon).
Qualifications: Prof Music Turin Academy (Italy) (has been teaching for over 20
years). Includes improvisation. Other style(s): classical.
"Classically trained, I have always wanted to play jazz and as I learn more about it
I teach more about it too - with lots of enthusiasm. I also get my students with
other musicians in schools to form small jazz groups".

Luck, Steven
(North East)
17 Braintree Gardens, Kenton, Newcastle upon Tyne NE3 3DL
07970 805243, steve@braintreegdns.demon.co.uk
Instruments taught: Piano, Keyboards.
Teaches 1 to 1. Teaches Associated Board Piano Exam. Age(s): under 11, 11
upwards. Area(s): reading, beginners, some knowledge, refresher, coaching.
Place(s): own home.
Qualifications: AB Grade 8; BA Hons (Music Education); Cert Ed FE (has been
teaching for 10-15 years). Other style(s): popular music, classical, world music.
"I am classically trained and have been teaching piano full time for 10 years. I
have also worked for various colleges teaching GCSE, BTec and Music Technology.
I have played in various bands (both jazz and rock) and compose. I have always
had a strong interest in jazz developed by a dissertation on early folk blues as part
of my degree. I can offer my students a broad musical education covering a wide
range of styles utilising a range of different strategies designed to make lessons
both enjoyable and stimulating."

Lusher, Don
(South East)
The Old Rectory, 104 Burdon Lane, Cheam SM2 7DA
020 8643 0749 tel/fax

Instruments taught: Trombone.
Teaches 1 to 1.
Workshops: small groups, large groups.
Qualifications: Experience (has been teaching for over 20 years). Includes improvisation.

Lynch, Sue
(London)
sue10lynch@hotmail.com
Instruments taught: Saxophone, Flute, Clarinet.
Teaches 1 to 1. Age(s): under 11, 11 upwards. Area(s): reading, beginners, some knowledge. Place(s): own home.
(Has been teaching for 5-10 years). Includes improvisation.
"I have run both adult and children's jazz workshops. Whilst able to follow pupils through grades if required, I prefer to set a course which is suitable to their needs. My main objective is to get people to enjoy playing music, either as an individual or within a group. Teaching methods include good sound production, technique on instrument, reading music, rhythm"

MacDonald, Laura
(Scotland)
PO Box 3743, Lanark ML11 9WD
07887 806795, 01555 860 595 home fax
jazzmac@hotmail.com, www.tommysmith.demon.co.uk/laura.htm internet
Instruments taught: Saxophone.
Berklee College music graduate. Teaches ear training and jazz improvisation. Prestwick Academy.

Mackworth-Young, Lucinda
(London)
28 Glebe Place, London SW3 5ZD
020 7352 1666, musicmindmovement@btinternet.com
www.musicmindmovement.btinternet.co.uk
Instruments taught: Piano.
Teaches 1 to 1. Teaches Associated Board Piano Exam. Age(s): 17 plus. Area(s): reading, beginners, some knowledge. Place(s): own home.
Qualifications: GTCL; LTCL (has been teaching for over 20 years). Includes improvisation. Other style(s): classical.
Introduces and starts classically trained pianists in jazz.

Magson, Jen
(North West)
11 Elmsworth Avenue, Levenshulme, Manchester M19 3NS
0161 225 6153, maxon@globalnet.co.uk
Instruments taught: Piano.
Teaches 1 to 1. Teaches Associated Board Piano Exam. Age(s): under 11, 11 upwards. Area(s): reading, beginners, some knowledge, refresher. Place(s): own home.
HE/FE, adults.
Qualifications: C and G 7307 Cert Ed in FE/AE; LTCL (has been teaching for 10-15 years). Includes improvisation. Other style(s): classical.

Maguire, Alex
(London)
43 Mulkern Road, London N19 3HQ
020 7281 0368, 07949 205196, alexmaguire@aol.com
Instruments taught: Piano.
Workshops: small groups. Speciality area(s): adult. Qualified music therapist (Dip.m.Th.) working with children with autism and adults with profound learning difficulties.
Schools: for 1-4 hours per week. HE/FE, adults. Guildhall School of Music and Drama plus other occasional institutions.
(Has been teaching for 15-20 years.) Includes improvisation. Other style(s): classical, other (Free improvisation).
Since the early 1980s has worked with Community Music. Also runs composers' rehearsal band. Private tuition since 1980. Other projects have included 'Access to Jazz' workshops in Norwich, Music Theatre at the Cockpit Theatre, Music for Dance in Amsterdam, Free improvisation workshop in Rotterdam, Music with deaf children in Newhams school for the Deaf, various multi-media courses at Dartington Hall, tuition at Guildhall, Learning difficulties Music and dance project in Leeds through Contemporary Music Network and regular tutor at Mid-Glamorgan Summer school.

Manby, Glen
(Wales)
104 Marlborough Road, Roath, Cardiff CF2 5BY
02920 487624 home tel
Instruments taught: Tenor Sax.
Teaches 1 to 1. Age(s): under 11, 11 upwards. Area(s): reading, beginners, some knowledge, coaching. Place(s): own home, pupil's home.
Workshops: Jazz ensemble, harmony, theory and repertoire at United Colleges of the World, Atlantic College St Donats and also Radyr Adult Education Centre, Radyr Cardiff.
"I work on the basis of hear-sing-play-analyse-remember, which should then devlop into hear-understand-play and then finally hear-play."

Mander, Derek
(South East)
47 Shelley Road, Chesham HP5 2EY
01494 771200, info@jazzworkshop.org.uk
www.jazzworkshop.org.uk internet
Instruments taught: Piano, Keyboards.
Workshops: Jazz Workshop, The Orchard Room, The White Lion, Amersham Road, Little Chalfont, Bucks.

Manington, Dave
(London)
6 Mattison Road, Harringay, London N4 1BD
020 8340 5598, 0961 956106, davemanington@hotmail.com
Instruments taught: Double Bass.
Teaches 1 to 1. Age(s): under 11, 11 upwards. Area(s): reading, beginners, some knowledge, refresher. Place(s): own home.
Workshops: Previously Woodbridge Special needs School. St Bedes School, East Sussex. Specialisation - Jazz Improvisation, Ensemble playing.

Schools:Primary, secondary. Adults and special needs.
"I have several years experience teaching specific techniques for bass and general improvisation, theory and harmony for all instruments and levels. I also have experience of teaching for special needs projects. As an active jazz musician myself I feel I'm able to teach all styles and levels as required."

Mansfield, Simon
(Yorkshire)
Oastler Centre, Co-op Buiding, Huddersfield HD1 2UA
Instruments taught: Trombone, Tuba.
Teaches 1 to 1.
Workshops: usually large groups. Speciality area(s): Primary, secondary, tertiary.
Schools: for 16+ hours per week. Primary, secondary. HE/FE.

Manship, Munch
(North West)
12 Honeywood Close, Holcombe Brook, Bury BL0 9RL
01204 883628 home tel
Instruments taught: Saxophone.
Teaches 1 to 1.
Workshops: small groups, large groups, classes (20+).
Schools: secondary (11-16), HE/FE, adults. LIPA Liverpool, Leeds College of Music.
Qualifications: Dip. Mus. (Has been teaching for 15-20 years.) Includes improvisation. Other style(s): popular music, classical, world music.
Runs Workshops (4 a year approx) at Colleges/Jazz festivals.

Mason, Janette
(South East)
10 Eton Court, Eton Avenue, Sudbury HA0 3BB
020 8900 2250, 0956 374677, FireBmusic@aol.com
Instruments taught: Keyboards, Piano.
Teaches 1 to 1. Teaches Associated Board Piano Exam. Age(s): under 11, 11 upwards. Area(s): reading, beginners, some knowledge, refresher, coaching. Place(s): own home.
Workshops: Previously, Group Improvisation Classes. Drill Hall, Chenies Street, London. Specialisation - Jazz Theory, Harmony, Improvisation, Keyboard skills.
Private tuition. Has conducted workshops for Lewisham Academy and Community Music over the last 10 years. "As a freelance musician/band leader in the jazz and popular music fields for the past fifteen years, I have a broad spectrum of skills and experience to bring to my teaching. I had a formal training in classical piano and studied jazz under Michael Garrick and at the Guildhall School of Music and Drama. I use a structured approach to learning and I also like to encourage self-expression through improvisation and composition and can facilitate group work on all instruments."

Massey, Aidan
(South East)
32 Woodlands Road, Redhill RH1 6HA
01737 215166, 07973 906964 mobile
aidanmassey@hotmail.com, www.ph_quartet.com
Instruments taught: Violin.

Schools:Primary, secondary. HE/FE, adults.
Qualifications: GTCL; LTCL; NTCL; QTS (has been teaching for over 20 years).
Includes improvisation. Other style(s): classical.
Head of String teaching at Surrey Youth Music and teaches jazz violin at Trinity College of Music. Teaches on the Benslow Music Trust weekends in February and Summer school at ESTA (European String Teachers Association).

Masters, Chris
(North West)
1 Hastings Avenue, Bispham, Blackpool FY2 0EU
01253 355421 tel/fax
Instruments taught: Bass Guitar.
Teaches 1 to 1. Age(s): 17 plus. Area(s): reading, beginners, some knowledge, refresher, coaching. Place(s): own home.
Workshops: Previously and currently, Jazz improvisation and Jazz development skills (own studio at home with small group of students). Specialisation - Developing Jazz mobility and improvisation skills.
Schools: Primary, secondary. Adults.
"By working alongside students in mastering and applying chord and scale alterations and amendments and their application to 'standard' vehicles, I am able to both enthuse the student to develop their technical skills as far as they can and then to experience the joy and satisfaction that creative playing will bring."

Mathieson, Ken
(Scotland)
20 Kyle Park Crescent, Uddingston, Glasgow G71 7DJ
01698 814 475 home tel
Instruments taught: Drums.
Teaches 1 to 1. Age(s): 17 plus. Area(s): reading, some knowledge, refresher, coaching. Place(s): own home, pupil's home.
Private tuition aimed at pupils wanting to improve their jazz time and Latin/Brazilian playing. "With experience of over 40 years playing jazz of all styles, I specialise in teaching jazz time-playing, its evolution and the importance of earlier styles in the evolution of later developments. In addition, a life-long love of Brazilian music and many years of playing it, enable me to teach phrasing on drums and various percussion instruments"

Mattos, Marcio
(London)
40 Sydner Road, London N16 7UG
020 7254 1351, 020 7503 8417 fax, 07982 783822 mobile
marcio@musiclay.freeserve.co.uk, www.musiclay.freeserve.co.uk
Instruments taught: Double Bass, Cello.
Teaches 1 to 1. Age(s): under 11, 11 upwards. Area(s): beginners, some knowledge, refresher. Place(s): own home.
Workshops: Available for workshops.
Workshops in Improvisation techniques. Also works with Free Improvising musicians to practise their ideas and techniques. Graphic scores.

McBride, Sean
(East Midlands)
Access to Music, 18 York Road, Leicester LE1 5TS
info@access-to-music.co.uk, www.access-to-music.co.uk
Instruments taught: Saxophone.
Teaches 1 to 1.
Qualifications: 25 years experience, PGCE, Access course (has been teaching for 5-10 years). Includes improvisation. Other style(s): popular music, classical, world music.

McCaughern, Danny
(East Midlands)
30 Victoria Street, West Parade, Lincoln LN1 1HY
dan@mccaughern.freeserve.co.uk
Instruments taught: Guitar.
Teaches 1 to 1. Age(s): under 11, 11 upwards. Area(s): reading, beginners, some knowledge, refresher, coaching. Place(s): own home.
Workshops: Previoulsy, Guitar playing in popular music, Lincoln Community Arts Centre. Composing Popular music, Summer School William Robertson School, Welbourne. Specialisation - composition (Popular and jazz); Improvisation.
Schools: Secondary. HE/FE.
"I do not specialise in jazz, but see jazz as a necessary study to enable musicians to realise their potential. I attempt to empower students with a holistic approach to music through practical and theoretical knowledge and develop listening skills, reading and writing skills and spirited performances."

McEwen, Bill
(South East)
57 Brookway, Lindfield, Haywards Heath RH16 2BP
01444 414427 home tel
Instruments taught: Piano, Keyboards.
Teaches 1 to 1. Teaches Associated Board Piano Exam. Age(s): under 11, 11 upwards. Area(s): reading, beginners, some knowledge, refresher. Place(s): own home, other (Teaches in two independent schools in West Sussex).
Schools: Primary.
Qualifications: Dip LM; LTABRSM. (Has been teaching for 15-20 years.) Includes improvisation. Other style(s): popular music, classical, world music.
"I have experience of a variety of styles including improvisation, for a professional ballet school, four years on cruise ships, bandleader and ten years full time teaching". Currently has a waiting list of pupils.

McKenzie, Paul
(London)
51 Osward Place, Edmonton, London N9 7EF
020 8884 0153 tel/fax, 07977 540312 mobile
Thesaxophone@workshop541.fsnet.co.uk
www.saxophoneworkshop.co.uk
Instruments taught: Saxophone.
Teaches 1 to 1. Age(s): under 11, 11 to 16. Area(s): beginners, some knowledge, refresher. Place(s): own home, pupil's home.
Workshops: Workshops cover wide range of techniques ie. Tone quality,

embouchure, tonguing, fingering via unison playing, discussion, Question and Answer and feedback. Aim is to improve your skills - read music with more fluency, improvise, understand scales, count time, posture, improve breathing techniques, embouchure and play with more rhythm. Cost: 90 minute workshop is £10 per individual, £40 for school workshops. Bring your own instrument.

Provide workshops in Primary and Secondary schools and for students taking GCSE and A Level music exams, covering all aspects of the music syllabus

Mealing, Adrian
(West Midlands)
The Croft, Old Church Road, Colwall WR13 6EZ
01684 540366, amealing@cwcom.net
Instruments taught: Percussion.
Qualifications: various. Other style(s): world music, other (Emphasis on Afro-Brazilian rhythms).

Meier, Nicolas
(London)
Flat 6, 5 Howitt Rd, Belsize Park, London NW3 4 LT
0207 449 9072, 7979 765 747 mobile
meiergroup@hotmail.com, www.meiergroup.com
Instruments taught: Guitar, Acoustic Guitar.
Teaches 1 to 1. Age(s): under 11, 11 upwards. Area(s): reading, beginners, some knowledge, refresher. Place(s): own home, pupil's home.
Workshops: small groups. Has taught on workshops with Deirdre Cartwright and held rock workshop in Chelmsford.
Qualifications: Diploma Boston Jazz Course (USA). (Has been teaching for 15-20 years.) Includes improvisation. Other style(s): popular music, classical, world music.
Graduated in Switzerland (Maths/Chemistry) but changed to music with a Diploma from Berklee School (Boston USA). Teaches whole range of styles of music and types of guitars, from electric rock to jazz.

Melville, Brian
(North West)
Linden House, Mawbray, Maryport CA15 6QT
01900 881 349, brianmelville@hotmail.com
Instruments taught: Piano, Trombone.
Teaches 1 to 1. Age(s): 11 to 16. Area(s): reading, beginners, some knowledge, refresher, coaching.
Workshops: small groups, large groups.
Schools: for 16+ hours per week. Secondary.
Qualifications: Certed (has been teaching for over 20 years). Includes improvisation. Other style(s): popular music.

Michael, Richard
(Scotland)
6 Dronachy Road, Kirkcaldy KT2 5QL
01592 263087, 01441 865 600, r.e.michael@cablenet.co.uk
Instruments taught: Piano.
Teaches 1 to 1. Teaches Associated Board Piano Exam. Age(s): under 11, 11 upwards Area(s): reading, beginners, some knowledge, refresher, coaching.

Place(s): own home.

Workshops: small groups, large groups, classes (20+). Previously, Associated Board - Edinburgh; Wigmore Hall London. Jazz Services West End Project - Newcastle. Jazz - Cornton Vale Women's prison, Stirling. Specialisation Jazz improvisation/Keyboard skills/composing and arranging.

Schools: for 16+ hours per week. Secondary. HE/FE.

Qualifications: Diploma in Musical Education Royal Scottish Academy Music and Drama (has been teaching for over 20 years). Includes improvisation. Other style(s): popular music, classical, other (Scottish Traditional).

Also teaches Composition/arranging. Member of Working Party and an Associated Board Jazz Examiner. Weekly rehearsals with the Fife Youth Jazz Orchestra in Kirkcaldy. Also specialises in improvising counterpoint on Church Organ. "I aim to be as simple as possible, to teach all ability ranges together or separately and to ensure each person attending my workshop leaves armed with as much information as possible to go away and play jazz."

Michael, Will
(South East)

20 Forge Lane, Headcorn TN27 9QH

01622 891686, pwmichael@themail.uk.com

Instruments taught: Piano.

Teaches 1 to 1. Teaches Associated Board Piano Exam. Age(s): under 11, 11 upwards Area(s): reading, beginners, some knowledge, refresher, coaching. Place(s): own home, pupil's home.

Workshops: small groups, large groups, classes (20+). QEH in 1999 for Associated Board and Music For Youth; May 2000 Wigmore Hall with Julian Joseph; and at Chislehurst and Sidcup Grammar School; termly sessions for Kent Music School.

Schools: for 16+ hours per week. Primary, secondary. HE/FE.

Qualifications: M A (Aberdeen University) P G C E (has been teaching for over 20 years). Includes improvisation. Other style(s): popular music, classical, world music.

"Students feel successful, from the most able to the other end of the spectrum. They love playing and always come back for more! My first student, 24 years ago, was Phil Bent (flute) and my current pupil is Jon Geyevu, who played at the Associated Board's National concert for High Achievers at the new Opera House in 2000."

Milburn, Philip
(South East)

1a Ruskin Road, Hove, Brighton BN3 5HA

01273 730707, philipmilburn@ukgateway.net www.lifemusic.org.uk internet

Instruments taught: Piano, Voice, Bass Guitar.

Teaches 1 to 1. Age(s): under 11, 11 upwards. Area(s): reading, beginners, some knowledge, refresher. Place(s): own home, pupil's home.

Workshops: small groups, large groups. Singing workshops in Brighton and London not specifically jazz. Includes group singing, voice work, songwriting, music improvisation, percussion, sound healing, performance skills (has been teaching for 10-15 years). Includes improvisation.

Currently teaches at Connaught Adult Education Centre (part of City College Brighton and Hove) "I do not only teach jazz, but all styles of music. I am a multi-instrumentalist, singer and workshop facilitator. My workshops are open to all levels of ability and experience and deal with music for fun, creativity, healing, self expression and community building."

Miles, David
(South West)

2 Salisbury Villas, Dorchester DT1 1JY
01305 266752 home tel
Instruments taught: Bass Guitar, Double Bass, Fretless Bass.
Teaches 1 to 1. Age(s): 17 plus. Area(s): some knowledge, refresher. Place(s): own home.
Workshops: small groups.
Schools: Secondary. Wimbledon High School (London) and St Anthony Convent (Dorset).
First jazz/rock guitarist at Kingston University (1974) and at Middlesex University (1977). Has taught at Central Poly, Poole College, Weymouth College, Exeter Arts Centre and many privately run workshops. Now teaches guitar/bass and jazz/rock ensemble at Sherborne School.

Miles, Matt
(London)

18 Belfast Road, Stoke Newington, London N16 6UH
020 8806 5305, 0976 272 490 mobile
Instruments taught: Electric Bass, Double Bass.
Teaches 1 to 1.
Has given a masterclass for the National Youth Orchestra.

Miller, Sue
(Yorkshire)

25 Norman Row, Kirkstall, Leeds LS5 3JL
0113 274 8425 tel/fax, 079 57 244 167 mobile
suem@charangadelnorte.co.uk, www.charangadelnorte.co.uk
Instruments taught: Flute, Tenor Sax, Piano.
Teaches Associated Board Piano Exam. Age(s): under 11, 11 upwards. Area(s): reading, beginners, some knowledge. Place(s): other (Yorkshire College of Music and Drama, Leeds and Froebelian School Horsforth Leeds).
Workshops: Cuban style and improvisation in a Cuban music context. jazz workshops at Yorkshire College of music; 1998 - onwards - Cuban music workshops with 10 piece band; weekly Cuban music Big Band at Yorkshire College of Music, Leeds: open to all.
Schools: Primary, secondary. HE/FE, adults.
"My interest is in improvisation and creativity whether it occurs in jazz, popular or world music. My own passion is for Cuban music, in particular Charanga which features a great deal of flute improvisation".

Miners, Richard
(South East)

6 Jensen Court, Hulse Road, Southampton SO15 2JW
02380 233863, 0780 840 3314 mobile
Instruments taught: Trumpet, Bass Trombone, Trombone.
Teaches 1 to 1.
Workshops: small groups, large groups, classes (20+).
Schools: for 16+ hours per week. Primary, secondary. HE/FE, adults.
Qualifications: PGCE (Music), B.A. (Hons) Music (has been teaching for 5-10 years). Includes improvisation. Other style(s): popular music, world music.

Mitchell-Davidson, Paul
(North West)

25 Bannerman Avenue, Prestiwch, Manchester M25 1DZ
0161 798 9604 tel/fax, 0797 9883516 mobile
pm-d@muse.telinco.co.uk, www.telinco.co.uk/pm-d internet
Instruments taught: Bass Guitar, Guitar.
Workshops: classes (20+). HND and Degree level.
Schools: for 12-16 hours per week. HE/FE. Salford University.
Qualifications: 30 years hands-on experience. (Has been teaching for 15-20 years.)
Includes improvisation. Other style(s): popular music, classical.
Teacher at the Royal Northern College of Music, annual jazz workshops. Jazz lecturer at annual Burnley jazz summer school.

Mitchell-Luker, Vicci
(London)

109 Lynton Road, Rayners Lane, London HA2 9NJ
020 8864 2896, 07974 557 809, Vicci@the-voice-school.co.uk
Instruments taught: Voice, Piano.
Teaches 1 to 1. Teaches Associated Board Piano Exam. Age(s): 11 upwards.
Area(s): reading, beginners, some knowledge, coaching. Place(s): own home, other (The Voice School).
HE/FE, adults.
"Having come to jazz in my late 20s after a rigid and rigorous classical training, I am aware both of the importance of a solid technique, reading and aural training and of relaxing to sink into the jazz idiom. Having spent time in struggling to achieve this myself I have come to an understanding of how to help students overcome some of the hurdles."

Moore, Alex
(Eastern)

86 Aldermans Drive, Peterborough PE36 AZ
alexmoore@hotmail.com
Instruments taught: Trombone, Trumpet.
Qualifications: G Mus PGCE (has been teaching for 10-15 years). Includes improvisation. Other style(s): popular music, classical.

Moore, Sarah
(London)

31 Weymouth Mews, London W1N 3FN
020 7580 4055, sarhauk@yahoo.co.uk
Instruments taught: Saxophone.
Teaches 1 to 1. Age(s): 11 upwards. Area(s): reading, beginners. Place(s): own home, pupil's home.
Workshops: small groups, large groups. Speciality area(s): adult. Performance workshops in schools with the band 'Transisters' which includes 5 women playing brass instruments. Specialist in World music and 'Street Band' music.
Schools: for 12-16 hours per week. Primary. HE/FE. City Lit., Hackney Community College - Pop and World Music course.
Qualifications: Certificate in Teaching Music to Adults - CMTA (has been teaching for over 20 years). Includes improvisation. Other style(s): popular music, world music.

Moran, Paul
(London)

1 Hill Court, Stanhope Road, Highgate, London N6 5AP
020 8482 5839 tel/fax, 07976 946680, moranfingers@aol.com
Instruments taught: Hammond Organ, Piano, Keyboards.
Teaches 1 to 1. Teaches Associated Board Piano Exam. Age(s): 11 upwards
Area(s): reading, beginners, some knowledge, refresher, coaching. Place(s): own
home, pupil's home.
Workshops: large groups. Has run workshops in Improvisation and Musical
Technology at the London Musical Institute.
Recently has played the piano for tuition of pupils in the new BBC TV series 'Fame
Academy' which included working with top vocal coaches. Has composed film
scores and TV themes. "Having worked for many internationally famous artists
(George Michael, Pete Townsend, Buddy Greco during 1999 UK tour at Ronnie
Scotts) in diverse areas, I can offer the student the benifits of immense and vast
experience".

Moy, Norman
(Scotland)

236 Rosemount Place, Aberdeen AB2 4XT
01224 462187 home tel
Instruments taught: Flute, Saxophone, Clarinet.
Teaches 1 to 1. Age(s): 11 upwards. Area(s): reading, beginners, some knowledge, refresher, coaching. Place(s): own home.
Workshops: Previously worked for Assembly Direct (Scotland) as a Tutor in improvisation in Dundee and Aberdeen. Specialisation - Improvisation and small combo
performance.
Schools:Secondary
"With the aid of simple motifs and scales I aim to get students improvising as soon
as possible. I do not smother them with too much theory until they are well on the
way to using their ears and fingers. Structure/harmony comes later."

Munnery, Paul
(South West)

Miller's Cottage, 7 Moorfield Avenue, Blakeney GL15 4DA
01594 516834 home tel
Instruments taught: Trombone.
Workshops: Aberystwyth Jazz Festival; Bude Jazz Festival Workshop -
Specialisation; Improvisation - mainstream styles.
Schools: Pre-school, primary, secondary, HE/FE, adults and special needs.
Qualifications: Certificate of Education; Member of the Institute of Personnel and
Training Development. (Has been teaching for 1-2 years). Includes improvisation.
Ex-management staff trainer. Interested in presenting courses in band manage-
ment, publicity, marketing, communications to adults. Also works in schools: practical and Jazz history/culture. Runs weekly workshops at the Dragon Hotel,
Montgomery. "My specialisation is taking groups of musicians at various stages of
competence and of all ages and through both individual and group tuition, getting
them to some level of performance ability. My workshops so far have maintained a
"ban" on written music. Many people who favour New Orleans, dixieland and swing
music, who have felt "left out" of most workshops offering "avant garde" tuition
have welcomed these workshops aimed at "classic Jazz" performance."

Murray, Angus
(South East)
377 Sandycombe, Kew TW9 3PR
020 8940 5498, 020 8332 0150 fax, 07973 145582 mobile
angus@jazzswing.co.uk, www.jazzswing.co.uk
Instruments taught: Piano, Voice.
Teaches 1 to 1. Teaches Associated Board Piano Exam. Age(s): under 11, 11
upwards Area(s): reading, beginners, some knowledge, refresher, coaching.
Place(s): own home, pupil's home.
Workshops: Chiswick summer Music courses 1994-98. Specialisation -
Improvisation/Jazz ensemble.
Schools: Primary, secondary. Kings House School, Richmond, Surre "Each pupil is
an individual who will have a unique undersatnding of life. Aside from the neces-
saary general musicianship/technique/improvisational skills needed, I try to
develop and encourage that inherent individuality".

Murray, Eliot
(Scotland)
115 Calderbraes Avenue, Uddington G71 6ES
07957 871924, ELAL94@aol.com
Instruments taught: Tenor Sax, Voice, Piano.
Teaches 1 to 1. Age(s): 11 upwards. Area(s): reading, beginners, some knowl-
edge, refresher. Place(s): pupil's home.
Workshops: Rhythm section, saxophone. Strathclyde Arts Centre (now Tramway)
Glasgow, Artsnet Jazz Orchestra, Advisory Service, Hope Street, Hamilton, South
Lanarkshire.
"In schools I teach all the rhythm section instruments, so I feel very confident
when it comes to adapting the parts to suit the individuals ability. As a jazz singer
I am not afraid to use my voice and always encourage pupils to do the same. I
also play many different types of music and believe that a proper study of soul and
funk styles is essential for any musician".

Murrell, Dave
(South East)
37 Woodland Rd, Selsey PO20 0AL
01243 602956, 07790 269411, dave.murrell@chichester.ac.uk
Instruments taught: Guitar.
Workshops: small groups, classes (20+).
Schools: for 16+ hours per week. HE/FE. Chichester College of Arts, Science and
Technology.
Qualifications: Cert.Ed. (Has been teaching for 15-20 years.) Includes improvisa-
tion. Other style(s): popular music.

Nash, Michael
(London)
122 Bray Towers, Fellows Road, London NW3 3JT
020 7586 7944
Instruments taught: Trombone.
Teaches 1 to 1. (Has been teaching for over 20 years). Other style(s): classical.

Nash, Phil
(South East)
13 College Street, Winchester SO23 9LX
01962 840833 tel/fax, phil@collegewinch.freeserve.co.u.k.
Instruments taught: Piano.
Workshops: small and large groups, classes (20+). Song-writing, arrranging, multi-track recording, technology.
Schools: for 16+ hours per week. Secondary.
Qualifications: BA (Hons) History, ARCM, LTCL (has been teaching for over 20 years). Includes improvisation. Other style(s): popular music, classical, world music,

Naylor, Patrick
(London)
224a Camden Road, London NW1 9HG
07949 668 249, patrick.naylor@cnwl.ac.uk
www.beebossrecords.co.uk
Instruments taught: Guitar.
Workshops: Organised workshops for Hampstead and Kensington Colleges..
"I have taught evening classes in all levels of guitar at Hampstead Garden Suburb Institute."

Neighbour, Pete
(Eastern)
The Mill House, Bradford Street, Bocking CM7 9AU
01376 331266, 07768 870881 mobile
Instruments taught: Alto Sax, Tenor Sax, Flute.
Teaches 1 to 1. Age(s): 11 upwards. Area(s): reading, beginners, some knowledge, refresher, coaching. Place(s): own home, pupil's home.
Workshops: Is involved with other musicians and Tunbridge Wells Jazz Club in running a jazz workshop for their music schools.
Schools: Secondary.
(Has been teaching for 10-15 years). Includes improvisation. Other style(s): popular music, classical.
"I aim to make playing fun - and hope that through enjoyment students will strive to explore all aspects of their chosen instrument and broaden their listening horizons."

Nelson, Deborah
(London)
245 Brookhowse Road, Catford, London SE6 3TT
020 8695 9764 home tel
Instruments taught: Piano.
Teaches 1 to 1. Teaches Associated Board Piano Exam. Age(s): under 11, 11 upwards. Area(s): reading, beginners, some knowledge, refresher, coaching. Place(s): own home, pupil's home.
Schools: Primary. Rushey Green Primary School, Culverley Road, Catford, London
Other style(s): popular music, classical.
"I teach jazz piano, usually as part of general piano lessons. I use the structure of the Associated Board Jazz Piano grades, whether the pupil chooses to take the exam or not. I also teach a via chord based approach - which is more hands on,

using the visual memory of keys played and by ear, going through popular music, gospel, soul etc. I have also taught singers who want to accompany themselves on the piano"

Nelson, Ian
(North West)
Fieldhouse School, Greenbank Road, Rochdale OL1 OHZ
Instruments taught: Trombone.
Teaches 1 to 1. Workshops: small, large groups. Specialist on Trombone technique, classical style. Schools: for 16+ hours per week. Primary, secondary. HE/FE. Rochdale Music Services.(Has been teaching for 5-10 years). Includes improvisation. Other style(s): popular music.

Newby, Richard
(South East)
40 Mill Road, Twickenham TW2 5HA
020 8255 9194, 020 8287 2041 fax, richard.newby@virgin.net
Instruments taught: Drums.
Age(s): 11 upwards. Area(s): reading, beginners, some knowledge, refresher, coaching. Place(s): own home, pupil's home.
Workshops: Drum workshops for jazz courses at Richmond Adult Community College on Saturday Morning.
Royal Academy of Music - drum tuning and maintenance workshop; Jazz workshops - Eddie Harvey and Andy Watson; Laurence Canty and Paul Dunne; Derek Nash and Sax Appeal; Guildhall School of Music Jazz Summer School - assistant in performance workshops. 18 years experience of performing on the London jazz scene. "All styles are taught thoroughly with an emphasis on musicality, posture and balance, creativity and relaxed control. I encourage students to think for themselves. I write my own worksheets using state of the art software. I use professional quality custom built equipment in my home studio."

Newman, Ron
(Eastern)
Withies, Harrow Green, Lawshall, Bury St Edmunds IP 29 4 PB
01 284 830830 tel/fax, Ron.newman2btinternet.com
Instruments taught: Piano, Keyboards.

Newton, Raymond
(North East)
6 Springwell Road, Sunderland SR3 4DG
0191 528 5879, 07970 441394 mobile
Instruments taught: Bass Guitar, Double Bass.
Teaches 1 to 1.
Workshops: small groups. Speciality area(s): adult.
Schools: Primary. Adults.
Qualifications: ARNCM, Cert Ed (has been teaching for over 20 years). Includes improvisation. Other style(s): popular music, classical.
Teaches the History of Jazz in Adult Education. Teaching experience at the University of Durham.

Nicholas, Julian
(South East)
8a Powis Square, Brighton BN1 3HH
01273 724515 tel/fax, 0771 358 1600 mobile
julien@melomania.co.uk, www.melomania.co.uk
Instruments taught: Clarinet, Saxophone.
Teaches 1 to 1. Age(s): under 11, 11 upwards. Area(s): reading, beginners, some knowledge, refresher, coaching. Place(s): own home, pupil's home.
Workshops: Composition, improvisation, rhythm, harmony. Previously Brighton Jazz Musicians Co-Operative. National Teacher Training for Access to Music, Improvisation. East Sussex Education Authority - Jazz in Schools. Currently South East London Schools - "Impro" - see separate entry. Specialisation - Composition, Improvisation, Performance, Rhythm. University of Glamorgan Jazz Summer School; Frydiant Summer School Czech.
Schools: Pre-school, primary, secondary. HE/FE, adults and special needs (people with learning difficulties)
"Having worked with jazz and commercial artists all over the world, I feel I bring an authentic, experienced foundation to the work. I have piloted training teachers in the National Curriculum through workshop composition, improvisation and performance.

Noble, Liam
(London)
31 Lily Road, London E17 8HY
020 8539 8349 tel/fax, 07971 583608, liam.noble@ntlworld.com
Instruments taught: Piano.
Teaches 1 to 1. Teaches Associated Board Piano Exam. Age(s): 11 upwards
Area(s): reading, beginners, some knowledge, refresher, coaching. Place(s): own home.
HE/FE.
"I see jazz as a tradition of looking to other forms of music for inspiration (Duke Ellington, Miles Davis and numerous contemporary musicians are indicators of this) as well as establishing a central vocabulary as a basis for improvising."

Norchi, Alan
(South East)
4 Olivier Way, Aylesbury HE20 1JG
anorchi@talk21.com
Instruments taught: Piano.
Teaches 1 to 1. Teaches Associated Board Piano Exam. Age(s): under 11, 11 to 16. Area(s): reading, beginners. Place(s): own home, pupil's home.
"Musicality; an emphasis on touch. Elaboration of the piano as a percussive instrument. Awareness of space and phrasing- Physical approach to playing - movement. Step by step towards improvisation. Jam sessions with pupil. Last part is always a jam. Kids love it."

Northover, Adrian
(London)
Flat 401, Oxo Tower Wharf, South Bank, London SE1 9GY
020 7401 3203, 020 8778 0375 home fax
age@adriannorth.worldonline.co.uk, www.theremoteviewers.com

Instruments taught: Alto Sax, Soprano Sax.
Teaches 1 to 1. Age(s): under 11, 11 upwards. Area(s): some knowledge, refresher. Place(s): own home.
(Has been teaching for 5-10 years). Other style(s): world music.
"For the past 10 years I have taught saxophone to adults at Hackney Community College and have developed a style of teaching that, whilst stressing the importance of technique (scales etc) emphasises learning tunes, using the ear and attempting to improvise, in order to encourage creativity"

Odell, Larraine
(Eastern)
Oak House, Church Road, Gt Yeldham, Halstead
01787 237653, larraine@rogerodell.co.uk
Instruments taught: Voice.

Odell, Roger
(Eastern)
Oak House, Church Road, Great Yeldham CO9 4PR
01787 237 653 tel/fax, 0771 2980070 mobile
roger@rogerodell.co.uk, www.rogerodell.co.uk
Instruments taught: Drums.
Teaches 1 to 1. Place(s): own home, other (Offers tutorials at his studio and on his website - www.drumatak.fsnet.co.uk).
Workshops:Schools: Secondary.
Tutorials on his website as well as drum tuition from home studio using the Guildhall School of Music Grade system with exams twice a year.

O'Higgins, Dave
(London)
61 Hargwyne Steet, London SW9 9RQ
020 7733 5156, 07973 349 605 mobile
o.hig@virgin.net, www.daveohiggins.com
Instruments taught: Alto Sax, Tenor Sax.
Workshops (Has been teaching for 15-20 years.) Other style(s): popular music, classical, world music.
In 2001 gave 20 Secondary school workshops arranged by JazzFM. Offers workshops to secondary schools (pupils with Grade 5) any instruments, no formal training necessary but must be willing to have a go! Has a great deal of experience of teaching summer courses, participating workshops and demonstrations at Primary and Secondary levels. Has taught on Summer Jazz courses - Guildhall, Royal Academy and Wavendon. Has acted as an external examiner for Royal Northern College of music, taught at Birmingham Conservatoire, University of Natal, South Africa and University of Cape Town. Was Director of a jazz project 'Jazz Squad' in Lincoln in 2000 which targeted primary and secondary schools as well as adult community organisations. This has generated other similar projects in Cambridge, Bournemouth and the Medway regions.

O'Neill, Bernard
(London)
43 Queens Road, Leytonstone, London E11 1BA
020 8532 8413 tel/fax, bernobass@aol.com
Instruments taught: Double Bass.

Forest School, Hampstead High and Greycoat Hospital School. Worked with Danny Thompson on Leigh-on-Sea Jazz Project (Access to Jazz). Musical Director of Liverpool Summer Music project.

O'Neill, John
(London)

103 South View Road, Hornsey, London N8 7LX
020 8341 2819, oneill.music@virgin.net
Instruments taught: Soprano Sax, Tenor Sax.
Teaches 1 to 1. Age(s): under 11, 11 upwards. Area(s): reading, beginners, some knowledge, refresher, coaching. Place(s): own home, other (Schools - Latymer School, Haselbury Road,Edmonton, London).
Workshops. Speciality area(s): large groups, primary, secondary, tertiary, adult. Has taught at Jazz Summer schools in the Czech Republic and Spain. Has also taught at Teacher Training Workshops on Jazz History and Improvisation for the London Borough of Ealing. Specialises in Jazz Improvisation, Jazz History, Harmony, Theory.
Qualifications: PGCE (has been teaching for over 20 years). Other style(s): classical, world music.
Has taught privately and in schools since 1980, as well as leading workshops and running a Youth Big Band. Has written five books - The Jazz Method for Saxophone/Clarinet/Flute/Trumpet (with Steve Waterman) 'Developing Jazz Technique for Saxophone' published by Schott with a CD included. "I emphasise the importance of the foundation techniques of woodwind playing, in particular breathing, tone and articulation. Reading skills and playing by ear are equally important and I teach both by a proven systematic approach which includes singing and clapping exercises. The emphasis is on the development of musicianship and of an open -minded approach which incorporates not just jazz but also world music and the classical tradition."

Orton, Ken
(West Midlands)

46 Coventry Road, Bedworth CV12 8NN
02476 315967 home tel
Instruments taught: Flute, Saxophone, Clarinet.
Qualifications: LLCM,TD (has been teaching for over 20 years). Includes improvisation. Other style(s): popular music, classical, world music.
22 years Local Education Authority, Independent schools and colleges from GCSE to A Level and diploma. Special interest in teaching complex odd meter rhythms.

Oswin, John
(Eastern)

8 Woodside Coourt, Woodside, Leigh-on-Sea SS9 4TF
07973 910680 mobile
Instruments taught: Piano.
Teaches 1 to 1. Teaches Associated Board Piano Exam. Age(s): under 11, 11 upwards. Area(s): reading, beginners, some knowledge. Place(s): pupil's home. Schools: Primary, secondary.
Qualifications: Cert in Music Education (Trinity); AB Grade 8. (Has been teaching for 15-20 years.) Other style(s): popular music.

Overon, Geoff
(East Midlands)
12 Somerville Road, Leicester LE3 2ET
Instruments taught: Guitar.
Teaches 1 to 1. Age(s): 17 plus. Area(s): refresher. Place(s): own home.
Workshops. Qualifications: MU Registered on Registry of Guitar tutors (has been teaching for over 20 years). Includes improvisation. Other style(s): popular music, other (Blues/Soul).

Pace, Paul
(London)
58 Besford House, Pritchards Road, London E2 9BJ
020 7739 3025 tel/fax, 07870 915682 mobile
paulpacejazz@hotmail.com
Instruments taught: Voice.
Teaches 1 to 1. Place(s): own home, pupil's home.
" I have attended several workshops, notably those of Mark Murphy. Coached by Claire Martin for two years. I teach basic performance skills and knowledge of repertoire. Enthusiatic supporter of 'Live Jazz', especially of audience friendly musicians able to convey the joy of the music. Mission to provide a "Genuine Jazz Room" where a largely non-jazz audience can experience the music as it should be heard (ie. Including a "Swinging" Rhythm Section) - I see a need to nurture and build an audience which otherwise receives little nourishment from mainstream culture."

Packham, Kit
(South East)
46 Livingstone Road, Caterham CR3 5TG
01883 370 737, 01883 370 733 home fax
kitpackham@supanet.com, www.onejumpahead.co.uk
Instruments taught: Saxophone.
Teaches 1 to 1.
(Has been teaching for 5-10 years). Includes improvisation. Other style(s): popular music, other (Blues).

Palmer, Matt
(East Midlands)
12 Brookside Road, Ruddington, Nottingham NG11 6AW
0115 921 1772, 0115 940 3534 fax, 07973 882235 mobile
Instruments taught: Clarinet.

Panayi, Andy
(South East)
2 Stonehouse Flats, Hartfield Road, Forest Row RH18 5DA
01342 824434 tel/fax, 07973 510872 mobile
apanyi@feltwell.co.uk, feltwell.co.uk
Instruments taught: Saxophone, Clarinet, Flute.
Teaches 1 to 1. Age(s): under 11, 11 upwards. Area(s): reading, beginners, some knowledge, refresher, coaching. Place(s): own home, pupil's home.
Workshops: Previous workshop: Grimsby International Jazz Festival - 'an Introduction to Jazz Improvisation'.

Schools: Primary, secondary. HE/FE, adults and special needs.
"Because of my experience performing with some of the best jazz musicians and my teaching, which I have done for 19 years I know what makes a jazz musician sound good. As well as the harmonic aspects in relation to jazz tuition, working on time, feel and rhythm is the key to really making it in jazz. I make my students work hard in these essential areas"

Parker, Christopher
(East Midlands)
308 Acre Lane, Northampton NN2 8PY
01604 843536, chrisparker@zoom.co..uk
Instruments taught: Bass Guitar, Guitar.
Teaches 1 to 1. Age(s): under 11, 11 upwards. Area(s): beginners, some knowledge, refresher. Place(s): own home.
Schools: Secondary.
(Has been teaching for 1-2 years). Includes improvisation. Other style(s): popular music.
"Jazz, Blues and Rock guitar - mainly fingerstyle, but also plectrum - with an emphasis on chord construction."

Parker, Eddie
(London)
22 Highfield Road, Wynchmore Hill, London N21 3HA
07950 701 703, impro@mdx.ac.uk
Instruments taught: Piano, Flute.
Teaches 1 to 1. Age(s): under 11, 11 upwards. Area(s): beginners, some knowledge.
Workshops:
"Teaching is as important as composing and playing". Lecturer in jazz composition at Middlesex University, and musical director of IMPRO (Integrated Music Project). Impro is a major education, training and performance project, "People Symphony" funded by the National Lottery through the National Foundation for Youth Music.

Parkinson, Brian
(North West)
21 Fairfield Lane, Barrow in Furness LA13 9AN
01229 823248 home tel
Instruments taught: Guitar, Bass Guitar.
Teaches 1 to 1. Private tuition. Works with 6th form bands.

Parr, Kenneth
(South West)
10 Burnley Close, Bradley Valley, Newton Abbot TQ12 1XB
01626 360931 home tel
Instruments taught: Saxophone.
Teaches 1 to 1.
Workshops: usually small groups.
Schools: for 8-12 hours per week. Secondary. HE/FE. Devon Youth Music.
Qualifications: DPLM, Cert Ed.. (Has been teaching for 15-20 years.) Includes improvisation. Other style(s): popular music, classical.
Kenneth Parr is a Director of Devon Youth Jazz Orchestra.

Parsons, Ian
(South West)
Carter Community School, Blandford Close, Hamworthy, Poole
Instruments taught: Clarinet, Saxophone.
Workshops Qualifications: G.R.N.C.M./P.G.C.E (has been teaching for 5-10 years).
Includes improvisation.
"I feel that I have been able to communicate my love of jazz to young people and I have been able to inspire confidence and enthusiasm in the talented young people that I have had the privilege to work with."

Peck, Mike
(South West)
Browns Park, Marhamchurch, Bude EX23 0HZ
01288 361565 home tel
Instruments taught: Piano.
Teaches 1 to 1. Teaches Associated Board Piano Exam. Age(s): under 11, upwards
Area(s): reading, beginners, some knowledge, refresher, coaching.
"I have been a professional musician since 1959. Since jazz is a very personal and individual art form, I prefer to teach on a 1 to 1 basis, from beginners to performance level."

Pells, Roger
(South East)
Misbourne Cottage, 15 Lexham Gardens, Amersham HP6 5JP
01494 726449 home tel
Instruments taught: Alto Sax, Tenor Sax.
Teaches 1 to 1.
(Has been teaching for 10-15 years).

Peploe, Brian
(Eastern)
7 Denton Close, Kempston MK42 8RY
01234 856973 home tel
Instruments taught: Alto Sax, Tenor Sax, Baritone Sax.
Teaches 1 to 1. Age(s): under 11, 11 upwards. Area(s): reading, beginners, some knowledge, refresher, coaching. Place(s): own home.
Workshops: Sax classes in schools and The Stables, Wavendon.
"For past 10 years worked alongside and observed most of the leading jazz educators on the Wavendon course but retired from that position at the end of 2000."

Perrin, Roger
(London)
84 Kingsbury Road, Kingsbury, London NW9 0AX
020 8205 3263, 07958 619 721, rogper@dircon.co.uk
Instruments taught: Piano, Bass Guitar, Saxophone.
Teaches 1 to 1. Area(s): reading, beginners, some knowledge, refresher. Place(s): own home.
Schools: Primary, secondary.
Qualifications: B Ed (Mus) and B A both from University of Melbourne.

Composer of 'Jazztet' series published by Studio Music London. Most of his compositions have been for small brass and sax ensembles with interchangeable parts. "My approach to jazz is music first, theory later. Students begin by playing simple tunes using simple scales and quickly get the feel for improvising."

Perrin, Roland
(London)

Basement Flat, 47a Waldram Park Road, London SE23 2PW
020 8291 2602, 078036 07578 mobile
rolandperrin@compuserve.com, www.oneblueplanet.co.uk
Instruments taught: Piano.
Teaches 1 to 1. Teaches Associated Board Piano Exam. Age(s): under 11, 11upwards. Area(s): reading, beginners, some knowledge, refresher, coaching. Place(s): own home, pupil's home.
Workshops: small groups. Previously at Morley College Summer Jazz weekend and Wavendon. Specialisation - theory into practice - the practical application of rhythmic, melodic and harmonic Jazz techniques.
Schools: for 4-8 hours per week. HE/FE, adults
Qualifications: BA in Music, Music Teacher's Certificate (has been teaching for 10-15 years). Other style(s): classical, world music.
Has taught jazz piano at Morley College for past 7 years. "I am very experienced at teaching adult beginners. That is beginners to jazz, not beginners to the piano."

Perry, Terry
(North West)

97 Raeburn Avenue, Eastham, Wirral L62 8BD
0151 327 1673 home tel
Instruments taught: Saxophone.
Teaches 1 to 1. Age(s): 11 upwards. Area(s): reading, beginners, some knowledge, refresher, coaching. Place(s): own home, pupil's home.
Schools: Special needs.
Qualifications: B.Ed. LRAM (has been teaching for over 20 years). Includes improvisation. Other style(s): popular music.
Since 1961 has had private pupils. "I have forty years experience of playing jazz in all styles from traditional to free form"

Peters, Pete
(North East)

44 Edward St, Bishop Auckland DL14 7DT
01388 605 909, 07790 049806, petepeters@yahoo.com
Instruments taught: Piano.
Teaches 1 to 1. Teaches Associated Board Piano Exam. Age(s): under 11, 11 upwards. Area(s): reading, beginners, some knowledge. Place(s): own home.
Schools: Secondary. Framwellgate Moor School, Durham.
Qualifications: Certificate in Education (has been teaching for over 20 years). Includes improvisation. Other style(s): popular music.
"Ex school teacher with 50 years practical experience in all styles of bands. Still working in bands but now freelance rather than resident. Entered many competitive local festivals with pupils who have never lost an event. Taught for many years (Jazz) and 24 years as a teacher in schools""

Phillips, Marlene
(North West)

Ivy Garth, Preston Patrick, Milnthorpe LA7 7PB
015395 67439, ejphillips@cix
Instruments taught: Piano, Keyboards.
Teaches 1 to 1. Teaches Associated Board Piano Exam.
Qualifications: LTCL/ATCL/LLCM (has been teaching for over 20 years). Includes improvisation. Other style(s): popular music, classical, other (Early music improvisation).
"I see jazz as part of a wide spectrum - historically - I also play early music; culturally - I am also a church musician and teach classical, pop etc. I compose music and encourage pupils to do the same"

Ponsford, Jan
(South East)

'Calliope' Eressos, Isle of Lesvos, 81105, Greece 00 30 225 305 2018
calliopehols@hotmail.com www.geocities.com/calliopehols
Instruments taught: Voice.
Teaches 1 to 1. Age(s): under 11, 11 upwards. Area(s): reading, beginners, some knowledge, refresher, coaching. Place(s): own home, other (Greece, Brighton, London).
Workshops: Very extensive workshop experience which has included Community Music (London and East), Middlesex Poly, Islington Adult Education, Studio Vox, Healing Sounds Festival and Greece. Specialisation - 'Free Your Voice', Breathing, Relaxation, Vocal Production, Harmony.
"Teach Orally/Aurally impaired through to Recording artists. I have been dedicated to music making for 25 years with a wealth of experience in performing, recording, composing, producing and teaching. I teach my own method with visualisation and power of positive thought techniques to help relax and bring out the best in students". Writing book on teaching.

Positive, John
(South West)

Chosen Lodge, 41a Albermarle Road, Churchdown, Gloucester GL3 2HE
01452 713159, johnpositive@chosenlodge.co.uk
Instruments taught: Piano.
Teaches 1 to 1. Teaches Associated Board Piano Exam. Age(s): under 11, 11 upwards Area(s): reading, beginners, refresher. Place(s): own home.
Qualifications: Ed Teaching Cert; BA (Open) Grade 8 piano, Grade 3 Jazz (Distinction) (has been teaching for over 20 years). Includes improvisation.
"My greatest asset as a music teacher is to be able to teach pupils how to practise. To make good use of their practise time pupils need to be set specific, achievable goals. As a qualified teacher (now retired) with experience in schools as well as 1 to 1 piano teaching, I guarantee good progress for child or adult learners if they will make time to practise. My own interest in jazz has developed since the publication of the Associated Board materials. It's all very exciting, and I believe that there is no better teacher than one who is keen to go on learning."

Potter, Sarah
(London)

18A Fawnbrake Avenue, Herne Hill, London SE24 OBY

Instruments taught: Piano.

Teaches 1 to 1. Teaches Associated Board Piano Exam.

Qualifications: Degree in Music (has been teaching for 3-5 years). Includes improvisation. Other style(s): popular music, classical.

"The basis of my teaching method is student centred. A good relationship is essential and I give plenty of encouragement and praise. Learning is taken at a pace
appropriate to the individual. I aim to set solid foundations in music learning where
theory (also in practice!), playing by ear, improvising in various styles, music reading, rhythm skills and composition are all part of weekly work"

Powell, Gary
(West Midlands)

7 Somerset Road, Handsworth Road, Birmingham B20 2JE

0121 523 3711, 07497 566654, gary-powell@breathemail.net

Instruments taught: Drums, percussion

Teaching experience in the USA and Canada.

Powell, Patricia
(South East)

76 Hurst Rise Road, Oxford OX2 9HH

01865 864 668, 01865 865 998 home fax

Instruments taught: Piano.

Teaches 1 to 1. Teaches Associated Board Piano Exam. Age(s): under 11, 11
upwards. Area(s): reading, beginners, some knowledge, refresher, coaching.
Place(s): own home.

Workshops: Blues and Improvisation in a Prep school - Dragon School Oxford.

Qualifications: B M Piano Perf; MM Piano Perf + Pedagogy; MA Oxon. (Has been
teaching for 15-20 years.) Includes improvisation. Other style(s): popular music,
classical.

"I teach improvisation, including jazz and blues alongside traditional Western classical as I feel the two art forms nourish one another and help to make a better all
round musician out of the pupils."

Preiss, Jonathan
(London)

12 Exeter Road, London NW2 4SP

020 8452 2075 tel/fax, 07968 167350, jwpreiss@cs.com

Instruments taught: Guitar.

Teaches 1 to 1. Area(s): beginners, some knowledge, refresher. Place(s): own
home.

Workshops. Speciality area(s): Primary, secondary, adult. Previous experience -
Dortmund Dance and Music (Indian/Jazz), Watford annual junior guitar ensemble
(classical, improvisation, composition) Highgate school assistant, Bath International
Guitar Festival adult intermediate workshop week, Killingworth School (Tyneside)
jazz workshop week.

Schools: Watford School of Music, Da Capo School (London), Pope John Primary, St
Marylebone School. In past Radlett Preparatory (Herts) Tring School (Herts),
Hemel Hempstead (Herts) Mary Ward Centre, Lambeth College.

Qualifications: GCLCM (Hons) Jazz Popular Music, Mmus (London) Performance and Related studies. Other style(s): popular music, classical, other (Brazilian).

Pretty, Adam
(London)

59a Prince George Road, London N16 8DL

020 7241 6366 home tel

Instruments taught: Clarinet, Saxophone.

Qualifications: Community Music Workshop Skills Cert (has been teaching for 5-10 years). Includes improvisation. Other style(s): popular music, world music. Teaches saxophone privately.

Priest, John Christopher
(South East)

1 Lowry Lodge, Harrow Road, Wembley HA0 2EA

020 8795 3154, 07712 388 731 mobile

Instruments taught: Piano, Keyboards.

Teaches 1 to 1. Teaches Associated Board Piano Exam. Age(s): under 11, 11upwards Area(s): reading, beginners, some knowledge, refresher, coaching. Place(s): own home, pupil's home.

Qualifications: Advanced Cert (Distinction).

"I draw on 30 years love and study of jazz, have highly developed academic skills (went to Cambridge University as a mature student studying Anthropology) and highly developed classical piano skills (last exam was Advanced Certificate with Distinction - now working towards the LRSM Performance Diploma). I have over 25 years of playing experience and 8 years of teaching. My experiences have generated excellent anaytical skills and interpersonal skills; high motivation/enthusiasm for jazz education; emphasis on rhythmic feel; versatile and responsive approach to each individual."

Pritchard, Malcolm
(Eastern)

Butterfly Lane, Elstree, Borehamwood WD6 3AF

Instruments taught: Piano, Clarinet, Saxophone.

Teaches 1 to 1.

Workshops. Schools: for 16+ hours per week. Primary, secondary at Haberdashers' Aske's School.

Qualifications: Dip. RCM (has been teaching for 10-15 years). Includes improvisation. Other style(s): popular music, classical.

Puddick, John
(Eastern)

Thorpe Hall School, Wakering Road, Southend on Sea SS1 3RD

Instruments taught: Keyboards.

Workshops: usually small groups.

Schools: for 16+ hours per week. Primary, secondary at. Thorpe Hall School and Southend Music School.

(Has been teaching for over 20 years).

Pullin, David
(Eastern)

2 Greenhills Road, Norwich NR3 3ET
01603 632308 home tel
Instruments taught: Double Bass, Saxophone.
Area(s): reading, beginners, some knowledge, coaching.
Workshops: Previously taught 'Improvisation and using modes' at Norwich Arts Centre. Specialisation: Improvisation./Composition.
Schools:HE/FE at Cambridge Regional College. Private tuition with some jazz emphasis. 'Approach to Improvisation' course covered chordal, linear, Modal and Free forms of jazz. "

Purcell, John
(South East)

447 Victoria Drive, Eastbourne BN20 8JU
01323 736644, 01323 508778 home fax
Instruments taught: Saxophone, Guitar, Piano.
Workshops: small groups. Teaches on GNVQ Performing Arts Course: Music and Business in the Performing rArts.
Schools: for 1-4 hours per week. HE/FE at Park College Eastbourne.
Qualifications: Not Formal (has been teaching for over 20 years). Includes improvisation. Other style(s): popular music.

Putson, Dave
(South East)

Poplar Mount, Belvedere DA17 6DL
01322 432608, bassplayer@joocypeach.demon.co.uk
www.joocypeach.com
Instruments taught: Bass Guitar.
Teaches 1 to 1. Age(s): under 11, 11 upwards. Area(s): reading, beginners, some knowledge, refresher. Place(s): own home, pupil's home.
Workshops: Runs 10 week Foundation and Intermediate courses. No specific starting dates - according to how many pupils held either at his home (up to 5 pupils) or at local school (over 5 pupils).
Schools: Secondary.
Qualifications: Musicians Institute Los Angeles (has been teaching for 5-10 years). Includes improvisation. Other style(s): popular music.
"My teaching approach to jazz is in part dictated by the course chosen (25 available on his website) and by the pupils preferred way of learning - which might be by listening first or from an academic approach or by playing and working back to technique. I provide information and encourage pupils to choose the genre/style. Aimed at all aptitudes: Accelerated learning for the absolute beginner through to point where student is able to understand form, structure and techniques. Course work provided each week".

Quinton, Neill
(London)

13B Sydner Road, Stoke Newington, London
020 7690 4262, neillnaylor@quinton35.freeserve.co.uk
Instruments taught: Piano.
Teaches 1 to 1. Teaches Associated Board Piano Exam. Age(s): under 11, 11

upwards Area(s): reading, beginners, some knowledge, refresher. Place(s): own home, pupil's home.
Workshops: Previously basic and intermediate level keyboards workshops for LB of Newham Adult and Youth Education Services. Workshop in the new academic year working with jazz singers and rhythm sections. Specialisation - jazz piano, Accompaniment for singers, Improvisation.
Schools: Secondary. HE/FE, adults.
"I aim to focus on the student's needs, rather than enforce a fixed path of jazz teaching. I have worked with children and adults, from complete beginners to accomplished musicians. Educated to post-graduate level, I have a thorough knowledge of musical theory and history and am comfortable with a variety of jazz styles."

Ramsden, Mark
(South East)
20 Beesfield Lane, Dartford DA4 0BZ
01322 863912, markurial@aol.com
Instruments taught: Saxophone.
Teaches 1 to 1. Age(s): 11 upwards. Area(s): reading, beginners, some knowledge, refresher, coaching. Place(s): own home, pupil's home.
Workshops. Specialisation - Saxophone, jazz improvisation.
Schools: Secondary. Adults.
Tutor at Munich Jazz School. Private lessons. Regular jazz workshops in Germany. "I encourage every student to find the unique music inside themselves."

Rawbone, Martyn
(South East)
49 Monkton Road, Minster, Ramsgate CT12 4ED
01843 822280, 07702 434615, mrawbone@hotmail.com
Instruments taught: Trombone, Piano.
Teaches 1 to 1. Teaches Associated Board Piano Exam. Age(s): under 11, 11 to 16. Area(s): reading, beginners, some knowledge. Place(s): pupil's home.
Schools: Primary, secondary.
Involved with Thanet Music Centre. "I combine experience of all aspects of Jazz playing: Big Band, Dixieland, Fusion with many years classroom teaching especially in the 7-11 age range. Thus I have a particular empathy with beginners taking their first tentative steps into improvisation."

Rayner, Alison
(London)
76 Hawksley Road, Stoke Newington, London N16 0TJ
020 7254 8935, 07973 799415 mobile
info@blowthefuse.com, www.blowthefuse.com/ internet
Instruments taught: Bass Guitar, Double Bass.
Teaches 1 to 1. Age(s): 17 plus. Area(s): reading, beginners, some knowledge. Place(s): own home.
Workshops: In the past has taught at the Glamorgan Jazz Summer School, Manchester and LIPA Jazz Summer Schools, Drill Hall Arts Centre, London Jazz Festival and Chard Festival of Women in Music workshops. Has been teaching at FE level for the past 8 years. Now only involved in 1 to 1 tuition.

Rendell, Don
(London)
23 Weir Hall Gardens, Edmonton, London N18 1BH
020 8807 7831, 0787 0905818 mobile
Instruments taught: Clarinet, Flute, Tenor Sax.
Teaches 1 to 1. Age(s): 11 upwards. Area(s): reading, beginners, some knowledge. Place(s): own home.
Workshops: Has been a tutor on many summer schools and colleges including Goldsmiths, Weekend Arts, JAWS, Guildhall School of Music and Drama.
Schools: Primary, secondary. Adults. Forest School, Walthamstow, London E17; Highbury Grove School, London N5; South Hampstead High School for Girls and since 1988 on the jazz course of Guildhall School.

Richards, Tim
(London)
111a Bovill Road, London SE23 1EL
020 8291 5221 tel/fax, tim@timrichards.ndo.co.uk
www.timrichards.ndo.co.uk
Instruments taught: Piano.
Teaches 1 to 1. Teaches Associated Board Piano Exam. Age(s): 17 upwards. Area(s): some knowledge, refresher, coaching. Place(s): own home.
Workshops: small groups. Speciality area(s): tertiary, adult.
Has taught in a wide variety of workshops including Dartington College of Art, Jazz Umbrella (Jazz Collective) Blackheath Concert Halls - Meantime Contemporary Jazz Orchestra, Premises (Recording Studio) Jazz Piano Week course. Specialisation: Jazz/Blues Piano and Improvisation all music styles.
Schools: for 4-8 hours per week. HE/FE
Qualifications: None (has been teaching for over 20 years). Includes improvisation. Other style(s): Blues
"I enjoy teaching as a natural sideline to my performing, composing and recording activities, I have 20 years experience of 1 to 1 jazz tuition, but still remember what it's like to be 'in the dark' about chords, improvisation etc.
I also enjoy running evening classes which I've been doing for about 15 years. I have a wealth of handout teaching material".

Richards, Tony
(West Midlands)
68, Woodside Road, Ketley, Telford TF1 4HE
01952 401688, 07778 751500 mobile
Instruments taught: Drums, Percussion.
Teaches 1 to 1. Age(s): under 11, 11 upwards. Area(s): reading, beginners, some knowledge, refresher, coaching.
Workshops: small and, large groups. Has run a very successful jazz workshop weekend at Ingestre Hall, in Sandwell for 40-50 instrumentalists.
Schools: for 16+ hours per week. Primary, Secondary. HE/FE, adults.
Qualifications: 'Industrial' Qualifications (recognised by LEA's) (has been teaching for over 20 years).
Includes improvisation. Other style(s): popular music.
Produced 'Basics to Jazz' a video which received very favourable reviews.

Richardson, Gerry
(North East)

9 Queens Road, Jesmond, Newcastle upon Tyne NE2 2PQ
0191 281 1263, gerry.richardson@cableinet.co.uk
www.gerryrichardsontrio.com
Instruments taught: Organ, Piano.
Teaches 1 to 1. Age(s): 11 upwards. Area(s): reading, beginners, some knowledge, refresher, coaching. Place(s): own home.
Schools: HE/FE.
Has taught improvisation, ensemble, keyboards, history and composition/arranging at Newcastle College on the B.Mus in Jazz popular and commercial music since 1987. "I tend to be very student based and design an individual programme to suit each student."

Richardson, Neal
(South East)

PO Box 2061, Seaford BN25 1NX
07801 230 610, info@impromptu.co.uk, www.impromptu.co.uk
Instruments taught: Piano, Drums.
Teaches 1 to 1. Age(s): 11 upwards. Area(s): some knowledge, refresher.
Place(s): own home.
Qualifications: BSc, Dipl Jazz and Popular music. Other style(s): popular music.
Teaching method based firmly around jazz harmony, covering common progressions, the cycle of 4ths, substitutions, blues and ear training "your ears are more important than your hands". His main teaching aim is to develop the ability "to be able to play anything you can hear in your head, in your own style". Has many years experience playing solo piano through to Big Bands as a professional musician.

Riley, Howard
(South East)

Flat 2, 53 Tweedy Road, Bromley BR1 3NH
020 8290 5917 home tel
Instruments taught: Piano.
Workshops: usually small groups, large groups, classes (20+).
Schools: for 4-8 hours per week. Adults. Goldsmiths College.
Qualifications: M.A., M.Mus M.Phil (has been teaching for over 20 years). Includes improvisation.
Founder of the jazz activities course at the Guildhall in 1970 and from then until 1990 also taught there. Since 1975 has also taught at Goldsmiths College: Contemporary Jazz Piano. 1971-80 taught at the Barry Summer School.

Riley, Lewis
(South West)

16 Riverside, Swallowfields, Totnes TQ9 5JB
01803 866242, rileymusic@beeb.net
www.totnesjazzcollective.org.uk internet
Instruments taught: Piano, Tabla.
Teaches 1 to 1. Age(s): under 11, 11 upwards. Area(s): reading, beginners, some knowledge, refresher, coaching. Place(s): own home.
Workshops: small and large groups. Previous jazz workshops - Exeter Phoenix,

Totnes Community College. Dartington International Summer School Jazz Course. Specialisation - Improvisation, Jazz Harmony, Ensemble playing. Schools: for 8-12 hours per week. Secondary. HE/FE, adults. Qualifications: Cert ED., B. Phil (Ed) Creative Arts in Education (has been teaching for over 20 years). Includes improvisation. Other style(s): popular music, world music.

Teaches jazz piano at Dartington College of Arts and University of Exeter. Freelance lectures and workshops at Universities, schools and Arts Centres. Has taken bands into schools for workshops and demos. 1996/97 Jazz composer in residence in East Cornwall schools. "I always try to meet individual needs and interests, rather than following a rigid syllabus. In workshop ensembles, I do not select, but take whoever is interested, and get them to improve their reading, ensemble, improvisation and rhythm skills, and to play 'as a band'.

Riley, Stuart
(North West)

2 Hazelbank Avenue, Withington, Manchester M20 3ES
0161 445 9851 home tel
Instruments taught: Double Bass.
Teaches 1 to 1. Age(s): 17 plus. Area(s): beginners, some knowledge, refresher, coaching. Place(s): own home.
Workshops: Previous taught at many weekly workshops at City College, Manchester, as well as eleven of their Jazz Summer Schools. International Jazz Summer School At LIPA. Specialisation - Improvisation, Arranging Group Interaction.

"Over 15 years experience of teaching Jazz in workshops, Summer Schools, 'formal' teaching of Jazz at beginner level, HND level and degree level. I have written programmes for jazz tuition from beginner to HND level and organised and directed 12 large scale Summer Schools. I currently teach at 1st and 2nd year degree level at Leeds College of Music, teaching ensembles, aural awareness, double bass and performance studies. I am a Jazz examiner for the Associated Board Jazz Piano examinations and Jazz ensemble examinations"

Ritchie, Stuart
(London)

48 Otterburn House, Sultan Street, Camberwell, London SE5 O XE
020 7708 0255, sturitch@yahoo.co.uk
Instruments taught: Drums.
Teaches 1 to 1. Age(s): under 11, 11upwards. Area(s): reading, beginners, some knowledge, refresher, coaching. Place(s): own home, pupil's home.
Workshops: Jazz, Rock, Blues, Funk, Organic Drumming at Aberdeen Arts Centre
"As a performer with 15 years professional experience and being self-taught, my observation of pupils (and myself) is that one is not necessarily encouraged to find their own voice. I think this is the most important aspect of individual development along with Music History, Technique, Posture, Relaxation and Energy Conservation"

Robinson, Eddie
(South West)

20 Aston Mead, Christchurch BH23 2SR
Instruments taught: Trumpet, Trombone.
Teaches 1 to 1. Age(s): 11 upwards. Area(s): reading, beginners, some knowledge, refresher, coaching. Place(s): own home.
"I have been playing jazz for 40 years and teaching it for 20. I have produced

players up to professional standard who have come through the ranks of jazz county youth orchestras. I cover all styles and lead the Bournmouth Jazz Orchestra and still perform in small group and Big Band situations. Lessons must be fun. I'm a qualified teacher. I cover: Basics for beginners (pentatonic scales), Rhythm keyboard, Backing - slow tempo"

Robinson, Joe
(South East)

32 Stanstead Crescent, Woodingdean, Brighton BN2 6TQ
joe@jrsounds.com, www.jrsounds.com
Instruments taught: Piano, Keyboards, Saxophone.
Teaches 1 to 1.
Qualifications: Guildhall School.
Currently visiting teacher of music at Roedean School, Brighton and Lancing College. Has taught keyboard skills at Chichester College jazz course, as well as private lessons.

Rodel, Chris
(London)

59 Rogers Road, London SW17 OEB
07788 667265, chris@crodel.freeserve.co.uk
Instruments taught: Double Bass, Bass Guitar.
Teaches 1 to 1. Age(s): 17 plus. Area(s): some knowledge, refresher. Place(s): own home.
(Has been teaching for 10-15 years).
Has taught Bass Guitar at Bass Institute. Private tuition.

Rose, John
(Eastern)

27 St Winifred's Avenue, Luton LU3 1QT
01582 613913 home tel
Instruments taught: Piano.
Teaches 1 to 1. Teaches Associated Board Piano Exam. Age(s): under 11, 11 to 16. Area(s): reading, beginners, some knowledge. Place(s): own home, pupil's home.
"I'm not sure I would say that I am distinctive as a jazz tutor - I've had no 'formal' jazz training. However, I do have a lot of experience in terms of improvisation and of 'traditional' piano teaching (I've given in excess of 10,000 piano lessons). I'm also taking the Associated Board Jazz exams and have gained distinction in grades 1 to 4"

Rose, Martin
(South West)

68 Field Barn Drive, Southill, Weymouth DT4 0EE
01305 774678 home tel
Instruments taught: Saxophone, Clarinet.
Teaches 1 to 1.
Workshops: small and large groups.
Schools: for 1-4 hours per week. Primary, Secondary.
(Has been teaching for 10-15 years). Includes improvisation. Other style(s): popular music.

Rosser, Pete
(South West)

26 Lansdown, Stroud GL5 IBG
01453 763 275, 07813 967364, peterosser@hotmail.com
Instruments taught: Guitar, Accordion, Piano.
Teaches Associated Board Piano Exam. Age(s): under 11, 11 upwards. Area(s): reading, beginners, some knowledge, refresher, coaching. Place(s): own home, pupil's home.
Workshops: Previously, weekly jazz workshop at Guildhall Arts Centre, Gloucester 1991 -1998. Street bands/Allcomer orchestras/Jazz in schools. Weekly jazz workshop at The Space, Lansdown, Stroud. Specialisation - Developing improvisation over jazz changes; composition through structured impro; songwriting.
Qualifications: PGCE Secondary Music Teaching (has been teaching for 10-15 years). Includes improvisation. Other style(s): popular music, classical, world music.
Has run jazz workshops, teaching at Star Centre in Cheltenham and various projects with the elderly, mentally ill and people with learning difficulties. "I am a composer/pianist/accordionist inspired by Jazz, Improvisation, World Music and contemporary composition, with 12 years experience of passing on inspiration to musicians and non musicians in most imaginable situations."

Royle, Ian
(North West)

3 Parsonage Road, Flixton M31 3PZ
0161 747 4073, 07957 858 821, ppimusic@telinco.co.uk
Instruments taught: Tuba, Trumpet, Trombone.
Teaches 1 to 1. Age(s): under 11, 11 upwards. Area(s): reading, beginners, some knowledge, refresher, coaching. Place(s): own home, pupil's home.
Workshops: Previously and currently Stockport MBC, Priestnall Centre, Mersey Road, Stockport, Reddish Vale School, Reddish,Stockport. Specialisation - Traditional Jazz, Big Band Jazz ensemble, small group mainstream and BeBop. Schools:Primary, secondary. HE/FE, adults.
"I played with traditional jazz bands in the early 60's, and then moved on to Big Bands. I later played with Jazz Educator John Brown (Leeds Jazz Music College). I was involved with the Stockport Youth Jazz Orchestra (Stagesound). I've 'helped out' Ian Darrington with WYJO. I assist with the A level jazz students at Sandbach School and have a number of private pupils"

Salisbury, Harold
(North West)

4 Grosvenor Place, Ashton-on-Ribble, Preston PR2 1ED
07866 309130 mobile
Instruments taught: Saxophone, Flute, Clarinet.
Teaches 1 to 1. Age(s): 17 plus. Area(s): beginners, some knowledge, refresher, coaching. Place(s): own home, pupil's home.
Workshops: Specialisation Jazz Improvisation - Theory and Ear.
(Has been teaching for over 20 years). Includes improvisation.
Private tuition. Inaugurated jazz classes at Salford CAT Music Centre (now University of Salford) and at Rossendale College of Further Education Music Annexe. "I teach the mid ground between Academic / Theoretical (Aebersold) and playing by ear (Peewee Russell)."

Samuels, Biddy
(London)

Flat 9, Markland House, Darfield Way, London W10 6UA
020 8964 5930 biddy@mhepo.co.uk
Instruments taught: Keyboards, Saxophone, Voice.
Teaches 1 to 1. Age(s): under 11, 11 upwards. Area(s): reading, beginners, some knowledge. Place(s): own home, other ().
Workshops: Zimbabwe National Music Camp - jazz workshops for all instruments in 1997/98 Specialisation - Afro-jazz, horn section work, composing and understanding the genre.
Schools: HE/FE, adults. Brent Adult and Community Education Services, Stonebridge and the Positive Age Centre in Kensington. Qualifications: Certificate in Music Teaching to Adults (Goldsmiths College). Keyboard workshops for Centre for Young Musicians.
"My strength is in building confidence in people of all ages and thus enabling them to master and de-mystify many skills, from playing or singing a melody to harmonising, improvising and composing. Afro-jazz is the genre I prefer to work in, and I like to convey something of the history and meaning of this music to my students".

Sanders, Gareth
(Wales)

County Hall, Haverfordwest SA61 1TP
Instruments taught: Saxophone, Clarinet.
Teaches 1 to 1.
Qualifications: PGCE Secondary Music (has been teaching for 3-5 years). Other style(s): classical.
Teaches the Pembrokshire Jazz Ensemble and Big Band

Sansbury, Brian
(Wales)

Pantyberllan, Bow Street, Aberystwyth SY24 5AR
01970 828470, 07779666415, sansbrian@hotmail.com
Instruments taught: Saxophone, Clarinet.
Age(s): under 11, 11 upwards. Area(s): some knowledge, coaching. Place(s): own home, other (schools as a peripatetic teacher)).
Workshops: In 2000 started various school bands including - Penglais School Big Band and a joint Big Band from Penglais School and Ceredigion County Big band.
Schools: Primary, secondary.
"I play regularly with a Dixieland jazz band (Aber Jazz) Was also a member of Welsh Jazz Orchestras in Cardiff and of a 70s top Welsh rock band. I have started off a County and Aber University Wind Band, County Wind Band, Three Counties Wind Band and County Orchestra"

Saunders, Hilary
(East Midlands)

91 Main Road, Wilford, Nottingham NG11 7AJ
Instruments taught: Piano.
Teaches 1 to 1. Teaches Associated Board Piano Exam. Age(s): 17 plus.
Workshops: Violin and recorder teaching.
Schools: for 8-12 hours per week. Primary,secondary. Adults.
Qualifications: GTCL; LTCL Scholl music LTCL piano (has been teaching for over 20

years). Includes improvisation.

"I am very keen to keep learning, listening and practising in order to keep up to date. I have several keen pupils of jazz styles I help them as much as I am able. I am not trained in jazz"

Scott, Andy
(North West)

224 Ways Green, Winsford CW7 4AR
07974 561889, lascott@cheerful.com, www.andyscott.org.uk internet
Instruments taught: Saxophone.
Workshops: small groups. Speciality area(s): tertiary, adult. Offers workshops based on his compositions for his band 'Sax Assault' at Royal College of Music, Guildhall and other universities as well as gigs and workshops with Dave Hassell.
Teaches at Royal Northern College of Music. Recently set up some saxophone workshop days aimed at both classical and jazz players with Rob Buckland and Mike Hall with a special guest (in 2002 Bob Mintzer)

Seabrook, Terry
(South East)

11 Bernard Road, Brighton BN2 3ER
01273 673914, 01273 298693 fax, 07970 mobile
terry@cubanabop.com, www.cubanabop.com
Instruments taught: Piano.
Teaches 1 to 1. Teaches Associated Board Piano Exam. Age(s): 11 upwards
Workshops: In the past taught a weekly Jazz Piano workshop and general workshops at Richmond Adult and Community College.
Qualifications: BA (Music). (Has been teaching for 15-20 years.) Includes improvisation. Other style(s): popular music, classical.
Teaches on Jamey Aebersold Jazz Summer Course at Richmond Adult and Community College.. Composer of 3 pieces in the Associated Boards' Jazz piano Grade Exams. Composer of 5 pieces for Rock School/Trinity College Piano Exams.

Seaman, Peter
(North West)

Wirral Grammar School for boys, Cross Lane, Bebington CH63 3AQ
0151 644 0908, 0151 643 8317 fax, 0797 036 2231 mobile
hm@wirralgrammar.demon.co.uk
Instruments taught: Guitar, Keyboards, Piano.
Teaches 1 to 1. Teaches Associated Board Piano Exam. Age(s): under 11, 11 upwards. Area(s): reading, beginners, some knowledge, refresher. Place(s): pupil's home
Workshops: small groups.
Schools: for 16+ hours per week. Primary, secondary. HE/FE, adults.
Qualifications: ALCM (has been teaching for over 20 years). Includes improvisation. Other style(s): popular music, classical.
"40 years as a professional musician and tutor covering all aspects of music. I have experience of working with duos, trios and quartets. Specialise in Latin American guitar"

Severn, Eddie
(West Midlands)
34 Gorseway, Whoberly, Coventry CV5 8BJ
02476 670 164, 02476 426 217 fax, 07968 826 729 mobile
info@eddiesevern.com, www.eddiesevern.com
Instruments taught: Trumpet.
Area(s): reading, coaching. Place(s): pupil's home.
Workshops. Speciality area(s): tertiary, adult. trumpet masterclasses.
A former student of the international trumpeter Bobby Shew, Eddie is constantly in demand both at home and abroad for his abilities as a trumpet clinician and jazz educator. A clinician for Edwards Trumpets and Taylor Flugelhorns he currently holds the posts of Jazz Musician in Residence at Napier University Edinburgh, Musical Director of the National Youth Jazz Orchestra of Scotland and Jazz Trumpet tutor at the Royal Scottish Academy of Music and Drama.

Sharkey, Andrew
(Scotland)
62 Reservoir Road, Gourock, Inverclyde
0141 576 8220, sharkand@hotmail.com
Instruments taught: Bass Guitar.
Teaches 1 to 1. Age(s): 17 plus. Area(s): reading, beginners, some knowledge, refresher. Place(s): own home.
"I place an emphasis on musical knowledge and ear-training, but always back these up with concrete examples which the student can relate to. I am always open to questions and willing to improvise a lesson, which is in the true spirit of the music."

Sharp, Tim
(London)
4 Deans Road, Hanwell, London W7 3 QB
020 8579 8642 home tel
Instruments taught: Piano.
Teaches 1 to 1.
Workshops: small groups, classes (20+).
Schools: for 16+ hours per week. Primary, secondary. HE/FE, adults.
Qualifications: LGSM, BSc, MSc (has been teaching for 10-15 years). Includes improvisation. Other style(s): popular music, classical, world music, other (Latin). ILEA qualified piano teacher. (Also qualified Humanities teacher).

Sharpe, Ian
(Yorkshire)
27 Ringstead Crescent, Sheffield S10 5SG
0114 266 4292 home tel
Instruments taught: Piano, Keyboards.
Teaches 1 to 1. Teaches Associated Board Piano Exam. Age(s): under 11.
Qualifications: Dip Mus Ed; ARMCM (has been teaching for 5-10 years). "I am a practicing jazz musician. playing piano in a dance orchestra (Glen Miller Style) as well as in a duo with a double bass player. This experience helps to enhance my music lessons. I was trained as a classical musician and this helps to inspire my pupils to develop self-discipline and a positive approach to practise"

Sharpe, Martin
(London)
16 Colson Way, Streatham, London
020 8696 9952, m-sharpe.maxsax.freeserve.co.uk
www.maxsax.freeserve.co.uk
Instruments taught: Piano, Saxophone, Clarinet.
Teaches 1 to 1. Teaches Associated Board Piano Exam. Age(s): under 11, 11 upwards. Area(s): reading, beginners, some knowledge, refresher. Place(s): own home, pupil's home.
Schools: Primary, secondary. Adults.
"I try to develop the improvisational skills of my pupils so that they can be creative with their music making."

Shepherd, Peter
(Eastern)
17 Marsh Lane, Hemingford Grey, Huntingdon PE18 9EN
01480 351664, mlcprs@aol.com
Instruments taught: Piano.
Teaches 1 to 1.
Qualifications: Amus LCM (London College of Music Diploma) (has been teaching for 3-5 years). Includes improvisation.
1 to 1 teaching over 4 years but only part of this was jazz.

Sherburn, Angela
(Yorkshire)
24 Brett Gardens, Beeston, Leeds LS11 6TS
07930 939321 mobile
Instruments taught: Piano.
Teaches 1 to 1. Teaches Associated Board Piano Exam. Age(s): 11 to 16. Area(s): beginners. Place(s): pupil's home.
Schools:Primary, secondary.
Qualifications: BA (Hons) in Music; 3 Diplomas in Music (has been teaching for 10-15 years). Includes improvisation. Other style(s): popular music, classical.
"As someone who has had to improvise on various styles since being a church organist at 13, then a schools pianist later on, I taught myself how to 'feel the groove' and improvise along with a melody, by adding good strong bass lines"

Siegel, Julian
(London)
63 Harcombe Road, Stoke Newington, London N16 0RX
020 7254 2438, mail@juliansiegel.com, www.partisans.org.uk internet
Instruments taught: Alto Sax, Soprano Sax, Tenor Sax.
Workshops: In past has led jazz workshops for Jazz Umbrella, Hackney Community College and at the Vortex (London). One of the founder members/tutors at the Jazz Umbrella East London Jazz project. Now concentrates on teaching at the Royal Academy and the Birmingham Conservatoire.

Silk, David
(South East)
Flat 1, 237 High Street, St Mary Cray, Orpington BR5 4AX
dave.silk@netway.co.uk, www.riverfrontjazz.co.uk
Instruments taught: Double Bass.
Workshops: In the past have been a tutor at Orton Hall, Grafham Water. The Hill
Abergavenny, Higham Hall, Cumbria.
Currently runs an 'art's performance class' to build confidence in stage performance at Level 2 to 4. Monday evenings Mycennae House, Blackheath every week

Silk, Rose
(South West)
14 Clover Mead, Taunton TA1 3XD
01823 252311 home tel
Instruments taught: Piano, Midi Vibes, Cello.
Teaches 1 to 1.
Workshops: small and large groups. Disabled people especially those with poor
vision or learning difficulties.
Schools: for 16+ hours per week. Primary, secondary. HE/FE, adults.
Qualifications: HND/BA (has been teaching for over 20 years). Includes improvisation. Other style(s): popular music, classical, world music, other (Religious Music -
western).

Silmon-Monerri, Joe
(North West)
Flat 15 Bankside Court, 49 Pink Bank Lane, Longsight, Manchester M12 5GA
0161 248 0250, 0161 225 6136 fax, jaasilm1@AOL.com
Instruments taught: Flute, Tenor Sax, Clarinet.
"Mainly self taught. A good ear for chords and limitless experience, are possibly
the best teachers in Jazz. After initial lessons on clarinet from Chick Purcell, I had
some brief periods when I did study music. I use music only as a guide and am a
slow reader. My forte is my ear. Although tenor was my best instrument for many
years, I find that the flute is now my favourite (possibly because I had a very good
classical teacher who forced me to make it 'sing"

Smith, Daniel
(London)
60a Fairhazel Gardens, London NW6 3SL
020 7624 7485, danbassoon@aol.com
www.danielsmithbassoon.com
Instruments taught: Clarinet, Saxophone, Bassoon.
Teaches 1 to 1. Age(s): under 11, 11 upwards. Area(s): reading, beginners, some
knowledge, refresher, coaching. Place(s): own home, pupil's home.
Qualifications: Several University degrees - extensive playing career (has been
teaching for over 20 years). Includes improvisation. Other style(s): classical.
Specialisation: Bassoon "I have an extensive background on all other wind instruments, having played in named bands, show bands, latin bands and jazz groups on
sax, clarinet and flute"

Smith, David S.
(Yorkshire)
21 Blackwood Rise, Cooleridge, Leeds LS 16 7BG
0113 230 1030, 0113 230 1010 home fax
davidsmith98@hotmaid.com
Instruments taught: Woodwind, Clarinet.
Teaches 1 to 1. Age(s): under 11, 11 upwards. Area(s): reading, beginners, some knowledge, refresher, coaching. Place(s): own home.
Workshops: Big Band workshops. Peripatetic woodwind tutor in Doncaster area. Also a course for staff in Sheffield at Birkdale school. Specialisation - how to teach children to develop improvisational skills, Blues, Modes and developing solos..
Schools: Primary, secondary. HE/FE, adults.
"I have had a diverse teaching and performing career which started with classical training. As a Saxophonist after graduating from University I have played on sessions for BBC radio, TV as well as many CD recordings. I regularly perform as a soloist with Big Bands and smaller ensembles but gain much satisfaction teaching others how to improvise and develop their skills to full potential. A number of my pupils have obtained Grade 8 Distinction but enjoyment of playing is my main target for students."

Smith, Harrison
(London)
1 Crescent Rise, London N22 4AW
020 8888 4844, harrisonsmith@blueyonder.co.uk
Instruments taught: Tenor Sax, Bass Clarinet, Soprano Sax.
Teaches 1 to 1. Age(s): under 11, 11 upwards. Place(s): own home.
Has taught at all levels in music colleges in this country and abroad. Covers reading, technique, theory, ear training, improvisation. Also uses a modified version of John Stevens "Search and Reflect" in improvised music workshops.

Smith, Malcolm
(London)
11c White Hart Lane, Wood Green, London N22 5SL
020 8881 6867, 07976 906795, mesmith@jazztrombone.com
Instruments taught: Trombone, Voice.
Teaches 1 to 1. Age(s): under 11, 11 upwards Area(s): reading, beginners, some knowledge, refresher, coaching. Place(s): own home.
Workshops: small groups. Speciality area(s): tertiary. Previously Brass Tacks Big Band, Walthamstow Borough. Currently Jazz harmony and ear training at City Literary Institute. Wavendon Jazz Summer School. Specialisation - Big Band, Brass, Vocals, Harmony.
Schools: for 4-8 hours per week. Secondary.HE/FE, adults.
Qualifications: LGSM (has been teaching for 10-15 years). Includes improvisation.
1993-96 Director of'Brass Tacks' Big Band. Since 1995 has been trombone tutor on Wavendon Jazz courses. Has aiso been involved in associated workshops and concerts in schools. "My teaching experiences extend through all levels and ages. My playing experience is also wide, covering all styles from New Orleans to contemporary. The combination of these elements makes me a very thorough teacher, who can communicate at different levels. My understanding of the whole jazz tradition enables me to cater for different tastes, and to examine different skills in a varied, interesting and enjoyable manner".

Smith, Tommy
(Scotland)

PO Box 3743, Lanark ML11 9PWD
07710 585231, ts@spartacusrecords.com
www.tommy-smith.co.uk
Instruments taught: Soprano Sax, Tenor Sax.
Teaches 1 to 1.
Workshops: small and large groups, classes (20+).
Schools: for 4-8 hours per week. Primary, Scondary. HE/FE, adults.Qualifications:
Doctor of Heriot-Watt University (Edinburgh). (Has been teaching for 10-15 years)
Includes improvisation. Other style(s): classical.
Teaches jazz improvisation, composition, Music Business, notation by hand,
ensembles - trios to sextet, arranging, jazz history, chords, scales. In 1999 The
Music of Duke Ellington - Scottish National Jazz Orchestra in Ayre. Course -
Listening, Inventing and Composition in Aberdeen.

Sneyd, Peter
(South West)

55 Bradford Road, Trowbridge BA14 9AN
01225 755439, petesneyd@blueyonder.co.uk
www.jazzfactory.co.uk
Instruments taught: Flute, Clarinet, Baritone Sax.
Teaches 1 to 1. Age(s): 11 upwards.Areas:reading, beginners, some knowledge.
Place(s): own home.
Workshops: small groups. Co-ordinator of Jazz Factory workshops at Wiltshire
Music Centre during term time.
(Has been teaching for 5-10 years). Includes improvisation. Other style(s): classi-
cal.
Co-ordinator of Wiltshire Youth Jazz Orchestra, Wiltshire Youth Jazz Festival.
Particularly interested in teaching improvisation to beginners

Snow, Barbara
(London)

283 Holmesdale Road, South Norwood, London SE25 6PR
020 8653 1715, 07956 447201 mobile
Instruments taught: Trumpet, Piano.
Teaches 1 to 1. Teaches Associated Board Piano Exam. Age(s): under 11, 11
upwards. Area(s): reading, beginners. Place(s): own home, other (In a school).
Schools:Pre-school, primary, secondary. Adults.
Has taught at the Lewisham Jazz Academy with Harry Beckett and has given Salsa
lectures. "I am very patient and I always put words to tunes to get the rhythm
across, which works every time"

Spencer, Piers
(South West)

University of Exeter, Heavitree Road, Exeter EX1 2LU
p.a.spencer@exeter.ac.uk
Instruments taught: Piano.
Teaches 1 to 1.

Workshops: small groups, classes (20+).
Qualifications: GGSM, ARCM, MTC, Dphil (has been teaching for over 20 years).
Includes improvisation. Other style(s): popular music, classical.
"I lecture on the history of Jazz as a tutor on the B.Mus (Jazz) course at Truro College"

Speyer, Loz
(London)

26 Montague Road, London E8 2HW
lozspeyer@onetel.net.uk
Instruments taught: Trumpet, Flugel Horn.
Teaches 1 to 1. Age(s): 17 plus. Area(s): reading, beginners, some knowledge, refresher. Place(s): own home.
Schools: Stoke Newington Community Association.
Qualifications: LGSM (Jazz performance) (has been teaching for 5-10 years).
Includes improvisation. Other style(s): popular music, classical, world music
"I teach from the starting point of enthusiasm, love of music and the desire to learn and communicate. Having these things myself, I can also generate them for others, whether individually or in groups. I teach a full range of practical approaches to improvisation (and music in general) including free expression, precision of harmony and rhythm, ear training, using the voice, sense of space and form: these approaches work for both near beginners and advanced players, the aim being to allow both freedom and precision of musicial self-expression".

Spiers, Stuart
(West Midlands)

Maple Lodge, 24 London Road, Shrewsbury SY2 6NU
01743 363016, stuart@spiers.net
Instruments taught: Saxophone, Clarinet, Flute.
Teaches 1 to 1. Age(s): under 11, 11 upwards. Area(s): reading, beginners, some knowledge, refresher, coaching. Place(s): own home, other (Schools/Adult classes/Workshops).
Workshops: Previously, Shropshire County workshops/schools. Currently runs monthly workshops at Prestfelde School. Specialisation: accepts all instruments, at all levels.

Spolia, Rajan
(South East)

12a The Wheatbutts, Eaton Wick SL4 6JH
01753 621 664, 07790 305942, fretless@btopenworld.com
Instruments taught: Bass Guitar, Guitar.
Teaches 1 to 1. Age(s): under 11, 11 upwards. Area(s): beginners, some knowledge, refresher. Place(s): pupil's home.
Workshops: small and large groups. Workshops have been as part of World music band.
Schools: Primary, secondary., HE/FE. Peripertetic teacher for the Berkshire Young Musicians Trust teaching in 10 schools throughout Berkshire. Mainly improvised jazz/Indian fusion.
"Not strictly jazz, more a fusion of Indian and improvised music"

Stacey, Peter
(Wales)
Tangraig, Pontsian, Llandysul, Ceredigion SA44 4UP
02920 641727, dr.pete@tinyworld.co.uk
Instruments taught: Tenor Sax, Soprano Sax.
Workshops: small groups.
Schools: for 1-4 hours per week. Adults. Cardiff University.
Qualifications: BA, PhD (has been teaching for 10-15 years). Includes improvisation. Other style(s): world music.
Interested in teaching music theory, harmony and improvisation.

Stanley, Christine
(Eastern)
5 Blinking Court, Recorder Road, Norwich NR1 1NW
07771 611657 mobile
Instruments taught: Organ, Keyboards, Piano.
Teaches 1 to 1. Teaches Associated Board Piano Exam. Age(s): 11 to 16. Area(s): beginners. Place(s): pupil's home.
"As yet I have only one pupil taking jazz exams and I am learning the syllabus along with him as my prior training has all been classical."

Steele, Jan
(South East)
1, St Anne's Road, Caversham, Reading RG4 7PA
0118 947 7170, 07718 347691, jan@metalworks.org
Instruments taught: Flute, Saxophone, Clarinet.
Teaches 1 to 1. Age(s): under 11, 11 upwards. Area(s): reading, beginners, some knowledge, refresher, coaching. Place(s): own home.
Workshops: Gamelan Workshops and also teaches Alexander Technique.
Schools: for 16+ hours per week. Primary, secondary. HE/FE, adults.
Qualifications: QTS(DES) (has been teaching for over 20 years). Includes improvisation.

Stein, Jon
(South West)
28 Stafford Road, St Werburghs, Bristol BS2 9UN
0117 909 5894, jon@stein39.freeserve.co.uk
Instruments taught: Piano.
Teaches 1 to 1. Teaches Associated Board Piano Exam. Age(s): under 11, 11 upwards. Area(s): some knowledge, refresher. Place(s): own home.
"Jazz is a language and can be learnt through listening, copying and ultimately, creating a new vocabulary. A teacher guides a student through this process. Ultimately learning to improvise fluently is a mind, body, soul experience where the player combines an understanding of music with technical facility on the instrument and a deep feeling for the music being made"

Stephens, Ian
(South East)
St Mary's Road, Swanley BR7 8TE
Instruments taught: Keyboards.
Teaches 1 to 1.
Workshops: usually classes (20+).
Schools: for 16+ hours per week. Secondary.
Qualifications: PGCE (has been teaching for 3-5 years). Includes improvisation.
Other style(s): popular music, world music.

Stepney, Roger
(South East)
61 Peartree Lane, Bexhill-on-Sea TN39 4PE
01424 844274 home tel
Instruments taught: Piano.
Teaches 1 to 1. Teaches Associated Board Piano Exam. Age(s): under 11, 11
upwards. Area(s): beginners. Place(s): own home.

Sterling, Andrew
(Eastern)
The Old Meeting Room, Main Road, Chelmondiston, Ipswich IP9 1DX
01473 780856 home tel
Instruments taught: Keyboards, Piano.
Teaches 1 to 1.
Qualifications: GLSM (has been teaching for over 20 years). Includes improvisa-
tion. Other style(s): popular music, classical.
"Teaches composition and improvisation in Jazz, Blues and Funk as a basis for
understanding music generally and building a solid keyboard technique."

Stevenson, Nick
(London)
23 Aldebert Terrace, London SW8 1BH
020 7642 8282, nickstev@westminster.org.uk
Instruments taught: Trumpet, Cornet.
Teaches 1 to 1. Age(s): under 11, 11 upwards. Area(s): reading, beginners, some
knowledge. Place(s): own home, pupil's home.
"'Many years experience as a performer and as a teacher"

Stewart, William
(East Midlands)
Access to Music, 18 York Road, Leicester LE1 5 TS
info@access-to-music.co.uk, www.access-to-music.co.uk
Instruments taught: Drums.
Teaches 1 to 1.
Workshops: small groups, classes (20+).
Schools:Primary, secondary. Adults.
Qualifications: OCN level 3, Drumset Certificate. (Has been teaching for 1-2 years).
Includes improvisation. Other style(s): popular music, world music.
Runs approx 4 workshops a year. Examples: Reggae Workshop at Bretton Hall -
Access to Music; Cambridge Regional College Access to Music.

Stopes, Ian
(Wales)

The Old Shop, Lower Street, St Asaph LL17 0SG
01745 582412 home tel
Instruments taught: Guitar.
Teaches 1 to 1. Age(s): under 11, 11 upwards. Area(s): beginners, some knowledge. Place(s): own home.
Qualifications: 20 years professional experience (has been teaching for 5-10 years). Includes improvisation. Other style(s): popular music.
Jazz improvisation workshops for the Welsh Jazz Society. Rhythm and expression workshops in schools in Clwyd and Gwynydd.

Stoysin, Branco
(London)

59a East Dulwich Grove, London SE22 8PR
020 8693 2398 tel/fax, www.jazzcds.co.uk
Instruments taught: Guitar.
Teaches 1 to 1.
(Has been teaching for 5-10 years). Includes improvisation. Other style(s): popular music, other (Brazilian).
Private tuition for all levels in jazz improvisation, chords, scales, modes and understanding of jazz. Also teaches Brazilian Sambas, Bossa Novas.

Strand, Arthur
(South East)

7 Grove Close, Nine Mile Ride, Wokingham RG40 3NA
Instruments taught: Acoustic Guitar, Bass Guitar.
Teaches 1 to 1.
(Has been teaching for over 20 years)

Strong, Barry
(Eastern)

10/12 Cameron Road, Seven Kings
01279 757041 home tel
Instruments taught: Keyboards, Piano.
Teaches 1 to 1. Teaches Associated Board Piano Exam. Age(s): 11 upwards.
Area(s): reading, beginners, some knowledge, refresher. Place(s): own home.
(Has been teaching·for 15-20 years.) Includes improvisation.
"Constantly studying and practising myself. I have a reputation for patience and aim to get students playing. Jazz beginners build from a simple basic solo as their knowledge grows"

Stuart, Don
(South East)

44 Windsor Road, Worcester Park KT4 8EW
020 8330 3075, 0956 541142 mobile
Instruments taught: Clarinet, Flute, Saxophone.
Teaches 1 to 1. Age(s): under 11, 11 upwards. Area(s): reading, beginners, some knowledge, refresher, coaching. Place(s): own home.
Workshops: small groups. "For over fifteen years has run various student bands

and jazz workshops. Currently, Jazz workshops at Merton Park Music Centre (London)
Schools: for 16+ hours per week. Primary, secondary. Adults.
(Has been teaching for 15-20 years.) Includes improvisation. Other style(s): popular music.
Many years experience of teaching including 12 years in Sutton: both junior and high schools. Has organised jazz ensembles for past 10 years which currently run every Tuesday/Thursday in Merton

Stuckey, Bob
(London)
9 Keystone Crescent, Kings Cross, London N1 9DS
020 7278 7246 tel/fax, stuckey@tinyonline.co.uk
Instruments taught: Organ, Piano.
Teaches Associated Board Piano Exam. Age(s): under 11, 11 upwards. Area(s): reading, beginners, some knowledge, refresher, coaching. Place(s): own home.
Qualifications: B.Mus (has been teaching for over 20 years). Includes improvisation. Other style(s): popular music, classical.
Private pupils. "Leading small groups through arrangements I have published 'Scales, Modes and Chords by key signature for Piano: this introduces a particular way of thinking about and practising scales. I try to promote the necessary understanding of chord symbols and syncopated notation for a pupil to be able to play through a lead sheet and improvise on it. I accompany the pupils on Bass (which the jazz pianist must understand how to interact with)."

Sutherland, Rowland
(South East)
21 Lytton Avenue, Enfield Lock, Enfield EN3 6EL
020 8361 4613 tel/fax, 078 5021 5687 mobile
rowlandsutherland@hotmail.com, www.rowlandsutherland.com
Instruments taught: Flute, Piccolo.
Teaches 1 to 1. Age(s): 11 upwards. Area(s): beginners, some knowledge, refresher, coaching. Place(s): own home.
Workshops for Flutes mainly one day events. Specialisation Flute or Horn Groupings.
Schools: for 1-4 hours per week. Secondary. Adults.
(Has been teaching for 10-15 years). Includes improvisation. Other style(s): popular music, classical, world music.
"I aim to instil technical grounding and provide musical guidance. I offer advice and try to inspire students. Create practise structures and set goals. Also cover posture and breathing. Develop aural capacity. Encourage self-learning"

Swift, Jeff
(Yorkshire)
349 Kirkstall Rd, Leeds LS4 2HD
Instruments taught: Guitar.
Teaches 1 to 1.
Workshops: small and large groups, classes (20+).
Schools: for 16+ hours per week. Primary, secondary. HE/FE, adults.
Qualifications: G Mus PGCE. (Has been teaching for 15-20 years.) Includes improvisation. Other style(s): popular music.

Sydor, Bob
(London)

12 Meadway Court, Meadway, London NW11 6PN
020 8458 5799, 0976 982 372 mobile
Instruments taught: Flute, Clarinet, Saxophone.
Teaches 1 to 1.
Workshops. Schools:Primary, secondary.HE/FE, adults.
Qualifications: 30 years experience (has been teaching for over 20 years). Includes improvisation. Other style(s): popular music.

Sykes, Tom
(North West)

68 Bescar Brow Lane, Scarisbrick, Ormskirk L40 9QG
0802 842521, tom.sykes@tesco.net
Instruments taught: Piano, Violin.
Teaches 1 to 1. Teaches Associated Board Piano Exam. Age(s): 11 upwards.
Area(s): reading, beginners, some knowledge, refresher. Place(s): own home, pupil's home.
Workshops: Improvisation workshops at Crosby Hall Educational Trust, Merseyside plus workshops for French Exchange students. These workshops are not available to the public, but information is available via LCC and Sefton MSS. Specialisation is improvisation, various levels and styles, and Jazz violin.
Schools: Secondary. HE/FE.
Qualifications: PGCE, LGSM (has been teaching for 5-10 years). Includes improvisation. Other style(s): popular music, classical, world music.
Has led/co-led improvisation workshops since 1991 working with Louise Elliott, Stan Barker and Mike Hall. Since 1993 has directed the Sefton Youth Jazz Orchestra as well as writing arrangements for them. Helps to run an annual rehearsal weekend. Has travelled abroad with two bands. "I have experience in working with students whose jazz abilities range from complete beginner to advanced, of all ages. I particularly like to use South African Jazz with beginners, because of its rhythmic and melodic appeal and simple chord sequences. As a violinist, I enjoy teaching jazz to string players, and encouraging those who are reluctant to try it"

Taggart, Robert
(South East)

35 Grove Lane, Kingston upon Thames KT1 2ST
020 8549 1183, 07930 562 254 mobile
Instruments taught: Keyboards, Piano.
Teaches 1 to 1. Teaches Associated Board Piano Exam. Age(s): 11 upwards
Area(s): beginners, some knowledge, refresher. Place(s): own home, pupil's home, other (Facilities at the Royal Academy of Music for external pupils.).
Other style(s): popular music.
"My approach develops harmonic and improvisational skills by encouraging aural awareness and wide listening. This is supported by reading skills, rhythmic development and a working knowledge of standard jazz repertoire. A careful approach to piano technique is integral to my teaching method, as is the development of an effective method of practise"

Taylor, Jon
(Yorkshire)
9 Slantgate, Kirkburton HD8 0QL
01404 604392, 07768 013937 mobile
Instruments taught: Flute, Saxophone.
Teaches 1 to 1. Age(s): 17 plus. Area(s): reading, beginners, some knowledge.
Qualifications: Diploma Light Music, LLCM. (Has been teaching for 15-20 years)
Includes improvisation. Other style(s): popular music.
Gives private tuition on jazz improvisation. Peripatetic at various schools including
Bradford Grammar. Leeds College of Music saxophone and woodwind tutor "I
attempt to inspire my students to play musically rather then get bogged down in
unnecessary harmony"

Taylor, Jonathan
(South West)
Ground Floor Flat, 87a Redland Road, Redland, Bristol BS6 6RD
0117 944 2048 tel/fax, jon.taylor3@virgin.net
Instruments taught: Keyboards, Piano.
Teaches 1 to 1. Teaches Associated Board Piano Exam. Age(s): under 11, 11
upwards Area(s): reading, beginners, some knowledge, refresher, coaching.
Place(s): own home.
Workshops: Five years experience of jazz and general music workshops for 'Live
Music Now' scheme across the UK - mainly for special needs and adults with learn-
ing difficulties. Has also run jazz workshops for instrumentalists - all ages and abilities in the South West. Specialises in jazz improvisation.
(Has been teaching for 5-10 years). Includes improvisation. Other style(s): popular
music, classical.
"I am an enthusiastic, experienced and well organised jazz piano teacher and
workshop leader. I have experience of teaching all levels of abilities and many different styles of music with improvisational content. Lessons are coherently structured and tailored to suit the needs of the individual"

Thomas, Nigel
(South East)
Ground Floor Flat, 9 Buckingham Road, Brighton BN1 3RA
01273 204031, joseph.robinson@lineone.net
www.nigelthomasquintet.co.uk
Instruments taught: Double Bass.
Teaches 1 to 1.
Several years experience of working in schools including work with students with
disabilities along side other musicians like Eddie Harvey and Dave Wickens.

Thomas, Peter
(London)
127 Ferndale Road, London SW4 7RN
www.petethomas.co.uk
Instruments taught: Saxophone, Flute.
Written and presented saxophone tuition video for Virgin Vision. Teaches part time
composition, arranging, jazz theory, performance, studio production at University
of Southampton

Thompson, Billy
(London)
14 Whitehall Gardens, Ealing Common, London W3 9RD
020 8992 5375, 07720 707 744 mobile
billy@thompsoundmusic.co.uk, www.billythompson.co.uk
Instruments taught: Violin.
Teaches 1 to 1. Age(s): under 11, 11 upwards. Area(s): some knowledge, refresher. Place(s): own home.
Has taught improvisation and jazz at the Liverpool Institute of Performing Arts (LIPA).

Thorpe, Tony
(North West)
143 Marsden Road, Burnley BB10 2QW
01282 456205, www.access-to-music.co.uk
Instruments taught: Guitar.
Teaches 1 to 1. Age(s): 11 upwards. Area(s): beginners, some knowledge, coaching. Place(s): own home.
Workshops: small groups. One day workshops, improvisation (Practical and Theory), History. Previously Improvisation (for Access to Music), Sheffield, Liverpool, Manchester, Blackburn. Currently runs workshops for Access to Music IMF course.
Schools: for 1-4 hours per week. HE/FE, adults.
Qualifications: IMF, OCNSEM. (Has been teaching for 1-2 years). Includes improvisation. Other style(s): popular music, other (Blues).
"I focus on effective timing/phrasing to capture feel and mood and liberate individual creativity and expression. I explain building complex structures from simpler ones, using voice-leading and interval-based chord theory. Students tell me they grasp more from me than some tutors, with 'finally I understand' a not uncommon remark"

Tilbury, Nigel
(London)
27a Bulwer Road, Leytonstone, London E11 1DE
020 8926 0304 home tel
Instruments taught: Drums.
Teaches 1 to 1.
(Has been teaching for 10-15 years). Includes improvisation. Other style(s): popular music, other (Rock and Fusion).

Tomkins, Trevor
(London)
14 Bellamy Street, London SW12 8BU
020 8675 1455 home tel
Instruments taught: Drums.
Workshops.
19 years experience of working in London schools/colleges including Goldsmiths College, West London College, Sussex University, London College of Music. Many projects for Education Authorities throughout the country. Currently Royal Academy of Music (BMus) Guildhall School of Music and Drama (Post Grad), Co-Director of Wavendon Jazz Courses.

Tomlinson, Jim
(London)
52 Albert Road, Alexandra Park, London N22 7AH
020 8889 6740 tel/fax, jwt251@aol.com
members.aol.com/jwt251 internet
Instruments taught: Clarinet, Saxophone.
Teaches 1 to 1.
Workshops: small and large groups. Runs secondary school age Big Band.
Schools: for 12-16 hours per week. Adults. London Borough of Haringey.
Qualifications: LGSM (has been teaching for 5-10 years). Includes improvisation.
Other style(s): popular music, classical.
Has taught in Harringay schools for 6 years. Introduces students to jazz at an early stage as part of a broad musical education. Encourages improvisation at all levels.

Tompson, Mike
(South East)
17 York Road, Brentford TW8 0QP
020 8568 4517 home tel
Instruments taught: Alto Sax, Tenor Sax.
Teaches 1 to 1. Age(s): 11 to 16, 17 plus. Area(s): reading, beginners, some knowledge. Place(s): pupil's home.
Private tuition using Jamie Aebersold tapes as basis for students to gain confidence in improvising. "I have been playing Jazz since the late 1960s (Blues, Standards, Latin, Jazz-rock etc) in a semi-professional capacity. I teach basic chords, scales and notes. I encourage students to jam with me, to use play-along CD's and to listen extensively to historic jazz performances"

Toussaint, Jean
(London)
Ground Floor Flat, 50 Crouch Hall Road, London N8 8HG
020 8347 8355 tel/fax, 07973 821 462, jtoussaint@bigfoot.com
Instruments taught: Saxophone.
Teaches 1 to 1. Age(s): 17 plus. Area(s): some knowledge, refresher, coaching.
Place(s): own home.
Workshops: usually small groups. Previously Jamey Aebersold (London), Glamorgan (Wales), Jordanstown University (Northern Ireland), Guildhall Sschool of Music and Drama, Jazz Rock and Studio Music, Summerr school (London). Currently Guildhall School of Music and Drama (London). Specialisation - Small band coaching, Theory and Harmony, Schools: for 4-8 hours per week. HE/FE, adults (21+).
Qualifications: Teach solely from professional experience (has been teaching for 10-15 years). Includes improvisation. Other style(s): popular music, other (jazz improvisation as applied to popular music).
Currently on the teaching staff at Guildhall School of Music and Drama (Jazz dept.) and the Studio Music Summer School. Also has private students. 'I know the value of a good teacher. Art Blakey taught me more in five years than I would have learnt in 10 or more without him. It was an amazing experience. I have tried to pass some of that on as a part time professor at the Guildhall School of Music and the Studio Music Summer School. My main focus is on performing, composing and recording. However, I am committed to also sharing that experience with a number of serious students willing to work hard."

Trahan, Linda
(Scotland)
Littlewood Cottage, Craigearn, By Kemnay
01467 643 490, 0777 998 5744 mobile
Instruments taught: Piano.
Teaches 1 to 1. Teaches Associated Board Piano Exam. Age(s): 17 plus. Area(s):
reading, beginners, some knowledge, refresher. Place(s): own home, other (Music
School). Schools: Primary (5-11), secondary (11-16), adults (21+).
Qualifications: ALCM; ICMA; Diploma in jazz at St Andrews University. (Has been
teaching for 1-2 years). Includes improvisation.
" Jazz music is my personal favourite! I have several pupils who have been taking
Associated Board Jazz grades, all have been successful."

Treiger, Norman
(London)
42 Holders Hill Avenue, Hendon, London NW4 1ET
020 8203 0718 home tel
Instruments taught: Piano.
Teaches 1 to 1. Age(s): under 11, 11 to 16, 17 plus. Area(s): reading, beginners,
some knowledge, coaching. Place(s): pupil's home.
Several years playing experience. Composes music. Ability to nuture talent in student and increase the level of talent and skill through his tuition.

Trevett, Julie
(South West)
2 Milton Mead, West Milton, Bridport DT6 3SQ
01308 485319, julie@rcussons.freeserve.co.uk
Instruments taught: Clarinet, Flute, Saxophone.
Teaches 1 to 1. Teaches Associated Board Piano Exam. Age(s): under 11, 11 to 16,
17 plus. Area(s): reading, beginners, some knowledge, refresher. Place(s): own
home.
Workshops: usually small groups, large groups. Speciality area(s): large groups,
classes (20+), tertiary. Previously and currently, 'Rubbish Band' Workshops -
Exeter University, and local schools and colleges. Specialisation - Jazz improvisa-
tion, Music and Dance, Rhythm Work.
Schools: for 16+ hours per week. HE/FE, adults (21+).
Qualifications: GDLM, LTCL (has been teaching for 10-15 years). Includes improvisation. Other style(s): popular music, classical, world music.
Runs workshops (approx 1 a month) on Free Jazz, percussion, samba, learner jazz.
"I focus on the individual and the confidence required to succeed with jazz improvi-
sation. I feel it is important to let everyone proceed at their own speed and give
them the right techniques to progress with confidence."

Trott, Malcolm
(East Midlands)
16 Crossley Close, Barrow on Soar LE12 8QL
01509 412984, 0589 815032 home fax
Instruments taught: Saxophone, Flute, Clarinet.
Teaches 1 to 1.
Qualifications: ATC Teaching Certificate (has been teaching for 10-15 years).
Includes improvisation. Other style(s): popular music, classical.

Tunley, Sarah
(Wales)

Steynton Road, Milford Haven SA73 1AE
Instruments taught: Piano.
Workshops: usually small groups, large groups, classes (20+). Speciality area(s): secondary.
Schools: for 16+ hours per week. secondary (11-16).
Qualifications: B.Ed (Hons) Music. (Has been teaching for 10-15 year. Includes improvisation. Other style(s): popular music.

Veltmeijer, Angele
(London)

Leyton, London E10 6EE
07973 334578, angelevelt@hotmail.com
Instruments taught: Midi Vibes, Woodwind, Keyboards.
Workshops: usually small groups.
Schools: for 8-12 hours per week. secondary (11-16), adults (21+).
Qualifications: Cert. Ed.. (Has been teaching for 15-20 year. Includes improvisation. Other style(s): popular music, world music.
Many years of experience of teaching woodwind. Teaches Intermediate Sax at Lewisham Academy, Composition and Midi sequencing at Tower Hamlets secondary school, Jazz at the City Lit.

Vergette, Marcus
(South West)

Coombe Farm, Highampton, Beaworthy EX21 5LJ
01837 810349 home tel
Instruments taught: Double Bass.
Teaches 1 to 1.
Qualifications: 20 years experience playing. (Has been teaching for 3-5 year. Includes improvisation.

Vicari, Andrea
(London)

212 Sherwood Avenue, Streatham Vale, London SW16 5EF
020 8764 6478 tel/fax, 07985 432255 mobile
a.vicari@talk21.com, www.jazzschool-dordogne.co.uk
Instruments taught: Piano.
Teaches 1 to 1. Teaches Associated Board Piano Exam. Age(s): under 11, 11 to 16, 17 plus. Area(s): reading, beginners, some knowledge, refresher, coaching. Place(s): own home.
Workshops: usually small groups, large groups, classes (20+).
Schools: for 16+ hours per week. pre-school, primary (5-11), secondary (11-16), HE/FE, adults (21+).
Qualifications: B.Mus/ P.G.C.E..
Teaches at Chelmsford Jazz Summer School and is Head of Jazz Studies on Pimlico School's special music course. Course director at Dordoyne Summer School

Wade, Tim
(South East)

2 St Paul Street, Brighton BN2 3HR
07711 963785, tbone@orange.net
www.rockin-in-rhythm.freeserve.co.uk
Instruments taught: Trombone.
Teaches 1 to 1. Age(s): under 11, 11 to 16, 17 plus. Area(s): reading, beginners, some knowledge, refresher.
Qualifications: GSND, Pdip (Jazz).
Graduate of the Guildhall School of Music, Tim teaches jazz trombone and improvisation. He also gives arranging classes and coaches the trombones at Brighton Youth Orchestra.

Wain, Janet
(East Midlands)

Access to Music, 18 York Road, Leicester LE1 5TS
info@access-to-music.co.uk, www.access-to-music.co.uk
Instruments taught: Keyboards.
Teaches 1 to 1.
Workshops: usually small groups.
Schools: for 1-4 hours per week. Primary (5-11). St Mary's School, Market Weighton.
(Has been teaching for 3-5 year. Includes improvisation.
Runs workshops 2 hours a week small group, fun times in school. 1 morning a week workshops over the Summer holidays for beginners 7 -15 years.

Waite, Glenn
(North West)

c/o Central Music Centre, Redgate, Formby L37 4EW
sefmss@rmplc.co.uk
Instruments taught: Bass Guitar, Tuba.
Workshops: One off workshops at Chesterfield High School and Birkdale Primary School.
Schools: Primary (5-11), secondary (11-16), HE/FE.
Qualifications: GHSM ARCM and PGCE. (Has been teaching for over 20 year. Includes improvisation. Other style(s): classical.
"I aim to encourage and enable young musicians to express themselves in the jazz language."

Waithe, Keith
(London)

20 Cantley Road, Hanwell, London W7 2BQ
020 8840 2831, 020 8992 2151 fax, 0776968 4638 mobile
keith.waithe4@virgin.net, www.keithwaithe.com
Instruments taught: Voice, Flute.
Qualifications: LRSM and PGCEA. (Has been teaching for over 20 year. Includes improvisation. Other style(s): world music.

Walker, Crosby
(Eastern)
30 The Hoe, Carpenders Park, Watford WD1 5AY
020 8428 7043 home tel
Instruments taught: Guitar, Bass Guitar, Keyboards.
Qualifications: None. (Has been teaching for 3-5 year. Includes improvisation.
Other style(s): classical, world music, other (Blues/Soul/Country).
Workshops to A Level music students in Jazz, Improvisation, Rock and Soul.
Individual tuition for Guitar. Was a full time teacher. Worked with Joe Loss organisation for 20 years.

Walkington, Julie
(London)
94 Palatine Road, London N16 8ST
020 7923 4994, 07966 540946 mobile
Instruments taught: Double Bass.
Area(s): beginners, some knowledge. Place(s): own home.
Workshops: Until recently was teaching with Adrian York on the Jazz FM workshops in a variety of schools. Taught at the Glamorgan Summer school in 2002..
She was a student at the Guildhall under leadership of Scott Stroman and occasionally attended jazz workshops led by Eddie Harvey and Frank Griffiths. Tutored on Cathy Stobart's Jazz Weekend, and attended as a student on Glamorgan Jazz Summer School led by Simon Purcell and Dave Wickens. Tutored amateur Big Band rhythm section for a CD recording.

Wallen, Byron
(London)
42 Commonwealth Way, Abbey Wood, London SE2 0JZ
07961 306627, byronwallen@aol.com, www.byronwallen.com
Instruments taught: Percussion, Trumpet.
Teaches 1 to 1. Age(s): 11 to 16, 17 plus. Area(s): beginners, some knowledge.
Place(s): own home, pupil's home.
Byron runs three different types of workshops. 1: Gamelan Workshops - these begin with teaching children pieces by memory and then showing them the structure and eventually the notation system. The number of students can vary from 4 to 16. Once the students have a general idea of the music they will be introduced to the more specialised, complex instruments such as the bonang, rebab (fiddle) and the suling flute. This will lead naturally into creative improvisation within the Gamelan. 2: Jazz and Improvisation workshops for all instrumentalists and vocalists. The jazz workshops are pitched at the level of the participants. At the most basic level, ear training, scale and chord combinations are covered. Following on from this, musicians will have the opportunity to develop listening and group playing skills. As well as the standard jazz repertoire, pupils are encouraged to write their own melodic lines and tunes that will be a vehicle for improvisation. 3: The workshops concentrate on the polyphonic interlocking xylophone music of the Bugandan and Basogan peoples of Uganda. The "Amadinda" orchestra consists of a large xylophone played by four people, three drums, a set of four panpipes and a vocalist. The amadinda provides the foundation of the musical activity, the other instruments reinforce this. Also explores the horn music of th Alur peoples of Nebbi in North West Uganda. This comprises five to twenty horns.

Walmsley, Beryl
(Wales)

2 Gwaun Coed, Brackla, Bridgend CF31 2HS
01656 680091 home tel
Instruments taught: Piano.
Teaches 1 to 1. Teaches Associated Board Piano Exam. Age(s): under 11, 11 to 16, 17 plus. Area(s): reading, beginners, some knowledge, refresher, coaching.
Place(s): own home.
"Lessons are fun, friendly, relaxed and encouraging."

Walter, John
(South West)

1 Magdalene Close, Totnes TQ9 5TQ
01803 864 538, john@drumcrazy.co.uk
www.drumcrazy.co.uk
Instruments taught: Piano, African Drums.
Workshops: usually large groups, classes (20+). Speciality area(s): large groups, classes (20+), primary, secondary, adult. Runs one-off workshops in schools, businesses etc. Around 20 per month..
Schools: for 16+ hours per week. pre-school, primary (5-11), secondary (11-16), HE/FE, adults (21+), special needs.
Qualifications: BEd. (Has been teaching for over 20 year. Includes improvisation.
Other style(s): world music.
Teaches 2 African drumming workshops a week in schools in Cornwall, Devon and Somerset. Specialisation is in percussion, bass and improvisation at all levels for very large groups "If you had an event with 500 people involved I would get them all drumming together - no limits" 'DrumCrazy' runs drum circles in school, conferences, festivals and community events. We work with groups of 30 - 200 at a time. The material is not culturally specific. We break down the barrier between audience and performer - everyone has fun."

Ward, Chris
(London)

c/o 8 Grove Road, Leytonstone, London E11 3AN
09758 407229 mobile
Instruments taught: Piano.
Teaches 1 to 1. Teaches Associated Board Piano Exam. Age(s): under 11, 11 to 16, 17 plus. Area(s): reading, beginners, refresher. Place(s): pupil's home.
Qualifications: BA Hons Music. (Has been teaching for 3-5 year. Includes improvisation. Other style(s): popular music, classical.
"I teach the student to recognise chord shapes with relevant terminology. The student can eventually play partially from music and by ear/charts."

Watkins, Michael
(East Midlands)

4 Reynard Way, Northampton NN2 8QX
reynard@argonet.co.uk, www.argonet.co.uk/users/reynard/ internet
Instruments taught: Saxophone, Clarinet, Bass Clarinet.
Qualifications: Open University Diploma. (Has been teaching for 1-2 year. Includes

improvisation. Other style(s): classical.

Alongside his musical training he brings experience of his management consultant work Occupational Therapy. He encourages and guides ensemble playing for adult developers. Organises musical playing events for amateurs with professional tutors - see courses. Has published music for the clarinet, saxophone and wind ensembles.

Watson, Andy
(Eastern)

64 Hill View Road, Chelmsford CM1 5RX

01245 258262 tel/fax

Instruments taught: Guitar.

Teaches 1 to 1. Age(s): 11 to 16, 17 plus. Area(s): reading, beginners, some knowledge, refresher, coaching. Place(s): own home.

Workshops: Previously, at St Andrews University Jazz Performance Summer School/Kent Music school Summer Jazz course/Numerous workshops around the UK for Arts Council of Great Britain and Local Education Authorities. Currently, Jazz Performance/Harlow College, Essex. Specialisation Improvisation Skills /Ensemble Playing skills/rhythm section. Schools: HE/FE, adults (21+).

Qualifications: ARCM, GDLM, PGCE.

Lecturer in jazz guitar at Leeds College of music. Teaches improvisation at Bretton Hall College/Harlow College. "I have a well developed method for teaching improvisation to musicians of all ages and abilities who have had little or no previous experience in this area. I have a substantial track record of professional performance experience as well as in solo and group teaching in schools and colleges from secondary to HE degree level."

Watson, Pete
(London)

338 Devon Mansions, Tooley Street, London SE1 2XQ

020 7207 0685, 07768 437154, pjnwatson@aol.com

Instruments taught: Accordion, Piano.

Teaches 1 to 1. Teaches Associated Board Piano Exam. Place(s): own home, pupil's home, other (schools).

Workshops: Jazz Umbrella workshops (see separate entry).

Includes improvisation.

Webb, John
(South East)

17 Panters, Hextable BR8 7RW

01322 664 947, 07941 386 357 mobile

Instruments taught: Drums.

Teaches 1 to 1. Age(s): under 11, 11 to 16, 17 plus. Area(s): reading, beginners, some knowledge, refresher. Place(s): pupil's home.

Schools: for 8-12 hours per week. secondary (11-16). Emanuel School and John Paul II school.

(Has been teaching for over 20 year. Includes improvisation. Other style(s): popular music.

Joined ILEA (Inner London Education Authority) Panel 1977. In the past has taught with Graham Collier on various Jazz Summer Courses.

Webb, Robert
(London)

70 Culverden Road, London SW12 9LS

020 8675 0335, webbmadd@britishlibrary.net

Instruments taught: Keyboards, Piano.

Teaches 1 to 1. Teaches Associated Board Piano Exam.

Workshops: usually small groups, large groups. Specialises in groups at Primary age and one-to-one at Secondary and upward. JazzULearn; Cat's Cradle Music School.

Schools: for 12-16 hours per week. Primary (5-11), secondary (11-16), adults (21+). Top Note Music School; JazzULearn; Cat's Cradle Music School.

Qualifications: Mmus (Surrey); BMus (Hons) (Lond) ISM registered teacher. (Has been teaching for over 20 year. Includes improvisation. Other style(s): popular music, classical, world music.

"I converted several young private keyboard pupils to the Jazz Piano syllabus in 1998. I founded the Jazz Piano Teachers' Association and have attended all major London workshops and seminars over the past year. My original jazz education came from Amancio Da Silva with whom I studied jazz guitar. Gave practical presentations for the ISM on Jazz Piano

Webster, David
(South East)

42 Alberta Road, Bush Hill Park, Enfield EN1 1JB

020 8357 9925 tel/fax, 077 74 605543, dave.webster2@virgin.net

Instruments taught: Drums.

Teaches 1 to 1. Age(s): under 11, 11 to 16, 17 plus. Area(s): reading, beginners, some knowledge, coaching. Place(s): own home, pupil's home.

Workshops: At school runs the School Big Band and Salsa group.

Schools: secondary (11-16).

Teaching in schools and examining for Guildhall School of Music and Drama. "I believe that when teaching an instrument you need a good cross section of styles, to be able to cross reference the whole musical field - in understanding jazz, you can also understand blues, funk, swing, and latin."

Weinreb, Paul
(London)

117 Mortimer Road, London NW10 5TN

07976 968 398, weinrebtarantula@aol.com

Instruments taught: Guitar, Piano.

Teaches 1 to 1. Age(s): 11 to 16, 17 plus. Area(s): beginners, some knowledge, refresher. Place(s): own home, pupil's home.

He is currently playing guitar with Claude Deppa's Five Funcky Fellas and Piano/Keyboards in 'African Jazz Explosion'

Weldon, Nick
(London)

24 Ryland Road, London NW5 3EA

020 7284 0226 tel/fax, 0797 140 9596 mobile

nick@jazzpiano.co.uk, www.weldon.demon.co.uk

Instruments taught: Piano.
Teaches 1 to 1. Age(s): 17 plus. Area(s): some knowledge, coaching. Place(s): own home.
Workshops: Previously at Wavendon Summer School - Beginners, Improvisation, Rhythm section. Bude Summer School, Glamorgan. Currently Wavendon Summer School. Specialisation - Group playing for all levels of ability, band coaching, specialist days for singers and for pianists. www.jazzschool.co.uk.
Schools: HE/FE, adults (21+).
As well as taking private students he is widely experienced in jazz workshops for all levels having had a long involvement with Wavendon All Music Plan, both as director of the Beginners Improvisation course and as a member of the Summer School teaching team. "I believe teaching to be an important part of the life of a musician. It is equally important to keep teaching in balance with playing. I have long and wide experience in passing on the jazz idiom, but I continue to flourish as a very active player on the British jazz scene. It is because of this balance that I teach effectively."

Wellard, Gordon
(London)
109a Victoria Park Road, Hackney, London E9 7JJ
020 8533 0851 home tel
Instruments taught: Drums.
Schools: Supply teaching at Primary schools covering jazz styles through nursery rhymes using a puppet.

Wetton, Carol
(West Midlands)
13 Baylie St, Stourbridge DY8 1AZ
01384 371859 home tel
Instruments taught: Piano.
Teaches 1 to 1. Teaches Associated Board Piano Exam. Age(s): under 11, 11 to 16, 17 plus. Area(s): reading, beginners, some knowledge. Place(s): other ().
Workshops: Group teaching at Rainbow Music Centre, Cradley Heath, West Midlands. (Pupils attend one hour per week) following AB Jazz Piano syllabus. Jazz Ensemble workshops. Specialisation - Improving performance and improvisation skills.
Schools: pre-school, primary (5-11), secondary (11-16), HE/FE.
"The Rainbow Music Centre aims to provide excellence in music education for all and jazz classes have become a popular and enriching part of the general syllabus. I do not claim to be a great jazz performer - I am self-taught from 'Jazz Piano from Scratch' but my students have achieved excellent results in AB Jazz piano and ensemble exams."

Whitehead, Tim
(South East)
5 Willowbank, Ham, Richmond TW10 7QY
020 8948 0687, 020 8948 3632 home fax
www.timwhitehead.co.uk
Instruments taught: Alto Sax, Tenor Sax.
Teaches 1 to 1. Age(s): 11 to 16, 17 plus. Area(s): reading, beginners, some knowledge, refresher. Place(s): own home.
Workshops: usually 1 to 1, small groups.

(Has been teaching for 15-20 year. Includes improvisation.
Currently teaches Intermediate and Advanced saxophone classes at the Weekend
Arts College (WAC) on a Sunday. Occasional visiting tutor at Trinity College. Has
composed two tunes for the Associated Boards' new jazz horn exams (launched
summer 2003) Previously has taught at Brunel University and run jazz workshop
for L.B. Hounslow

Whittaker, John
(Scotland)

48 Gartymore, Helmsdale
014312 821380 tel/fax
Instruments taught: Trumpet, Trombone.
Schools: Primary (5-11), secondary (11-16), adults (21+).
Qualifications: ARMCM (has been teaching for over 20 years). Other style(s): world
music.
As a jazz tutor I try to interest my pupils as someone would who has an interest in
jazz.

Wilding, Adele
(London)

07831 798 308 mobile
awilding@ukonline.co.uk, www.wildingandco.pwp.blueyonder.co.uk
Instruments taught: Voice.
Teaches 1 to 1. Age(s): 17 plus. Area(s): reading, beginners, some knowledge,
coaching. Place(s): own home, pupil's home.
Workshops: Previous workshops have included:- 'Introduction to Modal
Improvisation' Goldsmiths College - guest tutor for Louise Gibbs; 'Modal and Blues
Improvisation' Hertfordshire Youth Jazz Ensemble, St Albans Music School; 'Jazz
and Popular Singing Masterclasses' South Herts secondary schools, 'Introduction to
jazz vocal techniques and Improvisation' (Inset); 'Basic Approaches to Gospel
singing and Improvisation', Herts County Youth Choir. Specialisation - jazz based
techniques for singing and improvisation in jazz and other popular music styles,
use of modes in improvisation and performance techniques.
Schools: secondary (11-16), HE/FE, adults (21+). Peripatetic teacher.
"One important feature of my teaching is the use of 'modes' in improvisation.
Despite the explicit use of modes in traditional/folk and modal jazz styles, I feel
that modes are not fully exploited in mainstream music making. My modal
approach therefore introduces singers and musicians to the process of improvisation, in a relaxed and progressive manner. In addition to jazz, I relate improvisation to other popular styles, including pop, rock, Rhythm and Blues, Gospel and
Soul. As these styles are fundamentally jazz based, I feel that it is important to
inform pupils of this fact". Has recently contributed to curriculum developement in
Vocal Improvisation for the Federation of Music Services.

Willan, Eric
(East Midlands)

Access to Music, 18 York Road, Leicester LE1 5TS
info@access-to-music.co.uk, www.access-to-music.co.uk
Instruments taught: Trumpet.
Qualifications: LTCL, FTCC, Cert. Ed. (has been teaching for over 20 years).
Includes improvisation. Other style(s): popular music.

Williams, Ceri
(Wales)

94 Maple Road South, Sebastopol, Griffithstown, Pontypool NP4 5AR
01495 756020, 0779 010 5398 mobile
ceriwilliams@ceriwilliams.fsnet.co.uk
Instruments taught: Trumpet.
Teaches 1 to 1. Age(s): under 11, 11 to 16, 17 plus. Area(s): reading, beginners, some knowledge, refresher. Place(s): own home.
Workshops: Has organised with workshop with Lillian Boutte..
Currently in his 3rd year of a part time Masters degree (University of Wales) in teaching Special Needs and is developing some software to be used to produce either aural or visual effects for those with limited mobility.

Williams, Gareth
(London)

407 City View House, 463 Bethnal Green Road, Bethnal Green, London E2 9QY
020 7613 5254, 07931 341917, thetafia@aol.com
Instruments taught: Piano.
Teaches 1 to 1. Teaches Associated Board Piano Exam. Age(s): 11 to 16, 17 plus. Area(s): refresher.
Has taught at Jackson Lane Community Centre on jazz courses and summer school. GCSE tuition in schools.

Williams, Geoff
(South East)

84 Overdale, Ashtead KT21 1PU
01372 272170 home tel
Instruments taught: Piano.
Teaches 1 to 1. Teaches Associated Board Piano Exam. Age(s): 11 to 16, 17 plus. Area(s): reading, beginners, some knowledge, refresher, coaching. Place(s): own home.
Schools: secondary (11-16), HE/FE, adults (21+).
"As a professional performer over many years, I can offer practical experience as well as my natural enthusiasm for music."

Williams, John
(West Midlands)

Leasowes Bank Farm, Ratlinghope, Shrewsbury SY5 0SW
01743 790769 tel/fax, 07712 762 436 mobile
john@leasowes.freeserve.co.uk
Instruments taught: Bass Clarinet, Recorder, Saxophone.
Age(s): 11 to 16, 17 plus. Area(s): reading, beginners, some knowledge. Place(s): other ().
Workshops: Previously Advanced Jazz workshops for ILEA (1969 - 1983) Moberley Youth Centre. MU workshops at Bracknell International jazz Festival 1975/84. Currently Shropshire Youth Jazz Ensemble, (formed 1995 with Christine Bolton), Church Stretton School..
Schools: HE/FE, adults (21+).
(Has been teaching for over 20 years). Includes improvisation.
Directed masterclasses at Leeds, Salford, Marlborough Colleges, Westminster and Shrewsbury Schools. "My wide experience as composer, arranger, saxophonist and

MD extends beyond the jazz field and enables me to direct ensembles of varying instrumentation that include what some consider to be 'non jazz' instruments. As co-leader of the Shropshire Youth Jazz Ensemble I ensure that no one is excluded because their instrument 'doesn't fit'. This is demonstrated by the current line-up of flute, oboe, 4 clarinets, 7 saxophones, 2 trombones, violin and rhythm. The ensemble's flexible instrumentation has far more relevance today than the traditional 'Big Band' formula and is a response to the instruments that young people are actually playing."

Williams, Kate
(London)
17 Helena Road, London NW10 1HY
020 8450 9412 tel/fax, kw@kate-williams-quartet.com
www.kate-williams-quartet.com
Instruments taught: Piano.
Teaches 1 to 1. Teaches Associated Board Piano Exam. Age(s): under 11, 11 to 16, 17 plus. Area(s): reading, beginners, some knowledge, refresher, coaching.
Place(s): own home, pupil's home.
Qualifications: LGSM in Jazz teaching.
Private tuition since 1988. Has given jazz workshops for all ages including students at University of East Anglia. "Being trained in classical music and jazz means that I can be of particular use to students with some experience of classical playing who want to learn jazz. I have been teaching piano for 10 years."

Williams, May
(Wales)
St Michael House, St Michael Road, Abergavenny NP7 5AY
01873 855592, mayzmusik@yahoo.co.uk
Instruments taught: Piano, Keyboards.
Workshops: Started an adult jazz workshop.

Williams, Paul
(Eastern)
CIMA, The Old School, Ermine Street North, Papworth Everard
07788 834784, CIMA@educationcamcntygov.uk
Instruments taught: Piano.
Teaches 1 to 1. Teaches Associated Board Piano Exam. Age(s): under 11, 11 to 16, 17 plus. Area(s): reading, beginners, some knowledge, refresher, coaching.
Place(s): own home.
Workshops: Groups to prepare for Associated Board exams or coaching for gigs.
Schools: Mainly teach at Cambridgeshire Music School (based at Chesterton Community College, Gilbert Road, Cambridge).

Williams, Peter
(South West)
4 Christopher Drive, Chippenham SM15 3UT
01249 652248, 07930 420456 mobile
Instruments taught: Keyboards, Piano.

Williamson, Steve
(London)
7 Sutton Square, Urswick Road, London E9 6EQ
020 8985 3353 tel/fax
Instruments taught: Soprano Sax, Tenor Sax, Alto Sax.
Teaches 1 to 1. Age(s): under 11, 11 to 16. Area(s): reading, beginners, some knowledge, refresher, coaching. Place(s): own home.

Willmott, Peter
(North West)
71 Woburn Drive, Hale, Altrincham WA15 8NE
0161 980 3381 home tel
Instruments taught: Bass Guitar, Double Bass.
Teaches 1 to 1. Age(s): 11 to 16, 17 plus. Area(s): reading, beginners, some knowledge, refresher. Place(s): own home.
" Very wide experience of all types of professional music making over 30 years including the BBC Philharmonic (28 years) dance and Big Bands, jazz, pop, cabaret, asian fusion, celtic, rock and funk, which has equipped me to teach to the highest of standards. I also compose, arrange and produce."

Wilson, Jeffrey
(Eastern)
5 Church Green, Boreham Village, Chelmsford CM3 3EH
01245 450192 home tel
Instruments taught: Clarinet, Piano, Saxophone.
Teaches 1 to 1. Age(s): under 11, 11 to 16, 17 plus. Area(s): reading, beginners, some knowledge, refresher, coaching. Place(s): own home.
Workshops: Group individual improvisation and composition skills. Cornwall Music Services for Guildhall School and 2 local schools in Amiens France. Teach improvisation and composition class 'environ music' in Chelmsford. Runs workshops (1 per month) at Havering Music School, Guildhall School, National Association of Music Schools: Primary (5-11), secondary (11-16), HE/FE, adults (21+). Utrecht Conservatorium 3500 BM Utrecht Holland : Derek Rodgers Department of Initial Studies, Guildhall School of Music.
Qualifications: GRSM (Hons). (Has been teaching for 15-20 years.) Includes improvisation. Other style(s): popular music, classical.
Has taught at Junior Guildhall since '94. Studied with John Lambert and Herbert Howells at the Royal College and later with Gordon Jacob and Oliver Messiaen. Lectures in composition and improvisation at the Utrecht Conservatorium, Holland. Enjoys the experience of learnng and sharing in the art of music.

Wilson, Paul
(North West)
41 Phillimore Street, Lees, Oldham OL4 5B2
0161 652 2590, 0161 620 3901 fax, p.wilson@zen.co.uk
Instruments taught: Piano.
Teaches 1 to 1. Teaches Associated Board Piano Exam. Age(s): under 11, 11 to 16, 17 plus. Area(s): reading, beginners, some knowledge, refresher, coaching. Place(s): own home. "Three of my academic qualifications have had a jazz component (my particular area of interest is in the fusion of jazz elements into other styles). I teach the ABRSM piano syllabus and in addition have influenced several pupils for other jazz exams. So far all have gained distinctions or merit."

Wood, Fiona
(North East)
53 Teesdale Avenue, Penshaw DH4 7JA
0191 385 5144, 07967 530 776 mobile
Instruments taught: Clarinet, Trumpet, Piano.
Teaches 1 to 1. Teaches Associated Board Piano Exam. Age(s): under 11, 11 to 16, 17 plus. Area(s): reading, beginners, some knowledge. Place(s): own home, pupil's home, other ().
Workshops: usually small groups.
Schools: for 16+ hours per week. Primary (5-11), secondary (11-16), adults (21+).
(Has been teaching for 5-10 years). Includes improvisation.
Teaches at North East Music Academy (the only one in Sunderland) which covers all aspects of music. Jazz sector started in 2000.

Wood, James
(Scotland)
17 Glen Lyon Road, Kirkcaldy
01592 641031, 07779 829 114 mobile
Instruments taught: Keyboards, Piano.
Teaches 1 to 1. Teaches Associated Board Piano Exam. Age(s): under 11, 11 to 16, 17 plus. Area(s): reading, beginners, some knowledge, refresher. Place(s): own home.
Qualifications: LTCL (Classical) (has been teaching for 10-15 years). Includes improvisation. Other style(s): popular music.
"I mainly teaching classical piano. I don't consider myself a jazz educator. I have always had a personal love of jazz and have studied various courses on my own. I teach a handful of my pupils jazz, alongside their classical or pop if they express an interest in it. I Play in a jazz funk band and have experience in live performance and improvisation. Have put two pupils through the Associated Board Grade 5 jazz exams both of whom achieved a distinction".

Wood, Stephen
(South West)
10 Treveson Road, Pool, Redruth TR15 3PQ
01209 612 635 home tel
Instruments taught: Keyboards, Piano.
Teaches 1 to 1. Teaches Associated Board Piano Exam. Age(s): under 11, 11 to 16, 17 plus. Area(s): reading, beginners, some knowledge, refresher, coaching. Place(s): own home, other ().
Workshops: Speciality area(s): 1 to 1. Summer Jazz workshops at St Michael's School, Truro, Cornwall usually held July/Aug for 6 weeks.
Schools: for 8-12 hours per week. Primary (5-11), secondary (11-16), HE/FE, adults (21+).
Qualifications: Grade VIII Piano. (Has been teaching for 15-20 years.) Includes improvisation. Other style(s): classical.
"Experience as a professional musician in the '60s and '70s in Jazz Rock/Ethnic music scene. Composer of jazz and 'serious music'. An interest in the diversity of improvisational styles especially soloists and 'cross-over' music."

Woodhead, John
(West Midlands)
Finbrook, Dalehouse Lane, Kenilworth CV8 2JZ
024 7641 8150 tel/fax, 07710 215916
Instruments taught: Keyboards, Piano.
Teaches 1 to 1.
Qualifications: 50 years musicianship (has been teaching for 5-10 years). Includes improvisation. Other style(s): popular music.
Many years teaching jazz piano and harmony. Also assists at several schools on jazz syllabus.

Woods, Tony
(South East)
73 Isobel House, Staines Road West, Sunbury on Thames TW16 7BD
01932 780657, 07979 805454, towoods@lineone.net
Instruments taught: Clarinet, Saxophone.
Teaches 1 to 1. Age(s): under 11, 11 to 16, 17 plus. Area(s): reading, beginners, some knowledge, refresher, coaching. Place(s): own home, pupil's home, other ().
Workshops: Past workshops have included - schools in Sunbury for Spelthorne Borough; weekly workshops in Staines Old Town Hall. Current workshops for JAGZ (Jazz Club, Ascot) on Monday nights and Jazz Saxophone classes at Richmond Adult Education College. Specialisation - basic theory and developing ideas e.g. Motif development.
Schools: secondary (11-16), HE/FE, adults (21+).
Qualifications: GDLCM; LGSM (has been teaching for 10-15 years). Includes improvisation. Other style(s): classical, world music.
"As well as a strong love of the jazz tradition, I am fascinated by classical and folk musics from around the world. I'm sure this influences my teaching. I believe everyone has "something to say" and I try to bring out this creativity in the individual. All students need to work on technique, scales and harmony, but I also tend to stress the importance of rhythmic work."

Wyness, James
(Scotland)
8 Commercial Street, Edinburgh EX6 6JA
0131 5531617 tel/fax, egs.jimi@which.net
Instruments taught: Guitar.
Teaches 1 to 1. Age(s): under 11, 11 to 16, 17 plus. Area(s): reading, beginners, some knowledge, refresher. Place(s): own home.
Workshops: Previously ran the Belfast Jazz Workshop in the 90's. Specialisation - general ensemble skills..
"I run my own guitar teaching studio and have done for several years. I compose and play professionally and have a good knowledge of most musical idioms, including a working knowledge of electronic music. I have reliable working methods for teaching jazz guitar."

Yeboah, Kwame
(London)
Unit 2, Charles Despard Avenue, Battersea, London SW8
020 8510 0408, 0793 923 6635, kwameyeboah@hotmail.com
Instruments taught: Percussion, Piano.

York, Adrian
(South East)
25 Marksbury Avenue, Kew TW9 4JE
020 8878 3102, 020 8255 3105 fax, 07770 348 293 mobile
adrian-york@compuserve.com
Instruments taught: Keyboards, Piano.
Teaches 1 to 1. Age(s): 11 to 16, 17 plus. Area(s): reading, beginners, some knowledge, refresher, coaching. Place(s): own home, other (Jazz workshops in schools for Jazz FM).
Schools: secondary (11-16), HE/FE.
"With my background as a musical director I can enable students to develop their sense of time, rhythmic skills, inter-ensemble interplay, use of dynamics, improvisation skills and other performance related criteria. As a piano tutor I assess each student's skill levels and develop an educational package to enable them to become competent and creative".

York, Clive
(London)
72 North Hill, Highgate, London N6 4RH
07977 978542, clive@cliveyork.ssnet.co.uk
Instruments taught: Saxophone, Flugel Horn, Clarinet.
Teaches 1 to 1. Age(s): under 11, 11 to 16, 17 plus. Area(s): beginners, some knowledge, refresher, coaching. Place(s): own home, pupil's home.
"I am very relaxed and easy going. I have excellent communication skills. I can teach the very basics to a beginner or advanced theory/practice to an advanced player. I am a player who teaches rather than a teacher who plays, so as well as qualifications, I have a wealth of experience and can put technical details and ideas across in 'user friendly' terms."

Young, Jeffrey
(South East)
12 Henley Street, Oxford OX4 1ER
01865 245885, 078661 93320 mobile
Instruments taught: Piano.
Teaches 1 to 1. Teaches Associated Board Piano Exam. Age(s): under 11, 11 to 16, 17 plus. Area(s): reading, beginners, some knowledge, refresher. Place(s): own home.
Schools: secondary (11-16). Gothill House, Nr Abingdon Oxon OX13 6JL (Summerfields,Summertown Oxford).
Qualifications: Welsh College of Music and Drama - Grade 8. (Has been teaching for 15-20 years.) Includes improvisation. Other style(s): popular music, classical.
"I have been trained classically but perform improvised jazz regularly. This gives me a good knowledge of techniques and harmony and how to apply them in a practical way. It also allows for a flexible approach, whether teaching a child beginner or a classically trained adult wishing to try jazz."

Zakian, Laura
(London)
22 Bousfield Road, New Cross, London SE14 5TR
laurazakian@netscape.com, www.laurazakian.com
Instruments taught: Voice.
Teaches 1 to 1.
Workshops: usually small groups, large groups, classes (20+).
Schools: for 16+ hours per week. HE/FE, adults (21+).
Qualifications: Music Tutor training skills - Community Music (has been teaching for 5-10 years). Includes improvisation. Other style(s): popular music, classical.

Zegelaar, Art
(North West)
50 Devonshire Road, Liverpool L8 3TZ
0151 727 2593, art@artsound.com, www.artsound.com
Instruments taught: Piano.
Teaches 1 to 1. Teaches Associated Board Piano Exam. Age(s): under 11, 11 to 16, 17 plus. Area(s): reading, beginners, some knowledge, refresher, coaching.
Place(s): own home, other (ArtSound Music School).
Workshops: Speciality area(s): adult. Music Theory.
Schools: for 16+ hours per week. Primary (5-11), secondary (11-16), HE/FE.
Qualifications: ATCL Diploma in Music LTCL (Teaching) (has been teaching for 5-10 years). Includes improvisation. Other style(s): popular music, classical.
"A good classical training guarantees well co-ordinated movements. All my students learn to improvise in different keys and chord sequences."

Part III - Courses

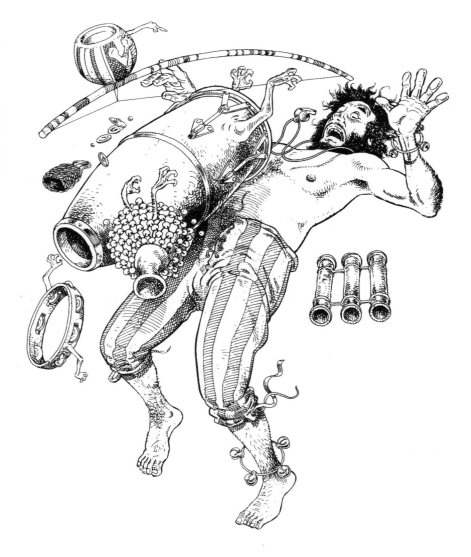

Airto Moreira
Seeds on the Ground / Budda BDS 5085

Abbrieviations

Qualifications

ABRSM	Associated Board of Royal Schools of Music
BA	Bachelor of Arts
BEd	Bachelor of Education
BMus	Bachelor of Music
BTEC	Business and Technology
GNVQ	General National Vocational Qualification
MMus	Masters of Music
NCBF	National Concert Band Festival (offer awards in form of medals)
NOCN	National Open College Network
NVQ	National Vocational Qualification
	(NOCN and NVQ are work based qualifications)
OCN	Open College Network – locally devised and/or nationally developed programmes
PGCE	Post Graduate Certificate of Education
QTS	Qualified Teacher Status

Organisations

FEFC	Further Education Funding Council
LSC	Learning and Skills Council – funds colleges, training providers, school sixth forms but no funds directly to teachers or students or for exams for the 16 and under
NCBF	National Concert Band Festival
NFMY	National Federation of Music for Youth
NQF	National Qualifications Framework
NTO	National Training Organisation
QCA	Qualifications and Curriculum Authority
TEC	Training and Enterprise Councils

Places

GSMD	Guildhall School of Music and Drama
LCM	Leeds College of Music
RNMC	Royal Northern Music College (Manchester)
RAM	Royal Academy of Music (London)
TCM	Trinity College of Music (London)

East

Full-Time

Anglia Polytechnic University

Jackson, Paul, Head of Music, Anglia Polytechnic University, Cambridge Campus, East Road, Cambridge CB1 1PT
01223 363271 Fax:01223 352935; 01223 363271 xt 2048 (box office);
pbritton@bridge.anglia.ac.uk (email); 01233 363271 (tel)

BA (Hons) Music (B.A. (Hons)

General Music with a Jazz Element - Aspiring Degree Level and Above -September - 3 Years
Academic year comprises two semesters, each one consisting of 12 weeks of teaching followed by time for revision and assessment. The aim is to provide all year one students with a common core of foundation studies in the principal areas of music (performing, composing, analysing), further foundation skills in writing and drafting, music technology and improvisation. Plus modular courses: performance, composition, music technology, jazz and music education and programmes in a variety of areas - non-western music studies, orchestration, stage performance and music therapy. Jazz is an available module in Year 2 and 3.

Peterborough Regional College

Park Crescent, Peterborough PE1 4 DZ
01733 767366 Fax:01733 767986;

Foundation Course in Music (Foundation Course in Music)

General Music - beginner - September - 1 year
Acts as a spring board for students with little formal background in music and can lead to a National Diploma in Popular music or AS/A Level Music. Students need to regularly bring their own instruments, practise amps or drum sticks as appropriate.

BTEC National Diploma Popular Music (BTEC National Diploma)

General Music with a Jazz Element - Semi-Pro or Amateur - September - 2 years
Course Content: Mandatory units include - Performing Arts in Context, Language of Music, Performing Arts Professional Practice, Special Subject Investigation, Aural Awareness, Performance Studies, Production Process, Production Project, Introduction to Music Technology, Composing, Applied Performance Skills, Arranging Techniques, Jazz and Contemporary Improvisation, Functional Harmony, Media Music Production, Music Publishing, Theory of Music (Associated Board Grades). Instrumentation or vocal lessons. Students must enter graded examinations on their chosen instrument as well as in music theory.

Intensive Music Studies (Music A Level)

General Music with a Jazz Element - Semi-Pro or Amateur - September - 1 year
An intensive one year A level in Music. Access to the college's performance programme (including orchestra, choir, music, theatre group) and the option to take

some modules of BTEC National diploma in Popular Music. Students are also provided with instrumental/vocal lessons and are required to enter for Grade examinations (Associated Board/Rockschool) as part of the course.

University of Cambridge
The Old Schools, Trinity Lane, Cambridge CB2 1TN
01223 337733 Fax:01223 332332
BA Music
General Music with a Jazz Element - Aspiring Degree Level and Above - September - 3 years
Degree covers history, analysis and compositional techniques. The aim of the course is to deepen understanding of music and its historical and cultural context, while ensuring that good skills are acquired in writing and the analysis of music. During the three years there is an increasing amount of free choice in the subjects as well as the opportunity to explore aspects of music that will probably be unfamiliar, like performance practice, early music, the psychology of music, and ethnomusicology. This allows development of skills at the same time as stimulating and satisfying individual interests. Year 2/3 modules include jazz.

Part-Time

CL Jazz
Batson, Ray, 26 Broadacres, Luton LU2 7YF
ray@nostab.freeserve.co.uk (email); www.cljazz.co.uk;
Jazz Improvisation Course
Jazz Only - Jazz Beginner - Crayford Manor House A.E. Centre - 10 weeks

Harlow College
Velizy Avenue, Town Centre, Harlow CM20 3LH
01279 506325
Jazz Performance class run by Andy Watson (musician)
Jazz Performance Workshop (Credits at levels 2 or 3)
Jazz Only - Semi-Pro or Amateur -
A practical one-day workshop with the emphasis on playing in a group and learning how to improvise jazz solos. You will need to be approximately grade 5 on your chosen instrument, and be able to read music. You will need to bring your instrument unless you are a drummer.

Melbourn Village College
Tookey, Val, Melbourn Village College, The Moor, Melbourn, Royston SG8 6EF
01763 260 566 www.nostab.freeserve.co.uk/Page2.htm;
Jazz Improvisation
Jazz Only - Jazz Beginner - Royston, Herts - September - 10 weeks
Every Thursday evening 7.30-9pm. Basic practical course in improvisation with reference to jazz theory. Age range 14 upwards. Each term cover five or six tunes - so possible to achieve a repertoire of 15 by the end of a year. Aim for a performance at the end of the course term. Tutor: Ray Batson

Workshop

Arts Centre

Jolly, Paul, Music Director, 65-67 Bute Street, Luton LU1 2EY
01582 419584 Fax:01582 459401; 07850 207346 (mobile); 01582 419584 (box office); 33jazz@compuserve.com (email); www.33jazz.com;

Big Band Workshop
Jazz Only - Semi-Pro or Amateur - Arts Centre, Luton - September - Alternate Sunday mornings 10.30 to 1.30 with subscription of £2.50 per session. Need basic music reading skills. There are a pool of about 30 players of all ages and a variety of experience.

Short Course

Benslow MusicTrust

Music Administrator, Benslow Music Trust, Little Benslow Hills, Hitchin SG4 9RB
01462 459446 Fax:01462 440171; info@benslow.org (email);

Big Band Weekend
Jazz Only - Semi-Pro or Amateur - 21/11/2003 - November - 3 days
Specialist coaching on a broad range of music, both original and arranged, under the supervision of Paul Eshelby. Aiming for a 17-piece ensemble and an 8-piece jazz combo, depending on recruitment. Applications welcomed from saxophone, trumpet, trombone, piano, bass, bass guitar, guitar and drum players of intermediate to advanced standard. Resident: £160 Non-Resident: £135

Sing Swing, Jazz and Barbershop
General Music with a Jazz Element - Jazz Beginner - 03/10/2003 - October - 3 days. Tutor - Mike Barrett. Discover close harmony singing through Barbershop songs and Jazz style in this course. You will need a pleasant voice and a good musical ear. Ability to read music is an advantage but not necessary. Resident: £155 Non-Resident: £130

Cambridge Jazz Course

Based at St Faiths School with easy access to central Cambridge. Tuition and Bookings organised by Rob Hall who is based in Scotland contact him at Jazz Course UK, 57 Laburnum Drive, Milton of Campsie, G66 8JS 01360 311 992 (office tel) admin@jazzcourse.co.uk

Course aimed at beginners in improvisation through to those that have some jazz experience. All chromatic instruments welcome. Course covers improvisation, learning music by ear, ensemble playing, on-the-spot arranging, jazz harmony, performance skills and more. Booking forms available on www.jazzandclassical.co.uk/cambridge

CL Jazz

Batson, Ray, 26 Broadacres, Luton LU2 7YF
ray@nostab.freeserve.co.uk; www.cljazz.co.uk;

Jazz Weekend Wicken House

Jazz Only - Jazz Beginner - Wicken House, Wicken Bonhunt, Essex - September - 3 days

Wicken House is a residential centre in the village of Wicken Bonhunt on B1038 (M11 from London exit 8 for Bishops Stortford; M11 from the North exit 9 for Saffron Walden). Course provides an opportunity for jazz performers and aspiring jazz musicians to meet in tutor-led groups, and rehearse for a performance. There are also ad-hoc late night jam sessions. Course begins 8pm Friday evening and finishes at 5pm Sunday. Cost in 2001 £95 to Ray Batson.

Colchester Jazz Co-operative

Paul Dawkins 01787 224 158 (contact tel) Weekly workshops held every Thursday at the Wilson Marriage Centre, Barrack Street, Colchester, Essex CO1 2LR. Fee £6

Jazz Weekend at St Albans

Bryce, Owen, 58 Pond Bank, Blisworth, Northants NN7 3EL
01604 858 192 (office tel) owen-iris@bryceo.fsnet.co.uk (email)
www.mysite.freeserve.com/bryceandjazz
Jazz Only. All Saints Pastoral Centre St Albans. 16/05/2003. 3 days
This jazz weekend course has been running since 1999 and will be repeated in 2004. One group, which mainly works in the Big Band idiom, ending with a jam session. Tutor: Owen Bryce. The Centre is situated in 70 acres of beautiful grounds. Applications to Iris Bryce at the above address.

Grafham Water Centre

Bielby, Laurie, c/o Grafham Water Centre, Perry, Huntingdon, Cambs PE28 0BX
01480 810521 (office tel) grafham.water@education.camcnty.gov.uk

Grafham Water Centre is set in its own grounds in the village of Perry, on the southern shore of Grafham reservoir, famous for its sailing, fishing and a wide variety of waterfowl. The Centre offers comfortable accommodation for up to sixty guests, has three lounges with superb views of the water, one of which has its own fully stocked bar! Wholesome home cooked food is on offer with vegetarians, vegans and other special diets catered for.

Accordian Jazz

Last weekend of May. Tutor: Bert Santilly. This course will concentrate on the practical aspects of playing jazz on the accordion, and will expand and reinforce your understanding of these through explanation of the underlying theory where appropriate. Area covered: playing chord studies of the pieces that form part of each session; understanding more about chords and chord symbols; using jazz scales; improvisation and developing your own style; developing bass and treble skills; accompanying soloists; arranging pieces.Cost: £110. Price includes accommodation, meals and refreshments.

Jazz Improvisation

Jazz Only 04/04/2003 April 3 days

Residential weekend devoted to mastering the principles of – and playing plenty of – jazz improvisation. The aim of the weekend will be to equip those participating, with the confidence, experience and ability to handle jazz improvising. It will be suitable for beginners and those who have made a start with improvisation and wish to pursue it further. A reasonable level of competence on your instrument is expected, but advanced technique and reading ability will not be required. To give everyone plenty of playing, the numbers on the course will be limited.

Cost: £110 Price includes accommodation, meals and refreshments. Booking forms and further information available from Laurie Bielby: 020 8458 2321

Jazz Weekend

Jazz Only. Last weekend of January 4 days

Welll established event offering a weekend of camaraderie playing jazz music as a group activity. The weekend has three different strands on offer:

Mainstream:Tutor: Laurie Bielby. Sessions cover blues, standards, great tunes by jazz composers/performers of all periods and songs that lend themselves well to solo and collective jazz improvisation. Suitable for competent instrumentalists needing an environment to get further into improvisation as well as for more experienced players wanting to develop their playing spectrum

Experimental: Tutor Martin Kemp. Explore interesting instrumental avenues of construction and form, with approaches whose starting points can vary from an idea-based improvisation to that of a tightly written arrangement.

Big Band: Tutor: Joshua Kemp. Tackles a wide variety of arrangements from swing and ballads to jazz/rock and challenging charts from the States. Chosen to develop essential reading and soloing ability within larger jazz ensemble, for both experienced players and competent instrumentalists. Enrollment form should indicate your main instrument, doubling instruments and your preference for which group you prefer to join.

Short weekend: £110; Long Weekend: £158. Prices include accommodation, meals and refreshments. Booking forms and further information available from Laurie Bielby: 020 8458 2321

Watford School of Music

Ellis, Phil, West Hertfordshire Jazz School, Watford School of Music, Nascot Road, Watford
01923 225531

West Hertfordshire Jazz School

Jazz Only - Semi-Pro or Amateur - Watford School of Music – 17/02/2003 - October - 2 days
Tutor: Rob Hall. Two 2 day jazz courses during the October and February half terms. Courses have an improvisatory approach. Students are of school age (minimum age 10 years) and must be a minimum standard of Grade IV or equivalent. Cost: £25 per course

Summer School

Benslow MusicTrust

Music Administrator, Benslow Music Trust, Little Benslow Hills, Hitchin SG4 9RB
01462 459446 Fax:01462 440171; info@benslow.org (email); www.benslow.org;

Big Band Summer School

Jazz Only - Semi-Pro or Amateur - 29/07/2003 - July - week
A wide range of repertoire will be covered in whole sessions and sectionals, under the supervision of Paul Eshelby, Nick Care and visiting tutors. Some solo coaching

by specialist tutors. Intermediate to advanced players of saxophone, trumpet, trombone, piano, guitar, bass, bass guitar and drums. The course runs along side the jazz singing course. Starts at 7pm on the first evening and ends after breakfast on the last day. There will be a 'Night of Jazz' on the Thursday night, free to course members. Resident: £290 Non-Resident: £245

Hot Fiddles

Jazz Only - Jazz Beginner - Benslow - 04/08/2003 - August - 4 days
Introduction to the art of jazz improvisation with particular reference to the history and tradition of 'Hot fiddle'. Tutor: Aidan Massey. Course material will start with a preview from Aidan's forthcoming book, providing an approachable beginning to jazz improvisation on the violin. It will explore the styles of the great jazz violinists, Stephane Grappelli, Joe Venuti, Stuff Smith and Eddie South, through a series of carefully progressive workshop sessions. Applications are invited from violinists of grade 4 standard and above. No previous knowledge of jazz techniques will be assumed, but there will also be challenges and inspiration for strings that can already swing!

Jazz Singing

Jazz Only - Semi-Pro or Amateur - 29/06/2003 - June - 1 week
Jazz singing. Tutor Sara Raybould. Vocal production, harmony singing and development of your own singing style. Gain experience from singing with a variety of accompaniments from single piano to Big Band. All participants are asked to bring and prepare a jazz ballad. Some contemporary singing experience necessary. This course is run alongside and collaborates with the Big Band course. Resident: £290. Non-Resident: £245

Banjo Summer School

Jazz only 11/07/2003 July weekend (3 days). Rhythm, jazz and ensemble playing, solo building, chord-melody, tremolo, duo-style, legato melody, harmony and other topics for all plectrum and tenor players. First steps to jazz and improvisation, which will be explained simply and fully with the aim to 'have fun'. Arrangement and interpretation of "progressively challenging music" at the centre of the course. Reasonable knowledge of the instrument and some playing experience required. Ability to read music an advantage but not essential. Resident £160 Non-resident £130

ABRSM Summer School at Benslow

2003 NO COURSE UNTIL 2004 due to Horn syllabus launch June 2003. Jazz Summer School is for teachers who have relatively little experience of jazz but who would like to learn more, develop their skills in a supportive group environment, and find out how to incorporate jazz into their teaching. An excellent way in to jazz playing and teaching for those who would prefer a residential programme and need something a little more intensive and challenging.

The course includes: daily warm-up: rhythm and singing workshops: an introduction to jazz history; group jazz piano lessons; jazz harmony; working in groups; and improvising

Chelmsford Borough Council

Chelmsford Spectacular, Arts Development, Chelmsford Borough Council, Civic Theatres, Chelmsford CM1 1JEG
01245 606973/606691

Chelmsford Jazz Summer School

Jazz Only - Semi-Pro or Amateur - 24/08/2003 - August - 5 days Usually near to

August Bank Holiday weekend. Small and large groups in workshops working on creative approaches to improvisation, rhythm, harmony and performance. 9:30 to 5:30 every day. All ages and standards. Musical Director Chris Batchelor (Brass) other tutors are Mark Lockheart (saxophone), Angela Elliot (vocals), Phil Robson (guitar), Andrea Vicari (piano), Dudley Phillips (bassist/composer), Nic France (drums/percussion), Martin Hathaway (brass). Takes place at New Hall School, Chelmsford. The fees are - Residential £262.50 (Concessions £194.25) full board. Non-residential £178.50 (Concessions £147.00).

Music Technology

Colchester Institute

Andrew Allen, Colchester Institute, Sheepen Road, Colchester, Essex, CO3 3LL. 01206 518000 Fax: 01206 763041, info@colch-inst.ac.uk, www.colch-inst.ac.uk

Foundation Degree in Popular Music

Start Month: September. Duration: 2 years. Requirements: Audition and interview.

CourseNotes: The course has been designed to provide the specific skills and knowledge required by those wishing to acquire competence in the area of either of two main directions: Music Technology or Performance. The programme is designed to allow students to focus on one of these areas while developing a sound knowledge of the other.

National Diploma in Music Technology

Start Month: September. Duration: 2 years.

The National Diploma in Music Technology is designed to provide a comprehensive grounding in the skills necessary to work in music engineering, production and computer composition. It is based on a combination of practical work and theoretical understanding. The main focus of the course is on using technology for the creation, production and presentation of music. The course prepares students for entry level work in the music industry and entry to higher education courses in music technology.

South East Essex College

Carnarvon Road, Southend-on-Sea SS2 6LS
01702 220400 Fax:01702 432320; marketing@se-essex-college.ac.uk
www.se-essex-college.ac.uk

HNC Music Production

2 years - Entry Requirements GCE A levels (one grade E), Advanced vocational certificate of education (AVCE), BTEC national certificate, BTEC national diploma, GNVQ; An access certificate with at least 12 credits at level three and four credits at level two OR equivalent work experience. If you are a mature student please contact the pathway leader in the subject concerned for individual consideration

Course is suitable for those with a music technology background who work in, or wish to work in, the creative and technical areas of the music industry. Includes a variety of modules, including: Analogue and signal processing; Synthesis and sampling; Production and technical practices.

East Midlands

Full-Time

Newark and Sherwood College

Friary Road, Newark NG24 1PB
01636 680680 Fax:01636 680681; enquiries@newark.ac.uk (email);
www.newark.ac.uk

BTEC First Diploma in Performing Arts (BTEC First Diploma)
General Music with a Jazz Element - Semi-Pro or Amateur - September - 1 year

South East Derbyshire College

Field Road, Ilkeston DE7 5RS
www.sedc.ac.uk; 0115 932 4212 (tel)

Weekly Evening Classes held at Cavendish Road, Ilkeston site.

BTEC National Diploma in Music Practice (Advanced)
General Music – September 2 years

BTEC National Diploma Popular Music (BTEC National Diploma)
General Music with a Jazz Element - Semi-Pro or Amateur - September - 2 years

Stoke on Trent College

Burslem Campus, Burslem, Stoke on Trent ST6 1JJ

01782 208208 www.stokecoll.ac.uk

BTec First Diploma in Performing Arts (Music)
General Music - September - 1 year
performance skills, the technology, marketing and group work needed to present a performance. There is an introduction to music technology and a musical knowledge element which enables students to study music theory, and styles of music. The course involves 9 separate units of study.

BTEC National Dip.Performing Arts (Music) (BTEC National Diploma)
General Music Semi-Pro or Amateur - September - 2 years
Main contents: Arts in Society, Production Techniques, Performance Workshop, Performance Project, Arts Administration, Language of Music, Music Performance Techniques, Orchestration, Composition, Recording Techniques, Music Technology, Music in Media, Singing for Performance, Keyboard

BTEC Higher National Diploma in Music (BTEC Higher National Diploma)
General Music - Semi-Pro or Amateur - September - 2 years
Contextual studies, research, art management, process and production, project realisation, professional practice, music performance. Students choose from a range of options including improvisation, music in the community, band studies, performance skills, aural perception, harmony and composition, keyboard skills, recording, notation, singing, acoustics, production analysis, audio recording, studio

production, modern composition, computer music production, songwriting. Work experience is incorporated into Year 2.

University College Northampton

Park Campus, Boughton Green Road, Northampton NN2 7AL
01604 735500 Fax:01604 720636; www.northampton.ac.uk

Joint and Combined Hons in Music (B A (Hons)

General Music - Aspiring Degree Level and Above - September - 3 years
No jazz bias but it welcomes students with "unconventional musical backgrounds" and qualifications. A range of choices from performance related, practical and historical modules are available. Performance involves individual instrumental lessons, lectures and seminars in performance theory, ensemble, and work on the Gamelan, the College's Javanese percussion ensemble. Historical Studies surveys a wide range of topics from the Middle Ages to the twentieth century to develop breadth of knowledge and understanding of historical method. Popular Music includes theoretical work in the nature and development of post-war popular music alongside group performance workshops. Music and Ideas examines music from western and non-western traditions to tackle fundamental questions about the nature of music and its social function.
In the second and third years you can continue with more advanced work in the subject studies covered at year one, or you can replace or supplement one or two of those areas with alternative modules in Gamelan (year 2 only). This involves advanced ensemble performance and looks at theoretical issues in nonwestern music. Creative Digital Music (years 2 and 3) develops competence with computer technology as a tool of creative experimental composition. Popular Music incorporates recording techniques and songwriting skills, while Music and Ideas explores areas like post-modern theory, the economics of music and music criticism. Performance focuses on historically informed approaches to mainstream repertoire and performance of contemporary music, and includesk collaboration with students taking the Composition modules.

University of Derby

Kedleston Road, Derby DE22 1GB
01332 622222 Fax:01332 294861; www.derby.ac.uk

BA Hons Popular Music and Music Technology

Music Technology - Aspiring Degree Level and Above - September - 3 years
Course covers live performance, the technology of the live event, the studio and the design of studio equipment; sound technology and MIDI applications, performance techniques and interpretation, session and ensemble musicianship, music in popular culture, studio equipment design and computer music production, dance music, video and audio production, music business and management, studio techniques, acoustics, musical applications programming, music theory, music industry and professional practice.

University of Nottingham

University Park, Nottingham NG7 2RD
0115 951 4755 Fax:0115 951 4756;

B.A. (Honours) Music (BA (Hons))

General Music with a Jazz Element - Aspiring Degree Level and Above - September - 3 years

Compulsory modules -Desktop Music Publishing, Language and Style I: Music to 1700, Tonal Analysis, Tonal Composition, Critical Thinking I, Innovation in 20th-century Music, Language and Style II: Music 1700—1900

Year 2 - Critical Thinking plus other modules including: Notation; Performance; Composition; Baroque Studies; Medieval Studies; Renaissance Studies; 20th-century Studies; Classical Music and Society; Jazz; Narrative and Emotion in Art and Music; Creative Orchestration; Film Music; and Romanticism.

Year 3 - Specialist modules include: Dissertation; Edition; Analysis; Composition; Performance, other options include a choice of up to four Research Seminars; Electronic Compositional Techniques; and Sound Technology and Recording.

MA in Musicology (MA)

Music Course Majoring in Jazz - Aspiring Degree Level and Above -October – 1 years or *2/3 years Part Time*

MA is for students wishing to complete their studies with a fourth year of specialised work, and also act as a thorough intellectual preparation for those who intend to work towards independent research. Tuition is by a mix of lectures, seminars and individual consultation/supervision. Covers a wide range of historical and stylistic genres, as well as a technical and critical approach. "intended to give students in-depth exposure to specific problems of interpretation, while also allowing ample room for personal initiative". Students are encouraged to develop their own research interests and enthusiasms. (Advanced performers may apply to be examined in 'Musicology with Performance', in which case a public recital is given in lieu of the final dissertation)

Research

The Music department has established research strengths in Composition, Analysis, Twentieth-Century music, English music, Opera, Jazz*, Film music, Medieval and Renaissance music and Notation, Transcription and Editing. The degrees offered are: AMusM and AMusD (Composition) and MPhil/PhD (Music Research or Composition.

* Darius Brubeck (from Natal University in South Africa) spent a year in the department

Teacher Training

Access to Music

18 York Road, Leicester LE1 5TS (0116 255 1936) info@access-to-music.co.uk (email) www.access-to-music.co.uk

Music Facilitator Course

Music course not specifically jazz. 1 year Qualification: OCNSEM

The successful completion of this course will enable you to teach on one of Access to Music's popular music courses and in some schools but further training is needed to lead to QTS (Qualified Teacher Status). Level 3 course is designed to give experienced musicians the opportunity to gain music facilitation/teaching skills and experience. There is also an option to acquire additional units designed to develop music theory, listening skills and key skills. It is a full time 35 week course (13 hours per week) tuition and workshops + workplace experience, usually at school/college with a minimum half day per week and a research project. It focuses on - education principles and understanding; national curriculum, classroom management, contribution to the delivery of GCSE music; lesson planning; monitoring and evaluation; improvisation and workshop skills; developing projects, assessment and feedback; management skills, self management, time management, finance management; developing a teaching programme and music literacy. Entry requirements - experienced musicians from both popular or classical backgrounds; motivation and commitment to work as a music facilitator/teacher; no requirement to read music; completion of a successful audition/interview.

Short courses

Launde Abbey Big Band Weekend
Bryce, Owen, 58 Pond Bank, Blisworth, Northants NN7 3EL
01604 858 192 (office Tel) owen-iris@bryceo.fsnet.co.uk
www.mysite.freeserve.com/bryceandjazz
November 16th to 18th 2003. Applications to Iris Bryce in Northants
Jazz weekend for two groups, one mainly Dixieland. Tutors: Owen Bryce and Bill Bates. When applying state which instrument you play (pianists are nearly always over subscribed). There is also provision for non-playing members on the course. Good accommodation and facilities.

Jazz Weekend Derbyshire
Bryce, Owen (contact details as above)
Jazz only. 04/07/2003. July. 3 days Alison House Centre, Cromford, Derbyshire
Owen Bryce leads 'largish' band. Bill Bates leads smaller group, mainly Dixieland repertoire. Applications to Iris Bryce at address in Northants.

Music Technology

New College Nottingham
Pelham Avenue, Mansfield Road, Nottingham, Notts, NG5 1AL.
0115 9607201 Fax:0115 969 3382; enquiries@clarendon.ac.uk (email);
www.ncn.ac.uk

Music Management and Promotion online
Location: On-line. Start Month: October. Duration: 30 weeks.

From anywhere in the world students will have the support of music business specialists and access to the Colleges department of Music and Music Technology via the internet. This 30 week course leads to an industry related qualification designed for musicians, DJ's and anyone else interested in entering or developing a career in the music industry. Up to the minute information on how to use the web for music business, putting on live events, contracts and legal aspects are just some of the topics covered in this revolutionary new course. Students will beed all course information and weblinks. There will be regular tutorials with the tutor via or telephone.

Music Production HND
Start Month: September. Duration: 2 years.

The course consists of the following modules: Studio Production, Research Process and Production Contextual Studies, Sound creation and manipulation, Modern composition, Acoustic computer Music Systems and Music Business

Music Tecnology and Industry Edexcel 1st Diploma
Start Month: September. Duration: 2 years.

The course will cover- Music technology, mixing, sequencing, multimedia, DJ mixing techniques, sampling, MIDI, music business and theory, key skills.

Newark and Sherwood College
Friary Road, Newark, Notts, NG24 1PB.
01636 680680 Fax:01636 680681; enquiries@newark.ac.uk (email)

BTEC National Dip in Musical Instrument Technology
Start Month: September. Duration: 2 years. Requirements: Including Mathematics and a relevant science subject plus music grades or a demonstrated interest in music. Qualification: BTEC National Diploma

BTEC National Diploma in Musical Instrument Technology: Designed for those who wish to develop a career in electronics associated with sound production and reproduction. Students also have the option of progressing to degree qualifications in Electronics and Music Technology. The Recoding Technology for this programme is based on the personal computer MIDI hardware and software. Electric Guitar making can be included as an option in year 2.

South East Derbyshire College
Field Road, Ilkeston, Derbys, DE7 5RS. www.sedmc.musicpage.com

BTEC National Diploma Music Technology
Start Month: September, Duration: 2 years. Qualification: BTEC National Diploma.

University of Derby
Kedleston Road, Derby, Derbys, DE22 1GB.
01332 622222 Fax:01332 294861

BA Hons Popular Music and Music Technology
Start Month: September. Duration: 3 years.

Integration of performance, composition, contextual study and music technology in each Level of the degree programme.

BSc Honours Music Technology and Audio System Design
Start Month: September.. Duration: 3 years. Qualification: BSc (Hons)

BSc Honours Music Technology and Audio System Design

London

Full-Time

Brunel University
see South East region

City University
Pearce, Andrew, City University, Music Dept, Northampton Square, London EC1V 0HB
020 7477 8271/8284 Fax:020 7477 8576; music@city.ac.ukg
www.city.ac.uk/music
Fees: £150/ £50 if unemployed.

B.Mus/BSc Hons Music (B.Mus/BSc (Hons))
General Music with a Jazz Element - Aspiring Degree Level and Above - September - 3 years
Broad based degree with a jazz related option within the Ethnomusicology module in the 2nd and 3rd years. Bias towards modern and intercultural music and Improvisation and Cognition to create an awareness of the music traditions of non-Western cultures. Offers a basic grounding in music's relationship with science and technology. First year includes – Music in Oral Cultures, Investigating Western Music, North Indian Classical music, Music, Sound and Technology, Composition, Instrumentation and Notation, Electroacoustic Studio project, Performance. Second and third years: students take a total of nine modules - five in their second year and four in their third year, as well as a major written project. Music department has Gamelan, oriental instruments and African drums. All students are given practical introductions to the library, library research methods, the use of computer networks, and the application of music notation software Final year major topic could be jazz. (Tutor - Gerry Farrell).

Music research department known for its work in Electroacoustic Music, Intercultural Music and Centre for Women and Gender in Music.

MSc/Diploma in Music Information Technology (MSc/Diploma)
Music Technology - Aspiring Degree Level and Above - September - 1/2 years
Covers key aspects of music production, storage and dissemination using digital technology.

Goldsmiths College
Jill Halstead, Admissions Tutor, Music Department, Goldsmiths College, University of London, Professional and Community Education, University of London, New Cross, London SE14 6NW
020 7919 7655(office tel); j.halstead@gold.ac.uk (email); www.goldsmiths.ac.uk

BMus Popular Music Studies

Waiting for validation. From Sept 2004 the music department at Goldsmiths will offer a dedicated undergraduate degree in Popular Music Studies (BMus). Experimentation and innovation will be at the centre of their teaching philosophy. The degree is structured to challenge students intellectually and creatively through engagement with the key theoretical, technical and philosophical approaches to popular music. Courses are grouped into four key areas: history and culture, creative, practical and technical studies. Students can choose to specialise in particular areas of interest at levels 2 and 3. Specific courses include performance, composition/songwriting, jazz and commercial music arranging, film music, improvisation, technology and production, music for mixed media and world music. The degree is designed to integrate theory and practice. Academically, an interdisciplinary approach will be taken, drawing from musicology, sociology and cultural theory. Specific courses include orality: folk and urban musics, music and identity, mass culture and the music industry, and the politics of sound. Final year students can choose to research a particular area of interest in an individual research project. Students are offered a range of career support and advice. Goldsmiths has strong links with the music industry and has frequent high profile lectures and workshops.

Guildhall School of Music and Drama

Stroman, Scott, Head of Jazz, Guildhall School of Music and Drama, Silk Street, Barbican, London EC2Y 8DT

020 7628 2571 Fax:020 7256 9438; info@gsmd.ac.uk (email); www.gsmd.ac.uk

Opened in 1880 in a disused warehouse in the City. It was the first municipal music college in Britain. It quickly outgrew the building and in 1887 moved to John Carpenter Street in a complex of educational buildings built by the corporation of London to house it and the City's two public schools. Originally tuition was on a part time basis but by public request full time courses introduced in 1920. Departments of Speech, Voice and Acting were added, with Drama added to its title in 1935. Moved to its present premises in London's Barbican in 1977 and is still owned, funded and administered by the Corporation of London. In 1993 a hall of residence was made available after the renovation and conversion of a courtyard which had originally been part of Whitbread's first brewery. Of the 690 full time students around 570 are undergraduate and postgraduate music students.

The Library's core subjects are music – (classical, jazz and world, musicology, music therapy), acting, theatre history, stage management and social history. The Audio-visual aisle has listening and recording facilities for CD, black disc, mini disc, DAT, audio cassette and radio, DVD video players. The IT aisle houses journal holdings, special collections and computer resources with a wide range of multimedia workstations. Each includes and internet access – (free to all full time students studying for degrees or diplomas), Microsoft Office, the ability to compose, arrange and print music scores and parts. Library staff give indivdual tuition and assistance to students who are unfamiliar with software. Further information about the library library@gsmd.ac.uk

BMus Hons Jazz Option(B Mus (Hons))

Music Course Majoring in Jazz - Aspiring Degree Level and Above - September - 4 Years

The Jazz Option offers a broad range of music study with a specialist emphasis on jazz. The content is similar to that followed by other students on the BMus course with skills being developed in a wide range of musical fields. The balance of study will be determined by the student's individual needs with support and advice from the Director of Music and the appropriate professors. Years 3 and 4 of the course allow students to specialise further. In addition to the BMus syllabus, the Jazz Option offers specialist training: Principal Study jazz lessons, small bands, Big Band, Jazz musical awareness/improvisation workshop, Jazz aural, Jazz keyboard skills, Jazz arranging, Jazz history, Jazz performance platforms, Rhythm class. Performance and communication skills are an essential part, with individual artistic development as important as the learning of the skills taught within the course.

Postgraduate Jazz Studies

Music Course Majoring in Jazz - September - 1 Year
This is a one-year intensive course for instrumentalists and singers who have already reached a high level of performance and are preparing to enter the field as professionals. The course is designed to train the whole musician through an aural approach and a broad curriculum to give students a solid foundation in perfor- mance, harmony, rhythm, improvisation, composition, arranging and studio record- ing. The course often hosts and performs with visiting artists. Recent visitors have included Randy Brecker, David Liebman, Kenny Wheeler, Billy Cobham, Kirk Lightsey and Carla Bley. Course components - Guildhall Jazz Band a large ensem- ble which performs and tours and leads workshops. Five times winner of the BBC Radio 2 Big Band competition; Guildhall Jazz Singers - vocal group with band; small jazz groups - regular mixed groups led by course tutors and visiting perform- ers; Improvisation - course emphasises fundimental techniques for improvisation and creative development; Harmony/ear training - a course to develop understand- ing, recognition and response to harmony; Composition/arranging - practical course in composition, arranging and orchestration for jazz ensembles; Jazz History and listening - study of the jazz tradition; Rhythm classes to develop time and rhythm skills; Studio/Recording workshops - recording, production techniques, sequencing and using computers; Individual study on first and second instruments, voice or specific topics. Selection is by audition, and the panel look for musician- ship and potential. Candidates are expected to have reached a reasonable level of proficiency in harmony and rhythm skills as a performer and/or writer. Closing Date for applications for September entry is mid January.

Institute of Education

Welch, Graham, Institute of Education, University of London, 20 Bedford Way, London WC1H 0AL
020 7612 6740 Fax:020 7612 6741; g.welch@ioe.ac.uk (email); www.ioe.ac.uk
World centre for the study of education and related areas.

MA in Music Education (MA)

Music Course Majoring in Jazz - Aspiring Degree Level and Above - October - 1/4 years
This course attracts musicians and music educators including music teachers in schools, conservatoires and universities, instrumental teachers, music advisers and music education consultants, music community and youth workers, music adminis- trators. The course is modular and can be taken *full-time or part-time over a period of one to four years. Alternatively, individual modules may be taken as independent short courses.* The aims are that students will enlarge their understanding of music itself, and of the various processes involved in musical per- formance, composition, listening, teaching, learning and other practices. Students examine the research and practice at the forefront of the field; being encouraged

to develop personal responses to issues and to become increasingly reflective as practioners.there are five modules - Aesthetics of music and music education; Psychology of music and music education; Sociology of music and music education; Curriculum studies and music education;Teaching popular music and world music. Students also write a Report or Dissertation in a special field of interest, under the guidance of a tutor.

International Trumpet Academy

Jonathan Eno, Principal, International Trumpet Academy, PO Box 32511, London W3 7FP
info@internationaltrumpetacademy.co.uk (email); www.internationaltrumpeta-cademy.co.uk

Diploma (diploma)

General Music with a Jazz Element - Aspiring Degree Level and Above - London - October - one year

Performance based course designed to give you the opportunity of becoming a professional trumpeter. Majoring in playing your instrument as well as solo and ensemble playing. Specialisms include Big Band, Latin, pop, show band, dance band, blues and jazz from guest tutors. Year is split into 5 terms (Oct/Dec; Jan/Feb; Mar/May; Jun/Jul; Aug/Sept). Included with the course is membership of Musicians' Union, International Trumpet Guild, ISIC (Student card), Ronnie Scott's Jazz Club, ITA Agency and a photo session with a London photographer for your personal portfolio

Lewisham College

Lewisham College, Lewisham Way, London SE14 1UT
0800 834 545 Fax:info@lewisham.ac.uk (email);

Access to Music (Access to Music Certificate)

General Music with a Jazz Element - Semi-Pro or Amateur- 1 year
Daytime, 15 hours per week, Next start date: September

Whether or not you have formal qualifications, this course offers pathways into both higher education and the music industry. Designed for musicians, both instrumentalists or singers aged 21 and over who already have some experience It provides a formal qualification, nationally recognised and meeting the entry requirements of degree-level courses. This is recommended as ideal for international students needing 15 hours of study for visa purposes.

There are 11 compulsory subjects: Aural skills, Composition, Improvisation, Keyboard skills, Midi technology, Music business/music in society, Music theory, Performance techniques (ensemble), Reading music, Solo performance, Studio skills. Some subjects are taught in lectures, or in smaller classes which always include some practical application. There is an emphasis on personal development through performance, with one-to-one weekly tuition on your instrument. Attendance is usually three days a week.

Entry to the course is by audition and interview. Experience of composition and/or performing is required, with performance of two prepared pieces, and a written short paper on what you hope to gain from the course and what your career plans are. Audition will include simple ear-training exercises and an interview with a teacher from the music department.

Asessment partly through assignments in each subject area. Credits at Levels 2 and 3 towards the 16 credits required for the qualification. Regular meetings with tutors help to plan studies and to discuss progress. Many students choose to go straight into the music industry, but the department also has a good record of progression into higher education. Also has good links with universities like Westminster, Middlesex, Rose Bruford and Thames Valley.

Fees for 2003-2004: Fee under 19: £0, Fee on benefit: £20, Fee not on benefit: £775, Fee international: £3,800

BTEC National Diploma Popular Music (BTEC National Diploma)

General Music with a Jazz Element - Semi-Pro or Amateur. Qualification: BTEC National Diploma Awarded by EdExcel. Daytime, 16 hours per week for two years. Next start date: September

Suitable for instrumentalist and vocalists with some previous experience who want to develop performance and composing skills and get an overview of the industry in general. This course is suitable for 16 to 19-year-olds as well as mature students.

There are 17 compulsory subjects: Composing, Freelance world, History of popular music, Keyboard skills, Listening skills, Live performance workshop, Music arranging, Music improvisation, Music in context, Music industry, Music performance process, Music performance project, Music performance techniques 1, Music performance techniques 2, Music theory and harmony, Sequencing and software, Sound recording techniques.

Individual tuition on your first instrument or voice and training to read and write music for a variety of performance situations. Band workshops will help develop your own and group compositions in a variety of different styles, including improvisation. Develop keyboard skills, learn how to arrange music and be trained in tape and MIDI (computer) technology.

Entry by interview and a short written pre-entry test with a demonstration of instrumental or vocal ability and sense of pitch and rhythm. Entry requirements - at least three GCSEs including English and Music (or equivalent, to be established at interview). Assessment is through assignments, exams and observation. Regular meetings with tutors to help plan studies and to discuss progress. On completion of this course, it is possible to progress to a higher education/music degree course, or on to other further education courses such as HND or multimedia courses.

Fees for 2003-2004: Fee under 19: £0, Fee on benefit: £20, Fee not on benefit: £775, Fee international: £3,800.

Popular Music foundation (Popular Music Foundation Certificate)

General Music with a Jazz Element - Jazz Beginner - September - 1 year Daytime, 15 hours per week Next start date: September

For singers or instrumentalists with a little experience wishing to develop skills as a performer, songwriter and arranger, the course offers pathways into further or higher education and industry.

Includes working as part of a group, performing in a variety of musical styles reading/writing music, understanding some music theory, using a computer to create music and backing tracks, historical and social roots of contemporary popular music. This course is recommended as being suitable for international students who need 15 hours of study for visa purposes.

There are nine compulsory subjects: Aural awareness, Composition, Group performance skills, Keyboard/fret board skills, Music and technology, Music in society, Reading music, Solo performance, Theory of popular music.

Course provides basic tools and information which will develop skills as a performer and songwriter, manage the personal dynamics of working as part of a group and learn about the attitudes and behaviour expected from professional musicians. Practical lessons provide opportunities to experiment and learn from mistakes. Classes in theory will teach the rules of music, including when and how they can be broken.

Entry by invitation for an audition, to demonstrate musical skills by singing or playing two pieces practised before auditioning, singing or playing along to a backing provided by the interviewer, copy (by clapping, singing or playing) rhythms, individual notes and melodies. Neccessary to convince the interviewer of commitment and enthusiasm to be able to make good use of one of the limited course places. Assessment takes place at regular times throughout the course as well as at the end. Assessment is based on live, public performances, recorded tracks, written tests, assignments and essays. Regular meetings with tutors to help plan studies and discuss progress.

Possible to progress to Level 3 Access to Popular Music course, or straight into higher education from the foundation course, or to Level 3 courses in sound engineering or music technology/production.

Fees for 2003-2004: Fee under 19: £0, Fee on benefit: £20, Fee not on benefit: £775, Fee international: £3,800

London College of Music and Media
Harvey, Eddie, Jazz Tutor, Thames Valley University, St. Mary's Road, Ealing, London W5 5RF
020 8231 3404 Fax:020 8231 2546;

B.Mus (hons) Performance/Composition (B Mus)
General Music with a Jazz Element - Aspiring Degree Level and Above - October - 3 years

Work within a wide range of music including classical, jazz and popular styles and have a realistic assessment of your aptitude and suitability for a variety of careers associated with music. Produce live performances, write original compositions of a high standard, demonstrate creativity and innovation in presentation skills, and be confident in evaluating stylistic and interpretative issues. Practical performance skills will also be much improved. Plan programmes (including professional quality programme notes) and be able to take performance and/or educational workshops from outline through to performance.

Develop an extensive knowledge of contemporary musics, with specialist expertise in your own choice of repertoire, giving an historical perspective to performances or compositional output; develop the ability to analyse repertoire, communicate with, lead and motivate colleagues and graduate with a strong portfolio of work.

First year - instrumental and ensemble studies, tonal structures and forms, the foundations of music history (classical/romantic) and cultural institutions.

Second year - continue instrumental and ensemble studies, be introduced to popular music, jazz, music arrangement and participate in music education workshops. There are opportunities to join placements in schools with performance partners.

Third year - further develop instrumental and ensemble studies, and tackles musical modernism and music beyond high modernism. Participation in a 20th century performance workshop and choose one option from a range of modules (a list is available on request).

Entry requirements: BTec National Diploma: Merit overall; Advanced GNVQ: Merit; Access: Pass. You will be invited to an interview at which you will be asked to present a portfolio of you work. Further requirements: Grade 8 standard on 1st study (instrument, voice, composition and conducting). All applicants for the BMus pathway will be required to attend an audition. Instrumentalists and singers: a 15-minute performance on 1st study of two contrasting pieces or three songs, and sight-reading/singing. Composers: the submission of a portfolio of works prior to the audition (including tapes if applicable) and a viva voce of 15 minutes based upon this work.

Dip in Higher Ed Popular Music performan (Dip in Higher Ed)

General Music with a Jazz Element - Aspiring Degree Level and Above - October - 2 years.
First two years of the BMus in Popular Music Performance

Mmus and PG Diploma in Performance (Postgrad. Dip/M Mus)

Music Course Majoring in Jazz - Aspiring Degree Level and Above - October MMus 1 year; PG Diploma 9 months *Full Time or Part Time*

Work on solo performance, as well as in chamber music, orchestral work and music theatre; workshops and masterclasses given by well-known visiting performers, like Vladimir Ovchinnikov, John Dankworth, John Lill, Martino Tirimo and Emily Beynon; encouraged to take part in our regular lunchtime and evening concerts; technological support, including a fully-equipped recording studio, video and electronic music facilities

Master of Music degree is designed for advanced performers who wish to develop practical skills at a professional level, while suppojrting this work with complementary academic study. Syllabus includes five modules: Instrumental studies on chosen instrument, voice or conducting skills. Assessed through public performance. Performance workshop through a masterclass approach. Work in small groups with an experienced performer to improve technique.

The Postgraduate Diploma concentrates solely on performance skills. Seen as a key part of the qualification, devoting more than 50 per cent of time to developing performance skills. Includes instrumental studies and performance workshop modules plus Ensemble Studies which provide the opportunity of developing interactive and self-directing skills. Taught through individual lessons, lectures, seminars, workshops and masterclasses, with assessment being through solo recitals, a portfolio or diary of work, critical evaluations, essays and practical demonstrations or viva voce.

Entry requirements: A first degree in music (specialising in performance, classical, jazz or popular) or substantial relevant prior experience. Audition required for this programme (overseas students may audition by video submission in exceptional circumstances). References will be required.

London Music School

The London Music School, 131 Wapping High Street,.London E1 9NQ
020 7265 0284 Fax:020 7488 3658; music@tlms.co.uk (email); www.tlms.co.uk
Founded in 1984 and it is now part of The Bass Centre Group of Companies, which

incorporates the Bass Centre, the Acoustic Centre, House Music Distribution and the London Music School. Their philosophy is "music education for the real world" and the aim is to graduate students to become professional musicians.

All courses run for 6 months (2 x ten week terms) approx. 400 hours. Courses commence in April and October and most have a jazz element.

Performance - Bass

General Music with a Jazz Element - Aspiring Degree Level and Above Course is for musicians who have at least 2 years playing experience.

"Designed by professional musicians to develop a music education program that endeavors to answer the question, 'what makes a player great?'

"You have to play in time and in tune. These are the essentials. At LMS we help you to develop these fundamental skills. However to be a GREAT PLAYER you need something special, you need style, originality, your own identity and above all the ability to move your audience. Over 6 months of intense playing and performance you will discover your true potential. Learn to perform a vast range of classic music, from Led Zeppelin to Prince, from Curtis Mayfield to The Manic Street Preachers. You will learn how to make music, why a groove works, how a song is structured and the principles of rhythm, melody and harmony. Making your own music is at the heart of the course at LMS. Many of our students form a band and by contributing to the writing and performance of new music often get the opportunity to play gigs in London venues. Regular visits from named musicians and key figures from the music industry who will host seminars, discussions and workshops. As a bassist you will cover: Feel and Groove, Time (various), Time and Groove, Fingerboard Harmony, Playing Technique, Ear Training, Harmony and Theory, Reading. You will also study various styles of music such as; Rock, Funk, Jazz and Latin. Places are limited"

Middlesex University

Michael Bridger, Head of Music, Middlesex University, Trent Park, Bramley Road, London N14 4YZ
020 8362 5684 Fax:020 8362 5684; www.mdx.ac.uk

Music (MUS) Middlesex University's music department is "internationally known for its informal and up-to-date approach to musical education. The Music Centre houses over 200 students from many nations and cultures, within a friendly and co-operative environment, studying on courses which are underpinned by clear musical and educational philosophies. The combination of informality and rigour produces high levels of achievement".

BA Hons Jazz (BA Hons)

Music Course Majoring in Jazz - Aspiring Degree Level and Above. October - 3 yrs
BA Honours Music (Jazz) *Three years full-time, five to seven years part-time*
Specialisation in jazz performance or composition. Tuition on a wide range of instruments with all students required to participate in jazz instrumental and/or vocal ensembles.

Specific entry requirements: Formal qualifications are not necessary if there is evidence of appropriate performing/composing experience. Initial selection is made on the basis of the application form, with successful candidates being called for audition and interview.

Year one - Stylistic Studies, Jazz Performance Basics, Elements and Concepts, Key Skills, Structure and Improvisation (elective)

Year two Stylistic Studies, Jazz Performance (or Composition), Jazz Harmony and Theory, plus choices from: Music, the Arts and Ideas, Music, Culture and Society, Musicianship Through Music Technology.

Year three - Stylistic Studies, Jazz Performance (or Jazz Composition), Post Bop, Salsa and Samba, Advanced Improvisation. Possible to opt for further vocational studies (Music Publishing, Music Business and Piano Pedagogy)

BA Hon Music and Arts Management

General Music with a Jazz Element - Aspiring Degree Level and Above - October - 3-7 years

Three years full-time, five to seven years part-time Designed for students who anticipate a career in music management, administration or the music business. Many of the programme's modules are shared with students from other music programmes, so that a wide variety of music may be covered. The Arts Management modules equip the student to make use of their skills in the community and music business environment. A wide range of arts practitioners and arts managers come to give sessions. There are also arts organisation based projects. Staff from the University's Business School collaborate with music staff in directing the programme.

Year one: Music Introductory, Arts Management for musicians, Key Skills, Studies in 20th century Music, Structure and Improvisation, Arts Administration for musicians.

Year two: Classical Styles and Techniques, Tradition and Innovation, Music, Culture and Society, Arts Marketing, Consulting to Arts Organisations. Plus choices from: Music, The Arts and Ideas, Jazz and Blues, Music, Culture and Society, Musicianship through music technology.

Year three: Workshop - Leaders in the Arts, Collaborative Arts Projects. Plus choices from: Advanced Stylistic and Historical Studies 1-4 (Baroque, late classical, Romanticism, Post-war), Music in Education 1 and 2, Commercial and Popular Music, Film Music. Proposition modules may be taken from year two, semester two onwards.

MA Music/Music Education

Music Course Majoring in Jazz - Aspiring Degree Level and Above - October - 1/2 years

One year full-time or two years part-time. Includes - Culture and Continuity in Music, Research in Music and Music Education, the Individual Voice in Music, Research in Music/Music Education (project preparation), Independent Project (Music or Music Education. All assessment is by coursework. In addition to essays and seminars, it is possible to include performance or composition elements relevant to each module's overall topics.

Attendance: The main teaching sessions are held in the evening in order to facilitate attendance by part-time students. Subject to final confirmation each year, the evenings involved are Monday in year one and Thursday in year two, with full-time students attending at both times. Individual tutorials, including instrumental tuition where this has been approved, may be arranged at other times and students are able to attend relevant modules in other programmes, or participate in ensemble rehearsals and concerts, in order to broaden their experience if they wish.

Roehampton Institute London

Roehampton Institute London, Whitelands College, West Hill, London SW15 3SN
020 8392 3232 Fax:020 8392 3148; enquiries@roehampton.ac.uk (email);
www.roehampton.ac.uk

B.Mus (Honours) (B Mus Hons)

General Music with a Jazz Element - Aspiring Degree Level and Above - September
- 3/7 years

Full time 3 years or part time 4 to 7 years. No specific jazz element but specialisation in years 2 and 3 can include Music Technology and Music therapy and the study of music from a variety of cultures including its history and function in different contexts. Opportunity to gain practical musical skills, skills in critical and lateral thinking and creativity. Most modules are assessed through course work or recitals.

Ensembles at Roehampton include a choral society, chamber choir, orchestra, Steel Pan band, Jazz band, and Gamelan. Over 20 visiting instrumental tutors. Students opting for the Performance modules receive one-to-one tuition.

Royal Academy of Music

Presencer, Gerard, Head of Jazz, Royal Academy of Music, Marylebone Road,
London NW1 5HT
020 7873 7338 Fax:020 7873 7374; jazz@ram.ac.uk (email); www.ram.ac.uk

Founded in 1822 by Lord Burghersh and granted a Royal Charter a few years later. By 1880 a system of metropolitan examinations for teachers had begun and the academy had over 340 pupils. In 1911 it moved to custom built premises in Marylebone Road. In 1935 the Junior academy was founded. They have expanded over the years to include the Jack Lyons Theatre, the Duke's Hall, the Thorn EMI Recording room and in 2001 new rehearsal and performances spaces were created along with a new 120 seater concert hall. They have introduced new courses including the Bmus degree course in conjunction with Kings' College London, the Mmus degree course and a two year postgraduate opera course. Many classical pupils went on to establish internationally recognised reputations - Sir Henry Wood, Harrison Birtwhistle, Sir John Barbirolli, Simon Rattle. The Academy runs a programme of public concerts often with the students playing with international artists. Facilities include rehearsal and performance spaces and new concert hall; good recording studio, well stocked library. There are also educational schemes to provide students with work opportunities in all aspects of the profession in London and abroad.

Jazz Department staff - Trumpet - Steve Waterman, Gerard Presencer, Chris Batchelor, John Barclay; Trombone - Mark Bassey, Hugh Fraser; Tuba - Oren Marshall; Saxophone - Martin Speake (Ensembles and History), Julian Arguelles, Iain Ballamy, Mark Lockheart, Tim Garland; Piano - Nick Wheldon, Huw Warren, Nikki Iles; Guitar - John Parricelli, Ed Speight, Phil Robson; Drum Kit - Trevor Tomkins, Martin France, Ian Thomas; Vibes - Anthony Kerr; Bass (electric and Acoustic) - Jeff Clyne Hon ARAM, Steve Watts, Paul Westwood, Michael Mondesir; Voice - Tina May, Norma Winstone; Flute - Eddie Parker, Andy Panayi; Early jazz - Keith Nichols; Composition - Armit Sen, Milton Mermikides, John Thomas. Associate Jazz Artists - Michael Gibbs, Ronan Guilfoyle, John Abercrombie, Karl-Heinz Miklin, Bernard Purdie, John Surman, John Taylor.

International Students There is an exchange programme with major institutions world-wide, a designated International Students Officer to support broad academic advice from tutors, a special "English for Musicians" course for students from abroad.

B.Mus. Jazz Performance and Composition (B.Mus Jazz Performance)

Jazz Only - Aspiring Degree Level and Above - 15/09/2003 - September - 4 years
The Academy's principal-study undergraduate Jazz Course is performance-based and is designed to provide a broad approach to all aspects of the music, as well as a personal focus on the needs and skills of each student. The course follows a modular scheme and leads to the award of a B.Mus (Performance) degree validated by King's College (University of London). In keeping with its declared intention to prepare students for the professional world, the B.Mus Jazz Course maintains close links with the Commercial Music Course and other Academy departments.

M.Mus (hons) Performance (Jazz) (M.Mus (hons))

Jazz Only - Aspiring Degree Level and Above - 15/09/2003 - September - 2 years
Offers performers of exceptional ability (who will normally possess a good honours degree) a principal study 'pathway' in jazz with a degree validated by King's College (University of London). In addition to the core programme students have the freedom to tailor a personalised curriculum from a range of specialist subject areas. Students are encouraged to generate new solutions to creative problems by developing an imaginative performance style. Balancing performance demands with academic study, the course stresses the need to develop analytical and interpreta-tive skills across historical periods, and apply them to performance. Embracing a range of stylistic developments, together with the materials of 20th century 'classi-cal' composition and aspects of non-western forms, the advanced student should be fully prepared upon graduation to make a genuinely individual contribution to the many spheres of jazz.

Post Graduate Diploma (Jazz)

Jazz Only - Aspiring Degree Level and Above - Royal Academy, London - 15/09/2003 - September - 1 year
One-year performance course is designed to focus on the creative development of the individual, helping to cultivate original jazz musicians. The main part of the course is with renowned jazz teacher/composer Pete Churchill, who will help the student to compile a portfolio of 5 octet pieces for an end of year concert. The portfolios must also be submitted for assessment. In addition to this, there is a weekly World Rhythms workshop with Barak Schmool and 45 hours of principal study lessons for the year. The objective of this course is to provide the space for highly proficient players to focus on their own direction.

Trinity College of Music

Barratt, Issie, Jazz Course Leader, Trinity College of Music, King Charles Court, Old Royal Naval College, Greenwich, London SE110 9JF
020 8305 4444 Fax:020 8305 9433; ebarratt@tcm.ac.uk (email); www.tcm.ac.uk

In August 2001 Trinity College of Music moved to the World Heritage Site of the Old Royal Naval College at Greenwich. The King Charles Court has been trans-formed and adapted to meet the diverse needs of a modern conservatoire. The site was once the Tudor Palace and home to King Henry VIII and Elizabeth I. Transformed into a Baroque building in Charles II reign. In the 17th century work was started by Sir Christopher Wren and Nicholas Hawksmoor to turn it into a Naval hospital, but by the last quarter of the 19th century it had become the Royal Naval College.

Facilities now include a Recording Studio with highest professional acoustic standards, a performance area large enough for a medium sized chamber ensemble and separate control room. The studio is connected to the Cobranet and can record from Trinity's larger performance spaces. There is a Keyboard Laboratory with 12 workstations; Composition Suite mainly for composition students involved with technology; Video conferencing and Cobranet potential for web-based real time composition and performance; Practise facilities for more than 80 teaching, rehearsing and practise rooms.

Scholarships at Trinity in Jazz Faculty - **Archer Scholarship** entitles a postgraduate to approximately £900 worth of lessons with a tutor/s of their choice, in return for which they must play with the college Big Band for six hours of rehearsals a week and all gigs. **Spike Robinson Scholarship** available through audition to a Baritone, Tenor or Alto Saxophone student - pays £1000 towards the recipient's fees (Bmus or Postgraduate) and in addition covers the cost of a week's accommodation in and flight to USA plus a year's Musicians' Union membership. The fund has been set up in memory of Spike Robinson, who died in 2001. He played equally in the UK and the USA (where he was born) and contributions to the fund, through a tax free Gift Aid scheme, have and will continue to come from both sides of the ocean and through donations from benefit jazz events.

The jazz faculty has an outstanding group of internationally renowned jazz musicians as tutors. To name a few in 2004, Double Bass – Mick Hutton, Geoff Gascoyne, Alec Dankworth, Steve Watts, Paul Westwood; Cello - Ben Davis, Drums - Martin France, Dave Wickins, Pete Zeldman; Drums (Workshop leaders) Mark Mondesir, Gene Calderazzo, Richard Pite, Trevor Tomkins; Guitar - Phil Robson, Dominic Ashworth, Dave Cliff, Mike Outram; Workshop leaders in Guitar Billy Jenkins, Jezz Franks, Mike Walker; Piano - Andrea Vicari, Nick Weldon, Phil Peskett, Pete Saberton; Stride Piano Keith Nichols; Saxophones - Julian Arguells, Iain Ballamy, Tim Garland, Mark Lockheart, Jean Toussaint, Russell van den Berg, Mick Foster; Trombone - Mark Bassey,workshop leaders Malcolm Earl Smith and Mark Nightingale; Trumpet - Steve Waterman, Mike Lovett; Trumpet (workshops) Henry Lowther; Vocal Coaching - Pete Churchill, Jacqui Dankworth, Don Greig, Victoria Newton; Violin "hot Club" Aidan Massey; Latin Violin Omar Puente

Trinity College Big Band - led by Bobby Lamb, provides an opportunity for students to study and perform works from the jazz repertoire. The Band meets twice weekly, presents public concerts around the country and abroad, broadcasts and makes recordings.

There is also a highly successful percussion group that includes jazz, Latin-American and World musics among its repertoire.

International Students - of Trinity's 550 students approximately 30% are from overseas. Initial contact is with Tutor for international students - 2002 Patricia Holmes (00 44 (0) 20 8305 3941) or write, or info@tcm.ac.uk. There is also an International Students Forum.

Disability and Special Needs College location is traffic-free and offers wheelchair access. Students with a physical disability are given priority in the allocation of rooms in the hall of residence, which were refurbished in 2002/03.

Students with a visual impairment will find a good level of understanding of their requirements at Trinity who work with the RNIB (Royal National Institute for the Blind) in providing various levels of support. This includes training in the use of specialist IT applications. Library facilities include some braille reference books, scanning, screen reading, optical character and voice recognition software, together with brailling facilities for text and music. CCTV magnification is also available for those with partial vision. Screen reading and voice recognition software is available for the use of students with dyslexia.

Issie Barratt, Head of the Jazz faculty, is a composer and a Baritone sax player. She has performed at leading venues - Ronnie Scotts, Birmingham Symphony Hall, the Royal Festival Hall and Glyndebourne International Opera House. Known for her commitment and collaboration with specific artists, she has written works for players from of all of the UK major orchestras. Recent compositions include the jazz opera Pandora's Box. In 2002 she had three world premiers.

BMus (Hons) - The Jazz Course (Bmus (Hons))

Jazz Only - Aspiring Degree Level and Above - September - 4 years
The jazz degree is intended to provide students with all the relevant skills in improvisation and composition - as required by 'the profession' whilst encouraging experimentation and individual freedom.

Entrance requirements available on-line

First and second year students are allocated a Principal Study tutor from the inhouse musicians. Third and fourth year jazz students may be able to study with different musicians of their choice.

Musicianship - classes to develop ability to reproduce sounds from aural sources and avoid relying on 'a collection of formulae and licks'.

Arranging and composition to provide a thorough grounding in jazz theory and orchestration. Contextual studies - seminars to investigate historical and stylistic developments in jazz and improvised music plus workshops to put into practice the repertoire, techniques and concepts. Seminars on the 'business of jazz'. Opportunities to develop ensemble and solo skills with faculty staff and visiting jazz musicians. Ensemble studies - weekly jazz ensembles include the Big Band, Contemporary Jazz ensemble, small groups led by staff members, Guitar ensemble, jazz choir, saxophone and brass ensembles. Students also form their own combos with rehearsal and gig opportunities. Performance opportunities - Tuesday evening gigs at college's Peacock Room - student bands with guest 'names' sitting in; termly gigs at Blackheath Halls; Monthly residencies at jazz clubs - 606 Club; residencies at London, Cheltenham and Greenwich Jazz Festivals; weekly jam sessions and monthly Big Band gigs in venues local to the college.

University of Westminster

University of Westminster, Headquarters Building, 309 Regent Street, London W1R 8AL
020 7911 5000 Fax:www.wmin.ac.uk

BA (Hons) Commercial Music (BA (Hons))

General Music with a Jazz Element - Aspiring Degree Level and Above - Harrow Campus - September - 3 years
Music production and the music business. Three main areas of study: music production; music business; and music sociology. Students can specialise in either music production or music business and law. Modules offered include: Performance and Style: the Contemporary Mainstream, Recording and Technology: the Contemporary Mainstream, Principles of Music Marketing, Law and the Music Market, The Anatomy of the Music Industry, Music Entrepreneurship Project, Music for Multimedia, Commercial Scorewriting and Arranging, Music Production for Theatre and Live Performance, Music Production for Broadcast Media and Film

Part-Time

Barking College

McDermott, John, Head of Schools, Barking College, Dagenham Road, Romford RM7 0XU
01708 770 000 Fax:01708 731067; switchboard admissions@barking-coll.ac.uk (email) www.barkingcollege.ac.uk

These courses are more about Performance in drama and singing than jazz musicianship.

BTEC Higher National Cert. In Performing (BTEC Higher National Cert.)
General Music - Semi-Pro or Amateur September - 1 year
This course is designed to give opportunities for the enhancement of performance skills in drama, dance and music and further training in arts administration to those seeking a career in the arts and entertainments industry.

BTEC National Diploma in Performing Arts (BTEC National Diploma)
General Music - Semi-Pro or Amateur - September - 2 years
A vocational course designed for students wishing to pursue a career in the performing arts. The course develops practical creative skills in Theatre, Dance, or Music, Theatre Design and a training in Arts Administration. The course is demanding and requires a high degree of commitment, energy and enthusiasm.

Birkbeck College

Birkbeck College, 26 Russell Square, London WC1B 5DQ
020 7631 6660 Fax:020 7631 6686; www.bbk.ac.uk

Certificate in Popular Music Studies (Cert. In Popular Music Studies)
General Music 2 to 3 years 1 evening a week

Origins of Popular Music

Theoretical course (not performance) which surveys popular music in the twentieth century, investigating the reasons for its explosive growth and phenomenal success. Traces the roots of styles such as the blues, jazz, pop, rock, reggae and others, along with the historical and social background to this profitable music of our time.

Blackheath Conservatoire of Music

Coombs, Stephen, Principal, Blackheath Conservatoire of Music, 19-21 Lee Road, London SE3 9RQ
020 8852 0234 Fax:020 8297 0596; info|@conservatoire.org.uk (email) www.conservatoire.org.uk

Practise rooms available 10-3pm Mon/Fri and 9-5pm Sundays. As well as their workshops they offer individual tuition in Piano, Singing, Guitar, Bass Guitar, Drumkit, Keyboards and Saxophone.

Big Band
Saturdays 15.30 to 17.00 with Kellie Santin. Meets for three sessions each half-term and open to players of Grade 4+. Existing conservatoire students can join by recommendation from their tutors, outside players should contact the tutor. Offer the opportunity for a number of different instruments to rehearse and perform a

large range of works from a popular Big Band repertoire.

Jazz Techniques

Jazz Only -11 sessions
Tutor: Ian East. Group one: for students with a basic/fair instrumental technique and with limited experience of jazz playing. (Saturdays 10.30 am - 12 noon) Group two: for students with some experience of jazz playing and a more advanced instrumental technique. (Saturdays 12 - 1.30 pm) Both groups provide tuition in harmony and musical techniques and lead students to apply this knowledge to their ensemble music making in a variety of jazz styles and jazz influenced musical techniques. Through improvisation, students develop a feel for the music and an understanding of their own responsibilities and duties in ensemble playing and creative music making. They also gain practical knowledge which can be applied in other situations. Spaces in both groups are limited and acceptance on the course will be influenced by the need to keep an appropriate balance of instrumentation in each group.

Jazz Singing

Thursdays 19.30 to 21.30; 11 sessions. Tutor Donna Canale. Course aims to improve vocal technique, increase awareness of different styles, give experience in performance technique and boost confidence. Each week learn a new song from scratch or practise one you already know, as well as exploring improvisation.

Junior Jazz

Saturdays 11.00 to 12.00 Tutor David Beebee. For young people aged 9 to 15 with a minimum standard of Grade 3 on their instrument. In groups of no more than five, offers an opportunity to explore the various musical techniques of jazz in a friendly environment. A variety of jazz styles covered as well as harmony, rhythm, improvisation.

City Lit Institute

Rhodes, Della, City Lit Institute, 16 Stukeley Street, London WC2B 5LJ
020 7430 0546 Fax:020 7831 8508;
www.city.ac.uk/music

City Lit has a highly regarded music department and the courses are booked up a long way in advance. Always contact the college to check availability of each course.

City Lit Big Band

General Music with a Jazz Element - An ensemble for proficient players who want to improve their reading and section work playing music from the classic era of Big Bands as well as contemporary and original arrangements. Finish date 5th July 2003. Saturdays 15.30 - 17.30 Band leader Simon Henry.

Introduction to Big Band playing

Jazz Only - Semi-Pro or Amateur - Stukeley Street London WC2 - Applicants must have a minimum of four years' playing experience to apply for the apprentice band. Good way to improve your sight reading and ensemble playing. Brass players particularly welcome. Saturdays 13.00 - 15.00. Band leader Simon Henry.

Jazz composition and arranging

Jazz Only - Aspiring Degree Level and Above – September – 33 sessions-
Advanced students with a good understanding of notation, jazz harmony and a reasonable ear. Includes preparing a lead sheet, ranges and transposition, writing

for small ensembles and rhythm section. Fri 13.30 - 16.00 Tutor Mark Bassey

Jazz Course Year 1, 2 and 3

Jazz Only - Semi-Pro or Amateur - Stukeley Street - September - 3 years
First year. 33 sessions - Tuesday 10.45 - 16.00. Tutor Angele Veltmeijer. First year students must ·have a good understanding of harmony and be prepared to develop existing reading skills - notation and chord symbols. Training in rhythm musicianship is an integral part of the course, and students must be reasonably competent on their instrument.

Second year - 33 sessions - Tuesday 10.45 - 16.00.) Tutor Malcolm Earle Smith students must have a good knowledge of jazz harmony, good reading skills and experience in playing jazz.. Third year - 33 sessions – Wednesday 10.45 - 16.00 –

Prospective students for Year 3 should have completed Year 2, or be otherwise well-versed in jazz harmony, sight reading and aural skills. The emphasis will be on playing, developing improvisation and applying theoretical understanding to practical situations. Tutors Della Rhodes and Mark Bassey

Jazz Harmony and Ear Training Level 1 and 2

Jazz Only - Semi-Pro or Amateur - Stukeley Street - September - 33 sessions
Level 1 September to July. Saturday 11 - 12.30 Tutor Malcolm Earle Smith. Involves guided listening to music forms concentrating on time, structure and root movement, harmonic progression, easy recognition of chord types, intervals and scales and modes.

Level 2 - September to December. Saturday 13.00 - 14.30 Tutor Malcolm Earle Smith For those who can already recognise basic intervals, diatonic 7th chords in sequence. It aims to develop aural, harmonic and rhythmic sense through studying jazz standards.

Jazz Piano Advanced

Jazz Only - Semi-Pro or Amateur - Stukeley Street - September – 12 sessions
January to March. Wednesday 20.00 - 21.30. Tutor Chris Wilson. Short course for experienced players to meet new challenges. Based on standard and unusual repertoire.

Jazz Piano Levels 1, 2 and 3

Jazz Only - Aspiring Degree Level and Above - September - 1 year
Level 1 - for students who have some pop piano training or equivalent skills this course will help you tackle the easier end of jazz piano repertoire Wed 18.15 - 19.45 Tutor Chris Wilson 23 sessions.

Level 2 - 12.30 - 14.00 Tutor Della Rhodes 23 sessions

Level 3 - covers interesting and unusual jazz pieces where you will need a thorough working knowledge of jazz harmony. Sat 12.30 - 14.00 Tutor Della Rhodes 10 sessions

Jazz Singers Workshop

Music Course Majoring in Jazz - Semi-Pro or Amateur - September - 33 sessions
For vocalists with experience of jazz and latin styles. This course will develop solo performance and technique. Take own repertoire. Sept - July. Monday 19.45 - 21.15. 33 sessions. Tutor Carol Grimes, Accompanist Issy Postill. Jan - July Sat 15.45 - 17.15. 22 sessions. Tutor Clare Foster, Accompanist Issy Postill

Jazz Singing Levels 1 and 2

Jazz Only - Semi-Pro or Amateur - Stukeley Street London WC2 - September - 23 sessions
Level 1 - for singers who want to improve their technique and solo performance,

and learn some standard repertoire. Aspects covered include style, phrasing, breath control, pitching, extending vocal range. Tutor Carol Grimes Accompanist Issy Postill.

Level 2 Sept - Mar. 23 sessions Monday 18.00- 19.30. Also May - July equivalent experience/ability. Sept - Mar Sat 10.45 - 12.15 Tutor Laura Zakian. Also Apr - July Mondays 18.00 - 19.30 (10 sessions) Tutor Carol Grimes

Jazz, soul and blues singers workshop

Jazz Only - Jazz Beginner - Stukeley Street London WC2 - September - 11 sessions Sept - Dec - Tutor Collette Meary, Accompanist Gabriel Keen.

Also Jan - Mar 11 sessions. Develop solo performance and vocal technique. New material available but students can contribute own repertoire.

Latin Percussion 1 and 2

Jazz Only - Jazz Beginner - Stukeley Street - September - 33 sessions September to July Saturday 14.00 - 15.30. Tutor Mike Bennett.

Level 1 - an introduction to trad latin rhythms - Afro-Cuban and Brazilian styles Rumba/Bembe/Samba/Baiao. September to July. Tutor Mike Bennett. Saturday 15.45 - 17.15.

Level 2 - more depth, developing hand techniques for congas /bongos and stick techniques for bell/timbales. Focus is on learning and playing as a group.

Saxophone Level 1 to 4

General Music with a Jazz Element - Semi-Pro or Amateur - Stukeley Street London WC2 - September - 1 year
Level 1 - beginners or students new to the instrument, other musical skills will be an advantage. Reading and improvisation included. Bring your own instrument. Wed 19.45 to 21.15 Tutor Sarha Moore £33 sessions also on Sat 14.15 - 15.45 Tutor Howard Cottle

Level 2 - at least one years experience on the saxophone and have some experience of performing. Emphasis on popular and jazz styles. Tues 20.00 - 21.30 Tutor Karen Betley

Level 3 - intermediate for students who can read, improvise and perform. Includes technical work and ensemble playing in a jazz/pop format. Sat 12.15 - 13.45 Tutor Joe Hatherill

Level 4 - experienced players can extend musicianship and performance skills in advanced workshop. Emphasis on ensemble and improvisation Tutor Joe Hatherill

Woodshedding (for pianists)

Jazz Only - Semi-Pro or Amateur - Stukeley Street - September - 10 sessions also April to July Wednesday 18.15 - 19.45. Tutor Chris Wilson. For intermediate/advanced jazz pianists who want to stretch their soloing. Course includes patterns/licks, organised around rehearsal backing in all 12 keys, at all tempi, in a variety of styles.

Woodshedding For All

Jazz Only - Jazz Beginner - Stukeley Street - January - 12 Sessions January to March Saturdays 13.00 - 14.30. Tutor - Malcolm Earl Smith. To explore, transpose and rehearse patterns of scales and chord tones relevant to improvising over jazz progressions. All instruments welcome although piano and guitar places are limited. Also May to July. Sat 13.00 - 14.30.

Goldsmiths College

Peyton Jones, Jeremy, Performing Arts Programme Co-ordinator, Professional and Community Education, Goldsmiths College University of London New Cross, London SE14 6NW
020 7919 7229/7200 Fax:020 7919 7223; j.peyton.jones@gold.ac.uk (email); www.goldsmiths.ac.uk

Certificate in Jazz and Popular Music Studies

1 year Start date: October Programme co-ordinator: Roger Cawkwell
Aims to prepare instrumentalists and singers with a background in jazz and popular music for work in the profession, or for further study in higher education. Entry is by audition and interview. You should be proficient on your main instrument, be able to read music and have a sound basic knowledge of music theory and harmony. Timetable: two classes per week, a General Musicianship Module and a practical class in either Performance and Ensemble or Music Technology

Certificate in Music Workshop Skills (Certificate)

Two years October start date. Primarily designed for competent musicians who wish to run workshops and pursue careers in community based music-making. The course is highly respected in the world of community arts with graduates having found work across a wide range of projects including Local Authority Arts Officers, working in prisons, with the physically and mentally disabled, as music therapists, on youth music projects. The programme combines the practical and theoretical aspects of music teaching together with learning through experience via a community

Diploma in Jazz and Popular Music Studies   Duration: 1 year.   Start date:

October. Programme co-ordinator: Roger Cawkwell. Offers more advanced study in jazz and popular music styles and their practical application. It is a natural progression from the Certificate in Jazz and Popular Music Studies and applicants should have at least the equivalent playing skills and the skills in reading, arranging, scoring, transcription etc as provided by the Certificate. The course includes further study of arranging and composition in a variety of styles, along with the development of advanced skills in playing, improvisation and musical direction and production. Classes are spread over 11 weekends throughout the year and include workshops and lectures.

Contemporary Jazz Piano (20 credits)

Jazz Only - Semi-Pro or Amateur - October - 20 weeks
Tutor: Howard Riley. Tuesdays 6.30 - 9.30pm. One of the longest running and most acclaimed jazz piano courses in London. Covers the technical, historical and expressive basis of contemporary jazz piano. over the last sixty years. You should have some previous piano playing experience in classical or popular or jazz music. Classical pianists who wish to play jazz are welcome. The practical approach, using two pianos for duet as well as solo playing, will enable you to start or (if you already improvise) develop as a creative contemporary jazz pianist.

Foundation Certificate in Music (College Certificate)

Music Course Majoring in Jazz - Aspiring Degree Level and Above - October - 1 year Colin Crawley Programme co-ordinator

Pre-degree level programme covering the study of classical, jazz and popular music styles. Wide range of options but each one providing a grounding and preparation for further specialisation. Core courses include musicianship training, study of classical and/or jazz and popular music styles and music history and analysis. In addition there are options in vocal and instrumental music, jazz and pop, composition, arranging, music technology, performance and world music. Students who successfully complete the Foundation Certificate will have automatic progression to the Certificate in Music Studies. The jazz and popular music courses and options provide progression to the Certificate in Jazz and Popular music studies.

Intermediate Jazz Piano
Jazz Only - Semi-Pro or Amateur - October - 30 weeks
Tutor: Tim Richards. Monday 8 - 9.30pm. This course is suitable for pianists with some previous experience of playing jazz and blues who wish to enlarge their repertoire and explore improvisation. Topics covered include; left hand styles, rootless chord voicings, two handed voicing principles, walking bass lines, chord/scale relationships, modal jazz, pentatonic, diminished and altered scales, II V I, building bebop lines, turnarounds, ear training, quartal harmony, transcription of solos and accompanying.

Jazz Piano Musicianship
Jazz Only - Semi-Pro or Amateur - October - 30 weeks
Tutor : Chris Kibble. Saturday 3.30 -5pm. Using the blues as a starting point, this course examines the basic concepts involved in playing jazz piano, from chord voicings to using modes, from improvising over 12 bar blues to playing simple jazz standards. Common structures are dealt with such as AABA form, rhythm changes and turn-around. You are encouraged to play together on several pianos in an informal atmosphere, which also includes listening to and playing along with recordings

Musicianship for Jazz and Popular Music
Music Course Majoring in Jazz - Semi-Pro or Amateur - October - 30 weeks
Tutor Jon Fell. Deals with the development of musicianship skills, aural perception and creative techniques as applied to popular and jazz repertoire. The course offers an introduction to composing and arranging in a practical setting, and so instruments should be brought to each session. This course is relevant to those preparing to audition for the Certificate in Jazz and Popular Music Studies.

Jazz Improvisation Workshop
Duration: 30 weeks Start date: October
Tutor:Colin Crawley. A practical course for players in contemporary popular and jazz styles which helps readers to become improvisers, and may also suit improvisers who want to take control of the direction and creation of their solos. This course also offers opportunities for arranging and ensemble playing and is open to all instrumentalists and singers

Musicianship for Jazz and Popular Music
Duration: 30 weeks start date: October Tutor Jon Fell

This course deals with the development of musicianship skills, aural perception and creative techniques as applied to popular and jazz repertoire. The course offers an introduction to composing and arranging in a practical setting, and so instruments should be brought to each session. This course is relevant to those preparing to audition for the Certificate in Jazz and Popular Music Studies

Guitar Basics Duration: 22 weeks Start date: October Tutor: Branco Stoysin. For guitar players who have recently started playing, this course aims to develop basic technique along with aural and music reading skills. You should have a basic familiarity with the instrument (at least three chords!) You must have your own instrument and time to practise.

Guitar Musicianship 1 Duration: 30 weeks Start date: October Tutor: Neil Luckett. For guitarists who want to develop their playing skills alongside music reading skills. Many musical styles are covered and attention paid to acquiring a secure technique in an informal atmosphere.

Guitar Musicianship 2 Duration: 30 weeks Start date: October Tutor: Neil Luckett Aims to further develop aural and music reading skills. It is for guitar players who have a basic grounding on their instrument and have been introduced to reading music notation.

Guitar Musicianship 3 Duration: 30 weeks Start date: October Tutor: Arthur Dick Aims to develop technical and creative skills in as many contemporary styles as possible. The following areas will be covered: chord construction and voicing, inversions, common bass line progressions, solo arranging. Attention is given to the guitar's role in ensemble, recording, rhythm playing and development of improvisation techniques. You should be prepared to develop sight-reading skills.

The History of Jazz and Pop Duration: 30 weeks Start date: October Co-ordinating tutor: Brian Priestley. Insight into the origins and development of jazz and popular music in America and Europe over the last 100 years. The aim of this module is to identify traditions and conventions and to investigate their development while acknowledging the frequent interjection of new ideas and innovative stylistic changes. External influences such as the media and recording industry, musicians unions and 'showbiz' will be considered and students will have the opportunity to see and hear a selection of recordings and video footage. Attendance of live performances in and around London is a recommended part of the course.

Intermediate Bass Duration: 30 weeks Start date: October Tutor: Anthony Caruana For bass players who have a knowledge of basic technique and an ability to read music and follow chord symbols. The course will aim to improve technique further in a number of contemporary styles and develop ability and confidence in improvising.

Saxophone Basics Duration: 30 weeks Start date: October Tutor: Nick Homes. Aimed at the beginner saxophone player this course covers reed/ mouthpiece/ instrument selection, breathing, embouchure, tone development and basic saxophone technique, how to organise practise time, reading music/chord symbols and the beginnings of improvisation. The music played during the course will draw on a variety of styles and will include both solo and various ensemble pieces.

Saxophone Musicianship 1 Duration: 30 weeks Start date: October Tutor: Nick Homes. Aimed at saxophone players with some prior experience this course covers further saxophone technique and developing your improvisation skills. The music played during the course will draw on a variety of styles and will include both solo and ensemble pieces.

Saxophone Musicianship 2 Duration: 30 weeks Start date: October Tutor: Nick Homes. Topics covered will include general saxophone technique, optimising a reed/ mouthpiece instrument setup, vibrato and tone development, improving music reading skills, how to organize practise time and improvising using chord symbols. The music played will draw on a variety of styles and will include both solo and various ensemble pieces.

Soul/Gospel Vocals Musicianship Duration: 30 weeks Start date: October Tutor: Mike King. For those singers who already have some experience, or who have completed the introduction course, this course further develops singing technique. A wide range of Gospel and RandB repertoire will be studied in some detail. The course focuses on building confidence and developing performance presentation skills.

Soul/Jazz/Gospel Vocals (Intermediate) Duration: 30 weeks Start date: October Tutor: Mike King A class for experienced singers of any style who wish to explore and develop soul, jazz and gospel technique. Music from all three genres will be explored and both traditional and contemporary songs learned and performed. Emphasis will be placed on understanding how to break down styles and how to listen. Techniques of pitch control, improvisation, interpretation and rhythm will be developed along with an understanding of harmony, tone and texture. The group will work towards performances

Hackney Community College

Wilson, Chris, Senior Lecturer, Hackney Community College, Central Admissions Unit, Shoreditch Campus, Falkirk Street, London N1 6HQ
020 7613 9320 Fax:0208 533 5922 (tel) www.comm-coll-hackney.ac.uk

Courses are held at a variety of locations throughout the Borough of Hackney. Autumn term Enrolment

African Percussion
Shoreditch Campus - September - 1 term
Beginners Wednesday 19.00 to 20.30 Tutor Isaac Tagoe. Intermediate course Tuesday19.00 to 20.30. Tutor Isaac Tagoe

Gospel Singing
Shoreditch Campus September - 1 Term
LOCN level 2 and 3 Wednesday 18.00 to 21.00 Tutor Andrea Robinson

Keyboards
Shoreditch Campus Room - September - 1 Term
Wednesday 10.30-13.30

Latin Percussion
Shoreditch Campus September - 1 Term
Thursdays 19.00 to 20.30

Saxophone
Jazz Only - Jazz Beginner - Shoreditch campus 13/01/2003 - January - 1 term
Proposed for 2003 according to numbers of pupils. Tutor Adrian Northover Tuesday 7 - 8.30pm

Hammersmith and Fulham Education

Hammersmith and Fulham Education, Community Learning and Leisure, Macbeth
Centre, Macbeth Street, London W6 9JJ
020 8846 9090 Fax:www.addison-singers.org.uk 020 8563 2185 Advice line

Addison Singers - Jazz Choir

Jazz Only - Jazz Beginner - Macbeth Centre London W6 - September - 10 weeks
20.00 to 21.30 Mondays. Tutor Keith Roberts. This choir, which is open to all,
explores well-known songs from the 1930s onwards. There are a variety of
approaches to develop group arrangements and fluency in jazz performance.
Recent repertoire includes 'Cabaret', West Side Story (Leonard Bernstein), Guys
and Dolls (Loesser), Cole Porter, Gershwin, Jerome Kern, Stephen Sondheim.

Addison Singers - Jazz Ensemble

Jazz Only - Semi-Pro or Amateur - Macbeth Centre W6 - September - 10 weeks
Mondays 19.00 to 20.00 Musical Director: Matthew Hough. Small Jazz Singing
Group. Entry by informal audition with the Musical Director. Repertoire includes
more complex jazz and popular music such as: Duke Ellington, Gershwin arange-
ments, classic jazz standards.

Addison Singers - Vocal Technique

General Music with a Jazz Element - Jazz Beginner - Macbeth Centre W6 -
September - 10 weeks
Mondays, 19:00 - 21:00. Tutor: Alice Hyde. Course covers warm-ups, breathing
exercises, scales, group and individual singing. Ideal for those wishing to improve
their singing or gain confidence and also for those who wish to sing a solo part in
the Jazz Concert or with one of the other choirs in the group. Repertoire (classical,
jazz and popular music by mutual arrangement with the Tutor). This class is not
suitable for beginners who should start with the Beginners Class. NB These classes
are very popular (maximum 10 people) and are allocated to the earliest sub-
scribers. Priority is given to other Addison Singers choir members for this group.
Early enrolment is advised to ensure a place.

Hoxton Hall

Hoxton Hall, 130 Hoxton Street, London N1 6SH
020 7684 0060 Fax:020 7729 3815; office@hoxtonhall.dabsol.co.uk (email);
www.hoxtonhall.dabsol.co.uk 020 7739 5431

Hoxton Hall has been a venue for professional and community theatre shows for
the past twenty five years, building strong links with the local community and
developing creative work of exceptional standard. It is situated on one of London's
vibrant East End market streets, which runs through an area rapidly establishing
itself as the new quarter for contemporary arts and media. This culturally diverse
area offers a variety of exciting bars and restaurants to explore and enjoy

Jazz and Latin Instrumental

Music Course Majoring in Jazz - Jazz Beginner - January - ongoing
Monday evenings. Tutor: Peter Cload. A workshop for a mixture of instruments to
play jazz and latin standards and originals and look at the ideas and theory behind
the compositions. A strong focus on improvisation and group playing leading to
performances and recording projects and collaborations with singers. Students

must be able to play an instrument - music reading skills are desirable but not essential.

Music Technology

Music Technology - Semi-Pro or Amateur - September - 1 year
Wednesday 11.00 to 16.00 Tutor: Peter Cload A one day a week, one year course which can be taken on its own or with other music classes (e.g. songwriting, singing). Learn live and recording sound engineering, how to use mixing desk and outboard equipment, creating computer music, hard disk recording, sampling and sequencing. The course also links technology with general musicianship such as scales and chords, rhythm, ear training and keyboard skills. Students are encouraged to work on their own creative projects. Entry is via interview.

Music 'Tutor Training' Course (NVQ level 3 Arts Development and Teachin)

Music Course Majoring in Jazz - Aspiring Degree Level and Above - Hoxton Hall - 01/05/2003 - May - 1 year
New course "for musicians who want to develop their practice and share their knowledge, whilst gaining a useful teaching qualification". Vocational course for one and half days a week Thursday 10.30 - 16.30 Tuesday 11 - 13.00.

Aimed at experienced musicians and existing teachers from all backgrounds (popular and classical) instrumentalists, singers, composers, songwriters and DJs who wish to develop their teaching/workshop leading skills for working with a variety of groups, ages and abilities in a range of contexts - 1 to 1, small and large groups in schools colleges and projects in the community, workshops and masterclasses. Course Director: Matt Lewis - an experienced teacher and workshop leader, professional instrumentalist and composer working in jazz, popular and contemporary music. Applications from those over 18 with access by interview and audition in March/April 2003. Send SAE for application pack

Morley College

Robert Hanson, Director for Music, Morley College, 61 Westminster Bridge Road, London SE1 7HT 020 7928 8501 Fax:020 7928 4074;

Advanced Jazz Workshop

Jazz Only - Aspiring Degree Level and Above - January - 28 weeks
For those who need tuition and experience beyond an intermediate course, possibly with a view to entering higher level courses. See the tutor on Mon 10 Sept 5.30 - 7.30pm. 198 Wed 6 - 7.30pm Paul Westwood Autumn: 11 wks from 19 Sept Fee: £37 Conc: £13 Spring: 10 wks from 9 Jan Fee: £35 Conc: £12 Summer: 7 wks from 17 April Fee: £24 Conc: £8 You must see a tutor before enrolling on this course.

Jazz Ear Training

Jazz Only - Jazz Beginner - September - 21 - 28 Weeks
Aural recognition of chords, progressions, intervals, rhythms and scales/modes, incorporating some acapella singing based on jazz standards. For any aspiring jazz instrumentalist. Ideally taken together with Jazz Harmony Level 1, but can be taken on its own. 1102 Tues 6 - 7.30pm Sara Dhillon Autumn: 11 wks from 18 Sept Fee: £38 Conc: £13 Spring: 10 wks from 8 Jan Fee: £35 Conc: £12 Summer: 7 wks from 16 April Fee: £26 Conc: £10 1103 Wed 2.30 - 4pm Sara Dhillon Autumn: 11 wks from 19 Sept Fee: £38 Conc: £13 Spring: 10 wks from 9 Jan Fee: £35 Conc: £12

Jazz Harmony Level 1
Jazz Only - Jazz Beginner - September - 28 Weeks
Develop a better understanding of scales, form, chords, standard harmonic progressions, keys, modes, etc. including detailed analysis of the more popular jazz
standards. Ideally taken together with Jazz Ear Training, but can be taken on its
own. Open to all instrumentalists. 1104 Tues 8 - 9.30pm Sara Dhillon Autumn: 11
wks from 18 Sept Fee: £38 Conc: £13 Spring: 10 wks from 8 Jan Fee: £35 Conc:
£12 Summer: 7 wks from 16 April Fee: £26 Conc: £10 Wed 4 - 5.30pm Sara
Dhillon Autumn: 11 wks from 19 Sept; Spring: 10 wks from 9 Jan Fee: £35 /£12

Jazz Harmony Level 2
Jazz Only - Semi-Pro or Amateur - September - 28 weeks
A follow-up to Jazz Harmony Level 1, includes voicings, scale derivations, analysis
of jazz standards etc. Open to all instrumentalists with knowledge of the basics of
jazz harmony. 1106 Wed 6 - 7.30pm Sara Dhillon Autumn: 11 wks from 19 Sept
Fee: £38 Conc: £13 Spring: 10 wks from 9 Jan Fee: £35 Conc: £12 Summer: 7
wks from 17 April Fee: £26 Conc: £10 You must see a tutor before enrolling on
this course.

Jazz Piano 1
Jazz Only - Jazz Beginner - January - 28 weeks
No jazz experience required but basic ability to play a keyboard is essential.
Practical and theoretical knowledge of jazz piano styles covered. 193 Mon 4 - 6pm
Roland Perrin Autumn: 11 wks from 17 Sept Fee: £51 Conc: £18 Spring: 10 wks
from 7 Jan Fee: £47 Conc: £17 194 Mon 6.30 - 8.30pm Roland Perrin Autumn: 11
wks from 17 Sept Fee: £51 Conc: £18 Spring: 10 wks from 7 Jan Fee: £47 Conc:
£17 Summer: 7 wks from 15 April Fee: £33 Conc: £12

Jazz Piano 2
Jazz Only - Semi-Pro or Amateur - September - 28 weeks
Some experience of jazz piano required. Improve playing and explore advanced
aspects of jazz harmony, rhythm and improvisation. See the tutor on Mon 10 Sept
5.30 - 7.30pm. 195 Wed 6.30 - 9pm Tim Richards Autumn: 11 wks from 19 Sept
Fee: £61 Conc: £20 Spring: 10 wks from 9 Jan Fee: £56 Conc: £19 Summer: 7
wks from 17 April Fee: £40 Conc: £13 You must see a tutor before enrolling on
this course.

Jazz Singing (Level 2 upwards)
Jazz Only - Semi-Pro or Amateur - September - 28 weeks
Improve your singing technique and understanding of jazz styles, and relate your
singing to a basic understanding of jazz harmony. Suitable for those who can
already sing a little. 1107 Tues 2 - 4pm Laura Zakian Autumn: 11 wks from 18
Sept Fee: £48 Conc: £16 Spring: 10 wks from 8 Jan Fee: £45 Conc: £15 Summer:
7 wks from 16 April Fee: £31 Conc: £11

Jazz workshop 1
Jazz Only - Semi-Pro or Amateur - January - 17 weeks
No previous jazz experience, but moderate ability on an instrument required. Music
reading desirable. Practical playing sessions in all aspects of jazz improvising and
style, theory, modes, chords. See the tutor on Mon 10 Sept 5.30 - 7.30pm. 197
Wed 7.30 - 9.30pm Paul Westwood Autumn: 11 wks from 19 Sept Fee: £48 Conc:
£16 Spring: 10 wks from 9 Jan Fee: £46 Conc: £15 Summer: 7 wks from 17 April
Fee: £31 Conc: £10 You must see a tutor before enrolling on this course.

Morley Big Band
Jazz Only - Semi-Pro or Amateur - September - 31 weeks
Improve playing standards and appreciation of jazz in the style of Basie and others. Conventional Big-Band line-up, playing mainly arrangements by the tutor. See the tutor on Mon 10 Sept 5.30 - 7.30pm. 1100VF Wed 7.30 - 9.30pm Tony Douglas Autumn: 11 wks from 19 Sept Fee: £48 Conc: £16 Spring: 10 wks from 9 Jan Fee: £45 Conc: £15 Summer: 10 wks from 25 April Fee: £45 Conc: £15 You must see a tutor before enrolling on this course.

Morley Jazz Orchestra
Jazz Only - Aspiring Degree Level and Above - September - 31 Weeks
For advanced players. We hope that both symphonic and jazz composers, including members of the orchestra, will write for us. See the tutor on Mon 10 Sept 5.30 - 7.30pm. 1101 Sat 10am - 12.30pm Gordon Rose Autumn: 11 wks from 22 Sept Fee: £59 Conc: £21 Spring: 10 wks from 12 Jan Fee: £53 Conc: £19 Summer: 10 wks from 20 April Fee: £53 Conc: £19 You must see a tutor before enrolling on this course.

Richmond Adult and Community College
West, Tim, Richmond Adult and Community College, Parkshot Centre, Parkshot, Richmond TW9 2RE
020 8940 0170 x 322 www.racc.ac.uk

Saturday Jazz School
Jazz Only - Semi-Pro or Amateur - Richmond- Parkshot - Jan / Apr - 10/13 Weeks
Saturday Morning Instrumental classes and. Afternoon Jazz Workshops. Three terms starting September. Not suitable for complete beginners but provides opportunities for students to develop their jazz playing techniques and perform in jam sessions and the end of term concert. Classes include: Computer music; Piano; Bass Guitar/ Double Bass; Drums; Saxophone; Jazz Guitar (Advanced and Intermediate); Brass Workshop; Jazz Singing (Foundation, Intermediate, Advanced and Masterclass); Jazz Workshop (Intermediate and Advanced)

Richmond upon Thames College
Richmond upon Thames College, Egerton Road, Twickenham TW2 7JS
020 8607 8305/8314 Fax:courses@richmond-utcoll.ac.uk. (email);

First Diploma in Performing Arts
General Music with a Jazz Element - Semi-Pro or Amateur - September - 1 year
During this course students will gain experience in devising, rehearsing and performing as either a drama or music specialist. The course is taught in a series of units which will vary from practical performance or production based tasks to projects and theoretical studies. Students will be assessed via a series of assignments leading to a qualification that can enable them to progress on to Higher Education or into the performing arts industries. As part of this course students will also be able to achieve an A level in Music Technology or Drama.

Music A and AS levels (A/AS Level)
General Music - September – 1 to 2 years
Students will be offered considerable choice in what they study and there is an opportunity for practical musicians to include a performance element on either

instrument or voice. Core skills studied are aural skills (dictation and analysis) and historical skills through the medium of specified musical works. Options are chosen from harmony and counterpoint, practical musicianship, recital compostition and project. The AS level is similar to the A level course but is assessed on 3 units rather than 5. Assessment is by exam and coursework depending on the options chosen.

Performing Arts A level (A Level)
General Music - September - 2 years
Modular course which encourages an integrated approach (there is a foundation module which looks at the language of performing arts and investigation work in drama, music and dance) An in-depth study of two disciplines - one in each year resulting in a performance. Each of the modules is separately assessed through performance and either course work or examination.

Roehampton Institute London
Whitelands College, West Hill, London SW15 3SN
020 8392 3232 Fax:020 8392 3148; enquiries@roehampton.ac.uk (email);
www.roehampton.ac.uk

PGCE Music part time (pgce)
General Music - Aspiring Degree Level and Above - Suthlands - September - 2 years

Sutton College of Learning for Adults
St Nicholas Way, Sutton, Surrey SM1 1EA
020 8770 6901 (office tel) scola@sagnet.co.uk (email)

Jazz only. September. 3 terms at Sutton Grammar School
SCOLA Jazz Ensemble is ideal for musicians wanting to improve reading and impro-visation skills, Taught how to read rhythms and improvise over chord changes in the Jazz idiom. The class meets on Wednesday evenings 19.30 -21.30 for three terms a year and is open to players of most instruments. Places are limited for guitar and bass/bass guitar. To benefit you should have played for about 2 years and know all the major scales. For more information please contact head of centre.

Workshops

Associated Board Jazz Development
Manager Marketing Dept, Associated Board Royal Schools of Music, 24 Portland Place, London W1B 1LU
020 7467 8210 Fax:020 7467 8258; mjames@abrsm.ac.uk (email);
www.abrsm.ac.uk

Getting in the Groove
Jazz Only - Jazz Beginner – Royal Northern College of Music, Manchester – Usually one day in May **postponed until 2004.**
A workshop is designed for piano teachers with little or no knowledge of jazz, Getting in the Groove will be a day spent exploring rhythm in jazz.

Beat Dis
Tabernacle Community Centre, Powis Square, London W11 2AY

020 7229 9329 (office tel) 020 7565 7810 info@beatdistrust.co.uk (email)
www.beatdistrust.co.uk

Beat Dis is a constituted association of professional jazz musicians committed to developing jazz as an art form, developing the audience and supporting emerging musicians. The goal in the British Jazz circuit is to allow everyone to enjoy real good quality jazz performed by up and coming musicians who are unable to perform in the larger venues.

Music Technology Course (Tony Thomas) - With access to industry standard hardware Beat Dis trains participants to the highest standards, giving them a real chance in the highly competitive multimedia industry.

Band Workshop Project (Brian Edwards) May - every Saturday for 10 weeks from 12.00pm till 15.00 at The Tabernacle Community Centre. Provide a basic platform and environment for participants in the community where they are encouraged to play alongside professional musicians. Aims to enhance participants' practical and theoretical skills whilst helping them achieve their own economic independence by teaching financial and administrative skills as well as Public Relations and Marketing.

As the main remit is working with young unemployed people, the aim is to equip them with the skills for employment in their chosen profession. AIMS - Practical and theoretical skills; development of a professional music repertoire; development of participants' ability to work as a performance team; experience of working within the realistic constraints of an arts discipline; development of career and educational opportunities.

Financial and Administration skills - an understanding of the economic environment within which the arts practice operates; marketing relevant to music promotion; understanding of industrial relations issues and legal requirements of public performance

Marketing - Develop ability to locate and establish professional relations with potential venues; enable participants to establish a connection and build an audience in venues not necessarily designed or equipped for music performance and promotion. Target group the North Kensington Community but will also consider participants from outside the area if possible to celebrate cultural diversity, enhance self esteem, break down isolation and promote awareness and appreciation of other cultures. Participants are aged between 16 - 40. Previous participants have been from a range of cultural origins including Australian, Aftican Caribbean, Asian, Moroccan, White British and a balance of gender.

Chats Palace Arts Centre

42-44 Brooksbys Walk, Hackney, London E9 6DF
020 8986 6714 Fax:020 8985 6878;

Workshops

Jazz Only - Jazz Beginner - September - 3 x 10 week terms
World jazz big band and world percussion courses available. Occasional one day jazz workshops are also run.

CIA Ltd

Irons, Janine, Director, PO BOX 665, Harrow HA3 5BE
020 8424 2807 Fax:020 8861 5371; 07958 918 453 (mobile); info@ciajazz.com (email); www.ciajazz.com

National Workshops 2003/2004
New Outreach and development programme lead by DUNE recordings artists to promote cultural diversity, equality of opportunity, life long learning, audience development and not forgetting the enjoyment and the appreciation of the music. The weekly jam sessions at the Jazz Café still continue every Sunday led by a core of musicians from Tomorrows Warriors. (See 'UK Jazz Organisations 'sections for details of the organisations aims and objectives).

Goldsmiths College
Peyton Jones, Jeremy, Music Co-ordinator, Goldsmiths University of London, Professional and Community, Education, University of London, New Cross, London SE14 6NW
020 7919 7229/7200 Fax:020 7919 7223; j.peyton.jones@gold.ac.uk (email); www.goldsmiths.ac.uk

African Drumming Workshop
Duration: 10 weeks - Start date: January. Tutor: Barak Schmool

Drawing upon the musical traditions of Senegal, Cameroon and Uganda, this practical course introduces African hand and stick drumming and singing. Participants will be given learning strategies that help to approach the music in a way authentic to its sensibilities, sources and context. Previous percussion experience is preferable but not essential.

Jazz Improvisation for Singers One Day Workshops
Tutors: Louise Gibbs / Anita Wardell

Two workshops per year usually in November and June. The November date offers an introduction for singers who want to learn about jazz styles and procedures, improvisation and working with a rhythm section. The June date is suitable for experienced jazz singers who wish to gain a deeper understanding of jazz vocals, explore more unusual jazz repertoire and improvisation techniques.

Jazz Improvisation Workshop
Duration: 30 weeks Start date: October

Tutor: Colin Crawley

A practical course for players in contemporary popular and jazz styles, which helps readers to become improvisers, and may also suit improvisers who want to take control of the direction and creation of their solos. This course also offers opportunities for arranging and ensemble playing and is open to all instrumentalists and singers.

Jazz Piano Weekend Workshops
Tutor: Tim Richardsrds 28/29 June 2003

Hands-on weekend courses held in April and July for pianists covering all aspects of jazz piano improvisation (chord changes, modal and free) in a practical way taught by two of Europe's leading jazz pianists. All you need is some previous piano playing experience. Whether you are a classical or popular pianist who has never played improvised jazz, or a jazz pianist who wishes to develop further musical insights, the practical approach using two pianos for duet as well as solo playing, will increase your improvising ability.

Latin Piano Weekend Workshop

Tutor: John Crawford

A weekend course, usually held in June for those wishing to develop their playing or have an intensive introduction to Latin styles as applied to the piano. The course is for any pianists of an intermediate level upwards. Afro-Cuban and Afro-Brazilian styles will be covered including Salsa, Samba and Guajira. Players will not need much knowledge of theory and harmony as the course will concentrate on rhythm, style and interpretation.

Modern Jazz Workshop

Duration: 30 weeks   Start date: October

Tutor: Howard Riley

This course provides experience of small group jazz performance for instrumental-ists in a very practical way. The emphasis is on improvisation, with each player performing in a small jazz group every week, using classic compositions from the jazz repertoire. It is preferable for players to have some experience of playing jazz and to be able to read a simple melodic line.

Songwriting Workshop

Duration: 8 weeks   Start date: April

Tutor: Steve Anthony

A workshop for aspiring and more seasoned songwriters wanting to know more about what makes a good song and wanting to hone their skills and try out ideas.

Introduction to Sequencing and Digital Technology

Start Month: October. Duration: 11 weeks.

Tutors: Jeremy Cox and Nic Bevan. 2.30 - 5.30 pm. This course will include an introduction to computer sequencing, composing with sampler and sequencer, multi-timbral synthesis, editing, advanced MIDI, effects processing, and post pro-duction techniques. Using Logic Audio sequencing software along with a simple mixing desk, sound module, sampler and effects unit you will have the opportunity to create your own composition using the techniques learned, and mix to DAT and cassette.

Introduction to Sound Sculpture Sampling and Digital Tech.

Start Month: May. Duration: 8 weeks.

Tutors: Jeremy Cox 14.30 -17.30.. This course is designed to introduce the new-comer to writing electronic music with samplers and digital audio. Using samplers, digital editing techniques and effects, the course will explore the concept of sculpt-ing sound through electronic manipulation. Students will be encouraged to use the sampler in a creative manner in combination with sequencing, editing and mixing to produce short original sound pieces.

Introduction to Studio and Recording techniques

Start Month: January. Duration: 11 weeks.

Tutors: Jeremy Cox. 14.30 -17.30. An introduction to multitrack recording, this course will cover the mixing desk, SMPTE and synchronisation, microphone placement and EQ, special arrangements for recording drums, vocals and instruments, using compressors, reverbs and other signal processing, basic mixing principles, and desk automation. You will have the opportunity to record and mix your own track with a final mix to DAT or CD.

Hoxton Hall

130 Hoxton Street, London N1 6SH
020 7684 0060 Fax:020 7729 3815; office@hoxtonhall.dabsol.co.uk (email); www.hoxtonhall.dabsol.co.uk 020 7739 5431

Hoxton Hall has been a venue for professional and community theatre shows for the past twenty five years, building strong links with the local community and developing creative work of exceptional standard. It is situated on one of London's vibrant East End market streets, which runs through an area rapidly establishing itself as the new quarter for contemporary arts and media. This culturally diverse area offers a variety of exciting bars and restaurants to explore and enjoy.

Singing 1
General Music with a Jazz Element - Jazz Beginner - 28/04/2003 - April - 10 weeks Monday 4.30-6.30pm Tutor: Virginia Firnberg. A supportive class for beginners who love to sing but feel a bit 'rusty'. Using simple breathing and vocal techniques as well as clapping and vocal rhythms, you will explore styles such as gospel, jazz, blues, folk and popular styles - part-singing and a capella singing. Occasional opportunities for some solo singing as well as optional performances. Guest instrumentalists will join in occasionally. Please talk to tutor before enrolling. Fees: £46.50+£8 membership, Concs: £6.50+£4 membership

Jacksons Lane

Wynyard, Melanie, Programmer, Jacksons Lane Community Centre, 269a Archway Road, London N6 5AA
020 8340 5226 Fax:020 8348 2424; 020 8341 4421 (box office); mail@jacksonslane.org.uk (email); www.jacksonslane.org.uk

Jazz Workshops
Jazz Only - Semi-Pro or Amateur – Jan/Feb - 6 weeks repeated during the year Workshops on Sundays 17.00 to 19.00 for instrumentalists of reasonable jazz experience. Course covers chord/scale relationships, chord function, the language of Be-bop, contemporary jazz and improvisation in different contexts. £25 (£22 conc)

Jazz Umbrella

Christiane, Kelvin, KC Music, 8 Stella Road, London SW17 9HG
07971 242864 (mobile); kelvin@kcmusic.co.uk (email); www.kcmusic.co.uk

Jazz Workshop
Jazz Only - Semi-Pro or Amateur - Chestnut Grove School, Balham SW London - Term time
Tutors: Kelvin Christiane plus others (including Mark Ingleby) Workshop/Jam session based at Chestnut Grove school, but aimed at adults with reasonable working knowledge of their instrument (bring your own). Every Wednesday evening during term time 19.30 to 21.15. Walking distance from Balham tube underground station.

Morley College

Hanson, Robert, Director for Music, Morley College, 61 Westminster Bridge Road, London SE1 7HT
020 7928 8501 Fax:020 7928 4074;

Getting the Feel
General Music with a Jazz Element - Jazz Beginner - 05/07/2002 - July - 3 days
A workshop in rock, pop, jazz and soul for singers with some experience, but not necessarily in these styles. Vocal technique, style and getting the right feel working with a pianist. Fri 6.30 - 9pm Laura Zakian and Sat 11am - 4pm Fee: £32 Conc: £16

Latin Jazz Fusion Workshop and Discussion
Music Course Majoring in Jazz - Jazz Beginner - July - 1 day
As part of a week of music from all over the world, this is a practical workshop which is guided by two Latin Jazz Fusion experts and framed by discussion of the global context. Fri 11am - 4pm Sarah Dhillon and Helen Simpson. Workshop fees per day: Mon and Fri: £16 Conc: £8 Tues/Wed/Thurs: £20 Conc: £10 Fee for the week £75 Conc: £83

Street Jazz Dance - an introduction
Jazz Only - Jazz Beginner - 06/07/2002 - July - 1 day
Learn some basic moves and a simple routine in the lastest dance style. Sat 11am - 1pm Irven Lewis. Fee: £6 Conc: £4

Serious

18 Chapel House, Hatton Place, London EC1
Dubbing The Jazz
The DJ workshop series was developed in 2000 with two of London's most innovative DJ's, Rita Ray and Max Reinhardt. Last year they took place in four different outer London boroughs - Croydon, Hounslow, Kingston and Waltham Forest - enabling young people from schools and youth groups to learn DJ skills, to work as a team and to experience jazz in its widest sense. Linking their experiences to live music events, the workshops ran in conjunction with the London Jazz Festival. This year, Serious will be working in Barking and Dagenham, Brent, Hounslow and Kingston.

Short Courses

Goldsmiths College

Peyton Jones, Jeremy, Music Co-ordinator, Goldsmiths University of London, Professional and Community, Education, University of London, New Cross, London SE14 6NW
020 7919 7229/7200 Fax:020 7919 7223; j.peyton.jones@gold.ac.uk (email); www.goldsmiths.ac.uk

Variety of music programmes and courses starting in September and covering many musical styles at a range of levels from beginners to degree and diploma levels and professional development for musicians and music teachers. Formal accreditation is available and there is guarenteed progression from one level to the next for those successfully completing an accredited programme. For more information and/or application form please contact Colin Crawley, Professional and Community Education, New Cross, London, SE14 6NW. Tel: 020 7919 7200

Harmony and Arranging for Jazz and Contemporary Styles (10 credits)

Music Course Majoring in Jazz - Semi-Pro or Amateur - 13/01/2003 - January - 11 weeks
Tutor: Colin Crawley. Mondays 2.30 - 5.30. This course studies the theory behind jazz and popular music's use of harmony: scales, extended chords, chord progressions and substitutions. Developing the ear and strengthening writing and arranging skills is a very important aspect of the course. Applicants to the course should be able to read bass and treble clef and have fluent grasp of chord formation.

Introducing Jazz Improvisation(for players)

Music Course Majoring in Jazz - Semi-Pro or Amateur - 29/04/2003 - April - 8 weeks
Tutor: Tim Richards. Tuesdays 7 - 9pm. A practical class for all instruments. This course is suitable for players who are already of a reasonable standard and wish to gain experience playing in a small jazz group. Help will be given with improvisation on a wide variety of standard jazz tunes including bebop, blues, swing, modal and latin styles. Topics covered include: Chord symbols/ Chord/scale relationships/ Using scales, arpeggios, pentatonic scales, patterns/ Jazz harmony/ Swing quavers and triplet feel/ Accompanying (for chordal instruments)/ Playing with a rhythm section/ Building melodic lines and constructing a jazz solo. All instruments welcome, including bassists and drummers.

Jazz Improvisation for Singers - 11 week course

Jazz Only - Semi-Pro or Amateur - 13/01/2003 - January - 11 weeks
Tutor: Anita Wardell. Mondays 6.30 - 9.30pm. An intensive course for experienced singers who wish to become more deeply familiar with jazz repertoire and vocal improvisation. You should be able to follow a song sheet. You should also be prepared to gain musicianship skills and vocabulary with the intention to make yourself a more complete musician. There will be an opportunityh to work towards live performance with jazz ensemble and a class recording session. Mondays 6.30 - 9.30pm

Latin Piano (Intermediate to advanced)

Jazz Only - Semi-Pro or Amateur - 30/04/2003 - April - 10 weeks
Tutor: John Crawford. Tuesday 6.30 - 9.30pm. For pianists of an intermediate level upwards who wish to develop a practical, working knowledge of the main Latin styles as applied to the piano. Afro-Cuban and Afro-Brazilian styles will be covered including Salsa, Samba and Guajira as well as the Argentinean Tango. Players will not need much knowledge of theory and harmony as the course will concentrate on rhythm, style and interpretation. Wednesdays 7 - 9pm

Music Reading and Writing

Duration: 10 weeks - Start date: April. Co-ordinating tutor - Amanda Vincent

This intensive course welcomes singers and instrumentalists who may be competent performers and have some basic knowledge of music but have poor music reading skills. Moving very quickly from first principles, this course teaches you to follow a score, sight sing, write down rhythms, melodies and basic harmonies as you hear them.

Sequencing and Digital Technology

Duration: 11 weeks. Start date: October. Co-ordinating tutor - Jeremy Cox

This course assumes a basic knowledge of sequencing and MIDI and covers composing with sampler and sequencer, multi-timbral synthesis, editing, advanced MIDI, effects processing, and post production techniques. Using Logic Audio sequencing software along with a simple mixing desk, sound module, sampler and an effects unit you will have the opportunity to create a final mix of your own composition.

Sound Sculpture, Sampling and Digital Technology
Duration: 8 weeks. Start date: April. Co-ordinating tutor - Jeremy Cox

Develops your skills in writing electronic music with samplers and digital audio. Using samplers, digital editing techniques and effects, the course will explore the concept of sculpting sound through electronic manipulation. You will be encouraged to use the sampler in a creative manner in combination with sequencing, editing and mixing to produce short original sound pieces.

Studio and Recording Techniques
Duration: 11 weeks. Start date – January. Co-ordinating tutor: Jeremy Cox

Develops your skills in the production of good quality recording. Covers multitrack recording, the mixing desk, SMPTE and synchronisation, microphone placement and EQ, special arrangements for recording drums, vocals and instruments, using compressors, reverbs and other signal processing, basic mixing principles, and desk automation. You will have the opportunity to record and produce a final mix your own track.

Islington Arts Factory
2 Parkhurst Road, London N7 0SF
020 7607 0561 Fax:020 7700 7229; www.cerbernet.co.uk./iaf
Dance Fusion
General Music with a Jazz Element - Jazz Beginner - 17/03/2002 - March - 3 months
Street Jazz
Jazz Only - Jazz Beginner - 15/04/2002 - April - 1 term
Jazz dance classes. Open to all levels. Mon 6.45 - 8pm

London Music School
London Music School, The
131 Wapping High Street
London E1 9NQ
020 7265 0284 Fax:020 7488 3658; music@tlms.co.uk (email); www.tlms.co.uk

Founded in 1984 and it is now part of The Bass Centre Group of Companies, which incorporates the Bass Centre, the Acoustic Centre, House Music Distribution and the London Music School. Their philosophy is "music education for the real world" and the aim is to graduate students to become professional musicians. All courses run for six months (2 x ten week terms), approx. 400 hours. Courses commence in April and October and most have a jazz element

Using MIDI Software
Music Technology - Jazz Beginner - October - 10 weeks
Using Midi Software - Wednesdays 7.15pm - 9.15pm Courses commence January, April, July and October Students should bring a note-book and pen to the class Suitable for beginners. Ten-week course suitable for beginners that provides essential experience in song construction using sequencers, samplers, loops, soft

synths and integrated virtual studio systems. Covering the industry standard Audio-MIDI applications Cubase VST, Recycle, Reason and Rebirth, students will gain the basic skills required to go on to study engineering, songwriting and producing or to compliment their own home-based recording activities.

Morley College

Hanson, Robert, Director for Music, Morley College, 61 Westminster Bridge Road, London SE1 7HT
020 7928 8501 Fax:020 7928 4074;

Jazz Piano for Teachers
Jazz Only - Jazz Beginner - 17/06/2002 - June - 5 weeks
For existing piano teachers who wish to extend their work into the new AB Jazz Piano syllabus, this course covering basic styles and techniques is taught by two contributors to the syllabus. 196VF Mon and Wed 6.30 - 8.30pm Roland Perrin and Tim Richards 5 wks from 17 June Fee: £56 Conc: £16

Music for Youth

Westland, Larry, Music for Youth, 102 Mount Pleasant, London SW18 1PP
020 8870 9624 Fax:020 8870 9935; mfy@mfy.org.uk (email); www.mfy.org.uk

Music for Youth National Festival
General Music with a Jazz Element - Semi-Pro or Amateur - South Bank Centre - 01/07/2002 - July - 5 days
Over 8,000 young musicians aged from 4-21 years come together to perform at Europe's largest youth music festival. Every kind of music will be performed from symphonic to steel, choral to folk, brass to rock, chamber to samba and Big Band jazz. Jazz takes place on Friday 11th July National Wind Band Festival, ABRSM Jazz Horn Workshops, National Jazz Festival at QEH, ABRSM Jazz Horns demonstrations (QEH Foyer)

Premises, The

Craik, Julia, General Manager, Premises Studios Ltd, 201/205 Hackney Road, London E2 8JL
020 7729 7593 Fax:020 7739 5600; info@premises.demon.co.uk (email); www.premises.demon.co.uk

Funding for the educational programme comes from Paul Hamlyn Foundation, News International, Foundation for the Sports and Arts with support from The Voice for the Gospel course. Also run DJ Mixing, MIDI Sampling and Sequencing, Women's Music and Technology courses.

Programme, The
General Music with a Jazz Element - Semi-Pro or Amateur - 6 months
For unemployed bands and vocalists. You can get onto the Premises programme and have free rehearsals, recording, business training for six months if you are 18-24. First band to join programme 'Campag Velocet' have now appeared on Later with Jools Holland as well as appearing on cover of NME. Applicants must have a serious commitment as the training course includes 12 hours a week rehearsal time + NVQ time spent at Hackney College. Runs in six month cycles. Auditions take place throiughout the year, dates on application.

Webb, Robert

70 Culverden Road, London SW12 9LS
webbmadd@britishlibrary.net (email);

Jazz Piano Development Course

Jazz Only - Jazz Beginner - 4 or 8 weeks
With enough enquiries - a minimum of four students - RW will run a course at any point in the year. Course will develop reading skills, comping, piano technique and composition. Students must be serious and consistent about learning.

Summer Schools

COMA

Toynbee Studios, 28 Commercial Street, Whitechapel, London E1 6LS
020 7247 7736 Fax:020 7247 7732; info@coma org(email); www.coma.org

Contemporary Music Summer School

General Music with a Jazz Element - Semi-Pro or Amateur - Bretton Hall, near Wakefield, West Yorkshire -26th July to 2nd August 2003 - 1 week
COMA is concerned with contemporary music rather than Jazz specifically. The summer school does cover - Developing rhythmic skills; Ethnic drumming for composing and performing; Percussion for composers; Improvising with percussion; Improvising with Sound and Video; Free Improvisation. The summer school offers "a friendly, non-competitive yet cutting edge approach to making music. Catering for all abilities from experienced to newcomer to contemporary music".

Guildhall Summer School

Heather Swain, Manager, Guildhall Summer School, Barbican, London EC2Y 8DT
020 7628 2571 (office tel) www.guildhallsummerschool.com
"The Summer School's famous team of British and American tutors, lead by Scott Stroman, have been together for over 15 years. Multi-skilled, open-minded, and the top performers and educators in the field, they are here to help you realise your own personal goals. "

Jazz and Rock Course

1 week Sunday afternoon 13 July to evening of 18 July. Everything is graded by ability and experience, and all abilities and instrumentalists/vocalists are welcome. Jazz and rock bands, vocal groups, classes, workshops, recording sessions, concerts and "the club" each night... it's a busy week.
Daily tuition sessions begin at 10.00am and continue through the day until the 5.30pm dinner break. The club runs each evening from 20.30 to 22.30 and there are also early evening gigs from tutors 19.00 to 20.00.

Singer's Weekend 12 and 13 July

Finishes with a concert on the Sunday night. This new workshop, led by Scott Stroman, Lee Gibson, Peter Churchill, and guests, works in a large group to prepare a programme of jazz, gospel, African and world music. No reading experience is necessary. Perfect for traditional choral singers who want to branch out to meet singers used to working by ear. Course times 10.00am - 17.00

Introduction to Jazz weekend of 12 and 13 July 2003Course Times 10.00 to 17.00 For students of any age with little or no jazz experience,course covers all the basics of harmony, rhythm, improvisation and ear training. Creative atmosphere, working mostly by ear.

Advanced Jazz Weekend 19 and 20 July 2003. For students on the one week course who wish to spend a few more days going deeper into harmony, improvisation, and performance. Finishes with studio sessions and a club concert on Sunday night.
Recording Engineering Beginners/Intermediate: 14 to 18 July studio recording techniques including microphones, mixing, processing, MIDI and production. Students record the many groups on the Jazz and Rock courses, run live sound for the "club" and produce the final concert
Improvisation for Strings All levels. 13th to 18th July 2003
Tutor Tanya Kalmanovitch (Canada) course includes swing, soloing, rhythm,, developing string instrument techniques, amplification, transcription, Irish traditional, South Indian classical, rock, blues, practise routines, jazz string technique.
Accommodation can be booked by completing an application form at the Barbican YMCA (10 minutes from the Guildhall School) in comfortable single or double student rooms - Single room, bed, breakfast and evening meal £35 per night Weekly* rate (7 days) £175 Double (shared twin room), bed, breakfast and evening meal £30 per person/per night. Weekly* rate (7 days) £145 per person.

Jamey Aebersold Jazz Summer School

Jazzwise, Jamey Aebersold Jazz Summer School, 2b Gleneagle Mews, London SW16 6AE
020 8769 7725 Fax:020 8677 7128;
admin@jazzwise.com (email) www.jazzwise.com
Summer School 2003
Jazz Only - Semi-Pro or Amateur - Parkshot Centre, Richmond Adult Community College - 27/07/2003 - July - 5 days
A world class jazz course led by Jamey Aebersold with expert tuition from Britain and America's finest jazz educators The course aims to help you to develop the musical skills that will enable you to become a more effective jazz improviser. You will leave at the end of the week with a greater understanding of the practical processes of creating jazz music and a clear idea of what to practise and how to practise. The course caters equally for beginners and experienced professionals by careful grading on the first day to determine your level of instrumental ability and your knowledge of music theory so that you can be placed in classes that will work best for you. There is no age limit - lower or upper. The course is accredited by the National Open College Network (NOCN). Tutors include – Sax: Mike Tracy, George Bouchard, Shelley Yoelin, Frank Griffith, Jean Toussaint; Guitar Dave Cliff; Trumpet Pat Harbison; Trombone Mark Bassey, Violin Stuart Hall, Voice Louise Gibbs; Piano Don Harle, Phil de Greg, Terry Seabrook; Bass John Goldsby, Bob Sinicrope; Drums Steve Davis.

Mediterranean Jazz Summer School

Fenner, Clive, 41A High Street, Wanstead, London E11 2AA
020 8989 8129 clivefennermjss@jazzsummerschool.com (email); www.jazzsummerschool.com
Cuba Jazz and Latin School
Jazz Only - Semi-Pro or Amateur - Havana, Cuba - 08/02/2003 - February - 2 weeks
Twelve days of workshops, rehearsals and performances with English (Cuban specialists) and Cuban musicians who are also skilled teachers. You will be given an introduction to key Cuban rhythms - Son, Rumba, Cha-cha and learn to play the percussion parts and traditional Cuban songs in these rhythms. This knowledge will then be applied to standard 'latin-jazz' repertoire. By the second week members

will learn to play modern Cuban jazz songs. The course and the accommodation all takes place in as self contained converted 15th century convent in the centre of old Havana. The convent has its own gardens, workshop rooms and a concert hall as well as a café restaurant.

Summer School
Jazz Only - Semi-Pro or Amateur - 16/08/2003 - August - 7 days
2003 is the eigth year and now extended to two separate weeks - 2nd week is 23 to 30th August. Location - a typical Languedoc village, Pezenas, 30 minutes from the sea and the mussel and oyster beds of 'Bassin de Thau'. Participants can book for one or two weeks. The course aims to develop performance and theoretical Jazz skills through small and large group workshops, constructed to meet learning needs and provide the opportunity to learn and play with others. Typical learning activities include * workshops, each group with rhythm section, front line and voice. During the week the groups study with each of the tutors. * Workshops with all students and tutors working together in the MJSS Big Band and MJSS Choir. * Specialist workshops for pianists, rhythm section, sax and brass, voice and guitar. * Opportunities to work on own material. * Evening club, performing workshop material, student material and 'Jam'. * Final night concert in the 'Grand Salle' to the public. * Learning programmes negotiated between students and tutors to meet students needs. The tutors include: Steve Berry, Pete Churchill, Nikki Iles, Martin Hathaway, Martin Speake. Accommodation and Prices: Ensuite double rooms £530 per person; single room with shared shower/wc £495 per person; Twin room for two single people £445 per person; all prices include tuition, break-fast, evening meal. Tuition only £250 per person.

Morley College
Hanson, Robert, Director for Music, Morley College, 61 Westminster Bridge Road, London SE1 7HT
020 7928 8501 Fax:020 7928 4074;

Summer Jazz Weekend
Jazz Only - Semi-Pro or Amateur -11/07/2003 - July - 3 days
In this concentrated period, ear training, harmony and rhythm will be studied using a 'theory through practise' approach, with an emphasis on improving improvisation skills. More details are available on a leaflet produced by the college. Please con-tact the Music Secretary before enrolling. Fri 6.30 - 9.30pm Sara Dhillon Sat and Sun 10am - 5pm Fee: £60 Conc: £30

Music Makers
David Andrews, 16 Whitsbury Road, Fordingbridge, Hants SP6 1JZ Tel/Fax 01425 654819; musmak1@aol.com (email)
Young Musicians Summer Coures (1) at King's College School Wimbledon July 14th to 18th 2003
Juniors 5-6 for children with no previous experience; Intermediate 7-10 for young instrumentalists to work in groups, singing, recorder playing and percussion in a range of styles from classical to jazz; Seniors 8-18 (Grades 2 to 8) for players of all orchestral and band instruments, who will be placed in groups according to abil-ity. The aim is to stretch each individual without being out of their depth. The daily programme will vary but course members may find themselves in a variety of rehearsal situations including - Brass and Wind ensembles, string groups, wind bands, jazz groups, improvisation workshops, chamber groups, sectional rehearsals and full orchestras. The course is non-residential. Booking is through David Andrews but the course is held in Wimbledon.

Music Technology

City University

Andrew Pearce, City University, Music Dept, Northampton Square, London, EC1V 0HB.
020 7477 8271/8284 Fax:020 7477 8576; music@city.ac.ukg (email); www.city.ac.uk/music

MSc/Diploma in Music Information Technology

Start Month: September. Duration: 1/2 years. Requirements: A degree or other recognised professional qualification is normally required. In certain circumstances work experience in a relevant field will be accepted. Qualification: MSc/Diploma

The course aims to inform students in depth about key aspects of music production, storage and dissemination using digital technology. It does not provide training for a specific area of employment, but seeks to cover a range of subjects that will be applicable to many types of employment. It is intended to meet the needs of recent graduates in music and the arts, business studies, computing and engineering who aim to work in the media, communications and the music industry; those already in employment who require additional theoretical support; teaching and lecturing staff who require in-service education.

Community Music

Alison Tickell, Community Music, 35 Union Street, London, SE1 1SD. 020 7234 0900 Fax:020 7403 2611; everyone@cmonline.org.uk (email); www.cmonline.org.uk

Certificate of Higher Education: Music Production

Start Month: September. Duration: 2 years. Requirements: No formal qualifications required: applicants need a proven interest in capacity to use music technology. Qualification: Cert of Higher Education

'Step Up'. Run in partnership with the University of Westminster this course is designed for musicians who thrive within a structured and formal learning environment. This is the only course of its kind in the country. Entry requirements based on musical skills as opposed to qualifications which enables young people from CM's access programmes to gain places. It represents a partnership between a third sector arts organisation and a university, with the majority of the course content written and delivered by CM.

CM Sound Start

Start Month: October. Duration: 1 year 2 days a week.

CM is a music training and production centre for young people near London Bridge. Sound Start set up in 2002 and is a new music and technology course for 16-25 year olds interested in learning music, production and music business skills. For those who want to produce their own music as a performer, DJ or producer. No qualifications or music training are necessary to apply and the course is free. It has been designed especially for those who want to study music but are not able to find the right course at school or college. The main requirement is a passsion for music and the desire to learn with other musicians. The course provides recording and performance opportunities and offersrecognised accreditation through the London Open College Network. All students will be given individual study support if needed and help to make the right move at the end of the course, including help with application forms, interview techniques, work placements and personal action plans Students from CM courses have previously gone to university, into the music business, trained as tutors and even become professional performers. Course Content Students will be taught at CM for up to 2 days per week covering music technology, music business awareness, keyboard skills, voice song writing, DJ and performance skills. The course runs from October to June. Sound Start is supported by Esmee Fairbairn Foundation, City Parochial Foundation and London Arts

Goldsmiths College
Jeremy Peyton Jones, Goldsmiths University of London, Professional and Community, Education, University of London, New Cros, London, SE14 6NW. 020 7919 7229/7200 Fax:020 7919 7223; j.peyton.jones@gold.ac.uk (email); www.goldsmiths.ac.uk

Creative Applications in the Sound Studio
Start Month: October. Duration: 30 weeks.

Tutors: Jeremy Cox and Nic Bevan. This course assumes some basic knowledge of studio recording and computer music techniques and is designed both for composers wanting to take the sound manipulation and recording creative process further and for those interested in developing their skills in recording techniques and sound synthesis and design. The course takes students through recording theory, sound synthesis and analogue/digital recording on to a recording project and preparation for mastering to CD. It will cover digital and analogue approaches, time code formats, mixing aims and techniques, sound synthesis and MIDI applications.

Hackney Community College
Chris Wilson, Hackney Community College, Central Admissions Unit, Shoreditch Campus, Falkirk Street, London, N1 6HQ.
020 7613 9320 (office tel)

midi tech
Start Month: September. thurs 6-8.30.

Haringey Arts Council
Keith Gillies, Haringey Arts Council, The Chocolate Factory, Unit 104, Building B, Clarendon Road, London, N22 6XJ.
020 8365 7500 Fax:020 8365 8686.

Multi Media Course- The Factory 21
Duration: 6 months

Sound Recording and Music Industry Programm Lvl 3
Start Month: September. Duration: 36 weeks.

This course is aimed at those with definite clear goals within the music industry who have some degree of prior knowledge/experience. The training is a direct follow on course from Level 2 and for those starting the course at this level it is essential to have a good working and theoretical knowledge of MIDI

Sound Recording and Music Industry Programme 1and 2
Start Month: September. Duration: 36 weeks.

Gives students the opportunity of spending time in a modern sound recording studio, to be introduced to the principles and practices in sound recording, mixing and mastering from both pre-recorded sounds and live performances. They will also cover both theoretical and practical Midi Recording

Hoxton Hall

Hoxton Hall, 130 Hoxton Street, London, N1 6SH.
020 7684 0060 Fax:020 7729 3815; office@hoxtonhall.dabsol.co.uk (email);
www.hoxtonhall.dabsol.co.uk

Dance Music Production
Start Month: May. Duration: 10 weeks.

Friday 11am-4pm Tutor: Dave Millea One day a week, 10 weeks course, repeated each term. Covers basic sound engineering and music technology, rhythm and counting, live playing, microphone techniques, multitrack recording, keyboard techniques, drum machine programming, synthesis, sampling, midi, mixing and mastering to DAT and CD. Use of Cubase, Logic, Recycle, Rebirth, Sound Forge, Wavelab and Vienna. Students must be keen on music and be able to commit to a one day per week schedule. All abilities welcome. Fees: £62+£8 membership Concs: £16 +£4 membership

Music Technology
Start Month: September. Duration: 1 year.

Wednesday 11-4pm Tutor: Peter Cload A one day a week, one year course which can be taken on its own or with other music classes (e.g. songwriting, singing). Learn live and recording sound engineering, how to use mixing desk and outboard equipment, creating computer music, hard disk recording, sampling and sequencing. The course also links technology with general musicianship such as scales and chords, rhythm, ear training and keyboard skills. Students are encouraged to work on their own creative projects. Entry is via interview. Fees: £46.50+£8 membership Concs: £6.50+£4 membership

London College of Music and Media

Eddie Harvey, London College of Music and Media, Thames Valley University, St. Mary's Road, Ealing, London, W5 5RF.
020 8231 2304 Fax:020 8231 2546; enquiries.lcm2@tvu.ac.uk (email);
www.tvu.ac.uk/lcmm

BA (Hons)DipHE in Music Technology
Location: Thames Valley University Ealing W5. Start Month: October. Duration: 3 years. Qualification: Dip in Higher Ed - Music Technology

BA(Hons)/DipHE in Music Technology Modes of study available Full-time On this pathway you will get the chance to gain a broad understanding of the variety of careers that are available in the music industry and valuable personal introductions, where possible. Our Careers in Music seminar programme offers an enjoyable and informal way for you to meet well-known composers, music agents, performers, recording industry executives, music copyright managers and others. The objective of this pathway is to ensure you acquire and develop skills that are appropriate to contemporary sound and music, pre- and post-production. We support students from a wide range of backgrounds with the proviso that you can demonstrate significant commitment to your area of interest when you apply. You will engage in the practical application of technology from a creative and theoretically informed base and on completion of the course are expected to be able to skilfully operate and control complex recording sessions and projects in high performance audio environments. During your first year study you will cover audio theory, be introduced to video, sound and multimedia, sound studio techniques and music technology (MIDI and synthesis). Your second year continues with sound studio techniques and music technology, but also focuses on digital recording, music in industry and creative sound. You will also need to complete a recording portfolio. If you continue to study for the BSc (Hons), the third year provides significant creative freedom and major opportunities for you to develop projects exploiting and developing your talents and audio production expertise. You will focus on music technology, but will also have the opportunity to see it in a broader context – including 'live' sound and post-production techniques, emerging technologies and standards, business survival, experimental sound and digital broadcast media. During your third year you will also complete a project. Mode: Full-time Location: Ealing Starting: October Length of pathway: Three year degree, two year DipHE UCAS Code BA (Hons) Music Technology UCAS code: W351 BSc/MusT DipHE Music Technology UCAS code: W350 DipHE/MuT UCAS website http://www.ucas.ac.uk Entry requirements: A Level: 8 points (2 A Levels at one sitting) BTec National Diploma: Merit overall Advanced GNVQ: Merit Access: Pass Further requirements: You will be required to attend an interview at which you will need to bring a portfolio of work either on audio cassette, DAT or CD. Visit days: Kate Pittman on +44 (0)20 8231 2092 Fax +44 (0)20 8231 2744 e-mail kate.pittman@tvu.ac.uk Further information: For further information, please contact learning.advice@tvu.ac.uk

Media Production Facilities

Media Production Facilities, Bon Marche Building, Ferndale Road, London, SW9 8EJ. 020 7737 7152 Fax:020 7738 5428; mpf@media-production.demon.co.uk (email); www.media-production.demon.co.uk

Analogue Sound Recording and Production

Start Month: September. Duration: 3 months. Qualification: Certificate.

Theory of Acoustic and Electromagnetic Waves: basis of acoustics; decibels; basic electrical principles; Principles of Magnetic Recording: record and produce equalisation and alignment hysteresis, bias, coercivity, print-through, crosstalk; Practical Operation of a Recording Studio: multitrack recording amd mixing processes; 24-track analogue tape recording with autolocator; digital and analogue mastering; Mixing Cconsoles: split and in-line designs; methods of operation and facilities offered; peak and VU metering; auxiliary sends and returns; inserts points; foldback; audio patchbays; master status switching; channel and monitor paths, group and stereo busses, intro to top of the range recording and mixing consoles (Solid State Logic, Neve, etc.) intro to computer-based automation systems including Amex Supertrue; Microphone Design and Characteristics: capacitor/condensor, electret, dynamic and ribbon designs; phantom power; practical application of microphone placement techniques; Outboard Effects and Signal Processing : digital reverbs, delays, and multi-effects processors; compressors and limiters, noise gates, side chains, graphic and parametric equalisers; software-based Virtual

Dynamics FX; Studio Monitor Systems: passive and active crossover networks; studio and control room acoustics; Basic Maintenance Techniques: first-line studio maintenance; Fundamentals of Synthesis: modular monophonic sythesisers to polyphonic, multi-timbral synths: digital and hybrid methods of synthesis; Introduction to Computers and MIDI in Production: the role of the computer in music production and recording; applications of MIDI; Introduction to Digital Audio: sampling theory; coding systems; conversion techniques; principles of storage; stereo digital sampling and editing; Business in the Industry: contracts; professional societies and associations, work conditions and opportunities. Tuition fees: £2750 + VAT. Registration fee: £100.This course is also the first module of the one year course.

Audio for TV/Film
Duration: 5 days

A five day introductory, practically orientated course in the audio post-production process for TV and film. The course is limited to 4 people, for those with some experience of professional recording, preferably in music-to-picture operations. Course materials include clips of TV programmes and films. Technical facilities include a fully-equipped 24-track studio with an automated Amek Mozart console, Otari and Tascam DA88 multitracks, Adam-Smith Zeta 3 synchronisers, VTRs, Fairlight FAME digital mixer/recorder/editor, featuring the MFX3 DAW with Amek Digital Mixing System and Sadie, referring to Dolby formats. The course aims to update existing skills and re-train candidates in current audio post production techniques, marrying sound-to-picture, editing and mixing to film and broadcast standards. This includes hard disk editing, utilising industry standard systems. The practical bias of the course aims to give an understanding of existing production requirements, integrated with computer-based techniques. The course is held at Media Productions in Brixton, South London. Course Fee: £650 + VAT

Creative Music Recording and Production
Start Month: September. Duration: 3 months. Qualification: Certificate.

This course is also the third module of the one year course and is therefore only suitable for those with considerable experience in multitrack studio operation and MIDI programming. Tuition fees: £2,750 + VAT. Registration fee: £100

Digital Sound Recording and Production
Start Month: May. Duration: 3 months. Qualification: Ceertificate.

This course is also the second module of the one year course and is therefore only suitable for those with experience in music production and multitrack recording. A basic knowledge of MIDI would also be required. Tuition fees: £6,350 + VAT. Registration fee: £100

One Year Diploma Course
Start Month: September. Duration: 1 year.

During the first module, Analogue Sound Recording and Production Techniques, students develop practical skills in multitrack sound recording and mixing, while also acquiring a solid foundation in the theoretical principles of audio. Hands-on experience is gained through operating the well equipped studio and digital programming suite. Students, working in small grouups under the guidance of an experienced engineer, actively participate in every aspecct of the multitrack recording and mixing processes. The second module, Digital Sound Recording and

Production Techniques, places a strong emphasis on digital technology and its applications in sound production, recording and post-production. Students attend seminars and lectures with specialists in all areas of digital audio, including computer-based MIDI music production, automated sound mixing and all forms of digital audio recording. Co-operation with various studios and manufacturers of pre-audio equipment allows Media to provide training in-house on a range of digital audio systems. The third module is Creative Music Recording and Production Techniques. The most practical term of the three encourages students to apply the knowledge and skills they have acquired in a creative way. Professionals share tricks of the trade and students develop their own music projects as well as with bands and individual artists. Sessions at other commercial sites provide practical experience of mixing and mastering techniques at the highest level. We examine employment opportunities in the industry and an introduction to audio post-production techniques is included. Tuition fees: £6350 + VAT. Registration fee: £100. This course has a modular format, each of 12 weeks duration.

SADiE 4 Day Course
Start Month: July. Duration: 4 days.

This course is aimed at those who need to develop an understanding of the SADiE PC-based digital editing and mastering system, predominant in radio production and general digital compiling, editing and mastering. Previous experience of the system is not essential, though knowledge of established audio editing techniques and Windows based software is advantageous. Candidates will gain a thorough working knowledge of the system, with an overview of hard disk editing concepts, advantages and limitations. Familiarisation of the SADiE's principal feaatures: - Analogue and digital inputs and outputs; Control windows, editing inc. Edit Decision Lists (EDLs), processing; File and disk management; Synchronisation, mixing and masterring to DAT/Exabyte/CD. Price £475 + VAT.

Premises, The
Julia Craik, Premises Studios Ltd, 201/205 Hackney Road, London, E2 8JL.
020 7729 7593 Fax:020 7739 5600; info@premises.demon.co.uk (email);
www.premises.demon.co.uk

Women's Music and Technology Week
Start Month: June. Duration: 5 days.

This five day workshop is aimed at women musicians and vocalists of all styles and standards and will be an intensive and enjoyable week of music tuition, sonwriting, structured improvisation plus hands-on experience and recording sessions in a 24 track recording studio. Cost: £125

The London Music School
London Music School, The, 131 Wapping High Street, London, E1 9NQ.
020 7265 0284 Fax:020 7488 3658; music@tlms.co.uk (email); www.tlms.co.uk

Combined Music Performance and Technology
Start Month: October. Duration: 6 month.

Full Time Combined Performance and Music Technology Course. Designed for musicians who wish to increase their playing ability, gain an understanding of music theory and learn the basics of sound engineering and using midi software. It is an integrated course that combines elements of the Performance Course and the

Music Technology Course. Music and Performance, Harmony and Theory, Sight-reading, Instrument or Voice Technique, Session Workshop, Song writing, 1 to 1 Tutorials, Music Technology, Studio Practice and Maintenance, Introduction to Cubase and Reason, Basic Sampling 1. Song to Film 2. Music Projects (Voice to Music and Music to Voice) Introduction to Mike Placement (all instruments and voice) Multi tracking Students who work throughout the course to develop their own songs will also have the opportunity to record one song to demo. As this course involves integrating with students who are attending full time courses in Music Performance or music Technology space restriction will mean that places are very limited.

Music Technology

Start Month: October. Duration: 10 weeks.

Courses commence January, April, July and October A comprehensive ten-week course aimed at those with a basic experience of Audio-MIDI applications. Offering 50 hours of full-on study, this course is particularly suitable for musicians, DJ's and tech-heads looking to enhance their knowledge of Cubase VST, Logic, Reason, Rebirth, Recycle and Peak and polish their songwriting and production skills. Students will be encouraged to work on their own musical projects with constant assistance from the teaching staff. All in all, this is a perfect opportunity for students seeking an intensive tuition program without commitment to a full-time course. 11am - 5pm Course Fee £650 LIMITED PLACES AVAILABLE (Bank Holiday Weekend 25th August 2001) TO BOOK YOUR PLACE CONTACT THE ADMISSIONS TEAM TODAY!

Music Technology and Engineering

Start Month: October. Duration: 10 weeks.

Basic Sound Engineering -Tuesdays 7.15pm - 9.15pm Courses commence January, April, July and October Students should bring a pen and note-book to the class. The course covers - suitable for beginners who wish to learn all of the basic principles of 24 track recording along with a thorough grounding in the art of audio engineering. Aspiring studio technicians and sound engineers as well as working musicians and DJ's will all benefit from this comprehensive over-view of the modern recording process. Core topics covered include: • Microphone placement (Inc Drums, Guitar, Bass and Vocals) The 32 channel mixing desk CD and DAT mastering, Vocal enhancement, Use of effects, Noise gates, compressors and limiters, Digital mastering, using cubase and peak, 24 track hard drive recording, Using Midi Software – Wednesdays 7.15pm - 9.15pm Courses commence January, April, July and October Students should bring a note-book and pen to the class Suitable for beginners The course covers A ten-week course suitable for beginners that provides essential experience in song construction using sequencers, samplers, loops, soft synths and integrated virtual studio systems. Covering the industry standard Audio-MIDI applications Cubase VST, Recycle, Reason and Rebirth, students will gain the basic skills required to go on to study engineering, songwriting and producing or to compliment their own home-based recording activities. ? Rebirth has been used on many hit records to recreate the 70s sound. ? Cubase is a standard industry software. ? Reason is one of the most important software releases of recent years. ? Recycle is a loop editing software. TUITION FEE FOR EACH OF THE ABOVE COURSES - £250.00

Music Technology Course

Start Month: October. Duration: 6 months.

Comprehensive program of Audio MIDI technology tuition in the UK, the London Music School's six month full time course offers intensive training in all aspects of modern studio recording, engineering and production. The course is broken up in to equal hours for computers and sound engineering and is module based. Key features covered by the curriculum include: Sequencing - how to use Logic and Cubase - the industry standards! MIDI and Audio Recording - How to record MIDI and audio on Apple Macintosh G3 and G4 or Atari. Studio and Live Recording - Record musicians as they play and perform in one of our live rooms, using 24-track studio equipment. Mastering - Delivering finished work on computer, DAT, reel-to-reel tapes and compact discs in all of the current industry standard digital file formats Microphone Techniques - Choose and place the correct microphones to optimise recording results. Sampling and Looping - In depth use of Akai and Emax samplers as well as Peak and Logic programs. Dance Music Software - How to use Rebirth, Recycle and Reason to make Dance tracks. Use of Effects - apply effects, delay, reverb, noisegates, limiters and compressors. Song Structuring and Lyric Writing - Examine and analyse song form and structure. Production Techniques - Experiment with song arrangements and recording concepts. Understanding SMPTE - synchronise Midi to Audio and then to Film using SMPTE time code. Equalisation and Fader Manipulation - use EQ and manipulate faders to achieve the best results possible. CD Cover and Label Design - Designing and producing CD labels and covers using Photoshop and QuarkXPress. Music for the Internet - compress and save audio files in RealAudio and MP3 formats. Studio Maintenance - maintain a safe, tidy and efficient working environment Career Advice - receive invaluable advice on career placement and development.

Using MIDI Software
Start Month: October. Duration: 10 weeks.

12 Students per year. Using Midi Software - Wednesdays 7.15pm - 9.15pm Courses commence January, April, July and October Students should bring a notebook and pen to the class Suitable for beginners. The course covers - ten-week course suitable for beginners that provides essential experience in song construction using sequencers, samplers, loops, soft synths and integrated virtual studio systems. Covering the industry standard Audio-MIDI applications Cubase VST, Recycle, Reason and Rebirth, students will gain the basic skills required to go on to study engineering, songwriting and producing or to compliment their own home-based recording activities.

University of Westminster
University of Westminster, Headquarters Building, 309 Regent Street, London, W1R 8AL. 020 7911 5000 (office tel)

MA Audio-Production
Location: Harrow Campus. Start Month: October. Duration: 1/2 years. Qualification: MA Audio-Production.

A new type of education programme for audio specialists, the MA in Audio-Production aims to develop students' creative abilities in audio covering music, sound, radio, television and film and multimedia. Course staff call on an impressive range of experience, from course leader Alan Fisher - musician, producer and engineer on projects including Take That, Bjork, Boy George, Frankie Goes to Hollywood and 808 State - to Quintin Hogg Research Fellow Dave Laing, one of the most significant writers on pop music in the academic world; plus Daniel Miller, Managing Director of Mute Records, has been appointed as external examiner to the course. Modules include: Recording and Production Process, Digital Audio, History and Theory of Audio Production, The Audio Production Industry, Audio Design for Broadcast Media and Film, Digital and Electronic Interface for Music.

Other

Guildhall School of Music and Drama

Silk Street, Barbican, London EC2Y 8DT
020 7628 2571 Fax:020 7256 9438; info@gsmd.ac.uk (email); www.gsmd.ac.uk
Music Therapy Diploma (DIPMTH 9GSMD-York))
General Music with a Jazz Element - Aspiring Degree Level and Above - September - 1 Year
Validated by the University of York. Aims to realise the full potential of students' individual musicianship and to apply this clinically with people with "learning disabilities, physical handicaps and neurology, mental illness, geriatric, emotional and social disorder in children and adults. It prepares students for employment in health, education, social and community service and private practice. The course is influenced by humanistic and psycho-dynamic approaches to therapy, although students are encouraged to develop a personal style of work". In addition to clinical and musical skills the course aims to develop a sensitive understanding of human relationships, an acute listening ability, creative and expressive musical playing, careful observation skills, peer-group learning skills, a strong questioning attitude, a willingness to examine one's own feelings and reactions. Course content - weekly lectures and seminars on psychology, theory of music therapy and academic studies; clinical lecture son disability, pathology and treatment; clinical tutorials on casework; experimental groups in music therapy, group dynamics and movement; up to four contrasting placements with adults and children in hospitals, schools and centres, supervised by qualified therapists; three weekly classes in improvisation, group improvisation, keyboard musicianship and clinical improvisation; individual lessons on Principal and Second study instruments. Clinical practice - external placement from the first week of training. One day a week throughout the course is dedicated to clinical practice. Students learn first by observation and then by taking their own cases with careful support and feedback from their placement supervisor and clinical tutor on the course.

Northern Ireland

Full-Time

Queen' s University
School of Music, Belfast BT7 1NN
01232 335105 Fax:01232 238484; 0289 066 5577 (box office);
B.Mus (B Mus)
General Music with a Jazz Element - Aspiring Degree Level and Above - September
- 3 years
Music schools' strengths are in historical musicology, composition and music tech-
nology. All students study Western Music, Fundamental Harmony and Techniques
and style with 2 or 3 modules chosen from World Music Culture, World Music
Society – no stated jazz module in any of the 3 years.

University of Ulster at Jordanstown
Humanities Faculty Office, Newtownabbey BT37 0QB
01232 366690 (enquiries); 01232 366354 (Faculty of Humanties
BMus with Hons (B.Mus. (Hons))
General Music with a Jazz Element - Aspiring Degree Level and Above - September
- 3 years
Course allows students to pursue the academic study of music together with practical training on one or two instruments, taught as an integral element. Distinctive
features of the course include the study of modern methods of analysis, composition in a wide variety of styles, the practical study of early music, knowledge of
information technology, and an emphasis on music of our own century including
popular music and jazz. Following a four-day assessment visit, the Higher
Education Funding Council confirmed that our teaching of music can be rated as
'excellent', providing educational opportunities at the highest level. Year 1 – all
modules compulsory and cover music history from early music, baroque, classical
studying important works up to the present day. Year 2 – historical and technical
modules and in performance students can choose popular American music 1900 -
39. Year 3 – modules cover late 19 early 20th century music complemented by an
advanced analysis course. All students complete a project and develop their performance to a higher level.

Music Technology

Queen' s University
Queen's University, School of Music, Belfast, N Ireland, BT7 1NN.
01232 335105 Fax:01232 238484; 0289 066 5577 (box office)

BSc (Hons) Music Technology

Start Month: September. Duration: 3 years. Requirements: BCC to include Computer Science or Mathematics or Music or Physics or Grade VIII Theory and Practical + GCSE Mathematics and Music. Qualification: BSc Hons Music Technology .

Music Technology is the study of the principles and practices of generation, processing and recording of musical sound and data. It combines musical knowledge and skills in acoustics, electronics and computer science. Students will learn how to operate equipment and computer software so as to produce the musical results, and they will also learn the principles which allow them to design new equipment or software, or to make innovative use of existing facilities. While Music Technology has only recently been recognised as a distinct subject, it draws on a long tradition and science of musical machines. Similarly, while a first degree in Music Technology was offered for the first time in 2000, the subject has been taught within Music degrees at Queen's for ten years and at Masters level for six years. The course is designed to give students knowledge of fundamental acoustics and psychoacoustics, fundamental music theory, and rudimentary electronics and computer science. Students will also learn how to distinguish musical and sonic features by ear, to use common studio equipment to record, diffuse, edit and process sound, and the fundamentals of how to use and program a computer. The course also covers uses of music technology in electro-acoustic music, and in the recording and new media industries. Students will have the opportunity of specialising in electro-acoustic composition, sound recording, or software development in their final year. It is hoped also to give students the opportunity of a work placement in a recording studio or some other appropriate business as part of the course. Some modules in Music or another related subject may be taken as part of the course.

Eire

Newpark Music Centre

Ronan Guilfoyle, Head of Jazz, Newpark Music Centre, Newtownpark Avenue, Blackrock, Co Dublin
00 +353 1 288 3740 (office tel) 00 +353 1 288 3989 www.newparkmusic.com
Professional Musician Training Course (PMTC) Jazz only Full Time - September to May 1 year – Certificate
Practical course specifically designed to prepare participants for a career as a professional musian. It is not specific to any one musical genre. Consists of 3 terms from September to May and in addition to 10 hours teaching a week, instrumental practice, composition and assignment time is required. Course includes - instrumental or vocal technique. Tuition availble for guitar, clarinet,violin, bass guitar, trumpet, trombone, voice, drums, percussion, saxophone, flute, piano, keyboard; piano as second instrument; coposition, harmony and ear training; jazz improvisation; technology. The Centre also plays host to IASJ Workshops which feature internationally known musicians as tutors.

Jazz Studies Dip (LGSM) jazz only – Full time - September - one year
Full time Licenciate Diploma in Jazz Studies from the Guildhall School of Music London. Admission by audition (early May each year) or by completing the certificate PMTC course. Course includes - Instrumental tuition on a chosen instrument following technique, tone production, set repertoire syllabus, transposition, sight reading; ear training covering general harmonic and rhythmic recognition; jazz improvisation; harmony arranging. Course runs from September to May.

Northern

Full-Time

Newcastle College

Birkett, James, Newcastle College, Faculty of Visual and Perf Arts, Rye Hill Campus, Scottswood Road, Newcastle upon Tyne NE4 7SA
0191 200 4000 Fax:0191 200 4729; jamesbirkett@btinternet.com (email); www.ncl.ac.uk

BMus(Hons) Jazz, Popular and Commercial Music (B Mus (Hons))

Music Course Majoring in Jazz - Aspiring Degree Level and Above - October - 3 years This practical degree course is the only one of its kind in the country. It provides in depth vocational training, which meets the technical and intellectual needs of successful musician. It is for dedicated musicians who have an advanced level of performance ability and would like to perfect their skills and technique.
Year 1: Instrumental studies, Ensemble studies, Music technology studies, Harmony and arranging, Keyboard studies, Aural studies, History, Critical studies
Year 2: Composition, Critical practice, Performance, Production (Optional), General Musicianship (Optional), Complementary studies, Electives
Year 3: Critical evaluation, Professional studies. A choice of two of the following, Performance, Production, Composition and arranging, Dissertation

In September 2003 Tim Garland was appointed as the Northern Arts Composer Fellow for the University. For details of his musical work see www.timgarland.com

University of Newcastle

Middleton, Richard, Music Department, University of Newcastle upon Tyne, Queen Victoria Road, Newcastle upon Tyne NE1 7RU
0191 222 6000

B.A. (Hons) Music (B.A. (Hons))

General Music with a Jazz option - Aspiring Degree Level and Above - September - 3 years
Year 1: music history, musical structures and processes, contemporary compositional techniques, performance and studio-based work. Modules on the roles of music in contemporary culture, including an introduction to the study of popular music. A large range of options available at Years 2 and 3.

Year 2: World music, musical analysis, plus your own package of options -historical and cultural studies - music and the Reformation; black music; the jazz age; world popular music. There are also practical options, typically including performance, composition, studio-based work, orchestration, and arranging and improvisation.
Year 3: music and culture with modules in music and cultural theory, music analysis plus a major specialist study (assessed through a dissertation, portfolio or recital) and at least one further option in historical and cultural studies. In years 2 and 3 you can take up to a third of your modules from other subjects offered by the University.

Part-Time

Newcastle College

Faculty of Visual and Perf Arts, Rye Hill Campus, Scottswood Road, Newcastle upon Tyne NE4 7SA

0191 200 4000 (office tel

September – 20 weeks – Saturday 09.00 to 16.00

Fame School (Level 1 - Foundation) Jazz Dance

If you're looking to get started in the Performing Arts and Entertainment Industries – as a singer, dancer, actor or as a pop performer – then this course is for you.

Fame School (Level 2 - Intermediate) Jazz Dance

If you're looking to get started in the Performing Arts and Entertainment

Northumbria University

Newcastle City Campus, Ellison Place, Newcastle upon Tyne, NE1 8ST
Tel: +44 (0)191 (0191) 227 4935 FAX: (0191) 227 3632:
ar.admissions@northumbria.ac.uk

Foundation Certificate in Jazz and Commercial Dance
September - 2 years, at Squires Building, Newcastle City Campus
Entrance by interview and audition. No formal qualifications are required and applications are welcomed from students with a broad-based interest in performance. Access course, aimed at mature students who wish to take the course for personal enjoyment, or as a route into employment or further study.

Dance styles include draw on the worlds of Broadway, Hollywood, West End musical and pop videos, the course is centred on choreography for theatrical/commercial performance. Course offers workshop sessions in commercial and jazz techniques

Year 1 - the first three units offer students workshops exploring approaches to commercial dance. Coached by professional dancers, these workshops will examine the fundamentals of the draft techniques of commercial dance for musicals, films and video through practical explorations of the basic principles of commercial dance techniques and choreography and through viewing of key works by major figures in the field such as Fred Astaire, Gene Kelly, Jerome Robbins and Michael Jackson. The first semester also includes the critical evaluation of professional examples of work in performance.

Year 2 - students develop a project in an area of personal special interest complemented by tutorial support and seminars.

COURSEWORK AND ASSESSMENT

In the first year, assessments are undertaken at two points in each semester and are based on a combination of critical evaluation of professional performance and successful completion of a variety of practical dance assignments.

In the second year, assessment is summative, based on the student's submission and performance of their individual project. It is possible to exit from the course after successful completion of the first year. An Intermediate Certificate will be awarded in this case. Applicants should note that successful completion of the course does not necessarily guarantee progression on to any of the higher level courses provided within Performing Arts.

University of Durham
Old Shire Hall, Durham DH1 3HP
0191 374 2000

M.Mus, PhD (M Mus/PhD)
Music Course Majoring in Jazz - Aspiring Degree Level and Above - October - 2-5 years
In most cases, students are registered for an MA by thesis and then, if their work progresses satisfactorily, they may apply for transfer to the M.Mus or PhD. If a student's native language is not English, he/she must be proficient in spoken and written English.

Short Course

Higham Hall
Higham Hall College, Bassenthwaite Lake, Cockermouth CA13 9SH
017687 76276 Fax:017287 76013; admin@higham-hall.org.uk (email);
www.higham-hall. org.uk

Jazz Workshop
Music Course Majoring in Jazz - Semi-Pro or Amateur - Highham Hall, Cumbria - August - 1 week
Designed for average to advanced players who wish to develop and improve their jazz and Big Band playing. The full spectrum of jazz is approached from duos to a 16 piece Big Band. Guidance during playing time,theory and instrumentation classes are included in the programme. Players of all instruments may apply but can only be accepted after discussion with the leader Len Phillips on 01322 521515 or 020 8850 1555

Landmark Recordings in Jazz
Jazz Only - Semi-Pro or Amateur - Cockermouth - October - weekend
Tutor Chris Howes s an experienced H H tutor who is well established in London as pianist, promotor, teacher and broadcaster. Selects stylistically varied performances which have made significant and influential leaps in both vocal and instrumental jazz during the first 80 years of the musics' recorded history. Each of the weekends seven sessions will contain the background story to the recording featured and some analysis of the music, its spirit and of the performer's development. Discussion, musical comparisons and archive video footage will be used. The seven recordings will include - Louis Armstrong West End Blues; Duke Ellington Far East Suite; Billie Holliday Strange Fruit; Miles Davis Kind of Blue; Frank Sinatra In the Wee Small Hours.

The Voice in Jazz
Jazz Only - Jazz Beginner - Higham Hall, Cumbria - May - 3 days
Chris Howes: examining ther voice in jazz through the ages - from African antecedents to High Art

Music Technology

Newcastle College

James Birkett, Newcastle College, Faculty of Visual and Perf Arts, Rye Hill Campus, Scottswood Road, Newcastle upon Tyne, Tyne and Wear, NE4 7SA. 0191 232 1718 (tel); 0191 232 1718; 0191 200 4000 Fax:0191 200 4729; jamesbirkett@btinternet.com

National Diploma in Music Technology

Start Month: October. Duration: 2 years. Qualification: BTEC HND.

A course both for singers and musicians who want to record music or create backing tracks, and for those seeking a career as a technology or production specialist in the music industry.

City College Manchester
Arden Centre, Sale Road, Northenden, Manchester M23 0DD
0161 957 1790 (admissions office tel); 0161 945 3854; www.ccm.ac.uk
No Jazz courses but offer BTEC certificate, diploma and HND in Music Technology

Music Technology BTEC National Certificate
Music Techology – September – 16 hours per week for 45 weeks
Offers a practical understanding of the recording studio and the integration of computers in the current music industry. Covers music production, MIDI sequencing and theory, sound recording, acoustics, keyboard skills, music industry studies plus DJ module or Musicianship module. Qualification is roughly equivalent to 2 A levels

Music Technology BTEC Diploma (BTEC Dip Music Technology)
Music Technology – September – 16-19 hours per week for 2 years 36 weeks per year. Provides a sound background knowledge in all main areas of music technology. Course is mainly hands-on with training in computer-based music systems and learning about the structure of the music industry. Basic music training, sound recording and music. Optional unit in year 2 includes music video production and composition as well as a two week work placement.

Music Technology BTEC HND
Music Technology – September – 16-19 hours per week for 2 years
Learn the techniques and technologies associated with the recording, composition and manipulation of sound and music. Topics (some are optional) musical studies, MIDI technology, acoustics, audio standards, technology workshops, electronics, computer music systems, recording and audio workshops, business administration, AV and Media application, new media technology.

Liverpool Community College
The Arts Centre, 9 Myrtle Street, Liverpool L7 7JA
0151 252 4300 Fax:0151 252 3000; www.liv-coll.ac.uk

Advanced Certificate in Jazz and Commerical Music (Advanced Cert in Jazz and Commercial Music (MOCN))
Music Course Majoring in Jazz - Aspiring Degree Level and Above - September – 1 year daytime, 17.5 hours per week, 33 weeks per year
Advanced course in jazz and commercial music covering instrumental and vocal performance, improvisation, sight reading, arranging, song writing, computer music skills, recording techniques, keyboard skills. This is preparation for BTEC HND in music and commercial music, a HNC in music Tutor Les Bolger 0151 252 4316

BTEC Higher National Certificate in Music
General music – September – 17.5 hours per week, 33 weeks per year, I year
Advanced course in commercial music, covering harmony, scoring for commercial mediums, improvisation, aural training, keyboard skills and performance skills. Qualification can lead to 2nd year HND in Music; degree course

BTEC higher National Certificate/Diploma in Music Performance
General music – September – daytime 15-25 hours per week over 30 weeks per year, 2 years to complete
Offers both classical and commercial music training. Students will be involved in lunch time and evening concerts. Music performance level 4

Liverpool Institute for Performing Arts (LIPA)
Mount Street, Liverpool L1 9HF
0151 330 3000 Fax:0151 330 3131; reception@lipa.ac.uk (email); www.lipa.ac.uk

B.A. (Hons) in Music (BA (Hons) Music)
General Music - Aspiring Degree Level and Above - September - 3 years
Year 1: Contextual Studies, Instrumental Performance, Music Creation, Music Production, Performance Project, Performance Skills, Professional Development,
Year 2: Advanced Instrumental Performance or Complementary Performance Skills, Advanced Music Creation, Ensemble Performance Skills, Music Production 2 Professional Practice and The Music Business, Public Performance Project
Year 3: Choice of 2: The Performer; Ensemble Performer, Composer, Songwriter, Producer; Final Research Paper
Performance modules include one-to-one tuition on your main instrument, ensembles, specialised ensembles e.g. Big Band/choir/guitar-orchestra and a cappella. In term three you apply the skills acquired in a performance project.

Cert in Higher Education: in Performing Arts for Disabled Artists (Cert in HE)
General performing arts- Semi-Pro or Amateur - September - 1 year
Specialist training in either acting, dance or music with the opportunity to study a secondary, complementary skill e.g. movement, singing or percussion.
Modules - ensemble skills, exploring general performance skills; Arts management and study skills plus Professional Development; Contextual Studies gives theoretical framework in which to work and explores the performing arts generally and also places Disability Arts within a political and social context; Opportunities For Disabled Artists aims to give support and advice on how to look for, apply and audition for other courses.

Royal Northern College of Music
Hall, Mike, Co-Ordinator Jazz Studies, Royal Northern College of Music, 124 Oxford Road, Manchester M13 9RD
0161 907 5200 Fax:0161 273 7611; 0161 907 5555 (box office); info@rncm.ac.uk (email); www.rncm.ac.uk

Although known for their classical music training the RNCM has opportunities for students to expand their skills and knowledge in jazz styles and improvisations, but within the context of an integrated course rather than as a specialist in jazz studies. The college has agreements for student exchanges with four USA music schools including the Manhattan School of Music as well as five conservatoires in Europe. The College in the centre of Manchester has its own on campus students accomodation. There are also four performance venues including the 600 seater Opera Theatre.

BA(Music)/Grad RNCM (BA/Grad RNCM)
General Music with a Jazz Element - Semi-Pro or Amateur - September - 4 years
A non-Honours degree course validated by the University of Manchester, but with fewer academic demands than the Honours course. The programme of practical

studies is identical to that for the Honours course but academic studies are normally completed by the end of Year Three. Jazz theory, improvisation and history of jazz taught. Option to perform in the Jazz Collective and/or RNCM Big Band.

Bmus (Hons) (B Mus (Hons))

General Music with a Jazz Element - Aspiring Degree Level and Above - Royal Northern College - September - 4 years

An Honours degree validated by the University of Manchester, designed for the practically-based musician wishing to pursue a course with significant academic content. Available to students wanting to major in academic studies, who wish to study in a conservatoire rather than a university. All students follow the same 'core' course units in the first year, in the second year there are choices within the history studies. In the third and fourth years students can explore a range of academic options and then elect to choose Jazz theory, improvisation, history of jazz. There is also an optional jazz element for performance in either the Jazz Collective and/or the RNMC Big Band. The Big Band has a recognised reputation, performing outside the college with guest performers that have included Julian Arguelles, John Dankworth, Guy Barker, Victor Mendoza, Tim Garland, Stan Tracey, Ed Thigpen. Tutors and visiting tutors include Steve Berry, Nikki Iles, Steve Waterman, Dave O'Higgins, Gerard Presencer.

Joint Music Course (Mus B (Hons)/GRNCM Dip)

General Music with a Jazz Element - Aspiring Degree Level and Above - September - 4 years

Designed for those with outstanding practical and academic ability, including composer-performers, this course is run in collaboration with the University of Manchester Music Department. Students follow the University's BMus (Hons) programme (normally completed at the end of Year Three) concurrently with the practical elements of the College's undergraduate programme (examined in Year Four). Succesful students receive both the University degree and the College's GRNCM Diploma. Numbers on this course are strictly limited (currently eight places per year). Intending applicants should consult the prospectus of the Univesity Music Department. Application must be made both to the University of Manchester (through UCAS) and directly to the College. Closing dates 1st October with auditions during Oct/Dec

University of Salford

Melling, Malcolm, Musical Director of Big Band, University of Salford, Faculty of Media, Music and Performance, Salford M3 6EQ
0161 295 5000 Fax:0161 295 5999; 0161 295 6136 www.salford.ac.uk

BA(Hons) Music

General Music with a Jazz Element - Aspiring Degree Level and Above - September - 3 years

This course embraces a wide spectrum of studies in both classical and popular music genres, covering options in Bands, Jazz and Popular Music and Music Technology. Composition and Performance. Composition is encouraged by the presence of experienced composers on the staff and Performance through the University ensembles and contact with club and performing venues around Manchester.

There is an additional foundation year for those insufficiently qualified for admission onto Year 1. The emphasis in the foundation year is on learning basic Study Skills, Harmony, Aural Training and a full programme of Performance. The academic slant of the course takes into account students interested in Classical, Jazz and Popular music specialisms.

The curriculum starts with core study areas - Composition, Performance, Analytical and Historical Studies. Year 2 onwards offers a range of options - Composition, History, Performance, Recording, Music Technology, Arts Administration, Latin Percussion and more.

All students are offered weekly 1 to 1 instrumental performance lessons with one of a large team of specialist tutors active as professionals in their own field. Students audition to join one or more of the University Ensembles - Brass Band, Wind Band, Big Band, Jazz and Pop Ensembles and Choir. Performance studies are backed up by a wide range of Masterclasses by visiting professionals in both the Classical and Jazz/Pop fields. These have included Tommy Smith, James Morrison, Bill Nelson, and Fred 'Thelonius' Baker.

BA Popular Music and Recording (BA)
General Music with a Jazz Element - Aspiring Degree Level and Above - September - 3 Years
Academic, theoretical and practical training in popular music and recording. Emphasis is placed on developing students' practical ability, critical awareness and creativity in the areas of music technology, composition and performance in the field of music criticism and analysis. The modular design of the course enables a degree of flexibility in the choice of second and third year options. On entry to the first year, students are directed towards Studio Performer or Studio Producer pathways through the course.
Year 1 - Core modules: Performance 1 (includes Ensemble Performance); Arranging, Compositional Studies; Critical Theory; Popular Music Style and Genre (1954-1969) and (1970-present); Rhythmic Awareness; Aural Perception. Choice of either Music Technology, Studio Production, Acoustics and Recording Theory or Session Musicianship and Introduction to Music Technology.
Year 2 - Core modules: Performance (includes Ensemble Performance and options in Group improvisation, Latin American Percussion); Compositional Studies Critical Theory, Optional modules: Music Video; African Music; Jazz Studies; Music, Audio and the Internet; Composition; Arranging; Musical Directing; Critical Theory Music Technology and Studio Production. Choice of either Music Technology and Studio Production or Session Musicianship.
Year 3 - Core modules: Business and Professional Practice, Optional modules: Composition; Arranging; Musical Directing; Dissertation; Performance; Music Technology and Studio Production. A critical evaluation module supports each specialist major elective.

MA/PgDip in Compositional Studies (Bands, Jazz and Pop) (MA/PgDip)
Music Course Majoring in Jazz - Aspiring Degree Level and Above - September - 18 months. *Available as part time over 36 months*
This course is designed to develop to an advanced level the creative and intellectual abilities of composers and arrangers specialising in contemporary music genres: jazz, brass and wind bands, popular music and electro-acoustic music. The taught element of the Diploma course consists of two compulsory and two specialist optional workshops plus one-to-one supervision in the preparation of a portfolio of compositions or arrangements. The strong team of composers and arrangers on the full-time staff is augmented by visiting specialists who conduct masterclasses and lead symposia in a programme of such events, running throughout the year. The final MA Stage of the award involves the completion of a dissertation (approximately 12000 words) and a commissioned work. Alternatively, a second commissioned work may be offered instead of the dissertation.

MA/Pgdip Performance (Bands, Jazz and Pop) (MA/Pgdip)

Music Course Majoring in Jazz - Aspiring Degree Level and Above - September -18 months FT or *36 months part time*

This course is designed to develop at an advanced level the practical and intellectual abilities of performers and conductors, particularly those specialising in contemporary music genres - jazz, brass and wind bands, popular music and, where appropriate, electro-acoustic music. The taught element of the Diploma course consists of two compulsory and two specialist optional workshops plus one-to-one supervision in the preparation of a series of progressively more demanding recitals. The strong team of instrumental specialists attached to the University is augmented by visiting specialists who conduct masterclasses in a programme of such events, running throughout the year. The final MA stage of the award involves the completion of a dissertation (approximately 12,000 words) or the delivery of a lecture-recital, integrating scholarly work and performance.

University of Liverpool

Liverpool L69 3BX

0151 794 2000 Fax:0151 7086502; www.liverpool.ac.uk

BA (Hons) Music /Popular Music (BA (Hons))

General Music with a Jazz Element - Aspiring Degree Level and Above - September - 3 years

The course is designed for students wishing to study popular and classical music in approximately equal proportion, and to investigate the relationships between them. It aims to provide students with an understanding of as wide a range of musics as possible. It also includes the option of practical instrumental or vocal study in classical idioms. Year 2 and 3 modules include popular music history (eg American music to 1950), music business (eg record companies), media (eg music journalism), music and daily life (eg gender and sexuality), studio composition.

MA in Popular Music Studies (MA)

General Music - Aspiring Degree Level and Above - September - 1/2 years

The syllabus consists of four core modules; four option modules and a dissertation. The four core modules are: Studying Popular Music, Popular Music in Daily Life, Textual Analysis and Semiotics and Topics in History. Option modules include: Music and the Media, Music Policy, Popular Music and the Politics of Place and Organisation and Structure of the Music Business.

MBA Music Industries

General Music - Aspiring Degree Level and Above - September - 1 or 2 years

The programme's main aim is to blend the best of a general understanding of how businesses work with a very specific understanding of how music businesses work. Alongside standard business modules, students take modules on the Recording Industry and Record Companies and Rights Ownership and Publishing. Further, they choose between elective modules on issues such as Artist Management and On-line Music. At every opportunity they benefit from the experience of established music industry figures. They are also encouraged to attend supplementary seminars on a wide range of topics - from dance music to venue management.

Part-Time

Nelson and Colne College
Nelson and Colne College
Scotland Road
Nelson BB9 7YT
01282 440200 Fax:01282 440274;

HND Popular Music and Sound Recording (HND Pop Music and Recording)
Music Technology - Semi-Pro or Amateur - September - 2 years
Year 1 - Popular Music Case Studies, Aural Training, Composition and Arranging,
The Music Business, Marketing and Enterprise, Music Performance Techniques,
Music Technology and Recording Studies, A Major Project.
Year 2 - Popular Music: Style and Genre, Critical and Theoretical Study of Popular
Music, or Performance Option and Aural Perception, Composition and Arranging, A
Major Project, Performance, Rhythmic Awareness or Acoustics and Recording
Theory, Session Musicianship or Music Technology and Studio Production.

University of Liverpool
Liverpool L69 3BX
0151 794 2000 Fax:0151 7086502;

Popular Music Flexible degree
General Music with a Jazz Element - Semi-Pro or Amateur – September.
Tailored to suit you, this new part-time degree offers the choice of daytime or
early evening courses with some Saturdays and summer school. You can study a
combination of your favourite subjects and if you are not quite ready for degree
level work, the Gateway course will give students the study skills they need. By
introducing students to popular music's complex socio-musical past and present,
the popular music units will encourage students to make a critical analysis of popular music's sources and influences, its performers and its vital place in social history. The units will encourage students to develop important anthropological, musicological and historical research techniques and creative abilities. E-mail:
flexible.degrees@liv.ac.uk for further information.

Workshop

Musicroots
Williams, Chris, Education, Band on the Wall, 25 Swan Street, Manchester M4 5JZ
0161 236 6627 Courses only
0161 834 1786 Mon-Fri Fax:0161 834 2559; 0161 8326625 (box office);
admin@bandonthewall.org (email); www.bandonthewall.org

***Spring term starts 28th April 2003 until 6th July - all courses 10 weeks.
Cost £90. £55 concessions***

Latin Percussion
Wednesdays 20.00-22.00. Tutor Chris Manis has played with members of one of
Cuba's finest rumba groups, and also Cuban Orisha singer Amelia Pedroso. He is

also a regular member of Orquestra Timbala, Apitos. Guides you through styles including rumba, son, Mozambique and songo. Conga- centred, but covering the other percussion instruments where relevant.

Jazz Improvisation (all instruments)

Jazz Only - Semi-Pro or Amateur

Tutor: Chris Williams. Weekly evening classes Tuesday 18.30-20.30 (elementary) Thursday 19.00-21.00 (advanced). Uses jazz standards to explore fundamentals of improvisation. Their programme states - "Chris Williams has been associated with this club since the early days, and has got to be one of the most inspirational jazz tutors around! Himself a top alto saxophonist, clarinettist and flautist, and a RCM graduate, Chris' understanding of the rudiments and repertoire of jazz is matched only by his ability to explain them in no-nonsense language. Oh, and he laughs a lot too"

Vocal workshop

General Music with a Jazz Element - Semi-Pro or Amateur

Mondays and Wednesdays 18.30-20.30 Tutor Mike Heath. Classes cover technique and repertoire in the jazz/gospel/pop/folk idioms.

Education Outreach Projects

Band On The Wall also run outreach projects designed to support the next generation of musicians and those who deliver community music projects. Funded projects are designed for people who may not have access to opportunities due to reasons of location, economic, gender or ethnic discrimination.

Summer School

Burnley Jazz Summer School

Worley, Kirk, Arts and Ents Officer, Burnley Mechanics, Manchester Road, Burnley BB11 1JA

01282 664411 Fax:01282 664431; 01282 664400 (box office); www.leisureinburnley.co.uk

Burnley Jazz Summer School

Jazz Only - Semi-Pro or Amateur - Burnley Mechanics, Burnley - 21/07/2003 July - 5 days

Built on a programme of daytime workshops, rehearsals and performances, the core philosophy of the course is to enable participants on their chosen instruments to improvise and improve. There are three categories to choose from, all of which depend, to some extent, on individual playing ability and experience.

1. The Essential Grammar of Jazz: introduces players to the fundamental rhythmic, harmonic and melodic techniques of improvisation, under the direction of Steve Berry.

2. Advanced Group work: tutor-led small bands that will work on appropriate repertoire agreed upon between tutors and participants.

3. Vocal Tuition: under the direction of Lee Gibson, singers will undertake a range of solo and group work, both accompanied and a cappella.

Owing to the popularity of categories 2 and 3, numbers have had to be restricted.

Additionally there will be an opportunity for course students to take part in either a Jazz Orchestra or Jazz Choir session, with a featured performance slot in the Friday evening 'Jam concert' in the main hall. There are also 'Stage Door Jam Sessions (Monday – Thursday evenings which will include performances by some of the Tutors and informal small groups formed by the students. Other tutors include: Mike Hall (sax/reeds), Nick Smart (brass), Paul Mitchell Davidson (guitar), Les Chisnall (piano), Dave Hassell (percussion) Cost: £110, £95 (students, unemployed and over 60s) – deadline for reservations (£15 non-refundable deposit) 2nd June 2003. For further information and application forms call: 01282 664400.

Music Technology

Accrington and Rossendale College
Accrington and Rossendale College, Sandy Lane, Accrington, Lancs, BB5 2AW.
01254 389933 (office tel)

Popular Music BTEC National Diploma
Duration: Two years

Opportunity to study music technology, operation of micro and computer controlled instruments, equipment and MIDI. Studio work: Recording and mixing. Composing/arranging, Sales, Management and promotions

Liverpool Institute for Performing Arts
Mount Street, Liverpool, Merseyside, L1 9HF. 0151 330 3000 Fax:0151 330 3131; reception@lipa.ac.uk (email); www.lipa.ac.uk

B.A. (Hons) in Sound Technology
Start Month: September. Duration: 3 Years. Qualification: BA (Hons) Sound Technology.

The B.A. (Hons) Degree in Sound Technolgy follows a modular structure, with dis-crete subject areas covered in each module. However, in keeping with LIPA's phiosophy of multi-skilling, students will need to complete all of the modules in years one and two, but have the opportunity for specialisation in a particular field by a choice of modules in year three. In the first year, students are introduced to basic operational and theoretical skills, with the focus very much on a multi-track studio environment. In addition, modules start to introduce some specialised areas of work, such as sound reinforcement, MIDI and sequencing. An important feature of the first year is a collaborative work module, in which students work with other students from the B.A. (Hons) Degree in Performing Arts programme on a variety of real life projects. The second year is concerned with further developing these technical skills and learning about other specialised areas of sound production, such as radio production, multimedia authoring and audio post production for tele-vision and video. In addition, students study topics such as business and manage-ment skills in the context of the audio and entertainment industries. By the third year, students will have accquired a high level of technical skill and discipline and will have been given the opportunity to use these by working on major practical projects, both collaboratively with other students and for external clients. In addi-tion, students are expected to complete a substantial dissertation on a subject in the sound technology field, supervised by a tutor.

Dipl.in HE: Theatre and Performance Technology

Start Month: September. Duration: 2 years.

This programme will provide you with the technical and professional skills that will enable you to develop and maintain a successful professional career as a specialist in one or more of the following areas: lighting, sound (for live performance), stage management, technical direction, production management and stage technology.

LIPA Dip: Pop. Music and Sound Technology

Start Month: September. Duration: 1 year. Qualification: Dip Popular Music and Sound Technology

This programme has been designed with two purposes in mind. First, it is geared twards those people who see themselves as musicians who wish to learn more about the technology of modern music production and recording and to improve their music skills, but do not wish to commit to three years of study. Secondly, the course can serve as foundation level for those people who may wish to register on a degree programme in either music or sound technology, but whose experience or theoretical knowledge is not quite sufficient for direct entry. This is a practical programme, although there is a minor component of written work, delivered by LIPA's team of musicans and sound technologists. Teaching and learning is delivered through a combination of whole group lecture sessions, small group practical workshops and occasional masterclasses by visiting practitioners.

Musicroots

Joe Splain, Band on the Wall, 25 Swan Street, Manchester, G Manchester, M4 5JZ. 0161 834 1786 Mon-Fri Fax:0161 834 2559; 0161 8326625 (box office); admin@bandonthewall.org (email); www.bandonthewall.org

Sound Recording

Start Month: April. Duration: 12 weeks.

Evening classes utilising the studio equipment at the Band on the Wall, covering the basics of recording and mixing and culminating with recording a concert in the venue. Cost £260; £200 concessions.

Nelson and Colne College

Scotland Road, Nelson, Lancs, BB9 7YT. 01282 440200 Fax:01282 440274

Lancashire Music Foundation

Start Month: September. Duration: 2 years. Qualification: Music Foundation Cert.

This programme offers a balance between modern music and technology, combining as it does the academic music study with the technical skills required by a professional musician. This is a two-year, double A level programme comprising study to A level in Music and Music Technology.

Music Technology A Level

Start Month: September. Duration: 2 years. Qualification: A Level Music Technology.

University of Salford

Malcolm Melling, University of Salford, Faculty of Media, Music, and Performance, Salford, G Manchester, M3 6EQ.
0161 295 5000 Fax:0161 295 5999

BSc Music, Acoustics and Recording

Start Month: September. Duration: 3 years. Qualification: BSc.

This course provides students with academic, theoretical and practical training in music, acoustics and recording, and is intended to serve as preparation for a career in the dynamic and rapidly transforming world of music and studio production and associated industries. The degree combines the study of applied acoustics with practical and creative studies in studio production, music technology, composition and arranging. Entry Requirements: A/AS level; CCC or AS equivalent, including mathematics and music. AS level candidates should offer a B in Mathematics. Advanced CNVQ: With overall distinction and an A level in mathematics. BTEC ND/NC: Two distinctions and two merits plus A level in mathematics.

Scotland

Full-Time

Aberdeen College
Gallowgate Centre, Gallowgate, Aberdeen AB25 1BN
01224 612000 Fax:01224 612001; enquiry@abcol.ac.uk (email);
Certificate in Foundation Music Studies (Cert in Foundation Music Studies)
General Music with a Jazz Element - Semi-Pro or Amateur - 06/09/2002 -
September - 1 year
This course will equip students with the skills and knowledge required to proceed
to an advanced music course at college or university.

Jewel and Esk Valley College
Campbell, Sarah, Course Co-ordinator, Jewel and Esk Valley College, Milton Road
East, Edinburgh EH
0131 660 1010 g.brockie@blueyonder.co.uk (email); www.jevc.ac.uk
HNC in Jazz Guitar
Jazz Only - Semi-Pro or Amateur - Edinburgh - September - one year
Aimed at anyone who would like to gain competence in performing guitar in the
jazz idiom. Students will gain experience in solo and ensemble performance and
develop an understanding of jazz harmony as well as gain an insight into studio
musicianship and music business enterprise. Students will be encouraged to
develop personal strengths and interests in different and original areas of music.
Modules Guitar Musicanship, Instrumental Study, Guitar ensemble, jazz composing
and arranging, aural and transcription, recording for musicians, jaz history, working as a jazz musician, music !aw and legislationSelection for the course is by audition and interview

Napier University
Severn, Eddie, Napier University Edinburgh, The Ian Tomlin School of Music,
Craighouse Road, Edinburgh EH105LG
0131 455 6200 Fax:0131 455 6211; www.napier.ac.uk
B.Mus/B.Mus (Hons) (B.Mus/B Mus (Hons))
General Music with a Jazz Element - Aspiring Degree Level and Above - October -
3/4 years
The B.Mus/B.Mus (Hons) Year 1 - Principal study instrument, voice oɼ composition,
history and composition styles of Renaissance and Baroque music, general music
skills, and free choice elective subject.
Year 2 - Principal study instrument, voice or compsition (normally the same as for
Level 1), history of Classical and Romantic music, Classical and Romantic compositional style, one optional subject chosen from: fretboard skills, jazz improvisation,
keyboard skills, music technology, subsidiary compostion/arranging, and free choic
elective subject.
Year 3 - Principal study instrument, voice or composition (normally the same as for
Level 2), history of 20th century music, 20th century compositional styles, projec-
cts. Two optional subjects chosen from: conducting, fretboard skills, jazz improvi-

sation, keyboard skills, music technology, light music performance styles, recital, subsidiary composition/arranging.

Year 4 - (honours) - options chosen from: Principal study instrument, voice or composition (normally the same as for Year 3), dissertation, analysis, honours recital, conducting, fretboard skills, jazz improvisation, keyboard skills, music technology, light music performance styles, subsidiary composition/arranging. Edinburgh quartet and Eddie Severn, jazz musician in residence.

M.Mus/Postgraduate Diploma - Jazz (M Mus/Postgraduate Diploma)

Jazz Only - Aspiring Degree Level and Above - October - 1 year

The Postgraduate Diploma/M.Mus programme in Jazz and Light Music is the first of its kind in Scotland. Napier University is the first Higher Education Institution in Scotland to appoint a Jazz Musician in Residence, Eddie Severn. He is programme leader and lecturer in trumpet, improvisation, composition, and ear training. He will also direct the Big Band. Currently, two jazz modules and one in light music performance styles, taught by Eddie Severn, are available to undergraduate students. Eddie Severn is professionally active nationally and internationally in jazz, both as a performer and as a teacher. He will be assisted by a team of part-time teachers, all of whom are active in jazz. Edinburgh is a major centre for the performance of jazz and, in its broadest sense, popular music. There is an annual Jazz Festival of international repute and a lively jazz scene during the rest of the year. Students who successfully complete Semester 1 will be awarded the postgraduate cerificate. Students who go on to successfully complete Semester 2 will be awarded the postgraduate diploma and students who successfully complete the diploma and dissertation will be awarded an M.Mus. Level 1/ Semester 1 - Jazz instrument of jazz voice; jazz harmony and improvisation. Semester 2 - jazz instrument 2 or jazz voice; jazz harmony and improvisation 2. Level 2/Semester 1 - Jazz composition and arranging1; history of jazz and light music. Semester 2- jazz composition and arranging 2; history of jazz and light music 2.

Perth College

Brahan Bldg, Crieff Road, Perth
01738 877000

BA Popular Music Performance (BA)

General Music with a Jazz Element - Aspiring Degree Level and Above - September - 3 years

Created by professional musicians with proven track records in the music business, this degree aims to produce talented graduates who can sustain a career in the growing music industry. It will equip them with the knowledge and confidence to influence and guide the industry's development, to analyse and bring about change, and to train others to do the same. Unique in covering all aspects of study for the modern musician, the course is suited for those who are serious about a musical career in a range of areas including performance, production and management.

Royal Scottish Academy of Music and Drama

100 Renfrew Street, Glasgow G2 3DB
0141 332 4101 Fax:0141 332 8901; registry@rsamd.ac.uk (email);
www.rsamd.ac.uk

B Mus (Performance) Hons

General Music with a Jazz Element - Aspiring Degree Level and Above - 4 years

Aimed at performers with exceptional potential to further develop and promote musicial performance abilities to the highest level. Weekly one and a half hour lessons focus on solo repertoire, ensemble classes, contemporary and early music classes, jazz workshops and specialist masterclasses are incorporated into a flexible and practical programme.

Note: for all second year BA (Music) and BEd students there is a one-term course in electroacoustic composition at the academy's studios.

Stevenson College

Bankhead Avenue, Edinburgh EH11 4DE
0131 535 4600 Fax:0131 535 4666; info@stevenson.ac.uk (email); www.stevenson.ac.uk

Degree Foundation in Popular Music (Foundation Cert)

General Music with a Jazz Element - Semi-Pro or Amateur - August - 1 year

For players or singers to improve practical skills, composition and arranging, music technology and jazz thory, harmony and improvisation. Entrance requirements - at least Grade 6 on chosen instrument plus an audition.

University of Glasgow

Glasgow G12 8QQ
0141 339 8855

Theses courses are included only because they have electroacoustic option (rather than jazz)

B.Mus Music (B.Mus)

General Music with a Jazz Element - Aspiring Degree Level and Above - October - 3/4 years

The BMus is a single-subject degree for those interested in pursuing a career in music, although it does not preclude other directions after graduation. It is designed as a comprehensive course for one year, followed by two years (General degree) or three years (Honours degree) in which your special interests are developed. Analysis, Harmony (both written and practical), Orchestration, Composition, History and Performance all play a part in the initial stages, leading to an opportunity to study Electroacoustic Composition, Notation, Performance Practice or other subjects, with a principal specialism such as History, Composition or Performance.

MA in Music (MA)

Music Course Majoring in Jazz - Aspiring Degree Level and Above - October - 2/4 years

The MA Music course caters for students who have some ability in music and an interest in its cultural background and technique. Courses such as Integrated Musicianship, Historical Studies, Composition and Music Technology are available in the first two years. Honours students have the opportunity to write a dissertation on a topic of their choice, present a portfolio of compositions, to study performance (subject to audition), or to choose from a very wide range of additional options, including Analysis, Historiography and Criticism, Electroacoustic Composition and Performance Practice. Should you wish to be considered for Honours you are required to take the Integrated Musicianship course in either your first or second year. MAstudents share classes and activities with BEng and BMus students to some extent.

Workshop

Fionna Duncan Workshops

Rae, Cathie, Alba Arts, 3 Preston Cottages, Preston Road, East Linton, EH40 3DS
Tel/Fax 01620 861000 admin@fionaduncan-workshops.co.uk

Fionna Duncan Vocal Jazz Workshops are a non-profit making organisation dedicated to making workshops accessible and affordable to everyone with an interest in vocal jazz. Offer 1, 2 and 5 day workshops and although their funding support finishes in September 2003 they will still run the 5 day workshops in 2004. Fund raising events still continue with next taking place on 20th May 2003. Jazz choirs have also been set up in Edinburgh, Glasgow and Aberdeen may follow soon.

Note: workshop prices may vary depending on how much they are subsidised by local authorities etc..

Vocal Jazz 5 day workshop

Jazz Only - Jazz Beginner - Edinburgh - 28/07/2003 - July - 5 days
Guest Tutor Sheila Jordan Cost: £400/350 (exclusive of accommodation) Glasgow 5 day workshop 1-5th July 2003 Fees £350/300 concessions The 5-day workshop provide intensive training and development: This workshop is aimed at complete beginners, intermediate students and professional singers in all fields of music

Physical and vocal warm-ups, Group singing technique and harmonies, Group dynamics, Listening exercises and harmonies, Rhythm work, Voice technique, Improvisation - techniques and creative expression, Jazz phrasing / expression, Setting songs keys / transposing, Working with a sound system / recording techniques, Ear training Song introductions and endings, Working with a band, Microphone technique, Performing with professional jazz musicians, Expression individuality, Performance technique, General development of self confidence. Individual written reports for each student and recommendations for further study

Vocal Jazz Workshop (residential)

12 and 13 April 2003 2-Day residential workshop in Garelochhead. £250 / £220 concession (includes 2 nights BandB Group Physical and vocal warm-ups, Group dynamics · Listening exercises and harmonies, Group Rhythm work, Group Improvisation - techniques and creative expression, Song introductions and endings, Group instruction on working with a band, Expression of individuality, Performance Technique, General development of self confidence, Question and Answer session, This workshop will be geared towards beginners and intermediate level students

Vocal Jazz Workshop

Last Saturday of the month in Edinburgh 29th March and 26th April 2003 Fee £40/35 Introduction to Vocal Jazz, Group Physical and vocal warm-ups
Group dynamics, Listening exercises and harmonies, Group Rhythm work
Group Improvisation - techniques and creative expression, General development of self confidence, Question and Answer session, Information on other workshops

Short Course

Jazz Course UK

Hall, Rob, Jazz and Classical Music Promotions, 57 Laburnum Drive, Milton of Campsie, Glasgow G66 8JS
07973 145976 (mobile); rob@robhall.co.uk (email); www.robhall.co.uk www.jazzcourse.co.uk

Jazz Course UK was set up in 1995 by saxophonist Rob Hall as a vehicle for promoting short courses and workshops for musicians with a focus on creative music making though improvised music

Glasgow - Tron Jazz Course

Jazz Only - Jazz Beginner - The Tron Theatre, Trongate - 08/08/2003 - August - 3 days

Jazz course at The Tron Theatre provides a valuable opportunity for musicians in the area to play and learn jazz in an intensive yet informal environment. The course is aimed at both beginner improvisers and those who have some Jazz experience already, although it is not for advanced improvisers. Applicants should have at least intermediate technical skills on their instrument/voice and any ensemble experience is useful although not mandatory. All chromatic instruments are welcome. Participants will gain experience in improvisation, learning music by ear, ensemble playing, on- the-spot arranging, Jazz harmony, performance skills and much more. Groups will be organised with up to 15 people with one tutor. Course runs from 10.00 to 16.00 on the first two days and 14.00 to 19.00 on the third day. Tutors - Rob Hall and Ged Brockie. Cost: £75 (10% discount when 2 or more places booked together).

Distance Learning

University of St Andrews

Younger Hall Music Centre, North Street, St Andrews KY16 9AJ
01334 476 161 Fax:01334 462 570; aem4@st-and.ac.uk (email);

Advanced Diploma in Jazz (Advanced Diploma)

Jazz Only - Semi-Pro or Amateur - November - 10 months

The aim of the Diploma is to increase the knowledge and extend the skills of jazz musicians. Special study days for Diploma students are held in St Andrews but there is also heavy emphasis on guided self-preparation, and a special project to be completed.

Scottish Certificate in Jazz

Jazz Only - Semi-Pro or Amateur - October - 10 months

The aim of the Certificate is to provide school teachers and others who have a substantial background in music with the means of extending their musical repertoire into the area of jazz. Players with some experience of jazz performance will benefit from the formal tuition offered, enabling them to gain a qualification in a subject which they may have already spent several years studying. Preparation consists in a series of study days held in St Andrews and will culminate in a residential weekend course. In between times students work from written and recorded material specially prepared by staff of the Music Centre. A special feature of this course is the additional 'contact days' when students can seek further advice and assistance on instrumental and theoretical techniques.

Summer School

Fife Jazz Summer Course

Michael, Richard, Fife Council Arts, Tower Block ASDARC, Woodend Road, Cardenden, Fife KY5 QNE
01592 414 714 (office tel)

Fife Jazz Summer Course

Jazz Only - Jazz Beginner - 07/07/2003- July - 5 days

Held at Balwearie High School, Balwearie Gardens, Kirkcaldy
Course Director - Richard Michael with guest tutors Pete Churchill (piano/voice), Maclolm Miles (saxophone) Fergus Andrew (trumpet) Jeremy Price (trombone) Robin Michael (piano) David Swanson (Drums)

Aimed at jazz enthusiasts with a basic grounding on your chosen instrument providing a range of opportunities including warm-ups, workshops, theory class, combos and singing. Masterclasses feature piano, bass and drums. Each rhythm player works with a combo in the afternoon sessions. Course is taylored to participants needs and abilities to development in a "pleasant, hard working and rewarding course". Course open to residential and non residential students with accommodation provided at Fife College Halls of Residence in Kirkcaldy. There are a limited number of places available. Application form available from Arts Development office.

Jazz Course UK

Hall, Rob, Jazz and Classical Music Promotions, 57 Laburnum Drive, Milton of Campsie, Glasgow G66 8JS
07973 145976 (mobile); rob@robhall.co.uk (email); www.robhall.co.uk www.jazzcourse.co.uk

Jazz Course UK was set up in 1995 by saxophonist Rob Hall as a vehicle for promoting short courses and workshops for musicians with a focus on creative music making though improvised music. Rob has been teaching jazz and improvisation since 1993 and is very experienced with all age groups including mature students. The courses are designed to combine the fun aspects of improvising music with the rewards gained through increased musical awareness.

Edinburgh Jazz Summer School

Jazz Only - Jazz Beginner - Edinburgh - 11/08/2003 - August - 5 days
Tutors: Rob Hall and Ged Brockie (Scottish Guitar Quartet). The Summer School is based at the Jewel and Esk Valley College and offers an opportunity to combine developing instrumental and vocal skills in playing, recording and performing Jazz, whilst enjoying one of the world's greatest and most diverse international arts festivals - the Edinburgh Festival. 4 nights accommodation on campus is included in the course fees (non-residential places are also available) plus there is an option to extend the stay for up to 2 extra nights. Amps and rhythm section equipment is

available. The course is aimed at intermediate to advanced instrumentalists and vocalists (prior improvisation experience is useful but not essential, all chromatic instruments welcome. Students on the course can expect a well structured programme focusing on improvisation, ensemble playing, performance and recording techniques, stylistic skills, Jazz harmony, composition and much more. There will be opportunities to perform in a public venue and to record a CD with fellow students. Cost: £375 (residential), £225 (non residential) * Launch discount: Book 2 places together and receive 10% discount. Printable application forms available online: www.jazzcourse.co.uk

National Youth Jazz Orchestra of Scotland

Hardy, Mike, Jazz Co-ordinator, National Youth Jazz Orchestra of Scotland, 13 Somerset Place, Glasgow G3 7JT
0141 332 8311 Fax:0141 332 3915; mikehardy@nyos.co.uk (email); www.nyos.co.uk

Summer Jazz Course

Jazz Only - Semi-Pro or Amateur - Strathallan School, Perthshire – 01/08/2003 - August - 5 days

Course aimed at students who have good technical skills on their instrument and have some understanding of chord symbols. As the teaching is personal and intensive, places are limited on an instrument and a number basis. Also offers students the opportunity to rehearse and perform with the National Youth Jazz Orchestra of Scotland. The orchestra will remain at Strathallan School immediately following the course for a further four days, developing their repertoire of music for public performance. Applications for the course close on at the end of November. Students will be invited to an induction day with the course tutors early in Spring. Course tutors - led by Simon Purcell (Professor at the Guildhall, London) rest TBC but past tutors have included Tom Bancroft, Phil Bancroft, Nikki Iles, Steve Watts, Julian Arguelles, Steve Watts, Laura Macdonald, Mario Caribe and Mike Walker. 2002 was the first year that young singers have been invited to join the course. "What we are trying to do here is to realise the creative potential of the students, and for that matter the tutors as well. We want to look beyond the traditional way of going about it, focusing on improvisation and on developing their own aesthetic, rather than just learning to play neat charts in a neat way" quote by course leader Simon Purcell

Music Technology

Jewel and Esk Valley College

Sarah Campbell, Jewel and Esk Valley College, Milton Road East, Edinburgh, Lothian, EH.
0131 660 1010 g.brockie@blueyonder.co.uk (email); www.jevc.ac.uk

Certificate in Sound Engineering

Duration: 1 year

Study areas covered are recording/mixing and editing sound and music, communication and basic electronics and computer applications

HNC Music and Audio Technology
Duration: 1 year. Requirements: NC Sound Engineering; BTech equivalent; appropriate professional experience.

The course allows students to develop the skills and techniques of recording and producing music and live sound. Study areas covered: Recording studio techniques, Live sound mixing, PA systems, Production techniques, Information technology, Freelance business skills and MIDI technology. Students learn on the College's state-of-the-art facilities, with the emphasis placed on hands-on practice.

NC Music and Music Technology
Duration: 6 months

This course is designed to equip musicians with the skills to enter further study or is an introduction to the music technology and related areas. The focus is on the performer in the popular music field. Ability in some of the following would be advantageous: basic computer skills, basic multitrack, basic music theory

University of Edinburgh
Alison House, 12 Nicolson Square, Edinburgh, Lothian, EH8 9DF.
0131 650 2423 Fax:0131 650 2425; Music@ed.ac.uk (email)

B.Mus (Hons) Music Technology
Start Month: October. Duration: 4 years. Qualification: B Mus.

The degrees of B.Mus and B.Mus (Hons) in Music Technology are designed to offer core knowledge in a wide and complementary range of musical and scientific disciplines. The courses in Music Technology, which form the basic thread of the degree through all years, offer practical experience in bringing those varied disciplines together in a creative context. The course is quite demanding, as it requires an equal commitment to both musical and technical strands. However, though a high degree of musical accomplishment is required at entry, no technological experience at all is assumed to start with. Due to the rather demanding nature of the course, there is less opportunity for course choices than in the B.Mus degree, but this is made up for by the amount of creative freedom given in the Music Technology courses themselves. These degrees are in no way training courses. They are designed ot give a broad, general background to music technology, to stimulate creativity and to confront issues of art and technology in uncompromising ways. The core knowledge in intended to give a background that is useful in many careers, including personal creative activity, and graduates have a good track record at finding employment in the recording, broadcast media and commercial music industries, as well as pursuing careers as artists, teachers, programmers and so one. Teaching takes place in six purpose-built studios, including an 8-track digital control room with recording studio, 16-track and 32-track digital studios, a real-time interactive studio equipped with video sensing, pitch trackers and various real-time controllers, a networked digital signal processing studio based on a Silicon Graphics computer, and a multi-media studio with facilities for animation, video and graphics editing and preparation of multi-media materials. There are also a number of interesting halls for live recording.

University of Glasgow

Glasgow, Lanarkshire, G12 8QQ. 0141 339 8855 (office tel)

B.Eng Electronics with Music

Start Month: October. Duration: 4 years. Qualification: B Eng.

The B.Eng course is intended for students who wish to acquire a professional quali-
fication in Electronics while pursuing an interest in the applications of electronic
and computer technology to aspects of music. Subjects taken in the Music
Department include:Acoustics and Studio Techniques: Music and Technology:
Practical recording and MIDI Processing : Sound Diffusion: Audio Programming :
Software Synthesis and Composition Systems.

South East

Full-Time

Bournemouth and Poole College

Bournemouth and Poole College of Further Education, Constitution Hill Centre, Poole BH14 0QA
01202 465 721

Advanced Studies in Music (Certificate in Advanced Studies in Music)
General Music - Semi-Pro or Amateur - September - 2 years
Part-time alternatives are available. Students study - composition and arrangement, computer music and music technology, multi-track recording, the history and analysis of music, project and dissertation work, harmony and counterpoint, listening and aural training, conducting and rehearsing techniques, practical work - including solo and group performing, choral and orchestral work. In addition, students follow two other subjects, normally at A level.

BTEC First Dip. In Performing Arts (Musi (BTEC First Diploma in Performing Arts)
General Music - Semi-Pro or Amateur - September - 1 year
According to skills, focus can be on individual instrument or music technology. Work in small groups and ensembles as well as seminars and lectures. Students taught through a combination of core and option modules with a strong emphasis on practical work. Topics include: - understanding music, music performance, performance project and technology in music. In addition, students will be encouraged to work towards ABRSM music theory grades.

BTEC National Diploma in Popular Music (BTEC National Diploma in Popular Music)
General Music - Aspiring Degree Level and Above - September - 2 years
This course will be delivered through a variety of learning environments, including: lectures, practical demonstrations, ensemble work, workshops and self-study. The course will develop a broad range of practical skills and knowledge in modular form including: - music performance and techniques, improvisation, aural skills, language of music, recording techniques, music technology, music in the media, music industry, together with playing and composing for a number of ensembles both inside and outside the College.

Bournemouth University

School of Media Arts and Communication, Talbot Campus, Fern Barrow, Poole BH12 5BB
01202 524111 Fax:01202 595530; srose@bournemouth.ac.uk (email); 01202 595371 (tel)

PGDip/MA Music Design for the Moving Image
General Music - Aspiring Degree Level and Above - September - 1 Year
Post-graduate course offering professional expert training in the art of composing

music for the media using Macintosh computers and MIDI equipment. Previous electro-acoustic experience not required but applicants should have a wide knowledge of musical styles and techniques, and be prepared to submit a portfolio of tapes and scores prior to interview.

Brunel University

Griffith, Frank, Director of Performance, Brunel University College, Uxbridge Campus, Faculty of Arts, Uxbridge UB8 3PH
01895 274000 x4495 frankgriffith@brunel.ac.uk (email); mustflg@brunel.ac.uk

BA Music - Single/joint honours (BA Music)

Music Course Majoring in Jazz - Aspiring Degree Level and Above - September - 3 years

Music can be taken as Single Honours or as Joint (Hons) where it can be combined with American Studies, Drama, English, Film and TV Studies, History. There is a strong tradition of 'practical' music making at Brunel with over 50% of module work and assesment being practical. Students also study the nature and meaning of music through analysis and critique, studying their social, cultural and political contexts. The full time course is split into 6 semesters (rather than 9 terms). *It can also be taken Part time over 4/5 or 6 years*. During the first year (Level 1) all modules are taken but in year 2 and 3, students can focus on areas of particular interest. Specially designed accommodation has teaching and practice facilities with a computer sequencing suite, audio equipment and two electronic studios, and a library of several thousand records, CDs and publications.

MPhil Jazz Studies (MPhil Jazz Studies)

Music Course Majoring in Jazz - Aspiring Degree Level and Above - September - 1 year

Prioritises the contemporary and the innovative. Its approaches are both theoretical and practice-based learning and research. Interdisciplinarity is a feature of much of the postgraduate student research programmes. Awards are available from the Arts and Humanities Research Board, and other funding bodies. Some of these funding packages cover tuition fees (at UK/EU rates) and living expenses for the duration of study; others cover the fees, or contribute in other ways towards the cost of study. In addition a number of Department bursaries (awarded by competition) meet some of the costs of fees in the first year of study.

Canterbury Christ Church University Coll

North Holmes Road, Canterbury CT1 1QU
01227 767700 Fax:01227470442; Admissions@cant.ac.uk (email); www.cant.ac.uk

BMus (Hons) Music (BA (Single Hons))

General Music with a Jazz Element - Aspiring Degree Level and Above - September - 3 years Full Time *available as part time 6 year course*
Offers opportunities to develop performance and compositional skills. Provides a thorough theoretical and practical underpinning of these two areas through a wide selection of optional courses. Year 1: Performance studies, Practical musicianship, Critical studies, Ensemble studies. Year 2/3: Theoretical and practical options which include Popular Music since 1950, Jazz and Popular Song, Electroacoustic Composition.

Chichester College of Arts, Sci. and Tech.

Kendon, Adrian, Director of Jazz Studies, Chichester College of Arts, Science and

Technology, Music School, Westgate Fields, Chichester PO19 1SB
01243 786321 Fax:01243 539481; adrian.kendon@chichester.ac.uk (email);
www.chichester.ac.uk/jazz.html
for further information on courses, contact the College

Access Diploma in Jazz (Access Dip in Jazz)
Jazz Only - Aspiring Degree Level and Above - September – 1 year
This course offers an intensive one year's formal training and is intended for those
students who are interested in the field of jazz and Afro-American music. It forms
the ideal course for those who wish to establish, consolidate or further their knowledge with a view to entering non-classical music courses at Higher Education level,
for those who are considering training for other positions in the music industry,
such as the retail trade, studio work, etc. and also for those who intend to become
practitioners in the field.

BTEC First Diploma in Performing Arts (BTEC First Diploma)
General Music with a Jazz Element - Semi-Pro or Amateur - September - 1 year
This course provides a nationally recognised vocational qualification for students
keen to pursue the study of rock and pop music. It will serve as an ideal prepara-
tion for students wishing to continue their studies on the National Diploma in
Popular Music.

BTEC National Diploma in Performing Arts (BTEC National Diploma)
General Music with a Jazz Element - Semi-Pro or Amateur - September - 2 years
This course is for anyone who has a real interest in one or more of the following:
Theatre, Dance, Stagecraft, and knows that there is more to the performing arts
than being on the stage and so is willing to learn skills relating to: Arts
Administration, Production Techniques, Stagecraft and Design.

Diploma in Jazz Studies (Dip. Jazz Studies)
Jazz Only - Aspiring Degree Level and Above - September - 1 year
This course offers an intensive one year's formal training and is intended for those
students who are interested in the field of Jazz and Afro-American music. It forms
the ideal course for those who wish to establish, consolidate or further their knowledge with a view to entering non-classical music courses at Higher Education level,
for those who are considering training for other positions in the music industrey,
such as the retail trade, studio work, etc. and also for those who intend to become
practitioners in the field.

HNC Jazz (HNC Jazz)
Jazz Only - Semi-Pro or Amateur - September - 1 year

HND Jazz/Popular Music (HND jazz/Popular Music)
Music Course Majoring in Jazz - Semi-Pro or Amateur - September - 2 years

Kingston University
Penrhyn Road, Kingston upon Thames KT1 2EE
020 8547 7149 Fax:020 8547 7118;
Jazz content varies and is optional

BMus (Hons) Music
General Music with a Jazz Element - Aspiring Degree Level and Above -
September - 3 years
Degree enables you to follow a broad musical training or to study an increasingly
specialised course in either music technology; music analysis, criticism and history;
composition; performance; popular musics; or educational and cultural studies in

music. Year 1 takes account of the wide variation of qualifications and previous experience by including a common core for all, which provides a solid foundation for your subsequent musical studies.

Year 2 - a core module that covers career management for musicians, also part of an interdisciplinary project with students from other schools in the Faculty of Art, Design and Music. BMus students take four specialist modules and choose option modules to either complement those of the specialist route, or add a broader context to their studies. Year 3 includes a major independent study within your chosen specialism. BMus students take five specialist modules.

Oxford Brookes University

Young, Michael, Oxford Brookes University, Music Department, Headington Campus, Oxford OX3 0BN
01865 484951 Fax:01865 484952; 01865 711082 (box office);
amp@brookes.ac.uk (email); www.brookes.ac.uk/schools/apm

BA (Hons) Music (BA (Hons) Music)
General Music with a Jazz Element - Aspiring Degree Level and Above - October - 3 years
Modules in Jazz, Improvisation, Composition and Popular music are available. These optional courses can represent a significant part of the degree programme. 1st year - Music Studies 1: Structure and Tonality, Music Studies 2: Skills in composition, Music Studies 3: Contexts for Repertoire, Introduction to Studio composition, University Music, 2nd/3rd year Ensemble Performance, Creative performance, Composition, Electroacoustic Composition, Text and Context, Music in Society 1 and 2, Opera and Politics, Early Music, Modernism: Music Analysis and Aesthetics, After Modernism: Music Analysis and Aesthetics, Understanding Jazz, Studying Popular Music: An Introduction, Musicology: Perspectives and Polemics, Independent Study: Solo Performance, Special Study in Contemporary Arts: New Collaborations

MA in Contemporary Arts and Music (MA)
Music Course Majoring in Jazz - Aspiring Degree Level and Above - September – 1 or 2 years
This is a unique postgraduate course offering a range of alternatives within an interdisciplinary framework. Applications from musicians with experience in improvisation and/or jazz are welcome. Artists, composers and performers specialise in their own chosen medium and also have the opportunity to collaborate with others, exploring interdisciplinary routes across art forms. Students are encouraged to conceive their work in terms of social location, audience relation and performance context. Taught by a team of artists, musicians and cultural theorists working and publishing nationally and internationally. The school enjoys a lively research culture which promotes collaborative projects between staff. The graduate environment is enhanced by excellent facilities for sound recording and electroacoustic composition, photography, video, bookworks, printmaking and 3D

South East Essex College

Carnarvon Road, Southend-on-Sea SS2 6LS
01702 220400 Fax:01702 432320; marketing@se-essex-college.ac.uk (email);
www.se-essex-college.ac.uk

HND Performing Arts Music Production
General Music with a Jazz Element - Semi-Pro or Amateur - September - 2 years
Awarding body EdExcel

Entry Requirements GCE A levels (one grade E); Advanced vocational certificate of education (AVCE);BTEC national certificate /BTEC national diploma /GNVQ
An access certificate with at least 12 credits at level three and four credits at level two OR equivalent work experience - if you are a mature student please contact the pathway leader in the subject concerned, for individual consideration.
Course to develop skills in music production based on hardware such as ADAT, DAT and DR8's as well as software including Pro-tools, Cubase and Cool Edit Pro.

BA(Hons) Music Production
Length of Course 1-year full-time
Entry Requirements - Relevant HND Mix of experience in live and studio settings
Range of modules relevant to the industry; Mix of specialist and core modules.
Work Placement forms an important component of this course.

University College Chichester
Bishop Otter Campus, College Lane, Chichester PO19 4PE.
01243 816002 admissions@chihe.ac.uk (email); www.chihe.ac.uk
BA (Hons) Music (BA (Hons) Music)
General Music with a Jazz Element - Aspiring Degree Level and Above - September - 3 years
All students are talented players, singers and composers, attracted by a pro-gramme that is designed for people who want to develop these skills
Entry by audition is an essential part of the selection process. 160 to 220 UCAS Tariff points OR a National Diploma OR an approved Access Course.
Aims to provide the skills to enable students to work independently as well as in groups, and the ability to collaborate with others. Practical skills in musical perfor-mance as well as creative skills in composing and improvising. Written and oral communication skills; problem solving; analytical skills; research skills.

University of Reading
35 Upper Redlands Road, Reading RG1 5JE
0118 931 8411 Fax:0118 931 8412; music@reading.ac.uk (email);
BA Music (BA)
General Music with a Jazz Element - Aspiring Degree Level and Above - September - 3 years
The study of music at Reading enables students to build on their existing skills in performing, composing, understanding and writing about music. Students will explore a diverse range of Western music and music making, from medieval polyphony through the romantic symphony and early 20th-century jazz to recent hip-hop. The project-based programmes offer numerous opportunities to develop a variety of practical and academic musical skills. There is an opportunity for special-isation in one of three areas: composition, performance or musicology (including analysis). Teaching is through lectures, seminars, small group teaching, individual tutorials and individual instrumental or vocal lessons. Project-based modules enable students to explore subjects in depth. A typical final year project would offer the opportunity to write about, compose in the style of and/or perform the music of an individual composer (or group of composers) or music of a particular style or genre.

University of Southampton

Highfield, Southampton SO17 1BJ
02380 595000 Fax:02380 593037; www.soton.ac.uk

BA (Hons) Music (BA (Hons))

General Music with a Jazz Element - Aspiring Degree Level and Above - September
- 3 years

The course has a core programme of musical studies in the first year and free
choice from a wide range of options thereafter. Students can study performance in
jazz styles during all 3 years of the degree. In the first year there is an
'Introduction to Jazz and Popular Music'; a performance module with 20 hours of
individual tuition plus a fortnightly 'Jazz and Pop' class. In the 2nd and 3rd years
units in Jazz Theory – a tonal and rhythmic theory of mainstream jazz of the
1940s and 50s, jazz improvisation solos, composition and arrangement, lectures in
theory and analysis. There is a 'performance tuition' unit and 'performance recital'
units. For students who have gained a high mark in Jazz theory and Orchestration
the Jazz Techniques course is available and covers the performance of jazz and
contemporary music. There are two student run jazz groups – University jazz
Orchestra www.soton.ac.uk/~sujo and a Jazz/Gospel choir 'Jazzmanix'
www.jazzmanix.org

MA in Performance(MA Performance)

Music Course Majoring in Jazz - Aspiring Degree Level and Above - September – 1
or 2 years

The MA in performance is offered in Jazz. It can be taken in either full-time mode
(over 12 months) or part-time (over 24).

University of Surrey

Guildford GU2 5XH
01483 300800 Fax:01483 300803; information@surrey.ac.uk (email);
www.surrey.ac.uk

B.Mus (Hons) (B Mus (Hons))

General Music with a Jazz Element - Aspiring Degree Level and Above -
September - 3 years or 4 year option includes a Professional Training year.
Performance, composition and the academic study of music have equal status in
the music department, so that programmes are well suited to those aspiring to a
professional career in any area of the music industry.
Western art music from ancient times to the present day still forms the basis of
the historical and analytical studies in the degree programme, but modules in popular and non-western music, music technology and jazz are also available, while in
the second and final years students may specialise in performance, composition,
musicology or conducting. Jazz Studies option in Year 3.

Bmus in Music and Sound Recording (Tonmeister) (B Mus in Music and Sound Recording)

Music Technology - Aspiring Degree Level and Above - September - 4 years
The course is aimed at those who are primarily concerned with the theory and
practice of sound recording, but who also wish to develop their musical knowledge.
Year 1 provides a solid foundation in the principles of sound recording and music.
Core subjects: Acoustics; Audio Engineering; Electronics; Electronics Practicals;
Mathematics; Operational Practicals; Recording Techniques; Harmony; Score
Studies; Understanding Music 1; Knowledge of Instruments. Available options
(from which you choose two) are: Analysis; Composition; Introduction to

Orchestration; Performance; and Understanding Music 2.
Year 2 Core modules are: Audio Engineering; Audio Laboratory; Digital Sound Synthesis and Processing; Electroacoustics; Recording Techniques (including practicals); Synthesis Basics and MIDI. You will also choose optional modules to the value of 40 credits from the Level 2 Music programme.
Professional Training
Gain experience by working in recording studios, broadcasting, audio consultancy, audio manufacturing, etc. University maintains contact with students through formal visits by Professional Training Tutors.
Year 3 Choose optional modules and pursue studies in: Audio Engineering; Audio Research Seminars; Recording Techniques Seminars; and Video Engineering; write a Technical Project, and submit a portfolio of your own recordings.
Therefore, in each year of the programme, students take a range of subjects from the list which the Music Department offers to its students in addition to their Sound Recording studies.
Career options include - television and radio engineering and production, pop and classical record production, equipment design, software engineering, audio systems maintenance, professional audio equipment support, freelance performance, teaching, lecturing, research (both academic and technical), arts administration, journalism and marketing.

Part-Time

Bournemouth and Poole College
Bournemouth and Poole College of Further Education, Constitution Hill Centre, Poole BH14 0QA
01202 205 205 www.thecollege.ac.uk
BTEC First Diploma in Performing Arts (Music)
September – 1 year
There are no formal entry requirements but some nstrumental skills are required. Entrance by interview and audition. There is a strong emphasis on practical work. In addition to solo and ensemble work studies include Music performance, Technology in music and Understanding music.

BTEC Higher National Cert. In Popular Mu (BTEC Higher National Cert. In Popular Mu)
General Music - Aspiring Degree Level and Above - September - 2 years
This course includes lectures, practical demonstrations, ensemble work workshops and self-study. Modules include: popular music history, ensemble studies, aural analysis, improvisation, music technology, recording techniques, business studies, composition and arranging, harmony and instrumental techniques. The course has a practical slant, and includes live performances at local venues and an additional sound recording qualification, with the opportunity to do a Rock School instrumental grade exam.

Evening Music Foundation (ABRSM Music Theory Grades)
General Music with a Jazz Element - Semi-Pro or Amateur - September - 1 year
Broad range of music areas including basic reading, advanced music theory, major/minor scales, key signatures, intervals, chords and inversions, diatonic harmony and analysis.

Canterbury Christ Church University Coll

North Holmes Road, Canterbury CT1 1QU
01227 767700 Fax:01227470442; Admissions@cant.ac.uk (email); www.cant.ac.uk

Certificate/Diploma in Music (Certificate in Music)

General Music - Semi-Pro or Amateur - September - 2 years (24 evenings per year 18.00 to 21.00)

The Certificate builds upon musical experience gained by the student in a variety of ways. Programme draws on the courses offered at Level 1 of the Single Honours Programme (see Full time BA course). Students will participate in departmental directed ensemble. Assessment is through the production of course work and examination. Diploma in Music - successful completion of the Certificate in Music allows students to study for a further two years part-time for the Diploma in Music. Building upon experiences and interests developed at Certificate level, the programme draws upon courses offered in the Single Honours Music Programme at Level 2 (see BA Music Full time)

Music Access Programme (Music Access Certificate)

General Music with a Jazz Element - Semi-Pro or Amateur - September - 1 year (one evening and one Saturday per week)

There are three main parts to the programme : - Performance (Development of Practical Skills and Theory to Grade V level). - Listening (Improvement of Listening skills) - Appraisal (Increasing Critical Awareness). For those unable to read music, notation at all levels will be taught. All students are expected to have private lessons in singing or on a solo instrument (these can be arranged through the College). Every student should be able to set aside half an hour daily to practise a solo instrument, and at least three hours each week for reading, listening and prepared work. In addition, there will be a weekly tutorial in Study Skills. The Music Access Programme is aimed at students wishing to ultimately apply for a place on a music degree programme.

Chichester College of Arts, Sci. and Tech.

Kendon, Adrian, Director of Jazz Studies, Chichester College of Arts, Science and Technology, Music School, Westgate Fields, Chichester PO19 1SB
01243 786321 Fax:01243 539481; adrian.kendon@chichester.ac.uk (email); www.chichester.ac.uk/jazz.html

for further information on courses, contact the College

A-Level Music (A Level Music)

General Music with a Jazz Element - Semi-Pro or Amateur - September - 32 weeks
Aural skills, harmony and composition, history and analysis, performance.

Crayford Manor House

Manley, Jan
Area Organiser, Crayford Manor House AE Centre
May Place Road East
Crayford DA1 4HB
01322 521 463 www.nostab.freeserve.co.uk/Page2.htm

Jazz Improvisation

Jazz Only - Jazz Beginner - Crayford Manor House, Crayford - A series of 7 meetings. Starting Saturday 25th January 2003

Saturdays 1-4.30pm but doesn't take place every week. Age range from 14 upwards. All levels of ability welcome but mainly a basic course which covers improvisation in a practical way with reference to jazz theory. Minimum of 9 students. Please mention the instrument you play when applying. Aim to hold a performance at the end of every term. Tutor: Ray Batson

North Kingston Centre
Hills, John, North Kingston Centre, Richmond Road, Kingston upon Thames KT2 5PE
020 8547 6700   adult.education@rbk.kingston.gov.uk (email);
www.kingston.gov.uk/learning/adulteducation

Blues into Jazz
General Music with a Jazz Element - Jazz Beginner - North Kingston Centre - 14/01/2003 - 11 sessions
New course. Commences 14th January 2003. 19.00 - 21.00 every Tuesday. Designed to 'remove the mystery which surrounds the ability to improvise when playing Blues or Jazz'. The sessions follow the musical path from basic country blues to jazz standards with a simple and logical method, which will help single line musicians (saxes, flute, guitar, violin) to develop an ability to improvise. Students need some basic technical playing ability on their instrument and the willingness to 'have a go'. Course is suitable for those new to jazz as well as for players wanting to explore the blues and its importance in the development of improvised music. It aims to develop and use a jazz vocabulary and communicate your own ideas within a band.

Queen Mary's College
Sheedy, Stephen, Principal, Queen Mary's College, Cliddesden Road, Basingstoke RG213HF
01256 417 500 Fax:01256 417501;

Playing Jazz
Jazz Only - Semi-Pro or Amateur - April - 10 weeks
Two courses - beginner and advanced. The courses cover: Improvisation skills, listening skills, chord theory, playing by ear, ensemble playing, hamony, instrumental role, key figures in jazz. The courses are taught through group and solo work plus workshop and practice sessions. The courses are bookable a term at a time and take place on Tuesday and Wednesday evenings 7 - 9pm.

University of Surrey
Guildford GU2 5XH
01483 300800 Fax:01483 300803; information@surrey.ac.uk (email);
www.surrey.ac.uk

M.Phil/PhD by composition (M Phil/PhD)
Music Course Majoring in Jazz - Aspiring Degree Level and Above -33 to 60 months (PT) - August -

M.Phil/PhD by research (M Phil/PhD)
Music Course Majoring in Jazz - Aspiring Degree Level and Above -33 to 60 months (PT) - August -
For both - proposals are particularly welcome in fields related to late 19th and 20th century aesthetics and analysis, and in popular music studies and critical musicol-

ogy, which are strong aspects of the Department's research profile Applicants will be required to submit evidence of creative potential as well as academic achievement. None of the research staff have a jazz or improvised music bias.

University of Sussex

Centre for Continuing Educatio, Gardner Arts Centre, Falmer, Brighton BN1 9RA 01273 685 447 Fax:01273 685 861 (bookings) (box office); www.sussex.ac.uk

Getting into Jazz - Beginners (18 credits)
Jazz Only - Jazz Beginner - Gardner Arts Centre University of Sussex - October - 15 workshops on alternate Saturdays 10-12pm. A workshop for musicians with little or no experience of playing jazz but who want a grounding in the elements of improvisation - rhythm, melody and harmony. Tutor - Geoff Simkins.

Getting into jazz - Intermediate (18 Credits)
Jazz Only - Semi-Pro or Amateur - Gardner Arts Centre - October - 15 alternate Saturdays 12.30 - 14.30pm. A course for musicians who have some basic experience of playing jazz (ideal for those who have already done the beginners course) and who want to study the music in greater depth. Tutor - Geoff Simkins.

Workshop

Brighton Musicians Jazz Co-Operative

Bailey, John, Organiser, Brighton Musicians Jazz Co-operative, 53 Springfield Road, Brighton BN1 6DF
johnbailey@yahoo.co.uk (email);

Workshops
Jazz Only - Semi-Pro or Amateur - Stamford Arms, Preston Circus, Brighton - Wednesday evenings
Jam sessions and workshops on a Wednesday 7.30pm upstairs at the Stamford Arms, Preston Circus, Brighton with local professional musicians running workshops. Pay MU teaching rates.

Jazz a Long a Weekend

Ayling, Derek, The New House, Sandy Balls Estate, Godshill SL6 2LA
01425 650770 hippotrain@btinternet.com (email);

Midsummer Jazz a Long a Weekend
Jazz Only - Semi-Pro or Amateur - Damerham, Hants - June - 2 days
A weekend allowing musicians of differing standards, experience and ability to play in a relaxed, friendly atmosphere. The emphasis is on chords, harmony, rhythm and improvising. The tutors are Mark Bassey, Alan Cook and Jim Phillips. The course takes place in an idyllic setting by the river, in the centre of the village of Damerham in Hampshire, near Fordingbridge in the New Forest. Cost £66

Jazz Platform

Lefrog, Thierry, Director, The Jazz Platform, c/o New Greenham Arts, 113 Lindenmuth Way, New Greenham Business Park, Newbury
dave.laing@ntlworld.com (email); www.jazzplatform.net NGA contact is Michelle Crumpen

Jazz Platform

Jazz Only - Semi-Pro or Amateur - New Greenham Arts, Newbury -
The Jazz Platform is held once a month on the SECOND FRIDAY of each month,
and provides an opportunity for amateur players to play live and network with
other musicians. Each evening is free (though there is an optional collection) and
starts with a workshop at 7.30pm. The main session starts at 8pm and continues
through to around 10.30. The platform attracts a wide variety of levels of player
and is open to anyone to play any type of improvised music. The numbers attending are typically 30/40. It provides a friendly and supportive environment with a
mixture of published jam numbers where anyone can join in. Some groups come
along to try out numbers and other groups are formed on the night! The Jazz
Platform recently ran a one-day tuition workshop tutored by Michael Garrick, and,
owing to its success are considering running another sometime later in the year!
See www.jazzplatform.net for more details

Jazz Workshop

Mander, Derek, 47 Shelley Road, Chesham HP5 2EY
info@jazzworkshop.org.uk (email); www.jazzworkshop.org.uk

Jazz Workshop

Jazz Only - Jazz Beginner – Sportsman,Croxley Green, Rickmansworth, Herts ongoing -
Every Monday 8-11pm at the Sportsman, Croxley Green, Rickmansworth, Herts.

The Jazz Workshop is an informal co-operative venture run by musicians for musicians. It has two main aims, which are primarily educational: - to introduce new
musicians to playing jazz; - to provide opportunities for existing jazz musicians to
play together to improve their ensemble playing. We attempt to do this by providing an opportunity for musicians new to playing jazz to try it out in an informal,
friendly atmosphere, with no 'schoolroom' feel. We are also providing an easily
accessible opportunity for more experienced players to get together to try out new
ideas, and practice their ensemble playing. Sponsored by Chiltern District Council.

Mill Arts Centre

Clarke, Deborah, Programming, The Mill Arts Centre, Spiceball Park, Banbury OX16
5QE
01295 252050 Fax:01295 279003; 01295 2790002 (box office);

Jazz Workshops

Jazz Only - Jazz Beginner - on going -
Jazz workshops for all ages and abilities. FREE on Tuesday evenings 21.00 to
23.00 Contact: Steve Cuttee

Ruskin College

Clarke, Natalie, Ruskin College, Walton Street, Oxford
01865 517832

Jazz Singing Workshop

Music Course Majoring in Jazz - Jazz Beginner - Ruskin College, Oxford - May - 8
weeks
Tutor: Alison Bentley. Aimed at improving the voice and experience of singing in
different styles. Students will practise breathing and vocal excercises for different
kinds of music - jazz, soul, gospel, blues and folk. Some repertoire will be sung in
harmony, but there is no need to be able to read music. Workshops take place on

Mondays 19.00 to 21.00.

University of Sussex

Centre for Continuing Education, Gardner Arts Centre, Falmer, Brighton BN1 9RA
01273 685 447 Fax:01273 685 861 (bookings) (box office); www.sussex.ac.uk

Jazz Band Workshop (24 Credits)
Jazz Only - Semi-Pro or Amateur - Gardner Arts Centre - October - 15 alternate
Saturdays 10.30 - 13.30pm. (Sub-titled - A Grounding in Theory and Practice)
Aimed at musicians who are experienced improvisers and who want to develop
their knowledge in a practical setting. Tutor - Geoff Simkins

Short Courses

Denman College

Marcham, Abingdon OX13 6NW
01865 391991 (office tel); 01865 391966

Jazz Course
Jazz Only - Semi-Pro or Amateur - October - 4 days
Tutor: Carl Attwood

Jazz Weekend at the Park

Kelly, Pat, BYJO, University of Reading, Bulmershe Court, Woodlands Avenue,
Reading RG5 4AN
0976 425995 (mobile);
Rehearsals are Sunday evenings throughout the year.

Jazz Weekend at the Park
Jazz Only - Semi-Pro or Amateur - South Hill Park, Bracknell - March - Weekend
Sat 10.00 to 18.00 Sun. 10:30 to 18.00 Tickets are £55 (£42) Music Union
Members £45, day tickets available. Further information Vivien Becher on extension 230. Bookings 01344 484 123. Jazz course consists of seminars, workshops,
masterclasses, covering solo, small and large ensembles, for all instruments and
voice, for all ages and all standards. Rhythm section and composition seminars.
Also - Open rehearsals - for Big Band and Jazz Orchestra players. Covers different
ways to rehearse a Big Band, rehearsing in sections, how to get the best out of
your arrangements and improvisation within a Big Band. Open to anyone on the
course, but designed especially for those who enjoy performing and like the discipline of a Big Band, but do not wish to take part in solo improvisation. Also - Jazz
Jam Session on Saturday night with jazz course tutors and other course members -
Big Band and small groups. Also - Gala Concert on Sunday night in Wilde Theatre
featuring tutors. Tutors include - Peter King, Tina May, Nikki Iles, Ian Thomas,
Mike Bradley, John Parricelli, Andy Cleyndert, Ben Castle, Peter Churchill, Stan
Sulzmann, Dave Cliff, Steve Waterman. Course

Summer School

Canford Summer School of Music

Binney, Malcolm, Course Director, Canford Summer School of Music, 5 Bushey
Close, Old Barn Lane, Kenley CR8 5AU
020 8660 4766 Fax:020 8668 5273; canfordsummersch@aol.com (email);
www.mikehall.co.uk/canford.html 0208 660 4766 (tel)
Tutors: Mike Hall; Gareth Huw Davies.
A journey through Jazz
Jazz Only - Jazz Beginner - August - 1 Week
Summer school lasts 3 weeks with jazz course in the second week. For instrumentalists with reasonable facility but not necessarily a great deal of jazz experience.
Features Workshops on solo, rhythm section and ensemble playing in a variety of
styles. Tutors are Mike Hall and Gareth Huw Davies. Students will be formed into
groups of different sizes and combinations offering opportunities to improvise, to
undertake in-depth work with individual tutors and, where possible, to give public
performances. Participants should have a basic command of their instrument but
no previous experience of improvisation is necessary. Musicians with classical skill
wishing to explore jazz for the first time are welcome. Because of the popularity of
the instrument, places for pianists will be restricted.

East Sussex Music Service

East Sussex County Council, County Hall, St Anne's Crescent, Lewes, East Sussex
BN7 1UE

Contact Suzanne Freeman on: 01273 472336 or
suzanne.freeman@eastsussexcc.gov.uk

7th July to 2nd August 2003

Provides music education for pupils throughout East Sussex, of every age and ability. Courses for strings, woodwind, brass, keyboard and percussion. Also, two new
courses that were introduced last year return in 2003 - 'East Sussex Jazz' and
'World Music' - for students who wish to improve their skills and experience with
jazz and improvisation, or to explore music from non-Western cultures using
authentic instruments. Once again, concerts for most courses will be held at the
end of each week, with many having the opportunity to perform at the Winter
Garden, Eastbourne.

Guest conductor for the Jazz course is Scott Stroman, Head of the Guildhall School
of Music and Drama and Director of the London Jazz Orchestra. Courses will run at
various venues in Eastbourne and Lewes. The concerts will take place at the Winter
Garden and St Saviour's and St Peter's Church, both in Eastbourne; St Mary in the
Castle, Hastings; and the Gardner Arts Centre, Falmer.

This annual event offers young musicians the opportunity to make music, and
enables real gains to be made in pupils' musical understanding and performing
skills - plus, students have the experience of studying and performing with others.

Jazz Academy

Garrick, Michael, Jazz Academy Resources, Contact address for booking - 12 Castle Street, Berkhamsted HP4 2BQ
01442 864 989 www.jazzacademyuk.com

All ages.

Summer Jazz 2003

Jazz Only - Semi-Pro or Amateur - Beechwood Campus Tunbridge Wells - 17/08/2003 - August - 1 week

Jazz for beginners, All instrumentalists, jazz singers and accompanists, string players, covering 85 years of Jazz Improvisation: 1917-2002.

"We don't pay that much attention to generation gaps at Jazz Academy (average ages 16-75): we're here to illuminate and pass on our experience, skills and great love of jazz…. only qualifications need to be a real curiosity, an ability to play or sing (in your own judgement) with reasonable facility and above all, an enthusiasm for sharing and learning with an open mind". Courses include instrumental tutorials, Illustrated jazz history, Ensembles, Harmony classes, Graded improvisation, Playalong sessions with tutor rhythm sections, Jazz beginners classes, Vocal groups, Opportunities for individual tuition, Composing and arranging. The Jazz syllabus from the Associated Board Royal Schools of Music can also be studied by those who may be interested. (Also run Xmas Swing 27-30 December 2003)

Kent Music Summer School

Kent Music School, Astley House, Hastings Road, Maidstone ME15 7SG

General enquiries 01622 691 212 Fax 01622 358 440
sseeds@kentmusicschool.org (email) www.kentmusicschool.org.uk

Kent Music School residential music courses for young musicians (8-19 years)are held each July in Kent. The purpose is to give students the opportunity to join in concentrated ensemble playing, away from the distractions of home and school. Anyone, regardless of where they live or are educated, can apply for a place. Courses are intended to be especially helpful to those preparing for GCSE and A level music, as a supplement to their studies.

Jazz Course - suitable for Grades 3 to 8 - held at Beneden School, near Cranbrook, Kent - Wednesday 23rd to Friday 25th July 2003

Jazz course provides opportunity to play jazz in the Big Band style with specialist tutors to help to develop improvisational skills. No audition necessary but placement is made after instrumental teachers' recommendation. Booking forms are distributed to all schools and Music Centres in Kent, but also available on-line from web address above. Deadline is end of February for July summer school.

Medway Jazz

Stubberfield, Harry, Medway Jazz Society, 43 First Avenue, Gillingham ME27 2LH

Summer School

Jazz Only - Jazz Beginner - Chatham Grammar School for Girls - July - 5 days

This year's summer school takes place from Monday 30th July through to and including Friday 3rd August 2001 at Chatham Grammar School for Girls. 45 minutes by train from London Victoria and 1 hour from Dover, the school is within easy access for anyone travelling either from Europe or the Home Counties. This year's school offers an exciting and intensive programme of Jazz study culminating in a performance at the end of the week. Most suitable for beginners and those of intermediate standard, the school offers tuition in improvisation techniques, ensemble playing, solo techniques, sound production, basic composition and arranging, musicianship, and rhythm and co-ordination. Running from 9.30am until 4.30pm daily, the school has its own resident trio for accompanying purposes and this year is actively encouraging singers to attend. Cost for the whole week is £125 or from £30 per day. Accommodation can be recommended if required. Tuition is provided by experienced professional performers and educators. Application forms are available from Jon Peel (Director) on 01795 843441 or Jazzdevelops@tinyon-line.co.uk. The added bonus of this school is that it takes place during the same week as the Medway Jazz Festival providing many opportunities during the evening to go out and enjoy yourself.

MUM (UK)
Dorothy Cooper, PO BOX 5063, Milton Keynes, Bucks MK5 7ZN
01908 670 306 Fax:01908 674 909 dcooper@mum-uk.demon.co.uk (email)
MUM(UK) Summer School at Desborough School, Maidenhead
10th August 2003 -7 days
Residential summer school at Maidenhead (address for bookings is Milton Keynes). Musical Directors: Jeff Clyne (bass), Trevor Tomkins (drums), Nick Weldon (piano), Dave Hassell (percussion). Tutors: Alan Barnes (saxes), Steve Waterman (trumpet), Mike Outram (Guitar), Malcolm Earle Smith (trombone), Jacqui Dankworth,Lee Gibson (vocals), Julian Cox (bass guitar). Course includes improvisation in Big and small bands, aural workshop, rhythm and harmony tuition. Concert with tutors on Friday and student performance on Saturday. Course fee: 2003, £420 includes accomodation, breakfast and evening meal and tuition. Accomodation single rooms.

Montgomery/Holloway Music Trust
Dorothy Cooper, PO BOX 5063, Milton Keynes, Bucks MK5 7ZN
Advanced Singers Summer School at Desborough School, Maidenhead
29th July 2003, 5 days
Musical Directors: Laurie Holloway, Jeff Clyne - bass, Matt Skelton - Drums, Anita Wardell, Jacqui Dankworth, Sara Colman - vocals, Malcom Edmonstone - pianist, composer, arranger. Other rhythm sections - pianist and guitar for students to work with. Concentrates on performance and accompanying techniques. Suitable for all styles of music, classical jazz, show performers, and for instrumentalists as well as singers.

Music Makers
David Andrews, 16 Whitsbury Road, Fordingbridge, Hants SP6 1JZ
Tel/Fax 01425 654819, musmak1@aol.com (email)
Young Musicians Summer Course (2) at Forres Sandle Manor School,
Fordingbridge, Hants. Week One 28th July to August 1st Week Two August
4th to 8th 2003
(This course is the same as the one held in Wimbledon but the Seniors group is split into Week One for Grades 2 to 6 and Week Two for Grades 6 to 8+ and these have a residential option)

Juniors 5-6 for children with no previous experience; Intermediate 7-10 for young instrumentalists to work in groups, singing, recorder playing and percussion in a range of styles from classical to jazz; Seniors 8-18 (Grades 2 to 8) for players of all orchestral and band instruments, who will be placed in groups according to ability. The aim is to stretch each individual, but not out of their depth. The daily programme will vary but course members may find themselves in a variety of rehearsal situations including - Brass and Wind ensembles, string groups, wind bands, jazz groups, improvisation workshops, chamber groups, sectional rehearsals and full orchestras.

Wavendon

Selvidge, Rachel, Wavendon All Music Plan Ltd, The Stables, Stockwell Lane, Wavendon, Milton Keynes MK17 8LT
01908 280 818 Fax:01908 280825; 01908 280 800 (box office) This famous Summer School usually held at the Dankworths' venue at *Wavendon Summer school is taking a break for 2003*

Music Technology

Bournemouth and Poole College

Bournemouth and Poole College of Further Education, Constitution Hill Centre, Poole BH14 0QA
01202 205 205 www.thecollege.ac.uk*BTEC National Diploma in Music Technology*
September – 2 years
General musicianship, aural skills, composing, music theory and keyboard skills as well as more technical topics such as recording techniques, music sequencing, acoustics, digital theory and multimedia. There is also a unit on how the music industry works. The course involves a lot of practical project work in well-equipped recording and technology studios, and includes an additional sound recording qualification

Brunel University

Frank Griffith, Brunel University College, Uxbridge Campus, Faculty of Arts, Uxbridge, Middx, UB8 3PH.
01895 274000 x4495; frankgriffith@brunel.ac.uk (email); www.brunel.ac.uk
BA (Hons) Creative Music and Technology
Music Technology 3 years full time
Covers acoustic and electronic compositional techniques, Film, TV, video music, signal processing, midi-sequencing and recording acoustics and psychoacoustics; sound sampling and editing; business skills; aural and musicianship training; analytical and critical skills. There are also specialist music options in world music, improvisation, modern music, music theatre, and ethnomusicology. In the final year, an independent project in an aspect of creative music technology will form a major part of 'your experience'. If students opt for the thick-sandwich route, they have the opportunity to spend a year gaining practical experience in a relevant profession, designed to equip them with skills that will be useful in a wide range of careers e.g.music professions, broadcasting, recording, digital studio engineering, multimedia and TV, video and film production.

Chichester College of Arts, Science and Technology
Adrian Kendon, Chichester College of Arts, Science and Technology, Music School, Westgate Fields, Chichester, W Sussex, PO19 1SB.

01243 786321 Fax:01243 539481; adrian.kendon@chichester.ac.uk (email); www.chichester.ac.uk/jazz.html

Music Technology (Sound Recording) Intermediate Award
Start Month: October. Duration: 30 weeks. Requirements: Open entry.

Wed 6.30-8.30 pm Microphones, mixing console, tape machines, recording, mixing techniques and editing, compressors and noise gates.

Music Technology Intermediate Award
Start Month: October. Duration: 30 weeks. Requirements: Open entry.

Mon 7-9pm MIDI sequencing using Applemac computers and Logic software or PCs and Cubase software

Cricklade College
Cricklade College, Charlton Road, Andover, Hants, SP10 1EJ.

01264 363311 Fax:01264 332088; info@cricklade.ac.uk (email); www.cricklade.ac.uk

AS Level Music Technology
Start Month: September. Duration: 2 years. Qualification: AA level Music Technology.

BRTE National Diploma in Music Technology
Start Month: September

Gateway School of Recording and Music Technology
The School of Music, Kingston University, Kingston Hill Centre, Kingston upon Thames, Surrey, KT2 7LB.

020 8549 0014 Fax:020 8547 7337; gatewayeducation@kingston.ac.uk (email)

Creative Music Technology (stage 2)
Start Month: May and Sept. Duration: 10 weeks.

This course is aimed at participants from the stage 1 course who would like to develop their skills further. It is a pre-requisite of this course to have completed stage 1. Further information available on request. Cost: £390.

Essentials of Music Technology (stage 1)
Start Month: May and Sept. Duration: 10 weeks.

This course provides a valuable opportunity to develop your practical skill and the-oretical understanding of music technology. This course is suitable for beginners. Cost: £390.

Higher Dip: Recording, Music Technology
Start Month: September. Duration: 2 years.

The aim of this course is to provide the student with a broad base of skills covering the three main subject areas of Recording, Music Technology and Music business

Studies. It is also possible to take modules of the course individually, subject to space, allowing for part time study of specific areas.

Studio Installation

Start Month: August. Duration: 1 day.

This one day seminar will be an ideal opportunity for those needing advice on installing a studio at home. The course will provide information on evaluating your needs, budgets, installation and equipment. Cost: £65.

Richmond upon Thames College

Richmond upon Thames College, Egerton Road, Twickenham, Middx, TW2 7JS.

020 8607 8305/8314 courses@richmond-utcoll.ac.uk. (email)

Music Technology (National Diploma)

Start Month: September. Duration: 2 years.

This is a practical course which aims to prepare you for a career in today's music industry as a sound engineer, programmer, musician, producer or indeed for progression to higher education.

Music Technology A and AS levels

Start Month: September. Duration: 1/2 years.

The courses offer the opportunity to study contemporary music production addressing that unique point where art meets science. Today's record producer has to deal with a variety of tasks ranging from arranging music to designing synthesiser sounds, recording a drum kit to applying special effects, sequencing (programming) music on computer to printing scores. All of these areas and much more are addressed in both A and AS. Most of the courses are assessed by practical submissions i.e. CD's of student's recordings, however AS includes a written paper and A2 includes a CD-ROM based production analysis. Pop, Jazz and classical genres are all addressed. Students will have access to the college recording studios and music production suite. The course is also supported by individual music tuition.

Recording Techniques

Start Month: September. Duration: 1 year. Qualification: BTEC advanced unit accreditation.

This practical course gives students experience in studio sound recording. Aspects covered include: microphone usage and placement, operation of a mixing console, multitrack recording, special effects and mixing. The course culminates with students producing their own full multitrack production on CD and leads to BTEC advanced unit accreditation.

Sussex Downs College

Sussex Downs College, Mountfield Road, Lewes, E Sussex, BN7 2XH.

01273 483188 Fax:01273 478561; info@lewescollege.ac.uk (email); www.lewescollege.ac.uk

BTEC National Diploma in Music Technology

Start Month: September. Duration: 2 years. Qualification: BTEC National Diploma in Music Technology

This two-year course is designed to prepare students for employment in the music industry or for Higher education. It covers all aspects of music technology and recording; an understanding of the music business - record companies, publishers, managers, agents, promoters, contracts and other legal aspects of the business, plus skills required for employment; live performance; compositions and arrangement. Students will be involved with the college record label which releases a minimum of two releases a year. The programme aims to enhance chances of a place in industry which is very competitive and often only provides irrregular and short term employment. For further information contact Trevor Jones on 01323 637511

University of Brighton

University of Brighton, Mithras House, Lewes road, Brighton, E Sussex, BN2 4AT.
01273 600900 Fax:01273 642825; admissions@brighton.ac.uk (email)

BA (Hons) MusicProduction

General Music with a Jazz Element - Aspiring Degree Level and Above - September -1 year

Offering a natural progression from the HND/C courses, the BA(Hons) top-up degree develops professional skills and specialist practice in a challenging context of leading-edge research and production. Recording, Multi-track Recording and mastering, MIDI Recording, Hard-disk Recording and Mastering, Synthesis and Sampling, Sequencing and Programming, History of Recording, Business, The Global Marketplace and Impact of New Media, Copyright Law, Music Business Agreements and Contracts, Business Organisational Skills and Marketing Methodology, Record Release (Compilation Albums), Performance, Twentieth-century Popular Music, Ensemble Skills, Performing Original Compositions, The Promoter, Solo Album, Songwriting, Lyric Writing, Composition.

BA (Hons) Digital Music

Music technology – 3 years (4 to 6 years Part time)
Course focuses on composition using computing and electronic instruments for areas like sonic design, multimedia, video, performance and the internet. It encompasses a wide range of musical styles. Candidates are expected to have a good grounding in musicianship and musical theory. Core elements such as sound studio work, computing, music theory and acoustics are supported by Historical and Critical Studies and a range of options.
Year 1 develops basic computing skills, involving virtual studio techniques and scoring, together with simple recording.
Year 2 - more advanced techniques including sound-to-picture applications (including synchronisation and dubbing), hard-disk recording and sound-sample manipulation.
Year 3 - students are encouraged to develop a strong portfolio of their own work.

Hons Music Production (HND top-up)

Start Month: September. Duration: 1 year.

This course is relevant to the development of many career paths in the world of music and music production. It develops practical skills in music technology, the music business, performance, songwriting and·music production.

Digital Music BA (Hons)

Start Month: September. Duration: 3/6 years. Qualification: BA (Hons) Digital Music.

4-6 Part Time. Course focuses on composition using computing and electronic instruments for areas like sonic design, multimedia, video, performance and the internet. It encompasses a wide range of musical styles. Candidates are expected to have a good grounding in musicianship and musical theory. Core elements such as sound studio work, computing, music theory and acoustics are supported by Historical and Critical Studies and a range of options. Year 1 develops basic computing skills, involving virtual studio techniques and scoring, together with simple recording. Year 2 - more advanced techniques including sound-to-picture applications (including synchronisation and dubbing), hard-disk recording and sound-sample manipulation. Year 3 - students are encouraged to develop a strong portfolio of their own work

HND Music Production

Start Month: September. Duration: 2 years.

This course is relevant to the development of many career paths in the world of music and music production. It develops practical skills in music technology, the music business, performance, songwriting and music production.

University of Surrey

University of Surrey, Guildford, Surrey, GU2 5XH.

01483 300800 Fax:01483 300803; information@surrey.ac.uk (email); www.surrey.ac.uk

BMus in Music and Sound Recording (Tonmeister)

Start Month: September. Duration: 4 years. Requirements: Typical A level offer – ABB. Qualification: B Mus in Music and Sound Recording.

The course is aimed at those who are primarily concerned with the theory and practice of sound recording, but who also wish to develop their musical knowledge.

Year 1 provides a solid foundation in the principles of sound recording and music. Core subjects: Acoustics; Audio Engineering; Electronics; Electronics Practicals; Mathematics; Operational Practicals; Recording Techniques; Harmony; Score Studies; Understanding Music 1; Knowledge of Instruments. Available options (from which you choose two) are: Analysis; Composition; Introduction to Orchestration; Performance; and Understanding Music 2.

Year 2 Core modules are: Audio Engineering; Audio Laboratory; Digital Sound Synthesis and Processing; Electroacoustics; Recording Techniques (including practicals); Synthesis Basics and MIDI. You will also choose optional modules to the value of 40 credits from the Level 2 Music programme.

Professional Training

Gain experience by working in recording studios, broadcasting, audio consultancy, audio manufacturing, etc. University maintains contact with students through formal visits by Professional Training Tutors.

Year 3 Choose optional modules and pursue studies in: Audio Engineering; Audio Research Seminars; Recording Techniques Seminars; and Video Engineering; write a Technical Project, and submit a portfolio of your own recordings.

Therefore, in each year of the programme, students take a range of subjects from the list which the Music Department offers to its students in addition to their Sound Recording studies.

Career options include - television and radio engineering and production, pop and classical record production, equipment design, software engineering, audio systems maintenance, professional audio equipment support, freelance performance, teaching, lecturing, research (both academic and technical), arts administration, journalism and marketing.

West Kent College

John Dodd, West Kent College, Brook Street, Tonbridge, Kent, TN9 2PW.

01732 358101 Fax:01732 771415; info@wkc.ac.uk (email); www.wkc.ac.uk

HND/C Music Production/Technology

Start Month: September. Duration: 2 Years. Requirements: A/AS level in a relevant performing arts subject or BTEC National Diploma

This course is aimed at those with at least four years experience in the music business in a musical or technical capacity. Areas of Study include: · Computer based music production · Sound Recorder · Acoustics · Electronics for Music · Music Business · Computers for the Music Business · Sound and Music for the Media The course is largely practical but with written work files accompanying each project. Assesment is continuous with written asignments in some areas.

South West

Full-Time

Bath Spa University College
Carter, Alan, Bath Spa University College, Newton Park, Newton St Loe, Bath BA2 9BN
01225 875875 Fax:01225 875444; 01225 873701 (tel) www.bathspa.ac.uk
BA /BSc Hons Education with PGCE (Music) (PGCE (Music))
General Music - Aspiring Degree Level and Above - September - 4 Years
Education studies for 3 years then 1 year primary PGCE course. Year 1: six modules - 2 education, 2 other subjects and two electives. Years 2 and 3: any combination of the education studies modules and the music course. Year 4: Primary PGCE.

City of Bath College
Avon Street, Bath BA1 1UP
01225 312191 Fax:01225 444213; enquiries@mkt.citybathcoll.ac.uk
www.hotbath.co.uk
BTEC National Diploma Popular Music (BTEC National diploma Popular Music)
General Music with a Jazz Element - Semi-Pro or Amateur - September - 2 years
The programme concentrates on four areas: Performance, Composition and Arrangement with Music Theory, the Technology of Music and the Music Industry. By choosing additional option units, students can specialise in a particular area. Individual performance skills on a variety of instruments will be developed, together with skills in the writing and arranging of popular music. Both will include expertise with the new digital technologies, and students will become familiar with recording studio practice.

Dartington College of Arts
Learning Resources Centre, Totnes TQ9 6EJ
01803 862224 Fax:01803 863569;
BA Hons Music (BA (Hons) Music)
General Music with a Jazz Element - Aspiring Degree Level and Above - September - 3 years
This is a 3 year full-time degree for dynamic, interactive musicians committed to exploring contemporary music styles including jazz, art music, pop, world and folk music. It offers maximum flexibility to develop different aspects of your musical ability, and the opportunity to place more emphasis on musicology. You engage with music through practical work and research, developing your interests and abilities in preparation for a professional career.

Truro College

Walker, Bill, Director of Performing Arts, Truro College, College Road, Truro TR1 3XX
01872 264251 Fax:01872 222360; 01872 264251 (box office); billw@trurocollege.ac.uk (email); www.kornwall.f9.co.uk

B.Mus Jazz (B Mus Jazz)

Jazz Only - Aspiring Degree Level and Above - Truro College - September - 3 years **2004 see next entry**
Bachelor of Music in Jazz Studies was developed in partnership with the University of Exeter to provide a comprehensive jazz degree program in the South West. The degree was designed to reflect a traditional approach to jazz studies while maintaining the view that successive generations of jazz musicians will diversify and expand the jazz language. A performance-oriented approach to jazz improvisation is stressed together with a substantial element of composition/arranging

University of Exeter

Undergraduate Admissions Officer, University of Exeter, Northcote House, The Queen's Drive, Exeter EX4 4QJ.
01392 263035 (Telephone:); admissions@exeter.ac.uk (email)
www.ex.ac.uk/music

Bmus in Jazz (B Mus Jazz)

September – 3 years
Degree course led by a team of experienced jazz performers and educators. It was previously taught in Truro, in partnership with Truro College, but in 2004 it will relocate to the Exeter campus, uniting it more closely with the University of Exeter's renowned American Music Collection. The degree provides progression opportunities in jazz performance, jazz composition and jazz scholarship.
Students take core modules in performance, jazz history, harmony/composition/arrangement, aural perception and transcription, and keyboard harmony before choosing specialisms at level 3.
The course has been designed historically: 1900-1944 (early jazz to the Big Band era) 1945-1969 (bebop to early fusion) 1970-present day (contemporary jazz) and aims to develop thinking musicians where the skills acquired in a traditional music degree are tailored for students wishing to specialise in jazz music.

Part-Time

University of Exeter

Northcote House, The Queen's Drive, Exeter EX4 4QJ
01392 263030 Fax:01392 263108; www.ex.ac.uk/music

BTEC Popular Music (Jazz) (BTEC National Diploma Popular Musix (Jaz)

Music Course Majoring in Jazz - Semi-Pro or Amateur - 2 years
The main areas of study will be: the language of Jazz, the music business, improvisation, composition, arrangement, aural perception, performance techniques, music keyboard skills, music technology and recording. In the first year of the course, students are entitled to individual tuition on one instrument for approximately 20 hours in the first year and 15 in the second. Students will be encouraged to take

part in the music activities on offer in the Department. They will need to bring their instruments from time to time.

Workshops

Bristol Jazz Workshops

Blomfield, Jim, 34 Heron Road, Easton, Bristol BS5 0LU
0117 951 0207   jim.blomfield@virgin.net (email);

Jazz Band Workshops
Jazz Only - Jazz Beginner - Kearney's Irish Bar, St Werburghs Bristol.

Bude Jazz Festival

Booking Office Bude Jazz Festival, c/o Bude Visitor Centre, The Crescent, Bude EX23 8LE
01288 356 360 (box office);

Jazz Workshops
Jazz Only - Jazz Beginner - Bude Jazz Festival - 26/08/2003 - 4 mornings
Four mornings during the festival week with participants of all ages, all skills grouped into bands, with tuition from Paul Munnery (runs his own band, 'Harlem') and other festival musicians. Book a place well in advance as there is a maximum of 48 places and a limit on instruments in certain categories (always too many saxophones). Bring your own instrument. Fee is in the region of £25 for all the four morning workshops. Contact Box Office number to reserve a place.

Furnish, Pete

24 Larksmead Way, Ogwell Cross, Newton Abbot TQ12 6BT
pfurnish@devon.gov.uk (email);

Workshops
Jazz Only - Jazz Beginner - half or full days.
Available to run half and whole day improvisation courses for all instruments including voice in the Teignmouth area. Subjects covered include Melody, Harmony, Rhythm and Intellect and these can be adapted to work with Jazz, Folk, World Music or Pop.

Middleton, Pete

38 Woodlands Road,. Buckland, Newton Abbot TQ12 4ER
01626 361 630

An informal audition process to assess playing levels. Every Monday evening from mid April 2003. Must be experienced on chosen instrument with an understanding of funk-jazz. Material to be covered George Benson/Crusaders. Small donation towards room hire costs with approimatley 12 places available. Check with Pete for start date confirmation and location.

Teignmouth Community College

Cox, Geoff, Teignmouth Community College, Everest Music Centre, Exeter Road, Teignmouth
01626 773370

Introduction to Jazz
General Music with a Jazz Element - Jazz Beginner - Teignmouth Community College - September - 10 weeks
All ages. 10 -12 am Sundays. £38 per term (£27 concessions) Autumn and Spring ten week term. Course leader Pete Furnish (Bass). Booking through the college. 30 places available.

Rhythm and Ensemble Workshop
Jazz Only - Jazz Beginner - Teignmouth Community College - October - 1 day
All day workshop 10am -5.30pm, concentrating on developing and improving skills and techniques of accompaniment, playing coherently in an ensemble. Sessions for particular instruments and group work. Tutors include - John Etheridge, Dudley Phillips, John Marshall, Rob Townsend. Full price £20 or concessions £15

Jazz Factory at Wiltshire Music Centre
Sneyd, Peter, 55 Bradford Road, Trowbridge, BA14 9AN
Contact Peter Sneyd - 01225 755 439
petesneyd@blueyonder.co.uk (email); www.jazzfactory.co.uk or
01225 860110 Fax:01225 860111; 01225 860100 (box office); enquiries@wiltsmusiccentre.fsnet.co.uk (email);

Jazz Factory workshops
Monday nights (term time only) in the Wiltshire Music Centre, Bradford on Avon between 19.30 and 21.30. Gives musicians of all ages the opportunity to play in a group and to learn jazz skills with professional tuition. Three groups - beginners (or truly terrified) for musicians who can produce a reasonable sound on their instrument, managing basic notes and simple tunes; Intermediate for players with some experience; and advanced instrumentalists. There is also a vocal group. Relaxed atmosphere with the emphasis on playing for enjoyment.

Play Jazz Weekend
26/27th July 2003 at Wiltshire Music Centre
A weekend of workshops for all instruments - Grade 3 to advanced -with groups for jazz beginners, intermediate and experienced players. Improvisation, rhythm and harmony workshops as well as a 'jamming' group. Tutors include Jason Rebello and Peter Sneyd and other leading jazz players. Sat 10.00 - 17.00 with informal evening performance, Sunday 10.00 - 17.00 with final concert starting at 16.00. Application forms also available from Wiltshire Music Centre

Summer School

Dartington International Summer School
Warren, Lisa, Manager, Dartington International Summer School, The Barn, Dartington Hall, Totnes TQ9 6OE
01803 847080 Fax:01803 847087; 01803 847077 (box office); info@dartingtonsummerschool.co.uk (email); www.dartintonsummerschool.co.uk
Due to extensive re-building work some courses. Are not available in 2003

Jazz /Jazz Improvisation Week 1
Jazz Only - Semi-Pro or Amateur - 26/07/2003 - July - 1 week
Week one: Directors Keith Tippett and Lewis Riley - Piano, Tutors - Julie Tippett -

Voice, Ben Clark - Drums, John Richards - Bass, Paul Dunmall - Saxophone. The course is open to all instrumentalists and singers, with or without jazz experience, exploring all aspects of jazz /jazz improvisation from the early 40's to the present day. No audition is necessary for this course, all are welcome regardless of age or standard; all you need is an instrument and to be serious about the music. It is possible to attend one or both weeks of the course.

Jazz and Gospel Choir

Music Course Majoring in Jazz - Jazz Beginner - 26/07/2003 - August - 1 week Director: Scott Stroman. Creating a performance (with band) of Scott Stroman's modern-jazz Mass, along with Gospel, African and jazz songs, will be focussed on by the ever-popular Jazz Choir. Everything here is learned "by ear" – daily sessions focus on developing a rich sound and strong rhythmic drive, harmonising by ear, and group improvising in a relaxed and uplifting environment. Singers of all ages and backgrounds required!

Rockshop

General Music with a Jazz Element - Jazz Beginner - 02/08/2003 - August - 1 week Director: Herbie Flowers.

Back by popular demand. Herbie and his team of top professionals, from the world of pop, rock and jazz, return to share their knowledge and experiences with musicians of all ages and standards. This course includes morning workshops on drums and percussion; electric and acoustic guitar; bass guitar and stand up bass; song writing and orchestration; keyboards; playing from chord charts; vocal and microphone techniques; improvisation; jazz, etc. Also 'supervised' band rehearslas, 'Acoustic' evenings. The 'Rockshop Big Band' will be on the lookout for five trumpeters, trombonists and saxophonists. Usual jive and jitterbug competition. Fabulous prizes! The 'Rockshop Choir' cordially invites all and sundry to come and learn a couple of numbers. The week culminates with everybody taking part in 'Rockshop's Big Night Out'.

Marlborough College Summer School

Kwiatkowski, Marek, Director of the Summer School, Marlborough College Summer School, Marlborough college, Marlborough SN8 1PA
01672 892388/9 Fax:01672 892476; admin@mcsummerschool.org.uk (email)
www.mcsummerschool.org.uk

Let's Play Jazz I

Jazz Only - Semi-Pro or Amateur – 28/07/2003 July - 5 mornings
Tutor: Colin Speight. Mornings 9.15 to 12.15

A course for those who have been playing an instrument for 3 or more years, know a few scales and can sight read a bit. Learn how Miles Davis, Charlie Parker and Duke Ellington improvised. Learn to improvise, understand a bit more about jazz harmony, but most of all enjoy playing with other course members.

Let's Play Jazz II

Jazz only. Semi pro or amateur. 28/07/2003. July afternoons
Tutor: Colin Speight Afternoons 13.50 to 16.30. Starts where course I finishes - it assumes that you know a few scales and how to apply them, have a basic understanding of jazz harmony and can improvise a solo with a jazz feel. More in depth study of harmony and its uses. The main aim of this course is to create, by the end of the week, a functioning band.

Music Technology

Bath Spa University College
Alan Carter, Newton Park, Newton St Loe, Bath, Avon, BA2 9BN.
01225 875875 Fax:01225 875444

BA (Hons) Creative Arts
Start Month: September. Duration: 3 years. Qualification: BA (Hons) Creative Music Technology.

Through module design, teaching and assessment, the student is encouraged to cultivate musicality and creative flair as well as practical knowledge. Thoroughly practical modules (including MIDI Music Production, Hard Disk Recording and Editing, Studio and Location Recording, and Digital Signal Processing) are studied within the context of the creative process and with an awareness of current contemporary musical thought. Entry Requirements: GCE A level, BTEC or equivalent award in Music Technology is preferred. Closely-related subjects (such as Music or Popular Music) are acceptable alongside demonstrable skill in some aspect of music technology.

Bournemouth and Poole College of FE
Constitution Hill Centre, Poole, Dorset, BH14 0QA.
01202 465 721 www.bpc.ac.uk

NCFE in Sound Recording
Start Month: September. Duration: 30 weeks, Qualification: NCFE in Sound Recording.

Topics covered include - sequencing using Cubase Software, the theory behind sound, microphones, dignal routing, 4-track recording, digital recording, compressing, gating and effects.

City of Bath College
City of Bath College, Avon Street, Bath, Avon, BA1 1UP.
01225 312191 Fax:01225 444213; enquiries@mkt.citybathcoll.ac.uk (email)

BTEC National Diploma Music Technology
Start Month: September. Duration: 2 years. Qualification: BTEC National Diploma Music Technology.

This course will allow students to develop skills in use of a Digital Recording Studio - engineering and production, MIDI music production, synthesis, computer music, sampling, hard disk recording, music-to-pictures, composition, music theory and the role that music technology plays in the Arts and Computer industries. The course is very practical with a lot of the work taking place in the Digital Recording Studio and Music Technology suite. Students will be mixing regularly with many musicians from varied backgrounds on a number of other courses in an exciting and dynamic department. Assessments take place at regular intervals to provide students with a clear understanding of how they are progressing on the course and to ensure that they can demonstrate the skills necessary to help them move into the Music Industry or Higher Education when they complete the course.

Wales

Full-Time

Bangor University of Wales
Bangor LL57 2DG
01248 382016 admissions@bangor.ac.uk (email);
BA/B.Mus Music (BA/B Mus Music)
General Music with a Jazz Element - Aspiring Degree Level and Above - October - 3 years

Music degree with a jazz module in year 2 that can be carried forward into 3rd year but this is not a main study option.
MA in Music Technology
MMus in Electroacoustic Composition
Modules for both degrees include - Electroacoustic Composition, Music for Film, the Media and Related Arts, Sound Recording and Editing, Music Technology
MPhil in Electroacoustic Composition
2 years full time *or four years part time*
Post graduate degrees allow students to follow their own supervised programme of research in composition
PhD in Electroacoustic Composition.
3 years full time or *6 years part-time*
Candidates with sufficient previous experience at Master's level may be allowed to shorten their period of registration.

Assessment is by submission of a portolio of compositions completed during the period of research. Composers may include non electroacoustic compositions in their portfolio if they wish. Candidates may also optionally submit a dissertation for all or part of their assessment.

Gorseinon College
Belgrave Road, Gorseinon, Swansea SA4 6RD
01792 890700 Fax:01792 898729; admin@gorseinon.ac.uk (email);
AS Level Music (A Level Music)
General Music with a Jazz Element - Semi-Pro or Amateur - September - 2 year
Music and Music Technology are a recommended double course for anyone thinking about a career in the music profession or sound / recording / media industries

Neath College
Neath Port Talbot College, Dwr-y-Felin Road, Neath SA10 7RF
01639 634271 Fax:01639 637453; Enquiries@ntpc.ac.uk (email); www2.nptc.ac.uk

A Level Music (A Level Music)

General Music with a Jazz Element - Semi-Pro or Amateur - September - 2 years
Entry Requirements: Students require a sound basic knowledge of musical notation, harmony, counterpoint and history, with practical proficiency on any one
approved orchestral instrument, voice, piano or organ. A GCSE (A,B,C) pass in
music with grade V1 Associated Board or similar on an instrument is desirable but
not essential.

Welsh College of Music and Drama

Castle Grounds, Cathays Park, Cardiff CF1 3ER
02920 640054 Music.admissions@WCMD.ac.uk (email);

BMus Jazz Studies Pathway (BMus).

Jazz Only. September. 4 yearsCo-ordinator Paula Gardiner
Jazz Studies is designed to equip students with performance and improvisation
skills across a wide range of styles within the jazz idiom., Principal study tuition,
currently available for saxophone, flute, guitar, piano, bass and drums, other
instruments by negotiation), is supported by regular practical group classes in ear-
training and harmony. Other regular sessions include listening / discussion and
transcription / analysis. The repertoire is studied within small groups and ensembles with regular performance opportunities. Additional specialist areas of study
include rhythm section clinics and front-line ensemble playing; not forgetting free
improvisation and the unique college Big Band, which rehearses weekly under the
inspirational leadership of Keith Tippett. Masterclasses and workshops undertaken
by visiting specialists.

Post Graduate Diploma in Music (Post Grad Diploma in Music)

Music Course Majoring in Jazz - Aspiring Degree Level and Above - September -
1/2 years
There are a number of specialist pathways two of which are Jazz Studies and Music
Technology. A special feature of the course is the development of the individual as
a performer. Students have personalised learning schemes and are encouraged to
develop an individual musical personality. Applicants should have, or expect to gain
before entry, a degree or a diploma. Mature applicants must satisfy the College
that they are of a satisfactory standard for entry.

Part-Time

Cardiff University

The Admissions Office, PO Box 494, Cardiff CF1 3YL
02920 874404 Fax:02920 874130; www.cardiff.ac.uk/learn

Jazz Improvisation (20 credits)

Jazz Only - Jazz Beginner - 38 Park Place, Cardiff - 10/01/2000 - January - 20
weekly sessions. Introduction for musicians with little or experience in jazz improvisation. Covers Blues, jazz standards and jazz-rock. Mondays 7-9pm. Tutor -
Stuart Earp. 20 credits.

University of Wales
Dept of Adult Continuing Education, Continuing Education Centre, University of Wales Swansea, Swansea SA2 8PP
Advanced Multi-Track Studio Sound Recording
Music Technology - Semi-Pro or Amateur - DACE Studio - September -
This course is available only to those students who have either successfully completed the basic Multi-Track Studio Sound Recording course, or who can display a high level of knowledge and experience in the recording industry. Applicants will need to be interviewed before their enrolment is accepted. Please ring Kathryn Harris on 01792 295787 for an interview time. Among the areas covered will be: advanced routing procedures, advanced use of dynamic and effects processors including side-chain, ducking, sampling etc. recording and editing audio on a computer using Cubase VST, editing and compiling on the hard-disc multi-track, midi time code synchronisation etc. The level of practical and theoretical tuition and assignments will be such as to demand a high level of commitment from the students.

Short Course

University of Wales
Dept of Adult Continuing Education, Continuing Education Centre, University of Wales Swansea, Swansea SA2 8PP
Jazz Improvisation (120 credits towards Higher Ed. Cert)
Jazz Only - Semi-Pro or Amateur - Steer Studio - September - 10
Tutor: Chris Haines. A course for those who can play their instrument and read music to a certain extent. All that is required is a desire to learn how jazz musicians do it and a willingness to practise. Blues, bebop and Bossas will be covered as well as other styles. Students will be taken step by step from simple modal tunes to the delights of the extended augmented chord. Students must bring their own instruments.
Jazz in Practice
Jazz Only - Jazz Beginner - Steer studios - September -
The course introduces students to jazz chords and their construction. Learn how chords fit together in common patterns and how to relate certain scales to chords in order to create a coherent solo over a sequence of chords. Tunes of varying tempos, styles and complexity will be analysed along with the approach to improvisation of well-known jazz soloists. There are keyboards available at the venue. Please bring other instruments.

Summer School

Aberystwyth Arts
Hewson, Alan, Director, Aberystwyth Arts Centre, University College of Wales, Penglais, Aberystwyth SY23 3DE
01970 622882 Fax:01970 622883; 01970 623232 (box office); aeh@aber.ac.uk

(email); www.aber.ac.uk/artscentre

International Summer School
Jazz Only - Semi-Pro or Amateur - Aberystwyth Arts Centre, Uni of Wales - 21/07/2000 - July - 10 days
Course tutor - Julian Nicholas with American classical composer and jazz pianist Peter Lieuwen. For varying levels of experience. Group and individual tuition within practical workshops.Two lots of week-long courses

Glamorgan Summer School
Giles, Gill, Course administrator, University of Glamorgan Summer School, Summer School Office, University of Glamorgan, Pontypridd CF37 1DL 01443 483261

Glamorgan Jazz
Jazz Only - Semi-Pro or Amateur - University of Glamorgan - 21/07/2003 - July - 1 for 2 weeks
Nightly jazz club session. Final performance on last night of both weeks. Singers welcome. Residential course. Dave Wickins and Assistant Organising Tutor: Simon Purcell. The curriculum features a wide range of practical group work - small ensembles, improvisation workshops and percussion classes, through to a Samba School, a Jazz Choir. The programme is flexible enough to allow each student to opt for classes appropriate to their specific needs and interests. The course has a friendly and uncompetitive atmosphere where all students, irrespective of age or ability are welcomed. Students will need some experience of chord symbols and an ability to read music would be helpful. Enthusiasm for jazz in its many forms is a good start and the flexible syllabus ensures that students derive maximum benefit from their studies. This course runs for two weeks and students can elect to attend one or both weeks. Accommodation en suite bedrooms. Special Projects in 2003 - Early Jazz with Malcolm Earle-Smith running an ensemble dedicated to classic jazz for both weeks. Free Improvised music with Alex Maguire exploring a range of approaches to free improvised music

Music Technology

Bangor University of Wales
Postgraduate diplomain Music Technology (Diploma)
Music Technology - Aspiring Degree Level and Above - October - 1 year
There are no BA and BMus in Music Technology or Electroacoustic Composition, but modules in these areas can be studied as part of a music degree

Core modules -Music for Film, Media and the Arts, Creative Sampling and, sequencing, Recording and Editing. Assessment is by written and practical projects. Students are encouraged to use technology for their own creative agenda, but options in arranging are available for those who are not primarily composers. Some projects are restricted to twentieth century popular genres

Gorseinon College
Belgrave Road, Gorseinon, Swansea, W Glam, SA4 6RD.
01792 890700 Fax:01792 898729; admin@gorseinon.ac.uk (email)

AS level Music Technology
Start Month: September. Duration: 2 years. Qualification: A Level Music Technology.

Year one concentrates on sound recording or computer sequencing skills, recording or creating a variety of high quality music performances. Students also arrange a classical piece using technology, and a pop or jazz style original piece, either through MIDI, or improvised through live recording sessions, or developed with a porta-studio, recording tracks one at a time. Year two comprises sequencing, recording and producing. Students will use close-mic and ambient micing techniques to produce a range of recordings, computer software to produce a range of sequenced music, and computer software packages for composing. Students should already be able to read music.

Neath College
Neath Port Talbot College, Dwr-y-Felin Road, Neath, W Glam, SA10 7RF.
01639 634271 Fax:01639 637453; Enquiries@ntpc.ac.uk (email); www2.nptc.ac.uk

A Level Music Technology
Start Month: September. Duration: 2 years. Qualification: A level Music Technology.

Entry Requirements: Students should have a basic knowledge of notation and harmony with practical proficiency an any approved instrument e.g. orchestral instrument, voice, piano, organ, classical/electric guitar, bass/lead guitar and drums and/or percussion. A GCSE pass in music and/or grade V1 pass/standard on your cosen instrument is desirable. Syllabus: this course is ideal for students who have an interest in music/computers, with a practical proficiency of grade V1 or above. Almost all the work is undertaken via the recording studio using the latest digital technology and computers. The college studio is one of the most advanced of its kind in Wales.

University of Wales
Dept of Adult Continuing Education, Continuing Education Centre, University of Wales Swansea, Swansea, W Glam, SA2 8PP.

Advanced Multi-Track Studio Sound Recording
Location: DACE Studio. Start Month: September.

This course is available only to those students who have either successfully completed the basic Multi-Track Studio Sound Recording course, or who can display a high level of knowledge and experience in the recording industry. Applicants will need to be interviewed before their enrolment is accepted. Please ring Kathryn Harris on 01792 295787 for an interview time. Among the areas covered will be: advanced routing procedures, advanced use of dynamic and effects processors including side-chain, ducking, sampling etc. recording and editing audio on a computer using Cubase VST, editing and compiling on the hard-disc multi-track, midi time code synchronisation etc. The level of practical and theoretical tuition and assignments will be such as to demand a high level of commitment from the students.

Multi-Track Studio Sound Recording
Location: Steer studios. Start Month: September.

This course introduces the techniques and equipment of the modern sound studio from the most basic level, progressing in stages to a point where the successful student should be able to work as an assistant Sound Engineer, or to engineer a session in a small recording studio. Among the subjects covered will be: use of microphones, understanding mixing-desks, routing procedures, basic recording techniques including drop-in/drop-out, effects processors, dynamic processors, mix-down procedures, midi sequencing set-ups etc.

Welsh College of Music and Drama
Castle Grounds, Cathays Park, Cardiff, S Glam, CF1 3ER.
02920 640054 Music.admissions@WCMD.ac.uk (email)

BMus (Music Technology)
Start Month: September. Duration: 4 years.

The main aim of the Music Technology Department is to provide a practical knowledge of the latest technology in an atmosphere that stimulates and encourages creative talent. The work of the department is conducted in a purpose-built suite of five studios, all interconnected and linked to the College performance spaces and the Internet. In addition, a professional state-of-the-art digital recording studio recently opened in the Anthony Hopkins Centre.

West Midlands

Full-Time

Birmingham Conservatoire

Price, Jeremy, Head of Jazz Studies, Birmingham Conservatoire, Paradise Place, Birmingham B3 3HG
0121 331 7207 0121 236 5622 (box office); conservatoire@uce.ac.uk (email); www.conservatoire.uce.ac.uk

Has a tradition of jazz education and performance which has now been formalised into a new course. Bursaries - there are no substantial bursaries offered by the conservatoire, but they are sometimes able to give some financial assistance to students in their 2nd and 3rd years. Students who have been offered a place students can ask for further advice. NOTE the deadline for applications is March of the previous academic year.

Jazz tutorial staff: Jeremy Price, Head of Jazz Studies and Trombone. Saxes -Julian Siegel, Jean Toussaint, Mike Williams; Trumpets – Martin Shaw, Neil Yates, Eddie Severn; Piano – Liam Noble; Bass – Arnie Somogyi; Guitar – Dave Cliff, Electric Guitar and Bass – Fred Baker; Drumkit – Gene Calderazzo; Composition – Mike Gibbs, Hans Koller + visiting musicians for masterclasses like Bobby Shaw and John Surman.

B.Mus (Hons) in Jazz (B Mus (Hons) Jazz)
Music Course Majoring in Jazz - Aspiring Degree Level and Above - September - 4 years

First study tuition is available in a wide range of disciplines including trumpet, trombone, saxophone, piano, guitar, bass and drums. There are both practical and academic classes, all of which are designed as a direct back-up to the area of jazz improvisation. Practical activities include a large proportion of small-group playing, as well as the Big Band and Jazz Orchestra. Performance workshop covers standard repertoire, world music and free improvisation and acts as a Masterclass forum for visiting artists. The academic content includes harmony, analysis of transcriptions and history. There is also a significant compositional element to be reflected in performance activities. There are optional activities to supplement core studies including World Music and Music Technology. Students can choose a final year option of musicological research. In the final year students are prepared for the music profession with classes covering contemporary issues in jazz, advice on the realities of a freelance career, personal finance, marketing and public sources of arts funding.

Postgraduate MMus/PgDip in Jazz Composition or Performance(Post Graduate Diploma) New in 2003/2004
Jazz Only - Aspiring Degree Level and Above - September - 1 or 2 years

The MMus/PGDip offers specialist study in: Performance or Composition. Includes one-to-one instrumental or composition tuition, regular masterclasses and workshops, small and large ensemble activities, jazz composers' ensemble, research seminars, jazz analysis and criticism, professional development. **PGCert in Jazz Performance** offers the first 5 elements of the MMus. Courses still subject to validation.

Coventry University Performing Arts

Leasowes Avenue, Coventry CV3 6BH
02476 418868 Fax:02476 692374

Music and Professional Practice BA (Hons) (National Diploma)
General Music - Semi-Pro or Amateur - September - 3 years
Music is a highly competitive field, yet opportunities exist for innovative, disciplined, and creative professionals. This course will expose you to performance techniques, and allow you to explore music technology and develop skills for survival as a freelance performing artist.

Provides an understanding of performance-related issues, to explore structure, style and instrumentation through analysis, demonstration and arranging, to devise creative workshops within the community, to examine the essential administrative duties for successful freelance work, and to gain an appreciation of historical context and complementary arts.

Modules include Performance Seminar, Production, Professional Practice, Theory and Aural, Instrumental Studies, Music Technology, Music/Performance Analysis, Historical/Cultural Studies, Music Arranging, Community Projects, Dissertation.

Students meet weekly for Performance seminars to monitor progress on their assignments

Kidderminster College of F.E.

Hoo Road, Kidderminster
01562 732268; admissions@kidderminster.ac.uk (email); www.kidderminster.ac.uk
01562 820811 (tel)

BTEC National Diploma in Music (BTEC National Diploma)
General Music - Semi-Pro or Amateur - September - 2 years.Core subjects: The music industry, Listening skills, Music in Context, Music Performance Process, Music Performance (major project). Optional subjects: Musical arranging, Aural skills, Composing, History and analysis of music, History of popular music, Music improvisation, Music performance techniques, Music theory and harmony, Special subject investigation, Sound recording, Computer music. Tom Bradley - Direct line 01562 732 234 or tbradley@kidderminster.ac.uk

BTEC National Diploma in Music Technology (BTec National Diploma)
General Music - Semi-Pro or Amateur -September – 2 years
Course covers: The Music Industry, Listening Skills, Sound Recording Techniques, Studio Production, Music in Context, Computer Technology and MIDI. Audio Engineering, Live Sound, Sound Creation and Manipulation, Keyboard Skills, Multimedia Production.

Music Technology and Studio Recording Level 2 & 3
Part Time Mondays 19.15 to 21.15

Music Technology OCN Level 2 & 3 P
art Time Mondays 19.15 to 21.15 Offer students the opportunity to use recording equipment and how it is possible to use it at home with a computer.Use microphones for recording and live use; understanding and using a mixing desk; basics of MIDI; using Cubase and Logic Software; audio recording on digital tape (ADAT);

PC and MAC computers; audio looping and sound manipulation; manipulating and re-mixing music

University of Birmingham

Harrison, Jonty, Dept Music, University of Birmingham, Barber Institute of Fine Art, Ring Road North, Birmingham B15 2TT
0121 414 5782 D.J.T.Harrison@bham.ac.uk (email);

B.Mus Single Honours (B.Mus)

General Music - Aspiring Degree Level and Above - September - 3 years
B.Mus covers musicology (music as an academic discipline), composition, and performance - both as an individual and in ensembles. The university is known for operas and international concert series, the students' own summer festival, New Music Ensemble and the annual Birmingham Early Music Festival. Their links with the City include instrumental lessons for all students at the Birmingham Conservatoire, the Birmingham Contemporary Music Group as ensemble in association, University concerts held in the internationally-acclaimed Symphony Hall, and access to open rehearsals from the likes of Thomas Adès and Sir Simon Rattle. Facilities include practice rooms, electroacoustic music studios, early instruments, computer workstations. This degree does not offer a jazz module. It does have an Electro-acoustic Music Studio.

University of Wolverhampton

Wolverhampton WV1 1SB
01902 321000 Fax:01902322680; enquiries@wlv.ac.uk (email); www.wlv.ac.uk

BA (Hons) Music (BA (Hons))

General Music with a Jazz Element - Aspiring Degree Level and Above - Walsall Campus - September - 3years
Core modules include: Dissertation (to qualify for honours), Music of the Early 20th Century, Musicology, Performance, Research Methods, Stylistic Composition, Specialist optional modules include: 20th Century American Music, Composition Conducting and Arranging, Editing Early Music, Ensemble Performance, Ethnomusicology, Music Technology, Orchestration

Part-Time

University of Birmingham

Harrison, Jonty, Dept Music, University of Birmingham, Barber Institute of Fine Art, Ring Road North, Birmingham B15 2TT
0121 414 5782 (office tel); D.J.T.Harrison@bham.ac.uk (email);

Certificate Higher Education Music(CertHE Music)

September - 2 years part time
Studies in Music - A comprehensive introduction to all aspects of music and music-making. Aural Skills 1 - A chance to develop the ear's responsiveness to sound. Harmony and Counterpoint - A practical exploration of harmony and counterpoint from Bach to Schubert. The modules for year two are: Music History Through Analysis - A survey of Western art music from the Late Renaissance to the Twentieth Century. Workshop: Compose and Perform - An exciting, hands-on intro-

duction to composition and performance. Students will be given the opportunity to create and perform their own works. Aural Skills 2 - A continuation of Aural Skills 1.

Diploma Higher Education Music (DipHE Music)
September – 2 years part time
Diploma is a qualification in its own right and is equivalent to the second year of a degree. The programme consists of modules, offering areas of specialisation to suit individuals' interests and strengths, and is designed to be studied through day-schools and evening classes. Modules (year one): - Performing, Arranging, Directing, Music Drama, Music Seminar i) Studies in Musicology I, Music semi-nar ii) Applied Harmony
Modules (year two): - Music Seminar i) Studies in Musicology II, - Music Seminar ii) Advanced Aural Skills, Music Seminar iii) Composing Today, Individual Project, Orchestration.

Summer Schools

Wedgwood Memorial College
Barlaston, Stoke on Trent
01782 372105 www.staffordshire.gov.uk
Jazz on a Summer's Weekend
Jazz Only - Jazz Beginner – 4th to 6th July 2003 - 3 days
Tutor: Chris Gumbley (teaches saxophone at Birmingham Conservatoire of Music)
The aim of the course, by giving a comprehensive picture of the elements of jazz and whilst having fun. The aim is to dispel the myth that jazz is a 'difficult' form of music-making that only an elite few can participate in. Beginners through to Intermediate

Music Technology

Birmingham Conservatoire
Jeremy Price, Birmingham Conservatoire, Paradise Place, Birmingham, W Midlands, B3 3HG.

0121 331 7207 Box Office:0121 236 5622; conservatoire@uce.ac.uk (email); www.conservatoire.uce.ac.uk

BSc Music Technology
Start Month: September. Duration: 4 yr. Qualification: BSc Music Technology.

Course Director - Ken Clegg. ken.clegg@tic.ac.uk Offered by the technology inno-vation centre of the University of Central England in partnership with Birmingham Conservatoire. The aim of this course is to prepare the Music technologists of tomorrow equally at ease in the recording studio and on the internet, in a multime-dia production and on location. The 5 themes are audio electronics, signals pro-cessing, multimedia technology, music technology and sound recording, music and critical studies. Students enrolled on this course will be encouraged to take an active role in all music technology related activities of the Conservatoire.

Keele University

Keele University, Staffs, ST5 5BG.

01782 584005/4/3 Fax:01782 632343; aaa30@keele.ac.uk (email); www.keele.ac.uk

BSc Electronic Music

Start Month: September. Duration: 3 years.

The Electronic Music course at Keele aims to provide musical training, encourage critical thinking and provide opportunities for specialisation (for example, in composition, performance, musicolgy or electronic music). The Modular base of the course allows students some flexibility in choice of topics and degree of specialisation. Full details of current courses and activities are available from the Music Department secretary.

Kidderminster College of FE

Kidderminster College of F.E., Hoo Road, Kidderminster, Worcs.

01562 748504; admissions@kidderminster.ac.uk (email); www.kidderminster.ac.uk

BTEC National diploma in Audio Productio

Start Month: September. Duration: 2 years.

Yorkshire

Full-Time

Barnsley College

Davis, Bob, Head of Music, Barnsley College, PO BOX 266, Church Street, Barnsley
01226 216475 music@barnsley.ac.uk (email); www.barnsley.ac.uk

BA (Hons) Contemporary Jazz (BA (Hons))
Jazz Major - Aspiring Degree Level and Above - Honeywell Site - 3 years
A new course focused on contemporary jazz, aiming to develop the strong
European tradition.
Year 1 - broad range of study (specialising in year three). Modules include
Composition and Arranging, Music Performance Techniques, Introduction to Music
Technology, Improvisation Techniques, History and Analysis.
Year 2 - Modules include: Musicianship (core), Composition, Arranging and
Orchestration, Music Performance Techniques, Music Technology, Improvisation
(core), History and Analysis, Music Business.
Year 3 - Choice of three modules (from a list) and students are expected to attain
a high level of specialisation.
Validated by the University of Sheffield.

BA (Hons) Creative Music Technology
Music Technology Degree level – 3 years
Year 1 six modules; Year 2 four modules; Year 3 specialise in one area plus two
modules as minor options.
The Department has five well-equipped digital studios and audio production facilities. There is the opportunity to participate in the operation of a newly-launched
College Recording Company, which is run by students as a professional organisation.
The course concentrates on both theoretical and practical work using computer
music software, synthesisers, samplers and synchronisation. Multi-media is
increasingly important to musicians, and enhanced CDs, games, multimedia
authoring and the Internet are covered. This module has a strong practical element
and it introduces you to animation, video graphics and authoring. Composing and
Arranging encourages understanding of the creative potential of Music Technology
in a range of styles.

Bretton Hall College

West Bretton, Wakefield WF4 4LG
01924 830 261 Fax:01924 830 521; bretton@bretton.ac.uk (email); www.bret-
ton.ac.uk

B.A. Music (B.A.(Hons))
General Music with a Jazz Element - Aspiring Degree Level and Above - September
- 3 years
Year 1 - Music theory: basic grounding in the grammar and forms of music, pro-

gressing to more advanced analytical skills. Music in History and Culture deals with 'contextual issues', examining the cultural and social functions of the concert hall, opera house and the church, and considering the way in which we approach history.

Years 2 and 3. In Composition, students explore a range of musical idioms up to the present-day and are encouraged to be active as composers from the outset. Individual studies can reflect student's own interests. Recent studies have included film music, Bartók, Popular Music in the Nineties, Lutoslawski and Jazz. These are often taught in mixed year groups. Students at Leeds benefit from a staff of international distinction. Teaching methods are tailored to meet learning needs: large lectures, smaller seminar groups, one-to-one tutorials. Examination is by coursework, including technology projects, dissertations, assessed essays, composition portfolios and recitals, and exams.

BA Popular and World Music
General Music with a Jazz Element - Aspiring Degree Level and Above -September - 3 years

Year 1 - Music in History and Culture, Understanding Popular styles, Music study skills, Practical skills, Introduction to the Science of Music, The Musician in Society – issues for the 21st century, Performance and elective module/s.

Year 2 – Approaches and analysis to Popular and World Musics, special studies (at least 1 of 3) performance, composition, music technology skills and techniques. Optional - Texts and Contexts, Special Study not already taken as a compulsory module, Projects in Performance.

Year 3 - Texts and contexts, dissertation; Optional – composition, performance, music technology, Projects in Performance.

Postgraduate Research
No jazz but offer Popular music, traditional music and ethnomusicology

Huddersfield Technical College
New North Road, Huddersfield HD1 5NN
O1484 536521 Fax:01484 511885; www.huddcoll.ac.uk

BTEC First Diploma Popular Music
General Music with a Jazz Element - Semi-Pro or Amateur - September - 1 year
The ability to play an instrument or sing would be useful on this course; however, applicants with a strong interest in music technology are also encouraged to apply. Those who play an instrument will be expected to attend an informal interview/audition, when you will be invited to demonstrate your playing skills. This course provides students with the opportunity to develop their musical skills and explore aspects of the pop music industry.

BTEC National Diploma in Popular Music
General Music with a Jazz Element - Semi-Pro or Amateur - September - 2 years
Course designed for those who wish to enter the commercial music business with particular emphasis on playing and performance. Course work covers - music industry, music technology, music theory, group and solo performance and awareness of cultural issues associated with popular music, listening skills, freelance world, performance techniques, arrangement, sound recording, keyboard skills, MIDI sequencing, live sound, history of Popular Music.

Leeds College of Music

3 Quarry Hill, Leeds LS2 7PD
0113 222 3400 Fax:0113 243 8798; 0113 244 5523 (box office); enquiries@lcm
ac.uk (email); www.lcm.ac.uk

Leeds College of Music is the largest music college in Britain with around 800 full time and two thousand part time students. Courses are for the beginner through to Post Graduate in all styles from classical, popular, Indian, contemporary as well as jazz and instrument making and repair. The degrees are validated by the University of Leeds and the Open University. The college has a partnership with the University, with which it offers joint degree courses in Music Technology. It also has close links with the Leeds Centre for Indian Music and Dance. The college occupies a new specially designed building with rehearsal and recording studios, workshops, teaching rooms, library and resource centre, recital room and bar. A 350 seat concert hall is nearing completion. It is situated in the centre of Leeds next to the West Yorkshire Playhouse and Yorkshire Dance Centre.

Access Course (Access Certificate)

General Music with a Jazz Element - Semi-Pro or Amateur - September - 1 year
The Access Course is designed for mature students who lack the formal qualifications they require to enter Higher Education degree or diploma programmes. Upon the successful completion of this course, the student may be able to progress to a degree programme in music.

Preliminary Course

General Music with a Jazz Element - Semi-Pro or Amateur - September - 1 year
For recent school leavers or mature students who need a transitional period before entering further Education, the Preliminary course is designed to build upon basic skills, giving the confidence to go on to further study.

BA (Hons) in Jazz Studies (BA (Hons)

Music Course Majoring in Jazz - Aspiring Degree Level and Above - September - 3 years
Course provides a broad base of skills and knowledge in jazz and contemporary music and from year two onwards, the opportunity to specialise in chosen areas. Three core areas of study - Performance, Composition and Historical, Critical and Analytical studies.
Performance - develop individuals with the guidance of teachers and ensemble coaches. Individual tuition in principal study with the opportunity to play in a range of college ensembles - Big Band, jazz combos, symphony orchestra, vocal groups and contemporary music ensembles
Composition - focus on contemporary composition and arrangement techniques to enable creation of new music in a range of jazz idioms.
Historical studies - examines principal developments in jazz history and the context in which they occurred, the relationship between jazz and other musical genres of 20th and 21st centuries.
Year One – three core areas plus fundimental principles, techniques and processes relating to performance, creation and study of jazz..Study improvisation and Latin percussion, together with aural training.
Year Two - three core areas plus two modules chosen from - Music Technology, Recording techniques, Electro-acoustic music, musical direction, Indian improvisation, advanced Latin percussion, twentieth century music.
Year three - choose to study either two major electives or one major and two minor elective from - Performance a Public receital, Composition - a portfolio of

original work and Dissertation an extended piece of research. Also con the two modules started in year two.

Leeds College of Music works closely with the Music Department of the University of Leeds, and this enables the student to draw upon a wider sphere of expertise and resources.

Entrance requirements - Two A levels one should be music, plus at least three other subjects at GCSE or O level grade C or above including English language and ABRSM grade VIII standard on at least one instrument. BTEC National Diploma applicants - as an alternative to A levels a relevant National Diploma with five merits in the second year is required. Entry to the course is via competitive audition held between November and February each year.

Dip HE/Bmus(Hons) Jazz with Contemporary Music (B Mus (Hons))
Music Course Majoring in Jazz - Aspiring Degree Level and Above - September - 4 years
Dip HE - 2 years full time. Bmus - 4 year full time.
This course is validated by the Open University, and builds on Leeds existing provision in jazz studies, developing this to embrace a wider range of contemporary musics. A significant feature of the full four-year BMus (Honours) course is that year three includes a part-time work placement, working with a community music project. The duration of the course enables you to focus on a broad range of contemporary music, without compromising performance standards and depth of study Offer core modules that include: Solo and ensemble performance, Composition and arranging, Harmony, Historical, analytical and critical studies
Year Three - 1st term includes: pedagogy and social psychology of music, placement preparation, ensemble musicianship work placement, which takes place in term 2.
Year Four - specialise in performance, with electives in composition and/or dissertation.

University of Huddersfield

Queensgate, Huddersfield HD1 3DH
01484 472003 Fax:01484 472656; music@hud.ac.uk (email); www.hud.ac.uk

MA Composition/Electro-Aoustic Com (MA/PgDip)
Postgraduate - October – 1 *or 2 years part time*
Emphasis is on Contemporary/New Music
Postgraduates work in a creative environment which is fostered by the provision of performance opportunities for composers, a music library well stocked with 20th century scores, recordings and books and four well-equipped electronic music studios containing a range of analogue and digital instruments. Postgraduates receive regular individual tuition from staff composers. Group seminars, which examine ideas and trends in significant 20th century works and electro- acoustic music. The annual Huddersfield Contemporary Music Festival provides an unparalleled opportunity to experience the most recent developments in new music. Students may work exclusively in electronic music, in acoustic music or in a combination of both. Opportunities exist to work in the area of concert music, stage and video music as well as other functional music.

University of Leeds

Dept. of Music, Leeds LS2 9JT
0113 233 2583 Fax:0113 233 2586; www.leeds.ac.uk
Since the merger in 2001 with Bretton Hall, the University has strengthened its position as a leading player in the provision of music, visual and performing arts.

B.Mus (Hons) in Performance (B.Mus.)

General music with a jazz element - Aspiring Degree Level and Above - September - 4 years
This performance centred degree aims to develop high standards of playing in the context of a strong understanding of history and theory. The third year of the four year programme is spent at one of a number of associated conservatoires in Europe and the USA focusing on performance

BA (Hons) in Music (B.A.)

General Music - Aspiring Degree Level and Above - September - 3 years
Available as Part time degree
Provides a foundation knowledge in history, theory, composition, technology and general study skills. Other areas like musicology, criticism and analysis are also introduced. Performance modules are available at all stages, although they are not compulsory. Students can be assessed as a soloist or as part of an ensemble. The final year offers the greatest scope to pursue your own interests, and undertake a dissertation on a chosen subject, composition portfolio, technology project or recital.

Master of Music (M.Mus)

General Music - Aspiring Degree Level and Above - September - 1 year or *24 months part time*
All M.Mus candidates are registered on a specific pathway - Composition; M.Mus Opera Studies; Performance; Music Technology; Critical Musicology; Historical Musicology.

University of York

Heslington, York YO10 5DD
01904 430000 Box Office:01904 433724; admissions@york.ac.uk (email); www.york.ac.uk

MA in Community Music (MA Community Music)

General Music - Aspiring Degree Level and Above - October - 2 years or *5 years part time*
Based on short course modules - core modules to be taken by all students - Core music skills; Workshop and communication skills; History and practice of community arts. Option modules (choose 3) Music and disability; World music; Music technology; Music and other arts; Arts Administration; Music Education. There is also a placement of 10 days contact with an outside agency, plus a dissertation of 10 - 12,000 words or an equivalent package including recordings and video. The course can be taken full time or part time. 'Community Music' covers musicians working outside formal settings - like schools, prisons, hospitals and evelopment of music in under resourced areas. It is seen as a growing career option as many orchestras and arts organisations are looking to extend their audience base into the community. Many arts organisations and Local authorities employ

Part-Time

Wakefield College

Kirtlan, David, Course Co-ordinator, Wakefield College, School of Music, Thornes Park Centre, Horbury Road, Wakefield WF2 8QZ
01924 789 8745 www.wakcoll.ac.uk

Course location : Thornes Park Centre

HNC Jazz Studies
September - 2 years - One day + one evening.
For instrumentalists and singers who have a good standard of performing skill and a particular interest in all aspects of jazz music and/or improvisation. The skills developed are relevant and responsive to the needs of the individuals who wish to go on to study music further or to pursue a career in music as either a performer or teacher. The course covers Performance Studies, Improvisation, Band/Ensemble Studies, Aural, Harmony and Arranging, History/Contextual Studies, Arts Management and Keyboard Skills

Workshop

Sheffield Jazz

Pete Lyons 0114 258 4935 and Chris Walker 0114 268 6850
www.sheffieldjazz.org.uk

Jazz Workshops
Held at King Edward's Upper School, Newbobuld Lane, Sheffield - Saturday 10.00 to 12.30
Tutors: Pete Lyons, Chris Walker, Jude Sacker, Graham Jones, Caroline Boaden and John Trier. These workshops are for anyone interested in playing jazz, no matter what instrument you play. It helps if you have some basic skills as the workshops are specifically for people interested in jazz improvisation- we are not able to cater for those who want a general introductory session. The best way to find out if it's right for you is to turn up and give it a try! Open to anyone to drop in. Just turn up on the day! At present there are three groups, new comers, intermediate and a self running group for experienced players. This year there will also be some special sessions, for which you'll need to book in advance. Cost: £6 or £3.50 (concessions).

Summer School

Leeds College of Music

3 Quarry Hill, Leeds LS2 7PD
0113 222 3400 Fax:0113 243 8798; 0113 244 5523 (box office); enquiries@leedscolmusic.ac.uk (email); www.lcm.ac.uk

Summer School - Jazz Big Band
Jazz Only - Semi-Pro or Amateur - 18/08/2003 - August - 4 days
Open to all jazz musicians, from those that have never played in Big Band before
to more experienced players seeking to improve their skills. Aim is for jazz instrumentalists to develop their skills and musicianship with four days of ensemble, Big
Band and improvisation workshops. Ability to read music is essential and a minimum standard of Grade V ABRSM or equivalent is required. There will be jam sessions in the evenings with a final informal Big Band concert on the last night.
Instruments required: alto, tenor, baritone sax (clarinet/flute as doubles only)
trumpet, trombone, piano, guitar, bass and drums. As there is a limit to the numbers of certain instruments it is best to book early. Guest tutors 2003 include Tony
Fisher, John Ruddick - leading trumpet player and Musical Director of the Midland
Youth Jazz Orchestra. Courses cost £130 each. For accomodation look at
www.leeds.gov.uk/tourinfo or contact Heather Wade for self catering student accomodation.

Summer school Jazz and Popular Vocal
Vocal course runs twice during the Summer School 14 - 17th and 28 - 31st July
2003. Tutors: Tina May, Anna Stubbs and Nicki Allen, plus support from members
of full-time LCM staff. The course provides four days of intensive coaching in jazz
and popular vocal performance for male and female singers over the age of six-
teen. As a proportion of the sessions will involve ensemble work, a basic music-
reading ability is desirable - about Grade IV ABRSM minimum. Course will cover -
techniques for jazz standards and popular music, performance with a pianist or
rhythm section, basic functional harmony for beginners, songwriting, confidence
building, improvisation - beginners to advanced, individual coaching, ensemble
vocal sessions, repertoire advice. Course price £130.

Summer School - Audio Technology
Summer school has two 4 days courses 28 - 31st August for Beginners and 4 - 8th
August for Intermediate level. Suitable for solo artists, groups, band managers and
sound engineers with groups, as well as people with a broader interest in music
technology. Limited places - contact Community Projects Manager 0113 222 3468.
Provides a practical insight into the techniques of audio technology. Course co-
ordinator is Paul Young who has worked with bands like Radiohead, Blur, Take
That, Nirvana and The Fall. Covers - simple PA systems, small gigs, choosing and
setting up microphones, Radio mics, Sound Pressure levels, mixing desks, EQ and
graphic EQ, stopping feedback, FX, speakers, dats, minidisks and computer backing tracks, live and studido recordings both analogue and digital. Handouts will be
given at each session to provide an ongoing source of reference.

Summer School – Saxophone course
21/07/2003 July 5 days
Suitable for both classical and jazz performers who have reached Grade V ABRSM
standard or equivalent. Course offers a week of intensive coaching in saxophone
performance led by Richard Ingham and Nick Turner (members of the Northern
Saxophone Quartet). Students will be coached in many forms of ensemble playing
and the week will conclude with an informal concert by the participants. Course will
cover e- full saxophone choir, peformance skills within chamber ensembles, masterclasses for soloists and ensembles, tuition in classical and jazz idioms, advanced
jazz styles, technique clinic, repertoire and playing skills forum, advice on reeds,
mouthpiece and doubling. Cost £130.

Music Technology

Huddersfield Technical College
New North Road, Huddersfield, W Yorks, HD1 5NN.
01484 536521 Fax:01484 511885; www.huddcoll.ac.uk

BTEC National Dip. In Music Technology
Start Month: September. Duration: 2 years.

A practical course for those wishing to pursue a career in the technological side of music, particularly in sound recording, synthesis and sequencing and studio management.

Leeds College of Music
3 Quarry Hill, Leeds, W Yorks, LS2 7PD. 0113 222 3400 Fax:0113 243 8798;
0113 244 5523 (box office); enquiries@leedscolmusic.ac.uk (email)

BTEC National Diploma in Music Technology
Start Month: September. Duration: 2 years. Qualification: BTEC National diploma.

BTEC National Diploma comprises 18 units and is equivalent to 3 A levels. It may be possible for students to study one AS level subject in each year, or to convert an AS in year one into an A2 in year two. This programme is more likely to be most suited to students who have decided that they want to study one field of music and have the intention to specialise from the outset. The National Diploma in Music Technology will give the student not only the basic knowledge and technical skills essential for the high-tech music industry, but also the opportunity to develop personal skills, enabling him/her to become more employable when he/she leaves College. Students will be encouraged to plan their own learning and relate this to what they want form their own career. They will be able to communicate more successfully at all levels and to present themselves more effectively. This course is studied on a modular basis, typically taking two years to complete. The modules studied are; Music Production, Sound Recording, Musicianship, Performance Workshop, Keyboard Skills, business Studies.

Summer School - Audio Technology
Start Month: August. Duration: 4 days.

Summer school has two 4 days courses 28 - 31st August for Beginners and 4 - 8th August for Intermediate level. Suitable for solo artists, groups, band managers and sound engineers with groups, as well as people with a broader interest in music technology. Limited places - contact Community Projects Manager 0113 222 3468. Provides a practical insight into the techniques of audio technology. Course co-ordinator is Paul Young who has worked with bands like Radiohead, Blur, Take That, Nirvana and The Fall. Covers - simple PA systems, small gigs, choosing and setting up microphones, Radio mics, Sound Pressure levels, mixing desks, EQ and graphic EQ, stopping feedback, FX, speakers, dats, minidisks and computer backing tracks, live and studido recordings both analogue and digital. Handouts will be given at each session to provide an ongoing source of reference.

Leeds Metropolitan University

Calverley Street, Leeds LS1 3HE
0113 283 2600 www.lmu.ac.uk

BSc (Hons) Creative Music and Sound Technology

Music Technology - Aspiring Degree Level and Above - September 3 years
Aimed at those who have an interest in working with technology in a creative sound/music context. It combines areas of music and sound technology in their broadest sense, including production aspects of music, with a secure underpinning in the physics of music and sound. The course has a strong practical and applications bias rather than being heavily analytical.

Year 1 -modules include, Audio Recording Techniques, Creative Technologies, Computer Based Composition, Introduction to Music Systems and Digital Audio.

Year 2 -modules include Studio Composition and Production, Music and Sound Synthesis, Acoustics and Psychoacoustics, and Electronics for Audio Systems. (Sandwich Year - students have the option of gaining relevant accredited work experience in an industrial environment. Usually a one year placement after year 2 and are required to build an extensive portfolio of their experiences and are visited in the workplace by a tutor)

Year 3 - emphasis of the course is on project work with an individual Dissertation and a group Project, with a music and/or sound production of professional standard which will be exhibited in a final year show. The project reflects their specialist path/area. The Enterprise module explores the business and commercial aspects of the music, broadcast and entertainment industries. This is intended to assist and help students to market and promote themselves and their work.

BSc(Hons) Music Technology

Music Technology – 3 years/sandwich year available as part time option

Year 1 - modules include Computer Based Composition, Creative Technologies, Creative Music Skills, Music Studies, and Audio Recording Techniques.

Year 2 - modules include Multimedia Design, Studio Composition and Production, Music and Sound Synthesis, Commercial Music, Production Analysis, the Music Industry, and Project Planning and Management.

(Sandwich Year - Students have the option of gaining relevant accredited work experience in an industrial environment. This normally takes the form of a one year placement after level 2 but other more flexible patterns of accumulating work experience can be considered. Students who undertake such work experience are required to build an extensive portfolio of their experiences and are visited in the workplace by a tutor)

Year 3 - project work where students produce an individual dissertation and a group project, and a creative music and/or sound production of professional standard to be exhibited in a final year show. The project reflects their specialist path/area chosen. Two modules choosen which allow the exploration in greater depth specific areas, complementary to their project or intended career. The Enterprise module explores the business and commercial aspects of the music, broadcast and entertainment industries and supports the development of students' portfolios.

Red Tape Studios

Moira Sutton, 50 Shoreham Street, Sheffield, S Yorks, S1 4SP.
0114 276 1151 Fax:0114 272 6562; cst@redtape.org.uk (email)

MIDI Programming

Start Month: September. Duration: 36 weeks. Qualification: NOCN Advanced Diploma in Music Technology.

Students per year: 16 An intermediate to advanced level course, with the majority of tutorials and self learning based around Studio 2, Studio 5, and the Project studios. By the end of the course students should be able to operate a significant amount of the equipment in the studios independently. The range of equipment is used regularly and will include analogue and digital consoles and multitracks, signal processors, sequencers, hard disk recorders, samplers and synths. The course is a good option for people who wish to acquire a strong grounding in studio practice generally, but have a leaning towards MIDI - for example as a programmer, composer, DJ or songwriter. There are opportunities to pursue personal projects, and to participate as programmer or assistant engineer in a wide variety of extended programming and recording sessions. The course is suitable for those who already use, or are considering setting up a MIDI or home, studio, have participated in recording sessions as a musician or observer, have helped out at a recording session or gig, have undertaken and completed courses in related subject areas You have acquired knowledge through self study in related subject areas. In total the course is 450 hours - 12.5 hours per week during days, evenings, and weekends. Students will have tutorials for 1 day per week from 10am to 6pm, and 4 hours of Resource Based Learning (RBL). There are 16 places available.

Sound Engineering

Start Month: September. Duration: 52 weeks.

Students per year: 16. An advanced level course, with the majority of tutorials and self-learning based around Studio 1 and ProTools. Extensive access is available to other facilities for personal and project work. By course completion, you should be able to operate all of Red Tape's facilities with confidence, and under session conditions. During the course students regularly record, mix and programme for a variety of bands and artists under the guidance of a producer, on both long and short term projects. Also responsible for directing assistant engineers during sessions. It is seen as a challenging and demanding course, which places the student in a position of responsibility to both client artists and their producers in real session conditions.

This course would suit students who have a MIDI or home studio with multitrack capabilities, have assisted in a recording or programming studio, have done Front of House or monitors at live gigs, have undertaken and completed courses in related subject areas, have acquired knowledge through self study in related subject areas.

In total the course is 450 hours - 12.5 hours per week during days, evenings, and weekends. Students will have tutorials for 1 day per week from 10am to 6pm, and 4 hours of Resource Based Learning (RBL).

University College Scarborough

University of Hull - Scarborough Campus, Filey Road, Scarborough, N Yorks, YO11 3AZ.

01723 362392 external@ucscarb.ac.uk (email)

BA (Hons) Creative Music Technology
Start Month: September. Duration: 3/ 4 years. Qualification: BA CMT.

The programme is structured so that, after successfully completing core modules in recording techniques and compositional study in the first year, you can choose from a range of options in the second and final years to develop your own pathway. Second-year options include Electroacoustic Composition, Composing for Film and Television, Composing for Dance on Film, Creative Studio Skills, Psychoacoustics and Studio Design, and Studies in Contemporary Music. Final-year options include Web Authoring for Musicians, Interactive Technology, Radio Production, Radio Drama, Installation Art and Sound, Studies in Popular Music, and The History, Criticism and Analysis of Song Writing, taken together with a year-long extended composition project, supervised on a one-to-one basis.

University of Huddersfield

Queensgate, Huddersfield, W Yorks, HD1 3DH.

01484 472003 Fax:01484 472656; music@hud.ac.uk (email); www.hud.ac.uk

B.A or BSc Music Technology
Start Month: September. Duration: 3/4 years.

BA/BSc(Hons) Music Technology

Year 1 - Principles of Synthesis, Hard Disk Recording and Processing, Music in the Computer Age, Introduction to Sound Recording, Sound Recording, Music Option, Mathematics for Technology, Introductory Electronics, Electronics, Software Design, Computing, Introductory Circuits, (Current options in music include Composition, Performance, Foundations of Analysis, Foundations of Musicology)

Year 2 - Digital Sound Processing, Sampling Techniques, Audio Technology, Introduction to CSound, Music Option, Object Oriented Programming, Computer, interfacing in C, Entertainment Electronics, Signals and Processes, Microcontrollers (Current music options include Music in Contemporary Culture, Music and the Moving Image, Popular Music)

Year 3 - Live Electronics, Studio Project, Sound Synthesis, Audio Processing, Digital Signal Processing, Elective Modules, Individual Project,

This three year undergraduale course aims to provide a critical understanding and training in which musical knowledge and skills are taught if conjunction with those of electronic engineering. It exists in two forms, as a B.A. and as a BSc. The B.A. has a bias towards music and the BSc a bias towards technology. Students will be expected to have previous experience and qualifications in both areas. A common first year will lead to specialisation on one field or the other in the second or third years. However, throughout the course all students will study both areas and will be expected to work on a range of inter-disciplinary projects. The aim of the course is not simply to educate students in two separate disciplines simultaneously, but to foster a genuinely inter-disciplinary approach. Musicians work best with technology if they have a firm grounding in the technology they are using. Engineers area better able to work in the fied of music technology if they understand the demands placed on that technology by musicians.

MA/PgDip Composition/Electro-Aoustic Com

Start Month: October. Duration: 1/2 years. Qualification: MA/PgDip.

Postgraduates join an active community of composers. A creative environment is fostered by the provision of performance opportunities for composers, a music library well stocked with 20th century scores, recordings and books and four well-equipped electronic music studios containing a range of analogue and digital instruments. Postgraduate composers receive regular individual tuition from staff composers, all of them with national and international reputations, This is complemented by group seminars, which examine ideas and trends in significant 20th century works and electro-acoustic music under the general heading 'Contemporary Musical Language'. In addition, the annual Huddersfield Contemporary Music Festival provides an unparalleled opportunity to experience the most recent developments in new music. Students may work exclusively in electronic music, in acoustic music or in a combination of both. Opportunities exist to work in the area of concert music, stage and video music as well as other functional music. The course arims to encourage postgraduates to develop their compositional techniques to achieve a degree of aesthetic maturity.

University of York

Heslington, York, N Yorks, YO10 5DD.
01904 430000 Box Office:01904 433724; admissions@york.ac.uk (email)

BEng / MEng Music Technology Systems

Start Month: October. Duration: 3/4 years. Requirements: A levels- ABC; A levels with AS - AB +CC. Qualification: B Eng / Meng Music Technology.

Students per year: 38. This is designed as an alternative to the MA in Music but taught within the MA. It is especially for students who prefer a less demanding course or whose progress during the MA falls below the standard required. The courses are not 'musical' in the sense that there is no formal development of performance skills, or any material in areas such as history, appreciation, harmony or counterpoint - likewise, the courses are not 'media-based' or 'studio-based'. The emphasis is on science, computers and technology in the context of musical applications. Nevertheless, in addition to the more technical material in areas such as synthesiser technology, MIDI, sampling, signal processing, and the like, studio and field recording techniques also form important strands in the course. There is also a considerable musical atmosphere - not only will students be expected to develop their skills in the technical aspects of recording, but they will also contribute through involvement in the musical activities which will provide the source material for the studio sessions.

MA/MSc/Diploma in Music Technology

Start Month: October. Duration: 1 year. Requirements: Class 1 or 11 first degree. Qualification: MA/MSc.

Electroacoustic music is one of the most demanding, rapidly developing and rewarding fields of work for the engineers and musicians of our time. The purpose of the course is to bring together musicians on the one hand, and hardware and software engineers on the other, to learn together about this new field and to make their own contribution to it. The course units are designed to give musicians a degree of technical appreciation, and engineers to a grasp of musical issues at an early stage.

Wakefield College

David Kirtlan, Wakefield College, School of Music, Thornes Park Centre, Horbury Road, Wakefield, W Yorks, WF2 8QZ.
01924 789 802 www.wakcoll.ac.uk

AS/A level Music Technology

Start Month: September. Duration: 2 years. Qualification: AS or A Level

Covers: Sequencing or Recording Arranging and Composing using Technology Listening and Analysing The Music A2 programme covers: Sequencing, Recording and Producing Composing using Technology Listening and Analysing The Music Department has three recording studios: an 8 track cassette based sketch book studio: 2 16 track digital. These are perfect facilities for the study of multitrack recording and mixing techniques, outboard equipment, signal path, mixing and remixing. In the PC computer suite students study MIDI sequencing in great detail together with MIDI theory, analogue and digital synthesis and sampling. The department uses Cubase VST software, Finale and PET.Entry qualifications: by audition but need to have four GCSE passes at Grade C with a good standard of theory, performance and composition work Attendance : Tues/Wed mornings.

BTEC National Diploma in Music Technology

Start Month: September. Duration: 2 years. Requirements: 4 GCSEs at grade C or above. Applicants will be required to demonstrate commitment to music technology at interview. Qualification: BTEC National Diploma.

Study MIDI systems,sequencing and audio recording together with traditional recording studio techniques, record production and sound for film and television. Learn the constraints and potential of music for internet and web based products. Listening skills will be sharpened in aural awareness and you will gain an understanding of the historical context of your work together with the essential skills needed to work in the industry. Course will also include Music theory and Harmony, Keyboard skills, Music Publishing, computer technology. Assessment is continuous throughout the course. Entry qualifications 5 GCSEs at Grade C or above plus Grade 3 Music theory. Interview required.

NCFE Sound Recording

Start Month: September. Duration: 36 weeks. Qualification: NCFE.

The NCFE Sound Recording course has been designed to meet the training requirements of a range of people; each sharing a common desire or interest in working in this field. The course was designed primarily to be delivered to any age or gender group and it was envisaged that candidates taking part would be of mixed abilities. The main components of the course are as follows: Introduction to Sound Recording, Consoles and multitrack tape machines, Microphones, Effects and Dynamics Processors, Computer Sequencing, Sampling

Word Hoard at the Media Centre

Word Hoard, Media Centre, 7 Northumberland Street, Huddersfield, W Yorks, HD1 1RL.

01484 483188 hoard@zoo.co.uk (email); www.wordhoard.co.uk

Composing and Recording

Start Month: May. Duration: 6 evenings plus 2 full days.

Practical course aimed at musicians, writers, singers, storytellers or anyone interested in how to make a recording of words and music. Tutors - Duncan Chapman and Keith Jafrate. Course runs from 1st May to 15th June 2003 with evening sessions 19.00 to 21.00 on 1st/8th/15th/22nd/29th May and 5th June plus two full days - 10.00 to 16.00 on the 14th and 15th June. With the tutors the group will partly compose and partly improvise a piece for recording. This will include writing text, creating arrangements and settings for them as well as the composition. The Word Hoard has in-house digital recording facilities and course members will receive the final CD recording at the end of the course.

Part IV: Youth Jazz Orchestras, School Bands And Rehearsal Bands

Cannonball Adderley
At the Lighthouse / Landmark 1305

East

Aylesbury Music Big Band

Nick Care, Aylesbury Music Centre, 1 North Cottages, Stockgrove, Leighton Buzzard, Beds, LU7 0BB (office tel 01525 237 401, nick@musictime.totalserve.co.uk) www.musictime.totalserve.co.uk Age range of members is 16 upwards. Prize(s) won: 13 National Awards. Bass - John Calvert, Guitar - Matt Calvert, Drums - Paul Toler/John Stevens, Percussion - Steve Mitchell, Piano - Simon Whittington, Alto Saxes - Jenny Hird/Sarah Hutchings, Tenor Saxes - Fran Hale/Catherine Kelly/Suzanne McSherry, Baritone Sax - Harry Stark, Trumpets - Toby Capell/Phil Cooper/Gladys Cropley/Jan Marchant/Alex Maynard/Adam Pleeth, Trombones - Phil Fellows/Howard Fielder/Dunc Hamilton/Daniel Taylor, Bass Trombone - Andrew Shilton. Have received 14 National and International Awards which have included BBC Radio 2 National Big Band Competition - 4 times, Daily Telegraph Young Jazz Competition - National winners twice, National Festival of Music for Youth - Outstanding Performance Award - 7 times, Outstanding Performance Award at Montreux International Jazz Festival. Have broadcast on TV and Radio and performed at Buckingham Palace, London Palladium, Royal Albert Hall and International Festivals. Guest musicians have included Kenny Baker, Django Bates, Chris Biscoe, Dave O'Higgins, Kenny Wheeler.

Bedford Contemporary Big Band

Brian Peploe, 7 Denton Close, Kempston, Beds, MK42 8RY
Age range of members is 16-70. Membership: Invitation only. Membership fees are payable. £1.50 per rehearsal.
Rehearsal: Alternate Wednesdays 20.30 - 23.00. Regular venue: Pub in Southill. Rehearsals all year round.
Public performances per year: 1-3.
The Bedford Contemporary Big Band has attempted to take the Best of the Big Band Era and combine it with some of the more contemporary sounds of today, while still retaining the overall Big Band concept. The Band has been fortunate in obtaining the services of Nigel Carter (lead trumpet with the BBC Big Band) as Musical Director since November 1996. Fund raise for charities through their performances.

Brian's Big Band (formerly Star Dusters)

Brian Peploe, 7 Denton Close, Kempston, Beds, MK42 8RY
Age range of members is 30-74. Minimum skills: Grade 6. Membership fees are payable. £1 per session.
Rehearsal: Tuesdays. Regular venue: George and Dragon Mill St Bedford. Rehearsals all year round.
Public performances per year: 4-6. Band originally formed in 1986. Occasional gigs,mostly charity fundraising. Originally a 40s re-creation band, now a more contemporary approach with a USA West Coast repertoire.

Hertford Youth Jazz Ensemble

Bob Power, Hertfordshire Youth Jazz Ensemble, County Youth Music Group, Wheathampstead Educ Centre, Butterfield Road, Wheathampstead, Herts, AL4 8PY (office tel 01582 830382, fax:01582 830383, bobpower@aol.com) Age range of members is 15-21. Minimum skills: Grade V. Rehearsal: Usually term time Sunday mornings-10-4pm. Public performances per year: 5-15. Recent events have included playing at a Conference in Brighton, the Royal Albert Hall in a schools gala 2000, and at the Millenium Dome. Also developing links with the Cornish Youth Jazz Orchestra.. HYZE directed by county staff. Works in Big Band format as well as in smaller groups and explore many styles, including latin and rock..

Cambridge University Jazz Orchestra (CUJO)
www.cujo.soc.ucam.org. University band for student members

Peterborough Youth Jazz Orchestra
Alex Moore, 86 Aldermans Drive, Peterborough, Cambs, PE36 AZ (office tel 01733 552707, fax:01733 552707, alexmoore@hotmail.com)
Grades 6 to 8 rehearse at Walton Comprehensive School on Mondays 18.00 to 19.30 and the Junior Orchestra Grades 3 to 5 at same school 17.00 to 18.00.

Redbridge Music School Jazz Orchestra
Jeremy Lewis, Redbridge Music Service, John Savage Centre, Fencepiece Road, Hainault, Ilford, Essex, IG6 2LJ (office tel 020 8501 3944, fax:020 8500 3893)
Age range of members is 13-18. Minimum skills: Grade 5 A/B. Membership: Invitation only. For existing members of the music school.
Regular venue: Music Service- John Savage Centre. Rehearsals only during term time.
Public performances per year: 1-3. clubs. Touring details: Czech Republic- July 2000.
Redbridge Music School Jazz Orchestra provides existing members of Redbridge Music Schools,bands,orchestras and choirs with an additional opportunity to play jazz. Rehearsals take place once a week in the Spring term which culminates in a concert. Pupils are invited to join on the recommodation of the teachers or ensemble conductors. Entry to RMSE is by an audition. Pupils must reside in or at school in the local borough of Redbridge.. Well known and produces a high level of performance, covering a wide repertoire in a fairly short season. Expect to play 30-40 numbers each season, from a library of approximately 300 charts. Two teaching staff are now involved - one conducts and the other provides input for smaller ensembles,working on improvisation..

Suffolk Youth Jazz Orchestra
John Seabrook, Castle Hill Community Centre, Highfield Road, Ipswich, Suffolk, IP1 6DG (office tel 01473 744187, fax:01473 255608)
Age range of members is 14 -2.
Rehearsal: 10am to 1pm Sundays.
An opportunity for young people to play modern, Big Band jazz and travel the country playing when they can

East Midlands

11th Session Music Workshop

Trevor Iles, 27 The Lawns, Collingham, Newark, Notts, NG23 7NT (office tel 01636 892587, trevoriles@hotmail.com)

Age range of members is 8-19. Minimum skills: grade 3. Membership: Open to all.

Rehearsal: Saturday mornings. Regular venue: yes. Rehearsals only during term time.

Touring details: Germany.

Boston Youth Jazz Orchestra

Lee Hextall, Sam Newsom Music Centre, South Street, Boston, Lincs, PE21 6HT (office tel 01205 313227, fax:01205 311478, music.boston@lineone.net) www.byjo.org

Touring details: Barcelona 1999.

Started in 1992 as part of the Lincolnshire County Council Music Support Service. From Swing through to Latin, Rock, Pop, Soul and Funk. Members from Boston College, Boston High, Boston Grammar, Kirton Middlecott, Spilsby and King Edward V1 Skegness Grammar, Sleaford St George's College. BYJO enjoys support from the parents and the local community. For the current line up see more information on the web.

Jazz Vehicle

John Crouch, North Kesteven School, Moor Lane, North Hykeham, Lincs (office tel 01522 881010)

Age range of members is 11-19. Membership: Open to all.

Rehearsal: Wednesdays 19.00 - 21.00. Regular venue: Yes. Rehearsals only during term time.

Music for Youth festival winners, EMI,.

Concerts.

Leicestershire Arts Big Band

Peter Lloyd, Leicestershire Arts in Education, Herrick Road, Leicester, Leics (office tel 01162 700850)

Age range of members is 9+. Minimum skills: AB 4/5 upwards. Membership: Open to all. Membership fees are payable. term fees as in evening classes.

Rehearsal: mon 5.30-7 7-8.45. Regular venue: yes. Rehearsals only during term time. Rehearsals all year round.

Public performances per year: 4-6. Competitions entered: BBC Big Bands - most promising jazz soloist. Touring details: France and Belgium.

Two bands A and B. Broadly based repertoire from Glen Miller to Stan Tracey. Band B is a pool of musicians aged from 9 upwards, no upper age limit.

London

Cardinal Vaughan Big Band

Scott Price, 89 Addison Road, London,, W14 8BZ (office tel 020 7603 8478 (school), mail@cvmsbigband.co.uk) www.cvmsbigband.co.uk

Public performances per year: 18+. Competitions entered: Touring details: France(1999) and Spain (2001).

Founded in 1996 by Scott Price and based at the Cardinal Vaughan Memorial School it has become an advanced ensemble with an extensive repertoire ranging from Duke Ellington and Count Basie to contemporary Big Band, including charts commissioned by the band. The band now has a residency at the Bull's Head, Barnes and played twice at the Cheltenham Jazz festival, reached the final of the National Festival of Music for Youth, performed at the the Royal Festival Hall, Barbican, Queen Elizabeth Hall and the Millenium Dome. Recorded CD 'The Heat's On' in 2002, played with jazz singer Salena Jones in October 2002 and also gave a world premiere of Frank Griffith work. Chart composed especially for them by Bob Mintzer (USA). Director - Scott Price

Enfield Schools Jazz Band

Mea Jenkins, Enfield Arts Support Service, Aylward School, Windmill Road, London,, N18 1NB (office tel 020 8807 8881, fax:020 8807 8213, mea.jenkins@enfieldartsupportservice.org.uk)

Age range of members is 12-18. Minimum skills: Grade V or equivalent standard/experience. Membership: Open to all. Membership fees are payable. £20.00 per term (average of 10 sessions a term).

Rehearsal: Monday 17.00 - 18.30 and 18.00 -19.30. Regular venue: Yes. Rehearsals only during term time.

Public performances per year: 1-3. Touring details: Tour to Spain 1998.

The Enfield Schools Jazz Band forms part of the Enfield Arts support service activities programme, offering opportunities for young musicians who either live in the Borough of Enfield or who attend an LBE school. The Enfield Schools Jazz Band draws advanced players from schools across the Borough, with regular term-time rehearsals leading to a variety of performance opportunities. The band is coached by specialist tutors and plays a variety of jazz styles including Swing, Bebop and Latin. Improvisation and development of creative musical skills are also features of rehearsal time.

Jazzworks

Andrew Hampton, 28 Harold Road, London, N8 7DE

Age range of members is 11. Minimum skills: Grade 4.

Rehearsal: Tuesday 4.15-5,15pm.

Public performances per year: 8. Competitions entered: Music for Youth finalists.

NYJO I

Bill Ashton, NYJO, 11 Victor Road, Harrow, Middx, HA2 6PT (office tel 020 8863 2717, bill.ashton@virgin.net) www.NYJO.org.uk

Age range of members is 11-25. Membership: Open to all. No fees.

Rehearsal: Saturday 10.30 - 14.00. Regular venue: Cockpit Theatre, Gateforth Street, London NW8. Rehearsals all year round. This is the best known Youth Jazz Orchestra in the UK and is very busy with performances throughout the year as well as recordings, radio and TV appearances. Bill Ashton (MD) also produces a magazine covering the activities of the orchestra which appears quarterly

Competitions entered: see notes.

NYJO1 performs 50 to 100 per year making records and Radio and TV appearances. Has produced some of the best jazz players in the UK. Rehearsals for NYJO I taken by Mark Armstrong and Bill Ashton Longest running orchestra (38 years)- three times voted best band.

NYJO II

Paul Eshelby, Cranleigh, 118 Preston Hill, Harrow, Middx, HA3 9SJ

Age range of members is 13-25. Minimum skills: Grade 6. Membership: Open to all.

Rehearsal: Saturday 10.00 to 13.00. Regular venue: Cockpit Theatre. Rehearsals all year round.

Public performances per year: 6.

Pimlico Jazz

Andrea Vicari, 212 Sherwood Avenue, Streatham Vale, London,, SW16 5EF (email a.vicari@talk21.com) www.jazzschool-dordogne.co.uk

Age range of members is 11-18. Minimum skills: Grade 1/2. Only open to children at Pimlico School.

Rehearsal: Thursdays 15.45. Regular venue: Pimlico School. Rehearsals only during term time.

Public performances per year: 4-6.

South London Jazz Orchestra

Paul Millington 07939 052 383. http://users.argonet.co.uk/users/ataylor/sljo Community band which is open to local people wanting to play Big Band Music. Started in November 1999 it had over a dozen public performances in 2001 with a long list of bookings for 2003. Rehearsals are on Wednesdays 19.45 to 22.00 at the United church, Red Post Hill London SE24. Open to saxophone, trumpet, trombone, guitar, keyboard, bass and drum players. New comers welcome – with or without experience. Friendly atmosphere with a wide age range. Have appeared at the 100 Club, county shows and fairs in South London. Musical Director is Bob Bridges

North East

251 Jazz

Kelvin Dennis, EAZ Music Initiative, Cooper Centre, Beech Grove, South Bank, Middlesborough, Cleveland, TS6 6SSU (office tel 01642 461 321)

Age range of members is 14-21. Minimum skills: Grade 3. Membership: Open to all. Membership fees are payable. £10 per term.

Rehearsal: Monday 5 - 6.15pm. Regular venue: City Learning Centre. Rehearsals only during term time.

Public performances per year: 6-8. Touring details: Disneyland, Paris (once a year).

There is a 'Friends of' scheme and money raised through raffles helps to buy music. Rehearsals are not every week for 251 as members drawn from 'Band of '78' which does rehearse weekly. 251 is the jazz part of the larger 'Band of '78'. Both bands perform on same evening programme. Aim is for involvement and fun rather than competitive. Repertoire is BeBop, Swing with an Art Blakey influence.

Band of 78

Kelvin Dennis, EAZ Music Initiative, Cooper Centre, Beech Grove, South Bank, Middlesborough, Cleveland, TS6 6SSU (office tel 01642 461 321)

Age range of members is 14-21. Minimum skills: Grade 3. Membership: Open to all. Membership fees are payable. £10 pa with concession rate.

Rehearsal: Monday 5 - 6.15pm. Regular venue: City Learning Centre. Rehearsals only during term time.

Public performances per year: 6-8. Touring details: Annual performance at Disneyland Paris.

Wind band formed in 1978. All members get a discounted entrance to the monthly jazz club at the Dickens Inn to see visiting front line musicians like Alan Barnes, Jim Mullen. Repertoire is more popular tunes than usual Big Band material.

Voice of the North Jazz Orchestra

Adrian Tilbrook, Jazz Action, 9 Dunbar Drive, Eaglescliffe, Stockton on Tees, Cleveland, TS16 9EG (office tel 01642 805016, fax:01642 805016, adrian@jazzaction.co.uk) www.jazzaction.co.uk

Contemporary jazz orchestra formed in autumn 1996 with the help of grants from Northern Arts. The orchestra was formed to enable professional and semi professional musicians in the region to rehearse and perform with the worlds leading jazz performers and composers. The Musical Director is John Warren. Based at the Arts Centre in Darlington the orchestra has performed to full houses at Sunderland, Newcastle upon Tyne, Whitehaven, Darlington, Hartlepool and Marsden Jazz Festival.

Northern Ireland

Ulster Youth Jazz Orchestra

Ken Jordan, Director, 29 Glendarragh, Belfast, BT4 2WB 028 9076 0403 (tel)
info@uyjo.co.uk (email) www.uyjo.co.uk F
Formed in 1993 afer a series of courses held by Ken Jordan at the Crescent Arts
Centre. The band has played in Austria, Holland, France and has played at many
Music for Youth Finals in the UK. In 2002. appeared in 3 gigs at the Guinness
International Jazz Festival in 2002 as well as a tour in Germany. Winners of the
'under 22' section of the BBC Band of the Year competition in 2002.
2002/03 line up -Alto Sax: Courtney Lewis, Adam Delaney, Sara Jane Dunn,
Shirley Brown, Jarlath Mulholland; Tenor Sax: David Howell, David McKee, Patsy
Farnan, Debbie Magill.
Baritone Sax: David Carville, Desi Egan; Trumpets: Nathan Simpson, Phil
Ferguson, Neil Doherty, Alan Dodridge, James Hamilton, Adam Lewis, David Lowry,
Maeve Geary; Trombones: Aimee Moorhead, Louise Ferguson, Robert McCormick,
Robin Todd, Matthew McCrum, Stephanie Reynolds, Andrew Cupples; Piano: Gareth
Lewis, Scott Flanigan; Bass: Carl Harvey; Guitar: Scott Jamison, Gavin McGrath;
Drums: Peter Comfort, Gerard Morgan, Colin Robb; Vocals: Julie Wilson.

North West

Ashton-on-Ribble High School Stage Band

Ian Gray, Lancashire Music Service, 84a Liverpool Road, Penwortham, Preston,
Lancs, PR1 0HT (office tel 01772 729331, graymusic@tinyworld.co.uk)

Age range of members is 11 -6. Membership: Open to all.

Rehearsal: Tuesday Lunch/Tuesday 6.00-7.30pm. Regular venue: Ashton High
School. Rehearsals only during term time.

Public performances per year: 12. Touring details: Eire, Holland.

Ashton-on-Ribble High School's Music Department promotes the ethos that the
musical life of the school is not just about the pupils: staff, parents, family, friends
and neighbours are all welcome. Music is meant to be shared and enjoyed..

Double B Jazz Orchestra

Dave Ellis, 14 Thatch Lane, Bramhall, Cheshire (email delliscomposer@aol.com)
www.davidellis-composer.co.uk

Age range of members is 22-68. Membership: Invitation only.

Rehearsal: Wednesdays. Regular venue: Five Ways Hotel, Hazel Grove.

Public performances per year: 12-14. Jazz and Social Clubs, Festivals.

Rehearsal Band that has a weekly residency in a pub, where band only get
expenses. Perform some commercial gigs. They have a very talented group of
young musicians currently in the band. Ron Darlington (tpt) runs King's School Big
Band Speciality is their own arrangements.

Frakture Big Band

Phil Morton, Frakture, PO Box 36, Wavertree, Liverpool, Merseyside, L15 9JD (office tel 0772 9371213, fax:0151 280 9628, office@frakture.freeserve.co.uk) www.frakture.freeserve.co.uk

Rehearsal: once a month. Regular venue: Sandon Room Bluecoat Arts Centre.

Started in 1998 by Phil Morton and Phil Hargreaves (then of Bonehouse) in conjunction with the first series of Frakture Concerts. Membership is flexible and can vary between 5 to 15, sometimes augmented by visiting musicians. The music can be completely improvised based based around some other structure - they once did a performance of one minute improvisations, interspersed with recorded examples of the genre and haiku. Past performances with bassist Simon Fell and singer Maggie Nichols. In 2000 performed a three hour improvisation in the colourscape tent at pier head Liverpool. In 2001 members of FBB performed the Dislocation Sermons by Dineah Allirajah and Phil Hargreaves funded by the Year of the Artist. As well as formal concerts, the FBB network often gives rise to other less structured performances and collaborations from within its ranks, often in collaboration with Bluecoat Arts Centre..

Jam Factory

Steve Berry, Room for Music, 51 Alexandra Road, Blackburn, Lancs, BB2 6DW (email steve@room4music.com) www.room4music.com

Age range of members is All. Membership: Open to all. Membership fees are payable. £2 per session; 50p concessions.

Rehearsal: 5.00pm Sundays. Regular venue: Yes. Rehearsals only during term time.

2001 now has 44 members, including all of Steve Berry's own children.

Jazzamatazz

Brian Melville, Linden House, Mawbray, Maryport, Cumbria, CA15 6QT (email brian-melville@hotmail.com)

Age range of members is 12-16. Minimum skills: Grade 3/4.

Rehearsal: Monday 15.15, Friday 13.15. Regular venue: St Joseph School, Workington. Rehearsals only during term time.

Public performances per year: 9-11. Keswick Jazz Festival. Touring details: Berlin, Dortmund.

School based band with a changing size band according interest from students. In 2002 only a quintet. Repertoire stage band arrangements and smaller ensemble jazz standards. Objectives - to encourage ensemble performance and improvising. Play every year at Keswick Jazz Festival and in the millenium year Jazz Action organised for two professional musicians to play with the band at the festival. 2001 band went to Berlin and played on a boat on a lake as well as at jazz clubs.

King's School Big Band

Ron Darlington, 94 Park Lane, Macclesfield, Cheshire, K11 6UA

Age range of members is 11-19. Minimum skills: Grade V. Membership: Invitation only.

Rehearsal: 16.00 -17.00 Monday main band and Thursday feeder. Regular venue:

yes. Rehearsals only during term time.

Public performances per year: 4-6.

Aim is to promote swing and jazz music at school level encouraging playing of written scores and improvising solos. Play to professional standards. The band is self-contained with sound system, drum kit, professional music stands. Funded by concerts given by the band which also has raised over £140,000 for local charities. Provides essential experience and has gained a good reputation for the school. Two CDs have been produced with extracts played on Jazz FM. The only school band to have taken part in the Wigan Youth Jazz Orchestra 25th celebration. Main band and a feeder band.

MF Horns

Ernie Garside, 2 Musbury Avenue, Cheadle Hulme, Cheshire, SK8 7AT (email ernie.garside@freeuk.com) www.erniegarside.com

Age range of members is 19-71. Membership: Invitation only.

Rehearsal: various. Regular venue: No. Rehearsals all year round.

Public performances per year: 18+. Jazz venues.

Northern Jazz Orchestra

Paul Rigby, 11 Aintree Drive, Lower Darwen, Blackburn, Lancs, BB3 0QU

Age range of members is 16. Minimum skills: Grade 5-8.

Rehearsal: Fortnightly Weekends.

Public performances per year: 18+.

The band plays modern contemporary styles and plays for private and commercial concerts

RNCM Big Band

Mike Hall, Royal Northern College of Music, 124 Oxford Road, Manchester, G Manchester, M13 9RD (office tel 0161 907 5200, fax:0161 273 7611, info@rncm.ac.uk) www.rncm.ac.uk

Rehearsal: Thursday afternoon. Regular venue: Royal Northern Music College. Rehearsals only during term time.

Public performances per year: 9-11. Approx 8 performances at RNCM others at festivals.

This band is one of two full sized orchestras at the RNCM open to all students at College. Experience in the orchestra helps students acquire performance skills and play alongside visiting top professionals. The Big Band performs regularly in Manchester and the North, as well as Cheltenham Festival, the QEH (London) and St David's Hall (Cardiff) and now have a national following. College also has a smaller Jazz Collective for those students who are not necessarily from the Wind/Brass/Percussion department (e.g. classical students studying piano wanting to play jazz). Participants from this collective can go on to join the Big Band The Collective gives at least 3 public performances a year in addition to appearances at internal college functions. In 2001/2 guest performers included - Digby Fairweather, Steve Waterman, Lee Gibson and Alan Ganley.

Rochdale Youth Big Band

Ian Nelson, Rochdale Music Services, Fieldhouse School, Greenbank Road, Rochdale, Lancs, OL1 OHZ (office tel 01706 750288, fax:01706 656043)

Age range of members is 14-21. Minimum skills: Grade V Associated Board. Membership by audition only. Membership fees are payable. £20 per year.

Rehearsal: Term time: Monday 6 -8 pm. Regular venue: Fieldhouse School, Greenbank Rd,. Rochdale. Rehearsals only during term time.

Public performances per year: 9-11.

Salford University Big Band

Malcolm Melling, University of Salford, Faculty of Media, Music, and Performance, Salford, G Manchester, M3 6EQ (office tel 0161 295 5000, fax:0161 295 5999)

Age range of members is 18/23.

Competitions entered: Prize(s) won: 1st prize BBC National Big Band.. Touring details: Russia, Germany, Crete, Iceland, Norway, Denmark.

Students mainly come from the University's Music department. Individual members of the band have also won prizes and there are regular guest soloists like Kenny Baker, Martin Taylor, Bobby Shew and Gary Cox. Ex-members have gone on to become top session players in London touring and recording with bands like the 'Brand New Heavies', 'Black Grape' and 'SuperGrass'. Current MD was lead trumpet with WYJO and then NYJO. He has toured and recorded extensively. From 1993 to 1998 he was MD for the Wigan Youth Big Band. Formed in 1974 by composer and arranger Goff Richards under the auspices of College Technology's Music Dept. Developed from a small rehearsal ensemble into a Big Band with a national reputation. New courses were introduced - the world's first BA (Hons) in Band Musicanship and the internationally acknowledged BA (Hons) in Popular Music and Recording.

Sefton Youth Jazz Orchestra

Glenn Waite, Sefton Youth Jazz Workshop, c/o Central Music Centre, Redgate, Formby, Merseyside, L37 4EW (office tel 01704 872773, fax:01704 833041, sefmss@rmplc.co.uk)

Age range of members is 15-19. Minimum skills: Grade 5. Membership by audition only.

Rehearsal: Monday 19.15 to 21.30. Regular venue: Central Music Centre Fornby. Rehearsals only during term time.

Competitions entered: Daily Telegraph 1989-94. Prize(s) won: NCBF Silver award, Music for Youth. Touring details: France, Germany and Belgium.

Members drawn from high schools in Sefton Borough. Performed with the Royal Liverpool Philharmonic Orchestra for one of their childrens concerts,recording a programme for Radio Merseyside and appearing on Granada TV during the celebrations at Liverpool's Albert Dock. Performed at the Nat Festival of Music for Youth on Londons South Bank and the Royal Northern College of Music. In 1996 they appeared alongside The National Youth Jazz Orchestra in Southport Theatre and at Wigan International Jazz Festival. In 1999 they released their first CD. Tours- The band has toured Belgium, France and Germany and vistied the euro conference of the International Association for Jazz Educators in Maastrict in 1992. Winners Nat Fest of Music For Youth- outstanding performance award at the 1998 National Festival. In the early 90s entered the young jazz competition sponsored by the Daily Telegraph and won several places culminating in winning the youth section award for the North West region in 1994. School pupils in Sefton area.

Sefton Youth Jazz Workshop

Tom Sykes, 68 Bescar Brow Lane, Scarisbrick, Ormskirk, Lancs, L40 9QG (office tel 01704 872773, tom.sykes@tesco.net)

Age range of members is 11-16. Minimum skills: Grade 3.

Rehearsal: Monday 18.00 - 19.00pm. Regular venue: Central Music Centre. Rehearsals only during term time.

Public performances per year: 5-10. Prize(s) won: Music for Youth Festivals. Touring details: Germany, France.

Feeder Band: Sefton Youth Jazz Workshop Workshop/Rehearsal Performance with NYJO Workshop/Rehearsal Performance with Soweto Youth Jazz Orchestra. Both bands are open (by audition) to pupils in maintained Sefton schools who play appropriate instruments. Sefton Youth Jazz Workshop aims to develop ensemble playing and basic improvisation using much South African Repertoire. Sefton Youth Jazz Orchestra is for slightly more experienced players using intermediate to advanced Big Band arrangements..

Shades Jazz Orchestra

Doug Whaley, 37 Turnstone Road, Offerton, Stockport, Cheshire, Sk2 5XT

Age range of members is 20 -. Membership: Invitation only.

Rehearsal: Monday 8.30. Regular venue: Yes. Rehearsals all year round.

Majority are soft promotions.

Sounds 18

Geof Kelly, Mellowtone, 11 Hutton Drive, Burnley, Lancs, BB12 OTR

Sounds 2000 Big Band

Jim Ashcroft, 119 Hinckly Rd, St Helen's, Merseyside

Age range of members is 18-65.

Rehearsal: Thursdays 20.30pm-23.00. Regular venue: Yes - The Orwell at Wigan Pier. Rehearsals all year round.

Public performances per year: 1-3. pubs. Competitions entered: BBC Big Band.

Wigan Jazz Club Big Band

Ian Darrington, Professional Development Centre, Park Road, Hindley, Wigan, Lancs, WN1 2NB (office tel 01942 255 227, ian.darrington@btinternet.com) www.wiganjazz.net

Senior band made up of graduates from the youth orchetra. Ian Darrington the MD is currently a teacher and advisor for Wigan Education Department with special responsibility for jazz education. He is the founder and director of the Wigan International Jazz Festival and co-founder of the Wigan Jazz Club. He has been the MD of WYJO for over 20 years and has held workshops in the USA, Europe and

Singapore. He was a clinician for the Daily Telegraph Young Jazz competition, working in schools and colleges. He has been advisor and guest MD at the Cork School of Music Big Band..

Wigan Youth Jazz Orchestra

Ian Darrington, Professional Development Centre, Park Road, Hindley, Wigan, Lancs, WN1 2NB (office tel 01942 255 227, ian.darrington@btinternet.com) www.wiganjazz.net

Public performances per year: 18+ festivals. Competitions entered: Radio Big Band competitions. Prize(s) won: Junior winners 89/91.Senior winners 1994/2000. Touring details: Touring in Europe/Far East and USA.

2000 Ian Darrington received the Humanity Award for Jazz presented at the International Association of Jazz Educators in New Orleans. Released 10 albums and a documentary video sold in 25 countries. Three week tour of Far East- in 1998 to celebrate 21 years Jan 2000 New Orleans 10 day visit to perform at the International Association for Jazz Educators Conference. March 2001 at the 25th anniversary 'Wigan Jazz Club salutes Youth Jazz Orchestra included seminars and concerts by leading US musicians and educators and youth jazz orchestras. Formed 1976 it is a training ground for young musicians performing music from 30s to 90s. Features music of Count Basie, Duke Ellington, Glenn Miller, Woody Herman, Stan Kenton, Les Brown, Ted Heath, Buddy Rich, Maynard Ferguson. Re-formed in 2001 and senior band WJCBB set up.

Scotland

Artsnet Orchestra

Colin Bowen, Advisory Service, Hope Street, Hamilton, Lanarkshire, ML3 6AF (office tel 01698 427373, fax:01698 429893, colin.bowen@southlanarkshire.gov.uk)

Age range of members is 15-18. Minimum skills: ab 5/6. Membership by audition only.

Rehearsal: Wednesday 16.15-18.15. Regular venue: yes. Rehearsals only during term time.

Public performances per year: 6-8.

The jazz orchestra is part of the Artsnet project which culminates in three performances in March each year. The projects involve drama,visual art and original music for the orchestra composed by local musicians. In total 350 children are involved in this area of school experience..

Balfron High School Jazz Band

Adrian Finnerty, 10 Brandon Drive, Bearsden, Glasgow, Lanarkshire, G61 3LN (email adrian.finnerty@totalise.co.uk)

Age range of members is 14. Minimum skills: Grade 3.

Rehearsal: Thursday 1.00pm.

Public performances per year: 2-4.

Bheim Braggie Brass

John Whittaker, Golspie High School, 48 Gartymore, Helmsdale, Sutherland

Age range of members is 10-78. Minimum skills: able to hold an instrument. Membership: Open to all.

Rehearsal: Monday 18.30-20.00. Regular venue: yes. Rehearsals only during term time.

Public performances per year: 4-6. Competitions entered: Falkirk Youth Jazz Festival 89. Touring details: France.

The band is a registered charity and is open to all. At the moment the band is short of players with vacancies at all levels and instruments. Repertoire is Big Band 40s style jazz using notated music with a vast repertoire of material.

Dundee Schools' Jazz Big Band

Martin Dibbs, 3 Morgan Street, Dundee, Tayside, DD4 6QE

Age range of members is 11-18. Minimum skills: Ability to find way around instrument/enthusiasm. Membership: Invitation only.

Rehearsal: Tuesday 4.45-5.45pm. Regular venue: Yes. Rehearsals only during term time.

Public performances per year: vary. County Music Concerts.

Edinburgh Schools Jazz Orchestra

Dan Hallam, 26 Marmion Crescent, Inch, Edinburgh, Lothian, EH16 5QY (office tel 0131 664 9793, fax:0131 659 5868, dan.hallam@btinternet.com)

Age range of members is 11-18. Minimum skills: Grades5-6 AB 3/4 training AB. Membership by audition only.

Rehearsal: Tuesday evenings. Regular venue: yes.

Public performances per year: 12-14. Competitions entered: see notes. Touring details: Sweden Switzerland Stockholm Jazz Festival Montrea.

Success in competitions from Oct 1994 to 2001: Boosey and Hawkes Scottish Band Festivals five gold, one silver and one bronze award. In Boosey and Hawkes National competition - four silvers and four golds. Two best performances in the Festival of British Youth Orchestras. Daily Telegraph Youth Jazz regional winners. Performances: seven appearances at the Edinburgh Jazz Festival, Fanfare for Europe in Edinburgh 1998, Millenium Dome in 2000, Peebles Jazz Festival, Borders Musical Youth Millenium Celebration in partnership with the Kneller Hall Military School of Music. Tours: Stockholm Jazz Fest, Montreux Jazz Festival, Compete at Falkirk Competition each year and Manchester Band Festival. Band aims to provide a quality jazz experience /education for young people.

Edinburgh University Jazz Orchestra

Paul Tippett, University of Edinburgh, Faculty of Music, University of Edinburgh, Alison House 12 Nicolson Sq, Edinburgh, Lothian, EH8 9DF (office tel 0131 650 1000)

National Youth Jazz Orchestra of Scotland

Mike Hardy, National Youth Jazz Orchestra of Scotland, 13 Somerset Place, Glasgow, Lanarkshire, G3 7JT (office tel 0141 332 8311, fax:0141 332 3915, mikehardy@nyos.co.uk) www.nyos.co.uk

Age range of members is 12-21. Minimum skills: Grade 5.

Rehearsal: Sat/Sun - monthly. Regular venue: Yes. Rehearsals all year round.

Touring details: Glasgow and Edinburgh Jazz Festivals, Lemon Tree.

The Scottish National Jazz Orchestra is unique in encompassing a diverse music programme with visiting world class international artists unlike any other jazz orchestra in Scotland. Formed in 1995 the SNJO has performed with many musicians that has included Dame Cleo Laine, John Dankworth OBE, Kenny Wheeler, Gerard Presencer, Bobby Watson, Guy Barker, Pete King, Joe Temperley, Norma Winston, Carol Kidd, Joe Lovano, Scottish poet - Edwin Morgan. During Duke Ellington's centennial year in 1999 the orchestra played his music extensively, performing the 'Nut Cracker Suite', 'Deep South Suite', 'Toots Suite', 'Far East Suite', 'Such Sweet Thunder', and 'Queens Suite' The Orchestra also plays the music of Gil Evans and Miles Davis. Each year the SNYJO commissions new and challenging works these have included jazz composers Kenny Wheeler, Chick Lyall, Gail McArthur, Steve Hamilton, Sebastiaan de Krom, and musicians from within the orchestra, plus classical composers Bill Sweeney and Sally Beamish. It operates on a Scotland wide basis. Annual Summer course.

Stewarton Academy Senior Jazz Ensemble
Stewart Forbes, 2 Moorfield Avenue, Kilmarnock, Ayrshire, KA1 1TS (office tel 01563 544386, stewartwforbes@strath.ac.uk) www.geocities.com/swforbes

Strathclyde University Jazz Orchestra
Stewart Forbes, Strathclyde University Jazz Director, 2 Moorfield Avenue, Kilmarnock, Ayrshire, KA1 1TS

South East

Berks, Bucks and Oxon Big Band
Sid Busby, BBO Big Band, Flint House, Fawley Court Farm, Marlow Road, Henley on Thames, Oxon, RG9 3AW (email sidbusby@aol.com) www.sidbusby.com

Age range of members is 20-60. Minimum skills: Grade VI.

Rehearsal: Thursdays in Jan/Jul and Sept/Nov. Regular venue: Clayton Arms.

Public performances per year: 15-17. Pubs, Art Centres.

Formed in 1986 as a rehearsal band and has a regular core of members, plus a long list of 'deps'. Rehearse every week but on the last Thursday of the month open to the public and ticket money is donated to charities in the region e.g. Alzheimers, Cancer research. Have raised over £150,000..

Bexley Youth Big Band
Dave Bowdler, Bexley Music Centre, 27 Station Road, Sidcup, Kent, SE18 1NT (office tel 020 8302 1456, fax:020 8300 6619)

Age range of members is 12-20. Minimum skills: Grade 3-4. Membership: Invitation only. Membership fees are payable. £5.00 per session.

Rehearsal: 2 per term. Regular venue: Bexley Music Centre.

Public performances per year: 4-6.

Uses American ensemble method of backing CDs. Band membership is by invitation only but if anyone is interested in joining from the Sidcup/Bexley area then contact the Music Centre.

Chislehurst and Sidcup Grammer YJO

Will Michael, 20 Forge Lane, Headcorn, Kent, TN27 9QH (email pwmichael@the-mail.uk.com)

Age range of members is 11-18.

Rehearsal: tues/thurs/fri lunchtimes.

Public performances per year: 1-3. Competitions entered: music for youth finals at QEH. Touring details: Italy 2001

Three bands at school all play Will Michael 's compositions and arrangements.

Forest Youth Jazz Orchestra

David Andrews, 16 Whitsbury Road, Fordingbridge, Hants, SP6 1JZ (email musmak1@aol.com)

Age range of members is 11-18. Minimum skills: Grade 3-4. Membership by audition only. Membership fees are payable. £50 per term.

Rehearsal: Friday 7.00-8.30pm. Regular venue: Fordingbridge Methodist Church. Rehearsals only during term time.

Public performances per year: 6. Fetes, festivals, churches etc.

A Big Band formed in 1998 run to give young musicians in the New Forest area the experience of playing and improvising in many different jazz styles and genres.

Hampshire Youth Jazz Orchestra

Hampshire Music Centre, director@hyjo.co.uk

Age range of members is <21. Minimum skills: Grade 6/7. Membership by audition only.

HYJO Formed in 1985 to showcase some of the best young jazz talent in Hampshire. Sponsored by the Hampshire Music Service and directed by Paul Stevenson since September 2000 the band aims to embrace as wide a range of jazz styles as possible - from the music of Duke Ellington, Buddy Rich and Maynard Ferguson to the contemporary work of Andy Sheppard, Chick Corea and the Brecker Brothers. Public performances per year: 6/7. Touring details: Short tour of Staffordshire, Prague and an appearance at the London Dome. Auditions are held every summer term.

HYJO2

The training band for the Hampshire Youth Jazz Orchestra, giving musicians the chance to experience the varied styles of jazz and study some of the techniques and skills involved. The age of HYJO II members ranges from 11 to 18 and the band draws upon players from schools and colleges throughout Hampshire.

Director is Richard Miners, a Brass peripatetic teacher for Hampshire Music Service.

In 1999 the band reached the finals of the National Jazz Festival and performed in the foyer of the Royal Festival Hall and in the Queen Elizabeth Hall, London.

Auditions are held every summer term

Also under the Hampshire Music Services are the following two bands:-

Romsey Area Youth Jazz Orchestra

Director: Shaun Moffat

Rehearse at The Mountbatten School, Romsey (Lantern Theatre) Wednesdays fortnightly, 19.30 - 21.00. Entry level: Grade 5 and audition

Winchester Area Schools Jazz Band (WAS-JAZZ)

Conductor: Ben Kill. Rehears at: The Henry Beaufort School, Winchester on Wednesdays, fortnightly from 18..45 to 20.45

Hounslow Youth Jazz Orchestra

Lee Neale, Hounslow Music Services, De Brome Building, 77 Boundaries Road, Hounslow, Middx, TW13 5DT (email info@houndslowmusic.fsnet.co.uk) www.hounslowlea.org.uk

Minimum skills: An interest in jazz and improvisation.

Rehearsal: Tues 16.30 in term time.

Public performances per year: 4-6. Touring details: Holland in 2000.

Play standard Big Band arrangements - Count Basie, Duke Ellington etc.

Hunterpierpoint College Jazz Band

Derek Austin, 6 Fairplace, South Road, Wivelsfield Green, W Sussex, RH17 7QR (email daustin@pavilion.co.uk)

Minimum skills: Grade 3 or 4.

Public performances per year: 4-6.

Ian Hamer and the Sussex Jazz Orchestra

Ian Hamer, 68 Rosehill Terrace, Brighton, E Sussex, BN1 4JL

Minimum skills: able to read. Membership: Open to all.

Rehearsal: Thursday 20.00-22.30pm. Regular venue: Branch Tavern London Road Brighton.

Public performances per year: 12. jazz clubs.

Players often recruited from students at Brighton University. Ian Hamer (trumpet) is the leader of this Big Band whose repertoire includes a lot of his own compositions as well as 'original contemporary' music by Paul Busby, Kenny Wheeler, Tubby Hayes, Stan Tracey, Wayne Shorter, Thad Jones, Lee Morgan, Freddy Hubbard etc.

Invicta Jazz Orchestra

Graham Standley, Kent Music School, Astley House, Hastings Road, Maidstone, Kent, ME15 7SG (office tel 01622 3588 430, fax:01622 358 440, gstandley@kentmusicschool.org.uk) www.kentmusicschool.org.

Age range of members is Adult. Minimum skills: No experience.

Rehearsal: Thursday 19.30-20.30.

Kent Youth Jazz Orchestra

Graham Standley, Kent Music School, Astley House, Hastings Road, Maidstone, Kent, ME15 7SG (office tel 01622 3588 430, fax:01622 358 440, gstandley@kent-musicschool.org.uk) www.kentmusicschool.org.

Age range of members is 13-24. Membership by audition only.

Rehearsal: Thursday 16.15-17.15. Regular venue: Rainham Mark Grammar School. Rehearsals all year round.

Frequent concerts are given throughout Kent and abroad. Jazz workshops are arranged to enable players to experience playing Big Band arrangements and to develop improvisational skills. These workshops are open to members of Kent Youth Jazz Orchestra and to non-members. Applications: Would-be members should contact the Kent Youth Jazz Orchestra Manager in Maidstone and they will be invited to join with the orchestra in rehearsal. An assessment will then be made regarding their suitability for membership..

MYJO (Merton Youth Jazz Orchestra)

John Mander, Merton Music Foundation, MMF Office, Chaucer Centre, Canterbury Road, Morden, Surrey, SM4 6PX (office tel 0208 8640 5446, myjo@mmf.org.uk) www.mmf.org.uk/myjo/

Minimum skills: Grade 5 upwards. Open to all young people in the LB of Merton.

Rehearsal: Wednesdays 19.30-21.30 (fortnightly).

One of the most important dates in MYJO's calendar is its performance at the Wimbledon Tennis Championships where it brings its Big Band sound to the Semi-Finals Day. Tours abroad to France, Switzerland and Norway and in 2003 will be touring the Ligurian coast of Italy. Established in 1994 and is the senior youth jazz orchestra of the Merton Music foundation to provide MYM members with jazz performance opportunities. Performs a varied programme of Big Band music like Herbie Hancock, Joe Zawinul, Duke Ellington and Count Bsie. Also contemporary charts from the National Youth Jazz Orchestra as well as compositions by its own band members. MYJO 1 (Senior band) MYJO 2 (Junior band) rehearse 18.15 - 19.15 Grade 3-5 required.

New Forest Big Band

Doreen Pullen, New Forest Big Band, 34 Charnock Close, Hordle, Lymington, Hants, SO41 0GU (email dpullen@btinternet.com)

Age range of members is Any. Minimum skills: Experienced no beginners. Membership: Open to all. Membership fees are payable. £1 per attendence.

Rehearsal: Thursday 19.30-21.30. Regular venue: St Marks Church Centre Pennington.

Repertoire from Big Band era..

Pendulum Jazz Orchestra (BYJO)

Pat Kelly, BYJO, University of Reading, Bulmershe Court, Woodlands Avenue, Reading, Berks, RG5 4AN

Age range of members is 11-51. Membership by audition only. Membership fees are payable. £20 per term.

Rehearsal: Sunday 2.00 - 5.30. Regular venue: Yes. Rehearsals all year round.

Formerly Berkshire Youth Jazz Orchestra (BYJO). Patrick Kelly founded BYJO for the pure love of the music and the necessity he felt to spread the word to young people. His enthusiasm and drive have taken the band to great heights of ability and creativity. BYJO is now known as "a prep college for young jazz musicians" and is certainly one of the finest young jazz orchestras in the country..

Strodes Big Band

Diane Maguire, Strodes College, High Street, Egham, Surrey, TW20 9DR

Age range of members is 16-60. Minimum skills: Grade 5 or equivelant. Membership: Open to all. Membership fees are payable. Fee approx £40 per term.

Rehearsal: Tuesday 7.30-9.30 pm. Regular venue: Yes. Rehearsals only during term time.

Public performances per year: 4-6. Touring details: France/Germany.

Current band members are keen to improve in all areas: performance, repertoire and presentation. Need more Trombonists to join (saxes over-subscribed).

South West

Beaminster Big Band

Thomas Forward, 36 Crock Lane, Bridport, Dorset, DT6 4DF Theakasandbeeb@com Membership: Open to all.

Rehearsal: Friday 12.45-1.15. Regular venue: yes.

Public performances per year: 9-11.

Bournemouth Youth Jazz Orchestra

Mike Hopkins, Bournemouth Youth Jazz Orchestra, 3 Bramley Road, Kinson, Bournemouth, Dorset, BH10 5LU (email jazizus@yahoo.com)

Age range of members is 12-19. Minimum skills: ABRSM or equivalent grade 5+. Membership: Open to all. Membership fees are payable. £51.

Rehearsal: Tuesdays 19.15 to 20.30. Regular venue: yes. Rehearsals only during term time.

Public performances per year: 4-6.

We draw on players between 12-19+ who are interested in playing Jazz and Big Band music. We play modern arrangements some with vocals. The rehearsals are aimed to be fun and productive. We aim to produce an excellent concert at the end of each term plus other concerts. Band members are encouraged to try their improvisational skills and play solos. We play Swing, Big Band, Funk, Pop, Rock. Playing is fun. MD is democratic in his appraoch and listens to ideas on interpreta- tion and choice of music..

Cornwall Youth Jazz Orchestra

John Austin MD Cardeuville, Breage, Helston, Cornwal TR13 9PL 01326 573 195 (home tel) OR Bob Peters, Highfields, Three Burrows, Blackwater, Cornwall TR4 8HT (home tel) 01872 560 990l

CYJO conceived in January 1982 at a concert given by the National Youth Jazz Orchestra in St Austell. Musical directors are Bob Peters and John Austin.

CYJO has become a familiar sight throughout the South West and has also made

appearances on TV's "Children in Need" and at Paddington Station in London to help Celebrate 100 years of the Great Western Railway.
Performed in Newbury, Torquay and in Manchester, twice winning the regional award in the Daily Telegraph Youth Jazz Competition. CYJO makes regular appearances in Cathedral Square in Truro every summer and also to their annual trip to the Bude Jazz Festival (August.)

Devon Youth Jazz Orchestra

Chris Brook, Exeter Phoenix (Exeter and Devon Arts Centre), Bradninch Place, Gandy Street, Exeter, Devon, EX4 3LS (office tel 01392 667055, fax:01392 667599, admin@exeterphoenix.org.uk) www.exeterphoenix.org.uk

Age range of members is 11-21. Minimum skills: grade V. Membership by audition only. Membership fees are payable. £140/year.

Rehearsal: Sat 10.00 to 16.00. Regular venue: St Thomas High School Exeter. Rehearsals only during term time.

Public performances per year: 9-11. wide variety within area. Touring details: Tour de France,Germany,Belgium.

Dorset Youth Jazz Orchestra

Lawrence Payne, Dorset Music Service, Carter Community School, Blandford Close, Hamworthy, Poole, Dorset (office tel 01202 678233)

Age range of members is 13-18. Minimum skills: Grade V1. Membership by audition only. Membership fees are payable. £51 per year.

Rehearsal: Sunday 10.00 to 16.30. Regular venue: Carter Community School. Rehearsals only during term time.

Public performances per year: 6-8. Touring details: France.

Dorset Youth Jazz Orchestra provides the opportunity to talented young(local) people to play in a Big Band that performs in a range of jazz styles such as swing,rock,latin,funk. They are able to play in a wide range of venues including tours abroad performing to a high standard.

Gloucestershire Youth Jazz Orchestra

Tony Sheppard, Gloucestershire Music Service, Colwell Arts Centre, Derby Road, Gloucester, Gloucs, GL1 4AD (office tel 01452 330300, fax:01452 541303, admin@gloucestshiremusic.co.uk) www.gloucestershiremusic.co.uk

Age range of members is 14-21. Minimum skills: Grade 6 Brass Grade 7 Saxes. Download audition forms from Music Service website.

Rehearsal: Monday 19.00-21.00 in term time. Regular venue: Chosen Hill School, Churchdown, Gloucs.

Public performances per year: 18+. Also play at Festivals and workshops. Touring details: Germany, Devon.

The band plays 30-40 gigs per year, an annual tour and has a regular monthly concert. Appearances at Cheltenham Festival Fringe, Three Choirs Festival, Stroud Festival, Hathcrop Castle, Sudeley Castle. CDs: Over the Rainbow (1996) and Moondance (1999). GYJO was formed in 1982 to provide enjoyable performance opportunities for talented young musicians living in Gloucestershire. The orchestra does a lot of live performances and regular rehearsal attendance and a lot of self-discipline is essential. The membership changes by approximately one third every year as students move on to College and University. Many of the members are multi instrumentalists doubling up on other instruments. Their reperetoire ranges from standard Big Band arrangements like Count Basie, Duke Ellington, Glen Miller and Stan Kenton, to more modern composers and arrangers (including jazz funk and Latin). Band performances are more than 30 per year. There is a thriving social life within the band who have their own student committee - where members can have their say.

Millfield Jazz Group

Patrick Benham, Redmeads, Wagg Drove, Huish Episcopi, Langport, Somerset, BA16 OYD (office tel 01458 444113, PB@millfield.somerset.sch.uk)

Minimum skills: Grade 3/4.

Rehearsal: Tuesday 17.00.

Public performances per year: 4/5. Prize(s) won: In mid 1990s regional finalists in Daily Telegraph.

The band is available to pupils of the school only. Repertoire swing-modern-latin-folk..

Millfield Prep School Swing Band

John Barton, School House, Doulting, Shepton Mallett, Somerset, BA4 4QE

Minimum skills: Grade 3. Membership: Invitation only.

Rehearsal: Tuesday lunchtime. Regular venue: yes. Rehearsals only during term time.

Public performances per year: 4-6. Cathedral.

This is a school band and does no outside recruiting. However the purpose of the band is to play a variety of material in various jazz idioms - swing, rock, latin and pupils contribute to the choice of material performed. This varies according to the nature of the venue.

Queen Elizabeth Big Band

Lawrence Payne, Dorset Music Service, Carter Community School, Blandford Close, Hamworthy, Poole, Dorset (office tel 01202 678233)

Queen Elizabeth Strutters Trad Band

Lawrence Payne, Dorset Music Service, Carter Community School, Blandford Close, Hamworthy, Poole, Dorset (office tel 01202 678233)

Salisbury Young Jazz

Christopher Holmes, c/o St Martins Junior School, Shady Bower, Salisbury, Wilts, SP1 2RG (office tel 01722 334032, fax:01722 334032)

Minimum skills: Grade 6. Membership: Invitation only. Membership fees are payable. £15 per term.

Rehearsal: Thursdays 6.00pm - 9.00pm. Regular venue: Yes. Rehearsals only during term time.

Public performances per year: 4-6. Fetes, concerts with other groups, social evenings. Touring details: Trip to Italy in 1998.

Shaftesbury Swing Band

Andy Baulch, Shaftesbury Swing Band, Shaftesbury Upper School, Salisbury Street, Dorset, SP7 8ER (office tel 01747 854498)

Age range of members is 14-80. Minimum skills: Grade 5. Membership: Open to all.

Rehearsal: Wednesday 6.30-8.30pm (term time). Regular venue: Shaftesbury Upper School, Music Block. Rehearsals only during term time.

Public performances per year: 10-30. Cruises, Festivals, Competitions. Touring details: Spain 1999, Italy 1996, France 1994, Canada 1992.

A community band for all to experience reading and performing music of 20th century in Big Band idioms, promotes high standard of development and a chance to tour every 2 or 3 years abroad. Free to join but tours are paid for by band members. Band is a mix of professionals, semi-professionals and amateurs.

Swing City Band

Jo Gurr, Purbeck View, Blandford Road, Corfe Mullen, Wimborne, Dorset (office tel 01202 600277, jokeonthesax@aol.com) www.scbb.org.uk

Age range of members is none. Minimum skills: good sight reading. Membership: Invitation only. Membership fees are payable. £20 per term.

Rehearsal: Sunday 9.30 -12.00. Regular venue: Birchwood School, Bishops Stortford, Herts. Rehearsals only during term time.

Public performances per year: 12-14. Competitions entered: Winner regional final Daily Telegraph Youth Jazz Comp.. Touring details: Paris,Luxembourg, Germany.

Offers students the chance to play alongside ex-pros in a good quality Big Band. Please note band located in Bishops Stortford- Herts. Formed in September 1993 by Jo Gurr a woodwind teacher for East Herts Music Service. Aim to provide good young brass rhythm and sax players the chance to play in a Big Band, developing their improvisation and reading skills. Since 1993 the band has been in demand for concerts and for charity fund raising events. They have supported Humphrey Lyttelton in concert and have raised over £10,000 for the Headway Charity with1940s style dances held three times a year in Colchester. In 2000 they played at Disneyland Paris.In 2001 first home tour of Dorset. Band is self supporting and all proceeds from dances/concerts go to pay for equipment and music. Each year several members go on to University or college and new talent is introduced into the band. Old Members return from time to time and swell the numbers. Available for bookings. Also contact Mike Barnard 01371 872350 or Bob Grimes on 01279 723327.

Three Counties Swing Band

Thomas Forward, 36 Crock Lane, Bridport, Dorset, DT6 4DF (email Theakasandbeeb@com)

Membership: Open to all.

Rehearsal: Wed 7.30-9.00pm. Regular venue: yes.

Public performances per year: 9-11.

Truro College Big Band

Larry Johns, Penrose, Halt Road, Goonhavern, Truro, Cornwall, TR4 9QE (email larry@kornwall.co.uk) www.kornwall.co.uk

Membership by audition only.

Rehearsal: Varieable. Regular venue: No. Rehearsals all year round.

Public performances per year: 18+. Pubs. Touring details: Vienne Jazz Festival.

There are four feeder bands with an average of Associated Board Music Exam standard 5/6 and 7/8.

West Moors Middle School

Ian Parsons, Dorset Music Service, Carter Community School, Blandford Close, Hamworthy, Poole, Dorset

Wales

John Henry's KoolKatz

Sarah Fowler, The Music Studio, 45a Cross Street, Abergavenny, Gwent, NP7 5ER (office tel 01873 859966)

Milford Haven School Jazz Band

Sarah Tunley, Milford Haven School, Steynton Road, Milford Haven, Dyfed, SA73 1AE (office tel 01646 690021)

Age range of members is 11. Minimum skills: Grade 4.

Rehearsal: Tuesday 3.30-4.30pm.

Public performances per year: 7. Prize(s) won: Daily Telegraph Young Jazz 92 and 93 (Regional). Touring details: Buffalo USA.

It is a school Jazz Band and we try to play in a variety of styles - pop, traditional, funk - to learn a variety of skills and to maintain interest. Most solos are written but we try to encourage improvisation.

Pembrokeshire Jazz Ensemble and Big Band

Gareth Sanders, Pembrokeshire Music Service, County Hall, Haverfordwest, Dyfed, SA61 1TP (office tel 01432 775202)

Minimum skills: grade 5/6. Membership: Invitation only.

Rehearsal: Termly residential weekend courses. Regular venue: no. Rehearsals only during term time.

Public performances per year: 12-14. Competitions entered: 2001 NCBF Regional Silver Award; Finals Bronze Award. Touring details: Ireland.

The Pembrokeshire Jazz Ensembels are run to provide pupils in the Pembrokeshire Music Service with the opportunity to play and perform jazz and popular music in a variety of contexts - concerts, dances, competitions and tours. The music the band plays varies from Big Band to funk and blues and will give the chance to perform solos from written to improvised.

West Midlands

Birmingham Conservatoire Big Band

Jeremy Price, Birmingham Conservatoire, Paradise Place, Birmingham, W Midlands, B3 3HG (office tel 0121 331 7207, conservatoire@uce.ac.uk) www.conservatoire.uce.ac.uk

MD is Jeremy Price.

Birmingham Schools Jazz Ensemble

John Ruddick, Midlands Youth Jazz Orchestra, New House, Marsh Lane, Hampton in Arden, Solihull, W Midlands, B92 0AH (office tel 01675 442050, john_g_ruddick@hotmail.com) www.myjo.co.uk

Age range of members is 11-18. Minimum skills: Grade 6. Membership by audition only. Membership: Open to all. Membership fees are payable. £25 per term.

Rehearsal: Monday evenings term-time. Regular venue: Yes. Rehearsals only during term time.

Public performances per year: 4-6. Competitions entered: Music For Youth. Prize(s) won: Highly commended by Music For Youth. Touring details: Holland.

Junior band that feeds members into the next level - the Senior band in the Birmingham LEA set up. Looking for good, keen players who live and are educated in Birmingham and who would like to play in a Big Band, learn to improvise and perform to a high standard and enjoy their music at the same time..

Brian Newton Big Band

Brian Newton, Hall Green, Birmingham, W Midlands

Rehearsal Band which offers a performance once a month to audience at their rehearsal (Monday evening) space in the Bulls Head pub. Band formed over 40 years ago and used to record at the BBC studios in London and perform in major towns in the Midlands. Brian Newton was given arrangements by Stan Kenton in the past and the band's repertoire also includes Count Basie, Shorty Rogers etc.

Dudley Music Services Big Band

Chris Jones, Dudley Music Services, Lawnswood Road, Stourbridge, W Midlands, DY8 5PQ (office tel 01384 813865, fax:01384 813866, cjones@saltwells.dudley.gov.uk) www.edu.dudley.gov.uk

Age range of members is 14-18. Membership: Invitation only.

Rehearsal: Tuesday 7-8.30. Regular venue: yes. Rehearsals only during term time.

Public performances per year: 6-8. Touring details: English cities. Canada in 2002.

The band plays groove music, encouraging creativity and enjoyment.

King Edward VI Big Band

Alison Allen, King Edward VI School, Frederick Road, Aston, Birmingham, W Midlands, B6 6DJ (office tel 0121 327 1130, fax:0121 328 7020)

Minimum skills: Grade VI. Membership by audition only.

Rehearsal: Thursday 15.45. Regular venue: yes. Rehearsals only during term time.

Public performances per year: 9-11. Touring details: France and Belgium.

Members are generally senior boys from school. Repertoire of Traditional through to Contemporary Jazz. Objective is to provide realistic Big Band experience.

Martineau Big Band

John Ruddick, Midlands Youth Jazz Orchestra, New House, Marsh Lane, Hampton in Arden, Solihull, W Midlands, B92 0AH (office tel 01675 442050, john_g_ruddick@hotmail.com) www.myjo.co.uk

Age range of members is to 81. Minimum skills: Informal. Membership by audition only. Membership: Open to all. Membership fees are payable. £4 per night.

Rehearsal: Tue evenings. Regular venue: Yes. Rehearsals only during term time.

Public performances per year: 1-3.

Originally set up as a night school class for adult jazz beginners and is now independent.

Midlands Youth Jazz Orchestra (MYJO)

John Ruddick, Midlands Youth Jazz Orchestra, New House, Marsh Lane, Hampton in Arden, Solihull, W Midlands, B92 0AH (office tel 01675 442050, john_g_ruddick@hotmail.com) www.myjo.co.uk

Age range of members is 9-25. Minimum skills: Grade 4-8 see notes. Membership by audition only. Membership: Open to all. Membership fees are payable. £27 per term. Rehearsal: Wed evening throughout year. Regular venue: yes. Rehearsals all year round.

Public performances per year: 18+. Competitions entered:

MYJO perform concerts in schools as a way to encourage the forming or development of a school jazz orchestra or set up workshops or rehearsals with existing school bands. Where there are no instruments a question and answer session can be arranged with a general talk about the history of jazz, improvisation, ensemble playing, styles of playing, use of chords etc. Help sheets are made available on the day. Three bands - MYJO 3 (ages 10-15) - Grade 4 level to join, MYJO TOO! (ages 14-20) Grade 6-8 and MYJO 1 (senior band) Grade 8+. Awards - BBC National Big Band Competition - Youth section 1979, 1980, 1986, 1988, 1990 Senior section - 1991, 1993, 1996, 1999 and 2002. Outstanding Services to Jazz at the 1991 IAJE conference, 2003 performed at IAJE conference in Toronto; winners of Dutch National Big Band Competition Touring - USA, Germany, Belgium, Switzerland, Russia, Netherlands, France and throughout UK. The band has worked with many outstanding musicians from the UK.

Sandwell Youth Big Band

Tony Richards, 68, Woodside Road, Ketley, Telford, Salop, TF1 4HE

Minimum skills: Grade 6.

Rehearsal: Saturday Morning.

Public performances per year: 6. local proms town hall.

Shropshire Youth Jazz Orchestra

Chris Bolton, Asterton Hall Farm, Asterton, Lydbury North, Salop, SY7 8BH

Age range of members is 18+. Minimum skills: Grade 3-4.

Rehearsal: 10-12 Saturday mornings.

Public performances per year: 4-6. Festivals, functions, South Shropshire Jazz Club.

Shropshire Youth Jazz Ensemble was set up 1995. Improvisation plays a very large part in the band and all students are taught and encouraged to improvise. Any instrument is considered - music is specially written for the band by tutors Chris Bolton and John Williams, as well as jazz standards..

Sneyd School Jazz Band

Julia Kendrick, Sneyd Community School, Vernon Way, Sneyd Lane, Bloxwich, W Midlands, WS3 2PA (office tel 01922 710298, fax:01922 473145, postbox@sneyd.walshall.sch.uk)

Age range of members is 13-18. Minimum skills: Grade 5. Membership: Invitation only.

Rehearsal: Tuesday 4.00-5.00pm. Regular venue: Music Room. Rehearsals only during term time.

Public performances per year: 12.

Styles - from Big Band to standards (Glen Miller, Cole Porter, Gershwin), from Movie Music to Modern Fusion. Modern and Traditional vocals.

Staffordshire Youth Jazz Orchestra

Graham Standley, Staffordshire Performing Arts, The Green, Stafford, Staffs 01785 278 271(office tel) graham.standley@staffordshire.gov.uk(email) www.sln.org.uk/music

Age range of members is 14-19. Membership by audition only. Membership fees are payable. £35/year.

Rehearsal: Fridays 18.15. Regular venue: yes. Rehearsals only during term time.

Public performances per year: 12-14. Festivals. Touring details: see notes.

Orchestra was established in 1973 under the name of Staffordshire Youth Big Band. In 1993, the Big Band was renamed Staffordshire Youth Jazz Orchestra The Jazz Orchestra now specialises in modern arrangements and the performers are required to cope with the challenging rhythmic and technical demands of their current repertoire. SYJO rehearses at the Green in Stafford. Members are drawn from all parts of Staffordshireand join as a result of competitive annual auditions. SYJO enjoys a demanding schedule and special events have included joint ventures with Devon Youth Jazz Orchestra, Hampshire Youth Jazz Orchestra, Don Lusher and the Northern Saxophone Quartet. In London they have appeared at the Royal Albert Hall, Royal Festival Hall and Symphony Hall and also performed with members of the BBC Philharmonic orchestra in a special Jazz Evening at the New Victoria Theatre, Newcastle. Recent concert tours the Czech Republic with performances in Prague and Karlovy Vary and in Malta including the island of Gozo. In July 2000, SYJO appeared for the fifth time in the National Jazz Festival held at London's South Bank before leaving for an eight-day concert tour of Malta. In December 2000, following a major sponsorship from McDonald's, SYJO gave the world premiere of a specially commissioned jazz suite at London's Dome. Staffordshire Youth Jazz Orchestra is one of 70 bands, orchestras and choirs that rehearse weekly under the management of Staffordshire Music Service

University of Warwick Big Band

Colin Touchin, University of Warwick Music Centre, Warwick Arts Centre, University of Warwick, Coventry, W Midlands, CV4 7AL (office tel 024 7652 3523, fax:024 7646 1606)

Membership fees are payable. £2/year.

Rehearsal: Thursday Eves 8.30pm-10.00pm.

Competitions entered: National concert Band Festival, Royal College of Music. Prize(s) won: silver award in the Open Big Band class. Touring details: UK and abroad.

A blend of high quality music making with a serious appetite for fun. Strong following in the Students Union. Regular gigs draw large crowds with band playing modern arrangements.

Walsall Jazz Orchestra

John Hughes, 36 Jesson Road, Walsall, W Midlands, WS1 3AS (email jh@jesson36.fsnet.co.uk) www.ostrichmusic.com

Age range of members is all.

Rehearsal: Thursday evening. Regular venue: Forest Community Centre, Walsall.

Public performances per year: 12-14. Festivals. Touring details: France and UK.

Orchestra plays original compositions by band members as well as Chick Corea and other contemporary jazz composers. Have played all around the Midlands and in 2003 will be appearing at Montreux Jazz Festival. Recorded 2 CDs 'Watershed' and 'Devil in the Detail'.

Walsall Youth Jazz Orchestra

John Hughes, 36 Jesson Road, Walsall, W Midlands, WS1 3AS (email jh@jesson36.fsnet.co.uk) www.ostrichmusic.com

Age range of members is 10-21. Membership: Open to all.

Rehearsal: Tuesday 19.00 -21.00. Regular venue: Yes. Rehearsals only during term time.

Festivals (Montreux, Lichfield, Birmingham etc). Competitions entered: BBC Big Band (Junior section) winners. National Festival of Music for Youth. Touring details: USA, Poland, UK.

Senior and Youth bands. Youth band builds on basics using - Ellington, Basie, Herman, Kenton and helps with improvisation - Modes, Blues. Players progress to Jazz Orchestra which is of professional standard, playing original material as well as arrangements of compositions by Chick Corea, Pat Metheny, Mike Gibbs. Improvisation in Jazz Orchestra is advanced. Both bands tour and have won both senior and youth sections of BBC Big Band competition. Ex-members include Julian Arguelles, Martin Shaw, Nick Purnell, Duncan Mackay, Tom Porter.

Yorkshire

Colin Yates Big Band

Colin Yates, 207 Hague Avenue, Rawmarsh, Rotherham, S Yorks, S62 7QA

Age range of members is 20-60. Membership by audition only. Membership: Invitation only.

Rehearsal: Fortnightly 20.00. Regular venue: Grange Park Golf Club, Rotherham. Rehearsals all year round.

Public performances per year: 12-14. Jazz Festivals.

Founded in 1971. Regular nucleus of members. Monthly concerts raises money for their music charts. Repertoire is Count Basie, Stan Kenton. Have appeared with a singer under the title of 'Sinatra All the Way'.

Document 1

Peter Fairclough, 150 Knowle Lane, Sheffield, S Yorks, S11 9SJ (email peter.fairclough1@btinternet.com)

Age range of members is 10. Minimum skills: A minimum level is required. Membership: Open to all. Membership fees are payable. Approx £35 per term (10 sessions).

Rehearsal: Saturday 10.00am-12.30pm. Regular venue: Bannerdale Centre, Bannerdale Rd, Sheffield. Rehearsals only during term time.

Public performances per year: 4. Festivals, Clubs.

Regularly perform at Sheffield Children's Festival and Music in the Sun Festival, Sheffield.. Document 1 is a band of secondary school age musicians who compose, rehearse, perform and record their own pieces of music. Enthusiasm to make progress and the ability to co-operate in a group of 15-20 are the qualifications.

Doncaster Jazz Orchestra

John Ellis, Doncaster Youth Jazz Association, Northern Jazz Centre, Beckett Road, Doncaster, S Yorks, DN2 4AA (office tel 01302 320002, fax:01302 320002, johnellis.donjazz@virgin.net) www.dyja.info

Membership fees are payable. Membership open to all. £1.50 per rehearsal.

Rehearsal: Mon 19.00-21.00;Wed 19.00; Thurs 19.30-22.15. Regular venue: Northern Jazz Centre. Rehearsals all year round.

The Association has three other orchestras - the Youth Orchestra, Swing Orchestra and the Youth Stage Band. These are graded bands all involved in a programme of rehearsals, concerts, workshops, master classes and foreign tours. Individual tuition is available on most instruments (Tuesday evenings and Saturday). There is a large library of jazz orchestral publications at all grade levels. Mostly UK and USA charts.

Duke Ellington Repertory Orchestra

Tony Faulkner, Leeds College of Music, 3 Quarry Hill, Leeds, W Yorks (office tel 0113 222 3400)

Started in 1990 by TF.

E.A.S.Y. Jazz Orchestra

Nigel Blenkiron, Scarborough Area Music Centre, c/o Sixth Form College, Sandy Bed Lane, Scarborough, N Yorks, YO12 5LS (office tel 01723 354042, fax:01723 367049) www.wiganjazz.net

Age range of members is 14-18. Minimum skills: Grade 5. Membership by audition only. Membership: Invitation only. Membership fees are payable. £32 per term.

Rehearsal: Saturdays 09.30-12.30 in term time. Regular venue: Sixth Form College.

Public performances per year: 12-14. jazz clubs. Competitions entered: NCBF National Bronze (01) NFMY. Prize(s) won: three NCBF national golds in mid/late nineties. Touring details: San Sebastian Jazz Festival/Wigan Festival.

The EASY bands aim to bring out the full potential of young jazz musicians in the eastern area of North Yorkshire via intensive rehearsals, gigging, masterclasses with jazz educators and professional musicians and festival appearances. Also has a junior band 'Jazz Train' which prepares musicians for EASY. The Eastern Area Schools Youth Jazz Orchestra was formed in 1977. They are linked to the Wigan Youth Jazz Orchestra.

Harrogate Youth Jazz Orchestra

Nigel Beetles, Harrogate Youth Jazz Orchestra, c/o Area Education Office, Ainsty Road, Harrogate, N Yorks, HG1 4XU (office tel 01423 700118, Nigel.beetles@virgin.net

Minimum skills: Grade 5/6. Membership by audition only.

Students are from around the area and rehearse on a Saturday morning and play at various venues throughout the year Senior ensemble offering opportunities to students wishing to explore jazz techniques and repertoire from Big Band to contemporary music. In 2000 chosen to work with Julian Joseph as part of BBC Music Live Festival. The band plays from a large library of music ranging from traditional Big Band standards to more contemporary music. HYJO consists of about 20 motivated students with a keen interest in jazz, funk and rock music.

Heckmondwike Big Band

John Hunter, Heckmondwike Grammar School, 5 Newbury Road, Rastrick, Brighouse, W Yorks, HD6 3PG (office tel 01484 719812)

Age range of members is 11+. Minimum skills: Grade 4.

Rehearsal: Thursday 3.30 pm - 4.45 pm. Regular venue: school. Rehearsals only during term time.

Public performances per year: 9-11. Marsden Jazz Festival 1999, Blackstone Music Festival. Touring details: Paris Spring 2001.

Kirklees Youth Jazz Orchestra

Simon Mansfield, Kirklees Music School, Oastler Centre, Co-op Buiding, 103 New St, Huddersfield, W Yorks, HD1 2UA (office tel 01484 426426, fax:01484 480490)

Age range of members is 14 +. Minimum skills: Grade V. Membership: Invitation only. Membership fees are payable. £12.50 per term.

Rehearsal: Saturday 11.15am - 12.15pm. Regular venue: Yes. Rehearsals only during term time.

Public performances per year: 4-6.

National Concert Band Festival and National Festivals 1995-1998. Projects with Barbara Thompson, Steve Berry, Grand Union Orchestra. The main objective of the group is to educate pupils through quality music. This involves section playing, band skills as well as improvisation. Aims to undertake one new project a year.

Manygates Big Band

Roger Scorah, Wakefield Music Service, Manygates Music Centre, Manygates Lane, Wakefield, W Yorks, WF2 7DQ (office tel 01924 303 306, fax:01924 303 306)

Minimum skills: Grade 4. Membership: Open to all. Membership fees are payable. £22 per term.

Rehearsal: Saturday 12 -12.50. Rehearsals only during term time.

Public performances per year: 4-6.

Approx 24 members from schools in and around Wakefield. Repertoire includes jazz favourites, Swing classics by Hal Leonard, Young Jazz Ensemble series by Warner Brothers. Objectives are to give pupils an experience of jazz and improvisation.

Ossett Music Centre Big Band

David Stephenson, 8 Glastonbury Avenue, Wakefield, W Yorks

Age range of members is 13-18. Minimum skills: Grade 4.

Rehearsal: Saturday 11.15-12.00. Regular venue: Yes. Rehearsals only during term time.

Public performances per year: 4-6.

Good average standard (Grade 5/6 Associated Board levels), with wide range of Big Band music, good fun!.

St Bernards Swing Band

Jonathan Cook, 23 Broom Terrace, Rotherham, S Yorks, S60 2TS (office tel 01709 828183)

Age range of members is 11-16. Minimum skills: Grade 3/4. Membership: Invitation only.

Rehearsal: Thursday 12.40-1.15pm. Regular venue: School. Rehearsals only during term time.

Public performances per year: 6. School Fetes/Hospitals/Local Community.

After 8 Jazz - an extension of school based activity - age 16-19. The band has progressed from the 'Hal Leonard' packs to playing Glen Miller arrangements and diversifying into jazz/rock music. We consider ourselves to be a very professional outfit and play at various events throughout the year in the local community. The students are asked to play a high standard and improvisation is encouraged at all levels.

Part V: Disability Arts Organisations

Dizzy Gillespie
Quintet of the Year – Jazz at Massey Hall / Original Chess Classics OJC 044

Artsline

54 Chalton Street, London NW1 1HS (T: 020 7388 2227; F: 020 7383 2653; Minicom: 020 7388 2227, access@artsline.org.uk) www.artsline.org.uk

Provider of disability access information to the arts, leisure and entertainment. They aim to promote equal access and participation for all disabled people within society. Campaign for the need to remove physical and attitudinal barriers that prevent equal access; encourage service providers to make their services accessible; work in partnership with other organisations to enhance their service; offer Disability Equality Training with follow-up support and evaluation; maintain a comprehensive database of access information to cinemas, galleries, museums, tourist attractions, theatres and other arts venues; provides advice to venues making improvements to their facilities and services.

Community Music East

Community Music East (CME) 70 King Street, Norwich, Norfolk NR1 1PG 01603 628 367 (office tel) www.cme.org.uk

Was established in 1985 to develop and run programmes for a range of disadvantaged people Trains practicing musicians in the necessary skills and techniques to become workshop tutors Develops core work with specific user groups Runs a public programme of workshops Squawk This is not specifically concerned with jazz or disability but can incorporate improvised music with people with disabilities.

CME Workshops and the Music Life Project (Email) sarah.abercrombie@cme.org.uk Norfolk's Youth Music Action Zone, the Music Life Project, started in January 2001. It was launched as part of a network and is managed by a consortium of five regional organisations. Community Music East; Norfolk Music Works, Creative Arts East, Benjamin Foundation, Mancroft Advice Project. Community Music East has targeted young people in disadvantaged communities to provide a series of music workshops:-Great Yarmouth, North Walsham, Norwich Central, Norwich Costessey, Norwich Mile Cross, Thetford, Wayland

Young people are able to write music and create their own music using a range of instruments such as guitars, drums and keyboards. This enables them to develop confidence, team building and communication skills. Younger children are using rhythm and percussion instruments to create stories and develop listening skills.

Drake Music Project

The Albany Theatre, Douglas Way, Deptford, London SE8 4AG (020 8692 9000; Fax 020 8692 5018, London@drakemusicproject.com) www.drakemusicproject.com

'Enables disabled people to make music through technology. From Hip Hop to classical, jazz to rock, it is a national charity that is committed to providing the opportunity for disabled people to explore, compose and perform their own music'.

BTEC Advanced Certificate

Drake Music Project Tutor Training offers three units in Disability Equality, Access Technology and Workshop skills plus a workshop placement. The course gives insight and hands on experience with technology like * E-Scape, Soundbeam, MIDIGrid and puts them into a creative context. Available at the Walsall, Bristol and Manchester centres.

*E-Scape is a computer software system which allows people to compose and play music without any external help, even if they are severely physically disabled. The organisation has regional centres:-

Milton Keynes Resource Centre

1 Fletcher Mews, Neath Hill, Milton Keynes MK14 6HW (01908 237 044; Fax: 01908 662 212, miltonkeynes@drakemusicproject.com)

Forest Community Centre

Hawbush Road, Leamore, Walsall WS3 1AG (01922 711866, Walsall@drakemusicproject.com)

Work in partnership with the Walsall Music Support Service and together they offer music sessions and performance opportunities to pupils of six special schools in the area. Training course available in 3 modules – Disability Awareness, Music Technology, Running Workshops – with a placement as part of the training. Total course time (exclusive of the placement) is approximately 200 hours. The fee is in the region of £1015. Contact Sue Balcombe for further details.

Claremont School

Henleaze Park, Westbury On Trym, Bristol BS9 4LR (0117 942 5096, annabatson@drakemusicproject.com)

Mancat

65-67 Lever Street, Manchester M1 1FL (0161 236 6330, Fax: 0161 236 7420, claireturner@drakemusicproject.com)

In the few years since this centre was opened Drake have set up workshops, collaborative projects and performances. Initially they formed a partnership with Manchester College of Arts and Technology to provide introductory music workshops for disabled people through the use of music technology. This has led to the inclusion in college courses and evening classes.

Edgar Hall

Chesser Avenue, Edinburgh EH14 1TA (0131 444 2608, Fax: 0131 455 7595, dmpscotland@drakemusicproject.com)

Unit 5 RDC

WIN Business Park, Canal Quay, Newry, Co Down (jonimccabe@drakemusicireland.com) www.drakemusicireland.com

Offer a one year training course for new tutors, which is designed to develop the skills required to deliver training to students in a workshop situation. The course has three stages

1. An 11 week intensive programme covering all of the accessible hardware and software in use in the project, composition, workshop planning and practice, disability awareness and health and safety

2. A semester of shadowing experienced tutors in workshop situations and identification of an area of research for a dissertation

3. A semester of tutoring in workshops and research in a chosen specialist area, leading to the presentation of a dissertation.

Firebird Trust

Burgess, Sybil, The Stables, Wellingore Hall, Wellingore, Lincoln LN5 0HX 01522 811 229 (office tel)

Music organisation working throughout the Midlands and East of England aiming to benefit local communities, in particular people whose access to the arts is limited through the expressive and creative power of music. Organise a large number of workshops in Day Centres, prisons, hospitals etc

Live Music Now

Alice Wilkinson, Director, 4 Lower Belgrave Street, London SW1W 0LJ (020 7730 2205; Fax: 020 7730 3641, London@livemusicnow.org) www.livemusicnow.org.uk

Founded in 1977 by Yehudi Menuhin and sets out to fulfil two aims :-

To promote the enjoyment and experience of live music amongst people who would not normally have access to it. To assist gifted young professional musicians at the outset of their careers.

Musical performances are organized throughout the UK and to achieve this auditions are held to recruit the widest spectrum of musicians whilst maintaining high quality of musicianship. Training and support is offered to newly accepted musicians on the scheme. Monitoring and evaluation of performances and workshops takes place. The young professional players work with children and older people, some with learning difficulties and others with physical and mental illness as well as prisoners, refugees and homeless people. The majority of the music is classical and folk but there are some jazz musicians included in their regular auditions. There are seven other branches in great Britain

National Disability Arts Forum

Mea House, Ellison Place, Newcastle upon Tyne NE1 8XS (T: 0191 2611 628; Textphone: 0191 2612 2237; F: 0191 222 0573)

Nordoff-Robbins

2 Lissenden Gardens, London SW5 1PP (020 7267 4496)

A two year postgraduate training course, held at the Nordoff-Robbins Music Therapy Centre in North London. It gives a full time professional training in Nordoff-Robbins music therapy and leads to the Master of Music Therapy (MMT) degree, awarded by the Centre with City University, London.

"The Nordoff-Robbins approach to music therapy developed from the pioneering work of Paul Nordoff and Clive Robbins in the 1950/60s. " It is grounded in the belief that everyone can respond to music - no matter how ill or disabled. Client and therapist improvise music together, building a creative musical relationship in which a therapeutic process takes place and change can be supported. The unique qualities of music as therapy enhance communication and can help people to live more resourcefully and creatively".

Training focuses primarily on developing clinical musical skills but also introduces other theoretical perspectives like - early infant development and psychodynamics. The course encourages integration of these concepts whilst thinking about the music therapy relationship. Study takes place in a multi-cultural environment, with placements in a wide variety of schools and community settings.

The course meets the requirements for State Registration in the UK and graduates qualify for membership of the Association for Professional Music Therapists (APMT). When qualified music therapists can go on to work in the fields of health, education, social services and the prison service, and many graduates also do research.

Qualified music therapists already holding the Diploma in Nordoff-Robbins Music Therapy can upgrade to the MMT by completing the dissertation requirements.

Assistance with the cost of fees is available in the form of Nordoff-Robbins Scholarships and interest-free loans.

Skill

Chapter House, 18-20 Crucifix Lane, London SE1 3JW (020 7450 0620; Minicom 0800 068 2422, skill@skill.org.uk; info@skill.org.uk) www.skill.org.uk

National Bureau for students with disabilities that promotes opportunities to empower young people and adults with any kind of disability to realise their potential in further and higher education, training and employment throughout the UK. They work in partnership with disabled people, service providers and policy makers; tutors, lecturers, student services or welfare officers, disabled student advisers, learning support co-ordinators, careers officers, disabled students and their families or enablers.

Their information service offers advice on applying to colleges, financial assistance while studying and a lot more.

It is a membership organisation that organises conferences and influences national policy about further and higher education.

Sonic Arts Network

Darryl Biggs, Communications Officer, The Jerwood Space, 171 Union Street, London SE1 0LN (020 7928 7337; Fax 020 7928 7338)

T10 Yorkshire Technology and Office Park: Paul Wright, Director of Education, Armitage Bridge, Huddersfield HD4 7NR (01484 660012; Fax 01484 660024; p.wright@sounded.demon.co.uk. www.sonicartsnetwork.org.uk

Sonic Arts Network is an events, education and information resource with members worldwide. Aim to raise awareness and innovate new approaches to sonic art by providing information and opportunity across the UK.

Founded as the Electroacoustic Music Association in 1979 their aesthetic principles are tied to those of a medium which has an experimental approach to sound and technology.

Their work in education has, since the 1980s, remained at the cutting edge of artistic and strategic creativity; and their support for new work through commissions, research and events has encouraged new developments in sonic art. They have acted as consultants to the Government's Qualifications and Curriculum Agency during the revision of the National Curriculum. Through composer led workshops the education section of the network explores the exciting ways that new technology can increase access to music.

Recent activities have included a 2 year collaboration with UK schools - at each level of the national curriculum - including special needs - to explore classroom strategies for integrating Information and Communication Technologies (ICT) into the music syllabus. This was alongside short artist residencies in the community, which explore collaborations between art forms, such as music and dance, music and photography, with an outcome in performance or installation by participating groups, and creative projects on the internet.

Pupils who do not normally respond to music are benefiting from a music project spearheaded by Rachel Stirland who was seconded to Sonic Arts by Kirklees local authority, has been trained and equipped to develop a highly successful and fully professional model of peripatetic music support for all special schools, using technology. By giving pupils ownership of sounds and musical material pupils' creativity is unlocked. Training is available for instrumental services from Sonic Arts Education Network.

Sound Sense

Kathryn Deane, 7 Tavern Street, Stowmarket, Suffolk IP14 1PJ (01449 673 990; Fax: 01449 737 649; info@soundsense.org) www.soundsense.org

National development agency for community music. They "promote the significance and value of community music, and assist the professional development of people practicing and participating in it".

It is a membership organisation and includes musicians; arts administrators; local authority arts officers; people working in multi-cultural arts; education officers; people working in health and social services; those working with young people, elderly people, disabled people, and many others.

They help and advise through the National Music and Disability Information Service, a database of thousands of contacts, and a library of books, reports and files, enabling them to answer a wide range of queries

Professional development includes organizing seminars, conferences, advice and support for community musicians across the UK. They publish a magazine *Sounding Board* featuring news, opinions, discussion and features on all aspects of participatory music-making and *Bulletin Board*, a newsletter

Publications, documents, articles and information - a range of materials advancing the uses and value of community music activities including information packs on *Community Music And Health*, and *Out Of School Hours* music-making and reports from area gatherings

Electronic information service (SSINFO) - containing contacts, news, funding, opportunities, diary dates, updated monthly, available by, on disc, and in archive form

Research and advocacy - in support of community music for central and local government, funding bodies, politicians and others

Articles and information about community music for newspapers, magazines and other media.

The Soundbeam Project

Tim Swingler, (Sales, Courses, Workshops), Unit 3, Highbury Villas, Kingsdown, Bristol BS2 8BY (0117 974 41 42 Fax: 0117 970 6241; e.tim@soundbeam.co.uk) www.soundbeam.co.uk

Soundbeam is a piece of sound equipment which makes the creation and exploration of sound possible for people with varied ability and mobility. "It has provided a source of empowerment, motivation and learning – and of fun, fulfilment and joy – in hundreds of centres worldwide".

Quotes

"All students moving within the beam are composing and playing live music instantaneously...on entering the beam, individuals are given the unique power to create qualities of sound which could otherwise only be realised by an accomplished musician"   *Penny Sanderson, Animateur*

"One of the wonderful things about the beam is that you can fine focus it, right down to the movement of a finger, so that even people who are almost totally immobile, produce some sound"   *Andy Hicks, Baytree school, Avon*

"One of the most exciting and stimulating tools we have worked with...drawing pople out of themselves and achieving creativity beyond the apparent limits of disability. Soundbeam turns musicians into dancers and choreographers into composers"   *Andrew Cleaton, Drake Research project*

Soundabout

Soundabout is a registered charity formed in 1997 with the aim of promoting musical work for children labelled as having profound and multiple learning difficulties, children for whom sound and music are of great importance but whose needs are not best served by the constraints of the National Curriculum.

Soundabout offers training tailored to the individual needs of special schools, ranging from group sessions using simple means (such as the resonance board) to individual/group work using electronic musical technologies – in particular – Soundbeam. They work alongside staff in the classroom using either high or technology methods or a combination. They also run conferences, workshops and in-service training days.

Soundability Courses

19-22nd May 2003

Four day course held at Oxon Hoath retreat in Kent, aimed at anyone wanting to find out more about Soundbeam and other technology, particularly for teachers in special education, day centre staff and community artists.

Delegates have the opportunity to devise their own curriculum from a range of options. No particular musical or technical skills required - just curiosity and enthusiasm.

Programme – presentations from experts in music technology and special needs, technical tutorials and creative sessions. Opportunities for delegates to talk about their own work.

Tutors include Phil Ellis – senior lecturer at Institute of Education, University of Warwick; Mark Newbold member of Soundbeam Project, testing software, designing and building circuits for ancillary equipment; Adrian Price has studied sound technology at Brunel College ((Bristol), singer and songwriter. Technical assistant for Soundbeam Project - Tim Swingler trained in social psychology and as a teacher. A founding member of the National Community Music Association and assisted in establishing Soundbeam Project in 1990; Edward Williams, world renowned composer of electronic scores, notably BBC TV's Life on Earth series.

South Hill Park Arts Centre

The Ark, Administrative Office and Dance Studios, Ringmead, Bracknell, Berkshire RG12 7PA (01344 483311; info@theark1.demon.co.uk)

Studio and Workshops - Migdal Or Chaalet, Ravenswood Village, Nine Mile Ride, Crowthorne, Berkshire RG45 6BQ (01344 755528)

The Ark

An organisation that provides a 'multi-sensory' environment in which people with disabilities can experience and participate in the arts at the highest level, unlocking creativity which could otherwise go unexpressed. Weekly workshops where highly motivated and widely-experienced, professional artists work in collaboration to provide a combined-arts programme. Two or three artists work with their user groups and their carers to motivate, inspire, empower and liberate all participants.

The artists include actors, composers, musicians, visual artists and choreographer. The jazz musician who has been involved for some time with the ARK is Alex Maguire – Internationally acclaimed jazz musician and composer, as well as a State registered Music Therapist who specialises in autism and forensic psychiatry.

The ARK has 180 users – adults and children who have moderate to profound multiple learning disabilities. Half their programme is dedicated to participants who live in the Bracknell Forest district, whilst the other half is shared by people in the Windsor, Maidenhead, Reading and Wokingham areas. They work closely with Social Services, Education and NHS Trust, residential care settings and the private sector.

The future development of the ARK will focus on the promotion and celebration of the work there – nationally – as an example of best practice. It is planned to develop a training programme with in-house residencies, Touring, Workshops, Video work.

Impro

Elaine Furness, Music Department, Middlesex University, Trent Park Campus, Bramley Road, London N4 4YZ 020 8411 5826; impro@mdx.ac.uk) www.impro.org

Impro was formed in 1997 with jazz composers and performers Eddie Parker and Chris Batchelor with Elaine Furness, whose background is in teaching and education project management. From 1997-2000 they worked on "Developing Musical Communities", Impro's response to the changing needs arising in the areas of music education, community music, professional development and performance. The pilot project in SE London worked with young people and their teachers and leaders in residencies leading to large-scale performances. This served as a model for future projects and led to a major award from Youth Music for their project 'People Symphony'.

The workshops with young people, some of whom have disabilities, concentrate on those skills and materials which make communal music-making possible, including innovative approaches to improvisation, composition and performance.

Professional and community performances provide a focus during each stage of the project. They consist of material generated and composed in the workshops and involve the professional development group, client groups and artists of international stature.

People Symphony *"provides an opportunity to encourage and foster understanding and respect amongst young people who have many different musical interests and cultures through creating musical frameworks where different skills and strengths inform and complement each other. While celebrating and encouraging respect for differences"*

The aim is to further develop innovative approaches, skills, concepts, materials and repertoire which make integrated music making possible. To this end we also want to target areas of need such as disabled groups, ethnic minorities and refugees, those showing an interest in alternative or marginal musical styles, older teenagers without instrumental skills, integrating these with formally trained and able-bodied groups.

Association of Professional Music Therapists
Mrs Diana Asbridge, 26 Hamlyn Road, Glastonbury, Somerset, BA6 8HT, Tel/Fax: + 44 (0)1458 834919, E-mail: APMToffice@aol.com

The Association of Professional Music Therapists (APMT) was established in 1976 to support and develop the profession. The association's members are qualified Music Therapists who have undertaken a recognised post-graduate training course in Music Therapy. The association holds a current register of practising Music Therapists. In June 1999, Music Therapy, along with other Arts Therapies became a State Registered profession

Max Roach
Sonny Rollins + 4 Original Jazz Classics / OJC 243

Overview Of Jazz Education In Europe From The Annual AEC Congress November 2001

The Association of European Conservatories (AEC) is over fifty years old with a membership of 160 higher education music schools. These include music conservatories, Universities with music courses, academies of music and high schools (Hochschulen). At the annual meeting in Groningen representatives from a variety of institutions participated in discussions in both large and small groups. Most of them were directors, deans and principals of music institutions. Most have a background in classical music. A number of the schools associated in the AEC do have jazz departments or are at the point of starting one.

Most of the AEC members that have a jazz department are also members of the IASJ. What is discussed and decided at meetings of the AEC affects professional music training in Europe, both classical and jazz. There were four main topics discussed in plenary sessions and the break-out sessions.

Music Education in a Multicultural European Society

During the last two years, with support of European funding through the Connect Program, various pilot projects have taken place in which a number of conservatories participated. By studying and putting into practice various forms of world music such as Indian raga music, African percussion music and Indonesian ketjak music, models of good practice were developed for European music education. It is my personal view that no matter how interesting these projects, it looks like the wheel of improvisation is again being re-invented by looking at world music. There are many examples of good practice if one looks at the teaching and learning of improvisation in jazz.

The effects of the Bologna Declaration

In 1999 the European Ministers of Education decided that by 2010 all higher education, including conservatories, must have reorganized their curriculum into a bachelors and masters degree structure. Culturally diverse as Europe is, this leads to many problems. The harmonising of all structures in the various countries is a difficult task. Because of the differences in traditions and policies it requires a willingness to change. However, someone remarked that what the Euro is for the financial world, the Bachelors-Masters structure will be for the music educational world. After all is said and done the official AEC point of view on the bachelors-masters issue is:

The adoption of a system based upon two cycles: undergraduate and post-graduate. The first cycle to be four years and should lead to a Bachelor's degree.

The second cycle to be two years and should lead to a Master's degree.

A system of credits such as the ECTS (European Transfer Credit System) should be established. In order to realize the AEC policy on this matter a Bologna Declaration Working Group was established. This working group will continue to implement the new pattern of education in the member schools. A few days before the AEC-Conference an interesting discussion on this topic started in the Digital IASJ Ongoing Dialogues. It is clear that every school of jazz, public or private, will be affected by the new structure.

Support scheme for talented young musicians

In the Netherlands the conservatories have set aside a substantial amount of money for the support of really talented young musicians. Once admitted to this program students receive close to full support for studying abroad, visiting master classes or participation in any practical activity that cannot normally be supported by the school.

The evaluation of 'MusicWeb'

This interactive website was developed in order to support the teaching of music theory and history. Implementing the possibilities of the MusicWeb in jazz education calls for an essentially different approach to the teaching of music theory. The use of a portal for all music theory related aspects could create sheer endless possibilities. Much depends on the capacity and willingness of the theory teachers involved in the MusicWeb consortium. At the moment the speed of the development varies in every school in Europe.

The AEC and the IASJ

It is clear that in Europe the institutions involved in professional music education are in a transit period. In Europe frontiers have changed, mobility has grown and society has become multi cultural. All these changes have an impact on the cultural life and inevitably on music education. It is important to be aware of the changes and interesting to see how traditional institutions such as conservatories react upon them. It is important for the IASJ to be involved in the process of change. Collaborating with the AEC could have advantages for the IASJ. The AEC might be the platform that can help realise the plans like the producing a book 'The History of Jazz in Europe', Jazz in general education, and the research on jazz improvisation. The AEC has good contacts in Brussels and has proven to be successful in receiving financial support from the various European cultural support programs. However, not all jazz schools or jazz departments in Europe are associated in the AEC. Especially the middle and south of Europe is not very well represented. The EMMEN network in which private jazz and also pop/rock schools are represented forms an addition to the AEC network of established institutions. In order to realize all kinds of plans brought forward in IASJ Meetings, collaboration with both EMMEN and the AEC seems to be the best policy to follow.

Walter Turkenburg

Chairman, IASJ (International Association of Schools of Jazz)

International Jazz Organisations

Australia

Australian Jazz Development
Eric Myers, New South Wales, Jazz Development Officer, Pier 5, Hickson Road, Millers Point, NSW 2000 (Tel: 9241 1349 Fax: 9241 3083, emyers@ausjazz.com) www.ausjazz.com

National Jazz Development Officer is Eric Myers who maintains the national database and publishes JazzChord. As well as the New South Wales office there are Jazz Development Officers in Queensland, Victoria, Western and Southern Australia. The Tasmania Jazz Co-Coordinator is helped by the four jazz societies in Tasmania. They all offer advice and services to assist jazz musicians, ensembles and organisations to achieve their objectives. Full addresses of each area office appear on their website

Austria

Austrian Music Information Centre
Helge Hinteregger, Stiftgasse 29, Vienna 1070 (Tel: 00 43 1 521 040, mica@mica.at) www.mica.at

One of the many International Music Information Centres that provide information on many genres of music. HH specifically covers jazz and New and Improvised Music. The website at present doesn't have an English translation service. Centre has a library and CD and photo archive which includes information on Austrian jazz and new music recordings and musicians.

Belgium

Les Lundis D'Hortense (Association of Belgian Jazz Musicians)
Laurant Poncin, Coordinator, Rue Paul Emile Janson 9, B-1050 Brussels (Tel:32 2 219 58 51 Fax: 32 2 219 14 36, ldh@jazzinbelgium.arc.be) www.jazzinbelgium.arc.be

A not for profit organisation whose main aim is the promotion of the current Belgian Jazz scene. Supported by the Ministry of Culture and Social Affairs

Denmark

Danish Jazz Federation
Christian Dalgas, Nytorv 3, 3 sal, DK 1450 Copenhagen, Denmark (00 45 33 45 43 00, info@dkjazz.dk) www.dkjazz.dk

Danish Jazz Federation is a non-profit organisation which aims to:-
• promote and support Danish jazz in Denmark and abroad
• collect and pass on information about Danish Jazz
• provide advice to jazz-related projects
• distribute government funds
• initiate various projects with the aim of maintaining a healthy jazz environment

Offer a variety of subsidies with the main aim being to support Danish Jazz musicians and venues. The Federation is primarily funded by annual grant from the Danish Music Council. It raises additional money for specific projects. The website includes information about the Danish jazz scene in general – venues, clubs and jazz festivals, jazz calendar, record labels, as well as information about their own activities.

Finland

Finnish Jazz Federation

Timo Vahasilta, PO BOX 54, 00101 Helsinki (Tel: 358 9 757 2077 Fax: 358 9 757 2067, info@jazzfin.com) www.jazzfin.com

The Finnish Jazz Federation was founded in 1966 as a national organisation for jazz musicians and enthusiasts. It now acts as an umbrella organisation for about 40 member societies. It supports its member societies by organising subsidised tours, giving travel support as well as advising those promoting jazz.

The FJF works throughout Finland and abroad. In collaboration with the Finnish Music Information Centre it produces a booklet on current information on the Finnish jazz scene.

France

IRMA

Pascal Anquetil, Jazz Information Centre, 22 rue Soleillet, Paris (Tel: 33 1 43 15 11 11 Fax: 33 1 43, panquetil@irma.asso.fr) www.irma.asso.fr

The Information and Resource Centre for Popular Music Forms (Centre d'information et de ressources pour les musiques actuelles - IRMA) is a not-for-profit organisation, which includes – the Jazz Information Centre, Traditional Music Information Centre - CIM, the Rock and Popular Song Information Centre - CIR.

IRMA aims to inform, guide, counsel and/or to enable people to follow specialised training courses.

Germany

Jazz-Institute Darmstadt

(See under Archives)
www.darmstadt.de/kultur/musik/jazz

Hungary

Hungarian Jazz Federation

Varosligeti fasor 38, Budapest 1068 (Tel: +36 1 479 5164 Fax: +36 1 479 5172, Steingruber.Zsusanna@eji.hu) www.hungarianjazz.hu

Provide data on Hungarian jazz musicians, promoters, record labels, education and festivals. Data appears on the Budapest Music Centre website.

Italy

Europe Jazz Network

Via Amalasunta 7, 48100 Ravenna (Tel: +39 544 405 666 Fax: +39 544 405 656, ejn@ejn.it) www.ejn.it

Started in 1987 as the first electronic networks in the arts. A not-for-profit association of promoters, musicians' associations, artistic directors and programming consultants in Europe working mainly in Jazz and Improvised music.
website has extensive information on European contacts for festivals, record labels, management agencies and musicians.

International Jazz Festival Organisation (IJFO)

Annika Larsson, Piazza Dante 28, Perugia 06122, Italy (T (0) 75 573 2432)
At the moment this international organisation is based in Italy but the chairman is Fritz Thom of the Vienna Jazz Festival. - fthom@viennajazz.org

In 2002 the original organisation (founded 20 years ago) expanded to include 12 major jazz festivals world wide. its members include Jazz Fest Wien (Austria), Montreal International Jazz Festival, Vancouver International Jazz Festival (canada), Pori Jazz Festival (Finland), Jazz a Vienne (France) North Sea Jazz Festival (Netherlands) Umbria Jazz (Italy), Molde International Jazz Festival (Norway), Festival de jazz Vitoria (Spain), Montreux Jazz Festival (Switzerland) International Istanbul Jazz Festival (Turkey) Monterey Jazz Festival (USA). The members do not compete territorially. The dates of the festivals allow for touring of common projects. These are developed at four annual meetings - at the IAJE conference (at a variety of locations), March at ILMC in London (UK), a September roundup (varying locations) and November with industry presentations in New York (USA)
In partnership with the International Association for Jazz Education the IJFO sponsors an international jazz award of $20,000. (see InternationalAwards)

Netherlands

Dutch Jazz Service

Keizergracht 462, 1016 GE Amsterdam (T +31 20 620 68 88 F +31 20 620 68 89, info@jazzdienst.nl) www.jazzserver.nl

website aims to "promote the Internationalisation of jazz and improvised music". It provides a platform for jazz musicians, venues and festivals to exchange information. It is a not-for profit organisation that aims to support jazz and improvised music in the Netherlands. Annually presents the VPRO/Boy Edgar Prize – jazz award for the Netherlands.

IASJ

Walter Turkenburg, Chairman, Juliana van Stolberglaan 1, 2595 CA The Hague, Netherlands (00 31 70 381 4251, servicebureau@iasj.com) www.iasj.com

The International Association of Schools of Jazz(IASJ) was established in 1989. It functions as a network of schools of jazz from all over the world. Students, teachers and representatives are connected through the IASJ. A large number of them meet during the Annual IASJ Jazz Meeting which takes place in a different country every year. Participants meet, play and network together for a week to establish potential life-long musical and personal friendships during the meeting. The IASJ Newsletter and the IASJ Website serve as a platform to disseminate the ideas and visions of the students, teachers and representatives of the schools involved in the IASJ. Through all the connections that the IASJ has in the jazz world, members benefit in many respects. Being a member of the IASJ enables students, teachers and staff to broaden their horizons through contact with colleagues from all over the world.

Activities

Holds an Annual IASJ Jazz Meeting in a different country each year, where participants from member schools come together to interact and communicate both musically and socially forming multinational ensembles which go beyond linguistic and cultural boundaries.

Encourages Regional IASJ Jazz Meetings.

• Has an ongoing student-to-student and teacher-to-teacher exchange.

• Publishes the IASJ Newsletter four times a year with pertinent information providing a network of communication and interaction.

• Produces recordings, videos and collections of compositions rendered by members of the IASJ.

• Continues to build a computerised database providing all participants with addresses for aid in travelling and working situations.

• Cooperates with other jazz organizations to do all that is possible to foster and encourage the growth of jazz.

Aims to:

• Facilitate high-level cross-cultural communication.

• Foster brotherhood and tolerance towards each other.

• Encourage individual creativity balanced with group interaction as is evidenced in the typical jazz group.

• Bring together a community and encourage a concept of jazz as inclusive music open to contributions by artists from all parts of the world whereby cultural differences combine to create new, innovative musical forms and styles.

• Expand the association to include musicians and schools from all parts of the world as jazz education continues to expand.

• Promote jazz and jazz education through audience and community development and the encouragement of funding and other creative financial resources thereby furthering playing opportunities and providing support for the world community of jazz artists.

Norway

Norwegian Jazzforum
Tollbugata 28, Oslo 0157 (T +47 2241 2010 F +47 2241 2004, nojf@notam.uio.no) www.jazzforum.no

Norwegian Jazz Association in Oslo is part of the forum in five regional jazz centres. The site provides information on clubs, festivals, musicians, concerts provided by each region. Also provide grant information to their membership

Poland

Polish Jazz Network
Cezary Lerski, 1820 S. Santa Fe St, Santa Ana, CA 92705, USA (00 1 714-850-2022 fax: 00 1 714-662-0405, info@polishjazz.com) www.polishjazz.com

A non-profit organization established in 2000 continuing on a mission to make the most of the Internet in promoting work of Polish jazz artists and jazz professionals. A volunteer organisation, to promote Polish jazz, encourage the exchange of jazz and to serve as a link between jazz fans and the international jazz community. They see themselves as the doorway to the world of jazz from Poland, offering the largest selection of Polish jazz on the Web. The website includes pages of Polish jazz artists, clubs, festivals, and links to other Polish jazz venues. You can listen to 24/7 Polish jazz radio, sample and buy jazz records, browse through jazz art galleries, chat with jazz fans, book your favourite artists. "We believe that jazz is one of the most important art forms of the 20th century; the form that embraces the spirit of independence, tolerance, resourcefulness, freshness and cosmopolitism. Jazz had conquered the world, and now it has become a truly global art form."

Russia

www.jazz.ru

Internet magazine covering jazz throughout Russia with Moscow and St Petersburg comprehensively covered. Staff based in Moscow with freelance contributors in cities in Russia, Europe, Israel and America. Only a small section in English at the moment but it includes festivals. CM is the Russian contributor to Downbeat in US.

Sweden

Swedish Music Information Centre
Box 37327, 102 54 Stockholm (T +46 8 783 88 00) www.mic.stim.se/svensk
Information about Swedish jazz musicians and bands

Swedish Jazz Federation
Nybrokajen 11, 111 48 Stockholm (T +46 8 407 17 40 F +46 8 407 17 49, kansli@swedejazz.se) www.swedejazz.se

Website lists clubs, festivals, record labels, bands, music organizations. The federation (SJR) is a not-for-profit organisation, which brings together Swedish jazz clubs. They try through cooperation with other organisations and local authorities, to improve conditions and develop opportunities for Swedish jazz.

USA

IAJE

PO BOX 724, 2803 Claflin Road, 66505 Manhattan, Kansas (00 1 785 776 8744, info@iaje.org) www.iaje.org

The International Association of Jazz Educators is a voluntary non-profit organisation (USA) aiming to ensure the continued growth and development of jazz through education and outreach. The International Association for Jazz Education (IAJE) serves 8,000 members in 40 countries. They "initiate programs which nurture the understanding and appreciation of jazz and its heritage, provide leadership to educators regarding curriculum and performance, and assist teachers, students, and artists with information and resources". The IAJE Annual Conference, held each January, is acknowledged as "the largest annual gathering of the global jazz community".

Jazz Journalists Association

PO BOX 90351, Brooklyn, New York, 11209 NY www.jazzhouse.org

The Jazz Journalists Association (JJA) is an international group of writers, editors, photographers, broadcasters, filmmakers, educators and media professionals who institute collegial and educational programs for the appreciation, documentation and promulgation of jazz. The goals of the Jazz Journalists Association are to promote high standards and respect for our works, to create a professional network, and to increase general interest in jazz. First gathering in Chicago in 1986, the JJA has held annual meetings, often timed to major festivals and jazz conventions JJA members debate hot jazz issues in public forums, team with musicians to teach jazz in schools, consult arts agencies and funders, mentor budding journalistic talents, hail new artists and labor to document jazz as it happens. Members include authors of jazz books, widely-published and exhibited photographers, internationally recognised broadcasters and pioneers of jazz in cyberspace.

All About Jazz

Michael Ricci, All About Jazz, 761 Sproul Road #211, Springfield, PA19064 - www.allaboutjazz.com

A website, part of which is dedicated to selling albums and is focused on America, but it states that it is "A site produced by jazz fans, for jazz fans". Includes information and opinions about jazz from the past and present, reviews of jazz from around the world, interviews with international musicians, biographies. The site is aimed at those new to jazz, as well as the aficionado. So it provides advice on building a jazz library, extensive archives of reviews and interviews, Jazz Timeline for checking major jazz developments in any one year, forums for expressing and exchanging opinions on issues relating to the music and the musicians.

Jazz Corner

Audioworks Group, 245 West 25th St, New York, NY 10001 (info@jazzcorner.com)
www.jazzcorner.com

website with links to a selection of American jazz musicians (except for inclusion of UK Double Bass player Peter Ind and his record label Wave) which lead to Biographies, Tour dates, Recordings, Photo Gallery, Management details. Site also has gig listings for many parts of USA as well as Canada, UK, Switzerland, Netherlands, France, Belgium and Italy provided by JazzValley (France). Interviews section with full length Real Audio features on individual musicians e.g four part profile on Bob Brookmeyer.

Thelonious Monk Institute of Jazz Performance

University of South California, 3443 Watt Way, Los Angeles California 90089-1102
www.monkinstitute.com

The website for the Thelonius Monk Institute has a web based jazz curriculum for 5th, 8th and 11th grade students (USA) available free to schools with download-able (in pdf) lesson plans. Examines the evolution of jazz styles – 'Jazz America's music' 'What is Jazz and what is not', Jazz recordings – including sound bites and some analysis, musical techniques

As well as the jazz education programmes available at Institute (see entry under USA courses) the institute runs a 'jazz in the class room' series, which visits schools throughout the USA and internationally. It offers a 'Thelonius Monk International Jazz competition', (Also see www.jazzinamerica.com)

.

International Jazz Awards And Competitions

Herbie Hancock
Sextant / Columbia 65681

Belgium

Jazz Hoeilaart

International Jazz Contest for Youth Orchestras
Albert Michiels, Jezus-Eiksesteenweg 47, 1560 Hoeilaart, Belgium (00 32 2 657 09 76, albert.michiels@pandora.be)

Began in 1979 within the framework of the festival of grapes and wine, with the aim of making talented young jazz musicians from Belgium and the Netherlands, better known. Since then it has grown to incorporate applications from over 50 different countries

Rules

Open to all nationalities

No restrictions on style or genre

Candidates must be born after the 15th June 1972

Deadline for applications before 15th June 2002 which must include a 30 minute tape recording + name and photo of group with details of the line up, address for correspondence as well as the names and addresses dates of birth and nationality of each of the musicians

Jury of well known jazz musicians will judge the recordings and select a maximum of 8 bands (plus 4 in reserve)

Finals to be held on 28 and 29th September 2002

Prizes – Money, Trophy for best soloist, CD recording of the four best groups, First prize winner also receives contracts for concerts in Belgium and abroad (Getxo Jazz Festival in Spain July 2003)

Organisers, VRT or other broadcasting stations as well as the CD producers will NOT pay any supplementary renumeration for the recording, filming or broadcasting of the contest

The groups will have at their disposal – an acoustic and digital piano, drum set, vibraphone, amps for bass and guitar and full PA equipment

Maximum playing time for each group is 40 minutes

For the finals only one line up allowed

Czech Republic

European Jazz Days

Pavel Svarc, Festival Secretariat CTA, Na Hajku 367, 180 00 Prague 8, Czech Republic (Tel/Fax 00 42 2 8482 6608, cta@iol.cz) www.clubta.cz

Applications to be made in writing by 31st December 2002 and should include a short history of the band, a good photo and a recent recording, programme for competition. Forms available from the website

Competetion for amateur bands in 3 catagories. 1. Jazz Band with 11+ musicians. 2. Jazz Band with 10 or less musicians. 3. Vocàl Jazz with rhythm section 7+ musicians.

Any style of jazz.

No limitation on composition, instruments or age range

Performance time limit is 20 minutes per band

Submission of at least one score of each composition to be played shortly before performance

Competition fee $90 per band

Applications in writing

Cash prizes for 1st/2nd/3rd winners in each category. International jury of musicians and teachers.

Travel and accommodation costs paid by participants

Competition is part of a festival and workshops (organised by International Association of Jazz Educators IAJE Canadian representative) and co-produced by Jezek's Music Conservatory and CTA (a concert and travel agency) with the winners appearing in the festival (24 - 27th April 2003). Festival events take place in National House of Vinohrady in Prague.

Denmark

Jazzpar Prize

Jazz Centret, Borupvej 66, DK-4683 Ronnede, Denmark (00 45 567 11 567, jazzpar@mail.tele.dk) www.jazzpar.dk

Musicians cannot apply, must be nominated. It carries a cash award of Danish Kroner 200,000 (approx US $25,000) and a bronze statue by Danish artist.

UK winners - Django Bates and Tony Coe.

International committee of acknowledged jazz authorities with non-voting chairman - Cim Meyer (Denmark) others Dan Morgenstern (USA) Brian Preistley (UK), Alex Dutihl (France) Filippo Bianchi (Italy) Erik Wiedemann, Boris Rabinow (Denmark). Panel considered more than 40 candidates in 2001. The prize can only be awarded to an internationally known and active jazz artist who is especially deserving of further acclaim.

Winner is focus for the Jazz Par Prize concert when the presentation takes place. It is recorded - available as CD and on radio and broadcast on TV followed by a tour.

Winner in 2001 Marilyn Mazur - a Danish percussionist, dancer and band leader. 2002 Enrico Rava - Italian Trumpet/Flugel horn; 2003 Andrew Hill - composer and pianist.

France

Martial Solal Jazz Piano Competition

Acanthes, Concours Martial Solal, 3 rue des Couronnes, Paris, France (00 33 1 40 33 45 35, ca@acanthes.com) www.acanthes.com

Open to high level jazz pianists of all nationalities born after October 6th 1967

1st Prize - Grand Prix de la Ville de Paris is 11000 Euro, 2nd 7500 Euro, 3rd Prize 4500 Euro, 4th Prize 3000 Euro. First round maximum of 15 minutes which will be an original composition by the contestant plus a rhythm section and a solo piece of a jazz standard. Second round maximum 30 minutes which will consist of a solo chosen from a set list of 16 pieces, a duo with a string or wind instrument, an original composition with a rhythm section. Final round maximum 30 minutes will include an original composition solo not more than 2.5 minutes, a piece arranged for an ensemble of 7/8 musicians with piano having a solo part, a jazz standard played with a rhythm section, a free solo improvisation. Final round takes place Oct 13th 2002.

Registration and Pre-selection - (see deadline) completed signed application form must include - recorded performance of minimum 10 minutes, photocopy of indentification i.e.passport, CV in French or English (max 2 typed pages) recent passport photo, entry fee - 65 Euros.

Monaco

Monaco International Jazz Soloist

Charly Vaudano, Academie de MusiqueFoundation, Prince Rainier III, 1 Boulevard Albert 1er, Monaco

Competition for all categories of instruments. Entry form available. Tape to include TWO jazz standards, ONE improvised number with a rhythm section and ONE "themed presentation". Three finalists will be chosen. Finals take place on 2nd June 2001 where musicians will have to perform three jazz standards of their own choice, from a list of 12 jazz themes which will be sent to finalists in advance. Soloists will be accompanied by a rhythm section. Prize money in 2001 is 8,000 FF; 6,000 FF; 4,000 FF with winner invited to join the jury for the following years' competition. Finalists are given accomodation costs for nights of 1st and 2nd June with a meal allowance. Winners in 1999 Peter Beets - Piano (Holland); Mika Kallio - Drums (Finland); Vladimir Karparov - Saxophone (Bulgaria) in 2000 Giovanni Guido - Guitar (Italy); Phil Abraham - Trombone (Belgium); Luigi Grasso - Saxophone (Italy).

Poland

Jazz Juniors Festival Award

Monika Molas, Jazz Juniors Festival Award, Stowarzyszenie Rotunda, Ul Oleandry 1, Krakow 30-060 (T +48 12 633 35 38 F +48 12 633 76 48)

International. Musicians in the band (2-9) must be under 25 with application forms plus a recording received by deadline. Recording should be no longer than 30 minutes and the band line-up should remain the same should applicants be short listed. Prizes awarded on condition of taking part in Laureates concert during the festival in December which will be judged by an international jury. Not open to soloists. Travel expenses not covered although accommodation is provided for finalists Deadline 10.11.2002

Final judging takes place during the festival 4-7th December 2002 held in the Rotunda in the Centre of Culture in Krakow, Poland. The aim is to provide opportunities for new young bands to be heard.

Spain

Getxo Jazz Competition

Getxo Cultural Centre, Urgull s/n, 48990 Algorta Getxo, Spain (Tel 00 34 944 914 080 Fax 00 34 944 912 139, kulturetxea@getxo.net)

Open to European groups of all musical styles of jazz. Four groups will be selected and perform during the festival (3-6 July).

Closing date for applications 23rd February 2002

Maximum Age: 30 for each group member

Applications to be accompanied by CD, photograph and Biogs

Each group selected will receive cash sum (Euro 900-1800) to cover travel etc

First Prize: 3000 Euro + trophy and CD recording; Second Prize: 1200 Euro + trophy; Best Soloist: 600 Euro + trophy

A CD will be recorded 'live' by the winning group during the two performances and the winning band will receive 10% of the sales.

Switzerland

Montreux Jazz Festival

PO BOX 126, Avenue du Chillon 70, Montreux, Switzerland (00 41 21 966 4445, saxcompetition@montreuxjazz.com) www.montreuxjazz.com

White Foundation World Sax Competition

www.whitefoundation.com

Applications close April 21st 2003

Open to saxophonists of any nationality born after January 1st 1973 (I.e. not over 30) who are pursuing a professional career and have never recorded as a leader for a major label.

Items to be sent with application

- A demo CD, mini disc or cassette with your name and contact details on item sent. Leave about 5 seconds between tracks. The recording must include 3 pieces of music (Total time 10 minutes) with the following :-
- One Standard from the Great American Songbook
- One composition by a jazz legend e.g. Monk, Coltrane, Miles, Rollins, Mingus
- Two photos of candidate with name written on the back
- A photocopy of the candidates ID card
- A CV (curriculum vitae - a maximum of 2 pages)

2002 was the first year for the Sax competition in association with Montreux Jazz Festival in the memory of the great saxophone players of the past and to encourage the stars of the future. The competition takes place in the Montreux Palace Hotel overlooking Lake Geneva.

Jury - under the patronage of Quincy Jones, panel will include Jean Toussaint

Details - Semi finals July 15th to 17th 2003; Finals 18th July 2003

4 finalists will perform (each contestant's programme a maximum of 30 minutes).

Candidates who have been short listed for the semi-final will be notified by May 9th 2003   Travel and accommodation to be covered by the candidate but the competition office can provide a list of hotels and youth hostels in the area.

First prize - recording contract, including studio editing, production, master and CD duplication; Henri Selmer Paris saxophone. Concert performance during the 31st IAJE conference in New York January 2004; Accommodation and concert performance during 38th Montreux Jazz Festival 2004; Performance at New York's longest running jazz concert series Jack Kleinsinger's Highlights in Jazz; Performance at BBC Radio 3 London Jazz Festival in November 2004. Jazzwise magazine will cover the competition and interview the winner

Second Prize - $1813 or 2042 Euro; Participation in IAJE conference in 2003 in Toronto

Third prize - $1208 or 1360 Euro

Shure Montreux Jazz Voice Competition with Universal Music

Open to all singers born after 1st January 1973.

Sponsors Shure, Universal Music in partnership with Bea Young Artist's Foundation.

Deadline for applications 21st April 2003. Semi-finals is a public performance in front of a jury between 15th and 17th July 2003. Finals (4 candidates) on 18th July 2003

First Prize $3700 (Euros 3250) Recording at Mountain Studios in Switzerland 19/20th July plus Performance at Montreux 2004 Festival (travel and accommodation paid) Performance at IAJE Conference in New York 2004 some expenses paid. Second Prize Cash $2220 (Euros 2110) Performance at IAJE New York 2004. Third Prize Cash $1480 (Euros 1408)

Montreux Solo Piano Competition

Address at Montreux Jazz Festival office

Open to pianists of all nationalities born after January 1 1973. Musical pieces must be piano solos only. Applications must include a demo CD/tape with good sound quality with two pieces of music one of which must be an own composition, the other either 'Very Early' by Bill Evans or 'In Your Own Sweet Way' by Dave Brubeck. Total time approx 10 minutes.

• Two photos of candidate (name on the back)

• Photocopy of candidates ID card

• CV + other relevant documents

• Application fee is non-returnable but will go to a charity fund

Deadline for application May 1 2003. Semi finals 8 to 10 July 2003. Finals (4 candidates) will take place on 11 July 2003

First Prize Performance at Montreux Festival 2004 (travel and accommodation paid) Performance at IAJE conference in New York 2004 (travel and accommodation paid) Recording of a demo

Second Prize Cash $3023 (Euros 3403) Performance at IAJE Conference in New York 2004. Third Prize Cash $1813 (Euros 2042)

USA

Betty Carter's Jazz Ahead
Kennedy Centre, www.kennedy-center.org/jazzahead
Application deadline December 20th 2002

March 20-28 2003

Jazz students in their teens and twenties are selected from an international applicant pool to spend a week in residency honing their musical skills with jazz masters culminating in performances of the participants original compositions at the Kennedy Centre.

Gil Evans Fellowship
IAJE, 2803 Claflin Road, Manhattan, Kansas 66502 USA (T; 00 1 785 776 8744)

Annual commission sponsored by Herb Alpert Jazz Endowment fund and IAJE. Aim is to identify an emerging jazz composer from an international field of candidates. The recipient is commissioned to compose a work in the jazz idiom for performance during the IAJE Annual conference. Commission is $2,500 with composer receiving two all-expenses-paid trips to the IAJE conference – one before their commission premiere and one on the year of the premiere. Started in 1990 it has helped launch the careers of such writers as Maria Schneider and Anthony Wilson

Applicants must be no older than 35 on or before October 15 2003. Three original compositions in a jazz idiom to be submitted by deadline – 15 October. Cassette tape ONLY of one of the compositions. CV of education, compositional achievements and professional experience. Plus a one page narrative explaining their goals in jazz composition. Application form from IAJE.

The International Jazz Award
Presented annually, in partnership with the International Jazz Festivals Organisation (IJFO) and the IAJE (at the IAJE Annual Conferencein January). The award, which includes a $20,000 (US$) prize, is designed to recognise international artists who have contributed significantly to the evolution of jazz. The first IJFO International Jazz Award was presented to Austrian keyboardist, bandleader, and composer Joe Zawinul at the 2002 IAJE Annual Conference and in 2003 Dave Holland (Double Bass) received the award.

International Songwriting Competition
Zero Governors Avenue 6, Medford, MA 02155, info@songwritingcompetition.com
www.songwritingcompetition.com

Annual competition that aims to provide the opportunity for both aspiring and established songwriters to have their songs heard in a professional international arena. 13 categories - new in 2003 is jazz/instrumental section. Cash and 'merchandising' prizes. Amateur and professional songwriters can apply. Completed application form must also include a 5 minute CD/tape plus $30 entry fee (additional song/s $20 each) lyric sheet for each song. Must be original work. Full rules on website as well as an application form. Deadline 15 September 2003

Julius Hemphill Composition Award

The Jazz Composers Alliance, Box 491, Allston, MA 02134, USA (JCAComp@aol.com)

Two categories large and small ensembles.

$1500 will be split between the top three composers in each category and music software,worth up to $500 donated by Mark of the Unicorn, will go to 6 finalists($2500 total cash prizes and 6 software prizes with a value of $3000.

The goal of the alliance is to promote the art of jazz composition and to honour the role composer Julius Hemphill had in the world of jazz.

Enquiries and entries should be mailed to Jazz Composers Alliance and should be postmarked no later than December 2003.

Entry Guidelines

Recording:casette tape or CDR. Remove or cover composers name.

Recording should only contain the piece being submitted. There is no time limit , but initailly no more than 8 minutes will be heard on listening.

Score or lead sheet

Short bio or resume. Include ensemble information. Please use 8.5 x 11 paper

Check or money order for $20, payable to the Jazz Composers Alliance

Materials will only be returned with SAE.

Multiple entries are allowed but must be under separate cover, with separate fee, biographies and recording. Do not put multiple entries on the same recording. There is no duration limit. Judging will be 'blind', by a panel including members of the JCA.

Category 1. composition for large ensembles; Category 2. small ensembles 1-7 instruments or voice.

Sisters in Jazz Collegiate competition (International)

Katherine Cartwright, San Jose State University of Music and Dance, One Washington Square, San Jose 95191-0095, California (T: 408 924 4649, katchie@bigfoot.com) www.katchie.com

Aims to support and promote more involvement by women in jazz education and performance. Female students compete by taped audition and the five winners form a jazz quintet (including piano, bass and drums) and receive an all expenses paid trip to the IAJE annual conference in January. They perform at the conference to audiences of jazz artists, students and people from the jazz industry.

Deadline November 2003

Thelonius Monk International Jazz Trombone Competition

Thelonius Monk Institute for Jazz, Smithsonian Institute, 225 Wisconsin Avenue NW Suite 605, Washington DC 20015-2014 (T +1 202 364 7272, info@monkinst.org) www.monkinstitute.com

Since 1987, the Thelonious Monk Institute of Jazz has developed a reputation for launching the careers of young aspiring jazz artists through its annual competition. Each year, more than $60,000 in scholarships and prizes are awarded to talented young musicians and composers. The scholarships help pay tuition for college-level jazz education studies; provide funds for private, specialized instruction; and support career development.

The competition focuses on a different instrument every year and features an outstanding all-star judging panel. Branford Marsalis, Pat Metheny, Herbie Hancock, Clark Terry, Dave Brubeck, Marian McPartland, and Diana Krall have all served as judges at past competitions. For the past seven years Vice President and Mrs. Gore have served as Honorary Chairpersons of the event.

Application form and rules available on-line

Deadline for applications 28.02.2003

Semi Finals 26th April 2003 with Finals on the following day both held at in Washington DC

1st prize $20,000 scholarship, 2nd $10,000, 3rd $5,000 plus a further two awards of $1,000.

Thelonius Monk International Jazz Composers Competition

Sponsored by BMI – world's largest performing rights organisation.

Deadline 28.02.2003

Results mailed to applicants by 26.03.2003

Performance of winning composition 27th April 2003

1st prize $10,000

Both competitions attract high profile press coverage appearing in publications from the New York Times to People magazine, covered by all the major networks as well as radio and the new interactive media. National Public Radio has presented 'one hour specials' of past competitions. Representatives from major jazz labels attend, recognising the opportunity to discover 'rising stars'.

Maria Fisher Founder's Award

Presented at the same time as the winners is the Maria Fisher Founder's Award

Awarded to an individual who has made essential and valuable contributions to jazz education and the jazz tradition. Winner in 2002 Wayne Shorter.

Application forms available on-line

International Archives

Australia

Victorian Jazz Archive
5 Mountain Highway, Wantirna, Victoria (T: +61 9800 5535, vjazarch@vicnet.net.au)   www.home.vicnet.net.au

Part of a national initiative collect and preserve Australian jazz material in all its forms also collects overseas material for the study in the reference library.

Austria

Institute for Jazz Research
Music University, Leonhardstrasse 15, A-8010 Graz (T:+43 (316)389 1203 F:+43 (316) 389 1266, gertraud.steinberger@kug.ac.at)   www.jazzresearch.org

Europe's oldest jazz research organisation also publish a yearbook and a newsletter

Belgium

La Maison du Jazz
11 rue sur le Foulons, B-4000 Liege (T:+32 4   221 1011 F:+32 221 4 2232, jazz@skynet.be) www.jazzaliege.be

Belgian jazz archives

Finland

Finnish Jazz and Pop Archive
Arabiankatu 2, FIN-00560 Helsinki (T: +358 9 757 0040 F: +358 9 757 0044, info@jazzpoparkisto.net) www.jazzpoparkisto.net

Director Dr Juha Henriksson. 272 personal anthologies (Finnish musicians or bands), sheet music (over 10.000) and hand-written sheet music (over 1000), photographs (10.000), interviews with Finnish musicians (over 230), recordings, mainly unpublished (5000 hours), videotapes (1500 hours) newspaper clippings (over 20.000), books, music magazines, concert programs, brochures, posters, etc

Germany

International Archives for Jazz Organ
c/o Jurgen Wolf, PO BOX 900709, Koln, D-51117 (T: +49 2203 932 881, jw@jwolf.com)   www.iajo.org

Private archive of Jurgen Wolf with 10,000 titles available in list form (no sound bites due to copyrights) also includes current world wide information about jazz organists by country with profiles, charts and new releases, newsletter

Jazz-Institut Darmstadt

Bessunger Strasse 88d, 64285 Darmstadt, Germany (00 49 (0) 6151 963 700, Fax: 00 49 (0) 6151 963 744, jazz@stadt.de) www.darmstadt.de

Opening hours Monday/Wednesday/Thursday 10 – 5pm; Friday 10 – 2pm;10 – 9pm

Europe's largest public reference archive on jazz. Holds specialised books, periodicals, sheet music, records, photographs, posters and other memorabilia. It is used by researchers, journalists, students, musicologists and the general public. In 1983 the city of Darmstadt bought the collection of a well-known German critic and producer Joachim-Ernst Berendt and since then other collections have been acquired. In 1997 the Institute moved to the "Bessunger Kavaliershaus". – originally an eighteenth century royal hunting lodge.

The recorded items are in the region of 40,000 in various formats – CDs, LPs, EPs, shellacks, cylinders, tapes which document the music from ragtime to free jazz and include jazz-rock, blues and spirituals as well as international 'world music'.

The photo and poster collection is one of the largest in the world; Sheet music includes transcriptions, fake books, band and orchestra scores. The book section especially focuses on jazz in America and Europe. Periodicals include Down Beat, Metronome, Jazz Hot, Jazz Podium. The Berendt archive includes, manuscripts for his radio shows, correspondence with musicians, and it gives an important insight into the development of jazz in post-war Germany.

Each year the Institute organises the 'Darmstadter Jazzforum' a discussion forum for musicologists and musicians. The institute also holds names and addresses on current research projects from all over the world; complete mailing lists with and internet addresses for world wide magazines.

Greece

Jazz Research and Promotion Centre

46 Tsami Karatassou Street, Athens GR-11742 (T: +30 923 8808 F: +30 924 1847)

Netherlands

Dutch Jazz Archive

Prins Hendrikkade 142, NL-1011 AT Amsterdam (T: +31 20 627 1708/1801 F: +31 20 428 8425, info@jazzarchief.nl) www.jazzarchief.nl

Collection includes 22,500 LPs, 2,500 CDs, 25,000 books, 1500 Videos. website in Dutch. Archive open weekday afternoons, publish a quarterly newsletter

Norway

Norwegian Jazz Archives

Tollbugt 28, N-0157 Oslo (T: +47 22 42 90 90 F: +47 22 42 90 91, info@jaz-zarkivet.no) www.jazzarkivet.no

Also available on-line is a joint project with the National Library of Norway a history and discography of jazz in Norway 1905 to 1998 Norwegian Jazz Base www.nb.no/norskjazz

Sweden

Swedish Jazz Archive

Norrtullsgatan 6, SE-11329 Stockholm (T: +46 8 340 935 F: +46 8 314 756 Postal address Box 16 326, svenskt.visarkiv@visarkiv.se) www.visarkiv.se

Folk Music Archive with a jazz department which collects material useful to researchers of Swedish jazz – interviews, recordings, notated music, books etc. Open to visitors weekdays 10 – 15.00 (May/Aug 10-14.30) and telephone enquiries

Switzerland

SwissJazzOrama

Museum Asylstrasse 10, CH-8610 Uster, Archive (and postal address) Im Werk 8, 8610 Uster (T: +41 1 940 1982 F: +41 1 940 1980, swiss@jazzorama.ch) www.jazzorama.ch

Museum documents the history of jazz in Switzerland plus special exhibitions, discussions, current publications, museum shop and bar. Archive contains recordings, books and ephemera and answers requests for jazz history information.

USA

American Jazz Museum

1616 East 18th Street, Kansas City, MO 64108 (T: 816 474 8463 F: 816 474 0074, awalker@americanjazzmuseum.com) www.americanjazzmuseum.com

Opened in 1997 and is the only museum devoted entirely to jazz. Includes interactive exhibits, a video juke box with over two dozen jazz videos, the facility to experiment in a studio-like environment, artefacts that detail Kansas City's contributions to jazz including exhibits on Louis Armstrong, Duke Ellington, Ella Fitzgerald and Charlie Parker. Educational programmes for school children.

American Music Centre

Suite 1001, 30 West 26th Street, New York, NY 10010-2011 (T: 212 366 5260 center@amc.net) www.amc.net

This is the official information agency for new American music including jazz with information on composers, musicians, scores, recordings and the industry

Blues Archive Mississippi Library(USA)

Greg Johnson, Blues Curator and Assistant Professor, Archives and Special Collections, J. D. Williams Library, University, MS 38677, Telephone: (662) 915-7753 Fax: (662) 915-5734; gj1@olemiss.edu, www.olemiss.edu

Based at the University of Mississippi and it acquires and conserves blues and blues-related materials, for scholars of the blues, African American studies, and southern culture. It houses over 50,000 sound recordings, 15,000 photographs; more than 350 videotapes; 3,000 books, periodicals and newsletters; and numerous manuscripts and ephemera. The archive is one of the largest collections of blues material in the world. It was established in 1984 and serves not only students and faculty within the University of Mississippi, but researchers worldwide.

Brubeck Institute University of the Pacific

3601 Pacific Avenue, Stockton, CA 95211 (T: 209 946 3970 F: 209 946 3972, jbdyas@uop.edu) www.brubeckinstitute.org

Dave Brubeck collection is one of the largest personal collections in the world it contains hundreds of published and unpublished compositions, original manuscripts, recordings, photos, press clippings and memorabilia. website has broad contents list and more detailed photo list.

Centre for Black Music Research

Columbia College, 600 South Michigan Avenue, Chicago, Illinois 606065-1996 (312 344 7559 Fax: 312 344 8029 cbmr@cbmr.colum.edu) www.cbmr.org

The Centre documents, collects and disseminates information about black music in all parts of the world and promotes understanding of the common roots of the music, musicians, composers of the 'global African diaspora'. Supports and originates study in areas of black secular and sacred music including jazz.

Chicago Jazz Archive

Regenstein Library, University of Chicago, 1100 E 57th Street JRL361, Chicago Illinois 60637-1596 (T: 773 702 3721 F: 773 702 6623 ucjazz@lib.uchicago.edu) www.lib.uchicago.edu/e/su/cja

Established in 1976 to collect and preserve materials of 1910s and 20s documenting the birth of Chicago-style jazz. Archive now tries to reflect all styles of jazz in all formats.

Eubie Blake National Jazz Institute and Cultural Centre

34 Market Place, Suite 323, Baltimore, Maryland 21202 (T: 410 625 3113 F: 410 385 2916 eblake847@aol.com) www.eubieblake.org

In 1984 the archive of the rag-time piano player Eubie Blake was donated to the City of Baltimore

Florida International University

Green Library, 11200 SW 8th Street, Miami, FL 33199 (T: 305 348 2461 F: 305 348 3408) www.fiu.edu/~library

Christobal Diaz Ayala donated his enormous Cuban music collection to the

University. It covers 1925-60. An extensive discography can be viewed and down-loaded from their site – look under digital recordings on main site or http://gislab.fiu.edu.SMC/discography.htm

Hamilton College Jazz Archive

Hamilton College, 198 College Hill Road, Clinton NY 13323 (T: 315 859 4071 mrowe@hamilton.edu)

Established in 1995. Collection of videotaped interviews with jazz musicians, arrangers, writers and critics. Main focus is on swing era and musicians associated with mainstream Jazz

Hoagy Carmichael Collection

Indiana University, Archives of Traditional Music, Morrison Hall 117 Bloomington IN 47405-2501 (atmusic@indiana.edu) www.dlib.indiana.edu/collections/hoagy

Collection of his personal items as well as those donated by his family including original music manuscripts, recorded interviews, films, photos, scrapbooks. In all over 3,000 items.

Institute of Jazz Studies

Dana Library, Rutgers University, Newark, New Jersey 07102 (T: 973 353 5595 F: 973 353 5944 eberger@andromeda.rutgers.edu) www.libraries.rutgers.edu/rul/libs/dana_lib/dana_lib.shtml

Considered to be the world's largest and foremost jazz archive. Founded 1952 by Marshall Stearns – a pioneer jazz scholar. Used by researchers, media, record companies, musicians and other archives.

Louis Armstrong Archive

Michael Cogswell, Director, Louis Armstrong House and Archives, Queens College, Flushing, NY 11367 (Tel: 00 1 718 997 3670. Fax: 00 1 718 997 3677) www.satchmo.net

Good site that provides information on the organisation, current educational and cultural programmes –(including exhibitions, musical performances for schools, presentations to schools and libraries). The site gives details about the House, the archives, membership, vital information for publishers wanting to use/reproduce visual and sound items and a very useful Frequently Asked Questions page. There is also a good biography of Louis Armstrong. The archive is located in the Benjamin Rosenthal Library on the Queens College campus in Flushing. Public opening hours Monday to Friday 10 to 5pm Saturday by appointment. Check before visiting.

Library of Congress/National Recording Preservation Board

c/o Motion Picture, Broadcasting and Recorded Sound Division, Library of Congress, 101 Independence Avenue SE, Washington, DC 20540-4698 (recregistery@loc.gov) www.loc.gov/rr/record/nrpb

An advisory group comprising a number of professional organisations and expert individuals concerned with the preservation of recorded sound.

Marr Sound Archives

Chuck Haddix, Sound Recording Specialist, University of Missouri, G11 Miller Nichols Library, 800E 51st Street Visiting hours 08.30-16.30 (001 816 235 2798, Fax: 00 1 816 333 5584, haddixc@cctr.umkc.edu) www.umkc.edu

The Marr Sound archive is part of the Special Collection department which holds nearly 250,000 recordings covering 6 major American experience areas – Historic Voices, American Popular Music, Vintage Radio Programmes, Authors reading their own works, Historic classical and operatic recordings and Jazz, Blues and Country.

The jazz collection covers all styles and the archive hosts 'Club Kaycee' a website devoted to Kansas City jazz history. It features photos, music and sound files, details on historic jazz venues and articles. On their web under the section 'People' - whole tracks of vintage Kansas City Jazz are available on real audio. See website for details of Access to the collection.

National Ragtime and Jazz Archive

c/o Southern Illinois University, Edwardsville, IL 62026-1063 (T: 618 650 2695 tdickma@siue.edu) www.library.siue.edu

Set up in 1974 and documents early recorded jazz and the lives of notable jazz musicians from the St Louis area. The basis of the archive is the John Randolph collection of 10,500 78rpm records. A funded Oral history project in the 1980s has added to the collection.

Paul Whiteman Collection

Williams College Library and Special Collections, Williamstown, MA 01267 (T: 413 597 2568) www.otis.cc.williams.edu:803/library/archives

About 4,000 orchestral jazz manuscript arrangements from 1920s, 30s, 40s as well as contemporary recordings

Smithsonian National Museum of American History

Washington DC 20560-0514 www.americanhistory.si.edu

In the Archives centre the American Music collection covers Big Band, gospel and folk. One the largest is the Duke Ellington Collection 1927-88 with thousands of scores, parts, recordings and photos, as well as his oral history collection and other collections relating to his life. There are also an Ella Fitzgerald and Benny Carter collection, materials on Woody Herman, Horace Silver, the Herman Leonard collection (120 photos) and the Ernie Smith Jazz Film collection which specialises in jazz dance material from 1894-1979.

University of North Texas

Music Library, PO BOX 305190, Denton, TX 76203-5190 (T: 940 565 2860) www.library.unt.edu/music/kenton

Band leader Stan Kenton bequeathed his entire orchestral library to the university. It includes over 2000 manuscripts and is supplemented by his publicist's collection of over 600 photos.

William Ransom Hogan Jazz Archive

Howard Tilton Memorial Library, Tulane University, 7001 Freret Street, New Orleans, LA 70118 Bruce Boyd Raeburn Curator Tel: 00 1 504 865 5688; Fax 00 1

504 865 5761 raeburn@mailhost.tcs.tulane.edu
www.tulane.edu/~lmiller/JazzHome.html

Collection of oral histories, recorded music, photos and film, manuscripts, clippings and books all relating to New Orleans Jazz. Also produce a newsletter. On-line River Boat jazz history

.

International Courses

Australia (++61)

Western Australian Academy of Performing Arts

(part of WA Conservatorium of Music), 2 Bradford Street, 6050 Mount Lawley, Western Australia (Tel: 9370 6594, j.hamilton@ecu.edu.au, waapa@ecu.edu.au) http://waapa.cowan.edu.au

Department offers a mix of jazz, contemporary music, music education (jazz) and creative technology courses and is "renowned for its innovative in-depth approach to teaching practice". The Academy offers the first Bachelor of Music Education for a Jazz Major in Australia, to enable new opportunities to jazz graduates previously only open to classically trained musicians. International exchanges are available to the best students with institutions like the Royal Academy (London UK) Miami University (USA) and Amsterdam School of Music (Netherlands)

Certificate IV in music (jazz)

One year full time course for students who want to develop their skills in performance and widen their 'musical backgrounds'. As well as principle and secondary study it includes jazz history, theory, concert practice, ensemble skills, aural training, large ensemble work, history of music.

Diploma of Contemporary Music

Two year full time vocational course aimed at producing performers for the commercial music industry

Advanced Diploma of Contemporary Music

One year course that continues on from diploma to further broaden skills including the study of jazz and jazz techniques

Bachelor of Music (Performance) Jazz

Three year degree constructed to prepare students for a career in performance and/or composition. First 2 years concentrate on core studies – instrumental studies, improvisation, electronic music; Music studies - history, style and analysis, aural training, composition and arranging; Performance – ensemble, concert practice, large ensemble.

Third year – specialise in chosen area of study. There is flexibility to change this at any time. Specialist streams – composition and arrangement, Performance, Vocal.

Batchelor of Arts (Jazz)

Three year degree which follows the same subjects as the Jazz Performance BA in the first 2 years. Third year students can study a wide range of minor units available throughout the university – like multimedia media or computing, to compliment core music studies Jazz Programme co-ordinator Pat Crichton

Elder Conservatorium of Music

University of Adelaide, 5005 Adelaide, Australia (Tel: 38 303 3828 Fax: 38 303 4423)

Jazz Programme Co-ordinator Bruce Hancock

Sydney Conservatorium of Music
109 Pitt Street, Level 2, 2000 Sydney, Australia (Tel: 2 9351 1252. Fax: 2 9351 1200. dmontz@greenway.usyd.edu.au) www.usyd.edu.au.

Jazz Programme Co-ordinator Dick Montz

Austria (++43)

Summer Outreach Programme
Hackl Studio Archengasse 11, A-6130 Schwaz, Tyrol, Austria (T: 5242 66245 F: 664 33 03 81 hacklmusic@netway.at) www.outreach-schwaz.at

Venue: Landesmusikschule, Schwaz 25th July for a month 2003

A collaboration between the Tiroler Landesmusikschulwerk/konservatorium and the New School (New York, USA) which started in 1990, where participants can audition for the Jazz and Contemporary Music Programme at the New School University (offering a BA in Jazz Performance with a focus on composition and arranging). Participants can choose their own combination of modules including a 3 day introductory series of classes for beginners (taught in German) where elementary instrumental skills are required.

There is a mixture of creative work, teaching of required skills, public appearances, insights into the music business, CD production and the latest technology. Styles include acoustic jazz, fusion, World music, classical, Hiphop to Drum 'n Bass and House.

Tutors are top musicians. Course includes one-on-one and group instrumental tuition (basics), ensemble coaching (network), music theory by ear tools), business matters. After the rehearsals there are performances at night, live and studio recordings, master classes with prominent performers, jam sessions, street concerts in the town center, concerts in open air at the Margreitner Platzl and a "high alpine" final celebration at the Gamssteinhaus at 5522 feet above sea level. Application forms available on-line

Graz Music University Institute 8 (Jazz)
Moserhofgasse 39-41, A-8010 Graz. (T: 00 43 316 389-3080. F: 00 43 316 425 386. Ingrid Windisch - Ingrid.windisch@kug.ac.at

Karlheinz Miklin, Head Jazz Studies http://www.kug.ac.at

This is the oldest music school and has university status. Batchelor of Music 4 years with a 2 year Masters course. Foreign students can start the course in English but special courses are available to learn German with an exam after one year. Entrance by audition at end of June. Terms are Oct to January and March to June. Students audition for at least one jazz ensemble and rehearse with this at least 3 hours a week

Bruckner-Konservatorium des Landes Oberosterreich
Jazz and Popular music, Christoph Cech, Wildbergstrasse 18, A-4040 Linz (T: 00 43 732 731306-0 or 600808-14. F: 00 43 732 731306-30)
http://www.ooe.gv.at/einrichtung/bildung/bruckons.htm

Konservatorium der Stat Wein
Abteilung, Jazz Robert Politzer, D'Orsaygasse 8, A-1090 Vienna (T/F: 00 43 1 3103928)
Conservatoire with a jazz department

University fur Musik und darstellende Kunst Wein
Abteilung 5, Popular music, A Vienna. Wolfgang Peidelstein (T: 00 43 676 518 2400, peidelstein@mdw.ac.at)
Jazz department is part of the Popular music course

Belgium (++32)
The majority of the jazz courses in Belgium are held in Dutch. They include the following

Music Conservatoire Liege
Rue Forgeur 14, B-4000 Liege
Improvisation course, not specific to Jazz.

Jazz Studio Tritonus
De Vrierestraat 17/19, B-2000 Antwerp, (Tel: 3 1 248 2448. Ondine.quackel-been@ping.be) www.jazzstudio.be
Private school. Jazz Programme Co-ordinator Maaver Weyler

Vlaams Conservatoire Antwerp
Desguinlei 25 B, B-2018 Antwerp, (T: (3) 244 18 00 F: (3) 238 90 17, secr@dptd.hogant.be)
Jazz Programme Co-ordinator Stefaan Debevere

Brussels Conservatoire
Jazz Afdeling, Regentschpsstraat 30, B_1000 Brussels (T: (2) 513 45 87)
5 year course Jazz and Popular music.

Gent Conservatory
Jazz and Light Music, Hoogpoort 64, B-9000 Gent. (T: (9) 225 15 15

Lemmens Jazz Afdeling
Herestraat 53, B-3000 Leuven. (T: (16) 23 39 67. lemmensinst@innet.be)
Teaching in Dutch. In collaboration with Antwerp Jazz Studio and the Halewyn Foundation has been running for almost 30 years, usually during the last week of July, in Dworp (south of Brussels) Teachers are European and American musicians

DWORP Summer Jazz Clinic

Halewynstichting, Le Grellelei 10, B-2600, Berchem. (T: (3) 239 66 02 F: (3) 218 99 58)

In Dutch and English

Conservatoire de Liège

14 rue Forgeur, B-4000 Liège. (T: 41 220 306, F: 41 220 384)

Jazz Programme Co-ordinator List Garret

Conservatoire Royal de Musique de Bruxelles

Jazz Department, Rue de la Regence 30, B-1000 Bruxelles. (T: 2 511 04 27, F: 2 512 69 79)

Maximum of 5 years. Two courses either Composition and Harmony or Performance with history, harmony, rhythm, groups and Big Band work. Course starts in October. Courses held in French

Canada (++1)

Banff Centre For The Arts

Box 1020, Station 23, Banff, Alberta T0L 0C0. (T: 403 762 6188, F: 403 762 6345. Jazz contact Karen Harper. Arts.info@banffcentre.ca) www.banffcentre.ca/music

Banff International Jazz Workshop

Now in its 30th year, the Jazz Workshop includes daily sessions with Dave Douglas; master classes and common sessions with all visiting artists; supervised small ensemble rehearsals; new compositions; unlimited opportunities for individual practicing and ensemble playing; and many opportunities for club and concert performances.

May 19 to June 7 2003 Application Deadline January 31st 2003

Saxophonists Mark Turner (May 19 - 24) and Mike Murley

(May 19 - June 7); clarinet Louis Sclavis (dates tbc); trumpeter/pianist Brad Turner (May 19 - June 7); pianist/composer Jason Moran (June 2 - 7);

Guitarist/composer John Abercrombie (May 26 - 31); cellist/composer Peggy Lee (May 19 - June 7); bassist James Genus (June 2 - 7); drummers Clarence Penn (June 2 - 7) and Dylan Van Der Schyff (May 19 - June 7).

The workshop "focuses on facilitating the creation of original music. By taking a broad look at great music of the past, visiting artists encourage the participants in fresh ways of thinking about music and music making. Visiting artists address composition, improvisation, ear training, rhythm studies, instrumental technique, and band leading. They also talk about their own music and how it is made; about life, the road, and the music business. A rigorous focus on musical techniques is combined with an emphasis on real world experience. In a non-competitive environment, visiting artists and participants explore their common passions for music, examining the tradition to find an individual approach to new music—looking at the past to create the future". There are small ensemble rehearsals, club and concert performances. The concerts are recorded.

Application forms available on-line with details of costs involved.

Long-Term Career Development Residencies

Autumn October/December 6; Winter January/March; Application deadline 2nd week of April

Composers, solo performers, ensembles, singers and jazz musicians can concentrate on personal artistic development in an interactive and supportive environment. The residencies are aimed at musicians already working in or about to enter the music profession as well as those on leave from academic or professional positions.

University of Toronto

Faculty of Music, University of Toronto, Edward Johnson Building, 80 Queen's Park, Toronto, Ontario, Canada M5S 2C5, General Enquiries (Room 145) T: 416 978-3750, Undergraduate Office (Room 108) T: 416 978-3740, Registrar: Jeannie Wang) www.utoronto.ca/music

BA Performance Jazz Studies four year course. Each student pursues an individual program of study with a private tutor. The course includes development of technical abilities, artistic concepts, methods of practice, improvisation and a study of repertoire in jazz and 'traditional' idioms. It is a blend of academic and performance to help students develop an individual voice in improvising, arranging and composing in a jazz context. Each student is assigned to two ensembles and performs between four and six concerts per year. The groups meet for an hour per week with a faculty member and for 2 hours independently. Course also includes History of Jazz, Improvisation, Jazz and Traditional Ear Training, Jazz and Traditional materials, Jazz arranging and composition, keyboard skills, Music as Culture, Studies in the European tradition.

Denmark (++45)

Nordiysk Musik Konservatorium

Ryesgade 52, DK-9000 Aalborg (T: 98 12 77 44. F: 98 11 37 63)

Rhythmic Music Conservatory

Dr Priemes Vej 3, FRedriksberg C, DK-1854 Copenhagen. (T: 31 23 24 52. F: 31 22 07 56. Head of Jazz Erik Moseholm)

Finland (++358)

Helsinki Pop and Jazz Conservatory

Hameentie ˋ35 A, FIN-00560 Helsinki (T: 358 9 777 12111. F: 358 9 728 7877. Jussi.saksa@hkiamk.fi) www.musicfinland.com/popandjazz

Founded in 1972 as an institute, becoming a conservatory in 1995. Participates in the staff and student exchange programme – 'Socrates'. Member of the IASJ and IAJE and a member of the Berklee International Network – a worldwide co-operative network. Guest tutors have included John Scofield, Ron McClure, Madeline Eastman, Mark Levine and Carlos Puerto.

Sibelius Academy

Jazz Department, PO BOX 86, FIN-00251 Helsinki (T: 358 9 405 4551. F: 00 358 9 405 4785. Anne.etelatalo@siba.fi) www.siba.fi/Yksikot/Jazz/english.html

Jazz department founded in 1983 and is the only university course for jazz in Finland. Offers a BA in Jazz (4 years) and an MA (5-6 years). Courses include workshops, Big Bands and Master classes as well as studies in main instrument, improvisation, harmony, ear training, arrangement techniques, history of jazz and the piano as a subsidiary instrument. Other options include composition, theoretical subjects and studio technology. Specialise in either performance or composition/arranging. It is also possible to carry on, after a Masters degree, to Post Graduate studies to Doctorate level. There is also a 'youth department' for those students at secondary school who show a jazz talent.

Entrance is by exam/audition in May with 6-8 places available each year. Head of the jazz department is the guitarist Jarno Kukkonen. Guest tutors from abroad offer master classes, which is seen as an integral part of the course. The Academy has its own record label – Jazz Weaver

France (++33)

American School of Modern Music

117 rue de la Croix Nivert, F-75015 Paris, (T: 1 45 31 16 07) www.american-schoolmodernmusic.fr

Head of Jazz Stephen Carbonara. Part time course spread over 5 years (8 to 10 hours per week) leading to a Diploma or a Certificate. As well as elected instrument tuition (2 hours per week) includes ear training, sight reading, jazz harmony and composition, jazz repertoire, arranging for Big Bands, improvisation in small ensembles. The school is a member of the Berklee College of Music International Network. This provides access to master classes (at all levels) by Berklee faculty tutors, who visit Paris regularly. Students at the school have priority for Berklee's International scholarships with the chance of an advanced placement and participation in international student exchange programmes. The school is also a member of the IASJ and IAJE who both organise international workshops and concerts providing an opportunity for students to play before large audiences and study with world-class musicians.

Registration – by entrance exam taken either from mid April to mid June or in last two weeks of September. Classes start early October. Fees for 2002/2003 range from 1647 Euros (for 6 hours per week) to 2561 Euros (for 10 hours per week) First year places limited.

Bill Evans Piano Academy

33 rue de Clemcen, F-75020 Paris (T: 1 43 49 17 00. F: 1 43 49 18 00, infos@bill-evans.com) www.bill-evans.com.

Head of Jazz Micu Narunsky

Offers 5 courses at 3 levels over 30 weeks in the year. Part time from 11 to 19 hours per week. Intensive course from 20 to 30 hours per week. Professional course (levels 2 and 3) from 15 to 30 hours per week. Part time course (at all levels) for those students who are also working from 5 to 10 per week. Training teachers 14 hours per week

Introductory Piano course

Levels 1 to 3 each have a core study of piano plus complementary courses in history of jazz, jazz piano, musical theory, rhythm, ear training and harmony with optional courses in Latin/Caribbean, Song, choral jazz, rhythm workshop, drumming for non-drummers

ARPEJ (Association recontre pour la pedagogie et l'enseignement du jazz)

29 rue des petites Ecuries, F-75010 Paris. (T: 1 42 46 26 48 F: 1 48 01 05 85, arpej@wanadoo.fr) http://perso.wanadoo.fr/arpej

ARPEJ is a school of Jazz, Salsa and Brazilian music

CIM School of Jazz

83 bis rue Doudeauville, F-75018 Paris (T: 1 42 58 55 62 F: 1 42 58 40 31) www.musiciens.com

Head of Jazz - Evelyn Rizzoli

Conservatoire de Paris

209 av Jean Jaures, F-75019 Paris (T: 1 40 40 45 45 F: 1 40 40 45 00 Conservatoire-paris-9@wanadoo.fr)

Head of Jazz - Gretchen Amusen

Institut Art Culture et Perception

32 Rue du CapitaineMarchal, F-72020 Paris (T: 1 40 30 91 95) www.jazz-iacp.com

First private jazz school in France. Focus is on instrumental improvisation through the work of the Orchestra, which performs 30 to 40 concerts per year. Takes 250 pupils from all over the world with 22 tutors

International Music School

4 rue de Faubourg, F-75004 Paris; (T: 1 42 71 25 07)

Germany (++49)

Cologne Music High school

Frank Haunschild,, Dagobertstrasse 38, 53668 Koln. (T: 00 49 221 91 2818-0, FrankHaunschild@compuserve.com)

Four year course

Greece (++30)

Phillipos Nakas Conservatory

41 Hippocratous Street, GR-10680 Athens (T: 1 363 4000 F: 1 363 3583)

Head of Jazz Leonidas Arniakos

Hungary (++36)

Feren Liszt Academy of Music
Bemmelweis U 12, H-1052 Budapest, (T: (1) 118 2044)
Head of Jazz Janos Gonda

Ireland (Eire)(++353)

Newpark Music Centre
10 O'Rourke's Park, Sallynoggin, Dublin (T: 1 285 3497)

Head of Jazz - Ronan Guilfoyle Music Centre established it's Jazz and
Contemporary Music Department in 1986 and is now recognised as the primary
centre for jazz and jazz related music education in Ireland. Full and part time
courses.

Professional Musician Training (Certificate Course). Practical course is specifically designed to prepare each participant for a career as a professional musician.
Structured into three teaching terms and runs from September to May. In addition
to ten hours teaching per week, instrumental practice, composition and assignments hours are required. Composition, Harmony and Ear Training, Jazz
Improvisation, Technology, IASJ (International Association of Schools of Jazz)
workshops, featuring internationally renowned musicians; ensemble
for 2fi hours per week, students play in a band, consisting of other course mem-
bers.The band is tutored for one session per week by both resident and visiting
tutors.

Licentiate Diploma course in Jazz. Full Time. 1 year
Auditions are held in May. Course runs from September to May
Admission to the diploma course can be either after successfully completing the
certificate course (Professional Musician Training Course) or through audition.
Course includes - Instrumental individual tuition on a chosen instrument - following
technique, tone production etc. and a set repertoire syllabus, ear training, improvisation, harmony andd arranging.

Jazz Improvisation. Evening classes. Tutors Ronan Guilfoyle and Tommy
Halferty.

Italy(++39)

Associazione Musicale Dizzy Gillespie
Via Ognissanti 4, 1-36061 Bassano del Grappa. (Tel/Fax (423) 545123)
Head of Jazz Lillian Terry

Associazione Sienna Jazz
Fotezza Medicea,, 1-53100 Sienna (T: (577) 271401 F: (577) 271404)
Jazz Co-Ordinator Franco Caroni

Centro Jazz
Torino Via Pomba 4, 1-10123 Torino (T: (11) 884477 F: (11) 812 6644)

Via Civico Corsi di Jazz di Milano
Corso Venezia 7, 1-20121 Milano
T: (2) 798729/(2) 7600 2714 F: (2) 799796 civijazz@galactica.it
www.scuolecivichemilano.it

Jazz Co-Ordinator - Enrico Intra

Ono Improvvisio
annaregio 3143 /P 1-30121 Benezia (T: (41) 720229)

Jazz Co-Ordinator - Giannantonio de Vinenzo,

Netherlands (++31)

DJAM
Postbus 92131 NL-1090 AC Amsterdam (T: (20) 665 63 38 info@djam.nl)
www.djam.nl

Conservatorium avn Amsterdam
PO BOX 78022 NL-1070 LP Amsterdam (T; (20) 527 7550 F: (20) 676 1506
info@cva.ahk.nl) www.cva.ahk.nl

Hogeschool voor de Kunsten Arnhem
Onderslags 9 NL-6812 CE Arnhem (T: (26) 353 5646 F: (26) 353 5643)

Head of Jazz - Michiel Braam

Hanzehogeschool Groningen /North Netherlands Conservatoire
Veemarkstraat 776 NL-9724 GA Groningen (T (50) 595 1300 F: (50) 595 1399
j.rol@pl.hanze.nl) www.hanze.nl

Head of Jazz - Joris Teepe

Royal Conservatory
Juliana van Stolbergplan 1 NL-2595 CA Den Haag (T: (70) 381 4251 F: (70) 385 3841)

Head of Jazz - Walter Turkenburg

Norway (++47)

Norwegian Radio Orchestra
Holger Gulbransen, Orchestral Director, NRK, 0340 Oslo (T: 00 47 2304 9036 F: 00 47 2304 8624) http://www.nrk.no/kork

Arrangers Workshop

Aimed at musicians under 35 who want to work with a Radio Orchestra for a week with their own arrangement or composition. In 2002 held in Oslo (previously in the Netherlands) with the Metropole Orchestra with John Clayton as workshop leader

Portugal(++351)

Associacao Filarmonica de Faro
Av. Da Republica 194-1 P, (T-8000 Faro T(89) 807050)
Head of Jazz - Furtado Joaquim

Flaluta de Hamelin/Centra de Ensino Musica de Braga
Rua Antonio Jose, Lisboa 80 Montelios PT-4700 Braga

South Africa (++27)

Centre for Jazz and Popular Music
University of Natal, Durban 4041, Director Darius Brubeck (T/F: 31 260 3385 brubeck@nu.ac.za) http://www.und.ac.za

Provides information on Durban's music scene, presents live music during term time, offers venue for meetings, educational projects, workshops and rehearsals as well as performances. Initiates visits from internationally known musicians, educational exchanges, international touring for senior students, musicians and staff; organises concerts, annual festivals and conferences; acts as band agency; co-operates with foreign embassies, patrons, commercial sponsors, Durban Arts Association, International Association of Jazz Educators, South African Association of Jazz Educators, Artworks Trust, Departments of Arts and Culture and Foreign Affairs; Fundraises for scholarships for jazz study, participation in overseas and local cultural events and to support itself.

In 1998 visitors from America, England, France, Germany, the Netherlands, Scotland and Switzerland performed and gave workshops at the music department at the University of Natal. Former students include Feya Faku, Lulu Gontsana, Victor Masondo, Johnny Mekoa, Zim Ngqawana, Concord Nkabinde, Melvin Peters, Bongani Sokhela, and many other active full-time musicians and teachers. UND jazz students have regularly attended and performed at the IAJE Conference in the USA.

Diploma in Music Performance (jazz)
The three-year Diploma is accessible by audition to students wishing to focus on performance in African Music and Dance, Classical Music or Jazz. The Diploma is designed for talented students who wish to concentrate on performance without having to take a full academic course load.

Historically, the Diploma in Music Performance was meant to give aspiring musicians, many of whom lacked the academic requirements to attend university, a chance to train as professional musicians, but over time it has become an access route to the B.Mus. (or even other degrees in the university). Students in both programmes (degree and diploma) receive individual tuition on their instruments. Jazz students study standard repertoire and the technique of improvisation in group classes constituted like jazz bands and normally join the NU Jazz Ensemble (big-band) or NU Voices (jazz choir).

BMus in Performance (Jazz)

BMus degree also includes a specialisation in Jazz Performance. The degree is a comprehensive musicianship programme which includes general courses in Music Theory and Perception and Music, Culture and History, as well as practical study in Jazz Performance, the experience of playing jazz in ensembles, the study of jazz and commercial arranging, more advanced work in jazz composition and arranging. There is also a M. Mus. in Jazz Performance.

Spain(++34)

Escuela de Musica Creativa
Pama 35, E-28004 Madrid (T: (1) 521 1156)
Head of Jazz - Joan Albert Serra

Escuela de Musica Virtelia
Ganduxer 117, E_08002 Barcelona (T: (3) 418 4719)
Head of Jazz - Francesc Llongueres

Estudio Escola de Musica
Rue Horreo 19, La Coruna, E-15702 Santiago de Compostela (T: (8) 156 1895)
Head of Jazz - Suso Antanes

Taller de Musicos
Requesens 5, E-08001 Barcelona (T: (3) 443 4346)
Head of Jazz - Lola Hueta

Sweden (++46)

Royal University College of Music
Box 27711 S-115 91 Stockholm (T: (8) 161801 F: (8) 664 1424)
Head of Jazz - Stefan Brolund

University of Goteborg School of Music
PO BOX 5439, S-40229 Goteborg; (T: (31) 773 4000 F: (31) 773 4030)
Head of Jazz - Gunnar Lindgren

Switzerland (++41)

Music School Luzern
Hami Haemmerli, Musical Director, Music School Luzern,, FAkultat III, Mariahilfgasse 2A, CH-6000 Luzern 5 (T: 41 41 412 20 56 hhaemmerli@mhs.fhz.ch)

Two year basic music course plus an additional 2 or 3 years for teaching or composition or performance. Qualification at the moment is a Higher Diploma which will change in the near future. Contact music school for an application form which should be returned with audio and written samples. Entrance after this is by audition usually held at the beginning of July

Jazz School Basel
Reinacherstrasse 105, 4053 Basel (T: 41 61 333 13 13, F: 41 61 333 13 14, bernhard.ley@jazz.edu Bernhard Ley) www.jsb.ch

Conservatoire de Montreux
Rue Eglise-Catholique 14, CH-1820 Montreux (T: (21) 963 6948)
Head of Jazz - Leonio Cherubini

Conservatoire Populaire de Musique de Geneve
35 Bd. Saint Georges, CH-1205 Geneve. (T: (22) 329 6722 F: (22) 329 6788)
Head of Jazz - Roland Vuataz

Ecole de Jazz de Musique Actuelle
Rue de Geneve 3, CH-1004 Lausanne; (T: (21) 320 9325)
Head of Jazz - Christo Christov

USA (++1)

California

Brubeck Institute
University of the Pacific, 3601 Pacific Avenue, Stockton, CA 95211 (T: 00 1 209 946 3970 F: 001 209 946 3972; jbdyas@uop.edu) www.uop.edu/brubeck

Undergraduate programme for exceptionally gifted students, also Summer Jazz Colony (a week-long program for exceptionally talented and motivated jazz students between their junior and senior year of 'high school').

BA in Jazz Studies at the University of the Pacific with courses in improvisation, composition, arranging, career management, small group performance, as well as the humanities.

Diablo Valley College
321 Golf Club Road, Pleasant Hill, CA 94523 (T: 925 605 1230 F: 925 605 1551, rsnyder@dvc.edu) www.dvc.edu/music
Director of jazz studies Rory Snyder

Large jazz department taking 400 students per term. Offers Music Industries Studies Certificate in Introduction and History of Jazz and rock music; Jazz theory and Improvisation; Jazz Workshop; Jazz Ensemble; Advanced Jazz Performance. Jamey Aebersold teaches a 2 day clinic in August. Visiting guest musicians have included Clark Terry, Joe Henderson, Don Menza, Louie Bellson, Michael Wolff, Bill Watrous.

The Jazz School

2087 Addison Street, Berkeley, CA 94704 (T: 510 845 5373 F: 510 841 5373 swing@jazzschool.com) www.jazzschool.com

Founded in 1997 for the professional musician or 'serious aficionado' looking for musical development. Quarterly terms – January 13 to 29th March; April 7 to 16 June; July 14 to August 24 2003. Quarterly registration fee plus course fees. Enrollment is on a first-come first-served basis. Also run workshops and seminars on Sundays. Application forms on-line

Stanford Jazz Workshop (Summer schools)

PO BOX 20454, Stanford, CA 94309 T: 650 736 0324 www.stanfordjazz.org

Founded in 1972 and a not-for-profit organization they aim to create an 'environment conducive to learning, experiencing and appreciating jazz by assembling a community that brings the best performers and teachers of jazz together with students of all abilities and backgrounds'.

Evening Summer Programme

June 23 to July 29th for listeners and musicians from 14 upwards, beginners (to jazz) to advanced levels. Six weeks of weekday evenings..

Jazz Camp

Ages 12-17 beginners to jazz to advanced Week one July 20-26th, Week two July 27-August 2nd

Jazz Residency

August 3-9th for adult musicians, beginners to jazz to advanced. Under 18s - by audition. Includes a Vocal programme

Jazz Weekend

Intensive August 7-10th adult instrumentalists. Tutors include Branford Marsalis (sax) Phil Woods (sax) Geri Allen (piano) Jeff 'Tain' Watts (drums) Robert Hurst (bass) Marcus Belgrave (trumpet) Harols Maybern (piano) Mundell Lowe and Jack Wilkins (guitar)

Thelonious Monk Institute of Jazz Performance

University of South California, 3443 Watt Way, Los Angeles California 90089-1102

One of the Institute's earliest goals was to create a unique college-level jazz program where the 'masters of jazz' could pass on their expertise to the next generation of jazz musicians in the way Thelonious Monk had done in his Manhattan apartment throughout the '50s and '60s. Launched in 1995 with the first class of seven students.

A select number of students are chosen from applicants (worldwide) by audition – direct enquiry line 213 821 1500. All of the students receive full scholarships, as well as stipends to cover their monthly living expenses.

Students receive personal mentoring, ensemble coaching and lectures but they also have unique opportunities to become involved in other learning situations e.g. students have traveled with performers like Herbie Hancock, Wayne Shorter to India, Thailand, Chile, Argentina.

Terence Blanchard is the Artistic Director and other tutors include Clark Terry, Jimmy Heath, Jackie McLean, Barry Harris, Wayne Shorter, Herbie Hancock, Ron Carter, Phil Woods, Slide Hampton, Curtis Fuller.

University of Louisville

Mike Tracy, Director of Jamey Aebersold Jazz Studies Programme
(miketracy@louisville.edu)
Actively recruit students world wide

University of Southern California

School of Music, Department of Jazz Studies, University Park Campus, Los Angeles
CA 90089-2991 (T: 213 740 3119 uscjazz@usc.edu) www.usc.edu/music
Degrees offered – Batchelor of Music BM, Master of Music MM, DMA, Graduate
Certificate. Courses provide a balance of teaching of traditional music and jazz per-
formance and a thorough grounding in the fundamentals of music.

Colorado

Lamont School of Music University of Denver

7111 Montview Boulevard, Denver CO 0220 (T: 303 871 6973. Malcom Lynn
Baker. mbaker@du.edu) www.du.edu/lamont
Five undergraduate degrees available in Jazz Studies and commercial music. Jazz
performance, composition and arranging. During a 3 year course (split into 10
week quarters) students join at least one jazz and one classical ensemble. Big
Band rehearses 4 hours a week

University of Northern Colorado

Jazz studies programme, 501 20th Street, Greeley CO 80639 (T:970 351 2577
info@arts.unco.edu) www.arts.unco.edu
Jazz Studies has been part of the programme since the music schools' inception in
1965. It is one of the few institutions in the USA offering a doctorate in Jazz
Pedagogy at Masters and Bachelor degree level. Classes include jazz history, jazz
planning and development, jazz administration, arranging, theory, improvisation.
They even have classes on jazz Grant Writing. Numerous opportunities to perform
are available through the small and large jazz ensembles both instrumental and
vocal.

As there is no undergraduate jazz major, students can select a balanced programme of traditional and jazz courses to provide the fundamentals of musicianship. Graduate students should already be accomplished jazz performers and wish
to learn teaching skills in the hope of becoming a tutor in a college/university.
There are 18 part time tutors and assistants, each of whom specializes in a specific
area of jazz.

Florida

University of Miami School of Music

PO BOX 248165, Coral Gables FL 3124 (T: 305 284 2241 F: 305 284 6475
kmoses@miami.edu) www.music.miami.edu

Jazz Programme Whit Sidener

Offer three Masters degree programmes in jazz studies

Jazz Performance - Instrumental or vocal: includes performance study, improvisation, jazz composition. Course finishes with a degree recital and a recital paper

Jazz Pedagogy - Combines jazz performance writing and analytical study with emphasis on educational methods and materials for jazz instruction. Course finishes with a written exam or a thesis.

Studio Jazz Writing - An advanced writing programme to prepare composers and arrangers for work in a variety of fields. Study includes instrumental, vocal and electronic writing techniques as well as orchestration practices as applied to small and large ensembles, symphony orchestras and computer based ensembles. Composition projects are rehearsed, recorded and critiqued. Final written project

Doctor of Music and Arts (Offered in Jazz Performance and in Jazz Composition) - Overall aim for jazz majors is to concentrate on tone development, musicianship, technical mastery of chosen instrument. Courses stress development of style, improvisation, jazz composition and arranging. Special sections on jazz theory and ear training are available. Approximately 36 jazz performing ensembles are available with many performance opportunities often with national/international guest artists.

University has 'state-of-the-art' recording opportunities in their own professionally equipped multi-track recording studios.

A joint programme between Instrumental Studio Music and Jazz and Music Education enables students to earn teacher certification in music education concurrent with the jazz major.

University of North Florida

4567 St Johns Bluff Road, S Jacksonville FL 32224-2645. (T: 904 620 2960)
www.unf.edu/coas/music

Chair of Jazz Studies Bunky Green

Offers a Bachelor of Music in Jazz Studies. Course includes music history, theory, improvisation, arranging, jazz fundamentals, small ensemble work and concert band
2002 winner of 6 Down Beat Awards. Their UNF Jazz Ensemble directed by Dr Keith Javors has its own website www.unfjazzensemble.com. The band and its musicians have won many awards and record on a regular basis as well as being invited to appear in international festivals that have included Montreux, North Sea and Viénne

University of South Florida

4202 E Fowler Avenue, Tampa FL 33620; (T: 813 974 4810 wilkins@arts.usf.edu)
www.arts.usf.edu/music

Jazz Programme - Jack Wilkins

Offer Batchelor of Music degree– Performance, Composition and Jazz Studies.

Each term visiting jazz artists present Master classes, rehearse and perform with student and faculty groups. In the recent past these have included Maria Schneider, Danny Gottlieb, Rufus Reid

Undergraduate and graduate scholarships are by audition, with applicants expected to perform a selection of standard jazz tunes – playing the melody and improvising.

Graduate teaching assistants and graduate fellowships are available to qualified graduate applicants. These come with a stipend and tuition waiver. Undergraduate international applicants are welcome with applications and credentials (transcripts and test scores) required for a decision with the following deadlines – for entry to Autumn semester (Aug) deadline March 1st; Spring semester for January entry deadline August 1st; Summer semester May entry deadline January 2nd.

Details of forms and regulations on their website

Illinois

Columbia College Chicago

600 South Michigan Avenue, Chicago IL 60605 (T:312 663 1600 F: 312 344 8078 hbaccus@popmail.colum.edu) www.colum.edu

Kentucky

University of Louisville School of Music

Belknap Campus, Louisville, KY 40506-0022 (T: 502 852 6907 or 6032, miketracy@louisville.edu) www.louisville.edu/groups/music

Head of Jazz - Mike Tracy

Louisiana

University of New Orleans Jazz Studies Division

PAC Building Room 108, New Orleans LA 70148. (T: 504 286 6039)

Head of Jazz - Corbie Johnson

Massachusetts

New England Conservatory of Music

290 Huntington Avenue, Boston MA 02115 (Tel: 610 585 1101 F: 610 585 1115 admission@newenglnadconservatory.edu) www.newenglandconservatory.edu

Chair of Jazz Studies and Improvisation Ken Schaphorst with a faculty of 35 leading jazz names from Steve Lacey to Bob Brookmeyer. Artist in Residence George Russell. Courses offered Bachelor's, Master's, Doctoral and Diploma programs in Jazz Performance, Jazz Composition and Contemporary Improvisation. Three jazz orchestras and 20 faculty coached small ensembles

Michigan

University of Michigan

School of Music, Dept. Jazz and Contemporary, Improvisation, 1100 Baits Drive, Moore Building, Ann Arbour, MI 48109-2085. Ed Sarath, Professor of Music. (T: 00 1 734 995 0239; sarahara@umich.edu) www.music.umich.edu

Offers undergraduate degrees in jazz and related idioms – Bachelor of Fine Arts in Jazz and Contemporary Improvisation; Jazz Studies; Jazz and Contemplative

Studies; Bachelor of Musical Arts; Dual Degree Programme. Graduate course – Master of Music in Improvisation. Sample curriculum:

BA in Jazz and Contemporary Improvisation - Includes one year of piano, private performance tuition, three terms with University Band, Orchestra or choir, 3 terms with jazz ensemble, three terms of Creative Arts Orchestra, three terms of ensemble chosen from Digital music, jazz or small jazz ensemble, two terms of music theory to include structure, primary tonal music, ear training, sight singing, written work in construction and composition and musical analysis, four terms of musicology exploring European and American music history, as well as sounds and concepts of world music traditions.

Admissions: Audition requirements available in detail for acoustic bass, drum set, piano, voice, woodwind, brass, vibes and guitar from Professor Edward Sarath 00 1 734 763 1321 or admissions office 00 1 734 764 0593.

New Jersey

Princeton University
Department of Music, Woolworth Centre of Musical Studies, Princeton NJ 08544-1007 (T: 609 258 4241 branker@princeton.edu) www.princeton.edu/-puje

Jazz ensemble programme has a variety of performing groups including – Art Blakey ensemble, Miles Davis ensemble, Monk/Mingus ensemble, Hard Bop ensemble, Avant Garde, jazz composers', concert jazz. High profile guest soloists from Jimmy Heath to Bobby Watson, private instruction faculty, Certificate in musical performance (jazz emphasis)

New York

Juilliard Institute for Jazz
Juilliard Admissions, 60 Lincoln Centre Plaza, New York NY 10023-6590. (T: 00 1 212 799 5000) www.juilliard.edu

Started in 2001 and is in collaboration with Jazz at the Lincoln Centre. Accepted 18 advanced jazz musicians selected by audition, tuition-free, pre-professional two year course leading to an Artist Dip. Application deadline 1st December

Manhattan School of Music
120 Claremont Avenue, New York, NY 10027 (T: 212 749 2802 ex. 2 F: 212 749 3025 admission@msmnyc.edu) www.msmnyc.edu

Offer jazz courses for double bass, electric bass guitar, guitar, trombone, saxes, clarinet

New School University
Jazz and Contemporary Music Program, 55 West 13th Street New York, NY 10011 (T: 212 229 5896 ex 302 F: 212 229 8936; Jazzadm@newschool.edu) www.newschool.edu/jazz

Director of Admissions Teri Lucas

Offer a BFA in Jazz Performance and in Composition and Arranging. Auditions take place in New York or during the Summer – August 10 in Schwarz in Austria (contact lucast@newschool.edu)

BFA Performance curriculum begins with a core of interdisciplinary studies which include theory, ear training, theory and performance, rhythm analysis, piano proficiency, sight reading, music history and liberal arts. Each students' curriculum is based on the results of their placement exams taken one week before the start of term.

Students can choose from a wide variety of elective courses – just a few are – Afro-Cuban Jazz Orchestra, Art Blakey and the Jazz Messengers Ensemble tutor Charles Tolliver, Blues - Junior Mance, Brazilian Jazz Ensemble - Richard Boukas, Charles Mingus ensemble - Andy McKee, Coltrane Ensemble - Reggie Workman, Ornette Coleman Ensemble - Jane Ira Bloom. For the Music Theory, Composition and Arranging course, the choice of elective subjects includes Composition and style analysis tutor Phil Markowitz who also teaches Chromaticism in Jazz, Introduction to Film scoring - David Lapato.

There is also a Vocal Performance degree course

International students make up a significant percentage of the Jazz programme which brings strong artistic and cultural diversity to the University. Entrance requirements are 12 to 18 credits. Application fee of $90 must be submitted with completed form and must be able to provide evidence that they have sufficient financial resources to attend. Admission can be either for the Autumn – deadline April 1st or Spring term – deadline November 15th. Entrance is by audition either taped or live. Tapes must be clearly labeled and contain 3 standard jazz selections performed with a rhythm section. One should be up tempo, one ballad and one blues. Applicants must submit a personal statement with a musical CV

Skidmore Jazz Institute Skidmore College

815 North Broadway, Saratoga Springs, NY 12866 (T: 518 580 5590 F: 518 580 5548) www.skidmore.edu

Co-ordinator of Jazz Programme Maria McColl

Two week intensive workshop for jazz students of all ages 29th June to 13th July 2002 includes concert series and Master classes

Wisconsin

Lawrence University

Admissions Office, Appleton, WI 54912 T: 800 227 0982
David.H.Stull@Lawrence.edu) www.Lawrence.edu

Index

Art Blakey
Moanin' / Blue Note 95324-2